CALLOWAY COUNTY PUBLIC LIBRARY
710 Main Street
MURRAY, KY 42071

Renaissance Clothing and the Materials of Memory

D0891329

During the late sixteenth century "fashion" first took on the sense of restless change in contrast to the older sense of fashioning or making. As fashionings, clothes were perceived as material forms of personal and social identity which made the man or woman. In *Renaissance Clothing and the Materials of Memory* Jones and Stallybrass argue that the making and transmission of fabrics and clothing were central to the making of Renaissance culture. Their examination explores the role of clothes as forms of memory that were transmitted from master to servant, from friend to friend, from lover to lover. But clothing was also an important form of wealth, stored up in good times and pawned or sold in bad times. Because of their financial value, clothes continued to circulate in the secondhand market and were disassembled into their constituent parts and reassembled in new forms. So while clothes were forms of material memory, they increasingly suggested that memory, personal identity, and social forms were vagrant and subject to restless change.

This book offers a close reading of literary texts, paintings, textiles, theatrical documents, and ephemera to reveal how clothing and textiles were crucial to the making and unmaking of status, gender, sexuality, and religion in the Renaissance. The book is illustrated with a wide range of images from portraits to embroidery.

ANN ROSALIND JONES, Esther Cloudman Dunn Professor of Comparative Literature at Smith College, works on gender ideology and women's writing in early modern Italy, France, and England. Her books include *The Currency of Eros: Women's Love Lyric in Europe, 1540–1620* (1990), an edition and translation of *The Poems and Selected Letters of Veronica Franco*, with Margaret Rosenthal (1998), and the forthcoming facsimile edition of *English Texts from the Querelle des Femmes, 1550–1650*, for the series the Early Modern Englishwoman, 1500–1750 (Ashcroft, USA).

PETER STALLYBRASS is Professor of English and of Comparative Literature and Literary Theory at the University of Pennsylvania. His writing includes *The Politics and Poetics of Transgression* with Allon White (1986/1990), *Subject and Object in Renaissance Culture*, co-edited with Margreta de Grazia and Maureen Quilligan (1996), and *Language Machines: Technologies of Literary and Cultural Production*, co-edited with Jeffrey Masten and Nancy Vickers (1997). His most recent book, *Marx's Coat* (1999), was published in Brazil and will shortly appear in an English version.

Cambridge Studies in Renaissance Literature and Culture

General editor
STEPHEN ORGEL
Jackson Eli Reynolds Professor of Humanities, Stanford University

Editorial board
ANNE BARTON, *University of Cambridge*
JONATHAN DOLLIMORE, *University of York*
MARJORIE GARBER, *Harvard University*
JONATHAN GOLDBERG, *Johns Hopkins University*
NANCY VICKERS, *Bryn Mawr College*

Since the 1970s there has been a broad and vital reinterpretation of the nature of literary texts, a move away from formalism to a sense of literature as an aspect of social, economic, political and cultural history. While the earliest New Historicist work was criticized for a narrow and anecdotal view of history, it also served as an important stimulus for post-structuralist, feminist, Marxist and psychoanalytical work, which in turn has increasingly informed and redirected it. Recent writing on the nature of representation, the historical construction of gender and of the concept of identity itself, on theatre as a political and economic phenomenon and on the ideologies of art generally, reveals the breadth of the field. Cambridge Studies in Renaissance Literature and Culture is designed to offer historically oriented studies of Renaissance literature and theatre which make use of the insights afforded by theoretical perspectives. The view of history envisioned is above all a view of our own history, a reading of the Renaissance for and from our own time.

Recent titles include

A complete list of books in the series is given at the end of the volume.

Renaissance Clothing and the Materials of Memory

Ann Rosalind Jones
Esther Cloudman Dunn Professor
Comparative Literature Program Smith College

Peter Stallybrass
Professor Department of English University of Pennsylvania

CAMBRIDGE
UNIVERSITY PRESS

CAMBRIDGE UNIVERSITY PRESS
Cambridge, New York, Melbourne, Madrid, Cape Town, Singapore, São Paulo

Cambridge University Press
The Edinburgh Building, Cambridge CB2 8RU, UK

Published in the United States of America by Cambridge University Press, New York

www.cambridge.org
Information on this title: www.cambridge.org/9780521786638

© Ann Jones and Peter Stallybrass 2000

This publication is in copyright. Subject to statutory exception
and to the provisions of relevant collective licensing agreements,
no reproduction of any part may take place without
the written permission of Cambridge University Press.

First published 2000
Fourth printing 2007

Printed in the United Kingdom at the University Press, Cambridge

A catalogue record for this publication is available from the British Library

Library of Congress Cataloguing Publication data
Jones, Ann Rosalind.
Renaissance clothing and the materials of memory / Ann Rosalind Jones and Peter Stallybrass.
    p.   cm. – (Cambridge studies in Renaissance literature and culture)
Includes index.
ISBN 0 521 78094 0 (hardback) – ISBN 0 521 78663 0 (paperback)
1. Costume – History – 16th century.
2. Fashion – History – 16th century.
3. Renaissance.
I. Stallybrass, Peter.   II. Title.   III. Series.
GT135.J66   2000
391′.0094′09031–dc21   99–055694

ISBN 978-0-521-78663-8 paperback

Cambridge University Press has no responsibility for the persistence or accuracy
of URLs for external or third-party Internet websites referred to in this publication,
and does not guarantee that any content on such websites is, or will remain,
accurate or appropriate.

In memory of our mothers,

Margaret Puchner Jones
(1918–1991)

Margaret Rosa Stallybrass
(1912–1999)

Contents

Illustrations

Acknowledgments

Full acknowledgments for a book like this would be longer than the book itself. It has taken us an unconscionable length of time to finish, and we couldn't have started or kept going without the help of colleagues (particularly at the University of Pennsylvania and Smith College), librarians, and friends. For help in discovering and gathering materials, we're deeply indebted to Mark Dimination, Kathleen Lynch, the late Ruth Mortimer, Michael Ryan, Dan Traister, Betsy Walsh, Laetitia Yeandle, and Georgianna Ziegler.

Renaissance Clothing and the Materials of Memory participates in a renewed attention to material culture, and we've been particularly influenced by the theoretical and historical work of Arjun Appadurai, the late Janet Arnold, Juliet Fleming, Patricia Fumerton, Marge Garber, Margreta de Grazia, Stephen Greenblatt, Anne Hollander, Meg Jaster, Barbara Johnson, Lisa Klein, Jean MacIntyre, Karen Newman, Stephen Orgel, Rosika Parker, Bill Pietz, Daniel Roche, Jane Schneider and Annette Wiener, Margaret Spufford, Joan Thirsk, and Elizabeth Wilson. The thinking that went into the collective volume *Subject and Object in Renaissance Culture* has been constitutive in the shaping of our book, and we're above all grateful for the work and generously critical comments of Margreta de Grazia.

We have been fortunate over the last ten years to participate in and organize conferences, lectures, and seminars related to the subject of this book. Above all, we should mention "Dressing the Renaissance Woman" at UCLA (thanks to Christine Junkermann, Sandy Rosenberg, and Tita Rosenthal); "History, Anthropology and the Renaissance Text," Birkbeck College, University of London (thanks to Lorna Hutson and Lisa Jardine); the conference on "Europa/Americhe: Sguardi Reciproci" in Genoa; the annual Renaissance conferences at the University of California, Santa Barbara (thanks to Louise Fradenberg and Patricia Fumerton); the Columbia University conferences on "The Material of Culture in Early Modern Europe" (thanks to Jean Howard, Caroline Bynum, and Robert DuPlessis) and on "Early Modern Economies" (thanks to David Scott Kastan and Martha Howell); the Harvard University conference on "Psychoanalysis and Historicism in Early Modern Studies" (thanks to Marge Garber and Carla Mazzio); the Folger Library's conference on "Material London c.1600" (thanks to Lena Orlin and David Underdown); "Veiling and Unveiling in Early Modern Europe" at the University of Michigan (thanks to Diane Owen Hughes, Pat Simons, and Valerie Traub); three "Attending to Women" conferences at the University of Maryland (thanks to Lisa Klein, Claudia Lazzaro, and Karen Newman); the conference on "Fetishism" at the University of Amsterdam (thanks to Webb Keane, Bill Pietz, and Patsy Spyer); our seminars on "Renaissance Fetishisms" at the Folger Shakespeare Library and on "Borrowed Robes: Clothes and the Renaissance Theater" at the Shakespeare

Association of America. We are above all grateful to the participants in these last two seminars. And we have benefitted in more ways than we can say or have been able to record from exchanges and comments when we presented some of this work at the following universities and colleges: Bristol, Cambridge, Columbia, Harvard, Georgia, Kansas State, London, Miami/Ohio, Michigan, Oxford, Princeton, Rochester, Southampton, Sussex, Vanderbilt, Vassar, and Wesleyan.

The writing and completion of this book was made possible by National Endowment for the Humanities fellowships at the Society for the Humanities, Cornell University (and by the uncommon humanity of Mary Ahl, Linda Allen, Aggie Sirrine, and Jonathan Culler) and by a Mellon fellowship at the Folger Shakespeare Library. All those who have worked at the Folger know the immense role that the staff and fellow readers play in Renaissance scholarship. We thank Carol Brobeck, Werner Gundersheimer, Richard Kuhta, Kathleen Lynch, Barbara Mowat, Andy Tennant, Betsy Walsh, Laetitia Yeandle and, above all, Georgianna Ziegler. The many readers who helped us with our project included Peter Blayney, Patrick Collinson, Katherine Duncan-Jones, Reg Foakes, Elizabeth Eisenstein, Andrew Gurr, Betty Hageman, Gil Harris, Natasha Korda, Laurie Maguire, David Miller, Bill Sherman, Bruce Smith, Ian Smith, Susan Snyder, Leslie Thomson, and Marion Trousdale. At the Folger, we are grateful above all for the wonderful comradeship we enjoyed with our fellow Fellows, Patricia Fortini Brown, Sue Lanser, and Jessie Ann Owens.

We have been fortunate with our readers. Stephen Orgel has been a consistently encouraging and challenging critic and an amazingly prompt and helpful editor. Josie Dixon has been supportive and helpful throughout. Karen Newman, Peter Holland, and Patricia Warner made excellent large and small suggestions, nearly all of which we have taken. And the book would have been weaker without the stringent criticisms of Michael Macdonald and Carol Rutter.

Friends, colleagues, and students who have helped in innumerable ways include Rebecca Bach, Crystal Bartolovich, Anne Barton, Pippa Berry, Greg Bredbeck, Ilana Blumberg, Rebecca Bushnell, Dick Corum, Julie Crawford, Stuart Curran, Hilary Dick, Drew Faust, Margie Ferguson, Judy Filc, Irene Fizer, Louise Fradenberg, Carla Freccero, Susan Frye, Swagato Ganguly, Stephen Greenblatt, Linda Gregerson, Kim Hall, Peter Hawkins, Margo Hendricks, David Hillman, Jean Howard, Martha Howell, Lynn Hunt, Margaret Jacob, Rayna Kalas, Webb Keane, Jim Kearney, John Kerrigan, Dominic LaCapra, Claudia Lazzaro, Sara Lennox, Sandy McClatchy, Jeremy Maule, Kerry Moore, Steven Mullaney, Stephen Nichols, Gerry O'Sullivan, John Parker, Karen Robertson, Amy Robinson, Jacqueline Rose, Marilyn Schuster, Marjorie Seneschal, Brenda Silver, Larry Silver, Dan Traister, Susan Van Dyne, Wendy Wall, Dan White, Michael Wilson, and Susan Zimmerman. We have learned a great deal from the textile historian Patricia Warner and the textile artist Nina Payne. And we have had excellent help from research assistants at Smith College; we thank Cameron Tims, Mina Nedialkova and Carolyn Tkach for for their inspired tracking down of illustrations, and Mina also for her useful suggestions about the manuscript as a whole.

It is a delight to acknowledge how much of this book has come into being over food and drink. Its beginnings were with Allon White at Curtis and Schwarz, with Jonathan Dollimore at the Café Lutécia, with Rachel Bowlby and Alan Sinfield at the Waldorf Café, with Margreta de Grazia in her kitchen, with David Scott Kastan in innumerable sports bars, with Anne Hillyer in Oregon and Massachusetts, with Bill and Margo Stallybrass in London and North Leverett. Since then, we have been challenged and stimulated at many shared tables, and we would especially like to thank for their ideas, friendship, and good cheer Michèle Barrett, Leyla Ezdinli, Will Fisher, Juliet Fleming, Marge Garber, Dave Glover, Jonathan Goldberg, Alvia Golden, Jody Greene, Jay Grossman, Barbara Johnson, Liza Jones, David Halperin, Betsey Harries, Peter Hawkins, Lisa Jardine, Cora Kaplan, Peter Kitchell, Sue Lanser, Claudia Lazzaro, Susie Lowenstein, Eliane Maillefer-Stallybrass, Randy McLeod, Jean MacRae, Michael Malone, Brenda Marshall, Jeff Masten, Paul Miller, Michael Moon, Randy Nakayama, Karen Newman, Stephen Orgel, Jessie Owens, Maureen Quilligan, Nina Payne, Donald Rackin, Phyllis Rackin, Jo Radner, Matthew Rowlinson, Mary Russo, Carroll Smith-Rosenberg, Vicki Spelman, Andrew Stallybrass, Wendy Steiner, Gary Tomlinson, Sasha Torres, Valerie Traub, David Wallace, Dan Warner, and Nancy Vickers. We hope that the many people we've doubtless forgotten to mention will forgive us.

Versions of parts of this book have appeared previously in two collections. We are grateful to Cambridge University Press for permission to reprint some of the materials in chapters 1, 4, and 10 and to Routledge for persission to reprint materials in chapter 8.

We dedicate *Renaissance Clothing and the Materials of Memory* to our mothers, the loving spirits who haunt this book, though neither of them lived to see it completed.

Introduction: fashion, fetishism, and memory in early modern England and Europe

Fashion

"Fashion," Elizabeth Wilson writes, "is dress in which the key feature is rapid and continual changing of styles. Fashion . . . *is* change."[1] Wilson is writing about modernity, but it was in the late sixteenth century that the word "fashion" first took on the sense of restless change. Indeed, "the fashion" as referring to "the mode of dress . . . adopted in society for the time being" is first recorded in the *Oxford English Dictionary* from 1568. As "fashion" begins to define the rapid shifting of styles in clothing, it does so largely negatively: fashion is "vnconfirmed"; it is "a deformed theefe"; it makes the wearer turn about "giddily." And yet its demands are inexorable. Not to obey fashion is to become oneself "stale, a Garment out of fashion."[2]

The innovative force of fashion was associated both with the dissolution of the body politic and with the exorbitance of the state's subjects. And this too was registered linguistically. "Fashion" extended its semantic field to include the sense of mere form or pretence ("worshipping God slyghtly for fashyon sake"). And at the very end of the sixteenth century, to "fashion" acquired a new meaning: to counterfeit or pervert. The Englishman's clothes, Thomas Dekker claimed, were not merely perverse but the epitome of treason:

> An English-mans suit is like a traitors bodie that hath beene hanged, drawne, and quartered, and set up in seuerall places: the collar of his doublet and the belly in France; the wing and narrow sleeue in Italy; the shorte waist hangs over a Dutch botchers stall in Utrich; his huge sloppes speakes Spanish; Polonia gives him his bootes; the blocke for his head alters faster than the feltmaker can fit him.[3]

As the clothes themselves condensed the geography of England's trading relations, they dismembered the body of the English subject. Critics of fashion nostalgically conjured up the "russet yeas, and honest kersie noes"[4] that had supposedly preceded the "traitor's body" constituted by foreign luxury goods.

There is nothing particularly surprising to us about this association of "fashion" with the world of expensive imports. But there was something surprising about the connection in the Renaissance. For "fashion" did not have changing styles of clothing as its naturalized referent; rather, it commonly referred to the act of making, or to the make or shape of a thing, or to form as opposed to matter, or to the enduring manners and customs of a society. It was thus the goldsmith's "fashion" (what would later be called "fashioning") which added value to the raw material that he worked upon. One could marvel at the "fassion" (form) of the earth and sky. One could note that "the seed . . . receiueth not *fashion* presently vpon the conception, but remaineth for a time without any figure."[5] Above all, in its verbal form, "fashion" had Biblical resonance. In the Geneva translation, Job says: "Thine hands haue made me, and facioned me wholy rounde about, and wilt thou destroye me?" And the Psalms repeat the notion that God's work is a work of fashioning: "Thine hands haue made me and facioned me"; "He facioneth their hearts euerie one."[6] The spelling of the Geneva Bible ("facion") emphasizes the derivation of "fashion" from the Latin *facio, facere*, to make.

But why, we should ask, did the notion of making come to bear both the glamor and the opprobrium of shifting styles of clothing? "Thine hands haue made me" – Job's response to God, but also and increasingly the response of the fashionable man or woman to his or her tailor. It has become a cliché that "the clothes make the man." Yet modern analysts of "fashion" have found it hard to think through the contradictory implications of the term. Focusing upon "fashion" as the rapid transformation of clothing styles, they have seen it above all as a dazzling play of surfaces. In doing so, they have repeated, even if to critique, the antithesis between clothes as the surface/outside and the person as the inside/depth. That antithesis is certainly not a new one. Indeed, it is embedded in classical theories of rhetoric in which the logic of the argument was its "body" and the figures of speech its "ornament" or "clothing." But this opposing of clothes and person was always in tension with the social practices through which the body politic was composed: the varied acts of investiture. For it was investiture, the putting on of clothes, that quite literally constituted a person as a monarch or a freeman of a guild or a household servant. Investiture was, in other words, the means by which a person was given a form, a shape, a social function, a "depth."

At the end of *Henry IV Part 2*, Hal, even before he is crowned, imagines the assumption of monarchy as the assumption of clothes: "Maiesty" is, he says, a "new, and gorgeous Garment" (5. 2. 44 [TLN 2930]). And then, seeing his brothers' sorrow at their father's death, he assumes that, too, as if it were a garment: "I will deeply put the Fashion on, / And weare it in my heart" (5. 2. 52 [TLN 2938–9]). One could, of course, take this as a sign of Hal's emotional shallowness. But such a reading effaces what is so challenging about the passage to a modern perspective: the notion that "Fashion" can be "*deeply* put on" or, in other words, that clothes permeate the wearer, fashioning him or her within. This notion undoes the opposition of inside and outside, surface and depth. Clothes, like sorrow, inscribe themselves upon a person who comes into being through that inscription.

To understand the significance of clothes in the Renaissance, we need to undo our own social categories, in which subjects are prior to objects, wearers to what is worn. We need to understand the animatedness of clothes, their ability to "pick up" subjects, to mold and shape them both physically and socially, to constitute subjects through their power as material memories. Memories of subordination (e.g. of the livery servant to the household to which he or she "belongs"); memories of collegiality (e.g. of the member of a livery company with his or her guild); memories of love (e.g. of the lover for the beloved from whom he or she receives a garment or a ring); memories of identity itself. For it is through the coronation service – the putting on of a crown and of coronation robes – that the monarch becomes a monarch. It is through the eldest son's ritual inheritance, publicly staged in church, of his father's armor, sword, and shield that the son "becomes" his father (the dead Earl of Arundel transformed into the living Earl of Arundel). It is through the putting on of tire and mantle that the boy actor becomes Cleopatra.[7]

Clothing is a worn world: a world of social relations put upon the wearer's body. "I will deeply put the Fashion on, / And weare it in my heart," says Hal. Sorrow is a fashion not because it is changeable but because fashion fashions, because what can be worn can be worn deeply. That the materials we wear work as inscriptions upon us is an insight more familiar to pre- or proto-capitalist societies than to fully capitalist ones. Anthropologists often have to learn how to understand their own latent care for such materials if they are to understand the cultures they analyze. Panetan, a Tubetube man, asked the anthropologist Martha Macintyre to explain the ring she was wearing, which had been her grandmother's; in response, he said:

When it was her ring it was to show that she was engaged, but you hold that ring to remember your Grandmother. You can look at it every day and keep her in your mind. It is the same with *mwagolu*, the hair necklaces our ancestors wore during mourning. You wear your ring and it shows people [something]. Our widows wore a *mwagolu* and it shows – it reminds – herself and others who look at it.[8]

Clothing (by which we understand all that is worn, whether shoes or doublet or armor or ring) reminds. It can do so oppressively, of course. Why, for instance, should women alone have to recall the dead? But, whether oppressively or not, memory is materialized. Both ring and hair necklace are material reminders, working even when what is recalled is absent or dead. And if they remind others, they also remind the wearers themselves. This is the significance of Hal's "put[ting] on" of sorrow: sorrow will permeate him only if it acts with as much force as mourning clothes.

It is Hal's view, not Hamlet's, that we need to understand if we are to make sense of the constitutive function of clothes in the Renaissance. Hamlet, in a saying which is all too familiar, "know[s] not seems."[9] His mourning garments "seem" but he has that within, he claims, which passes show. But even Hamlet has been misheard in our haste to find a modern subject, untrammeled by the objects that surround him. "'Tis not *alone* my inky cloak," says Hamlet, that shows grief. His grief nonetheless takes the material form of that very cloak. If he claims something in addition to his mourning clothes, those clothes are still a necessary part of his memorializing of his father. But Hamlet's appeal to inner depth, because of its very "obviousness," has less to tell us about clothes in the Renaissance than Hal's notion of "deep" wearing.

In *The Anatomie of Abuses*, Phillip Stubbes captures both Hamlet's sense of the literal superficiality of clothing and Hal's insistence upon the depth of the superficial. Stubbes reviles extravagant apparel as superfluous, a waste of money, a drain upon the English economy. But he dedicates such passion to apparel because it is a superfluity that has the power to constitute an essence. The physical presence of clothes makes them, in his view, more dangerous (more inward, one might say) than the inward workings of corruption. He writes:

Pride is tripartite, namely, the pryde of the hart, the pride of the mouth, & the pryde of apparell, which (unles I bee deceiued) offendeth God more then the other two. For as the pride of the heart & the mouth is not opposite to ye eye, nor visible to the sight, and therefor intice not others to vanitie and sin . . . so the pride of apparel, remaining in sight, as an exemplarie of euill, induceth the whole man to wickednes and sinne.

Pride of the mouth, Stubbes continues,

is not permanent (for wordes flye into the aire, not leauing any print or character behinde them to offend the eyes.) But this sinne of excesse in Apparell, remayneth as an Example of euyll before our eyes, and as a prouocatiue to sinne.[10]

Clothes, unlike the working of the spirit, leave a "print or character" upon observer and wearer alike. And, when excessive, they visibly imprint "wickednes and sinne." Through its ability to "print or character" the wearer, exotic clothing "*transnatureth*" English gallants, "making them weake, tender, and infirme."[11] Clothes give a nature to what previously had no nature; they take an existing nature and transnature it, turning the virtuous into the vicious, the strong into the weak, the male into the female, the godly into the satanic.

Not understanding this "transnaturing" power of clothes, modern commentators (pursuing the purified "spiritual" logic of a later culture) have been puzzled and embarrassed by the central Protestant conflict of Elizabethan England: the vestiarian controversy. According to this later logic, reformers should have been worrying about theology and the nature of the sacraments, not about what clothes the priest should or should not wear. Yet it was precisely the latter question that most exercised radical reformers in later sixteenth-century England. For the priest's clothes were not a matter of indifference, a question of social decorum; rather, the surplice and square cap that Archbishop Parker insisted upon were attacked as the materializations of the Whore of Babylon at the heart of the Church of England. Such vestments were, according to Miles Monopodios, the soldier-hero of a dialogue written by the puritan Anthony Gilby, "worse than lowsie: for they are sybbe [closely related to] the sarcke of Hercules, that made him teare his owne bowels a sunder."[12] Like Hercules's shirt, vestments would poison the wearer, corrupting his inner faith at the same time as they branded him with "the popes liverie."[13] Dr. Turner not only argued that no parishioner should listen to a priest who wore such livery; he also made an adulterer do penance wearing a "popish" square cap and trained his dog to bite the caps of visiting bishops off their heads.[14]

If the radicals believed that Catholics and Satanists placed "all their religion in hethen garments, & Romish raggs,"[15] they themselves saw such clothing as a form of transnaturing. They thus agreed with those whom they opposed on the animating and constitutive power of clothes.[16] As Edmund Spenser observed in *A View of the State of Ireland*: "mens apparrell is commonly made according to their conditions, and their conditions are oftentimes governed by their garments . . . there is not a little in the garment to the fashioning of the minde and conditions."[17] For Milton, the "free" and reformed subject could come into being only if one first discarded the "polluted cloathing" of Catholic ceremony.[18] And in *Areopagitica*, he wrote:

I fear yet the iron yoke of an outward conformity hath left a slavish print upon our necks; the ghost of a linnen decency yet haunts us.[19]

Clothing has the force of an iron yoke, enforcing conformity; clothing has the ability to leave a "slavish print"; clothing is a ghost that, even when discarded, still has the power to haunt.

The rapid development of "fashion" (as we now understand that term) in the Renaissance has obscured the sense in which clothes were seen as printing, charactering, haunting. The centrality of clothes as the material establishers of identity itself is apparent in the early modern institution of livery, the custom whereby people were paid for their services not in cash but in goods, especially clothing. Livery included food and drink; livery cupboards, also known as "dole cabinets," were built to contain the allowance of food and drink given to people working in a household each night. (One from about 1500, now at the Victoria and

Albert Museum, has an openwork wooden front to allow air to circulate around the edibles inside.) But cloth or clothes were so essential a part of such payments that the term came to have the predominant meaning of clothing that identified its wearer as the servant of a particular household or member of a particular liveried group.

Livery acted as the medium through which the social system marked bodies so as to associate them with particular institutions. The power to give that marking to subordinates affirmed social hierarchy: lords dressed retainers, masters dressed apprentices, husbands dressed their wives. But livery, as it dignified the institutions to which it identified people as belonging, also dignified the participants in such institutions. This mutually supportive interplay of loyalties is what was seen as being at risk by writers attacking sartorial anarchy, the tendency of modern Englishmen (and women) to dress as free-floating individuals rather than as representatives of groups defined by shared labors or loyalties. When Stubbes's Spudeus denounces vestimentary disguise, he does so because it is adopted to elevate single agents rather than to affirm the corporate entities that confer genuine social identity:

And as for . . . priuat subjects, it is not at any hand lawful that they should weare silks, veluets, satens, damasks, gould, siluer, and what they list . . . except they being in some kind of office in the common wealth, do vse it for dignifying and innobling of the same. But now there is such a confuse mingle mangle of apparell in *Ailgna* [anagrammatically, Anglia], and such preposterous excesse thereof, as euery one is permitted to flaunt it out, in what apparell he lust himselfe, or can get by anie kind of meanes.[20]

Stubbes wants to reserve sumptuous dress as the proper dignity of high office. He deplores the existing situation in which

it is very hard to knowe, who is noble, who is worshipfull, who is a gentleman, who is not: for you will haue those, which are neither of the nobylitie gentilitie nor yeomanry, no, nor yet anie Magistrat or Officer in the common welth, go daylie in silkes, veluets, satens, damasks, taffeties and such like, notwithstanding that they be both base by byrthe, meane by estate, & seruyle by calling.

Stubbes wants clothes to place subjects recognizably, to materialize identities for onlooker and wearer alike. But he is forced to recognize what he deplores: that clothes are detachable, that they can move from body to body. That is precisely their danger and their value: they are bearers of identity, ritual, and social memory, even as they confuse social categories.

We began by noting that "fashion" as it is now conceived is above all about change. The connection between fashion and change emerged in the Renaissance, and was registered in such phrases as "shifting fashion" and "changing fashion." But fashion-as-change was in tension with the concept of fashion as "deep" making or as enduring cultural pattern. Renaissance "anthropology" developed as the collecting of the manners and customs of other societies. In 1520, Johann Boemus published a small but highly influential book entitled *Omnium gentium mores, leges, & ritus*; in 1555, this was translated into English as *The fardle of façions, conteining the aunciente maners, customes, and lawes, of the peoples enhabiting the two partes of the earth, called Affrike and Asie*.[21] To write about "aunciente" manners and customs was to write about "*façions*." And what characterized such fashions was the supposed fact that, far from shifting, they endured. These "deep" fashions were portrayed in terms both of customs and of costumes. The travel writer recognized the alien by their clothes. But that, of course, presumed that the alien had a particular style of clothing. A society remembered itself visually and tactilely through what it distinctively wore, through its habits.

"Habit" (both clothes and "habitual" behavior) is at the furthest remove from the emergent meaning of "fashion." While the latter came to characterize the lability of an elite, the former suggested the persistence of cultural patterns. As Daniel Defert argues:

> To confuse the meaning of habit [*l'habit*] in the sixteenth century with that of fashion [*la mode*] is an anachronistic illusion. Habit has the original connotation of *habitus*, which implies work upon the body. The serious expression of a judge or the reticence of a virgin, the hairlessness or the tattoos of an Indian, body piercing or asceticism, are all part of the *habit-habitus* which defines the mode of being of established groups and not the free choice of individuals.[22]

Clothing, as "habit," implies a cultural way of life. This was perfectly clear in relation to the "habits" that monks wore. As Defert notes:

> No sixteenth-century French dictionary defines [*habitus monasticus*] simply as "garment." The *habitus monasticus* designates the rule, the way of life, from which the garment cannot be disassociated: *l'habit-habitus* makes the monk . . . The garment is a rule of conduct and the memory of this rule for the wearer as well as for others.[23]

Indeed, anticlerical proverbs warning against the equation of monks' gowns with their behavior (for example, Rabelais's "L'habit ne faict poinct le moine" in his first Prologue, or Queen Katherine's "They should be good men . . . But all Hoods make not Monkes," in Shakespeare's *Henry VIII*[24]) made their point only by denying the antithetical assumption that costume and custom were mutually determining.

One can locate the determining features of "habit" in many early modern societies. Jennifer Wearden, for instance, has fascinatingly traced the clothing of Siegmund von Herberstein, sent by Ferdinand I, the Holy Roman Emperor, as an ambassador to Süleyman the Magnificent in 1541, after most of Hungary had been annexed to the Ottoman Empire. At the Ottoman court, von Herberstein was given a special gown of cloth of gold in which to be presented to the sultan. The gown was both a mark of honor and "a pledge of security." It thus points to the significance of clothing in the constitution of the social, since it was given to him as a gesture of incorporation. Such gowns had traditionally been worn by the sultan himself, so the transfer of the gown was an assimilation of the recipient to the body politic through the medium of the sultan's own body. In a book published in Vienna in 1560, von Herberstein memorialized this transfer by including a woodcut of himself in the gown that the sultan had given him.[25]

But in von Herberstein's gown, one can see the complex intertwining of fashion-as-social-incorporation with fashion-as-transformation. The gown was of Turkish cut, so von Herberstein was being reshaped by the *habitus* of the Ottoman court. Yet the gown itself was hybrid, since it was made from red Italian velvet dating from about 1500. An almost identical piece of velvet is now displayed in the Victoria and Albert Museum. The Ottomans had, indeed, been trading with Genoa since the fourteenth century and ambassadors from the West brought European velvets to Istanbul where they were highly valued. Two splendid kaftans of the late sixteenth and early seventeenth centuries in the Topkapi Sarayi Museum are made of Italian velvet. A kaftan attributed to Osman II (1604–22) is made from a velvet of about 1540, which is probably Italian although influenced by Spanish design, and a similar fabric appears in the gown worn by Eleanora of Toledo when she was painted by

Bronzino about 1544. The history of von Herberstein's gown reminds us of the limitations of a European-focused history that, even as it traces the hybridization of Europe itself through colonialism and trade, imagines its "Others" as "uncontaminated," without history. The latter view was, indeed, the founding myth of anthropology and was in turn to become the founding myth of tourism. The Other is imagined as eternally itself (Turkish, or Navaho, or Ashanti), subject to the mobile and restless observation of the European observer: the Other is changeless, outside of fashion; the European is the marker and bearer of fashion and of historicity itself. Against such an opposition, the gown that Süleyman presented to von Herberstein simultaneously records both the workings of fashion that brought Italian velvets to the Ottomans even as they brought silks, carpets, and other textiles from the Ottoman empire to Europe, and the rituals of incorporation, obligation, and memory.[26]

But such relatively equal gift-exchanges between powerful allies and antagonists were not, of course, the only models of exchange. Conquest, colonization, and slavery also provided the material base for radically unequal "exchanges," in which the appropriated goods were deliberately stripped of their "memories," memories that testified to violence and oppression. In place of such memories, the European colonizers manufactured their own myths of the "exotic," myths which memorialized the supposed heroism of the merchant adventurers (often, like Drake, pirates and slave traders) even as they purified the appropriated goods of the "unheroic" labors of their manufacture.[27] These unequal "exchanges," which tainted and haunted materialization, were one of the causes of an increasing uneasiness among the colonizing powers toward materiality itself. For paradoxically, as Europe imported goods from Asia, Africa, and the Americas in ever greater quantities, it increasingly asserted the detachment of the European subject from those goods. From this new perspective, to attach too much signficance to the power of clothes was to fetishize them – to endow "mere" objects with a power that would increasingly be appropriated as the sole prerogative of subjects.

Fetishism

In the introduction to his important book on *Material Culture and Mass Consumption*, a book that attempts to restore the significance of things to the making of culture, Daniel Miller writes: "an approach to modern society which focuses on the material object always invites the risk of appearing fetishistic, that is of ignoring or masking actual social relations through its concern with the object *per se*."[28] It is extraordinary that, in a book about the necessity and inevitability of objectification, Miller still seems embarrassed before actual objects. We are here at the end of a long trajectory that situates us as subjects (or rather, "individuals") whose interest in objects (including clothes) is characterized by disavowal. To care about things is to appear "fetishistic." Nowhere have antithetical political positions had more in common than in the denunciation of the materialism of modern life and of our supposed obsession with "mere" things. The force of that denunciation depends upon the assumption of a place before the fall into materialism, a society where people are spiritually pure, uncontaminated by the objects around them.[29]

The denunciation often draws either explicitly or (as with Miller) implicitly upon Marx. For was it not Marx who analyzed how an obsession with "material objects" effaced "actual social relations"? The answer is: no. No one has been less embarrassed by material makings than Marx. Marx's critique of capitalism is not a critique of "materialism."[30] Marx, of course, famously developed a theory of fetishism, but it was a theory of the fetishism of the *commodity*, not of the *object*. For Marx, the commodity comes to life through the death of the object. What defines a commodity always lies outside any specific object, and depends upon the equating of a specific quantity of paper cups with a specific quantity of coal or diamonds or academic books. Only if one empties out the "objectness" of the object can one make it readily exchangeable on the market. A shoe manufacturer who is obsessed with the particular shoes that he makes is almost certainly a failed capitalist. Capital needs to pursue profit and thus to detach itself from any particular object so as to transfer itself (to adopt Marx's animistic language) from one style of shoe to another, or from shoes to paper cups or armaments, as the market dictates. Capitalism could, indeed, be defined as the mode of production which, in fetishizing the commodity, refuses to fetishize the object. In capitalist societies, to love things is something of an embarrassment. Things are, after all, "mere" things. To accumulate things is not to give them life. It is because things are not fetishized that, in capitalist societies, they remain theoretically lifeless.[31]

To oppose the materialism of modern life to a non-materialist past is not just wrong; it actually inverts the relation of capitalism to prior and alternative modes of production. As Marcel Mauss puts it in *The Gift*, his founding book on pre-capitalist exchange, objects in such exchanges can be "personified beings that talk and take part in the contract. They state their desire to be given away." Things-as-gifts are not "indifferent things"; they have "a name, a personality, a past."[32] Similarly, in the livery economy of Renaissance Europe, things took on a life of their own. That is to say, one was paid not only in the "neutral" currency of money but also in material that was richly absorbent of symbolic meaning and in which memories and social relations were literally embodied. Yet new forms of trade, colonial conquests, and political and religious conflict within Europe put increasing strain upon these forms of embodiment, finally leading to the radically dematerialized opposition between the "individual" and his or her "possessions." As Igor Kopytoff notes, "this conceptual polarity of individualized persons and commoditized things is recent and, culturally speaking, exceptional."[33]

One aspect of this dematerializing polarity was the development of the concept of the "fetish." In a series of brilliant articles, William Pietz has traced the etymology and the function of the concept in early modern Europe.[34] Pietz argues that "the fetish, as an idea and a problem, and as a novel object not proper to any prior discrete society, originated in the cross-cultural spaces of the coast of West Africa during the sixteenth and seventeenth centuries."[35] The word "fetish" derives from the pidgin *fetisso*, which may be traced to the Portuguese *feitiço* (meaning "magical practice" or "witchcraft"). *Feitiço* has its root in the Latin *facticius*, meaning a manufactured as opposed to a natural object. "Fetish," like "fashion," is derived from the Latin *facere*: to make.[36] There was, as Pietz argues, a long history of distrust of the "made"; Pliny used the term *facticium* to mean "artificial" in the sense of "made to deceive," "factitious." This distrust was elaborated and reinforced by the Church Fathers, who associated *facticii* with idolatry, and hence, by extension, with witchcraft. Pietz notes, though, that the prior history of *facticium* cannot account for its specific emergence within Portuguese West Africa in the

Renaissance to define "the problem of the social and personal value of material objects."[37] For the *fetisso* marks less the earlier distrust of false manufactures (as opposed to the "true" manufactured wafers and images of the Catholic Church) than a suspicion both of material embodiment itself and of "the subjection of the human body . . . to the influence of certain significant material objects that, although cut off from the body, function as its controlling organs at certain moments."[38] The *fetisso* thus represents "a subversion of the ideal of the autonomously determined self."[39]

Moreover, the fetish (in contrast to the free-standing idol) was from the first associated with objects worn on the body – leather pouches, for instance, worn around the neck, containing passages from the *Koran* (37). In 1625, the Cape Verdean trader Andre Donelha met a young African, whom he called Gaspar Vaz, on the Gambia river. To the "distress" of Donelha, Vaz, "a good tailor and button-maker," was wearing "a Mandinga smock, with amulets of his fetishes around his neck." Vaz claimed to be doing so because he wanted to inherit from his uncle, who believed in "the Law of Mohammed." To show his own belief in "the Law of Christ Jesus," he "took off his smock, beneath which he wore a doublet and shirt in our fashion, and from around his neck drew out a rosary of Our Lady" (38). No doubt, the clothes functioned as livery for Vaz, who became Donelha's interpreter. The contrasting garments materialized conflicting cultural and religious identities. Yet there is a surprising overlap between the so-called "fetishes" and the Catholic rosary. Both focus power in a worn object. At the same time, the naming of the the African amulet as fetish disavows the "fetishistic" quality of the rosary. The concept of the "fetish" was thus developed literally to demonize the power of "alien" worn objects (through the association of *feitiço* with witchcraft), while at first preserving the notion of the sacramental object. It was not, in Donelha's view, mistaken to attribute spiritual powers to an object; rather, it was necessary to distinguish between legitimate and illegitimate objects.

By the late 1590s, the Dutch began trading with the Guinea coast and, after the organization of the Dutch West Indies Company in 1621, they displaced the Portuguese. But the Dutch were Protestant. For them, there was no distinction between African fetish and Catholic sacramental object. In 1602, Pieter de Marees wrote of the Akans as having "divers Wispes of straw about their Girdles, which they tie full of Beanes, and other Venice Beades, esteeming them to be their Fetissos, or Saints."[40] Marees called the beads "*Paternosters*," explicitly conflating African "fetish" and Catholic rosary. Marees also refers to the "Ceremonies of their Idolatrous Fetissos":

they hang a Net about the bodie [of their children], like a little shirt, which is made of the barke of a tree, which they hang full of their Fetissos, as golden Crosses, strings with Coral about their hands, feet, and neckes, and their haire is filled full of shels.[41]

The Dutch thus attacked "fetishes" for being, like the objects of Catholic worship, "idolatrous." That is, the fetish was said to personify and spiritualize "dead" matter (although in doing so it might indeed incorporate the demonic). At one level, then, the critique of the fetish became an extension of Protestant attacks upon Catholicism. There had been an extraordinarily intense period of iconoclasm in the Netherlands in 1566, and iconoclasm, like the attack upon vestments, was central to Protestantism throughout Europe.[42] "Idols" were pulled down in churches, the Catholic sacrament itself derided as idolatrous.

Protestants saw idolatry as permeating everday life in the "over-reverence" for "mere" things.[43] The extreme form of such reverence was the devotion to relics, many of which took the form of "fetishes" that had been and could be worn. In 1535, the English reformers disposed of "the vincula S. Petri, which women put about them at the time of their delivery"; "S. Thomas of Canterbury's penneknyff and his bootes"; the Virgin's girdle "which women with chield were wont to girde with"; the "singulum of S. Bernard . . . sometimes lent for pregnant women"; the combs of St. Mary Magdalen, St. Dorothy, and St. Margaret.[44] In 1604, John Reynolds denounced the wedding ring as itself an idol.[45] There was a potentially democratizing impulse in these attacks upon the church's materializations, since they were aimed at the power of an elite to embody its own powers and memories to the exclusion of all others. For it was only the church that could sacramentalize an object, as it was only the priest who could "make" the sacraments themselves. But the attack upon such elite sanctifications slid into a critique of the animating powers of *all* objects. Moreover, as such animations were attributed to a corrupt ecclesiastical hierarchy, they were also and increasingly attributed to the "fetish"-worshipping African. The concept of the "fetish" thus emerged as the colonizing subject simultaneously subjugated and enslaved other subjects and proclaimed his own freedom from material objects.

This disavowal of the object has often been read as merely a ruse. In this view, colonial entrepreneurs proclaimed their detachment from objects, while "fetishistically" collecting them. But this constant repetition of "fetishism" as a category of abuse repeats rather than illuminates the problem. For colonial entrepreneurs did not, at least after the early stages, fetishize objects; on the contrary, they were interested in objects only to the extent that they could be transformed into commodities and exchanged for profit on the market. We need, then, to understand the economic, as much as the religious, motivation of the concept of the fetish. The Dutch, like the Portuguese before them, were intent above all upon finding gold in Africa. As Pietz notes, they discovered it in three states: as gold dust, as lumps of ore, and as the golden *fetissos* worn on the body. It was above all in relation to these latter forms of gold among the Akan ("cast into elaborate and varied animal, vegetable, and mythic forms") that European "fetish" discourse developed. What the concept of the "fetish" marked in economic terms was the site of a crisis in value. For, on the one hand, these fetishes were viewed by Europeans as "trifles" or "toys" and even as peculiarly valueless. Thus Nicolas Villault claimed that the fetishes of the Gold Coast were "inanimate things, and most often so filthy and vile that one would not wish to touch them." [46] On the other hand, if they were made out of gold, they were precisely what the Europeans were in search of. And yet the Akan did not distinguish between their fetishes primarily on the basis of "market value" (gold as against beads or leather). Their interest in the power of the inanimate did not, indeed, seem to be about "value" at all as Europeans understood the concept. Hence, Akan fetishes, even when they were golden, were often composed of a mixture of metals of which gold was only one. As a result, " 'Fetiche Gold' became associated with 'false gold' used in commercial fraud."[47]

The "fetish," then, came into being as a term of religious and economic abuse. As a term of economic abuse, it posited the Akan as a people who worshiped "trifles" ("mere" fetishes) and "valuable" things (i.e. gold) alike. This meant that they could be "duped" (goods that the Europeans considered valueless – beads, for instance –

could be exchanged for "valuable" goods). But it also implied a new definition of what it meant to be European: that is, a subject unhampered by fixation upon objects, a subject who, having recognized the true (i.e. market) value of the object-as-commodity, fixated instead upon the transcendental values that transformed gold into slaves, slaves into ships, ships into guns, guns into tobacco, tobacco into sugar, sugar into gold, and all into an accountable profit. What was demonized in the concept of the fetish was the possibility that history, memory, and desire might be materialized in objects that are touched and loved and worn.

A by-product of this demonization of the fetish was the impossible project of the transcendental subject, a subject constituted by no place, no object – by nothing worn. "The Word *Fetish*," John Atkins wrote in 1737, "is used in a double signification among the *Negroes*: It is applied to dress and ornament, and to something reverenced as a Deity."[48] The transcendental subject of modernity, on the other hand, "knew the value of things" – that is, disavowed any but a financial investment in objects. Clothes could be "fashion" – detachable and discardable goods – but they were less and less likely to be fashionings, the materializations of memory, objects that worked upon and transformed the body of the wearer. The sixteenth and seventeenth centuries, the period of our study, are of particular interest in the history of clothing because clothes were still material mnemonics in metropolitan centers even as they were becoming the commodities upon which international capitalism was founded.

Renaissance clothing

Renaissance Clothing and the Materials of Memory explores the contradictory implications of "fashion" as "deep making" and as circulating goods. The first part of this book, "Material subjects," explores the function of clothes in the constitution of Renaissance subjects. In chapter 1, "The currency of clothing," we explore clothes as payment and as stored and circulated wealth. Servants, whether aristocratic attendants upon the monarch or the poor workers for a yeoman, usually received less of their income in cash than in material goods and benefits: lodging, food, cloth and clothing. Payment in cloth and clothing was a form of bodily mnemonic, marking the wearer's indebtedness to master or mistress. The liveried body, even though the livery was rarely marked as such, stitched servants' bodies to their households. Such clothes were "habits" in the sense that they were persistent material reminders of status and of incorporation. But because of their economic value, clothes could be traded for cash at the pawnbroker or fripper. The value of clothes, then, pointed in antithetical directions: on the one hand, they materialized social status and indebtedness; on the other, they were circulating commodities.

In chapter 2, "Composing the subject: making portraits," we return to the value of clothes to argue that portrait paintings were often supplements to the specific clothes that the sitter wears. That is, whereas portraits have often been seen as founding the interior self, we contend that they display a self that is constituted through investiture. At the simplest, aristocratic clothes were commonly far more expensive than even a full-length portrait by Van Dyck, and portraits were frequently painted to commemorate an occasion, such as a wedding, for which new and costly clothing had been bought. Moreover, the faces of the sitters were often sketched in haste, whereas the clothes were sent to the studios, where they exhibited

CALLOWAY COUNTY PUBLIC LIBRARY
710 Main Street
MURRAY, KY 42071

a patience that their sitters had rarely if ever shown. If the sitters' clothes materialized their status, though, they also inscribed other forms of memory: the memory of the dead, marked by the mourning clothes of the living; family memories (such as the "C4" jewel that Queen Anne so often wore to commemorate her father, Christian IV); the memory of the beloved (through a glove worn in the hat or a locket held open); religious memory (such as an inherited cross, materializing the sitter's Catholicism); memories of incorporation (such as the "livery" that marked Sir Robert Shirley as Persian ambassador). The sitters are permeated by what they wear.

In "composing the subject," the act of material memorialization is arrived at through a collaboration between sitter and artist that itself depends upon a range of hybrid material forms (paints made from Mexican beetles or from lapis lazuli; clothes made from a variety of imported textiles). In chapter 3, "Yellow starch: fabrications of the Jacobean court," we turn to the fears that such material fabications engendered. If a person could be permeated by the material memories of what he or she wore, how could one construct a national subject from "foreign" materials? In the violent attacks upon yellow starch in the early seventeenth century, we trace the xenophobic fear of a subject undone by the contagion of foreign fashion, a fashion that is depicted as Catholic, effeminate, demonic, and poisonous. The poison of yellow starch is above all attributed to the manufacture of women.

In the second part, "Gendered habits," we turn to the relations between women's manufactures – spinning, weaving, needlework – and the attempts to produce "femininity" through the repeated habits of the body. We move here from "habits" in the sense of what is worn to "habits" in the sense of embodied disposition. In chapter 4, "Arachne's web," we explore the tension between the social insistence that women play a crucial part in the production of textiles, above all through spinning, and the fears that women will weave their way into the social fabric, a fear that we explored in the previous chapter. In Velázquez's painting, commonly known as *Las Hilanderas* ("The Spinners"), what is the relation between the plebeian spinners in the foreground and the mythological splendor of the tapestried room in the background? And what do Renaissance commentaries on the myth of Arachne and Minerva tell us about both the relegation of female labor to the uncelebrated work of spinning (Arachne as spider) and the creation of social memory in the narrative weavings of Minerva?

Chapter 5, "The fate of spinning: Penelope and the Three Fates," analyzes transformations of the story of Penelope in the Renaissance as a means of exploring the changing relations between spinning and weaving as forms of women's work. As weaving became dominantly a male profession, Penelope was recast as a spinner rather than a weaver. As a consequence, her woven narrative was displaced by praise for her spinning, the repetitive habit through which she came to embody a wifely industry both virtuous and meaningless. But the fate of Penelope in these retellings is contradicted by the myth of the Three Fates, in which spinning, far from being meaningless work, is the foundation of the social fabric.

In chapter 6, "The needle and the pen: needlework and the appropriation of printed texts," we analyze comparable tensions within needlework. Like spinning for poor women, needlework was the expected labor of aristocratic women, a supposed cure for idleness. But while needlework was often imagined, like spinning, as a bodily habit that inculcated virtue through meaningless repetition, elite women stitched their own versions of the social and political realm into the textile narratives they made. These narratives were usually taken from engraving and pattern books, but in choosing specific models (such as Judith and Holofernes or the Gunpowder Plot) women reworked and transformed the imagined boundaries of the domestic and the political, the private and the public.

In the third part, "Staging clothes," we bring together the preoccupations of the first two parts of the book in an examination of the function of clothing in the English professional theaters. On one hand, we return to the concerns of chapter 1, exploring the relations between livery and the circulation of clothes; on the other, we explore how gender, class, and memory are materialized through worn habits. In chapter 7, "The circulation of clothes and the making of the English theater," we argue that the accumulation and circulation of clothes were constitutive features of the professional theater. The professional companies also offer us an extraordinary insight into the significance of the trade in secondhand clothes, since they recycled clothes from the court, the church, and the city. But while the companies participated in the profitable circulation of clothes, they staged plays that as frequently emphasized clothing as forms of material memory. The companies spent large sums of money on clothes, but again and again they staged the haunting power of a ring, a handkerchief, a detached piece of clothing to connect the present to the past, the living to the dead, the present to the absent. The theater embodied the antithetical possibilities of clothing: as commodities which, in the form of props, took on only temporary meaning during the life of a performance and which could be discarded and replaced; as the imagined materials of memory itself.

In chapter 8, "Transvestism and the 'body beneath': speculating on the boy actor," we turn to the question of the dressing and undressing and the naming, unnaming, and renaming of the boy actor. It is as if the clothes literally re-member the actor's body, "transnaturing" it, as the anti-theatricalists claimed. Indeed, on the professional stage, the gender of the boy actor is usually marked by the donning of specific clothes. In a woman's clothes, he becomes Viola; in a man's, Cesario. Names emerge from prosthetic parts, the clothes that gender and regender the imagined body beneath. The theater plays with the problem of that body, above all in undressing scenes where the attachable parts that constitute a gendered identity begin to be detached. But if the body beneath can be imagined as male, it is also portrayed as permeable, open to transformation by the materials which it assumes and which, in turn, shape it.

In chapter 9, "(In)alienable possessions: Griselda, clothing, and the exchange of women," we address in a different context the problem of dressing and undressing. We here examine what it means to be clothed by the hands of another. The story of Griselda was probably the most popular story of the Renaissance, told by Boccaccio, retold by Petrarch and Chaucer, and performed on the stage. Griselda, a poor peasant, is married by Walter, a prince. But this is possible only because he has first "translated" her, reclothing her as a suitable bride. Later dismissing her, he strips her of her courtly clothes and sends her home in her own undergarment. Dressing and undressing are embodied forms of naming and unnaming. But in the Admiral's Men's staging of *The Pleasant Comodie of Patient Grissill*, Griselda's gray gown, the garment of which she was stripped to reclothe her in courtly livery, hangs upon the stage as a counter-livery, a material mnemonic of her former self.

These material mnemonics are at the center of chapter 10, "Of ghosts and garments: the materiality of memory on the Renaissance stage." We here explore the persistence of the clothes of the dead as material forms of haunting. This is related to the wills in which the dying bequeathe gowns, doublets, petticoats, hose, rings to the family, the friends, the lovers they leave behind. What is the burden of these material memories? Who receives them? How do the living step into the shoes or assume the mantle of the dead? At the same time, the dead themselves return to the stage either in the "ghostly" clothes that they now wear, the sheets which are the shrouds in which they were buried, or, like Achilles and Hamlet's father, in the armor in which they lived. We conclude by looking at the ways in which memory itself is figured as and through permeable cloth and impermeable metal, torn shroud and burnished armor.

Throughout *Renaissance Clothing*, we focus on the making of the human subject through the worn things that shape the body and work as material mnemonics. Yet these worn things can be transferred from body to body; they can be appropriated or stolen. As memories, their meaning is neither given nor fixed. Even crown jewels, the symbols of royal splendor, can lose their magic by being turned back into pawnable commodities. But at the same time, the most worn-out piece of clothing can materialize an absent lover. Our argument is that fabrics were central both to the economic and social fabrication of Renaissance Europe and to the making and unmaking of Renaissance subjects.

Part 1

Material subjects

1   The currency of clothing

Between 1530 and 1609, 11,201 people were apprenticed to eleven major companies (including the main victualling companies) in the City of London. During the same period, 19,913 people (nearly *twice* as many) apprenticed with four of the major cloth and clothing companies (the Clothworkers, the Drapers, the Haberdashers, and the Merchant Taylors).

Between 1550 and 1609, the number of apprentices in the five major victualling companies increased by 132 percent; in the Merchant Taylors, the number increased by 496 percent.[1]

The Broker (skorning to bee called Vsurer) will lend none money, at ten in the hundred, vpon bond or securitie, but (for sooth) Sir if you will bring a pawne worth double the summe you desire, and make a bill of Sale, you shall haue halfe, or sometimes the third of the value thereof . . . *Item*, deliuered to Mistris Spendthrift vpon a bill of Sale, the first of *Ianuarie*, 1618, for a Taffata Peticote, a Beuer Hat, Gold Band, Yellow Feather, a Fanne, a payre of Silke Stockings, Garters, and Roses, -- 3 ll.

Item, for the bill of Sale -- 1s.
Item, for renewing the Bil euery three moneths ------------------------------------ 3s.
Item, for Sir *Huighes* office --- 1s.
Item, for nine moneths interest at 8d. the moneth for the pound -------------- 18s.
------------------------------ *Summa tot.* ------------------------------ 01 ll.---03s.---00d.[2]

Livery and the non-monetary economy

In fully developed capitalist societies, most people are paid in money, through the dole, scholarships, wages, salaries, and so on. In such economies, it is hard to reimagine a society where people were paid in things as much as in money. The "things" in early modern Europe were immensely varied, ranging from food to plate, from land to candles, from fuel to lodging. Among these things, cloth and clothing had a particular significance, suggested by the way in which "livery," which originally meant all sorts of non-monetary payment including food, lodging, and hay for horses came increasingly to be applied to gifts of cloth or clothing. And in its narrowest sense, livery came to mean not just clothing but *marked* clothing, which incorporated retainers and servants into the social body of their master or mistress. On the one hand, such marking could be seen as a privilege, giving protection and security, but from the late fifteenth century marked livery came to be seen by many as an unacceptable form of subordination. In the seventeenth century, Sir Thomas Overbury describes a "Servingman" as "*a creature, which though he be not drunk, yet is not his owne man. He tels without asking who ownes him, by the superscription of his Livery.*"[3] The servitude of livery is emphasized by Milton in *Samson Agonistes*, when the Philistines clothe the defeated Samson "[i]n their state Livery," thus making "thir dreadful enemy thir thrall." And Joseph Hall preached, "Doe wee not laugh at the groome that is proud of his Masters horse, or some vaine whiffler, that is proud of a borrowed chaine? So ridiculous are we to be pufft vp with that, whereof we must needs say, with the poore man, of the hatchet, *Alas master it is but borrowed.*"[4]

By the sixteenth century, the livery system in its narrowest sense – that is, the dressing of retainers in the identifying livery of their household – was rapidly breaking down. Indeed, the Tudor monarchy attempted, with considerable success, to erase the "badges of factious dependance," replacing them with royal badges (the Tudor rose, the Beaufort portcullis, the red rose of Lancaster). These marks of allegiance to the monarch were used to adorn clothes, to make up jewelry, and to display on doorways, chimneys, ceilings, and in windows.[5] But even these forms of marked livery declined during the sixteenth century.

The decline of marked livery, though, should not obscure the extent to which payment in things remained central to early modern economies throughout Europe. At Elizabeth I's court, "watching" liveries were distributed from the Great Wardrobe and "summer" liveries directly from the Exchequer, and they could take the extravagant form of scarlet cloth, gold spangles and gold embroidery.[6] One can get a sense of the economic significance of court liveries by comparing the value of salaries with that of the "gift" of clothes, textiles, and clothing accessories. The highest wages for women at court, for instance, were for the Ladies and Gentlewomen of the Privy Chamber and Bedchamber. In 1589, these women were paid either £33. 6s. 8d. or £20 (of the three Bed Chamberers, Lady Cobham received £20 and Lady Carew and Blanche Parry £33. 6s. 8d. each).[7] The clothes, jewels, and materials that they were given were undoubtedly worth much more than their wages. Gifts of clothes by Elizabeth to the women attending on her included her own purple velvet gown, given to Mary Howard, her own French gown and kirtle, refashioned for Lady Anne Russell, six yellow satin gowns with green velvet and silver lace, a French gown of black velvet with laces of Venice silver, eleven identical gowns made of crimson velvet, blue taffeta, murrey satin, and 42lb. 4oz. of lace.

There are fuller livery accounts for a woman known as Ippolyta the Tartarian, who was possibly a child, but more likely a dwarf. In 1564, she was granted a "Gowne & kirtle of damaske gardid withe velvett drawne oute with sarceonett with poyntynge Ribande lined with cotton fustian and linnin Item one other Gowne and kirtle of grograyne chamlett garded with velvett poyntynge Ribande Item one other gowne of clothe And a kirtle of grograyne drawne out with sarceonett as afore."[8] The accounts for the *other* items of clothing (smocks, thread, a scarf, a hat, etc.) given to Ippolyta in 1564 have survived, and they amount to £15. 8s. 10d. Not only does this total not include the figure for the expenditure on her gowns and kirtles, but it also does not include additional clothing like furs (she was given five dozen black coney skins in 1569).[9] In other words, the livery of Ippolyta the Tartarian must have cost significantly more than the wages of Lady Cobham for a year's work. We can only guess at the cost of Lady Cobham's clothes.

Nor was the expenditure on Ippolyta in any way atypical. If we turn to the Italian jester, Monarcho (mentioned in *Love's Labour's Lost* as "[a] Phantasime, a Monarcho, and one that makes sport / To the Prince"),[10] we find that in 1569, the year of his arrival at court, he was not only granted an elaborate costume but also had his gown and jerkin furred by Adam Bland, the queen's skinner, with twelve fox skins and 151 lamb skins. In 1574, Monarcho's new gown was furred "with twelve white fox and forty-six hare skins, powdered with sixty black genets tails."[11] In addition to livery, other gifts of clothing to court entertainers were frequent. In 1575, William Shenton, a court fool, received, over and above his livery, "sixe Shirtes: two quilted nighte Cappes and sixe peire of Showes," as well as bedding.[12] The Folger Inventory of the queen's clothes in 1600 notes clothes "Taken as Fees" (including a robe of purple velvet of the Order of the Garter) as well as a much larger list of clothes, buttons, and jewels lost or stolen.[13] Recent work like Janet Arnold's on the Elizabethan court demonstrates that gifts of apparel were a constitutive gesture of social organization.[14] Clothing was more binding than money, both symbolically, since it incorporated the body, and economically, since a further transaction had to take place if you wanted to transform it into cash via the fripper or broker.

"Livery" in the broad sense – that is, the payment of dependents in food, lodging, and clothing – continued well into the nineteenth century. Karl Marx's servant, Helene Demuth, was never given a regular wage, and she lived mainly off non-monetary "gifts."[15] And the poorer you were, the more significant was livery as a crucial part of your income. The accounts of the Berkshire farmer Robert Loder in the early seventeenth century show that he paid yearly salaries of £1. 4s. for a boy, 30s. for a maid, and £2 for a shepherd; but Loder calculated that he spent about £10 a year for each member of the household on food, clothes, and perquisites.[16] Similarly, Ralph Josselin, a seventeenth-century clergyman, paid his servants an average of about £2. 10s. a year, but he spent about £10 a year for their food and clothes.[17] When John Dee engaged Lettice as his maid, he paid her the high salary of four nobles, but he still supplemented this with "an apron a payr of hose and shoes," while Thomas Hollis gave his servant "some old clothes and a suit of laced clothes, now too little for me" so as "to induce him to continue like a faithfull and attentive servant."[18] Sir Ralph Verney paid Luce, his wife's chambermaid, £3 a year, although she was a gentleman's daughter. Bess, the other servant who stayed with Verney during his exile in France, was paid only £2 a year, but in 1646 Verney bought her a pair of "trimed gloves" that cost £1. 5s. or more than half her year's wages.[19] While new clothes were a crucial part of the payment of servants, so also were hand-me-downs. As Sara Mendelson and Patricia Crawford remark,

One of the main perquisites maidservants and female labourers received from employers was their cast-off but still highly-valued clothes. Among many items of clothing and linen in her will, Celia Fiennes made several bequests to female servants: "Let my washer woman have my cotton night gown and one paire of ordinary couch sheets and ordinary apron."[20]

Of course, livery in the form of cloth or clothes was only one of the material forms in which wages were supplemented. One gets a detailed insight into the nature of the "supplementary" economy in the Earl of Salisbury's attempts to put the King's Works (responsible for royal building) on a clearer financial footing in 1609. The investigation that he ordered came to the conclusion that Simon Basil, the King's Surveyor, made only a small percentage of his annual wealth from his salary. Basil was paid £45. 12s. 6d. a year. The new provisions attempted to make him "fully" salaried at £284. 5s. 10d. a year (a raise of over 500 percent), on condition that he gave up his alternative sources of income. These were reckoned as £73 a year for food and lodging; £12. 13s. 4d. for livery; £73 for dead men's pay (that is, nonexistent workers' wages which Basil claimed and pocketed); £80 for the surplus building materials that Basil ordered and sold off on the side. It is quite extra-ordinary from a modern perpective that Basil was not accused of corruption. In fact, Salisbury's 1609 Orders draw up similar accounts for the Comptroller (paid £27. 7s. 6d. but with a presumed income of £145. 6s. 10d.), for the Master Mason (paid £18. 5s. but with a presumed income of £103. 12s. 10d.), for the Master Carpenter (paid £18. 5s. but with a presumed income of £113. 7s. 6d.), for the Paymaster (paid £36. 10s. but with a presumed income of £139. 18s. 4d), and for the Purveyor (paid £12. 3s. 4d. but presumed to be making £57. 15s. 10d.). In other words, most of the officers of the King's Works were presumed to be making four to six times their official salaries. Moreover, it is almost certain that these are underestimates, and that many of their earlier practices of making money continued in reduced form after the new salary scales came into effect.[21] Indeed, to call the additional ways in which the officers of the King's Works made money "supplementary" reverses the actual economic situation in which it was the salaries that were supplementary.

Within the non-salary economy, livery was only one form of income, and its economic significance varied dramatically. Bess's livery (of which the gloves that Verney gave her were only a part) made up a far higher percentage of her income than Simon Basil's livery (even though his was valued at over £12, or more than six times Bess's annual wages). But servants' liveries (in the broad sense) were often worth more than their official wages. In 1673/4, Sir John Nicholas paid £7. 15s. 0d. for his "mens wages," whereas for "Liverys" for his coachman, groom, and two "footeboys," including not only display clothing but also daily necessaries like shoe repairs, he paid £27. 6s. 1d.[22]

The "value" of livery, though, cannot be fully calculated in monetary terms. Livery was a form of incorporation, a material mnemonic that inscribed obligations and indebtedness upon the body. As cloth exchanged hands, it bound people in networks of obligation. In most modern societies, dominated by neutral exchanges of money, the creation of bonds, of debts, and of liberties through the physical medium of clothes appears increasingly strange. We are rarely connected in any personal way to our employers by our wages, any more than we are personally connected to the supermarket through the plastic cards or the pieces of paper and metal with which we trade. In a livery society, though, things take on a life of their own.[23] Payment is made not only in the "neutral" currency of money but also in material which is richly absorbent of symbolic meaning and in which memories and social relations are literally embodied.

The material mnemonics of livery are central to Renaissance accounts of Genesis. Indeed, such accounts often analyzed the origin of clothes in the garden of Eden as the founding of a livery system. Adam and Eve vainly tried to clothe themselves in fig leaves. But they were reclothed by God: "Vnto Adam also and to his wife did the Lord God make coates of skinnes, and clothed them."[24] In *Paradise Lost*, Milton describes how Christ pities Adam and Eve "[b]efore him naked to the aire":

> As Father of his Familie he clad
> Thir nakedness with Skins of Beasts.[25]

Milton sees Christ as fulfilling the same function that Robert Loder assumed for his family and servants: the clothing of his "Familie" in livery.

For Milton, the livery that Christ gives is a "robe of righteousness," but it was equally common to see the skins of dead animals which Adam and Eve assume as the livery of death – the memory of an inescapable debt. As Gervase Babington put it, "The beginning of apparrell is heere to bee noted, that it was when wee had sinned, and so is vnto vs at this daye no otherwise, then if an offender should weare an halter all his life in remembrance of his fault."[26] While commentators argued over just what these clothes were a memorial to, they all agreed that they were livery. Genesis 3. 21, Lancelot Andrewes writes, is "the opening of Gods warehouse, and giving thence his liverie aparrell." Adam and Eve "came hereby into Gods favor, by wearing his liverie they became his servants, and so of his household: They are of the Princes house, to whom he giveth bread and cloathing."[27] The garden of Eden is, for Andrewes, no different from a Renaissance prince's court: both model relations of domination and subordination through inscriptions upon the body. Yet the material mnemonics of livery increasingly confronted the marketplace of circulating fashions, in which "the Princes house" also played a dominant role.

Circulating clothes

"Over a period of five years from 1608 to 1613, James I bought a new cloak every month, a new waistcoat every three weeks, a new suit every ten days, a new pair of stockings, boots, and garters every four or five days, and a new pair of gloves every day."[28] The clothes of the monarch were a miniature industry in themselves, but the king was also at the center of a much larger engine of fashion: the court. One can calculate the power of this engine both through the detailed expenditures of individuals and through the Office of the Wardrobes. In 1610, the Earl of Rutland spent £53. 15s. on crimson velvet and ermine, while, in the same period, the Earl of Salisbury "was buying crimson cloth of tissue at £4. 12s. a yard, figured satin at 22s. a yard, and velvet at 26s. a yard." "Twenty years later," Lawrence Stone writes, "a relatively modest peer like William Lord Spencer was spending £14. 15s. 3d. on a scarlet cloak, £1. 14s. on a pair of carnation silk stockings, and £22. 16s. 2d. on a black taffeta suit and cloak." And if luxury textiles were expensive, embroidery and jewels were even more so. In 1634, Lord Spencer paid £33. 8s. for a black satin suit and cloak. The silk twists to embroider his clothes cost a further £15 and the embroidering cost £28. 16s. (at 2s. a day for 288 days). In 1612, the embroidery for a masquing suit cost £84, while the embroidery for Henrietta Maria's confinement beds came to £675 in 1630 and £772 in 1631.[29]

The records of the Office of the Wardrobes give a picture of astronomic increases in expenditure in the early seventeenth century. In the last four years of Elizabeth I's reign, the average annual expenditure was £9,535. Under Lord Dunbar at the beginning of James's reign, expenditure increased nearly fourfold to a yearly average of £36,377. Sir Roger Aston, Master of the Wardrobes from 1606 to 1612, reduced the yearly spending to £28,492, only for Lord Hay, who took over the office in 1612, to increase expenditure again. Here are the *low* estimates for Hay's expenditures:

1612–13:   £65,999. 1s. 2d.
1613–14:   £45,109. 18s. 6d.
1614–15:   £36,934. 0s. 0d.
1615–16:   £43,163. 0s 0d.[30]

Lionel Cranfield, to whose moneylending and pawnbroking activities we return below, took over as Master of the Wardrobes in 1617 by underbidding Lord Hay.

Cranfield claimed that he could run the Wardrobes for £20,000 by cutting out extravagance and graft. The official fees for running the office were £221. 13s. 4d. a year, but Cranfield estimated that Lord Hay had in fact been making £4,000 a year, i.e. nearly twenty times his salary. Cranfield was astonishingly successful in cutting back on expenses and he seems to have tried to do away with the regular system by which profits came in the form of "excess" material goods and kickbacks. In other words, he appears to be, and in many way was, a modern bureaucrat. But this needs to be set against the fact that everything he saved under £20,000 he pocketed – which resulted in an astounding personal profit of £7,000 a year. One can only guess, then, what Lord Hay was really making.

It is clear from Cranfield's personal accounts that, on a radically reduced scale, he was also taking the usual perks. Although he claimed that most of "the rich cloths and handfuls of cloth" that came his way he "did forbear to take," he took £2,000 of unused black cloth from Queen Anne's funeral and sold it, and he admitted to accepting "cloths" and "stuffs" as well as "monies." Moreover, in his private jottings, especially for the 1630s, he refers to the sale of luxury textiles, including rich cloth of tawny damask, cloth of gold, cloth of silver, and black velvet, and it seems probable that these were some of his perks from the Wardrobes.[31]

Two features of the Office of the Wardrobes' records are worth stressing. First, they allow us to see how some of the richest courtiers made their profits. Even Cranfield, who was trying to introduce a "modern" accountancy system, never pretended to be living off his salary. He was not expected to, nor could he possibly have done so. But while he made his profits largely in the form of money, even he hung on to the material perquisites that accounted for so much of Lord Hay's wealth: the accumulation of textiles, expensive thread, clothes, and jewels. Secondly, this accumulation employed, directly or indirectly, a small army of spinners, weavers, drapers, mercers, tailors, embroiderers, goldsmiths, and importers. The court was, indeed, an engine for the transformation of London. As Lawrence Stone notes,

The phenomenal growth of London was largely due to its unique role as a centre for luxury goods and professional services . . . It was alleged that the number of mercers in London rose from 30 to 300 in the second half of the sixteenth century. By 1618 there were 148 foreign tailors in London, and nine years later many Scottish tailors were to be found in Westminster.[32]

We can also begin to account for the extraordinary increase in the number of apprentices being trained as Merchant Taylors between 1550 and 1609, an increase of 496 percent.[33] Elizabeth I spent large amounts on clothes and jewelry both for herself and as marks of favor, but she was restrained in comparison to James I in the first half of his reign.[34]

The currency of clothes depended in the first instance upon the economic value stored up in the materials from which they were made. This was, as we noted above, central to the functioning of livery. Clothing, as a form of material memory, incorporated the wearer into a system of obligations. But it was also a real form of payment. Renaissance clothes were piecemeal assemblages of parts, every part exchangeable for cash until completely worn out. (Even when worn out, linen provided the valuable rags used to make paper.) Livery as a memorializing system can be set against both the circulation of clothes outside the structures of court, household, and guild and the translations of materials from one garment to another, from overgarments to undergarments, from gold to gold thread back to gold again. Inventories, wills, and pawnbroking records constantly remind us not only that clothes were transmitted, but that they could be disassembled into their parts.

In *Patterns of Fashion*, Janet Arnold shows in photograph after photograph the myriad eyelet holes through which laces were passed to attach hose to doublet, sleeves to kirtle, busk to bodice, codpiece to hose, one part of a "body" to another part to make "a pair of bodies" (i.e. a bodice).[35] The intricacies of lacing meant that dressing and undressing were social processes that required (especially for the rich, although not for them alone) other pairs of hands. It is no mere fiction that Desdemona needs the hands of Emilia to undress, that Macbeth needs Seyton to put on his armor. The *work* of dressing and undressing was itself a constant reminder of the significance of clothes in the daily makings and unmakings of the body. In 1646, Mary Verney wrote anxious letters to her husband, in exile in France, about the possible loss of her "chamber maide," Luce Sheppard. Without such a maid, she would not be able to travel to France to see her husband as there would be no one capable of dressing her. In fact, Mary Verney had another servant, Bess, but Bess was of a different class from Luce (who was a gentleman's daughter), and not trained in the complexities of aristocratic fashion: "I cannott take Bess next to me because I know she cannott starch and beside I know she can neavor learne to dress me. I am in a great straight."[36] Dressing and undressing the fashionable was a major undertaking.

The time-consuming nature of dressing was the cause of satire levelled specifically against women. In *Lingua*, Tactus (touch) tries to assert his own status by putting on a pageant of Venus and Cupid, kissing and touching each other. But Venus isn't ready for her part:

fiue houres agoe I set a douzen maides to attire a boy like a nize Gentlewoman: but there is such doing with their looking-glasses, pinning, vnpinning, setting, vnsetting, formings and conformings, painting blew vaines, and cheekes, such stirre with Stickes and Combes, Cascanets, Dressings, Purles, Falles, Squares, Buskes, Bodies, Scarffes, Neck-laces, Carcanets, Rebatoes, Borders, Tires, Fannes, Palizadoes, Puffes, Ruffes, Cuffes, Muffes, Pussles, Fussles, Partlets, Frislets, Bandlets, Fillets, Croslets, Pendulets, Amulets, Annulets, Bracelets, and so many lets, that yet shee is scarce drest to the girdle: and now there's such a calling for Fardingales, Kirtlets, Busk-points, shoo-tyes &c. that seauen Pedlers shops, nay all Sturbridge Faire, will scarce furnish her: a Ship is sooner rigd by farre, then a Gentlewoman made ready.[37]

This is, of course, misogynist exaggeration, despite the irony that it is a boy who is being dressed. Yet the satire suggests many of the elements that did indeed go into the construction of a lady. What it effaces is the fact that many of these labors were equally crucial to the construction of a gentleman, who, no less than a lady, required the attendance of others. His ruff must be pinned to his pickadil; his sleeves must be laced or pinned to his doublet; lace cuffs had to be pinned to the bottom of the sleeves; his hose must be laced to his doublet. Moreover, there was a steady increase in the number of men's buttons during the sixteenth century. M. Channing Linthicum notes records for "five dozen [buttons] to a jerkin; four and a half dozen to a doublet; two dozen to a cloak; seventeen to thirty-six dozen to a cassock, often with a corresponding number of buttonholes."[38] Nor were such labor-intensive fastenings the monopoly of the court. Indeed, in Middleton and Rowley's *The Old Law*, a courtier mocks old men's fashions (which bring fashion into disrepute), claiming that "[t]hey love a doublet that's three hours a-buttoning."[39]

Buttons, pins, points (laces usually with a metal tag at the end), ribbons, and hooks and eyes held detachable parts together. In the seventeenth century, hooks and eyes were increasingly used instead of points to attach men's hose to their doublets, and no doubt this made dressing somewhat less dependent on the labors of others (although the attachments had to be made at the back as well as at the front and sides). In *Dick of Devonshire*, an anonymous play probably written in 1626 or shortly after, the servant Buzzano claims that "Taylors are ye wittyest knaves/ y^t live by bread":

In old time gentlemen would call to their men, & cry, come trusse me; now ye word is, Come hooke me; for every body now lookes so narrowly to Taylors bills (some for very anger never paying them) that the needle lance knights in revenge of those prying eyes, putt so many hookes & eyes to every hose & Dubblet.[40]

Buzzano is here mocking the shift from trussing with points to using hooks and eyes, claiming that the move to a greater simplicity of dressing has been sabotaged by tailors, "the needle lance knights," who pad out their bills with a proliferation of fastenings.

Clothing was a composition of detachable parts, so garments could be disassembled. In the Stowe Inventory of Elizabeth's wardrobe, there are multiple entries for gold or jeweled buttons and aiglets, as well as entries for a cap band and for "Sondrie Parcells," including "one parte of a furre of Sables for a night gowne" and (crossed out) "one paire of Lawne sleeve of Cutworke."[41] And in the inventory of Lady Jane Stanhope's apparel, made in 1614, there is a separate category of "Boddis and sleues" (each bodice recorded as "a paire of boddis"), while linings, facings, lace and other emboidery of gold and silver are carefully noted.[42] The piecemeal nature of clothing is fully apparent both in the clothing parts that Philip Henslowe accepted as pawnbroking pledges and in the way he describes "complete" garments. The pledges include a pair of embroidered sleeves, embossed with gold; an embroidered waistcoat in five pieces; the lining for a shag cloak; a piece of taffeta for an apron; a remnant of green cloth; five pieces of linen; cloth for a petticoat, lace, and a piece of tuft taffeta; a silk fringe and braided lace; twenty-six silver buttons. These are the parts out of which clothing could be assembled.

On the other hand, Henslowe records "complete" garments in terms of their parts. He lists a cloak of silk grosgrain lined with velvet and "layd" with buttons; a murrey-colored cloak lined with serge, "layd" with three laces and faced with pinked taffeta; a woman's gown embroidered with lace of silk and gold; a "fayer" black cloak with four broad laces, faced with branched velvet; a woman's gown embroidered with lace and spotted with bugels; a violet cloak, "layd befor" with buttons, "don a bowt" with lace, and faced with serge; a "crane colerd" fustian doublet, embroidered with three laces of black silk and gold.[43] These descriptions were so detailed, no doubt, for the sake of differentiating between pledges. But they simultaneously record the detachable parts out of which clothes were constructed. Above all, for the more valuable garments, they emphasize the significance of gold and silver "lace."

"Lace" today usually means decorative cloth made of white linen. But in the

Renaissance, there were three quite different clothing parts that went by the name of "lace" or "laces": embroidered linen for collars, cuffs, and handkerchiefs (i.e. what we now call "lace"); "laces," made of ribbon, braid, or leather, sometimes with gold tips at the ends (whence the name "points"), used for tying clothing together; and, most important of all in inventories, decorative braids of gold and silver that were added to outer garments.[44] In Henslowe's list in our previous paragraph, every reference to "lace" is to these latter decorative braids. It is this form of lace that Elizabeth I referred to when she commanded her tailor, Walter Fyshe, to make a gown for Fraunces Vaughan with "one brode and two narrowe lases of venice silver," and that is recorded in her gift to Lady Elizabeth Drury's daughters of clothes "laced alover with silver lace."[45]

"Lace," in this sense, was made by spinning gold or silver wire around a core of silk thread. The Company of Gold and Silver Wyre-Drawers, first incorporated in 1623, later received a coat of arms. The arms bear the tools of the company's trade, supported by an Englishman, holding in his hand a hank of silk, and an American Indian wearing an Eastern crown (representing gold).[46] The value of this lace was directly proportionate to the quantites of gold and silver used. Astronomic quantities were used by Henry VIII at the Field of the Cloth of Gold both for clothes and for tents and pavilions.[47] But this was no one-off expense. Italian merchants were paid large sums for importing cloth of gold, made from gold thread. And we have records for the expense of gold and silver in specific garments. In 1536–7, Henry VIII paid the gold-drawer £8. 7s. for "Pypes and Pyrles" of gold to embroider a lady's gown, and in 1553, the embroiderer William Ibgrave presented his accounts for work on a jerkin, a doublet, and a pair of hose: he charged £18. 13s. 4d. for the silver used and £9. 15s. for the labor.[48] In addition, clothes could have pieces of gold or silver sewn on to them. John Parr, one of Elizabeth's embroiderers, attached "hanging spangles," "a garland of silver purle," and "hanginge spangles, pincht plate, spangles" (all forms of gold or silver) to clothes.[49]

Lace was thus a material constituent of the currency of clothes. This currency at first depended entirely upon imports, and Italian cloth of gold and silver dominated the market. But in 1545, Andrew Schultz brought the art of making gold and silver wire to Augsburg, and in 1592, Frederick Hagelscheimer began to prepare spinnable gold and silver thread in Nuremberg. From Germany, the art spread to France and England. Mary Forest claimed that she and others had been apprenticed to a Frenchman, Jean Rosineall, who resided in London in 1596, while in 1611, a Frenchwoman was brought to London to teach apprentices to make gold and silver thread under the patronage of the Countess of Bedford.[50]

From 1616 to 1624, a full-fledged crisis arose due to the increase in production of gold thread. The Goldsmiths' Company complained that their craft was being undermined; a group of monopolists (most notoriously Mompesson) was variously supported and attacked by James I and Parliament; and proclamations were in turn enforced and repealed against the making of gold and silver thread as "a great waste and consumption of Coyne and Bullion of the Realme." Thomas Violet, appointed Surveyor of the Manufacture of Gold and Silver Wyre and Thread in 1636, estimated the annual value of the gold and silver used in the industry as £100,000.[51] So valuable was gold lace that one of the goldsmith's tasks was to extract the gold from it when it was no longer of any use for trimming clothes. Even cheaper forms of "lace" (i.e. lace without silver or gold) were a major expenditure. Henslowe records these braids in his pawnbroking records, and he often numbers them. A kirtle has "j bellemente lace"; a cloak has "vj frenge laces"; a petticoat has "iij laces."[52] The value of clothes was thus directly connected to the expense of the materials from which they were made. Because of their value, the materials often had long and complex afterlives.

Even the court, although an engine of new fashions, stored up, recirculated, and translated its old clothes. In 1617, the Earl of Dorset had "all his Old Cloths in purple stuff" translated into furniture fabric. And a note in the 1619 inventory of his clothes states that two caparisons (coverings for horses) were used to make a canopy and to cover a chair, stools and cushions in the Long Gallery at Knole.[53] In *Gone with the Wind*, Scarlett O'Hara, in what appears to be a simple reversal of Dorset's translation of his clothes into fabric, pulls down "the moss-green velvet curtains" of Tara to make a new dress in which to see Rhett Butler. But the differences are as important as the similarities. Margaret Mitchell is trying to conjure up a scene of gentry impoverishment, in which the "normal" routines of fashion have been dislocated.[54] It is a sign of Scarlett's desperation that she has to turn curtains into clothes. Dorset, on the other hand, is simply obeying the norms of his society, in which fabrics were reused by rich and poor alike.

In the Renaissance, even monarchs stored up and recirculated clothing. In 1559, Elizabeth gave to the brother of Montmorency "valuable clothes which had belonged to King Edward her brother," and clothes originally belonging to Edward VI and Mary are recorded in the Stowe inventory in 1600. As Janet Arnold further notes, Elizabeth remodeled her own clothes both for her own use and as gifts. She kept a gown that she had been given by the Earl of Warwick for twenty-five years, during which time it was spruced up several times with additional embroidery and three new borders made by John Parr. In 1577, she gave one of her kirtles to Mary Scudamore without alterations, and she made many other gifts of her own clothes to her ladies-in-waiting.[55] Scaramelli, the Venetian Secretary, wrote that, after Elizabeth's death, her clothes were taken over and remade by Anne of Denmark:

In the late Queen's wardrobe [Anne of Denmark] found six thousand dresses, and though she declared that she would never wear cast clothes, still it was found that art could not devise anything more costly and gorgeous, and so the Court dressmakers are at work altering these old robes, for nothing new could surpass them.[56]

Elizabeth's old clothes were also recirculated as masque costumes. In 1603, Arbella Stuart wrote that Queen Anne "intendeth to make a mask this Christmas, to which end my Lady of Suffolk and my Lady of Walsingham have warrants to take of the late queen's best apparel out of the tower at their discretion."[57] The office of the Revels also played a prominent part in the recirculation of old clothes, translating materials from one garment to another: in one entry, hanging sleeves were translated to headdresses and undersleeves, and "ageyne from thence in to Shoes."[58] Both inside and outside the court, from courtiers to servants and actors, cast-off clothes and jewels circulated as reused parts, as gifts, as livery.

Pawnbrokers

"Cast" clothes could circulate as gifts or livery, but they could also be exchanged for cash. Pawnbrokers played a crucial role in the exchange of clothes and jewels as commodities. The word "pawn" itself probably derives from the Latin root *pannus*, meaning cloth or rag. (The French "*pan*" which meant a skirt also meant a pledge.) Before the advent of the modern bank, men and women of every class *stored up wealth in clothes*. Modern scholars have failed to understand that clothes were an important way to store wealth because they have failed to imagine what people without bank accounts did with the money they had. As Robert Lopez notes, gold and other forms of "money" were often worn as clothes and jewels.[59] This currency of cloth and gems could, when necessary, be exchanged for cash.

As the surviving records throughout Europe show, every social class pawned goods.[60] This is surely the most notable shift between the Renaissance and today, when it is mainly the poor who turn to pawnbrokers. In Renaissance Florence, borrowers included patricians, notaries, bakers, weavers, and secondhand dealers; in Bruges, the Count of Flanders pawned the crown jewels and the Countess of Bar a gold coronet to the same pawnbroking business that had rules about what they would and would not accept from weavers; in Nivelles, the clientele included barons, knights, burghers, the lower clergy, craftsmen, and tenants; in Sienna between 1483 and 1511, the clientele included a tailor, a book publisher, a stationer, priests, doctors, lawyers, members of the patriciate, and eleven women, including a nun and the daughter of a dyer. One also gets a sense of who was trying to use pawnbrokers by noting what could *not* be pledged. In Bruges, it was forbidden to lend money on church ornaments and vestments (this seems to have been a widespread prohibition). Despite the prohibition, a dalmatic from St. Walburge was in fact used as a pledge. In Louvain, students were forbidden to pawn their school texts. In Troyes, one could not pawn agricultural instruments.[61] But the important point is the wide variety of the pawnbrokers' clientele, and the fact that it included the elite.

In England in 1297, Edward I borrowed 4,600 li. from the Lombards on the security of jewels and plate worth 7,015 li. (an unusually small pledge for such a large sum, but princes were often given special deals in return for political favors and protection). Edward III pawned the great crown of England to Simon de Mirabello, and was charged 35 percent interest.[62] Forty percent and above seems to have been a commoner rate. James I himself had to pawn goods. The best known of his jewels was the "Three Brethren." It had been made for John the Fearless, Duke of Burgundy, but it was captured by the Swiss from his grandson in 1476. In 1506, the town of Basel sold it to the Fuggers, who tried unsuccessfully to sell the jewel first to Charles V and then to Ferdinand I. Henry VIII tried to buy it, but it was Edward VI who completed the deal. The jewel finally arrived in England in 1553 after Mary had ascended the throne. Elizabeth wore it in the Ermine portrait and James I in his hat. Hitting hard times, James I had the largest diamond removed in 1623 and he pawned the entire jewel in 1625. It was last heard of in Rotterdam in 1650. James also pawned the "Mirror of Great Britain" (a jewel commemorating the "union" of England and Scotland) in 1625.[63]

Some of the wealthiest Jacobean merchants and financiers acted as pawnbrokers and also pawned goods themselves. Thomas Myddelton, a member of the Grocers' Company, made his fortune trading in sugar with the Low Countries and became Lord Mayor of London in 1613. He operated as "a pawnbroker in the grand manner," his favorite securities being gold and jewels, possibly because his brother, with whom he worked closely at times, was a member of the Goldsmiths' Company and could appraise pledges and sell them off if unredeemed.[64] Sir Arthur Ingram, merchant and moneylender, lent the Earl of Nottingham £1,680 on the pledge of a diamond ring. In this case, the pledge may scarcely have covered the loan, since Ingram's partners were reluctant to make the deal. But Ingram was correctly banking on political leverage and on the immense financial gains that could, and would, result from his court connections.[65] In spite of Ingram's own wealth, he borrowed £100 from his friend and fellow moneylender, Lionel Cranfield, upon the pledge of a jewel. Cranfield records in 1623 that the money lent to Ingram is to be repaid "with interest."[66]

As rewards for his indispensable services at court, Cranfield himself was made Master of the Wardrobes, Master of the Court of Wards, and Earl of Middlesex. He had made his fortune as a usurer and pawnbroker, accepting as pledges land, industries (like coalmining), and monopolies, but, like smaller brokers, he also accepted moveable goods. From Sir Richard Gargrave, for instance, he took jewels as a pledge. More astonishing is the fact that Cranfield, one of the wealthiest men in England, had to turn to the pawnbrokers himself. In 1625, immensely rich in lands and goods, he was nevertheless "shorter of ready cash than he had ever been in his life." He sold a "rich bed" for £1,000 and pawned jewels and plate. In 1626, perhaps with some hyperbole, he wrote that he could not "provide food for [his] wife and family without pawning and selling [his] plate and household stuff." Despite Cranfield's work as a moneylender, he, like the aristocrats to whom he lent cash, stored up wealth in lands and goods.[67]

Why were even the rich so often strapped for cash? In the first place, there were no deposit banks in England. Those who accumulated money had to store it themselves, like the Duchess of Somerset who, when she died in 1587, had £5,200 in gold in her closet or like Sir John Oglander, who, in the early seventeenth century, kept £2,400 in gold hidden in a hole in his parlor and another £220 in gold in a box in his study.[68] In pre-capitalist societies, and even in transitional societies, such hoarding tends to be seen as both miserly and pointless. What good does gold do lying around when it can be enjoyed in the form of food or clothes or land or buildings or any of a hundred forms of sociability? When there is no capitalist banking system, such hoarding tends to bring social *dis*credit, whereas conspicuous consumption, by sharing the wealth around, brings credit.[69] The Countess of Shrewsbury, who was lavish in her expenditure, was not atypical in being constantly low on cash. In 1610, she wrote a desperate note to her agent to "gett what you can into your handes," because she did not know "which wayes to turne me."[70] Cranfield met with little sympathy when, in 1624, he was accused of mismanaging the Wardrobes and accepting bribes, and sentenced to the Tower during the king's pleasure, a fine of £50,000, and banishment from court.[71] His very failure to spread the wealth around by cutting back on expenditure at court meant that he had little social credit. He was cast in the guise of the miser and usurer that his society despised, even as he was accused (correctly) of making massive personal profits.

Yet even Cranfield did not usually hoard money, preferring to transform it into land and goods. In 1623, he recorded that he owned "black cloths in Mr. Venn's hand" worth £1,400, plate, jewels, and "household stuff" worth £8,000, and "cloth of gold and stuffs" worth £800, while he sold jewels worth £2,000 to Sir Peter Van Lore. In 1624, he calculated that his wife's jewels were worth £5,000, his hangings and household stuff £3,000, and his "cloth of gold, stuffs, velvets" £1,000, but he still had to pawn plate to John Williams for living expenses. And in 1630, he not only sold two jewels for £1,600, goldstuffs and gilt for £500, and a rich bed and two carpets for £1,000, but he also noted down, without giving their value, that his "stuffs" were at the pawnbroker.[72] Clothes and jewels were an exchangeable currency even for the wealthy, who were often cash poor.

The wealthy usually stored more of their money in clothing accessories (above all, in jewels) than in cloth. But even they used clothes as pawns. In 1593, William Lord Vaux was unable to attend the House of Lords because he had pawned his parliamentary robes and the broker refused to lend them back unless the principal was paid as well as the interest.[73] The rich pawned clothes, and they could also acquire clothes from the pawnbroker. Thomas Verney, the scapegrace son of Sir Ralph, was in constant financial difficulties and in 1638 he wrote to his father that he had "hardly any clothes left, neither bands, ruffs, shirts, boot-hose, boots, or anything else but is upon my back." He continues:

Ther is a sute of cloths come to me, but never a coat with it, it will be very unseemlie for mee to wear my sute, and never a coat but one sorey thing, which I bought about two months agoe, att a broker's, and some say as it is your old coat that you gave to your man, and I confess that it is very like yours, and as farr as I know it was yours; therefore I pray doe but judg of the goodness of it.[74]

In Thomas's account, there is a splendid interweaving of the social and the economic in his attempt to blackmail his father into sending him not only a coat but also "2 paire of gloves, 2 paire of linen stockings, 2 paire of plaine boothose topps, 2 paire of woolen boothose and three handkerchiefs." The possiblility that the coat he is wearing went from Sir Ralph to his servant, from the servant to the broker, and from the broker to Sir Ralph's son is clearly meant to impugn the father's reputation, materially debased in the circulation of his coat. One can perhaps understand how Sir Ralph would have understood Thomas's threat by comparison to Picasso's much later fear of material contamination: "He was deeply offended, for example, when [Françoise Gilot] gave an old jacket of his to the gardener at Vallauris, where they were living, and warned her unreasonably that this act would transform him, Picasso, into an ugly old man."[75] But if Thomas's threat was based upon the magical properties of clothes, his father was as aware as his son that clothes were also financial currency, and that any new clothes he sent Thomas were likely to end up, like his servant's, at the broker's to pay for gambling debts.

Although clothes and jewels could be exchanged for money, they never realized their full value as pledges. Pawnbrokers rarely lent as much as 60 percent upon a pledge, and then usually on more costly pledges for which they had a sure market or upon pledges (from princes and courtiers) which might be accompanied by political favors. In general, it was commoner to lend 20–50 percent of a pledge's value, although there were wide variations even within a given business. The pawnbroker Fripper in *Your Five Gallants* proclaims that "our pawne is euer thrice the value of our mony vnles in plate and Iewells," while Velvet Breeches in Robert Greene's *A Quip for an Vpstart Courtier* (1592) complains that the pawnbroker will lend only £3 on a pledge worth £10, and then charges interest at 12d. in the pound per month, plus 4d. a month for renewing the pawn ticket. And pawns on which the interest was not paid could be lost completely:

[I]f you breake but your day set downe in the bill of saile, your pawne is lost, as full bought & sold, you turnd out of your goods & he an vnconscionable gainer: suppose the best, you keep your day, yet paying sixteen pence a month for twenty shillings, you pay as good for the lone as fower score in the hundred . . . [T]he poore Gentleman paies so deere for the lauender it is laid vp in, that if it lie at a Brokers house hee seemes to buy his apparell twice.[76]

The less valuable the pawn, the higher the rate of interest. Cloth Breeches claims that he has "knowne of late when a poore woman laid a siluer thimble that was sent from her friends for a token to pawne for six pence, & the broker made her pay a halfpenny a week for it, which comes to two shillings a yere, for sixpence."[77] This is, of course, a satirical account, but pawnbroking records show that Cloth Breeches is not exaggerating. In 1596, Elizabeth Crowcher borrowed 24s. from John Cleaborough upon the pledge of a gown. She was charged 8s. interest for eight months, representing an interest rate of 50 percent.[78] In the nineteenth century, it was calculated that the interest rate on a 6d. pledge redeemed the same day would amount to 3,000 percent.[79]

European pawnbroking records from the fourteenth to the nineteenth century show that, for the average business, clothing was by far the commonest pledge. Here, for instance, are the kinds of object pledged over five days in 1417 in Pistoia, listed as percentages:

Clothing and apparel: 57.5 percent
Jewelry: 11.2 percent
Tools, agricultural implements: 11.2 percent
Arms and armor: 8.8 percent
Bedding: 7.5 percent
Kitchenware and household utensils: 2.5 percent
Calf skins: 1.3 percent[80]

More than 70 percent of these pledges are objects worn upon the body (including jewelry and armor as well as clothes in the narrower sense). The only detailed record of an early pawnbroking transaction that survives also concerns clothes. In 1465, Patrick Home, archdeacon of Tyndale in Scotland, was passing through Bruges, where he pawned "*tres togas foderatas, unam rubeam, aliam brunam, terciam nigram, et unum caputium nigrum, unam foderaturam de bevere, unicam tunicam de worset, unam bursam de panno deaurato et unum coopertorium blavii coloris.*" When Home returned to Bruges two years later, he tried to redeem his pawned clothes, but they had been sold.[81]

In the three sets of pawnbroking accounts of Philip Henslowe, somewhat sporadically covering the years 1593 to 1596,[82] clothes again form the majority of pledges, although the business also accepted pledges like ear-picks and pewter pots.[83] Clothes (and a small quantity of cloth) account for 62.2 percent of his pledges; another 13 percent is for clothes and household goods, clothes and plate, or clothes, household goods and plate; household goods (mainly linen) account for 12.2 percent; and "plate" (mainly in the form of rings) accounts for 11.5 percent.[84] Despite changes in fabrics (above all the massive increase in cotton), industrialization, and the consequent reduction in the value of clothes, clothing still accounted for more than 75 percent of the total pledges in an 1836 survey of English pawnbrokers, with metal goods (including watches, rings, and medals) a mere 7.4 percent, and bibles 1.6 percent.[85] As late as the 1950s, Tony Curtis and Jack Lemmon pawn their overcoats in *Some Like It Hot*, although the film comically recalls the earlier time of Prohibition.

Clothes can be pawned only if the broker has a market for the unredeemed pledges. And indeed, Henslowe sent Goody Watson clothes that he now called "my owne" and required that she sell them at the prices he set.[86] Just how sure Henslowe was of a market in secondhand clothes is demonstrated by the sums he was prepared to pay for them. If we recall that the cost of admission to the public playhouses was 1d., we get some idea of the value of even the smaller items of clothing for which Henslowe lent money: 10s. lent "vpon a payer of blacke sylke stockenes of goody streates"; 10s. "vpon a velluatte cappe"; 6s. "vpon a lynynge of shage for A clo[a]cke"; 6s. "vpon A dublet & A payer of breches ffor A chylld."[87] The *pawn* value of a pair of silk stockings, then, was enough to pay for seventy-two visits to the theater (which means that the stockings themselves probably cost as much as 144 to 216 cheap theater tickets). At the higher end of the market, Henslowe lent £3. 10s. to Mr Crowche "vpon his wiffes gowne"; £5 for "A womones gowne of branched damaske & lyned throwghe wth pincked tafetie & layd wth a lace of sylke and gowld"; £3. 10s. "vpon A sylke grogren gowne garded wth veluett & lyned wth saye of m^{r}. Burdes"; £4 "vpon ij payer of fyne sheates & a tabell cloth & a towell & a sylke quylte."[88]

Henslowe created a banking system in clothes in a variety of ways. Most obviously, he lent money to the sharers of the professional theater companies so that they could buy clothes. But he also pawned and sold clothes either directly himself or through agents. Henslowe's use of women agents as the collectors of pawns is, in fact, entirely typical. The middlemen who bring the clothes of women to the pawnbroker in Middleton's *Your Five Gallants* are men but this theatrical casting is surely only for effect in a play that emphasizes the "handling" of women by men.[89] In reality, the day-to-day circulation of household goods was, as Natasha Korda has argued, the work of women. As Korda points out, we need to rethink our concept of an all-male theater in relation to the number of women involved in the making of linen undergarments, the stitching and repairing of clothes, the pawning and selling of secondhand clothes.[90]

Henslowe employed at least three women as agents (Goody Watson, Mrs. Grant, and Anne Nockes, his nephew being the only man he employed), and he did business by our calculations with fifty-nine named women as compared to thirty-five named men.[91] The presence of women in the overall running of pawnbroking is suggested by other evidence as well. In London in the 1600s, Alice Singer, having received several pounds from a lodger, "leant [it] to a Neighbour of hers vpon a good quantitye of plate pawned and engaged for her money."[92] In Salisbury, Edith Pines was owed £15 upon pawns in 1625 and Agnes Masters, a butcher's widow, was described in 1631 as "a coman carrier of cloathes and other things about the towne to sell and to pawn."[93] A century and a half later, in Paris, we find a clear division of labor between the richer pawnbrokers and frippers, usually men, and the poorer street pawners, buyers and sellers of secondhand clothes, usually women. In 1767, after the police had organized the *revendeurs* and *revendeuses* (the street collectors and sellers of secondhand clothes) into a "free craft," they recorded 1,263 women as against 486 men, 800 women and 250 men selling old clothes and secondhand linen.[94] Henslowe's records also show that pledges were far more often of women's than of men's apparel. Of his pledges in 1593 that we were able to identify as male or female clothing (some of them undoubtedly repeats), thirty-one items were men's and eighty-two items were women's.[95] Women, then, played a particularly important role in the circulation of clothes. For all the ideological conflation of women with the domestic, in reality their wealth consisted of portable property that moved across the imaginary boundaries separating "public" from "private" space.[96] As women's clothes circulated, so too did women as frippers and as pawnbrokers' clients.

Yet the fact that clothes went so frequently to the pawnbrokers recalls that, however much they circulated, they were imagined as returning home. The distinction between selling and pawning clothes was that in the latter case, the clothes were usually reclaimed. Such clothes oscillated between being commodities, with a calculated cash value, and being the materials of comfort, of status, of pleasure, of memory. The pawnbroker, in other words, lived on the social cusp between the world of material memories and the intermittent but persistent need for ready cash.

"Garment[s] of memory"?

In *Poems and Fancies*, Margaret Cavendish implicitly compares her writing to the tapestry that Arachne weaves in her competition with the goddess Minerva. But what Cavendish is "spinning with the brain" is not a tapestry but a "Garment of Memory" that may "lapp up [her] Name, that it might grow to after Ages."The garment will establish who she is: "I cannot say the Web is strong, fine or evenly Spun, for it is a Course peice; yet I had rather my Name should go meanly clad, then dye with cold."[97] In the Renaissance, clothes were material mnemonics, the bearers of names. Yet as bearers of names, clothes inscribed conflict. Whose name is materialized in cloth? The name of the spinner, the weaver, the tailor, the giver of livery, the previous wearer, the present wearer? The name of the silkworms, the cattle, the sheep from which the materials of clothing come, as Lear suggests when he calls clothes "lendings"? In Genesis, Adam and Eve, as we noted above, attempt to clothe themselves, however humbly, with figleaves. But they are not allowed to take possession of themselves through an act of self-tailoring. The garments of skin that God gives them in place of their figleaves rename them as liveried servants, at the very moment that they are expelled from Eden, the household's inner sanctuary. But outside Eden, they will find new forms of clothing that will rename them, even as they rename themselves through new acts of investiture.

One function of clothes was to name, unname, rename. But these material mnemonics were also a form of economic currency. A petticoat or gown was made of silk or wool, it could be embroidered with silk, it could have gold lace added to it. Its specific value was calculated by the tailor and recalculated by the pawnbroker in the different stages of the garment's life-cycle. Clothes, in other words, were closer both to a second skin, a skin that names you, and to money than are the clothes that we wear today. The tension between clothes as mnemonics and clothes as cash is one of the most fertile sources of cultural analysis in the Renaissance. Dramatists, preachers, lawyers, merchants, courtiers, artisans act out and meditate upon that tension. At the end of the period that we explore in this book, Richardson made the tension central to the most popular novel of the eighteenth century, *Pamela*. Pamela, a servant, is paid in clothes both by the lady for whom she works and, after her death, by her son, Mr. B. Pamela understands, though, that to accept clothes from her employers is to be refashioned by them. They will mark her as owned. What would it mean to be possessor of oneself, the novel suggests, if not to buy one's clothes with one's own money and to dress oneself? Pamela writes to her parents:

My master . . . has given me a suit of my lady's clothes, and half a dozen of her shifts, and six fine handkerchiefs, and three of her cambric aprons, and four Holland ones. The clothes are fine silk, and too rich and too good for me, to be sure. I wish it was no affront to him to make money of them . . .[98]

To the extent that these clothes are material reminders, it is an "affront" to treat them as exchangeable commodities. "[T]o make money of them" is imagined as dangerously close to putting Pamela's employers on the market and circulating them as currency. Yet Pamela, for all her fears, reminds us that clothes could always be tranformed into ready cash. And her resistance to being liveried leads her to a new sense of the advantages of the market in her fashioning of herself.

The notion that clothes could escape circulation was, by and large, a fantasy. As we have seen, the crown jewels could be pawned; an aristocrat's ceremonial robes could be pawned; a priest's cloak could be pawned; a worn-out doublet or a pair of sleeves could be pawned. Money was transformed into things; things were transformed back into money. It was in things that the Renaissance stored up material memories, but it was also those things that would, when need required, become commodities again, exchangeable for cash.

2 Composing the subject: making portraits

In chapter 1 we looked at the tension between clothes as circulating wealth and as material memory systems. In this chapter, we attempt to show the ways in which economic value and social memory could reinforce each other. Portrait paintings now tend to be valued for capturing a subjectivity prior to and unconstrained by the marginal things – clothes, jewels, fans, gloves, landscape – that surround the face. We want the sitter's face and the painter's psychological insight to tell the story. But in the Renaissance sitters' faces were often glimpsed only in passing and "their" hands were frequently the hands of a studio model. The sitters' clothes, on the other hand, were often carefully sketched to record their color and material or they were actually sent to the studio where they could have their "portrait" made at the painter's leisure.

We argue further that many Renaissance portraits were supplements to rites of passage in which large sums of money had been spent on clothing and jewels. A portrait was usually a relatively minor expense in addition to the money that had gone into the buying of clothes and props by sitter and painter alike. Such paintings often functioned as material representations of the more fleeting but more costly props that had transformed a monarch into an icon, a courtier into the queen's champion, an English aristocrat into a Persian ambassador, a citizen into a gentleman. We examine here the function of clothes and jewels in the construction of the elite subject. As an English proverb put it, "We are all Adams sons, silk onely distinguisheth us."[1]

Clothing the subject

An important moment in the invention of the modern individual is the psychological interpretation of painting, and above all the psychologizing of the portrait. This psychologizing moment emerges in the Renaissance in Italian theories of artistic production which were disseminated throughout Europe, and which were used to distance the "gentlemanly" profession of painting from the artisanal and the mechanical (the work of embroiderers, goldsmiths, tapestry makers, for instance). We should not be surprised, then, when Nicholas Hilliard in *A Treatise concerning the Arte of Limning* Englishes such views. "Of all things," he writes, "the perfection is to imitate the face of man kind." And to imitate the face requires an understanding of the "variety of looks, and countenance" of the sitter.[2] The portrait, and above all the miniature, focusing upon the face of the sitter, would seem to be the ideal medium for the triumph of individual subjectivity over the distractions of the material world.

Yet what is most striking about Hilliard's *Treatise* is that, after belatedly repeating the arguments of Italian humanists, he proceeds to give a minute and technical description of how to paint a miniature in which the preparation of paints, the representation of clothes and jewelry, and the understanding of the relations between gems and color are the overwhelming focus of attention. Moreover, as Patricia Fumerton notes, the face in a Hilliard miniature is quite literally the *background*,[3] a background which is then made to support variable and complex depictions of hair, ruffs, jewelry, clothes, and other objects. Edward Norgate in *Miniatura*, written between 1648 and 1650, praised the way in which Hilliard and his follower, Isaac Oliver

have in readiness a dozen or more Cards ready prepared, and grounds laid of severall Complexions. And when they were to drawe any picture by the Life, I have seene them choose a Card, as neare the complexion of the party as they could, ever remembering to choose one rather too faire, then too broune, for in this Art of Lymning, there is noe heightning in the face, but the ground it selfe serves for heightning.[4]

The sitter's complexion is constituted by a wash of "carnation" (a flesh color) upon vellum that precedes the appearance of any sitter. The face itself, beautifully defined though the eyes, nose, mouth, and above all hair, could be completed more rapidly than the painstaking work of depicting a ruff, buttons, pearls, or jewels.

In Hilliard's miniatures, the relation between face and costume is, indeed, the reverse of what our term "portrait" would suggest: the costume, not the face, is privileged. For instance, Hilliard prepared three grades of white pigment. The coarsest was to be carnation for the sitter's complexion; the intermediate white was for painting linen; the finest was reserved for representing satin.[5] Sittings were given over largely to the representation of features and hair, but in the representation of textiles and jewels Hilliard elaborated new and extraordinarily time- and money-consuming techniques. He painted the lace of ruffs, for instance, line for line by dribbling white lead onto the vellum surface, the paint being so thick that the lines were raised up from the background, "each one casting its own small shadow."[6] And in the 1590s he began replacing the plain blue background of the conventional miniature with a curtain of red satin, the material represented by a thin mixture of red lake (an expensive red pigment), the shadows being created by a thicker mixture of lake floated onto the still wet surface. More complex still were the techniques by which Hilliard represented individual jewels. He created a pearl, for instance, by dribbling on a raised hemisphere of white lead, which was then shadowed and finished with silver paint on top. Diamonds were made by painting and burnishing a ground of reflective silver paint over which he applied transparent blacks and grays.[7]

These portraits, then, are as much the portraits of clothes and jewels as of people – mnemonics to commemorate a particularly extravagant suit, a dazzling new fashion in ruffs, a costly necklace or jewel. While the modern connoisseur searches the faces for a revealing feature or for the identity of the sitter, the pictures themselves give a minutely detailed portrayal of the material constitution of the subject: a subject composed through textiles and jewels, fashioned by clothes. Hilliard's portraits repeat through the costly and diverse pigments of the miniaturist the costly and diverse materials worn by the sitter. Thus, his miniature of George Clifford, third Earl of Cumberland, while it may give a detailed representation of the face, is most "individual" in its representation of the specific suit of Greenwich armor, armor which is now in the Metropolitan Museum of Art, finely chased with Tudor roses, fleurs de lys, and true lovers' knots (Figs. 1 and 2). The armor itself

Fig. 1. Nicholas Hilliard, miniature, *George Clifford, 3rd Earl of Cumberland*, c. 1585

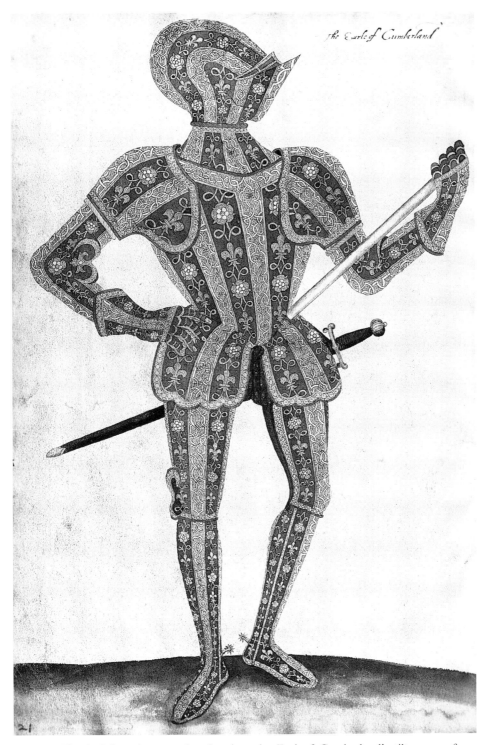

the Earle of Cumberland

Fig. 2. Ink and watercolor drawing, the Earl of Cumberland's tilt armor, from *Almein Armorers Album*, 1590 constitutes the role of the Earl both as naval commander and as knight in the Accession Day tilts.[8] It is the armor, not the face, that tells the story. Cumberland succeeded Sir Henry Lee as the queen's champion in 1590, and a later miniature of him by Hilliard shows him in a different suit of Greenwich armor, a splendid tunic covered with jewels, and the jeweled glove of his mistress pinned to his hat.[9] The single glove calls out to its other half, pairing him to his royal mistress, confirming his new position.

Similarly, Isaac Oliver's miniature and William Larkin's full-length portrait of Richard Sackville, third Earl of Dorset, tell us less about the earl's character than about his wardrobe. In the Oliver miniature, dated 1616, Dorset wears the "watchet [bright medium blue] silke stockings embroadered" and the "Bullen hose of Scarlett and blew velvett the panes of Scarlett laced all over with watchett silk silver and gold lace and the puffs of blew velvett embroadered all over with sonnes Moones and starres of gold" that were carefully recorded in "An Inventorie of the rich wearing Apparrell" of the earl in 1617 (Fig. 3). While the clothes constitute Dorset as one of the most fashionable of James's courtiers, the armor at his feet and the plumed helmet upon which he rests his hand proclaim his pretensions to be, like Cumberland, by profession a knight. Larkin's portrait equally commemorates specific, recorded clothes: a "doublett of Cloth of silver embroadered all over in slips of sattin black and gold"; a "Cloake of uncutt velvett blacke laced with seaven embroadered laces of gold and black silke and above the borders powdred [sprinkled] with slipps [floral motifs] of sattin embroad[ered] with gold and lyned with shagg of black silver and gold."[10] Portraits frequently derived from or were supplementary to the sitter's clothes. The clothes and jewels were inordinately expensive; by comparison, portraits were relatively cheap. £25 was the usual price for a Van Dyck portrait; Hilliard's miniatures, to the extent that they involved his goldsmith's skills in "clothing" them in jeweled boxes, might cost considerably more.

Royal weddings, like that of the Elector Palatine and Princess Elizabeth in 1613, which led to lavish aristocratic spending on clothes, also led to a spate of portraits to record that finery. It is probable that Larkin's portrait of Dorset records the clothes that he had made for that specific wedding. Sir John Finnett, the Master of Ceremonies, wrote to Mrs. Carleton about Princess Elizabeth's wedding: "The bravery and richese of that day were incomparable: gold and silver laid upon lords', ladies', and gentlemen's backs were the poorest burthen; pearls and costly embroideries being the commonest wear . . . but above all the King's Favourite, Viscount Rochester, and Lord Hay, Lord Dingwell and Lord Dorset dazzled the eyes of all who saw the splendour of their dress."[11] The portrait thus refers to a fleeting event even as it memorializes the sitter's specific clothes for that event.

The clothes, that is, provide a specificity that the faces do not. This is particularly true in the case where faces became repeated patterns, while the clothes were given a detailed specificty. As Roy Strong notes of the paintings in the orbit of Larkin, "[t]he sheer quality of the painting of dress and accessories is nowhere brought home more forcefully than in the case of repetitions. The face in the Countess of Somerset now in the National Portrait Gallery is the dull work of an assistant, but the lace is painted with all the care of any in one of the full autograph portraits."[12] In fact, the complexity of putting a name to a face has become notorious. Many of the identifications of Renaissance sitters are unclear or have been contested. Larkin's

Fig. 3. Isaac Oliver, miniature, *Richard Sackville, 3rd Earl of Dorset*, c. 1616

picture of Richard, third Earl of Dorset, was later inscribed wrongly with the name of Edward Sackville (the fourth Earl), whereas a contemporary portrait of Edward also by Larkin was wrongly inscribed as a portrait of his brother Richard.[13] A miniature from the circle of Nicholas Hilliard was firmly identified in van der Dort's inventory as a "Picture of Prince Henry upon an ovall redd Curteine ground Card in a white silver and gilded Armor his left hand in a gantlet houlding the dame [same?] at his side, and on his right side upon the Table standing a head peece wth a white feather Bush."[14] When a new inventory was made in the late seventeenth century for James II, the picture was identified simply as "a limning of a man," although the "gilt armour to the waste" was still specified.[15] The painting is more clearly identified by the description of the armor than by the name of the sitter.

It is also striking how frequently portraits were named after the clothes of the sitter rather than after the actual sitter. As Christine Junkerman has shown, Titian's painting now called *La Bella* has provoked an ongoing argument among art historians as to whether it is the portrait of a courtesan or an aristocrat.[16] But the argument is anachronistic. The Duke of Urbino simply refers to it as a painting of a woman *che ha la veste azzura* ("wearing a blue dress"). Although the dress itself is splendid, its splendor does not confirm that it was worn by either a courtesan or an aristocrat. For even if one could not afford to buy such splendid clothes, one could rent them. In 1494, the Milanese Pietro Casola marvelled at the clothes of Venetian women, even of those who could not afford them: "I said also those who cannot afford [them], because I was told that many of them hire these things." When, nearly two centuries later, Samuel Pepys sat to have his portrait painted by Hayls, he rented a gown of figured silk.[17] The portrait thus records a figure of greater splendor than Pepys himself could cut in his daily life. Moreover, painters themselves often had a store of expensive garments in which they clothed their models. We know that this is true in the case of Vermeer because an inventory made after his death records some of the costumes which make repeated appearances in his paintings.[18]

The significance of clothes is suggested by the ways in which portraits were inventoried in the Renaissance. If, indeed, the name of the sitter (often wrongly ascribed) is a common method of inventorying, so also is the dress of the sitter. The inventories of the Earl of Leicester's collection in the 1580s refer to "A counterfet of a gentlewoman in crimson and yellowe satten and a gowne of black velvet trimed with golde and silver lace," "A little picture of a stranger with a chaine of perle about his neck," "A counterfet of a gentlewoman in a petecote of yellow sattin." Even when the identity of the sitter is recorded, it is frequently accompanied by costume information ("my Lord Admirale in black armor"; "the Earl of Lestars picture in a yet [jet] box draune in his Cloake with a Cap and Fethar") or even by information about the "clothing" of the painting – that is, about the curtains that often hung before a painting and might be more valuable than the painting itself ("The historie of Cookery in a frame of woode all gilt aboute the border with a curteine of silke"; "One of my lord with a little curteine of green sarcenett").[19] A painting that would become for a later period a form of psychological revelation could oscillate in the Renaissance between being a representation of a person, a genealogical record, a portrait of clothes, and a valuable object (frame, curtain) in its own right.

Even when painters did record a person, they were frequently involved in the composition of the person as well as the painting. That is, their paintings recorded their own work as jewellers, goldsmiths, and designers of armor, work which they then inscribed upon their sitters' bodies. Nicholas Hilliard, for instance, was a goldsmith (as were Botticelli, Verrocchio, Ghirlandaio, and Robert Peake), he was the son of a goldsmith (as were Dürer and Charles I's Serjeant Painter, John De Critz), and he married a goldsmith's daughter. He was apprenticed to the goldsmith Robert Brandon from 1562 to 1569 and was liveried as a member of the Gold-smiths' guild in 1571; his son Laurence, also a miniaturist, was in turn apprenticed as a goldsmith and became a liveried member of the guild in 1605.[20] We know that Nicholas and his brother John, also a goldsmith, made jewels and rings, including "a rose of gold enameled wt a diamond in it, and a pearle hangynge at it," "A litle rynge wth a parrett vpon it," and "a litle rynge of gold wt an emerald peane [i. e. heraldic sable] in it."[21] Hilliard was involved, then, in the dressing and ornamenting of people who might then be depicted in the ornaments with which he had dressed them. His paintings and miniatures could thus do double duty: as representations of his sitters and as advertisements for his skill not only as a painter but as a goldsmith.

Moreover, miniatures actually turned the sitters into jewels – both in the sense that they were set down in gold, silver, lapis lazuli, lake, and other expensive pigments and in the sense that the painting itself was set into a "jewel" – a box of ivory or ebony or a more elaborate jewel of gold, enamel, and gems. Hilliard, as a goldsmith, was responsible not only for the picture but also for its casing. In 1610, he was paid £20 by Lord Salisbury for "Christall sett upon twoe pictures"; in 1612, he was paid £12 for a case of gold with blue enamelling for a miniature of Prince Charles; in 1615, he was paid £35 for adding diamonds to the case of a picture of James I.[22] Within the miniature, as we have noted, the face was literally the background, the clothes and jewels the foreground; but in terms of both space and expense, the visual representation was often in turn subordinated to the "fore-ground" of the frame. Indeed, the miniature as a portable object, an ornament to be worn, may be said to have derived from its frame. Pierra Sala, in about 1500, had his love poems illustrated and sent them to his mistress in an elaborately painted and gilded case, decorated with both their initials, for her to wear at her girdle.[23] It was probably from such cases as these that the cases of miniatures derived.

In combining the arts of jeweler and painter, Hilliard was following in the footsteps of the painter he most admired: "the most excelent painter and limner *Haunce Holbean*, the greatest Mter truly in both thosse arts after the liffe that euer was."[24] It was Holbein who introduced Renaissance styles and themes into English jewelry, and his designs were rapidly adopted by London goldsmiths, including Henry VIII's goldsmith, Cornelius Hayes or Heyss, a Flemish master who was naturalized in 1523; Robert Amadas, Master of the Jewel House from 1526 until 1532; and Holbein's friend, John of Antwerp, who had settled in London in 1515 and who witnessed Holbein's will in 1543.[25] Holbein's new and distinctive pendants, brooches and medallions are depicted again and again in his paintings. In his portrait of a lady aged twenty-one, for instance, Holbein depicts a medallion in which Lot is being led away from Sodom by an angel, while his wife is turned into a pillar of salt. Holbein's design for this medallion survives in his sketchbook of nearly two hundred jewelry designs. Similarly, he designed the enamel crucifix that Sir Thomas More wears in his portrait at Knole.[26] Holbein's paintings are thus a record and an advertisement for the latest style in jewelry, a fashion for which he himself

was responsible. And his particularly neat and exact method of painting enabled
him to record jewels, textiles, and colors in the most precise detail.

This emphasis upon the constitution of the subject through the "supplements" of
dress would seem to be contradicted by the fine series of portrait drawings that
Holbein made on his two visits to England. In these drawings, the face is sketched
with exquisite precision in black, white and colored chalks and, usually, black ink.
The costumes, by comparison, are usually hastily sketched in, with little or no color.
In reality, the sketches were what a 1547 inventory calls "paternes for phisioneamyes": that is, they were the outlines of faces which would then be transferred to
panel either by pricking or by tracing. These patterns facilitated repeated versions of
the face, which could be traced as easily by an assistant as by the master himself.[27]
The faces, then, could be easily transferred and repeated, but this was not true of the
costumes and jewels, which required the painter and his assistants to use paint to
differentiate not only specific dyes but also specific textiles. The specificities of dress
are often made clear in Holbein's sketches, even when the actual drawing is vague.
On the sketched costume of William Parr, first Marquess of Northampton, for
instance, Holbein wrote *wis felbet* ("white velvet"), *burpor felbet* ("purple velvet"),
wis satin ("white satin"), *Gl* (for gold), *MORS* ("death" on a jewel, as part of a
motto). The same sketch contains on the left-hand edge a series of detailed
depictions of the silver-gilt jewels which embroider the Marquess's hat and of the
medallion (almost certainly designed by Holbein) which hangs from the Marquess's
neck.[28] The same sketch depicts the traces of the fur that lines a slashed sleeve. Other
sketches note in the margins the ornamental fretwork of a headdress, the embroidery
of a collar, the pins in a shoulder-piece, an ear-iron.[29] And careful attention to
textiles and colors is recorded in notes for *atlass* ("silk"), *rosa felbet* ("pink velvet"),
dam ("damask"), *rot damast* ("red damask"), *Dofat* ("taffeta"), *silbe* ("silver"),
karmin ("carmine").[30] It may be that the more detailed the dress notes on the
sketches are, the less precisely the costume is painted in the finished portrait. A *lack*
of costume notes may imply that Holbein had access to his sitter's costume and
jewels and could paint them at his leisure. The sitter, on the other hand, particularly
when he or she was an aristocrat, may well have been impatient of the time
consumed in sittings. Costumes were, no doubt, particularly rewarding to paint.
They showed no signs of impatience; they memorialized and advertised Holbein's
own work as a designer of jewels.

The matter of painting

In addition to painters' work in recording details of dress, a more formal continuity
existed between the making of textiles and the making of paintings: the use of color.
Color itself seems now so obvious a part of painting that it has been difficult to
analyze. The obvious is, of course, what tends to be overlooked: we cannot see
things (as Wittgenstein observes) because of their familiarity. Yet the complex
technique whereby a painter begins with the buying, preparation, and application of
pigments is clearly set out in Hilliard's *Treatise*. Hilliard defines the miniaturist as
the master of pigments. He needs to use water from a clear spring or juice pressed
from black cherries; to have a grinding stone of crystal, serpentine, jasper, or hard
porphyry; to have a supply of gum arabic; and to wear silk clothes so as not to
spread dust or hairs. He needs to understand that the five unmixed colors derive

from gems: murrey (reddish purple) from amethyst; red from ruby; blue from sapphire; green from emerald; yellow from topaz orient. He needs to know how to make velvet black by burning ivory in a crucible; how to burn and grind cherry stones, date stones, peach stones; how to grind lake with gum arabic; how to make carnation; how to mix pink with massicot and ceruse so as to make a light green.[31] The miniaturist, like the dyer and goldsmith, mediated between the wealthy client and a world-trade system in dyes, pigments, and metals.

The connection between painters and colors was, indeed, formalized in the fact that all painters in London were officially supposed to belong to the Company of Painters-Stainers, a company that was responsible for illustrating documents, for coloring heraldic banners, for making the decorations for revels and pageants, as well as for what we now call "painting." (Like other painters' guilds in Europe, the Painters were originally part of the Saddlers Company, much of their work consisting of adding color to harnesses.) While the Painters-Stainers helped to support the world trade in pigments and dyes, they attempted to suppress the internationalization of their craft: their dislike of the domination of court painting by foreigners who were not, and could not be, members of the company (including Holbein, Mytens, and Van Dyck) found official expression in their petition to Charles I in 1627 against such "aliens." It was because of the guilds' power that Van Dyck, like the King's Men, took up residence in Blackfriars, a "liberty" within the city, and hence not subject to the guilds' decrees.[32] The guildsmen's complaint gave a nationalist focus to the issue of identity and representation: how could the depiction of an *English* court be given over to the hands of Germans, Flemings, and Italians? And how could the aristocrat's body be a national body if it was composed of French, Italian, Spanish, and Dutch fashions, if it was "dyed in grain" by indigo (meaning, literally, "Indian substance"), cochineal (from Mexico), and other "foreign bodies," if it was clad in Russian and American furs, in Persian silks, in Italian textiles, in jewels from India, Peru, Mexico and Africa, in feathers from every port of trade? Equally, what did it mean that the English court was "composed" by artists using pigments from India, Persia, Africa, and, increasingly, the Americas?

The actual cost of a painting still depended (in Hilliard's case to an extraordinary degree) upon the cost of the materials employed. Hilliard notes, for instance, that "the darkest and highest *Blewe* is *Vltermaryne* of *Venice* of the best, I haue payed iij s viij d a Carret wch is but fower graines, xj ll x s [£11 10s] the ounce" and that consequently the painter will sometimes have to substitute "smalt" [an inexpensive deep blue made from crushed glass] or "blue bices."[33] Not only did the cost of materials determine the cost of a painting, but the difference in cost *between* pigments defined the hierarchies of people and objects represented within the painting. The advantage of a painting, as Michael Baxandall perceptively notes in his analysis of fifteenth-century Italian painting, was that it was "both noticeable and cheap: bells, marble paving, brocade hangings . . . were more expensive."[34] Yet the cost of paintings depended on the materials the painter used, and the painters' contracts that Baxandall studies usually stipulate the quantity and quality of ultramarine that the patron desires. For example, Domenico Ghirlandaio's contract for *The Adoration of the Magi* on 23 October 1485 called for ultramarine "of the value about four florins the ounce."[35] Gold and silver were the most expensive and difficult materials the painter or limner used, but ultramarine came next in price, being made from powdered lapis lazuli from the Levant.

These expensive materials were in turn used to determine the significance of a particular subject. This hierarchy through color is clear enough in the gold halos of Christ and saints, but less clear to a modern viewer in the ultramarine mantle of the Virgin or in the ultramarine of the gown that St. Francis gives to a poor soldier in Sassetta's panel in the National Gallery, London.[36] Marcia Hall has argued that not only specific colors but specific pigments identified their subjects: the finest ultramarine was used (if the patron could afford it) for Christ and the Virgin; Peter usually wears a yellow ochre robe; Simon wears a vermilion robe over a malachite vestment. James, like Christ, wears a blue robe over a red vestment, but James's red is an orangish vermilion in distinction to the purplish red lake of Christ.[37] And Hall notes that Duccio constitutes the divinity of a body by the use of gold striations added to the blue vestments of Christ and the Virgin. Moreover, in Duccio's *Christ Healing the Man Born Blind*, the "blues are scaled hierarchically, the less precious materials applied to the Apostles on a relative scale of importance, with Peter's a paler echo of Christ's, and John's still paler."[38]

During the Renaissance, the emphasis upon precious pigments was partially displaced by an emphasis upon the particular artist's skills. Gold, for instance, moved from the center of the panel or canvas to the frame or, in the case of miniatures, to the borders of the vellum. Alberti, in his treatise *On Painting*, praised the painter who could represent gold through the use of yellow and white pigments:

There are painters who use much gold in their pictures because they think it gives them majesty: I do not praise this. Even if you were painting Virgil's Dido – with her gold quiver, her golden hair fastened with a gold clasp, purple dress with gold girdle, the reins and all her horse's trappings of gold – even then I would not want you to use any gold, because to represent the glitter of gold with plain colors brings the craftsman more admiration and praise.[39]

But the English miniaturists, partly no doubt because of the overlap between their work and that of goldsmiths, continued to emphasize the significance of expensive and exotic materials. A miniature was simultaneously a painting and a jewel. If an aristocrat like Richard Sackville, whom we examined above, was composed by his tailors, embroiderers, and goldsmiths from the costly scarlet, blue, watchet, silver, and gold of the dyer's and goldsmith's trade, Isaac Oliver's miniature composes him from the costly pigments of lapis lazuli (for the blue of the trunkhose) and azurite (for the stockings).[40]

Antony Van Dyck broke with the Holbein/Hilliard/Oliver tradition of representing the English court through the minute particulars of costume and surrounding objects. But it is worth noting that in effecting this break, his painting quite literally lost value. That is, an expensively cased miniature by Hilliard or Oliver was worth considerably more than most full-scale canvases by Van Dyck.[41] The materials themselves were of greater value than anything the painter could add to them. At the same time, Van Dyck, while reducing the percentage of expensive pigments for the large canvases he had to fill, continued to use them. A cross-sectional sample of the sky in Van Dyck's portrait of Elena Grimaldi reveals that he (and/or his assistants) used an underlayer composed of chalk, smalt, lead white and a small amount of red lake.[42]

Red lake was extremely expensive to make, being based until the sixteenth century upon various species of *cocci*, an insect found on oaks particularly in Portugal, Spain, Tunisia, and Asia Minor. Only the female insects could be used, just before they laid their eggs in May and June. Dried and crushed, they produced a dye called "kermes," "grain" (since the insects themselves looked like, and were often believed to be, grains), or "scarlet." In mid-fifteenth-century Flanders, kermes cost 38 1/2 d groot per pound, compared to 1 1/3 d groot per pound for madder, the most common alternative red used in dyeing.[43] From the 1560s, kermes began to be replaced throughout Europe by cochineal, a scale insect growing on cacti in Mexico and resembling the Mediterranean *coccus*. Cochineal was more powerful than kermes and could also be harvested up to six times a year. But such was the demand for cochineal that it increased to four times its original price on the Amsterdam market between 1589 and 1642.[44] It is almost certainly the Mexican cochineal which provided the basis of Van Dyck's red lake, since Judith Hofenk-De Graaff has demonstrated by chemical analysis that cochineal, having been introduced into Europe in the 1520s, had fully displaced kermes in textile dyeing by 1580.[45]

The top layer of paint composing the sample of sky in Van Dyck's portrait of Elena Grimaldi is made from a thin mixture of smalt, lead white, and the very expensive ultramarine (which, as we noted above, had been reserved in Italy in the fifteenth century for such figures as Christ and the Virgin Mary). Van Dyck thus continued to use the extravagant pigments of previous court painters in England, although he increasingly cut costs by thinning the depth of paint. The thickest areas of paint on one later canvas (*A Genoese Noblewoman and Her Son*) is "only one sixth the thickness of the paint in [his] earlier Italian painting."[46] Moreover, in this later painting, Van Dyck used only smalt where before he had used the expensive ultramarine, with the consequence that the sky is now paler and grayer than intended because of the fading of the inferior pigment.[47]

Even though Van Dyck, following Rubens, cultivated a *sprezzatura* style that distanced the painter from the minute attention to detail of the embroiderer and the goldsmith, the sitters whom he portrayed were carefully composed of heterogeneous materials. According to the Paris art collector, Eberhard Jabach, who sat to Van Dyck three times, the artist began with a sketch of the face, followed by a drawing of the figure and clothes in white and black chalk. He then gave this second drawing to his assistants, and their task was to paint the sitter's clothes, which had been sent to the studio for the purpose. Hands were added later, and they were not those of the sitter but of models specifically employed for the purpose.[48] In this, he followed earlier painters like William Larkin. As Roy Strong notes, Larkin's hands "are always stylized outlines which are so repetitive that it would be reasonable to surmise that the tracings of the standard poses existed in the workshop."[49] In contrast to Larkin, Van Dyck gave carefully differentiated forms to hands, but the specificity is that of the model rather than the official sitter.

At the same time, Van Dyck often reclothes his sitters, at least in part, adding accessories, jewels, drapery that belonged to the studio rather than the sitter. The painting is thus a making of the sitter as much as a representation. The Countess of Sussex, for instance, while disliking Van Dyck's representation of herself ("the face is so big and so fat that it pleases me not at all"), did not object to the artist's additions to her splendor: "he has made [the painting] . . . too rich in jewels I am sure, but tis no great matter for another age to think me richer than I was."[50] Yet it remains true that Van Dyck, by relegating the costume of his sitters to his assistants while he focused upon the face, helped to establish a more Cartesian subject of portraiture: a subject, that is, who is most truly him or her self when imagined as prior to or even separate from the heterogeneous materialities that compose that subject.

Hybrid subjects

From the perspective of the Cartesian subject, the hybridized subject of earlier Renaissance portraiture will be repeatedly found lacking. Even Holbein's *The Ambassadors*, a picture widely praised, is criticized for its supposed flaws of composition. G. H. Villiers, for instance, in his useful account of the painting, writes:

It must be frankly admitted that as a composition *The Ambassadors* leaves something to be desired. It would certainly be unfair to describe our picture as "Astronomical instruments on a table, with portraits of an ambassador and a bishop," but it would not be devoid of all justification. The spectator's eye is directed not to the two portraits but to the elongated skull, which is unduly prominent in the foreground, and to the instruments and globes on the table occupying the centre of the panel. The two men, who have been compared to the supporters of a coat-of-arms, give the impression of being somewhat cramped and awkwardly placed at the extreme edge of the picture.[51]

Villiers's criticism is repeated by John Rowlands in his description of the *Portrait of George Gisze* in the most recent complete catalogue of Holbein's paintings. Rowlands writes that Holbein

obviously delighted in showing his unbeatable skill in recording such a prodigious variety of acutely observed detail. Because he was uniquely accomplished in representing all this, he has, in so doing, almost submerged his sitter. As a portrayal of Gisze's character the painting is one of Holbein's less expressive efforts.[52]

What dismays both Villiers and Rowlands is the fact that Holbein pays as much attention to objects as subjects. If "character" is what Holbein is representing, then why all this attention to the merely "supplementary" features of books, carpets, writing instruments, astronomical instruments? Villiers, in fact, does address these features, even though he cannot make sense of them within a portrait. Rowlands, on the other hand, having already decided that "character" is what counts, pays the briefest of attention to the actual composition of the portraits and to the materials (the clothes, the jewels, the objects) which compose most of the surfaces of Holbein's work. For Rowlands, only the face can give "character"; the rest is distraction.

Yet Villiers's ironic retitling of *The Ambassadors* (itself a modern invention) as "Astronomical instruments on a table, with portraits of an ambassador and a bishop" actually allows us to see more of what Holbein displays than the usual title does. In fact, the name *The Ambassadors* depends upon the belated, if persuasive, identification of the sitters by Mary F. S. Hervey in 1900 as Jean de Dinteville and Georges de Selves.[53] Before Hervey's identifications, the painting showed two anonymous men; the objects, by contrast, were carefully inscribed in ways that make them specifically identifiable.

"Identity" is thus clearer in the case of the objects than of the subjects. And the objects refer us back to the *making* of identities – the transnational labor through which subjects and objects alike come into being. On top of the table in the center of the picture are a range of astronomical instruments, many of which Holbein had already painted in his 1528 portrait of Nicholas Kratzer, the German astronomer of the English court. In this portrait, Holbein depicted Kratzer in the process of making a ten-sided sundial. This sundial reappears, now completed, in his 1533 painting. Kratzer, in other words, is portrayed in the act of making the professional instruments which constitute him as an astronomer.

The other objects that Holbein depicts are equally specific. The mosaic floor at the bottom of the panel depicts the floor in the Sanctuary of Westminster Abbey, the work of Italian workers in the thirteenth century. The open hymn book is that of Luther, published in 1524 with music by Johann Walther, the Kapellmeister to the Saxon court. The book of mathematics is *Eyn Newe unnd wolgegründte underweysung aller Kauffmanns Rechnung* ("A new and well-grounded Instruction in all Merchant's Arithmetic") by Peter Apian, who was professor of mathematics and astronomy at Ingolstadt in Bavaria. The terrestrial globe on the bottom shelf of the table represents a globe made by Johann Schoener of Nuremberg, showing "the line between Spanish and Portuguese possessions in the New World, as laid down by the Borgia Pope Alexander VI." Holbein has copied, in part or in whole, 109 of the inscriptions on Schoener's globe, including the names of continents, countries, cities, seas, gulfs, rivers, and divisional names (the Arctic Circle, the Tropic of Cancer). He has added to Schoener's globe nineteen names, including "Polisy," the name of the family estates of the Dintevilles in France. The celestial globe on the top of the table in the painting depicts one made by Peter Apian (who also wrote the book of arithmetic); his globes were renowned for their precision and their beauty.

Yet even Hervey, in her profoundly impressive work of research on both sitters and things in the paintings, attempts to subordinate the objects to the sitters: "The objects selected for illustration precisely represent the pursuits and occupations most in vogue at the time in France."[54] Yet it is only the sitters' clothes that relate them to France. Jean de Dinteville, on the left of the picture, is a lay aristocrat, and as such wears the *robe courte*; George de Selves is a bishop and wears the *robe longue* of ecclesiastics and lawyers.[55] Moreover, Dinteville wears around his neck the Order of St. Michael, otherwise known as the *Ordre du Roi*, which was instituted by Louis XI in 1469.[56] With the exception of the clothes, the objects belong not to the French world of the visiting ambassadors but to Holbein's Anglo-German circles in London. They quite literally belong to that world: to the court astronomer, Nicholas Kratzer; to the German merchants and craftsmen of the Steelyard in London, whom Holbein had frequently painted; to his own studio. *The Ambassadors* is thus an extraordinary record of the work of German scientists, craftsmen, writers, and musicians. While painting two aristocrats, Holbein meticulously details the non-aristocratic labor through which that aristocratic world is made.

The painting also records a world system constituted by trade, migration, and colonialism. The sitters are French, but they are painted by a German at the English court. Holbein's terrestrial globe pays particular attention to France (although he adds four names to Spain and three to Germany, including "Saxonia," where Johann Walther was Kapellmeister) but they are surrounded by German objects and they stand upon an English mosaic floor made by Italian craftsmen. Nor is Europe the only region represented. Holbein, indeed, has always been well known among carpet historians – so well known that his name has been given to a particular kind of Middle Eastern carpet: "the Holbein carpet." It is a so-called Holbein carpet which Holbein carefully depicts in the center of his panel, clothing the table. In fact, these carpets had been previously represented in Italy by Rafaellino del Garbo and Domenico Ghirlandaio. They came from what is now a part of Turkey: north-western Anatolia, probably in the Bergama district. And they were highly valued, both in Turkey and in Europe.[57] They continued to be made and traded throughout the sixteenth century, and one of the last English representations of such a carpet appears on the table in the picture of *The Somerset Conference* (1604) in the National Portrait Gallery, London. As the carpet inscribes the interconnections of world trade, so too does the terrestrial globe portrayed in Holbein's painting, with North at the bottom. Africa is in the center of the globe and, because of the globe's inversion in the painting, Europe is below it, Asia to the left, and the Americas to the right.

While the carpet implies the hybridization of Europe by Asia, the globe implies Europe's mythic imperial claims to control the East. To the East of Egypt, Holbein paints on the globe the inscription "Habesch . . . esbiter . . . nnes." These are the last visible words before the globe is first obscured by shadow and then entirely cut off from our view by the ermine lining of Dinteville's surcoat. Holbein's inscription refers to the inscription on Schoener's globe: "Habesch [this region contains] presbyter Joannes." The name of "Prester John" (*presbyter Joannes*) refers to a mythical Christian emperor of fabulous wealth and power who, according to the stories that circulated in twelfth- and thirteenth-century Europe, supposedly ruled large parts of the far East. Cesare Vecellio's *Habiti antichi et moderni di Diverse Parti del Mondo*, first published in 1590, locates Prester John in Africa but makes the same explicit imperial claim for him: he is the very first figure to be represented and he is shown, like the page and the assistant who are portrayed next, holding a cross.[58]

The name of "Prester John" had been revived in the winter of 1532–3, just months before Holbein painted *The Ambassadors*. A Portuguese man, calling himself David King of the Ethiopians or Prester John, presented letters to Charles V and the Pope, declaring that he was descended from Queen Candace, who is named in the Acts of the Apostles. As material proof of his claims, he showed them a crucifix of gold. He asked for "some excellent artificers and 2000 Arquebusiers whom he would use in a war against the Turk in Egypt, when his Holiness would compose the differences in Western Parts, and join all Christian Princes for recovery of the Holy Land." It was reported in England that this "Prester John" was a tool of the Portuguese in their attempt to gain a monopoly over the Eastern trade in spices, silks, and dyes.[59] "Prester John" thus implied, depending upon one's perspective, the past achievement and the present hope of a universal Christian empire or the factional infighting between the emergent nation-states of Europe. It is surely the latter perspective which is suggested by Holbein's reduction of "presbyter Joannes" to ". . . esbiter . . . nnes." For if the instruments of astronomy and navigation imply the integration of a world system, such an integration is denied by conflicting colonial claims. Those conflicting claims are carefully marked by the longitudinal line added down the entire globe, with the clearly inscribed words: "Linea Divisionis Castelloru[m] et Portugallen," the division of lands in the New World between Spain and Portugal. The division of nations is repeated by the division of religions: George de Selves, on the right of the picture, was a Catholic bishop; yet it is Luther's hymn book which lies open.

The embassy of the two French ambassadors to England was partly an attempt to heal such religious divisions, but the painting itself offers little in the way of consolation. Half-hidden in the upper left-hand corner of the picture, truncated by the green drapery, there is a silver crucifix, itself increasingly a symbol disputed between Catholics and Protestants.[60] What are we to make of the deliberate obscuring of the crucifix in the composition? Moreover, an emblem of musical harmony, a lute, is prominently displayed on the bottom shelf of the table, but one of its strings is broken, perhaps in allusion to Alciati's emblem of a broken lute ("*Unaque si fuerit non bene tenta fides,/ Ruptave (quod facile est) perit omnis gratia concha/ Illique praecellens cantus ineptus erit*" ["And be there one ill-tuned or broken string,/ Easy mischance! all grace of music dies,/ And disconcerted is the concert fair"]). Alciati makes clear the *political* significance of this emblem in his address to the Duke of Milan: all it takes is for one Italian ruler to refuse alliance for the harmony of Italy to be dissolved.[61] The painting's artifacts, that is, while themselves both the products of and the preconditions for new forms of transnational trade, present this global economy less in terms of a utopian process of integration than in terms of conflict and dismemberment.[62]

But most striking of all in *The Ambassadors'* inscription of discord is the anamorphic skull which seems at first to be an ugly flaw in the painting, defacing the bottom of the canvas. As John Berger surely rightly suggests, the distortion of this skull creates a radical disjunction in the painting.[63] It is literally impossible to hold the skull in focus at the same time as the sitters and the other objects. By inserting this disjunctive perspective into his painting, Holbein seems to be rejecting both the material details which he has so meticulously represented and his own techniques for appropriating that materiality. Yet at the same time the anamorphosis brilliantly demonstrates another new element in the repertoire of the modern painter: the skull is not the making but the unmaking of a person, but the anamorphosis is a representation of Holbein's own skill – his skill at unclothing the human figure, yet animating, through a deliberately distorted perspective, the remaining skull.

What emerges from Holbein's double portrait is not the interior life of the two ambassadors. Rather, it is the construction of the portrayed subject through prostheses, the attachable/detachable parts, the clothes, furniture, books, scientific and musical instruments that animate the subject. It is as if the anamorphic skull celebrates the opposing power of the painter: the power to strip the subject of those prostheses, and finally of the skin itself (as if skin were just another prop to identity, another set of clothes). To the extent that the subject is composed, the subject can be discomposed, decomposed, disassembled.

Portrait painters composed identities for their sitters not only by concentrating on the nuances of faces but also by combining an international range of substances for artwork, material objects, and garments to represent those sitters' positions in a world of complex economic and political circulation. Aristocratic sitters appear to have played an active role in employing painters to represent them in such positions, to compose an identity for them out of the objects that signaled their participation in different cultures. Men at court, wearing exotic fancy dress, played parts in royal masques, but their roles as foreigners – Irishmen turned civil, for example, as in Jonson's *Irish Masque* – were temporary: the costume was worn for one or two evenings and then retired from public life. Courtiers attempting to establish more durable intercultural identities for themselves had themselves painted in foreign clothing that was neither fanciful nor exotic. Such garments, coming from colonies and kingdoms near at hand and from across the seas, provided material evidence of their wearers' interaction with England's "others," or, indeed, their partial or total incorporation into such otherness through dress. In our concluding analysis of three portraits of Englishmen in foreign costume, we trace out the processes of identity formation at work in Elizabethan and Jacobean portraits that make their sitters' "outlandishness" explicit.

In 1594, Marcus Gheerhaerts painted Captain Thomas Lee, an English "soldier of fortune," who, by the date of the portrait, had been serving English interests in Ireland for close to twenty years (Fig. 4).[64] In Gheerhaerts' painting, Lee is strikingly bare-legged and barefoot. He wears a linen shirt hoisted up around his hips and carries a spear with a wooden handle, a pointed metal helmet, and a round, fringed shield at his back. All these details of dress and undress signify Irishness. Art historians such as Roy Strong have pointed out that Lee's clothes and accoutrements correspond to prints of the Irish soldier in contemporary costume books, including Abraham de Bruyn's *Omnium Paene Gentium Imagines* (1577) and Jean-Jacques Boissard's *Habitus variarum orbis gentium* (1581), and that the portrait also draws on images of Irish warriors in written English accounts of the country.[65] Chambers remarked in his biography of Lee that the lightweight costume and bare legs are "obviously well adapted to bog-trotting." But English prints and drawings from the 1580s, in which Irish warriors wear leggings and shoes, suggest that Lee's portrait may put particular emphasis on atypically bare legs.

At the same time, however, Lee's portrait includes emphatically English details of dress. His linen shirt is embroidered with Tudor roses; he wears an elegant, military-looking open velvet doublet; he carries weapons more sophisticated than those of the Irish, a snap-haunce pistol and a sword at his waist. Irish warrior and English gentleman, but over-armed for an Irishman and startlingly underdressed for a courtier: why did Lee have himself represented in these clothes and weapons?

One answer might be that the painting records a costume Lee wore at the Ditchley entertainment staged by his uncle Sir Henry Lee to honor Elizabeth in 1592. As Elizabeth's Master of the Armoury and former Champion, the older Lee also organized Accession Day tilts, one of which included wild Irishmen in costumes similar to Thomas Lee's in the portrait.[66] But there is no proof that Thomas Lee performed in masques or tilts (he was in Ireland throughout 1592). His political situation in 1594 suggests, rather, that Gheerhaerts followed Lee's wishes that he compose a *strategically* hybrid identity for him. Lee wears a kind of double livery, composed of garments and objects from both sides of the English–Irish border, designed to constitute him as part Irish through experience in the country, but not entirely Irish – and for that reason a useful servant to the colonizing crown.

In 1594 Lee was in London to defend himself against accusations of treason in his dealings both with Irish chieftains and with Anglo-Irishmen loyal to England.[67] He had established a friendly relationship with the native chief of Ulster, Hugh O'Neill, Earl of Tyrone, and he had been feuding since the 1580s with Thomas Butler, Earl of Ormonde, now Royal Deputy to Ireland. Deprived of his twenty-four horsemen in 1583 as a result of this and other raids and quarrels, Lee had also married an Irishwoman from whom he separated after she betrayed his plan to attack an Irish enemy, who, once informed of the plot, killed one of Lee's followers. But Lee had also impressed Elizabeth and her councillors by negotiating for a truce with Tyrone in 1593, and he had performed a spectacular military feat – entering the deep ford of Golune – during an attack on Tyrone's rivals, for which action he was praised by both Tyrone and the English leader Henry Bagenal. Lee apparently felt that these

Fig. 4. Marcus Gheerhaerts, *Captain Thomas Lee*, 1594

successes would support his complaints against English deputies in Ireland and convince Elizabeth to restore him to favor. Similar expectations probably prompted his completion of *A Brief Declaration of the Government of Ireland*, a tract he had begun during his parleys with Tyrone, in which he argued that English policy should be to right the wrongs suffered by royal officers in Ireland but also to establish good relations with Tyrone and the other northern lords.

The 1594 portrait uses costume as Lee used his political compositions, which later included a tract dedicated to Cecil, *The Discovery and Recovery of Ireland, with the Author's Apology*. Lee's mixed costume defends his usefulness as a long-term inhabitant of Ireland who is also an informant devoted to England: the bare Irish legs and minimal armor are precisely what make dazzling exploits in the queen's service possible, just as his long association with Tyrone makes him a canny advisor to those who would dominate Tyrone's enemies in Ireland. The motto inscribed above Lee's right arm in the painting, "Facere et Pati Fortia," comes from a speech attributed by Livy to Mucius Scaevola, the early Roman hero who defeated Tarquin Porsena's attempt to restore his own tribe to power:[68] "to do and endure mighty things" signals Lee's promise that he, too, will contain the uprisings of previously defeated enemies of the new imperial state.

What the Flemish painter performs, then, is not primarily the study of a face; rather, it is Lee's body, garments, and weapons that speak. The portrait assembles Lee as a public figure by assembling objects from both of the cultures with which he claims familiarity: the linen shirt and wooden spear of Ireland in tension with the elegant doublet and the English pistol. What Lee is *not* wearing is equally significant. The bare legs differentiate this ford-wading warrior from Elizabeth's silken-hosed courtiers, as the wooden-handled spear aligns him with rough-and-ready counter-insurgency rather than the elaborate courtly performance of ritual tilts. Through a complicated visual rhetoric, the portrait employs bi-national sartorial objects to identify and defend Lee as an Englishman gone Irish and *therefore* a meritorious defender of the realm.

England's colonial projects were turned not only toward the West but toward the East by the time Anthony Van Dyck painted William Feilding, the first Earl of Denbigh, soon after 1632. The English East India Company, founded in 1600, was fast consolidating the voyages in search of dyes and dyeing techniques that had earlier been organized by the Russia Company (1553–1603) and by individual entrepreneurs.[69] In 1579, for example, Richard Hakluyt had sent the dyer Morgan Hubblethorne to Persia, to study the processes of carpet and silk dyeing and to bring back as much anil, a shrub that produced blue dye, as he could, "to enrich your country"; in 1582 Hakluyt instructed fellow Englishmen in Turkey and Constanti-nople to bring back not only anil but "all other herbes used in dy[e]ing," and, if possible, to bring back native dyers of wool and silk as well.[70] After the East India Company was founded in 1600, its members imported dyes and textiles in a much more massive, systematic way, building factories on the southern Persian coast and in Calcutta, for example, where they established monopolies on the production of local textile workers making silk and printed cottons.[71]

Feilding, the husband of Susan Villiers, the sister of James's favorite George Villiers, the Duke of Buckingham, was created Master of the Great Wardrobe and Earl of Denbigh in 1622. From 1631 to 1633 he traveled on the East India Company's ships, visiting Persia and India with letters of introduction to the Shah and the Great Mogul from King Charles. The trip was not an official diplomatic mission, however; Feilding explained in a letter to his son that his was not a state visit but a private voyage, undertaken "to better my understanding."[72] Van Dyck's painting, done after the earl's return in 1633, before the artist departed for the Netherlands in 1634, obviously commemorates Feilding's three years in the East, from which he brought back jewels, seventeen pieces of "Mesapotamia cloth," and "a pagan coat."[73]

In his portrait, Feilding wears a rose-pink silk *paijama* with a narrow gold stripe, a Hindu Indian style (Fig. 5). He is not dressed entirely in an Indian mode, however. His lace-trimmed shirt, leather purse, and black shoes are European, and the tight buttoning of the pajama coat over his chest and its opening above the waist corresponds to 1630s English fashion for men. He is dressed, in fact, in the combination of local and European garments that early seventeenth-century Europeans in India wore to sleep in and to relax.[74] Yet his accoutrements and setting construct him as explorer. His rifle, mentioned in an early inventory of the painting as a "fowling peece" and probably made in France or the Netherlands,[75] like the sword strap and hilt at his left side, marks him as ready for any animal or human encounter. One possible narrative implied in the painting is that the earl's next step will be to draw a bead on the parrot, a source of the feathers so valued for European costumes.[76] Feilding's dark-skinned young servant, dressed in an ornate turban and a yellow satin robe, looks up at him respectfully; the wild landscape, including the parrot in a palm tree and a snowy mountain peak in the distance, suggests both the exotic flora and fauna and the physical challenges the Englishman confronts in this Eastern land.

Later commentary on the painting demonstrates the ambiguities of Feilding's hybrid costume. Originally, the portrait could have signalled English trade not only with Europe and Asia but also with the New World: in Van Dyck's underpainting, the earl was holding in his left hand a wide-brimmed black hat, the "castor" made of beaver fur.[77] Such hats, made of felt based on the silken underfur of beaver pelts acquired by Englishmen trading first with Russia and then with Native Americans up and down the Atlantic coast, were popular throughout the early seventeenth century; King James and Henry, Prince of Wales, owned many.[78] The elimination of the hat from Van Dyck's painting emphasizes its allusions to Indian and Persian realms instead.

But even these allusions could be, and were, read in contradictory ways. The guide or servant boy, for example, was variously identified in later inventories. In an early one, the maker and subjects of the painting are listed as "Vendick My Lorde Denbeigh & Jacke."[79] Had Feilding brought the boy back with him from his travels and given him an English nickname? If so, the younger sitter doubles the earl's hybridity: renamed in a new country, he poses for a Flemish painter, with his English master, in the costume of his native land. His turban is Persian in style. Cesare Vecellio, whose woodcuts of Asian costume were first published in 1590, shows such cross-wrapped headgear on his "Persian nobleman" and "Persian captain," and a seventeenth-century gouache of a Muslim encampment, painted by the Indian artist Govardhan, contrasts a Hindu holy man's circularly wrapped turban to the crisscross-wrapped turban of a Muslim traveler with a parrot in a cage.[80] Feilding's companion wears a turban very similar to the Muslim's, though more sumptuous. But a later inventory, made between 1641 and 1649, calls the boy

Fig. 5. Anthony Van Dyck, *William Feilding, 1st Earl of Denbigh*, c. 1632

"a Blackamore"; a 1712 list names him "a tawny Moor"; and an eighteenth-century traveler to Hamilton, the Denbigh estate, heard a guide describe Feilding in this painting as "the Governor of Jamaica," apparently interpreting the boy as a Caribbean mulatto.[81] Whenever the painting was viewed, the boy played the role of identity marker for Feilding, establishing him as explorer or colonial official in the eyes of English viewers. The changing readings of Feilding were thus co-extensive with changing interpretations of the boy.

As Kim Hall has argued in relation to other seventeenth-century portraits in England, the black figure operates as ennobling supplement, as a necessary prop that defines the white figure as white and as master – in this case, as master of all he surveys.[82] Family legend has it that the painting represents Feilding lost in the Eastern forest; critics remark on his gesture of "mild surprise" and his "lurching" step.[83] His hatlessness also gives him an unusually informal quality, compared to the elaborate beaver and velvet hats usually worn or held in seventeenth-century portraits of aristocratic men. But Feilding's and his servant's costumes nonetheless construct him as a figure of authority and power: at ease in Indian *déshabille* but also armed and alert. While the portrait of Thomas Lee uses shirt, spear, and nudity – a significant *lack* of clothing – to position the sitter both inside and outside the Irish territory that the painting suggests he commands by reason of his marginality, the portrait of William Feilding juxtaposes his mixed Anglo-Indian costume and the "exotic" dress of his servant to compose him as an English traveler "bettering his understanding" in a way perfectly suited to the commercial interests of England's trading corporations in the East.

A more radical undoing of Englishness itself is suggested in Van Dyck's portrait of Sir Robert Shirley in Persian clothes (Fig. 6). In the painting, Shirley is dressed in a tunic with gold and silver embroidery and a cloth of gold cloak, embroidered with figures and flowers. He wears a turban and carries a bow in his hand. The portrait, we would argue, points toward the extent to which identity itself was more a matter of livery than of nationality or race. Robert was the third son of Sir Thomas Shirley, Treasurer in the Low Countries. In 1598/9, Robert and his brother, Anthony, accompanied the Earl of Essex on a mission to Persia. Robert remained there, marrying Teresia Khan, a Circassian Christian noblewoman. Alastair Laing provides the following biography:

> In 1607/8 he left Persia to negotiate alliances with European princes against Turkey on behalf of Shah Abbas the Great. He was well received by Sigismund III of Poland and Pope Paul V, and was first knighted, then created a count palatine, by the Emperor Rudolph II. Shirley was in England from 1611 to 1612/13, but found himself opposed by the Levant merchants. He began a second series of missions at the end of 1615, and spent from 1617 to the summer of 1622 in Spain; on 22 July he arrived in Rome, where he was received by Pope Gregory XV. While in Rome he encountered Van Dyck, whose 'Italian' sketchbook contains a whole set of quick pen sketches of Shirley, his wife and his suite.[84]

To us, and probably even within fifty years of its painting, the portrait looks like the epitome of orientalism – the dressing up of an English aristocrat in the exoticism of the East.[85] But this is clearly not how Shirley saw himself, nor how Van Dyck meant to record him. In a sketch for the painting, Van Dyck carefully notes down various clothing details ("*drapo duro*," "*de colori differenti de veluto*"), but the clothes are not "costume" in the modern theatrical sense. They are the clothes of a man whom Van Dyck records as "*Ambasciatore di Persia in Roma*" – a Persian ambassador,

Fig. 6. Anthony Van Dyck, *Sir Robert Shirley*, 1622

rather than an English aristocrat in fancy dress. The painting thus records a livery rather than a costume – the livery that absorbed and transformed Sir Robert Shirley into the Persian ambassador, the deep making that came from surface inscriptions.[86]

It is a mark of our own Eurocentric perspective that we find it hard to imagine that for Shirley the journey to Persia was a journey toward "higher" forms of technology and civilization – toward fabrics and dyes and embroideries that surpassed anything he had seen in Europe.[87] As Philip Curtin notes:

The "European Age" in world history had not yet dawned [in the sixteenth and early seventeenth centuries]. The Indian economy was still more productive than that of Europe. Even the per capita productivity of seventeenth-century India or China was probably greater than that of Europe . . . Europe's clear technological lead was still limited to select fields like maritime transportation, where design of sailing ships advanced enormously through the sixteenth and seventeenth centuries. Otherwise, Europe imported Asian manufactures, not the reverse.[88]

One might say that the long history of the silk routes was only just coming to an end, a history that looked toward the East for technical developments above all in cloth. At the same time, the very notion of "Europeanness," that is, of a bounded region defined by its imagined cultural and technological superiority to Asia, Africa, and the Americas, was only just coming into being. Shirley could become Persian to the extent that he had never imagined himself as "European" or "English" in the first place, but rather as an aristocrat. (Nicholas Canny's work on the popular classes suggests even more strikingly their lack of a given national identity during this period. There were, for instance, massive desertions by English troops in Ireland, many of whom seem to have happily changed sides or settled down to live in Ireland. In other words, they did not consider themselves irrevocably, or even deeply, "English."[89]) At the level of the elite, the persistence of a livery system made possible the change of allegiance through a change of clothes.

And this was a deep, not a surface change. When Robert Shirley entered the Shah's service, he did so by putting on his clothes, which incorporated him into the body politic of a non-European, non-Christian state. As Thomas Fuller noted, "as if his clothes were his limbs, [Shirley] accounted himself never ready till he had something of the Persian habit about him."[90] It was through the Persian habit that he acquired the habit of being Persian, a habit that endured even after he believed that he had lost the Shah's favor. The clothes permeated Shirley, reconstructing his interiority through external livery. At the same time, his livery was not fixed. When he traveled as Persian ambassador through Europe, he acquired and wore clothes that proclaimed his multiple allegiances. In Florence, he was given a gold chain to wear by the duke; in Rome, where Pope Paul V gave him the title of Count of the Sacred Palace of the Lateran, he wore a gold crucifix in his turban to manifest his religious beliefs.[91] But in England, such local hybridizations of the Persian ambassador's loyalties seemed insufficient. Shirley's refusal to discard his Persian clothes infuriated James I. James read the refusal (correctly) as Shirley's assertion of his allegiance to the Shah over his allegiance to his "own" monarch.

Yet by 1757, when George Vertue saw Van Dyck's painting of Teresia, Robert Shirley's wife, the clothes no longer seemed constitutive. To the eighteenth-century viewer, this was simply a painting of "the lady Shirley in fantastick habit."[92] The subject of the painting was necessarily prior to the clothes that he or she wore. For Vertue participated in a social formation in which the cultural and material opposition between person and thing, subject and object, the individual and his or her possessions, had become a given. From that later perspective, the history of portraiture could only ever be a history of faces, faces as the outward and visible sign of an inward invisible state. What an earlier tradition of portraiture reveals is the extent to which even our faces are fashioned, the extent to which the *persona* (originally a mask used in a dramatic performance) precedes the person.

3 Yellow starch: fabrications of the Jacobean court[1]

In chapter 2, we analyzed the function of clothes in the making of portraits. We argued that textiles, armor, jewels, far from being the supplements to a preconceived self, were the material forms out of which a hybrid subject was fashioned. Hybridity itself, though, was a repeated cause of suspicion and alarm. If the aristocrat was fashioned from foreign textiles, did that mean that he or she was fashioned as a traitor, ever ready to follow the supposedly vagrant habits of Italy or France or Spain? If one was permeated by what one wore, did that mean that one was permeated by the material forms of heresy? This was certainly the claim of many radical Protestants during the sixteenth-century vestiarian controversies. Idolatry was rampant not only in the sacrament and in Catholic images but also in the bodily inscriptions of vestments that were the livery of antichrist. In other words, if the body could be composed through clothes, it could also be decomposed.

In this chapter, we turn to the fear of the decomposing body. In the Jacobean fashion of yellow starch, radical Protestants detected a new form of the antichrist's livery. If starch itself decomposed the body politic by turning food into luxury fashion, the yellow with which it began to be dyed was attacked as a stain that "transnatured" men into women, the godly into papists, the English into the foreign.

"Policies, dissimulations, treacheries, witchcraft, conjurings, charmes, adulteries, poysonings, murderings, blasphemies and heresies"[2]

The 1650s saw an extraordinary flood of publications about the reign of James I. A striking feature of these histories is that they ignore altogether the reign of Charles, as if his trial and execution had not been the central political event of the century. Where one would expect to find a narrative of Charles's failures and tyranny, one finds instead a meditation on the court corruptions of James, as if it were he, and not his son, who was the immediate cause of civil war. It is equally surprising that a single event dominates most of these accounts: the murder of Sir Thomas Overbury. Surprising, because although most modern historians mention his murder, it has become one of the better-known byways of James's reign without being seen as the beginning of a highway that led to revolution and the overthrow of a monarch and of the monarchy itself. Yet that is precisely how Overbury's death appears in these accounts.

In 1651, the publisher Michael Sparke produced a compilation of his own making called *Truth Brought to Light and Discovered by Time or A Discourse and Historicall Narration of the first XIIII yeares of King Iames Reigne*. The top of the title page shows Truth and Time pulling back curtains to reveal a diminutive and dead King

James. Below, the figures of Memory and History, recording the truth that will be brought to light, frame the central panel: a coffin out of which a large tree grows, whose fruit is scrolls and books. The facing page has a poem explaining the title page, and the final stanza explains the central panel:

> *At last, i' th' midst, thou may'st a* Coffin *spie,*
> Wherein a murthered-Corps *enclos'd doth lie;*
> On which, a Light *and* Urn, *thou plac'd may'st see,*
> *And in the midst to grow a* spreading Tree,
> *Full fraught with* various Fruits, *most* fresh *and* fair,
> *To make* succeeding Times *most* rich *and* rare.[3]

Truth, the poem claims, not only tramples Error, but also tames "Death, Kings, Crowns, Scepters." Monarchy in fact is depicted *as* death; life, on the contrary, rises up from the tomb of the murdered Overbury, a tomb which offers up the fruits of truth.

Any doubts that the "murthered-Corps" is that of Overbury are dispelled by "The Lively Portraicture of Sir Thomas Overbury" that appears in some copies on the opening prior to the title page. The prominence given to Overbury is extraordinary, given that Sparke's book covers fourteen years of James's reign, and that Sparke divides those years into four parts, in only one of which does Overbury play a significant role. Why is the portrait not of James I, whose reign is to be narrated? Not only is the portrait of Overbury; it is accompanied by a caption which, to the modern eye at least, resolutely situates him in the role of a private man, at the furthest distance from court politics:

> A mans best fortune or his worst's a wife:
> Yet I, that knew nor mariage peace nor strife,
> Live by a good, by a bad one lost my life.

> A wife like her I writ, man scarce can wed:
> Of a false friend like mine, man scarce hath read.

This seemingly cryptic caption would have been clear enough in the seventeenth century, for it refers to one of the most sensational publication successes of the period: the numerous and ever-fatter editions of Overbury's turgid poem, *A Wife* (to which were appended his and other people's "characters," as well as an ever-growing number of elegies to the author and of puffs for his poem). In reusing the portrait and verses that predate 1622, Sparke self-consciously introduces the "private" life of Overbury into the middle of the "public" events at the center of James's reign. Overbury will live through his *Wife*. But he has also been murdered by a wife: Frances Howard, Countess of Somerset, newly married to Robert Carr, James's favorite and Overbury's patron.

The bare outlines of the story of Overbury's death, as it had come to be narrated by those hostile to the court, are reworked in Sparke's account. In 1606, the fourteen-year-old Frances Howard was married off to the fifteen-year-old Earl of Essex. In 1613, Frances Howard and her family requested an annulment of the marriage on the grounds that it had not been consummated. After a virginity test, the countess was given a divorce by a royal commission by a majority of seven to five. The annulment was granted on 25 September 1613. On 3 November Robert Carr, the king's favorite and Overbury's patron, was created Earl of Somerset. On 26 December, Frances Howard married him at court. The marriage of Robert Carr,

Earl of Somerset, and Frances Howard, now Countess of Somerset, was the cause of elaborate celebrations: Campion's *The Somerset Masque* on 26 December; on 27 December, Jonson's *A Challenge at Tilt*; on 29 December, Jonson's *Irish Masque* (repeated again on 3 January); on 1 January, a tilt. On 4 January, the court moved to the Merchant Taylor's Hall, to be fêted by the Lord Mayor with two masques (including Middleton's *Masque of Cupid*) and a play, and on 6 January, the court went to Gray's Inn to see the *Masque of Flowers*, paid for by Francis Bacon. The wedding, in other words, was the stimulus for a wide range of court-, city-, and Inns-of-Court-sponsored literary patronage, including poems by Chapman and Donne justifying the divorce and praising the marriage.[4] After his fall, in fact, Somerset was attacked even for his literary interests. Having been "elected of the council," he had, Sir Edward Peyton wrote in 1652, "furnished his library onely with twenty play-books and wanton romances, and had no other in his study."[5]

Sir Thomas Overbury, previously inseparable from his patron Somerset, played no part in these literary celebrations. Overbury explicitly opposed Somerset's marriage to Frances Howard, and, perhaps by an elaborate plot of Somerset's, also fell into disgrace with James. On 21 April 1613, he was imprisoned in the Tower, where he died on 15 September, three months before the wedding. In 1615, rumors began to circulate that Overbury had been poisoned in the Tower, and the rumors were followed by the arrest and execution of four people either close to Frances Howard or in charge of Overbury's imprisonment. Finally, in May 1616, the Countess of Somerset and then the Earl were tried and found guilty of conspiring to poison Overbury. Yet despite the fact that they were both found guilty, James pardoned them, leading to speculations that Somerset still held some power over James and was possibly in a position to blackmail him.

According to Richard Codrington in his 1646 biography of Essex, Frances Howard's divorced husband, the poisoning of Overbury stemmed directly from his writing *A Wife*. While the Somersets' marriage opened up patronage to a wide range of writers, Overbury's writing led to the end not only of his patronage but of his life. Codrington claims:

> At that time [of Frances Howard's divorce from Essex] there was a gentleman of excellent understanding, Sir Thomas Overbury by name, who, being beloved by the Earl of Somerset, did compose a poem intitled, "The Wife," to dissuade the Earl of Somerset from this marriage; but the lady, conceiving that it did reflect upon her honor, did so prevail with the Earl, that she turned his love unto hatred, and wrought his hatred unto so great a height, that nothing but the death of Sir Thomas Overbury would satisfy their revenge.[6]

We do not know of any evidence to substantiate Codrington's implausible claim.[7] But our interest is not in what we find plausible but in what a wide range of writers in the 1650s (as well as, to a lesser extent, in the 1640s) thought central to an understanding of the political events of their century.[8]

Increasingly significant to such an understanding was the figure of Sir Thomas Overbury, not perhaps in his own life a particularly likeable or even principled man, but in his death gaining ever greater renown: as poet ("Others by Children lengthen out their life / Thou onely art eterniz'd by thy *wife*"[9]); as male victim of a female plot; as Protestant martyr of the Catholic or crypto-Catholic Howard family;[10] as private citizen destroyed by the machinations of a corrupt court. In short, he came to be represented as a republican hero: a critic of the court and monarchy; an opponent of government by "effeminate" favorites ruled by their wives; a staunch defender of the reformed church against Catholicism; an English patriot fighting against Scottish and pro-Spanish courtiers. This interpretation bears little relation to any account that might have been given of Overbury in 1613 at the time of his death. But it was the account that was written into truth by the successive publications of *A Wife* with its accompanying elegies, and by the publication of "secret" histories of James's reign, from the anonymous pamphlet *The Five Years of King James* (1643, but incorporated into Sparke's 1651 *Truth Brought to Light*), to Anthony Weldon's *Court and Character of King James* (1650), *A True and Historical Relation of the Poysoning of Sir Thomas Overbury* (1651), Sir Edward Peyton's *Divine Catastrophe of the Kingly Family of the House of Stuarts* (1652), *A Cat May Look upon a King* (1653), Arthur Wilson's *History of Great Britain, being the Life and Reign of King James I* (1653), Francis Osborne's *Historical Memoirs on the Reigns of Queen Elizabeth and King James* (1658) as well as his scurrilous unpublished play on the Somerset marriage.

In fact, the attack on the Somersets opened the way to a direct critique of the monarchy. Somerset had indeed been elevated from a Scottish commoner to the English aristocracy by James himself. And James had also pushed for the Essex divorce and had later pardoned the Somersets for Overbury's murder. But by the 1650s, the rumor that Frances Howard had been the lover of Prince Henry (James's son, and for many a Protestant hero in contrast to his father) and that she had poisoned him had been transformed into the story that James had poisoned his own son out of jealousy; that James had in turn been poisoned by his next favorite, George Villiers, Duke of Buckingham, and his Catholic mother and wife; that "his minions and favorites rule the kingdom in the name of the king"; and that, being a Scot, James had in any case no right to rule England ("indeed it was the wonder of those Statesmen who had experience of the gallantry of this Nation, that a *Scot* should enjoy the Crown without resistance").[11]

But above all, the destruction of the monarchy was now justified as a purging of the earlier sexual "corruption" of James's court. "The holy state of *Matrimony*," it was claimed, had been "made but a *Maygame*"; "great persons" had "prostitut[ed] their bodies to the intent to satisfie their lusts"; "lawful marriages were divorced or multiplied"; "masques and plays at Whitehall were used onely for incentives of lust" and "the courtiers invited the citizens wives to those shews, on purpose to defile them"; courtiers like Lord Roos had fed their affections "upon the barren and loathsome apples of Sodom."[12] And the Scottish James and his wife, the Danish and Catholic Anne, were, it was now claimed, the fount of all sexual corruption. Anne was "a virago" who, during her marriage to James, "found others to satisfie her unruly appetites"; she had been "more like a bawd than a discreet mother" to her own son; her death was caused by a skeleton in her womb which "prove[d] she was with childe, and that physicke had destroyed it, and so the skeleton remained; which was laboured to be purged away, but all in vain, rotted in her."[13] James himself was a tyrant whose antiwar policy was a plot "to luxuriate the people"; his love to his favorites "was as amorously conveyed as if he had mistaken their Sex"; his kissing of his favorites "after so lascivious a mode in publick, and upon the Theatre as it were of the World," wrote Francis Osborne, "prompted many to imagine some things done in the *Tyring-house*, that exceed my expressions no less than they do my experience."[14]

The first remarkable thing about the publications attacking James in the 1650s is that they give the Somerset marriage, the poisoning of Overbury, and the sexual "corruption" of James's court priority of place in the events leading to the overthrow of the monarchy.[15] The second feature of these accounts is the extraordinary importance they attribute to fashion, and above all to yellow starch, in the unfashioning of godly rule.

"The infection of a yellow band"[16]

Commonwealth attacks upon Jacobean fashions and yellow starch were bolstered by the publication in the 1650s for the first time of certain plays that Middleton and others had written some thirty years earlier. In 1652, "A Comedie" called *The Widdow*, attributed to the hands of Jonson, Fletcher, and Middleton, was published in London. Martia, a young woman, appears disguised as a man in *The Widdow* and, toward the end of the play, she wears the clothes of Brandino, a judge. Brandino, arresting her for the theft of his suit, declares that he will not "wear those clothes again," contaminated as they are by him/her. The judge's clerk, Martino, comments:

That Suit would hang him [i.e. Martia], yet I would not have him hang'd in that Suit though, it will disgrace my Masters fashion forever and make it as hatefull as yellow bands.[17]

It is not just the hanged person who is disgraced but the fashion of the clothes in which he is hanged. To hang Martia in the judge's suit would be to discredit the judge's own style of clothing, as "yellow bands" had previously been discredited. The reference to "yellow bands" is to collars of holland, lawn, cambric, or linen, dyed with yellow starch, that had been fashionable in the 1610s and 1620s, when the play was written, but which do not appear in court wardrobe accounts after 1625. "Yellow bands," then, would seem to be a reference lost not merely on a modern reader but on many, if not most, readers by the middle of the seventeenth century, when the play was published. But in fact "yellow bands" had made an extraordinary comeback in the 1650s, not as an item of apparel but as a textual effect. Their fame depended upon the belief that Anne Turner, a friend and confidante of Frances Howard, when found guilty of assisting in the poisoning of Overbury, had been hanged in November 1615 in a band and cuffs dyed with yellow starch.

Contemporary accounts give extraordinary attention to the claim that Mrs. Turner had invented yellow starch, or at least introduced it into England. Her trial depended upon the sensational accusations that she had been bawd to Frances Howard, Countess of Somerset, when the countess was married to the Earl of Essex; that she had practiced witchcraft with magicians and conjurors, including Simon Forman; that she had made wax models both to secure the love of Somerset and to make the Earl of Essex impotent; that she had solicited poisons from the apothecary Francklin; and that she was, in the words of Coke, the Lord Chief Justice, "a whore, a bawd, a sorcerer, a witch, a papist, a felon, and a murderer."[18] Yet despite the wide range of gossip which her execution provided, the contemporary accounts seem as concerned about the execution of yellow starch as about the execution of a poisoner. James Howell wrote to his father in 1618 that, although the Earl and Countess of Somerset had escaped Coke's death sentences,

yet the subservient Instruments, the lesser Flies could not break thorow, but lay entangled in the Cobweb; amongst others Mistress *Turner*, the first inventress of *yellow Starch*, was executed in a Cobweb Lawn Ruff of that color at *Tyburn*; and with her I believe that *yellow Starch*, which so much disfigured our Nation, and rendered them so ridiculous and fantastic, will receive its Funeral.[19]

Howell, in other words, seems less concerned with the sensational crime for which Anne Turner had been prosecuted than with the elimination of the "*yellow Starch*, which so much disfigured our Nation."

Howell was not alone in focusing upon yellow starch, even at the expense of poisoning and witchcraft. Sir Simonds D'Ewes also focused upon the yellow starch, although in his account, Mrs. Turner had worn it at her trial, while the hangman had worn it at her execution:

Mrs. Turner had first brought up that vain and foolish use of yellow starch, coming herself to her trial in a yellow band and cuffs; and therefore, when she was afterwards executed at Tyburn, the hangman had his band and cuffs of the same color, which made many after that day of either sex to forbear the use of that colored starch, till it at last grew generally to be detested and disused.[20]

It may well be that both Howell's and D'Ewes's versions are confused. John Castle wrote to James Miller in the very month when Mrs. Turner was hanged, and he does not mention either Mrs. Turner or the executioner wearing yellow starch. He claims, on the contrary, that Mrs. Turner used the occasion, like Mary Magdalen, to turn her back upon her sins and to denounce "painted pride, lust, powdered hair, yellow bands, and all of the rest of the wardrobe of court vanities."[21] But in Castle's account, as in those of Howell and D'Ewes, it is yellow starch and "the wardrobe of court vanities," rather than poisoning and witchcraft, that appear to be on trial. Why this extraordinary emphasis upon what looks, to a modern eye, like a peripheral issue?

Just how central this issue of yellow bands remained, even after the fashion had died out, is suggested by the fact that, the year before the publication of *The Widdow* in 1652, two books appeared which addressed not only the murder of Overbury but also yellow starch. The first was the anonymous *A True and Historical Relation of the Poysoning of Sir Thomas Overbury*; the second was Michael Sparke's *Truth Brought to Light*, which not only focuses upon Mrs. Turner, but also foregrounds her execution in "The Epistle to the Reader":

were there now in these times such Sentence and Execution performed, as the then Learned Lord Cook gave on that fomenter of Lust, Mistris Anne Turner, whose sentence was to be hanged at Tiburn in her yellow Tiffiny Ruff and Cuffs, being she was the first Inventer and wearer of that horrid garb. Were there now in these daies the like upon such notorious black-spotted Faces, naked Brests and Backs, no doubt but that ugly Fashion would soon there end in shame and detestation, which now is too vainly followed: For never since the Execution of her in that yellow Ruff and Cuffs there hanged with her, was ever any seen to wear the like.[22]

There are several notable features of Sparke's account. First, Mrs. Turner's "invention" of yellow starch merits a significant place in a "discourse and Historicall Narration of the first XIIII yeares of King Iames Reigne"; second, the hanging of Mrs. Turner is interpreted as simultaneously the hanging, and eradication, of the fashion which she introduced (cf. the clerk's claim in *The Widdow* that to hang Martia in the judge's suit "will disgrace my Masters fashion for ever, and make it as hatefull as yellow bands"); third, "shame, infamy and misery" are said to originate in "vanity and adultery."

Sparke was, perhaps, drawing upon Humphrey Mill's attack upon "Night-

Walkers," which had been published in 1640. Sparke, like Mill, uses yellow starch (which had disappeared by the late 1620s) as a stick to beat the continuing fashions of exposed breasts, black spots, and patches. Of the use of patches by "Night-Walkers," whether prostitutes or women of high fashion, Mill had written:

> Who taught thee't? was't a witch, a whore or devill?
> For such are forward'st in all kind of evill.
> (The poysoning witch that did to Tiburne march,
> Was held the first that brought up yellow starch).[23]

But whereas Mill uses Anne Turner's importation of yellow starch to attack London's night life, Sparke uses it as the epitome of all the evils of the monarchy and the court.

For Sparke, as for Mill, yellow adulterates the wearer's body, masculinizing women and effeminating men. But it also, he suggests, transforms Protestant into papist, patriot into traitor, the human into the monstrous or the demonic. Sparke's focus upon yellow starch, then, is not a displacement of witchcraft and poisoning but a condensation of them. Fashion, like witchcraft, is imagined as an illicit form of making. As Karen Newman remarks,

In the notorious Lancashire trials of 1612, clay pictures and images were frequently adduced as evidence of *maleficium*. Witchcraft involved injury, doing harm; but my emphasis here is on the etymological force of the word, its root in the verb *facio*, to make, construct, fashion, frame, build, erect, produce, compose. The fashioning of such images at once suggests the power and danger of mimesis.[24]

The word "fashion" is also derived from *facio*. The accusation that Mrs. Turner had invented yellow starch was an accusation of evil making, *male-ficium*, a making which introduced *faction* (also derived from *facio*) into the body politic, dismembering it through the act of molding and remaking it.[25] "Vanity," then, is seen not as some marginal vice but as the process by which the kingdom is remodeled in a demonic image. It is a form of magic in which the "fashioned" person is permeated by the materials and dyes which he or she has touched. In Richard Niccols's *Sir Thomas Overburies Vision* (1616), the ghost of Mrs. Turner returns to demonstrate the connection between fashion, the foreign, and the satanic:

> First pride array'd me in her loose attires,
> Fed my fond fancie fat with vaine desires,
> Taught me each fashion, brought me ouer-seas
> Each new deuise, the humorous time to please:
> But of all vaine inuentions, then in vse
> When I did liue, none suffer'd more abuse
> Then that phantasticke vgly fall and ruffe,
> Daub'd o're with that base starch of yellow stuffe:
> O that my words might not be counted vaine,
> But that my counsell might find entertaine
> With those, whose soules are tainted with the itch
> Of this disease, whom pride doth so bewitch,
> That they doe thinke it comely, not amisse:
> Then would they cast it off, and say, it is
> The baud to pride, the badge of vanity,
> Whose very sight doth murder modestie,
> Ye then detesting it, they all would knowe,
> Some wicked wit did fetch it from belowe,
> That here they might expresse by this attire

> The color of those wheeles of Stygian fire,
> Which prides plum'd ofspring with snake-powdred haire,
> About their necks in *Plutoes* Court doe weare.[26]

Yellow starch is "baud to pride," "the badge of vanity," and it "doth murder modestie." It is also the color of hell's fires. Yellow, in fact, had long been associated not only with satanic flames but also with the clothes that Judas wore. In Giotto's *Betrayal of Christ*, for instance, as Judas embraces Christ, he covers him in his yellow robes.

But if Mrs. Turner's use of yellow starch is satanic, it is at the same time one of the "vaine desires" that are fed from "ouer-seas." The implication that foreign fashions dismember the body politic was a commonplace. Thomas Dekker, for instance, claimed that "an English-mans suite is like a traitors bodie that hath beene hanged, drawne, and quartered, and is set vp in seuerall places."[27] To fashion oneself through alien clothes was to factionalize both one's own body and the state. The materiality of the foreign cloth and dye effected a material dis-location, fracturing the wearer's body into conflicting kingdoms. In *Notes from Blackfryers*, first published two years after Mrs. Turner's execution and reprinted in 1619 and 1620, Henry Fitzgeoffrey satirized the "foreignness" of the gallant who attends the theater:

> Knowest thou yon world of fashions now come in
> In *Turkie* colors carued to the skin,
> Mounted *Polonianly* untill hee reeles,
> That scornes (so much) *plaine dealing* at his heeles.
> His Boote speakes *Spanish* to his *Scottish* Spurres,
> His Sute cut *Frenchly*, round bestucke with Burres.
> Pure *Holland* is his Shirt, which proudly faire,
> Scornes to out-face his *Doublet* euery where.
> His Haire like to your *Moor's* or *Irish* Lockes,
> His chiefest Dyet, *Indian* minced Dockes.
> What Countrey *may-game* might wee this suppose,
> Sure one woo'd thinke a *Roman* by his *Nose*.
> No! In his *Habite* better vnderstand,
> Hee is of *England* by his *Yellow Band*.[28]

To recognize the Englishman by his yellow bands is to recognize him as a traitor: following the fashions of the executed Mrs. Turner, he follows fashions which are foreign, papist, and effeminating (because invented by a woman).

In fact, yellow starch condensed into the detail of a fashion accessory a whole series of histories of the "foreign." To take the question of color first. The yellow coloring that distinguished Mrs. Turner's bands and ruffs came from saffron, derived from the dried stigmas at the top of the pistils of crocus flowers. Throughout the sixteenth century, saffron dye was associated above all with the Irish. Saffron had been imported to Ireland, possibly as early as the tenth century, either from Spain or from the Middle East. The dyestuff was expensive, because it took so long to pick the thousands of stamens necessary to produce it, but the Irish were dyeing linen with saffron in considerable quantities by the early sixteenth century.[29] Saffron-dyed linen was, indeed, targeted as a form of excessive luxury from the beginning of English attempts to control the country. In 1536, Henry VIII, in an effort to suppress what was seen as Anglo-Irish as well as native extravagance, forbade his subjects in Galway to wear saffron in their "shirts, smocks or any other garments," and he extended the prohibition to the rest of the country the next year.[30]

Paradoxically, saffron was also seen as a sign of poverty, of the uncouth roughness of people who owned too few clothes and harbored vermin as a result. Edmund Spenser thought the Irish had adopted the dye from Spain because it was used there to prevent "that evil which cometh of much sweating and long wearing of linen."[31] Fynes Morryson, reporting on his Irish travels, was more specific: because the "wild Irish," a very "lowsie people," wore their shirts constantly, never removing them until they fell apart, their shirts were "colored with saffron to avoid lowsieness, incident to the wearing of foule linnen."[32] The Venetian ambassador, Ludovico Falier, supported (or repeated) this explanation in a report to his Senate that the Irish "wear a shirt steeped in saffron [*zafferanata*] on account of the lice."[33] Several English commentators also remarked on the fact that the Irish used urine to intensify the dye. William Camden in his history of Britain quotes William Good, a priest and schoolmaster in Limerick, on the technique: "Their way is not to boil the thing long, but to let it soak for some days in urine that the color may be deeper and more durable," and Camden himself remarks that when Shane O'Neill visited Queen Elizabeth, his bodyguards wore shirts that had been dyed with saffron or "infected with human urine."[34]

As a culturally freighted color, saffron yellow linked luxury and contaminating waste; at the same time, it was seen as originating with England's traditional enemies, Spain, Ireland, and France,[35] all seats of "the whore of Babylon." In a lengthy attack on yellow starch, Thomas Stoughton captured the ambivalent status of the saffron dye. It was a product of "the common school of all vanitie" – "except only in Ireland, where they saffron all their wearing linnen (as some report) for the auoiding of that vermin, that do most abound in that country." Yet those who in England plead thrift are unmasked both by the fact that they do not "yellow also their other wearing apparel" and also by the fact that they are "in all other things . . . most prodigall, most riotous."[36] In "inventing" yellow starch, Mrs. Turner had installed the whore of Babylon at the heart of the English court.

A further twist was given to the attack on yellow starch as an attack on the court by the fact that saffron was as commonly used in Scotland as Ireland. In other words, in treating saffron as a characteristic of the "debased" Irish, one could also implicitly attack the Scots who now, English "patriots" complained, ruled England. As Lindsay of Pittscottie wrote in 1573, the "wild Scots" were "cloathed with ane mantle, with ane schirt saffroned after the Irish manner." And Robert Gordon claimed in his account of Scottish fashions at the time of the Battle of Glenlivet in 1594 that "next the Skin they wear a short linnen Shirt, which the great men among them sometimes dye of saffron color." Later, in 1703, Martin Martin wrote in *A Description of the Western Islands of Scotland*: "The first Habit worn by Persons of Distinction in the Islands was the *Leni-Croich*, from the Irish word *Leni*, which signifies a shirt, and *Croch* [from "crocus"], Saffron, because their Shirt was dyed with that Herb."[37]

Saffron dye was associated both with the foreign (whether Spanish, French, Irish, or Scottish) and with a woman (Mrs. Turner), and this association was equally true in the case of starch. To begin with, women were the producers of linen. Throughout early modern Europe, while men were usually the tailors of men's and women's clothing alike, women were responsible for the making and starching of linen undergarments. Thus the clothes that were closest to the skin were fashioned by women. If it was a woman who supposedly introduced yellow starch in England, it was also supposedly a woman and a "foreigner" who had introduced starch itself. According to John Stow in his *Annales of England*,

In the third yeere of the Raigne of Queene Elizabeth, 1562, began the knowledge and wearing of Lawne and Cambricke, which was then brought into England by very small quantities, and when the Queene had Ruffes made thereof, for her own Princely wearing, there was none in England could tell how to starch them, for untill then all the Kinges and Queenes of England wore fine Holland in Ruffes, but the Queene made speciall meanes for some Dutch woman that could starch, and Guilliam's wife, was the first starcher the Queene had, and himselfe was the first coachman.[38]

While the Dutchwoman Gwillam Boone became starcher by appointment to Elizabeth, Dinghen ven der Plasse, a Flemish refugee, set up a starching business in London in 1564 and, according to Stow, charged English women £4–£5 to show them how to starch and a further 20s. to show them how to prepare starch.[39] In fact, starch made from the sap of cuckoo-pint (the wild arum plant) had been used before this, but it blistered the hands and, until the fashion for starched ruffs, there had been little call for it. Now, with the invasion of Dutch fashions in ruffs, there was a corresponding demand for starch.

But this new fashion (as all "fashion") was bitterly decried by Protestant "patriots" like Phillip Stubbes. For Stubbes, indeed, ruffs and starch were the very emblem of the subjugation of "Ailgna" (England) not only to foreigners but to Satan:

But wot you what? the deuil, as he in the fulnes of his malice, first inuented these great ruffes, so hath hee now found also two great stayes to beare vp and maintaine this his kingdome of great ruffes (for the deuil is king and prince ouer all the children of pride) the one arch or piller wherby his kingdome of great ruffes is underpropped is a certaine kind of liquide matter which they call Starch, wherin the deuill hath willed them to wash and diue his ruffes wel, which when they be dry, wil then stand stiffe and inflexible about their necks.[40]

To later editions of *The Anatomie of Abuses* (first pubished in 1583) Stubbes added a story that literalized the connections between starch, women, and Satan. According to this "true" tale, a "gentlewoman of Eprautna" (i. e. Antwerp) was invited to a wedding on 27 May 1582. Unable to find anyone "(so curious and daintie she was) that could starche, and sette her Ruffes," she invoked the devil, who appeared, "transfformyng himself into the forme of a young man." He set her ruffs, kissed her, and then broke her neck, "her bodie beyng Metamorphosed, into blacke and blewe colors." At her funeral, when four men were unable to lift her coffin, they opened it and "founde the bodie to be taken awaie, and a blacke Catte verie leane and deformed sittyng in the Coffin, setting of great Ruffes, and frizlyng of haire, to the great feare, and wonder of all the beholders." In this extraordinary story, the gentlewoman is metamorphosed into her own "accessories" (frizzled hair and ruffs), attended on by a familiar in the form of a cat. And when Philoponus has finished his story, Spudeus recasts it as a tale less of Satan's than of women's witchcraft, the outcome of "*Cyrces* cups" or "the *exorcisms* of *Medea*."[41]

If starch was seen by militant Protestants as simultaneously foreign, effeminating, and demonic ("the *Diuells* Idoll" as Sir Poule Either-side calls it),[42] it was also attacked for enriching the nobility at the expense of the poor. Being made from bran, starch turned potential food into fashion for the elite. And while the monarchy turned this new product into a source of profit, selling the monopoly on starch to Sir John Pakinton in 1598, it also recognized that starch was a potential source of civil unrest. In October 1595, a period of serious dearth, a crowd in Cheapside made a carman unload the starch he was carrying. And a royal proclamation the next year declared that

her majesty, being informed of an abuse greatly tending to make a scarcity of corn meet to make bread by making of starch within the realm, doth straightly command that no manner of person shall make any starch of any corn or bran of corn grown within the realm, or that is or shall be brought into the realm, nor wittingly sell or utter any such starch except such as hath been made by virtue of her majesty's letters patent.[43]

Again, in 1607 (the probable year in which *Coriolanus* with its account of grain riots was written), the starch industry was attacked in Parliament for wasting wheat and causing food shortages.[44] But despite (or because of) such protests, which were probably fostered by merchants trying to reorganize the trade, the Royal Commission set up to regulate starch in September concluded, the following year, by granting the monopoly on starch to the Earl of Northampton. Northampton was not only the most active member of the Howard family, he was also the uncle of Frances Howard, later to be Countess of Somerset. A life-long Catholic, he was the recipient of money from Spain, and deeply implicated in the murder of Overbury, although he died before his part in the affair could be investigated. From the perspective of Protestant critics, starch, the invention of foreign women, had been given over into the hands of the least "English" of James's English councillors. Moreover, while Northampton was meant to be helping to finance the monarchy, he was making a killing from starch himself. Promising to pay James £333. 6s. 8d., he sublet the farming of starch for £3,000. In fact, it was upon starch, together with grants of land, that Northampton's new fortune rested. But, because of continued complaints about the shortage of grain in 1609–10 and the deep unpopularity of Northampton with the active Protestant faction in Parliament, his monopoly in starch was revoked by Parliament in January 1610 and, on 22 August of that year, there was a royal proclamation absolutely prohibiting the making of starch.[45] Needless to say, starch continued to be made in large quantities, but the constant attempts to regulate or ban it suggest its political volatility. By the 1610s, it had become associated in the eyes of militant Protestants with the foreign, the demonic, the "Catholic."

Yellow starch had in fact been put on the stage and mocked in Thomas Tomkis's *Albumazar*, a comedy performed at Trinity College, Cambridge, on 9 March 1615 before an audience that included not only James I but many of the Howard faction. The most significant absence from the performance was Queen Anne. She was a bitter opponent of both Somerset and the Howards. Given that this state visit was arranged by the university's Chancellor, the Earl of Suffolk, Frances Howard's father and Somerset's father-in-law, it is not surprising that it was rumored that she had deliberately not been invited. According to John Chamberlain, there were at the play "few or none present, but of the Howards or that alliance as the Countesse of Arundell with her sister the Lady Elizabeth Gray: the Countesse of Suffolke with her daughters of Salisburie and Somerset, the Lady Walden and Henry Howards wife."[46] Yet before this audience, the foolish gallant Trincalo, "choicely neate" in his clothes, his language "drawne from the Plaies I see at the Fortune, and Red Bull, where I learne all the words I speake and vnderstand not," appears in a collar starched yellow. And the transformation of food into fashion is alluded to in Armellina's mocking greeting: "*Trincalo*, what price beare's wheate, and Saffron, that your band's so stiffe and yellow?"[47] Such a scene treads dangerously close to an outright attack upon the fashions of the court, even if the attack is indirect because aimed not at aristocrats but at their apes.

The most sustained attack upon colored starch appears in Middleton and Rowley's masque, *The World Tost at Tennis* (1620), where the social target is unspecified, or rather is presented in the guise of the growth of factions and generalized deceit. In the masque, "The fiue Starches: White, Blue, Yellow, Greene, and Red" are presented by Jupiter as the corrupters of a happier time:

> Pride brought in
> Forgetfulnesse of goodnesse, Merit, Vertue,
> And plac'd ridiculous Officers in life;
> Vaine-glory, Fashion, Humour, and such toyes
> That shame to be produc'd.
> The phrenzie of Apparell, that's runne mad,
> And knowes not where to settle Masculine painting;
> And the fiue Starches, mocking the fiue Sences,
> All in their diff'rent and ridiculous colors,
> Which for their apish and fantastique follies,
> I summon to make odious, and will fit vm
> With flames of their owne colors.[48]

The five Starches enter and compete over which is the most ancient vice, finally leaving after dancing. Jupiter responds to their exit:

> These are the youngest Daughters of deceit,
> With which the precious time of life's beguil'd,
> Fool'd, and abus'd; Ile shew you straight their Father,
> His shapes, his labours, that has vext the world
> From age to age, and tost it from his first and simple state,
> To the foule Center where it now abides.[49]

Simplicity then enters, to mourn the corruption of the world by the Starches' father, Deceit, who smells "abominably" of "controuersies, Schismes and Factions" and in whom one can find "forty Religions together."[50] Colored starch, then, is the progeny of Deceit, which only a monarch who follows Simplicity can undo.[51]

By contrast, Jonson in his later work attempted to defuse the political potency of yellow starch. For the Christmas celebrations of 1616, performed after the execution of Anne Turner but before the trials of the Somersets, Jonson wrote "Christmas his Masque." The mumming begins with Christmas himself, who introduces his ten children, the first of whom, appropriately enough for the season, is Misrule. Misrule wears a "great yellow Ruffe like a Reveller," later claiming that he "doth not like his suite: he saies the Players have lent him one too little, on purpose to disgrace him." While yellow starch is the garb of a reveller, this is the licensed revelling of Christmas. The satanic infection that militant Protestants discovered in the fashion is recuperated as festive play. In fact, in his masque Jonson is revisiting a topic that he had developed more fully in *The Devil is an Ass*, performed the same year as the masque. The climax of *The Devil is an Ass* is a scene in which Fitzdottrel fakes demonic possession. The case of possession is probably based upon the case of John Smith of Leicester, who pretended to be possessed and was responsible for the hanging of nine women on 18 July 1616. James himself took an interest in the case and unmasked the fraud in August, after Smith had accused six more women. Merecraft tells Fitzdottrel that "A Boy o' thirteene yeere old made [the devil] an *Assel* But t' other day" (5. 5. 50–1). Fitzdottrel's fraudulent possession, then, is a faking of a faking.

But Jonson adds a curious element to Fitzdottrel's "possession." As he foams at the mouth (with the help of soap), he raves "*Yellow, yellow, yellow, yellow*, etc." (5. 8. 74). Sir Poule Either-side, the foolish Puritan justice investigating the proceedings, knows immediately how to interpret Fitzdottrel's single word:

> That's *Starch*! the *Diuells* Idoll of that color.
> He ratifies it with clapping of his hands.
> The proofes are pregnant.   (5. 8. 75–7)

Jonson had already mocked Puritan horror at starch in *The Alchemist*. There, Subtle confers with Tribulation and Ananias, respectively pastor and deacon of Amsterdam, about what the matrons of the church may or may not do: whether they

> May lay their haire out, or weare doublets:
> Or haue that idoll *Starch*, about their linnen.   (3. 2. 81–2)

To which Ananias responds, "[i]t is, indeed an idoll" (3. 2. 83).[52] In *The Devil is an Ass*, Fitzdottrel's "ratification" of Sir Poule's interpretation of "yellow" as the color of "the *Diuells* Idoll" by clapping his hands is in fact taken from an earlier case of "possession," also alluded to in the play (5. 3. 6): that of Thomas Darling, supposedly possessed and exorcised by the Puritan preacher John Darrel. Samuel Harsnet, who exposed Darling in *A Discouery of the Fraudulent Practices of Iohn Darrel*, quoted a ballad that mockingly claimed of Darling that

> *He shewed the manner of our Fardingales,*
> *Our Buskes, and Perriwigges, Masks, and Vales,*
> *And by clapping of his handes,*
> *Hee shewed the starching of our bandes.*[53]

For Jonson, as for Harsnet, the Puritan obsession with fashion and with starch is absurd. In *The Devil is an Ass*, to the supposed absurdity of starchphobia Jonson adds the new phobia against *yellow* starch. Writing after the execution of Anne Turner, Jonson can still find nothing but comedy in the notion that the Devil might inhere in an item of fashion.[54]

Yet Jonson's critique of the attack on yellow starch is perhaps politically defensive.[55] For he was responding to a literature that, following Mrs. Turner's trial, was increasingly directed at the court itself, imagined as subjugated by women, by Catholics, by foreigners. Mrs. Turner was a Catholic; the Earl of Somerset was a "foreigner," being, like the monarch, Scottish, and having received his fashionable training in France; and the Countess of Somerset was a Howard, and thus allied to the pro-Spanish faction. Through them, so it was claimed, a fashion that had, with some success, been prohibited on the borders of that fiction, "Great Britain," emerged as high fashion in Westminster, from where it was re-exported both to the provinces and to Ireland. The English court had, so its opponents implied, itself become the chief perpetrator of alien modishness. Barnabe Rich, one of the most violent denigrators of the Irish, nevertheless came to see the Irish as the corrupted victims of English fashion. In *The Irish Hubbub*, the prefatory letter of which is signed "Dublin the 24. of Iune 1618," so disgusted is Rich with English fashions that he represents himself as borrowing an Irish mantle. In his earlier writings, the mantle had been the very sign of civil disobedience; but now, since it "carrieth no shew of pride," the mantle, although still a "disguised manner," may more readily suggest "inward vertue" than a "more glorious garment."[56] Rich represents yellow starch as already having unmanned the English:

Our mindes are effeminated, our martiall exercises and disciplines of warre are turned into womanish pleasures and delights: our Gallants thinke it better spend their lands and liuings in a whores lap, then their liues in a martiall field for the honour of their Countrey. Wee haue conuerted the coller of steele to a yellow-starched band.[57]

Like tobacco, yellow starch "was first brought into England by some man of little vertue"; but now, base women, "proud and new upstart changelings," have corrupted the Irish: "They be these that haue filled *Ireland* so full of new fashions, by their strange alterations in their Ruffes, in their Cuffs, in their huffes, in their puffes, in their muffes, and in many other vanities, that *Ireland* was neuer acquainted withall, till these women brought them vp."[58] Thus, in Rich's view, even if a "man of little vertue" had first imported yellow starch to England, its effeminating contagion was the doing of women.

Moreover, yellow starch, like contagion, could not be simply executed as Mrs. Turner had been. One of the most curious features of the majority of both contemporary and later accounts of Mrs. Turner's execution is that they claim that, with her death, the fashion for yellow starch had also died. In Howell's letter (quoted above), the eradication of yellow starch is a hope; but in the accounts of D'Ewes, of the authors of *The Widdow*, of the 1650s writers like Michael Sparke, and of modern historians and critics like Beatrice White and David Lindley, that hope is translated into accomplished fact. According to them, the ignominy of Mrs. Turner directly led to the ignominy of yellow starch. But Rich (and a range of other testimony) directly contradicts this view. Indeed, according to Rich, Mrs. Turner's deathbed renunciation of yellow starch, far from discrediting the fashion, helped to circulate it even more widely:

in the place where shee was executed, . . . before the whole multitude that were there present, she so bitterly protested against the vanitie of those yellow-starcht bands, that her outcryes (as it was thought) had taken such impression on the hearts of her hearers, that yellow starcht bands would haue been ashamed (for euer after to haue shewed themselves about the neckes, either of men that were wise, or of women that were honest) but wee see our expectation hath failed vs, for they beganne euen then to bee more generall then they were before.[59]

Yellow starch had, in fact, become fashionable only shortly before the marriage of Somerset and Frances Howard. In Jonson's *The Alchemist*, entered into the Stationer's Register in 1610, Subtle speaks of "my-lords goose-turd bands" (4. 4. 50), and blue starch had been common before that.[60] But from 1614, yellow starch became a familiar target of satirists. In that year, Richard Niccols wrote an epigram attacking "a rusticke Asse" who "late a yellow band he carried downe / To make himselfe more noted in the Towne." But because he has also adopted the latest style of boots and spurs, in place of shoes, no one even notices "the fashion of his yellow band." Niccols also attacks three women in a coach, sitting like "Furies," whose "yellow colored bands, and strange attire / About their neckes, appear'd like wheeles of fire."[61] In 1615, Richard Brathwait attacked "Parasites" who had become "Poettasters" (was he attacking those like Campion, Jonson, Donne, and Chapman who had celebrated the marriage of the Somersets?) and who wrote sycophantically in praise of any absurd fashion:

> not a saffron band,
> But like a roaring boye, can make thee stand
> And yeeld obseruance to him.[62]

And Brathwait's "The Ape of Fashion," belatedly published in 1658 and rekindling the attack on James's court, begins "Fashion thou art mine Idol." But by now we should scarcely be surprised to find out just where this idol-worship leads:

> Twelve yeers and more I have a Trav'ler been
> In France and Italy, where I have seen
> Variety of fashions, whose rich fraught
> I now, at last, have to my Countrey brought;
> For I was he that did the first discover
> Your Saffron yolkie band, and brought it over.[63]

In 1616, Robert Anton raged against the *"sur-reuerence fashion"* of saffron, that turned *"Gentilitie"* into "some painted *whoore"*:

> where are those
> That had more *honour* in their *minds* than *clothes*;
> Great *Caesars* court did shine with warlick *hands*;
> Ieer *Atlas*. Ieer, and laugh at *yellow bands*,
> That now do *staine the times*.

Now, Anton writes, the *"mortalitie* of *pestilence"* rises from the *"muckhill* of [upstarts'] prides" and

> each phantastick corner of the *land*,
> Stinkes with *infection* of a *yellow band*.[64]

In 1619, John Heath wrote against a fashionable woman who, scornful of the fact that she had been imitated by mere citizens, hit upon the device of dyeing her hair and her collar:

> But *Lusia* now doth such a fashion follow,
> Whose Hayre is Flax, and Band as Saffron yellow,
> That there's no Citizen, what ere she be,
> Can be transformed so like an Owle as she.[65]

In 1621, Joseph Martyn wrote "To Flaua of her yellow Band," claiming that the yellow of her collar showed the ripeness of her vice:

> Yet *Flaua* this excuse hath still at hand;
> Most braine-sicke men do weare a yellow band.[66]

The dates of these satires show that if the fashion for starch shortly preceded the Somersets' marriage and their disgrace, it survived for several years after those events.

Paintings from the same period tell the same story. The Suffolk collection, now housed at the Ranger's House, Blackheath, depicts the Countess of Suffolk, Frances Howard's mother, in a band that has been starched yellow. A portrait of Lady Dorothy Cary in the same collection depicts her not only with yellow ruff and cuffs but also in an Irish mantle, as if to flaunt the unEnglishness of the Howard faction. Both these elaborate and magnificent full-length portraits by William Larkin were painted before the disgrace of the Howard faction. Indeed, it is probable that the paintings commemorate either the marriage of the Princess Elizabeth to the Elector

Palatine or, more likely, the marriage of Frances Howard herself to the Earl of Somerset. The point of such portraits was often to commemorate the extraordinary outlay on clothes at such festivities. In the portrait of Frances Howard at the National Portrait Gallery, she also appears in a yellow ruff. What is extraordinary, though, is that Paul van Somer's portrait of Queen Anne, an opponent of Somerset, painted in 1617, two years after the supposed humiliation of yellow starch, depicts her in a ruff and cuffs that have been dyed with saffron. The queen is also wearing other fashions of the "*hic mulier*," the very fashions of Frances Howard herself: short hair, plumed high hat, low-cut dress.[67] In fact, the inventories of the court wardrobe reveal that yellow starch was used at least into the middle years of the 1620s, when Rubens depicted the wife of the Duke of Buckingham (the replacement to Somerset in James's favors) with a yellow-dyed lace trimming at the yoke of her bodice and with yellow-dyed cuffs.[68]

One can further trace the actual demise of the fashion for yellow starch to the mid-1620s in *Alba Amicorum*. These were scrap-books used mainly by German travelers, composed of the signatures of famous people, heraldry, quotes and mottos, and small fashion pictures of the places they visited. These fashion pictures were clearly the work of professional workshops in London, Paris, Venice, and so on, because the designs are repeated from book to book. In the *Album Amicorum* of Tobias Oelhafen, who traveled to France, Geneva, and London in 1623–4, the woman identified as "An English Ladie" is depicted with falling collar and cuffs dyed with yellow starch. The same years, Georg von Holzschuer visited Switzerland, France, and England, and he has the same design of the English lady with yellow starch. Joachim Kammerer, who probably visited two to four years later, collected the same picture in his book, but his lady's collar and cuffs are no longer dyed yellow. The fashion had passed.[69] But while it lasted, to the despair of its critics, it was adopted by every faction at court.

Indeed, just across from the portrait of Frances Howard in yellow starch in the National Portrait Gallery, there is a portrait of George Villiers with collar and cuffs dyed yellow.[70] Buckingham had been expressly groomed as a rival to Somerset by the Protestant faction at court, led by the Earl of Pembroke and the Archbishop of Canterbury, George Abbot. The rise of George Villiers, the son of a Leicestershire gentleman, was meteoric. On 23 April 1615 (St. George's Day), he was knighted; on 4 January 1616, he was made Master of the Horse; in April 1616, he was appointed a Knight of the Garter; and in July he was given the lands of Lord Grey of Wilton, who had been found guilty of treason, and created Viscount Villiers. In early 1617, he was made Earl (later Duke) of Buckingham and appointed to the Privy Council.[71] The portrait of him in the National Portrait Gallery shows a very youthful Villiers in the full robes of a Knight of the Garter. The portrait was probably painted in 1616 to commemorate his new position. It was painted, in other words, in the same year as the conviction of Somerset and, retrospectively, can be seen as marking the displacement of the Scottish favorite, assimilated to the pro-Catholic, pro-Spanish Howards, by an English favorite, promoted by the anti-Catholic, anti-Spanish faction. Yet Buckingham is depicted, like Frances Howard, wearing yellow starch; and he is depicted a year after the supposed "death" of the fashion with the execution of Anne Turner.

Yellow starch, in other words, was a generic court fashion, worn by men and women alike, both before and after the trial of the Somersets. By associating yellow starch with the Somerset/Howard faction, though, critics of the court were able to attack the continuing "corruption" of the court, under the guise of attacking a discredited faction and a discredited fashion. And Buckingham would rapidly come to be seen as another Somerset, particularly after he journeyed to Spain with Prince Charles in an attempt to arrange a marriage with the Spanish Infanta. The return of Charles unmarried in 1623 was the occasion for massive popular celebrations, and Buckingham was widely accused of having used his "best tricks with Catholicks / to bring our Prince to Spaine."[72] In fact, Buckingham's mother and his wife had converted to Catholicism in 1623, and Buckingham's failures as a military leader were implicitly blamed upon his mother in an anonymous lampoon:

> Could not thy mother's masses, nor her crosses,
> Nor yet her sorceries prevent these losses?[73]

When Buckingham was murdered in 1628, his assailant, John Felton, was "uniformly hailed as 'stout' and brave, the opposite of the effeminate, foppish coward Buckingham." Felton had, from a radical Protestant perspective, overthrown "Treason, ambition, murder, pride, and lust," the very corruptions of which Somerset and Frances Howard had been accused.[74] Buckingham, like the Somersets, was a creature of the court, attacked as effeminate, crypto-Catholic, pro-Spanish, and suspected of using poison to murder James I. He too had been "infected" by yellow starch.

We would argue, then, that anticourt rhetoric deliberately put together contradictory claims: first, that yellow starch was the exclusive wear of the Howard faction and was a sign of their sexual and religious depravity; second, that yellow starch fell immediately from fashion with the execution of Anne Turner in 1615; third, that yellow starch was the transsexualizing fashion of a wide range of courtiers and courtesans, roaring boys and country imitators, continuing well into the 1620s; fourth, that yellow starch was the fashion of Queen Anne herself and of the Duke of Buckingham, the king's favorite after the fall of Somerset. To this series, we can add a fifth contradictory element. As Stephen Orgel has shown, the Dean of Westminster, with James's encouragement and approval, attacked women who wore "masculine" fashions. Taking this to include yellow starch, the Dean refused to admit any "Ladies and gentlewomen" wearing yellow ruffs into the pews of his church. James was prevailed upon to explain to the Dean that "his meaning was not for yellow ruffs, but for other man-like and unseemly apparel."[75] Orgel goes on to ask, given that Queen Anne herself wore such "masculine" apparel, was the Dean's attack upon such clothes also an attack upon the queen, partially licensed by James himself, since Anne had set up her own independent household and followed an independent line in religion and politics from her husband? We can push this argument further. If James claimed that he did not mean to attack yellow starch, how can we explain his outburst on his way from Whitehall to Westminster to open Parliament in 1621? According to Sir Simonds D'Ewes, "looking up to one window as he passed, full of gentlewomen or ladies, all in yellow bands, he cried out aloud, 'A p – take ye! are ye there?' at which being much ashamed, they all withdrew themselves suddenly from the window."[76] Was it that James, like the satirists, feared and detested the fashions which his own court generated? Or did he fulminate against the appropriation of those fashions outside the privileged domain of the court?

Whatever James's own attitude, the attack on yellow starch provided a focus for the development of an anticourt rhetoric that was not limited to a critique of the Somerset/Howard faction. That is, to the extent that satirists, preachers, and parliamentarians (like D'Ewes) derided yellow starch as a condensation of the "foreign," the "Catholic," the "whorish," the "satanic," they found a means of attacking a court in which yellow starch continued to be a dominant fashion, a fashion patronized by both the queen and by the king's favorite (for all James's own protestations against yellow starch). It was this discourse, emerging in the 1610s, that would openly flourish in the 1650s as the rationale for the overthrow of the monarchy. In yellow starch, republican theorists found a fashion accessory that combined all that they detested in the court: its permeability by the "foreign" and above all by Catholic influences; its vanity, pride, and sexual corruption; its supposed fashioning (like starch) by the hands of women. But in the process, they left a troubling legacy within republican ideology, a legacy in which a radical class politics was generated at the cost of profoundly conservative gender, sexual, religious and nationalist politics, as if all evil could be attributed to women, to those who chafed at the confines of marriage and heterosexuality, to Catholics, to the Spanish or the French or the Irish or the Scots.[77]

This conservative republicanism also naturalized English virtue, as if it was embedded in pastoral wool and cloth production and contaminated by the workings of culture in the form of "fashion." In the process, nostalgic republicanism profoundly mystified England's own technological history. For England had traditionally been the European outpost for the raw material of cloth production (wool and unfinished cloth), while the necessary but more sophisticated processes that transformed unfinished cloth into dyed and finished cloth had been carried out in the Low Countries and Italy. Finished cloth had for centuries been reimported to England, because England did not have the technological skills to produce it. To the extent that the English began to acquire those skills during the sixteenth and seventeenth centuries, it was through the immigration of dyers and cloth finishers from the Low Countries and France, with a corresponding increase in the knowledge of the "mysteries" of dyeing and finishing. In other words, England desperately needed to acquire the very techniques of coloring and fashioning cloth that were derided in the coloring and fashioning of people.

In 1616, the year of the Somersets' trials and convictions, Thomas Tuke, "Minister of Gods Word at Saint Giles in the Field," published *A Treatise against Painting and Tincturing of Men and Women*. For Tuke, such body-painting was equally the characteristic of Medea ("a notable Sorceresse," who "deuised these arts") and of the barbarous Scots (who "used to paint ouer their bodies"): witchcraft and the Scot, implicitly brought together in James's court.[78] For however wicked such painting had been in the past, it had reached its apotheosis in the present and, as Tuke's appendix claims, in the fruit of such painting: ambition, pride, adultery, witchcraft, poisoning, and murder. Painting has culminated in the poisoning of Overbury, the witchcraft of his murderers, and the fashions of Satan. And yet, Tuke claims, Mrs. Turner, the instigator of these fashions, showed the way by renouncing them at her death:

One of the offenders [marginal note: "Mistress *Turner* executed at Tiburne the 14. of Nouemb. 1615"] hauing made a profitable vse of her arraignment and conuiction, did confesse to the glorie of God, being truly humbled by hearty repentance, that she was hainously guilty of the murther of Sir *Thomas Ouerburie*, and was iustly condemned for the same, detesting her former life in poperie, pride and sensualitie, and exhorting the assistants with much earnestnes to leaue off their yellow bands, and of garish fashions, the very inuentions of the diuell. I wish that her words might take impression in those that heard them, and her example serue others for instruction.[79]

But, in "The Pictur of a Pictur, or, The Character of a Painted Woman" (drawing upon the model of the poisoned Overbury's "characters"), Tuke decries the painted woman as "her owne *creatrisse*," who ignores the example of the repentant Mrs. Turner:

Rather than she'll leaue her *yellowbands*, and giue ore her pride, she wil not stick to deny that Mistr. *Turn.* spake against them, when she died. Her deuotion is fine apparel deere bought.[80]

Although Mrs. Turner's repentance appears as a possible model for the redemption of the court, she is at the same time the very origin of the court's corruption.

Indeed, the charge that women had effeminated and quite literally bewitched men was powerfully conjured up in the trial of Mrs. Turner. Here, according to her accusers, there were a series of interconnected bewitchments: first, Mrs. Turner had caught Frances Howard up in sorcery; then, Mrs. Turner and Frances Howard had together cast spells on Essex and Somerset; finally, it was implied that, via James's favorite, they had contaminated the royal family and the king himself. Michael Sparke, in his preface to *Truth Brought to Light*, claims that pride in dress was the first step in a series of events leading to public catastrophe ("observe what was begun here with vanity and adultery, ends in shame, infamy and misery") and establishes Mrs. Turner as the origin of the entire scandal: she is first described as "that fomentor of lust," then as "the first inventor" of "that horrid garb," the yellow cuff and ruffs (Sparke, sig. A2). Her desire for money is defined as the source of her sexual and necromantic villainy alike: "in prodigality and excess most riotous," in debt as a result of her "expectations and extreme pride" after the death of her doctor husband, she fell "into evil courses: as to the prostitution of her body to common lust, to practice sorcery and inchantments" (Sparke, p. 414). Sparke calls her "facinorous," a word related by etymology to both "fashion" and "faction." He writes: "she is apt to enter into any evil accord, and to entertain any evil motion, be it never so facinorous." "Facinorous" comes from the Latin *facinus, facinoris*, meaning "deed" but particularly "a bad deed, outrage, villainy, crime"; the word had come to mean "atrociously wicked," but here it is specifically associated with the etymological sense of "fashioning," "making."

Mrs. Turner's sins, that is, are imagined as interchangeably sexual and sartorial. In making fashions, in dressing others in her clothes, she subjugates them to her licentious will. *Truth Brought to Light* gives a vivid account of the ways in which her trial revolved not around the charges for which she was brought before the court (that is, assisting in the poisoning of Overbury) but for the unrelated "charges" (of which she did not technically stand accused) of using enchantments, procured from Simon Forman and other "sorcerers," so as to make the Earl of Essex, Frances Howard's first husband, impotent. Sparke writes: "pictures in wax are made, crosses, and many strange and uncouth things . . . At last they framed a picture of wax, and got a thorn from a tree that bore leaves, and stuck [it] upon the privity of the said picture" (Sparke, p. 417). Witchcraft as sympathetic magic requires dressing the victim: the naked Essex, in miniature, has a minimal but powerful external costume imposed upon him. Evidence presented at the trial mentioned further enchantments in the form of costumed bodies. A figure drawn in parchment and labeled "Corpus" had fastened to it a little piece of the skin of a man: Essex in effigy, the skin itself turned into a maleficent item of clothing.[81] And Mrs. Forman testified that Mrs. Turner had come to her after Dr. Forman died, asking for objects from her husband's study, including a wax model of a figure "very sumptuously apparelled in *silkes* and *sattins*, as also one other sitting in the form of a *naked woman, spreading* and laying *forth* her *haire* in a *Looking-glasse*" (Sparke, p. 137). What were these models that horrified and fascinated the crowd at Mrs. Turner's trial? The royalist William Sanderson, attempting in the 1650s to discredit what had become the republican account of the trial (itself a central means for justifying the overthrow of a corrupt court) claimed that these supposedly demonic forms were simply the tools of Mrs. Turner's trade, the doll-sized mannequins through which dressmakers transmitted new clothing styles in miniature: "I was present at their Arraignments, and the pictures, puppets for magic spells were no other but several French babies, some naked others clothed; which were usual then, and so are nowadays, to teach us the fashions, for dress of ladies' tiring and apparel."[82]

But despite the plausibility of Sanderson's account, it scarcely addresses the "republican" critique: namely, that fashioning, and in particular fashioning by women, is already a form of enchantment or *male-ficium*. For Sparke, Mrs. Turner's very means of bewitchment were her techniques as a dressmaker and a fashion innovator. Making garments, making models, making men: this was the logic according to which she was accused of corrupting Somerset as well as Frances Howard. The accusation posited clothes not as surface style but as cause and evidence of deep transformations. *Truth brought to Light* describes Somerset's obsession with dress not only as a symptom of his infatuation with the countess but as the source of a series of metamorphoses leading to a strange slide from extravagant masculine dress to déshabille normally belonging only to women:

the corruption remains to brand him in the forehead for his ill living: his modesty becomes eclipsed, his behaviour light, his carriage unseemly in his place; nothing so costly, no tyre so uncouth, but at all costs and charges he obtains it for the increase of favor; new fashions are produced, that so he might shew more beautiful and fair, and that his favor and personage might be made more manifest to the world; and for this purpose yellow bands, dusted hair, curled, crisped, frizzled, sleeked skins, open breasts beyond accustomed modesty, with many other inordinate attires, were worn on both sides to the shew of the world; so that, for the increase of dishonest appetites, they were abundantly practised and praised. (Sparke, p. 418)

The syntax of the list leads toward a hermaphroditic body: beginning with Somerset, the list moves from yellow starch to curled hair to bared breasts as though they were all the male courtier's attributes, holding back the verb that tells us that "both sides" wore such fashions. And the "effeminating" of Somerset marks the development of a lechery that can sexually subordinate him to men and women alike. If his clothes mark his attraction to Frances Howard, they also mark him as the object of James's desire. Somerset and Buckingham alike, according to Francis Osborne, in their desire to become "*Burning-glasses*" interposed between the king and his subjects, "labour to resemble women, in the effeminacies of their dressings," though "in w[horish] looks and wanton gestures they exceeded any part of Womankind."[83]

Strikingly, in the account of the effeminacy of Somerset, the focus is upon his head and neck rather than the lower body – as if gender was more a question of the visible parts than of the "private" parts. Gender, as Thomas Stoughton argued, is proclaimed through the visibility of the head. And the fashioned distinctions of male and female have, he claims, been unfashioned by the latest Jacobean styles:

How therefore haue men and women changed their sexe (as much as they can) one with another? Men wearing long haire like vnto women, and women cutting off their haire like vnto boyes, or beardlesse yong men, wearing nothing thereon but hats . . . Oh monstrous, oh monstrous.[84]

Similarly, Barnabe Rich claims that curled hair and yellow starch both effeminate men:

And from whence commeth this wearing, & this imbrodering of long lockes, this curiositie that is vsed amongst men, in freziling and curling of their hayre, this gentlewoman-like starcht bands, so be edged, and be laced, fitter for *Mayd Marion* in a *Moris dance*, then for him that hath either that spirit or courage, that should be in a gentleman.

But amongst all the rest of these ill becomming follies, that are now newly taken vppe (me thinkes) these yellow starcht bandes should bee euer best suited, with a yellow *Coate*.[85]

Gender is here constructed through collar and hair. In fact, as early as 1581 in *Riche his farewell to Militarie Profession*, Rich associated effeminization with the head and with ruffs: "Howe many Gentlemen shall you see at the present day, that . . . in the setting of their Ruffes, and the freshing of their haire, are more new fangled and foolish then any curtisan of Venice."[86]

Yet the same prosthetic devices (yellow starch, frizzled hair, exorbitant and unseemly clothes) that supposedly effeminate Somerset are depicted by the court's critics as masculinizing the Countess of Somerset. Somewhere between the early 1610s and the early 1620s, Simon van de Passe engraved two states of the bust of the countess (Figs. 7 and 8). In the first version of the engraving, she wears a full, crimped coiffure; the significant changes in the second version are that her hair has been cropped short and that she is wearing a broad-brimmed, feathered hat.[87] What is perhaps most apparent to a modern viewer, though, in both states of the engraving is the almost full exposure of the breasts, not, as David Lindley has rightly argued, a sign of her particular wantonness but the common court fashion of the mid-1610s and one which Queen Anne herself had adopted. Why, then, this attention to details of the head? What are we to make of the re-engraving that gives Frances Howard short hair and a wide hat and feather?

To the extent that gender was constructed through visible prostheses, the head was given particular attention. Moreover, in women's regendering of the head, the very symbol of patriarchal authority (the head as emblem of the king, the father, the husband) is appropriated by women. In 1614, Richard Niccols, who two years later published *Sir Thomas Ouerburies Vision*, reviled the man-woman. She could be told, he wrote in *The Furies*, by her head: "The head is mans, I iudge by hat and haire."[88] In fact, as early as 1576, George Gascoigne had derided women's masculinizing of their heads: women, he claimed, were "masking in mens weedes," wearing "high copt hattes, and fethers flaunt a flaunt."[89] And in 1619, in *A Sermon of Apparell*, the defining features of the "halfe man halfe woman" were that s/he had "a *polled head*" and that she was "wagging a *Feather* to defie the *World*."[90] The man-woman of the 1610s, then, emerges less from the hybridization of her lower parts (skirts/breeches) than from the hybridization of the head.

This is made quite explicit on the title page of *Hic Mulier: or, The Man-Woman* (1620): on the left, a barber polls Hic Mulier's hair; on the right, Hic Mulier looks at her head in a mirror, to see herself wearing ruff, broad-brimmed hat and feather

Fig. 7. Simon van de Passe, engraving, first version, *Frances Howard, Countess of Somerset*, 1618–20

Fig. 8. Simon van de Passe, engraving, second version, *Frances Howard, Countess of Somerset*, 1618–20

(Fig. 9).[91] And in the anonymous *Two Wise Men and All the Rest Fooles*, Levitia, Parvagracio proclaims, is "not a woman . . . tis a maremaide, halfe a dog, halfe a woman." Levitia's crime is to be wearing "a yellow band about her necke" and to have on her head "periwigs of dogges haire white." The scandal of the regendering of the head by "short haired Gentlewomen" – "poled rigs, ramps, and Tomboys" – is explicitly sexualized by Thomas Stoughton. Such women, he claims, cut their hair so that "they may be taken for yong men in long coates, the rather because some of them also weare boots and spurres, and short swords by their sides, that being so taken they may also be bed-fellowes to such yong men, and so play the harlots with them, as holy Pope *Ioane* did."[92]

In reworking his engraving of the Countess of Somerset by giving her cropped hair and a hat, Simon van de Passe is keeping her up to date with the changing fashions of the Hic Mulier, the man-woman. Yet it is not surprising that David Lindley, in his excellent work on contemporary and later figurings of Frances Howard, fails to understand the reworked engraving as depicting a man-woman, because in both its states, as we noted above, the Countess's breasts are almost fully displayed. And while Lindley finely observes that a later engraving by Martin Droeshout, in which a woman is explicitly being purged of "manliness," is modeled on the second state of van de Passe's engraving, he suggests that the image has been cut loose from its reference to Frances Howard, since she was accused of "sexual voraciousness," not manliness.[93] But Lindley is assuming a modern notion of the "manly." In fact, *Hic Mulier: or, The Man-Woman* (1620) takes the defining features of the man-woman to be not only "the cloudy Ruffianly broad-brim'd Hatte, and wanton Feather" and the "most ruffianly short lockes" that figure so conspicuously in the second version of the Countess but also "the lasciuious ciuill embracement of a French doublet, all vnbutton'd to entice." Similarly, "Hic Mulier," as s/he appears in *Muld Sacke: or The Apologie of Hic Mulier*, notes that men-women are conventionally defined as "deformed monsters," formed "by cutting their haire, wearing French doublets, hauing open breasts and false bodies."[94] In other words, the exposure of a woman's breasts, far from being a sign of femininity, is figured as a mark of sexual aggression and a usurpation of male prerogative.[95]

At the same time, *Hic Mulier* traces the fashions of the man-woman to two specific sources: Mrs. Turner and Frances Howard, "the lowest despised creatures that Record can giue testimonie of," the one "cut from the Common-wealth at the Gallowes" (Mrs. Turner), the other "well knowne" (Frances Howard, with a Biblical pun upon "known"): "From the first you got the false armoury of yellow Starch . . . From the other, you have taken the monstrousnesse of your deformitie in apparrell." Mrs. Turner is represented as the active source of illegitimacy: "for to weare yellow on white, or white vpon yellow, is by the rules of Heraldry basenesse, bastardie, and indignitie." But it is specifically from the Countess of Somerset herself that every fashion of the man-woman is said to come. And such fashions are simultaneously oversophisticated and barbarous (a form of "apish inciuilitie").[96] The pamphleteer equates all the elements of this costume, from feathered hat to naked breasts, with aggressive masculinity; sexual voraciousness is conceptualized here as in itself masculine, even as it emasculates men. The repetition of "ruffianly" insists on the masculinity of women dressed so seductively. Repeated throughout "Hic Mulier," "ruffianly" puns upon "ruff." The ruff of the female "ruffian" conjures up the power of women to initiate fashion and to fashion men. Deriving from the Italian

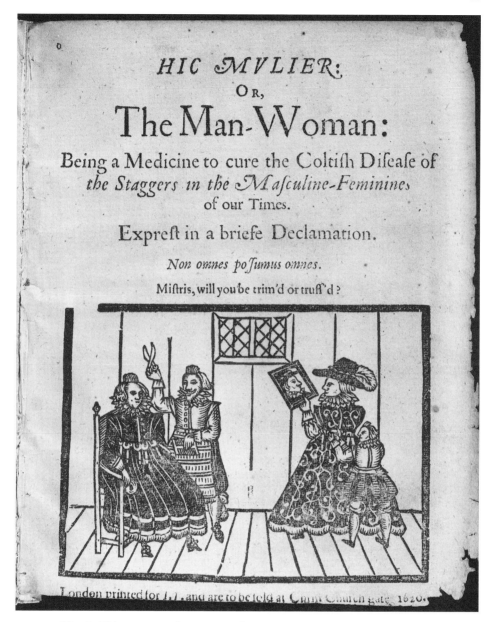

Fig. 9. Title-page woodcut, Hic Mulier: or The Man-Woman, 1620

noun *ruffiano*, meaning a male pander, "ruffian" here conjures up both the masculinizing of women and the eruption of alien others into the English state:

What can bee more barbarous, then . . . to mould their bodies to euery deformed fashion . . . and their hands to ruffianly and unciuill actions . . . : If this bee not barbarous, make the rude *Scithian*, the untamed *Moore*, the naked *Indian*, or the wild *Irish*, Lords and Rulers of well gouerned Cities.[97]

As molders of their own and others' bodies, as, in the case of Mrs. Turner, dressmakers,[98] women can transform themselves into men and men into women, dislocating gendered and national identities alike in the circulation of prosthetic devices.

In fact, the Countess of Somerset circulated as an image both inside and outside England in and after her life. On 2 March 1615, a portrait of the Countess was presented by Sir Thomas Roe to the Great Mogul. Was this a version of the portrait in the National Portrait Gallery, in which she wears a low-cut dress and yellow starch? So captivating was her image that Francis Osborne, in the *True Tragicomedy*, which he wrote in the 1650s to denounce the Somersets' marriage, puts in a special plea for preserving it. In the play, Frances Howard spends her time with Anne Turner, Dr. Forman, and other conjurors, plotting her escape from her first husband and appearing in the clothes of a "waistcoateer" or prostitute.[99] But in the "characters" that Osborne prefaced to the play, Osborne attacks the "rabble" who have "bespatter[ed] her fame" and who have attributed to her (rather than Anne Turner) "the invention of yellow starch." Defiling the Countess of Somerset (an undertaking in which Osborne himself played no small part) appears here as the sport of those who would magnify the vices of others so as minimize their own. He continues:

I hope [the Countess of Somerset's] more innocent picture may be allowed still to adorn the cabinet of our Princes, as it doth at this day that of the Great Mogul to whom it being presented by Sir Thomas Roe did so far advance his conversion as to confess, God was more immediately among the Christians than Mahometans, else they could never produce such angelical shapes.[100]

Frances Howard is presented here no longer as poisoner, witch, and agent of the devil, but as angelic shape and sacred image. In fact, the fascination of the image appears to have confused Osborne. It was not Frances Howard's picture that the Mogul was so drawn to but the image of an unkown woman whom Roe "loved dearly."[101]

The "fascination" of and with Frances Howard and Anne Turner was, in fact, double-edged. They were inscribed as the epitome of the court and as the fount of all corruption, a corruption stemming from the agents of Satan – women, Catholics, foreign fashions. In his derisive epitaph on Frances Howard, "Upon our Ages MESSALINA, insatiat Madona, the matchless English-COROMBONA," Richard Brathwait took up both the image of Messalina (the adulterous wife of the Emperor Claudius) and of Vittoria Corombona, about whom John Webster had published *The White Devil* in 1612, a year before the poisoning of Overbury and the annulment of Frances Howard's first marriage. Webster's Vittoria provides Brathwait with a model for understanding Frances Howard's "foreign" vices, foreign vices which she has nonetheless made English:

> Weake in Grace, but strong in Will.
> Honours blemish, *Hymens* stayne,
> Virtues poyson, Beauties baine . . .
>
> Painted Idol, Arts-new-creature,
> Ladie in a Pages feature.[102]

But what Brathwait does not capture is that Webster's Vittoria is also the court's most radical critic. She dies not repenting her sins, but attacking the court in which she lived:

O happy they that never saw the Court
Nor ever knew great Man but by report.[103]

If Webster could be turned by Brathwait towards misogynist and sexually conservative ends, he could also provide a different way of interpreting the "man-woman":
as the estranged perspective from which one could begin to demystify the rule of
princes.

Vittoria was, like the Countess of Somerset, sexually unconstrained, and she was,
like Anne Turner, at first only a humble dweller on the fringes of the court. Before
her death, Turner, unlike Vittoria, repented. But perhaps David Lindley moves too
rapidly to criticize the conservatism of such repentances.[104] True, Turner *did* repent,
and indeed took the sacrament of the Church of England, having previously been a
Catholic. But her "repentance" had such a powerful effect upon later accounts
because it was at the same time a devastating assault upon the court. Like Vittoria,
she declared that it was her service to aristocratic "greatnes" that had brought her to
"a dogged death"; she reviled the king's servants for "mallice, pride, whoredom,
swearing, and reioising in the fall of others"; she denounced "the wardrobe of court
vanities."[105] Anne Turner's "confessions," in other words, legitimated other radical
denunciations of the court. And even the pity that some felt for Frances Howard
had its radical aspect.[106] While James denounced the monstrous regiment of women,
Lady Leedes declared that "she would speak treason, because the King declared that
most women were atheists and papists."[107] The public staging of the trials of Anne
Turner and Frances Howard, like the public staging of Vittoria Corombona's trial
in *The White Devil*, put the court as much as the "man-woman" on trial.

But even the denunciations of the "man-woman" opened up the power of women
to fashion as well as to be fashioned. The power of the man-woman is imagined as
proceeding from two contradictory sources: the "natural" (but un-naturing) display
of "open breasts"; the "unnatural" construction of "false bodies."[108] But what are
"false bodies"? In early modern England, "bodies," far from pointing towards a
unitary physical presence, bifurcated in antithetical directions: on the one hand,
"bodies" as flesh, bone, muscle; on the other, "bodice" (the modern spelling of what
is simply the plural of "body," as "dice" is the plural of "die"), formerly usually
written as either "bodies" or "a pair of bodies" (the latter because it was constructed
by lacing together two pieces of material). The "bodice" is/are the materials which
construct a body, as if the made "bodies" preceded any physical body and gave
shape to it.[109] The "false bodies" of the man-woman, then, are made bodies, the
bodies that the bodice makes. Barnabe Rich writes that tailors ("*Idol-makers*" and
"the *diuels enginers*") now "make the whole world with their new inuentions."
Tailors have become "*Body-makers*" that "swarm through all the parts of London"
and are "more sought vnto then he that is the *Soule-maker*."[110] The fashioners
(those who, according to their detractors, "mould their bodies to euery deformed
shape") make gender, make nationality, make nature itself. The now-dead metaphors of habit (clothing and custom), of costume/custom, of bodies/bodice were
given vital and conflictual force in the narrations of the Overbury affair. Yellow
starch, fashion dolls, the wearing of broad-brimmed hats and feathers by women –
these can only seem trivial now, in a dematerialized regime that coined the
demonized concept of "fetishism." But in the trials of Mrs. Turner, of the Countess
of Somerset, of the Earl of Somerset, these very "trivia" were the site of conflict over
definitions of the body and the body politic.

Part 2

Gendered habits

4   Arachne's web: Velázquez's *Las Hilanderas*

The preliminary and most basic stage of making clothes and all other textile goods in the Renaissance was the manual spinning of fibers. Thread, whether linen, wool or silk, was the basis of simple and luxurious fabrics alike, and all of it, until the industrial revolution at the end of the eighteenth century, passed through the fingers of spinners. The greatest number of these spinners were women. Boys and men spun, as well; in spinning schools and workhouses, they, too, were set to the distaff. And in rural areas throughout Europe, poor farmers, when their agricultural day was over, sometimes joined their wives in the nocturnal work of spinning.[1] But the gender ideology reigning throughout Europe defined spinning as women's work, indeed, as the work of women of all classes. For women of middling and upper ranks, however, the value of spinning was less practical than moral: it was praised as evidence of chaste industriousness. As a crucially necessary activity, on one hand, and a sign of feminine virtue on the other, this primary textile work was represented in a wide range of cultural forms in which earlier spinning stories were rewritten in relation to new social formations specific to the Renaissance. In this chapter, we trace out how the mythological figure of Arachne was transformed by social anxieties produced and managed through the early modern identification of femininity with spinning.

Arachne textrix

About 1654 Diego de Velázquez painted a canvas later called *Las Hilanderas* ("The Spinners") or *La Fabula de Aragne* ("The Fable of Arachne") (Fig. 10). *The Fable of Arachne* was given as the title of the painting in a 1664 inventory of the possessions of a Spanish nobleman and courtier, Don Pedro de Arce. Sometime after 1711, the painting was willed to the royal collections, where it was inventoried in 1772 after it had been expanded by the addition of painted canvas strips on all four sides, including a top panel depicting a golden arch (Fig. 11).[2]

The two titles given to this painting after Velázquez's death signal the hierarchical habit of thought that divides artistic work into separate spheres, a "low" realm of quotidian, habitual labor and a "high" realm of mythological themes and allegorical interpretation. The title *Las Hilanderas* addresses the foreground of the painting. Barefoot and poorly dressed, working in semi-darkness, surrounded by raw wool and a basket for the finished yarn on the viewer's right and a pile of finished fabric on the left, three women assisted by two others comb, spin, and wind wool. The title *The Fable of Arachne* refers to the background where, on a raised platform rather like a brightly lit stage, a scene of elegantly dressed women includes a figure in a classical helmet who is looking at a tapestry. The two titles (and subjects) of the

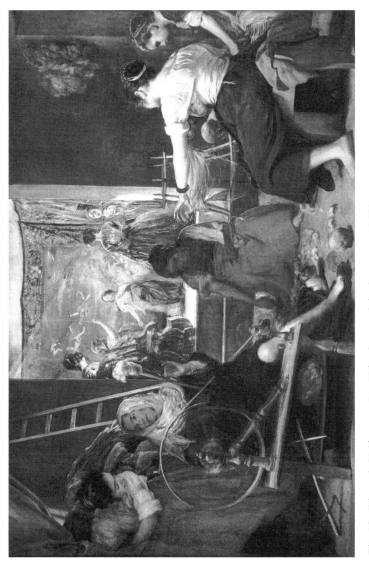

Fig. 10. Diego de Velázquez, *Las Hilanderas*, original canvas. c. 1654

Fig. 11. Diego de Velázquez, *Las Hilanderas*, expanded canvas

painting name the process by which spun and woven objects – objects belonging to material culture in its most literal sense – have been the site of an ideological divison: on the one hand, manual labor; on the other, the elevated world (literally elevated in the painting) of classical myth and its visual representations. Such a division is not only anachronistic in relation to the monetary value that textiles and paintings had in the Renaissance, when woolen tapestries cost far more than canvases painted with oil; the contrast between the titles of the painting also reveals the dematerializing logic through which a physical product – the wool yarn produced by women's labor – has been subordinated to work done by men in this period: the workshop tapestry, the painting in oil. In addition, the subject of Velázquez's painting and the history of its later naming typify a systematic process in early modern gender ideologies: through a shift from work to "virtue," the textile labor extracted by grim necessity from lower-class women spinners was displaced by a moral ideal prescribed for higher-class women.

What are Velázquez's women spinners doing, exactly? The foreground of the painting shows the various stages of the process clearly. The woman in the center of the scene is reaching down for a clump of wool, which she will card – comb, to part and line up the fibers – with the carder in her left hand; the white-coiffed woman at the left has attached a carded hank of wool to the top of her distaff and is pulling out fibers from it to feed onto the spinning wheel in front of her, which will even it into thread and wind it onto a reel; the woman with her back to the viewer is winding finished thread from a reel or skeiner into a ball.[3] These spinners collaboratively manufacture (in the early, literal sense of "make by hand") the staple material for cloth of all kinds: the thread from which it is woven.

In Spain, the making of woolen cloth occupied men and women alike, although in separate spheres. Male shepherds herded highly valued merino sheep south and then north each year in a migration carefully controlled by a powerful network of guilds (the "Mesta"), which also supervised the production of woolen cloth, according to strict rules governing the care of flocks and the techniques of urban men's labor in weaving workshops.[4] But wool yarn, the basic substance required for work in cloth and tapestry workshops, was produced by women working at home, as participants in a cottage industry or putting-out system in force throughout early modern Europe. With or without the spinning wheel at which Velázquez's white-coiffed older *hilandera* sits, women in towns and in the countryside spun wool into thread, which was purchased in bulk by merchants, who sold it to clothmakers and to tapestry workshops in the cities.

The background scene of Velázquez's painting, and the title it was given by a seventeenth-century collector, led later critics to emphasize the more elaborate, woven textile form represented in the painting, focusing on the brightly lit background scene in which Minerva judges Arachne's tapestry. Painting this kind of classical topic, Jonathan Brown has argued, would have accredited Velázquez as a learned humanist painter rather than a mere craftsman.[5] The painting has been read, accordingly, as a statement of the superiority of art to craft. Madlyn Kahr, for instance, argues that

Las Hilanderas . . . transmits a message with brilliant clarity: art exists to remind us there is something beyond our earth-bound daily labors. While it occupies physically but a small part of the world, art is more vivid, more colorful, more exciting – thus, in a sense, larger than life.

Art is sublimation. It heightens sensibility, expands consciousness. And though life ends, art endures.[6]

But Kahr resolutely ignores the problems that the picture raises. First, it is difficult to imagine that many viewers would discover the story of Arachne and Athena in this painting, were it not for the early catalogue entry. The illuminated scene in the background follows none of the previous artistic conventions for depicting the story. There is no competition between the spinner and the goddess; there are no looms; we do not see Arachne being transformed into a spider; and there are five, not two, figures in Velázquez's *mise-en-scène*, four of them clearly women, the fifth an ambiguous figure wearing a helmet, identifiable as Athena only after one has decided that it is the story of Arachne that is being depicted. In other words, Velázquez goes to great lengths to disguise the story, if indeed it is this story that he is depicting.

This indistinct treatment of the myth is the more curious because Velázquez had a detailed familiarity with a previous painting of Arachne, done by Rubens for the Torre de la Parada.[7] Rubens's painting, along with others of his Ovidian cycle, had been copied by Juan del Mazo, and the copies were hung in the "pieza principal" of the Alcázar. This is the room that Velázquez depicts in *Las Meninas* (painted during the same period as the *Fable of Arachne*), and del Mazo's copy is dimly visible above Velázquez's own head in that composition. But there is no significant resemblance between Rubens's portrayal of the story of Arachne and that of Velázquez.[8] Rubens, like earlier engravers of the scene, shows Minerva striking down Arachne with her shuttle. Arachne lies imploringly at the feet of the goddess. Behind Minerva, two women are standing within a large loom. Both the action and the furniture of Rubens's composition clarify the story he is telling, even though, unlike some of the earlier engravers, Rubens does not depict Arachne metamorphosing into a spider. The only resemblance between Rubens's and Velázquez's representations is that they both display in the background a tapestry of the rape of Europa, one of the subjects of Arachne's tapestry in Ovid's account. Otherwise, Velázquez radically departs not only from Rubens's depiction but from all previous depictions of the myth.

Equally striking, even if we accept *The Fable of Arachne* as the title of Velázquez's painting, is the reversal of priority he gives to the mythological realm and to the scene of the woolworking women. Jonathan Brown, for instance, notes Velázquez's decision "to depict a casual genre scene in the foreground, while placing the narrative subject at the rear, in flagrant disregard of the conventional requirement to subordinate secondary incidents to the primary action."[9] The alternative title of the painting, *Las Hilanderas* ("The Spinners"), is not simply a mistake, then, registering the failure of the viewer to know the key to the painting. On the contrary, the actual organization of the painting seems to encourage such a "mistake," subordinating mythology to a scene of female labor.

Kahr, like many other analysts of the painting, reverses Velázquez's act of subordinating the high to the low. For these analysts, the laboring women have the role of suppliers of mere "stuff," the raw material from which Minervan, Arachnean, and painterly *oeuvres* are made. Yet such commentary stresses the painting's metaphysical implications by erasing the painting's structure. Why, it seems fair to ask, did Velázquez juxtapose the two kinds of activities that give the painting its alternative names? And why does the scene of the spinners take up so much of the foreground of the painting and contain details so much more distinct – the figure of the woman dressed in white, winding wool, for example – than those in the recessed scene of the tapestry viewing?

The painting is not historically realistic, in the sense of representing an actual tapestry workshop. During the seventeenth century, tapestries were mainly imported into Spain from the Low Countries or made in workshops supervised by Flemish designers.[10] Although a small tapestry workshop in Madrid, first established in Calle Santa Isabel by the tapestry master Antonio Ceron, was active in the late sixteenth and early seventeenth century, it was a man's workplace: Ceron employed four male weavers and eight male apprentices.[11] Art historians of the early twentieth century, following the 1772 inventory of Madrid's royal holdings, have accepted its identification of the Santa Isabel tapestry workshop as the setting for the painting, but textile practices in the 1650s, particularly the exclusion of women from men's workshops, make such an assumption dubious.[12] The wool yarn spun at home by women made its way into tapestry ateliers through merchant middlemen, who sold it to masters for use by their male dyers and weavers. It is highly unlikely that women spinners would have occupied the same factory space as male tapestry weavers.

What Velázquez does is to juxtapose two temporally and physically separate stages of the process of tapestry making, the production of yarn and the display of the finished tapestry, in a way that insists on the importance and interest of the women's work. He puts his emphasis not upon the higher-paid activities of men (dyeing and weaving) but upon the most poorly paid female labor. Velázquez includes no looms or male weavers. And his virtuoso play with the texture of the wool, in tufts, yarn, and balls, and the sheen with which he depicts the rapid spinning of the wheel focus the viewer's eyes upon the spinner and her companions.

Female labor underpins the making of tapestries; it also literally underpins the making of Velázquez's own painting. For the painting is on canvas, a material woven of linen, a fiber also spun by women in its first stages.[13] Although the techniques of linen making belonged to a major urban industry in the Low Countries, women working at home also grew, soaked, combed, and spun the flax and hemp from which painters' canvas was made.[14] At the same time, it was women's work to sew strips of canvas together when painters wanted a larger field than single pieces of the textile permitted. Antonio Palomino, who came to the Spanish court eighteen years after Velázquez died, wrote a treatise on oil painting, *El Museo pictorico y la escala optica*, in which he explains this gendered division of labor: "Sewing the canvas is more women's work than men's, [so] it is necessary for the artist to tell them which stitch they must use to join the pieces."[15] Women, then, performed the practical basic labor of joining the strips of fabric that constructed Velázquez's canvas.

In contrast to the processes by which Velázquez's canvas was made, later readings of the painting have emphasized allegories of virtue and vice over women's labor in textile production. The subordination of such labor to moralizing and allegorical interpretation is not just a product of modern art history, however. It was itself formulated in the Renaissance reception of classical literature, and specifically in Renaissance allegorizations of the story of Arachne and Athena. Such transparent allegory is resisted in Velázquez's painting. Yet he was working against the dominant tradition.

Ovid's tale of Arachne was to have a life of its own in the Renaissance. And Ovid, like Velázquez, foregrounds the material processes of spinning and weaving in Book 6 of *The Metamorphoses*. The poem pits the mortal Arachne and the goddess Athena against each other, but despite their difference of status, they are described as sharing the same manual techniques of weaving. Ovid introduces Arachne, the daughter of parents of low birth, as famous throughout Lydia for her skill as spinner and weaver both, and he describes her spinning in detail:

> sive rudem primos lanam glomerabat in orbes,
> seu digitis subigebat opus repetitaque longo
> vellera mollibat nebulas aequantia tractu,
> sive levi teretem versabat pollice fusum,
> . . . scires a Pallade doctam.[16]

> whether she was winding the rough yarn into a new ball,
> or shaping the stuff with her fingers, reaching back
> to the distaff for more wool, fleecy as a cloud,
> to draw into long soft threads, or giving a twist
> with practiced thumb to the graceful spindle,
> . . . you would know that Pallas had taught her.

These acquired skills prompt Arachne to call on Minerva to compete with her, in a challenge to divine power and to age hierarchy.

Ovid describes the action that opens the contest, each woman's dressing of her loom, by attributing the same manual dexterity to mortal and goddess alike. Because he has presented Arachne as the possessor of textile skills so vividly in the earlier passage, and because no superhuman power is implied in his closely focused narrative of the technique whereby vertical warp and horizontal weft are set up by both pairs of equally skilled hands, his first lines on the contest stress the human skill displayed in loom-work:

> haud mora, constituunt diversis partibus ambae
> et gracili geminas intendunt stamine telas:
> tela iugo vincta est, stamen secernit harundo,
> inseritur medium radiis subtemen acutis,
> quod digiti expediunt, atque inter stamina ductum
> percusso paviunt insecti pectine dentes.   (Ovid, 6.53–8)

> Without delay they both set up the looms in different
> places and they stretch the fine warp upon them. The web
> is bound upon the beam, the reed separates the threads
> of the warp, the woof is threaded through them by
> the sharp shuttles which their busy fingers ply, and
> when shot through the threads of the warp, the notched
> teeth of the hammering slay [comb] tap it into place.

In Ovid's narrative, Arachne's defiance of her divine superior in no way undermines her skill. Rather, the material details and concrete vocabulary emphasize the interplay of hands and machines (the looms).

Each woman's tapestry represents scenes that imply a particular view of the relations between gods and mortals and also between men and women. Minerva's web supports divine order – her own. Her subject is the moment at which Athens was named after her, the result of her triumph in a contest that pitted her against her brother Neptune. Their rival claims to be the patron deity of Athens are judged by the rest of the gods, headed by Jove as king of the gods, "a royal figure." Athena represents herself in her masculine military mode, with spear, helmet and aegis, although the images she sets at each of the four corners of her web identify her with female divine power: Juno is specified as the agent of a Pygmy queen's transformation into a crane and the Trojan Antigone's change into a stork. In the central judgment scene, Minerva represents herself giving Athens the olive branch, signifying peace and fertility, to convince the city to choose her over her brother. Ovid concludes his description of her tapestry by mentioning the olive branches she weaves into its border.

But Minerva's actions in regard to Arachne are neither just nor peaceful. Arachne's tapestry is flawless; Ovid tells us that neither the goddess nor Envy could find anything to criticize in it (6.129–30). Yet Minerva, rather than giving the prize where it is due, envies Arachne's "success," tears the girl's cloth to pieces, and hits her four times on the head with a spindle. When Arachne hangs herself out of indignation at this treatment, the goddess uses Hecate's potions to return her to life, partly out of pity, Ovid says, but also to set her up as a monitory example for generations to come: "Hang there still," she says, and may all your kin to come also exemplify "the law of punishment." As defender of divine justice, Minerva produces a textile art designed to support heavenly order and to take credit for the stability of the city that chose her as patron. But her behavior toward Arachne contradicts the principles that her tapestry upholds.

Recent critics have argued that Ovid puts a subversive spin on his version of the myth not only by making Arachne deserve to win the contest, contrary to earlier versions of the story, but also by treating her tapestry more sympathetically than Minerva's. Leonard Barkan comments, "Minerva's work is as much a straw man as it is a woven cloth. As an aesthetic and an account of metamorphosis, it exists in order that Ovid may shed its sharp moral and aesthetic rules."[17] The order of the narrative affirms this interpretation: by setting the mortal woman's work after the goddess's tapestry, the poet gives Arachne's text the last word, and through the sheer quantity of Arachne's twenty-one images of male gods transforming themselves into beasts in order to rape mortal women, he allies himself with the irreverent weaver. He uses Arachne as a narrator within the narration, as a medium through which he can depict celestial crimes ("caelestia crimina," 6.131) yet – at least in theory – escape the kind of judgment Minerva imposes on such blasphemous representation. Although Ovid ends the story by leading his heroine to a suitably dire end, the theme of her work as weaver has supplied him with a double opportunity: to expose the undignified sexual exploits of the male gods and to compose verbal tapestries himself – that is, to write skillful ekphrases of textile skill. He rounds off his representation of Arachne's web by describing its border in two lines that bring closure to the weaver's work and to his own. Arachne's border represents the ivy that was an emblem of poetic fame: "Ultima pars telae, tenui circumdata limbo, / nexilibus flores hederis habet intertextos," 6.127–8 ("The last part of the web, surrounded with a narrow border, / contains flowers intertwined with ivy, woven together").

Ovid, then, figures Arachne as a self-made woman, distinguished not by divinity or rank but by command of her craft. His detailed description of her tapestry also demonstrates that her skill and sense of design are fully equal to Minerva's. Both interweave colored and golden threads so subtly that the blending is invisible (6. 61–6); each works out a form of composition perfectly suited to her subject, one classically balanced, one tumultuous and crowded. Even the final lines of the episode do justice to the art of Arachne, surviving as a spider:

> in latere exiles digiti pro cruribus haerent,
> cetera venter habet, de quo tamen illa remittit
> stamen et antiquas exercet aranea telis. (6.143–5)

> the slender fingers clung to her sides as legs;
> the rest was belly. Still from this she ever
> spins a thread; and now, as a spider, she exercises
> her old-time weaver-art.

Ovid leaves his reader warned of the gods' power to punish presumptuous mortals, but also reminded of the continuing virtuosity of weaving as ancient and modern métier.

Rereading Arachne

Ovid's version of the myth was radically reinterpreted by the English writer George Sandys in his elaborate commentary, *Ovid's Metamorphosis Englished, Mythologized, and Represented in Figures* (1632). Drawing on a range of earlier discourses (including the interpretations of Dante, Boccaccio, and Christine de Pizan), Sandys uses a range of classical texts to provide allegorical interpretations of the myth. By selecting from a range of ancient and early modern symbolic conventions, he reads the rapport between the tapestries and their makers in ways that make Ovid seem to side unequivocally with Minerva. The humanist commentator assembles a network of "information" that judges Arachne as political and moral outlaw and dismisses her craft as trivial female fiddling.

A central agendum in Sandys's commentary is to extol Minerva as a representative of political as well as divine order. What Ovid represents as an almost equal battle between two female characters competing with the shuttle Sandys reads as a profound threat to hierarchies of class and gender. One way he justifies the outcome of the contest is by drawing on another myth related to the founding of Athens: the response of Athena and Neptune to the citizens' vote to choose a patron deity:

The *Athenians* therefore put it to the Balloting: where the men were for *Neptune*, and the women for *Minerva*; who carried it by only one pebble. Whereupon incensed *Neptune* surrounded most of their territories: . . . but after, appeased by thus punishing the women – That they should have no voice in publique decrees, that their children should not carry their names, nor themselves be called *Athenians* – , . . . *Neptune* was more easily reconciled to Minerva, both having in *Athens* one Temple, wherein an Altar was erected to *Oblivion*. (Sandys, 218) [18]

The bond reestablished between the divine brother and sister is made possible by the denial of political, familial, and civic rights to women. And although the temple is built to celebrate the male and the female siblings' willingness to forget their previous enmity, its name implies that the possibility of women taking a part in the governing of the *polis* will also be forgotten. In contrast to Arachne's tapestry, which assures that posterity will remember gender injustice in the form of male gods' rapes of mortal women, the chapter Sandys adds to Athenian history paradoxically justifies the denial of the women citizens' vote as the basis of harmony for the "democratic" city.

Above all, Sandys reads Arachne not as a craftswoman or an artist but as a subverter of class hierarchies. Accordingly, he represents her allies as malcontents intent on disrupting social hierarchy. "Profane Arachne," he writes, insisting on the distance separating mortals and divinities, "sets forth the rapes and adulteries of the gods" (220). He revises Ovid's remark that Envy found nothing to reproach in the tapestry ("non illud carpere Livor / possit opus," Envy could find no fault in that work, 6.129–30) by assigning a new motive to Envy: the goddess rightfully censors an act that typifies underlings' pleasure in hearing gossip about their superiors: "Minerva teares in peeces what envy could not but commend, because it published the vices of great ones, and beats her with the shuttle to chastise her presumption" (Sandys, 221). Ovid's concluding comment, that the outcome of the contest caused a furor throughout Lydia and beyond, is taken by Sandys as evidence of the inconstancy of the common people. He concedes Arachne's skill as a weaver only in connection with the mob tendency always to make a martyr of a member of the lower orders: "The common people who envy the eminent, and pitty those whom they envied in adversity, storme at the ruine of so excellent an artizan" (Sandys, 221). According to this reading, Arachne deserves punishment as a traitor because she reveals the secrets of the gods and stirs up sentiment against her betters.

Sandys combines both kinds of accusation – that Arachne is dangerous as an unruly woman and as a political agitator – in his final comment on the frame she weaves for her tapestry:

These personages, with the places, being woven to the life by Arachne, she incloseth the web with a trail of Ivy; well suting with the wanton argument and her owne ambition. [Ivy is] Worne in garlands at lascivious meetings; and climing as ambitious men, to compass their owne ends with the ruine of their supporters. (221)

To justify his criticism of Arachne's frame, Sandys appeals to classical representations of revelry: the ivy garland at the drinking festival. But he excludes other possible interpretations, for example, the association of ivy with poets. A recent editor of *The Metamorphoses*, William Anderson, suggests that Ovid links poetic endeavor generally and his own in particular with Arachne's ivy by assigning her border motif an aesthetic prestige that equals Minerva's olive branch.[19] But Sandys, focusing on the vine as a destructive parasite, narrows the range of meanings that both classical and Renaissance discourses assigned to ivy. A deeply ambivalent symbol in the Renaissance, ivy could signify and condemn amorous languor: in Barthélemy Aneau's *Picta Poesis* [1552], a tree trunk covered by ivy represents a man destroyed by the lust of his female lover.[20] But it could also figure amorous devotion and political loyalty: in England, Robert Dudley addressed an impresa to Queen Elizabeth in which he was figured as a vine clinging to an obelisk, with a motto affirming their mutual interdependence: "te stante virebo" ("you standing, I will flourish").[21] Sandys's concern for social hierarchy, however, forecloses all readings except the one that condemns Arachne's ivy as evidence of her ambition and envy.

Sandys's final strategy is a shift to *ad feminam* argument: he points to Arachne's ivy border as proof that her argument is "wanton." The logic of Aneau's emblem, in which the vine represents the effeminating effect of a woman's lust on her lover, perhaps enters into his interpretation here, but the crucial issue is libel and censorship. Arachne's publishing of "celestial crimes" is a crime in itself. However skillful she may be as a weaver, she oversteps the bounds when she exposes male gods' sexual adventures to mortal view. To displace lust from Jove, Neptune, Apollo, and Bacchus onto the mortal woman, Sandys reads Arachne's narrative against her, as a revelation of *her* character rather than the character of the *gods*. His treatment of the mortal weaver repeats the strategy of the kind of judge who, in rape trials, interprets a woman's accusation of a man as proof that *she* is prey to indecent fantasies. Wanton actions by men, divine or mortal, are transformed into signifiers of the wantonness of the woman who exposes them.

Sandys's commentary on Ovid not only devalues Arachne's final gesture, the ivy skillfully interwoven with flowers, to support a verdict of female ineptitude. He also effaces Arachne as textile worker by allegorizing her metamorphosis into a spider so as to dismiss the actual labor of spinning: "uselesse and worthlesse labors are expressed by the spiders web" (221). Women's textile work, elevated to divine status by Athena's participation in it, is here flatly dismissed as the seventeenth-century commentator rewrites the virtuosity attributed to both contestants in Ovid's weaving war as "uselesse and worthlesse labors." The material labor of weaving and the stories that Arachne pictures forth are displaced by allegories that elaborately transform material product and sign into emblems of political pride and malice.

But the paradox of Sandys's critique of Arachne is that he suggests the political potency of Arachne's weavings (weavings which can infuriate the gods) even as he implies the futility of her labor. This paradox is in fact inscribed in the contradictory perspectives on the spider into which she is transformed. On the one hand, it is a radical diminution. As George Turberville wrote of Arachne:

> The Spider shewes the spite
> 　　that she (good wench) abid,
> In token of hir pride shee hanges
> 　　at roufe by rottin thrid.[22]

But at the same time, Arachne, like a spider, is made the epitome of a potent resentment:

> With venim ranck and vile
> 　　hir wombe is like to burst,
> A token of hir inwarde hate
> 　　and hawtie minde at furst.

Like her rival, Minerva, she is seen as capable of unfashioning and refashioning the state, as she unfashions and refashions the gods through her weaving.

While Sandys, like most Renaissance commentators, fears and derides Arachne's power, he is contending with an alternative tradition, stemming from Ovid, in which the emphasis is not upon Arachne's pride or malice but upon her skill in fashioning. Describing a splendid bed curtain, for instance, Joseph Beaumont writes that it has

> 　　a Texture of so fine a thread,
> That neat *Arachne* might the Spinster seem,
> Whose matchless art is so distinctly read
> In every line, that thence it takes its name:
> 　　We call't *Aranea*, a Net whereby
> 　　I catch the purest winged Beams that fly.[23]

Arachne's work, far from being, as Sandys would have it, "uselesse and worthlesse labors," is a "matchless art," an art whose fineness can be "distinctly read / In every line." Here, Arachne is imagined, like the maker of the bed curtain, as both spinner

("Spinster") and weaver of a "Net." The story that the net tells, though, is not a narrative of the gods but a display of her skill in creating "a Texture of so fine a thread." Where Sandys attacks Arachne for her narrative text, Beaumont praises her for her material texture. But Beaumont's praise of the textile skill of the "neat *Arachne*" was frequently transformed back into praise of her narrative skill in her figurative appropriation as poetic muse. In 1599, Thomas Storer presents to "the Worshipfull M. Ion Hewson, Chaplaine to Her Maiestie" "such a web as I could frame," which "My Muse *Arachne*-like presents to thee."[24] And John Beaumont, in a puff for Francis Beaumont's *Salamacis and Hermaphroditus*, curiously conflates Minerva and Arachne, both equally striving for "illustrous glory," but with Minerva, rather than Arachne, "[s]pinning in silken twists a lasting story" of the "loues of the gods," goddess and mortal spinner alike figuring Francis Beaumont's skill in weaving his poem "[w]ith fine Mylesian threds."[25]

More surprising, given this emphasis upon Arachne's skill both as maker of the finest thread and upon her skill in weaving narratives of the gods, is her metamorphosis into the emblem of a simpler, purer age, before human society had been corrupted by silk and dyes. William Browne, like John Beaumont, conflates Arachne and Minerva, but he subsumes all trace of their conflict in the contrast between the golden age in which they lived and the present fallen age of fashion, mixed dyes, and transnational trade:

> Happier those times were, when the Flaxen clew
> By fair *Arachnes* hand the *Lydians* knew,
> And sought not to the worme for silken threds,
> To roule their bodies in, or dresse their heads.
> When wise *Minerua* did th' *Athenians* learne
> To draw their milk-white fleeces into yarne;
> And knowing not the mixtures which began
> (Of colors) from the *Babylonian*,
> Nor wooll in *Sardis* dyde, more various knowne
> By hues, then *Iris* to the world hath showne:
> The bowels of our mother were not ript
> For *Mader-pits*, nor the sweet meadowes stript
> Of their choise beauties, nor for *Ceres* load
> The fertile lands burd'ned with needlesse *Woad*.
> Through the wide Seas no winged Pine did goe
> To Lands vnknowne for staining *Indico*;
> Nor men in scorching clymates moar'd their Keele
> To traffique for the costly *Coucheneele*.
> Vnknown was then the *Phrygian* brodery,
> The *Tyrian* purple, and the Scarlet dye,
> Such as their sheep clad, such they woue and wore,
> Russet or white, or those mixt, and no more.[26]

In Browne's account, gone not only is the strife between Arachne and Minerva but the sense that either of them used their skills to weave subtle tapestries. The political story that, even if demonized, is at the center of Sandys's account is transformed into an arcadian account of a *polis* ignorant of trade. Corruption is imagined as coming from the growing and harvesting of plants for dyes; from the searching of the world for indigo, cochineal, purple, scarlet; from the cultivation of silkworms.[27]

The materiality of spinning

In contrast to both Sandys's demonizing of Arachne and Browne's pastoralizing of her, Velázquez's *Fable of Arachne* explores the interrelation between the lowest paid form of female manual labor (spinning wool) and the most expensive forms of courtly production (tapestries). In fact, one of the problems that the painting presents, if one accepts that it *does* depict the story of Arachne, is the identification of Arachne herself. Is she the woman in the middle of the group of five women in the background scene? If so, she is presented at her moment of triumph, having equalled the skill of Minerva. She stands in front of one of her own tapestries, depicting the crimes of the gods. The particular tapestry in Velázquez's painting represents the rape of Europa, which is copied from Titian's painting of the myth, a painting which was at that time in the Alcázar, whose rooms Velázquez had been employed to remodel and redecorate.[28] If this is Arachne, she stands with her body toward the viewer, facing Minerva to her right. Minerva's right arm is raised. In admonition? Pointing to Arachne's work? But there is nothing clearly to identify the central woman in the background scene as Arachne. There is no loom near her, although she does seem by her dress (mantle and robe) to belong more to the mythological world of Minerva (mantle, robe, and helmet) than to the fashionable contemporary Spanish world of the other three aristocratic women.

But Arachne could equally be identified as the woman spinning in the left foreground of the painting. Attention is carefully drawn to her by the woman on the extreme left, who pulls back a heavy red curtain so as to reveal the woman spinning. And we should recall that if Arachne was famous for weaving her tapestries, she was equally famous as a spinner. Ovid describes how the nymphs would leave their vineyards to watch Arachne working with distaff and spindle and winding her yarn into a new ball.[29] And in a marginal gloss to *The Silkewormes, and their Flies*, Thomas Moffet characterizes her as a "most famous *spinner* in Lydiae."[30] Or should we identify Arachne with the woman in the right foreground, upon whom the light falls as she turns away from us, winding finished thread into a ball? Or are Arachne's labors split between these figures, so that she is both part of the foreground world of manual labor and part of the background world of courtly display? But even in the courtly scene, the figure one might identify as Arachne inscribes the plebeian world from which, as Ovid emphasizes, she comes ("de plebe suoque"). The rolled-up sleeves of her smock mirror the rolled-up sleeves of the smock of the woman winding thread in the right foreground. The two worlds, then, are not simply opposed. Indeed, the courtly display is dependent upon the manual labors depicted in the foreground, but it is a display reflected not in Arachne's clothes but in her splendid tapestry and in the clothes of the other women included in the scene.

Jonathan Brown, analyzing the details of the tapestry, builds on earlier critics' recognition that the fluttering cupids and waving woman are copied from Titian's "Rape of Europa." Arachne, that is, gestures not toward her own masterpiece but toward a man's. Brown argues that Velázquez treated the subject in this way in order to raise his own status as a painter. By stopping the narrative before Minerva changes Arachne into a spider, the scene focuses on the moment when the mortal woman's weaving is seen to equal that of the goddess. The implication is that human artistry is divine: "Titian is equated with Arachne, and Arachne could 'paint' like a god" (253). Brown argues that Velázquez allied himself with Titian, earlier the favorite painter of both the Spanish kings who employed Velázquez, because Titian had been honored with gifts and titles by both kings. In Brown's interpretation, then, an upward displacement of gender and of material occurs in the substitution of Titian's Europa in oil for Arachne's scene in wool.

But despite the acuity of Brown's analysis, it is not quite right. It is *not* Titian's painting that we see in Velázquez's painting, but a tapestry copied from Titian. This is perhaps not just because of the requirements of the fable (Arachne was a spinner and weaver, not a painter) but also an acknowledgment of the hierarchies of courtly production. For despite the aesthetic value that Philip IV (like Charles I in England) attributed to the work of Titian, *literal* value was materialized far more in tapestries than in paintings. As Lisa Jardine notes in an important corrective to twentieth-century aesthetic hierarchies, "painting was an inexpensive form of luxury decoration, compared with tapestry."[31] Charles V, the great-grandfather of Philip IV, spent a massive sum commemorating his victory at Tunis in tapestries. The designs alone, from Jan Vermeyen, cost 1,900 Flemish pounds, and the actual tapestries, using "the best and finest Lyon thread" as well as "Granada silks" in sixty-three colors and gold and silver thread, came to about 15,000 pounds, including 6,637 pounds for silk thread alone. The buying of the materials was supervised by Maria of Hungary herself and the financing was organized by the merchant Jakob Welser. Being easily portable, the tapestries were a moveable form of courtly splendor, carried between Brussels, London, Toledo and Antwerp.[32] Similarly, for all Charles I's connoisseurship of painting, it was in tapestries that he invested most. Between 1625 and 1640, the Exchequer paid £7,830 for paintings (£3,000 alone for Rubens's ceiling in the Whitehall Banqueting House), compared to £17,541 for tapestries.[33] The fact that almost half of the cost of Charles V's Tunis tapestries was spent on thread emphasizes just how much of the cost of luxury textiles was derived from the production of primary materials.

In depicting Arachne's tapestry, then, Velázquez's painting stages not the triumph of the painter's skill but the transformation of the painter's design (here, Titian's) into the more luxurious and costly world of textiles. Velázquez himself was keenly aware of the significance of textiles and of other costly goods in the production of the court and the courtier. As a painter, Velázquez was a manual laborer, hardly different from the spinners who occupy the foreground of the *Fable of Arachne*. He knew this to his cost. From 1650, he had been preoccupied with gaining admission to the Order of Santiago, thus winning acceptance as aristocrat and courtier. Although he received a royal nomination in 1658, he was turned down by the Council of Military Orders, whose rules excluded "those who themselves or whose parents or grandparents, have practiced any of the manual or base occupations here described . . . By manual or base occupation is meant silversmith or painter, if he paints for a living, embroiderer, stonecutter, mason, innkeeper, scribe, except for royal secretaries." The Council rejected Velázquez's genealogy, despite the fact that he presented 148 witnesses to testify that he was of noble blood. Only after he had received two papal dispensations was he finally "ennobled by the king and admitted to the Order of Santiago on 28 November 1659."[34] Having been admitted, despite the resistance of the Council, Velázquez proceeded to transform himself into the aristocrat he claimed to be. He did this through his clothes and deportment, and, if Antonio Palomino is to be believed, he did so entirely successfully. Palomino describes Velázquez's appearance at the meeting of Philip IV and Louis XIV six months after his admission to the Order of Santiago:

Don Diego Velázquez was not the one who showed that day the least consideration for the adornment, gallantry, and finery of his person; for in addition to his gentlemanly bearing and comportment, which were courtly, not to mention his natural grace and composure, he was distinguished in dress by many diamonds and precious stones. It is not surprising that in the color of his cloth he was superior to many, for he had a better understanding of such things, in which he always showed very good taste. His whole costume was trimmed with Milanese silver point lace. On his cloak he wore the red insignia [of Santiago]. At his side was a very fine rapier with silver guard and chape, with exquisitely chased designs in relief made in Italy. Round his neck was a heavy gold chain with a pendant badge adorned with many diamonds, on which was enameled the insignia of Santiago, and the rest of his apparel was worthy of such a precious decoration.[35]

In other words, Velázquez made every possible use of the arts of the weaver, the dyer, the jeweler, the goldsmith, and the armorer to achieve the position from which his status as a mere painter, a worker with his hands, had debarred him. In fact, to transform himself into an aristocrat, he had to make the absurd claim that he had never painted for money at all.

But if Velázquez's "bearing and comportment" were an attempt to suggest a "natural grace and composure," his *Fable of Arachne* stages a radical denaturalizing of courtly splendor. For the painting depicts the primary processes of carding, spinning, and winding the threads that will create the materials for tapestry and clothes alike. Even the raw product, before it has been manufactured, is conspicuously displayed. On the right wall above the winder's head is hung a mass of sheep's fleece, its dull color and rough texture providing a striking contrast to the gleaming, multicolored tapestry in the scene behind.

The contrast between the makers of the raw material of cloth and the wealthy women in the background, distanced from spinning as labor, provides a richly revealing optic for a range of Renaissance texts. In conduct books, poems and plays, and in popular and elite visual representations, Sandysian strategies were deployed to interpret other myths, as well. Homer and classical fables were subjected to readings that dematerialized women's textile work in order to produce a feminine ideal of behavior, an elite ideal that obscured women's economic labor in a cloth-based society by transcendentalizing spinning into a symbolic exhibition of virtue. The power of Velázquez's painting is its power to rematerialize the processes through which the symbolic is manufactured.

5   The fate of spinning: Penelope and the Three Fates

Spinning, as we showed in the previous chapter, was the foundation of a cloth economy. At home in the evenings and in free moments between farmwork, house-keeping, and child-minding, poor women worked with their distaffs and spindles or at their spinning wheels to earn extra income. Prior to the invention of spinning machines in the eighteenth century, every piece of cloth made in Europe, whether of linen, wool, silk or cotton, was woven of thread that had been spun by human hands – in the great majority, by the hands of women. As Alice Clark remarked, "It requires some effort of the imagination to realize the incessant industry which the duty of clothing her own family imposed on every woman, to say nothing of the yarn required for the famous Woollen Trade."[1] In this chapter, we look at the actualities of spinning in poor women's lives and then at its representation in early modern writing and images in order to trace out the ways in which threadmaking, economically crucial, was elevated into a moral ideal in the construction of middle-class femininity. We will look as well at how the centrality of spinning was acknowl-edged, both positively and negatively, in Renaissance interpretations of particular ancient spinsters: Homer's Penelope and the Three Fates.

The culture of spinning

Homespun wool and flax were in enormous demand in early modern Europe. Six to eight spinners' output was needed to supply one weaver for a day's work.[2] But spinning was not particularly profitable. Prices paid for spun thread were very low, especially in England. Kenneth Ponting reports that Tudor spinners averaged 3 to 4 pence a day, hence an average of 21 pence, less than two shillings, for a six-day week, compared to a London artisan's average weekly wage of six shillings.[3] Since a pound loaf of bread cost a halfpenny,[4] wool-spinning provided at best a meager living wage. The prices paid for linen thread were so low that no one could support herself as a flax-spinner alone. A mid-seventeenth-century writer in Norwich estimated that a woman might make up to a shilling and 8 pence a week for spinning flax all day, but by this time, this was far from a living wage.[5] A woman had to have other income in order to profit maximally from spinning, "a tertiary occupation," as Clark calls it.[6] The most profitable way to spin was to buy wool at the local market, spin it at home, and keep the yarn until the market price was good. Women who made yarn in this independent way, withholding it from the market until a moment to profit arrived, got a higher price for their thread than those who spun every day on commission, working the wool supplied to them by clothiers (wholesalers who bought a year's supply of raw wool at a time) at prices the clothiers set themselves.[7] In practice, spinners for the cloth market profited from a systematic inconstancy in their labor. In the realm of gender theory, however, as we shall see, spinning was equated with constancy.

Even though spinning for profit called for interruptions in making and selling thread, for many women producing the primary material for clothing was a life-long bodily habit, in the sense of a *habitus*, or complex of customs and activities involving practical know-how and ongoing calculations of physical and social kinds.[8] Spinning was a manual ritual based on steady repetition, a work technique that imposed an order upon the body and developed specific skills of the eye and hand. To spin wool, once it had been tied in a carded (combed) bundle onto the usually two-pronged wooden pole called a distaff or rock, the spinner had to have a feel for the hank of wool with which she began: the strength, smoothness and elasticity of the fibers determined how fast she could pull and twist them into thread. Flax, too, required sensitive handling with finger and thumb; the spinner had to wet it to to remove gummy matter remaining from the soaking of the flax-plant fibers and to produce a smooth, flexible thread, which she kept pliable by dampening it with saliva or water from a cup attached to the wheel.[9] Spinning wheels, the "great wheel" for wool and the fly or Saxony wheel for flax, quickened the process by increasing the speed with which thread could be wound onto bobbins, but merchants objected to the use of spinning wheels because they thought that the treadle established a speed that prevented women from stopping to smoothe out lumps in the thread.[10] To the extent that the middlemen responding to weavers' fluctuating demands for wool set the price they were willing to pay countrywomen for their yarn, earning a living through spinning was a hard economic practice for poor women, not a fixed moral virtue.

But spinning for a livelihood was not necessarily an isolated or isolating practice. Although early modern aristocratic households and church authorities eventually discontinued the medieval practice of attaching women's textile workshops to manors and ecclesiastical estates, in northern Europe, village and city women, young and old, gathered together on winter evenings in *Spinnstuben*, public spinning rooms where they gossiped, sang, and told stories, and they defended this culture against interference by male authorities.[11] In France, in spinning schools and silk workshops headed by women, sixteenth-century orphan girls learned profitable trades: to work with wool and linen and to unwind the cocoons of silkworms. Natalie Davis, drawing on a late fifteenth-century text that records the customs of spinning women, *Les Evangiles des quenouilles*, argues that the work culture of spinners celebrated the power of textile craft and allowed relative independence to the producers of thread.[12]

Certainly, the spinning women depicted as exchanging popular beliefs in *Les Evangiles* see their techniques as having magical properties, prophetic, malign, and beneficent. The first thread spun in a day, hung across a door, is said to have the power to predict the first name of the man the spinner will marry (it will be the same as that of the first man to pass through the door).[13] A spinning woman standing by the roadside presages serious harm to a man on horseback, who ought to turn back unless she is willing to put her distaff behind her; flax left on a distaff from Saturday to Monday will never make pure white cloth, which is why German women's linen is never as white as Frenchwomen's; warts can be cured by binding them with thread spun by a woman in the labor of childbirth; homespun linen sheets freshly laid on a bed contain an angel.[14] Davis also suggests that spinners' workshops headed by women sometimes broke down class divides: "The domestic work culture provided a kind of vertical identity beween mistress and female worker, which could sometimes be used by the former to hurry along the work process and sometimes by the latter to slow it down" (180).

Spinners' work was represented as being valued by both sexes alike. It was a stock feature of folk tales that a peasant girl's textile virtuosity could win her a desirable husband. In one of the tales collected by the Grimm brothers, "The Cast-Off Remnants," when a young man about to marry a girl who hates spinning discovers that her maid has made herself a dress from the remnants of flax his fiancée has extravagantly thrown away, he marries the maid instead.[15] Another, more intricate tale, "The Spindle, the Shuttle and the Needle," magically balances several oppositions. In it, a prince marries a young orphan girl who can spin and weave with supernatural efficacy, because he sees that she is both poor and rich: humble by birth but able to spin golden thread and weave beautiful carpets. After making her his queen, that is, raising her to the status of a noblewoman freed from the necessity of spinning for a living, he none the less preserves and exhibits the spinning tools she no longer uses: "The spindle [and] shuttle . . . were kept in the Treasure House and held in high esteem."[16] In other tales, "Frau Holle," the patron saint of spinners, guides young and old women to exploit the art of spinning to marry as they desire. It is significant, as Jack Zipes points out, that the negative associations of words such as "spinster" in the sense of "an old maid" and the German *spinnen* meaning "to babble in a crazy way" developed only in the eighteenth century, when women were being driven out of spinning as it was taken over by factories equipped with the new spinning machines invented by James Hargreaves in 1764 – that is, when women were losing not only the wages but the respect that hand textile work had brought them.[17]

Folk tales often register the power of spinning women, but they suggest as well that the work took a heavy toll. The pain and even bodily distortion caused by a lifetime of spinning are vividly pictured in the Grimms' tale, "The Three Spinners." In it, the low-born heroine, who has no skill at spinning, is helped to win the prince by three women who appear to her to spin the three rooms of flax that she has been assigned by the queen. One of the spinners has a flat, splayed foot, from pressing the treadle of her wheel; one has a huge, drooping lower lip, from licking thread to smoothe it; the third has a splayed thumb, from twisting thread onto reels. Invited to the royal wedding, as the queen-to-be has promised them they will be, they explain how they came to be so misshapen. Their final boon to the heroine is that the prince, horrified by their appearance, swears that his young wife will never touch a spinning wheel again.[18] The tale concludes, "Thus she was relieved of the wretched task of spinning flax."

"The Three Spinners" exposes a class difference, which we will explore further, between the fact of spinning as a poor woman's necessary occupation and its use as a sign of diligence (capable of deceptive use, as signs are) in discourses aimed at constructing a model of femininity for higher-ranking women. The new queen in the Grimms' tale, by not forgetting what the three spinners have contributed to her success, assures her own dispensation from the obligation to labor as they do. The tale speaks of the material and even the magical usefulness of spinning and, at the same time, of the desire to be free of it – as does the tale of the orphan turned queen, whose spindle becomes a demonstration object in the state treasury. Indeed, as Maria Tatar points out in a study of spinning throughout the Grimms' tales, such tales about liberation from the task would have been told by women who *were* spinning as they narrated and listened to them. She concludes that spinning "occupies a highly ambiguous status . . . It can take the form of both a blessing and a curse."[19] In magical tales, spinning helpers – good fairies, wise old crones, Rumpelstiltskins – save heroines through miraculous intervention, but spinning also "deforms the body and dulls the mind." Of "The Three Spinners" in particular, Tatar concludes, "By imprinting the bodies of the three spinners with the trademarks of toil, the tale makes it eminently clear that beauty and hard work are incompatible."[20]

Spinning as ideology

Magical rather than practical thinking predominated in the conduct books of early modern Europe, whose writers aimed to convince high-born women that textile work and beauty could go together, via an equation between spinning and the idealized simplicity of the good woman who spun. But the negative aspects of spinning registered in folk tales were obviously felt among women of the elite, as well: the phrasing of many injunctions to spin suggests that male writers were trying to forestall their female audience's resistance to being assigned this duty. Ruth Kelso reads in humanists' recommendations their sense that they might be preaching to the unconvertible: "The most unquestioned housewifely art for the gentlewoman of any rank was needlework, with spinning and weaving still recommended though obviously out of fashion since advisers spoke of them as a cause already lost."[21] Paraphrasing Juan Luis Vives's remarks on textile work in *The Instruction of a Christian Woman*, she points out that he seems to be answering the practical argument that women who could afford to buy cloth did not need to spin woolen thread to make it.[22] In his citations of ancient and Christian writers who insisted that spinning was the duty of all women, however high born, Vives argued from an ethical rather than a commercial premise: the goal of textile work is avoiding sin, not producing a usable or saleable product. A good example is his comment on St. Jerome's advice to the wealthy Roman noblewoman Demetrias:

St. Jerome counselleth the holy virgin Demetrias to eschew idleness. And therefore when she hath done her prayers, to go in hand with wool and weaving, that by such change of works the days seem not long. Nor he bade not that she should work because that she was in any poverty, which was one of the most noble women in Rome, and richest; but that, by the occasion of working, she should think on nothing but such as pertaineth unto the service of our Lord.[23]

Thomas Salter, too, translating Giovanni Bruto's 1555 *Institutione di una fanciulla nata nobilmente* as *A Mirrhor mete for all Mothers, Matrones and Maidens, intituled the Mirrhor of Modestie* (London, 1579), wrote to forestall the objections of high-born girls: "I wish our Maiden, not onely to know all maner of Nedlewoorke, meete for a Maiden; but also all that whiche belongeth to the Distaffe and Spindle, not thinkyng it unseemely to any of what estate or degree so ever."[24] Such an objection is raised explicitly in women's voices, although probably not by a woman writer, in the pamphlet entitled *The Women's Sharp Revenge*, published in London in 1640. In this long text, most likely written by John Taylor, "Mary Tattlewell and Joan Hit-him-home, Spinsters" protest the injustice whereby sons are sent to grammar school and then to the university, but daughters, though temperamentally well suited to learning,

> have not that generous and liberal education, lest we should be made able to vindicate our own injuries: we are set only . . . to the wheel to spin a fair thread for our own undoings; or perchance to some more dirty and debased drudgery.[25]

But it is unusual to find spinning linked to debased drudgery in male-authored texts of this period.[26]

More typically, the Dutch moralist Jacob Cats wrote verses recalling better days when no class status exempted a woman from spinning. Like many moralists, he invoked the Old Testament model of the good wife in Proverbs (31: 10–31). But he recognized at the same time that wealthy women oversaw their daughters and maids spinning rather than do it themselves:

> Choose, oh young lady, the spindle over the game.
> Search old times and all past life;
> The richest young lady spun, the mother could weave;
> The princess of the country, the highest in rank,
> Handled wool or pure white flax.
> Consider the esteemed woman described by Solomon,
> She is motivated by the sheer pleasure of spinning;
> *She makes her family* turn the spindle
> For the good of the house, in the service of her husband.[27]

The commitment to spinning as a symbolic value led other conduct book writers to make contradictory claims about it, as well. Like Cats later, Francesco Barbaro in his *De Re Uxoria* (Florence, 1416) conceded that the main responsibility of aristocratic women was to oversee the spinning of their servants rather than to do it themselves, but at the same time he held up a classical model of female textile virtue irrelevant to the division of labor in wealthy households of his time. Barbaro acknowledges that the duties of a woman like Ginevra Cavalcanti, to whom he dedicated his book on the occasion of her marriage to Lorenzo de' Medici, will really be to hire good stewards and promote deserving maids. But he goes on to invoke an episode from early Roman history to exemplify the universality of women's duty to spin:

> So that a wife's duty might be commended to posterity, there were affixed to the bronze statue of Gaia Caecilia, the daughter of Tarquinius, a household slipper and a distaff and spindle, so that these objects might . . . signify that her diligent work at home ought to be imitated by future generations.[28]

This inconsistency typifies humanist discourse on ideal femininity: the scholar's devotion to classical sources works against his project of writing a practical guide for a patroness from the contemporary elite.

The central issue for Barbaro, as for Vives and English conduct book writers, was the fear of gentlewomen's idleness. As Patricia Crawford remarks in her study of sixteenth- and seventeenth-century prescriptions for needlework in England, "A woman who was utterly uselessly employed – as was Penelope, weaving and undoing – was virtuously employed."[29] Richard Brathwait's advice in *The English Gentlewoman* (1631) affirms this attitude: "Chuse rather with Penelope to weaue and unweaue, than to giue Idlenesse the least leaue."[30] Anxiety over women's idleness led to a conflation of two different systems of value, economic and moral, in Anthony Fitzherbert's *Book of Husbandrie* (London, 1555). At first, in the context of a discussion of flax and linen making, he asserts the moral value of spinning over its limited practical profit: "lette thy dystaffe be alwaye redy for a pastyme, that thou be not ydell. And undoubted a woman cannot get her livinge honestly with spinning on the dystaffe, but it stoppeth a gap and must needs be had."[31] But he goes on to argue that spinning wool has substantial economic value. Even a wife who has no wool of her own, he says, "may have a conuenient living" by spinning clothmakers' wool for them. Fitzherbert tries in vain to maintain a single standard toward women's work because spinning itself is split: wool brings shillings and pence, flax brings profit only of a moral kind.

A similar conflation of the ethical and economic values attributed to spinning occurs in John Evelyn's 1685 portrait of an old village spinster in his memoirs. Evelyn was writing more autobiographically than prescriptively in this text, but the earlier conduct book writers' nostalgia persists in his account of the spinster's virtuous poverty. He approves of his subject's working life as a sign of her spiritual state, reflected in her infrequent speech and simple clothing as well as her ceaseless labor:

[She] lives on foure pence a day, which she getts in spinning: She says she abounds, and can give almes to others, living in strange humility and contentednesse, without any apparent affectation or singularity; she is continually working, or praying, or reading, gives a good account of her knowledge in Religion . . . ; is not in the least given to talke; wonderfull modest, and of a simple, not unseemly behaviour, . . . clad very plaine, but cleane and tight.[32]

Evelyn plays down the hard facts of the spinner's life (she would be dependent upon her parish were it not for the "little hermitage my Lady [Clarendon] gives her rent-free") in order to celebrate her exemplary virtue, even as he claims that she is one of a kind: "In summ, [she] appears a *Saint* of an extraordinary sort, in so religious a life as is seldom met with in Villages now a daies."

In fact, spinning was not extraordinarily but frequently an economic necessity. As Merry Wiesner has shown, the spinning wheel was considered an essential tool for poor women in German cities. When a Frankfurt family's household was broken up in bankruptcy proceedings, the wife was allowed to keep her wheel, presumably because she was expected to survive, however narrowly, by spinning.[33] Legal codes explicitly enforced spinning as a women's task: women convicted of crimes were forced to spin. This is why "spinninghouse" became a synonym for "prison" in Northern Europe and in European colonial territories.[34] Wiesner records the case of a woman thief in Memmingen who was so sick that she was moved from the prison to the hospital. But once she had arrived there, she was chained into a position in which she could still spin.[35]

Wayne Franits, however, has shown that Dutch painters depicted upper-class women at their spinning wheels in order to represent an ideal of feminine diligence; the wheels are a symbolic convention rather than a record of actual practice. In Holland by the seventeenth century, he points out, only one in five households listed spinning wheels in their inventories, and to own one was not necessarily to use it.[36] Cornelia Moore argues that in Germany as well as the Low Countries, burgher concern about idleness was the motive for exhortations to women to spin. Citing humanist moralists such as Konrad Bitschin and Jakob Wimpheling, she points out that although they name royal women and even the Virgin Mary as exemplary spinners, "There is never any mention of the end product of all this handiwork. Its mere busy-ness appears to be sufficient."[37]

There was, then, a conflict at the heart of representations of spinning. On the one hand, it was recognized as the absolute precondition for all textile production and as the required labor of poorer women. On the other, it was an ideological program for the production of virtuous femininity across class lines. Consequently, it was recommended for aristocratic and middle-class daughters as the necessary *habitus* that produced "woman," while the actual work of producing thread was trivialized or ignored.

Unraveling Penelope

The most famous of literary female textile workers in the Renaissance was Penelope, in Homer a skilled weaver rather than a spinner. But even in the case of this more sophisticated labor, weaving a shroud for Odysseus's father Laertes, the "work" is a simulation. In *The Odyssey*, Penelope, surrounded by importunate suitors, promises that when the shroud is completed, she will choose a new husband; every night she unravels what she has woven during the day so as to remain loyal to her husband, Odysseus. One reading of this plot of the *Odyssey*, a Renaissance reading affirmed in several versions of Homer's faithful wife, is that female virtue is constructed through work without an outcome. The *appearance* of industry is what Penelope aims for and what guarantees her chastity for the three years before her subterfuge is discovered. The Renaissance appropriation of Penelope as a model of female virtue knots together idealizations and contradictions that expose the gap between the material processes of textile production and the versions of "woman" produced by ideological labor.

In fact, Renaissance poets often drew less upon Homer's account of Penelope than upon Ovid's letter from Penelope, the first epistle of the *Heroides*, as the basis for their versions of the faithful wife. And in *Heroides* I, Ovid's Penelope speaks of both spinning *and* weaving. This Penelope complains that if Paris had drowned before he reached Menelaos's kingdom, she would not be lying cold in a deserted bed, nor would "the hanging web" ("pendula tela"), that is, the partly woven shroud, be tiring her widowed hands.[38] Here, she is clearly referring to her Homeric task as weaver. But the Ovidian Penelope is also conceptualized as a spinner: she imagines Odysseus telling some other woman what a rustic wife he has by saying that her greatest concern is "not to allow wool to remain rough," that is, unspun ("quae tantum lanas non sinat esse rudas," line 78). The context of this remark – the wife's fear that her absent husband is somewhere mocking her lack of sophistication – emphasizes the rough simplicity attributed to spinning as the first stage of textile work.

The Ovidian account thus opens up for Renaissance poets the possibility of rewriting Penelope as spinner rather than weaver. What is gained by this change? Most crucially, it redefines femininity itself in terms of the most basic of textile processes. That is, it cuts and restitches *The Odyssey* by simplifying Penelope. In *The Odyssey*, Penelope's weaving is associated with cunning, shrewdness, foresight, the devising of plots, the ingenuity required for social resistance.[39] Homer uses the words *mêtis* and *dolos*, cunning and trickiness, to characterize her plan for fending off the suitors. As John Winkler points out, in so far as Homer's Penelope spins, it is by analogy to the poet himself: she "winds up balls of tricks," *dolous tolupeuô* (*Odyssey*, 19. 137). Like Homer, Winkler argues, Penelope works at the "clever designing of interdependent tensions, the warp and woof of crossed purposes and inimical purposes."[40] Indeed, one derivation suggested for the name "Penelope" is the Greek *pene*, meaning "loom" or "woof." And Nancy Felson-Rubin points out two Indo-European roots that associate weaving as a physical act with physical speed, mental agility, and strength: *webh*, meaning "to weave" and "to move quickly," and *teks*, from which the Greek *tekhne* is derived, meaning "to shape with an axe" and "to weave, "to fabricate."[41]

Precisely because of Penelope's cunning, classical commentators were not unanimous in their admiration for her. One scandalous Roman reading of her character, Servius's commentary on the *Aeneid*, had it that she slept with all (*pantos*) 108 suitors, the god Pan being the result.[42] As I. D. Jenkins has shown in a study of weaving women in ancient Greece, female textile work was crucial to the survival of men's households, but as an intricate, learned skill, "the incomprehensible dexterity of the female art of weaving provided a natural metaphor for the art of deception; the more *poikilos* (elaborate) the fabric, the more *poikilos* (cunning) it became."[43] The darker possibilities of women's power through textiles are also figured in Helen, weaving the story of the Trojan War into a tapestry in *The Iliad*; Clytemnestra's two tapestries in *The Oresteia*, the purple one on which she encourages Agamemnon to walk and the robe in which she and Aegisthus pinion him to stab him in his bath; and Euripides's Medea, who sends a poisoned robe to her rival, Jason's new wife. The "devious intent" attributed to such anti-heroines, Jenkins suggests, reveals "masculine anxiety about a task which, paradoxically, men themselves give their women to do" (115).

Weaving, whether by women or men, could not go forward without spun thread. Yet spinning was contrasted to weaving as a less ambitious, more repetitious task. In the classical world, the spinning and weaving of wool went together. It was the job of servant women overseen by aristocratic mistresses, though it was also a privileged activity of high-ranking women, for example, the two Athenian girls assigned each year to help priestesses of Athene make a *peplos* for her statue in the Parthenon.[44] But weaving, separated from spinning, was increasingly becoming a man's craft in early modern Europe. During the Middle Ages, women worked at weaving wool as well as silk, but by the middle sixteenth century they had been forced out of most of the clothworking guilds throughout Europe.[45] At the same time, spinning was celebrated in the attempt to produce an ideal woman valued for her "simplicity." By emphasizing spinning as an antidote to the kind of plotting and planning carried out by Penelope as weaver, early modern moralists and poets reversed the Homeric equation. In their work, they present spinning as a guarantee of the *absence* of feminine shrewdness, as a habit that forecloses the possibility of willful or lascivious thoughts loosed by idleness.

The association of spinning with a more narrowly defined femininity may explain a peculiarity of several literary treatments of Penelope in Renaissance literary English texts: her weaving is transformed into spinning. Rather than attribute to her the potentially deceptive technique of Penelope as weaver or the complex technical skills that now belonged mainly to male professionals, writers gave her the simpler work of spinning. An anonymous translation from *The Heroides*, "The beginning of the epistle of Penelope to Vlisses, made into verse," published in the second edition of Tottel's *Miscellany* (1557), clearly positions Penelope as spinner rather than weaver. This Penelope, wishing like Ovid's Penelope that Paris had drowned before he arrived in Greece to meet and abduct Helen, complains not of the hanging shroud that she weaves and unravels but of the nights she spends alone with her distaff:

> O that the raging surges great that lechers bane had wrought,
> When first with ship he forowed seas, and Lacedemon sought,
> In desert bed my shiuering coarse then shold not have sought rest,
> And whiles I cast long run[n]ing nightes, how best I might begile,
> No distaff should my widowish hand have weary made the while.[46]   (lines 5–18)

The distaff of the final line imposes upon the Homeric/Ovidian discourse of the poem the figures of virtuous spinning wives and widows repeatedly represented in Renaissance conduct books and genre paintings.

While Penelope's weaving is not erased in Peter Colse's 1596 pamphlet, *Penelope's Complaint: or, A Mirrour for wanton Minions*, it is minimized and systematically linked to spinning. The title page of the pamphlet implies that Colse's text is a translation from Homer ("Taken out of Homers Odissea, and written in English Verse"[47]), but Colse's telling anachronisms transform Penelope into an exemplary Renaissance heroine. He gives Penelope the spinning wheel, which arrived in Europe only in the Middle Ages, and he represents her spinning flax to make linen, which in ancient Greece was usually imported from Egypt.[48] One of the first complaints of Colse's Penelope is that by marrying "a knight that Armes had bore," she doomed herself to solitude; Ulysses' "martiall mind / And courage stout" soon took him away from "*Venus* court" (B2v). If she had avoided such a marriage, she says, she would have avoided the preliminary stage of woolworking. Spinning, using two different techniques – the wheel, used by a sitting woman, and the drop spindle, used most often in ancient times by a standing woman – is mentioned three times in four lines:

> With distaffe thus I neede not drudge,
> Nor yet with wheele have worne my hand:
> Nor want of sleepe neede I thus grudge,
> Nor tired thus a-twisting stand.   (B3)

In a later passage, "Her answere to the wooers," Colse's Penelope specifically mentions her tapestry, which she admits she has finished. But in her speech, she moves quickly past her completion of the woven woolen cloth of the tapestry to focus on her spun linen ("tow," strictly speaking, was dry flax roughly prepared for spinning). Colse uses his heroine's work as spinner to make a transition to her lines in praise of Ulysses, shifting from the more complex to the simpler textile skill in order to affirm her status as the faithful wife:

> Sweete Lordings though my web be wrought,
> And al my towe be readie spun,
> Another doubt comes to my thought,
> You know, what worth *Ulysses* won:
> You know he was a worthie knight,
> And got him honour for his might.   (G3)

Penelope's Complaint departs from its classical model in protesting the miseries of marriage rather than celebrating the Ithacan couple's reunion. But while Colse's poem is sympathetic to Penelope as bereft wife, it constructs a Penelope far less skillful and cunning than Homer's. The virtue of Colse's Penelope is inscribed in her function not as a weaver of tapestries but as a spinner of tow.

Penelope's textile skill is similarly limited to spinning in the silk-weaver Thomas

Deloney's 1597 prose romance *Jack of Newberry*, celebrating the Tudor master weaver who rose from poverty to riches. As Joan Pong Linton points out, the first ballad inserted in Deloney's text represents Jack's London workshop as staffed by male weavers and by women spinners, whose good cheer and attractive appearance "gloss over the economic displacement of women," that is, the exclusion of actual women from the profitable trade of the weavers' guild, an exclusion that had occurred throughout the sixteenth century.[49] Jack's "pretty maids," Deloney writes, were never idle, "But in that place all day did spin" (lines 17–18). Linton also points out that in the "Weauers Song" performed by Jack's men for King Henry VIII, Deloney rewrites the myth of Penelope to justify men's "monopoly on weaving" (reinforced in 1511, for example, by an edict prohibiting women from clothworking guilds) as a source of peaceful stability.[50] This song turns Penelope into a spinner rather than a weaver by clearly splitting her work from that of the ancient weavers of Ithaca. Indeed, Deloney adapts the refrain of the song to set up this amicable division of labor as a contrast to the conflict at Troy:

> But while the Greekes beseiged Troy,
> Penelope apace did spin,
> And Weauers wrought with mickle ioy,
> though litle gaines were coming in.
> For loue and friendship did agree,
> To keep the bands of amitie.   (31)

Following the same logic, Deloney goes on to position Helen of Troy not as the weaver described in the *Iliad*, producing a rich and intricate tapestry picturing the events of the Trojan War, and not even as a spinner, but as a woman who should have been the performer of an even simpler process yet. Immediately after its lines on Penelope, the song presents a wishful image of Helen as a carder, that is, a comber of wool into the manageable hanks of fiber needed before spinning can begin:[51]

> Had Helen then sate carding wooll,
> (whose beauteous face did breed such strife)
> She had not been Sir Paris trull,
> nor caus'd so many lose their life.

Simplicity and virtue, attributed to Deloney's women workers through their transformation into spinners and carders, guarantee their chastity while reserving the profitable public labor of weaving for men.

A broader, quasi-generic link connecting spinning as female virtue to homespun textile work is typified in several Renaissance texts that tend toward pastoral. In Robert Greene's trio of prose tales, *Penelopes Web* (1587), Penelope maneuvers "in the Court of *Ithaca*," but even there, she exemplifies the virtuous avoidance of idleness recommended by Brathwait. Greene revises Homer to present her weaving as a defense against idleness, already begun before her "pollicie" prompted her to make the completion of her work the precondition for her choice of a suitor:

She therfore beguyling time with labour, hauing begun a web wherein she spent the day to keepe her selfe from ydlenesse, knowing that *otia si tollas periere cupidinis arcus* ["take away leisure and Cupid's bow is broken," a citation from Ovid's *Remedia amoris*], gaue answer, that when her work was finished she would make a choyce of some one of them for her husband.[52]

Greene also supplies Penelope with a maid, Vgenia, who praises her for her contentment in humble household work, which the maid takes as an admirable sign of her mistress's devotion to Ulysses:

In deede, quoth Vgenia (for so was her second mayd called) when I see maiestie a contented copartner with labour, and a resolute farewell to ease: the chosen companyon to a Queene, I cannot thinke but that Loue is a great Lord, that in a womans affections worketh such straunge effects. (154)

In the tale that follows, told by Penelope, the heroine Barmenissa leaves an opulent court for a humble cottage and supports herself by textile work – she is adept with her needle as well as her wheel – until her erring husband recognizes her worth. The link that Greene establishes between his frame story and this first tale, then, ties Penelope to rustic retirement and spinning as virtuous labor.

A similar pastoral logic, through which a high-ranking heroine's willing descent down the social ladder into rustic simplicity is emblematized by her expertise as a spinner, shapes Michael Drayton's adaptation of Ovid to English history in his *Heroicall Epistles* (1619). In his "Epistle 23," he presents Lady Geraldine Fitzgerald as a latter-day Penelope, writing to Henry Howard, Earl of Surrey during his travels on the Continent. When Geraldine begins to describe the dwelling to which she plans to retire in the wandering Surrey's absence, it is a retreat signaled not only by the noblewoman's departure from gilded halls but, as we might expect, by the technology of the distaff rather than the loom:

> Till thou returne, the Court I will exchange
> For some poore Cottage, or some Country Grange,
> Where to our Distaves, as we sit and Spin,
> My Maide and I will tell what things have bin . . .
> And passe the Night, while Winter tales we tell
> Of many things, that long agoe befell.   (lines 163–71)[53]

Drayton here invokes the traditional link between spinning and storytelling (as in "spinning a yarn"), but in a way that reinscribes his Renaissance Penelope as a humble country spinner, incapable of *mêtis*.[54]

The model of woman-as-spinner is inscribed even in so sophisticated a form as the court masque. In Ben Jonson's *Hymenaei*, written to celebrate the marriage of Frances Howard to the Earl of Essex in 1606, the masquer representing Frances Howard was accompanied by two pages, "the one bearing a *distaffe*, the other a *spindle*," and costumed in virginal white, wearing "on her back, a weathers fleece hanging down: Her *zone*, or girdle about her waste of white wooll, fastened with the *Herculean* knot."[55] Jonson gives Reason the following commentary on the costume of the bride, which he models on ancient Roman custom:

> . . . that she should not labour scorne,
> Her selfe a *snowie fleece* doth weare,
> And these her *rocke* and *spindle* beare,
> To shew that nothing, which is good,
> Giues checke vnto the highest blood.
> The *Zone* of wooll about her waste,
> Which in contrarie circles cast,
> Doth meet in one *strong knot*, that binds,
> Tells you, so should all married minds.   (lines 186–95)

Costumed in this exemplary fashion, which ties spinning to chastity, the masquer representing Frances Howard resembles Barbaro's statue of Gaia Caecilia: both are made to embody a virtue inscribed in terms of the supposed pastoral simplicity of spinning. In fact, as we showed in chapter 3, Frances Howard's life was a radical undoing of such pastoral simplicities. By the time of her trial in 1615, the public eye was focused upon the intricacies of her fashions and fashionings instead.

The link between pastoral simplicity and the virtues ideologically assigned to women spinning was also made in texts that celebrated Englishness in terms of local textile production. John Jones, for example, in his 1579 London household manual, *The arte and science of preserving bodie and soule*, gave women a patriotic as well as pious duty. To spin well was to defeat rival nations:

The labours that be both decent and profitable for gentlewomen are these . . . as spinning of Wooll on the greate compasse Wheele, and on the rocke or distaffe, wherewith I would not that any should be so daintie, as to be offended thereat but rather to commende and use them as an ornament, and benefit of god bestowed upon oure flourishing countrey, surpassing all our princely neyghbours.[56]

Jones's invocation of English superiority in fine spinning was already nostalgic in the late 1570s, when domestic production of wool and exports to Europe were coming to the end of a long period of growth. Beginning in the middle sixteenth century, under James, and after the Restoration, the English wool trade declined radically. The industrial recession of the seventeenth century, combined with politically motivated Continental embargoes on English wool and the use there of wool from Ireland and Spain, as well as locally driven but wrongheaded clothiers' demands that exports of raw wool should be stopped so that English workers alone could profit from finishing it, led to much lower prices for local wool, to much less wool-raising, and consequently to less opportunity for spinners.[57] In this troubled context, Gervase Markham opened his *English Hus-wife* (first printed in 1615) with an image of the good housewife as a model of homespun simplicity, wearing and eating local rather than imported products, which she has tended and prepared herself. Moral perfection and nationalist loyalty are bound together in Markham's model, in which inward – that is, domestic – self-control is explicitly made to parallel economic self-sufficiency, the independence of the English as a nation:

Let . . . the Hus-wife's garments be comely, cleanly and strong, made as well to preserve the health, as adorne the person, altogether without toiish garnishes, or the glosse of light colors, and as farre from the vanity of new and fantastique fashions, as neare to the comely imitations of modest Matrons . . . Let her dyet . . . be apter to kill hunger than revive new appetites, let it proceede more from the provision of her owne yarde, then the furniture of the markets; and let it rather be esteemed for the familiar acquaintance she hath with it, than for the strangeness and raritie it bringeth from other Countries.[58]

But by 1615 this prescription was thoroughly impractical. For most rural families in England, sufficient farmland to raise flax and wool for an individual household was no longer available, given the increase in large-scale planting for local markets and the shift in land use from sheep grazing to grain-growing. As Susan Cahn points out, "The ideal of self-sufficiency remained normative but was less and less normal."[59]

The model of the home-bound female spinner, producing thread for her own family's consumption, effaced not only the economic strategies of aristocratic marriages, as in the masque for Frances Howard, but even the ways in which the low-paid work of the thousands of women who spun for money was increasingly caught up in an unstable global textile system. Ideological efforts to mold female virtue through textile work were themselves spun out of a local economy in transition, a nation constructing its identity by closing its borders to imports at the same time that it was trying unsuccessfully to insert its woolen cloth farther and farther into the world trade system.[60] To be a good woman was to spin like Penelope – who also, however, used deception to protect her husband's house and bed. To be a good Englishwoman in the early seventeenth century was to take on an even more contradictory assignment: to collaborate with English patriotism as it rejected international imports during a period in which the local wool trade was actually declining. During the fifteenth and early sixteenth centuries, Englishwomen had provided spun yarn to an industry in expansion, but by 1600 textile virtue was more than ever a moral ideal rather than an economic reality. No traditional or new moral constants invoked to define the virtuous bourgeois daughter or wife guaranteed that the cloth trades would continue to sustain threadmakers as they spun.

Spinning fate

The danger of Penelope's weaving is implicit in what she weaves: the shroud of her father-in-law, Laertes. It is as if she holds the power of life and death in her hands (as Clytemnestra does in her weavings). Making a shroud, Penelope figures Laertes's death. As she unwinds her weaving every night, she asserts her ability to make and to unmake, to prefigure death and to restore life. In the act of unmaking, that is, she reduces weaving to spinning, returning the web of material returned to its material constituent: thread. Even as Renaissance rewritings of Penelope as spinner rather than weaver attributed a reductive simplicity to her, they also centralized the fundamental technological process out of which all cloth was made. The connection between the making of thread and the making of life is still embedded in the expression "the thread of life." In making thread, women founded social life. Spinning is one of the primary processes through which nature is made into culture; the stems of the flax plant and the wool of sheep are "cooked," fermented and hot-water washed, to be transformed into thread; thread is then used to weave a swaddling gown for a naked infant. As a woman spins thread to clothe a baby, she sustains its physical life and also places the child in a social system of clothing. The threads she spins will cover the body of the child, shape it, and be internalized as tactile memory and social form. And such external threads define how fragile the line is between biological life and death – a line as fragile as a thread that, at any moment, can be cut.

Christianity had essentialized the connection between women and spinning by depicting the fallen Eve as spinner while the fallen Adam dug with a spade, an assignment of work given a radical twist in the proverbial question: "When Adam delved and Eve span, / Who was then the gentleman?" But the opposition of Adam's digging to Eve's spinning was also a way of naturalizing a gendered division of labor. In the late sixteenth or early seventeenth century, an Englishwoman represented Eve as mother and spinner on an embroidered pillow cover decorated with scenes from Genesis (Fig. 12).[61] In the upper left rectangle of this embroidery, Adam is digging up tree roots while Eve holds her breast for a nursing infant with her right hand and supports her distaff in the crook of her right elbow, combining the two activities with apparent (though implausible) ease.

The distaff ideologically associated women with domesticity by associating them, through gestation, with the making of the thread of life. The Virgin Mary, for

Fig. 12. Needleworked pillow cover, silk on linen, Eve spinning, c. 1600

instance, was sometimes depicted as spinning out the thread of life in her womb. In a Rhenish painting of about 1400, Mary draws a thread from the distaff at her left, a thread that crosses the light-surrounded infant revealed in her womb, while Joseph looks on from her right.[62] (Fig. 13). Prints by the early seventeenth-century French engraver Jacques Bellange include an Annunciation (based on Dürer's "The Sojourn in Egypt") in which Mary sits by a basket containing a reel and two balls of yarn, and a domestic scene including the swaddled Christ child, in which she spins while a Cupid-like young angel holds her distaff.[63] The sacred gestational power attributed to spinning in such images shifts to a more social register in representations of Saint Elisabeth of Thüringen, an aristocratic woman who insisted on sharing the spinning carried out by her fellow nuns, strengthening the convent community by participating in its textile work. Saint Elspeth, as she was called in the North, is shown in a 1511 print by Hans Baldung Grien holding a distaff, thread and spindle that link her to five other spinning women even as she wears a halo that distinguishes her from them (Fig. 14).[64] The link between spinning and the production and support of life is built into the metaphor of the English word "lifespan," which relates the length of a life to the length of a spun thread.[65]

Women spun life into being, but they were also viewed, as Penelope reminds us, as the weavers of shrouds and the caretakers of the dead. The ambivalence felt toward such power is strikingly captured in the mythology of the Moirae or Fates. In early Greek myth, the three Fates, the daughters of Necessity, were described as engaged in the production of thread that determined how long a man or woman would live. Clotho ("the Spinner"), at the moment of birth, spins out the thread of each human life; Lachesis ("the Measurer") calculates its length; and Atropos ("The Inexorable," literally, she who cannot be turned aside) cuts it off.

An extended description of these "fatal sustren," as Chaucer called them in *Troilus and Cresseyde* (3, 734), occurs at the end of Plato's *Republic*. In Er's

Fig. 13. Erfurt master, *Mary at the Distaff*, c. 1400

narration of what he saw in the afterlife, he begins with the primary implement of hand spinning, the drop spindle, an elongated cylinder attached to the bottom of a length of thread in the making. The weight of the spindle helps to pull the fibers down into a twisted thread, and the spinner winds her finished thread, as she completes it, around the spindle.[66] In Plato's tale, this implement provides the

Fig. 14. Hans Baldung Grien, engraving, *Saint Elisabeth*, 1511

structural basis of the cosmos. In a pure column of brilliant light, Er says, souls about to be reborn see how all the revolving firmaments are held together.[67] Necessity (Ananke) holds a spindle, fitted with a hook and shaft of adamant and a whorl, a spherical weight made of wood or clay, set below the spindle to even out its turning. Within this whorl, eight smaller whorls, each a planet, turn, all held in place by the spindle's shaft, which is their axis. Because these whorls turn at independent speeds, some seem to move in different directions, from the outermost sphere of the fixed stars to the moon, the sun, Venus, Mercury, Mars, Jupiter, and Saturn. A siren stands on each of these circles, singing a single note; together, the eight notes produce a full scale, the music of the spheres. Er continues:

Round about, at equal distances, were seated, each on a throne, the three daughters of necessity, robed in white with garlands on their heads, Lachesis, Clotho and Atropos, chanting to the Sirens' music, Lachesis of things past, Clotho of things present, and Atropos of things to come. And from time to time Clotho lays her right hand on the outer rim of the spindle and helps to turn it, while Atropos turns the inner circles likewise with her left, and Lachesis with either hand takes hold of outer and inner alternately. (355)

In this intricate fantasy, the Fates control the movement of the heavenly spheres as well as the course of human lives.

One version of the Fates' genealogy makes them subject to Zeus, their father by Themis, as in Hesiod's account (*Theogony* [lines 904–5]). But Hesiod also calls the Fates daughters of primordial Night (line 217), without naming a father. There is a second, even more threatening account of the power of the Fates: as daughters to Necessity via parthenogenesis, they precede Zeus. These contradictory genealogies underlie the episode in *The Iliad* in which Hera warns Zeus that he will set a dangerous example to the other gods if he saves his son Sarpedon from the death the Fates have decreed for him. Zeus assents; that is, he obeys the Fates' command (16. 435–70). Similarly, in Aeschylus's *Prometheus Bound*, Prometheus equates "the steersman of necessity," stronger than Zeus, with "the triple formed fates and the remembering Furies" (line 501); in Aeschylus's *Eumenides*, the Furies invoke the Fates as their sisters, "steering spirits of law, / goddesses of destiny" (lines 961–2).[68] As givers, measurers and takers away of life, their power is absolute. It takes precedence over any desire of human beings or, however uneasily, of Olympian deities.

In Roman myth, the Moirae were equated with the minor birth goddesses, the Parcae, and were often represented as predicting the birth of a child at wedding ceremonies or blessing a new-born infant. But Augustan writers still represented them as ruling over the gods, including Jove. In Ovid's *Metamorphoses*, Jove explains to Ceres that he cannot bring back their daughter Proserpina from Hades because the "decree of the Parcae" warns against it (5. 532). Ovid also explains, in the context of Julius Caesar's assassination, that none of the gods who wanted to protect him could resist the Fates' "iron decrees" (15. 781, 799–800). Catullus, in *Carmina 64*, writes a vividly ambivalent description of the Parcae, who come "to utter truth-telling chants" at the wedding of Thetis and Peleus. Though beautifully dressed in white robes fringed with red, they are old women with "palsied gesture" and "feeble limbs" (lines 305–9). But despite their frailty, they are attributed absolute power as the inventors of gods', men's, and women's fates. All three hold distaffs and spindles and, as they predict the birth of Achilles and the destructiveness of the Trojan War, they sing a refrain in unison: "Run, drawing the woof-threads, spindles, run" – that is, spin out the threads that will be used to weave the prophecy of Troy's fall.[69] In Catullus's poem, the Fates' song elicits both terror and admiration. Their refrain is simultaneously the textile that the Fates weave and the text that Catullus writes. The Fates, then, came to figure not only women's power over physical life and death but the power of writers and painters to depict life and death.

More important for our study, they also figured the power of life and death materialized in the making of thread. This ambivalent power of the Fates was reworked in Renaissance painting and writing. From 1621–5, Peter Paul Rubens produced a series of paintings for Marie de' Medici, the widow of Henri IV. Rubens began the cycle with a panel entitled "The Destiny of Marie de' Medici," in which the lower three figures are the Fates, young, full-bodied nudes in seventeenth-century coiffures. Clotho, at the top, holds a distaff; Lachesis, with her back to the viewer, spins a thread down to Atropos; Atropos draws the thread down to a spindle. But here, to overcome the power of the Fates to determine the death of Marie, Atropos has no scissors: in her left hand she holds the thread coming from above, from her right she dangles only a spindle.[70] The life the three Fates spin for Marie has no end: through her fame and her commemoration by her artists, she will live forever.

The originality of Rubens's revision, which might well be seen as a triumphant denial of the ancient goddesses' supremacy over life and death, is all the clearer compared to other visual treatments of the Fates near in time or contemporary with the Medici cycle. The Dutch painter and engraver Hendrik Goltzius published several versions of the Fates. In a print dated 1587, following other mannerist artists, he presented the Fates as elegant young nudes who resemble the three Graces more than the fatal trio of Greek myth, although he positions them in a rocky landscape and sets Atropos's scissors right at the center of the circular composition.[71] In a later print engraved by Jan Muller from a drawing by Goltzius, the three figures are sharply differentiated by age. Atropos, following the account in Hesiod, is oldest – in fact, a grim, dark figure with a bony face averted from the viewer and a hanging, desiccated nipple (Fig. 15).[72] She uses a knotted arm and massive hand to hold her scissors poised at the thread held between the garlanded, maidenly Clotho and the fresh-bodied Lachesis, who wears her hair bound up in the style of a married woman.

Goltzius was following the visual tradition of Atropos as terrifying eldest sister, as it appears earlier in Hans Baldung's 1513 print "Die drei Parzen," in which the different ages of the Fates are linked to their different degrees of erotic desirability (Fig. 16).[73] In Baldung's print, a little girl picks a flower of the kind held by the young, wavy-haired, smiling Clotho at the right (possibly following an earlier literary treatment of the Fates by Pausanias, who likened Clotho to celestial Aphrodite because of Aphrodite's power over generation);[74] on the left, Lachesis, in a married woman's coif, looks calmly out at the viewer, holding the thread and a spindle. But Atropos, set behind Clotho, has a bony, ruggedly muscled body and a crone's scowling face framed by wildly flowing hair. She looms up at the top of the composition above Clotho, energetically bending forward to hold her shears to the thread just as it leaves the distaff held by the contrastingly benign-looking younger woman. Baldung, a student of Dürer, worked in a German context less courtly than Goltzius' milieux, and his print – or at least his Atropos – has a kind of popular savagery very different from the Dutch artist's Italian-influenced images. But both artists give their Atropos full and frightening power. There is no effacement of her shears, and her age reinforces her link with death.

Even in the courtly context of François I's Fontainebleau, Atropos retained her danger. In a complex, intriguing print engraved by Pierre Milan of what were probably Rosso Fiorentino's costume designs for a court masque of the middle

Fig. 15. Hendrik Goltzius, engraving, *Parcae*, c. 1587

1530s, three figures of different size are arranged in a line in profile, facing toward
the viewer's right (Fig. 17).[75] The smallest woman, wearing light torso armor, puffed
sleeves, a garland and crown, and a youthful mask, pulls apart a hank of flax; the
middle one, a bit taller with a matronly mask, coiffure and body, winds thread from
a reel into a ball. The third figure, taller than the other two and dressed in flowing
robes and a nun-like headdress, wears a sunken-eyed mask and is raising two hanks
of wool, apparently yanked apart, high in the air. None of the three figures carries
out the spinning task traditionally assigned to each Fate. They are not usually

Fig. 16. Hans Baldung Grien, engraving, *Die drei Parzen*, 1513

Fig. 17. Pierre Milan, engraving after Rosso Fiorentino, *The Three Masked Fates*, c. 1545

described or represented breaking flax or wool prior to setting it on the distaff, although Rosso might have seen Roman tomb paintings in which this was the case.[76] The middle figure in the print is holding a spinning implement, but one used after thread has been spun from a distaff: the reel onto which finished thread is woven. David Acton identifies the figure on the right as Atropos, the middle one as Lachesis and the one at the left as Clotho, but this seems unlikely. Some ancient writers, including Hesiod and Plato, identify Atropos as the smallest of the sisters but they also say that she is the oldest and the most powerful. Rosso's youngest Fate is more likely Clotho, and his tall, imposing oldest Fate, though she lacks the fatal scissors, has the frightening energy that earlier and later prints assign to Atropos. Acton suggests, in fact, that her upraised hanks of wool recall Jupiter's lightning bolts. They do seem a possible displacement of the rupture of the thread of life from the end of the spinning process to its beginning, but if this is the case, the figure is definitely Atropos. In the context of courtly and popular prints assigning her greater age and greater ferocity than her sisters, Rosso's menacing Jovian woolbreaker shows the persistence of the ancient equation between the third Fate and death.

This equation is visualized with startling simplicity in Valeriano Bolzani's *Hieroglyphica*, a massive collection of Latin commentaries on ancient symbolic imagery first published in Lyon in 1556 and frequently thereafter, including an edition of 1602. In Book 48, in a section on the meanings of the distaff and spindle, Bolzani discusses the three Fates, mentions Gaia Caecilia as a typical Roman bride carrying the distaff and spindle to indicate her new status and duties, and devotes a section to the spinning tools' association with death (*mors*).[77] Of the two images on this page, one of an isolated distaff and spindle is set at the top right of the section entitled MORS (Fig. 18). It is hard to imagine a starker illustration of the synecdoche through which the tools of spinning were used to symbolize the Fates' power over life through death.

M O R S.

, ſtaminibus abruptis, mortis
int, vulgata quam citauimus
diximus, ſuum vnicuique rei
iomine, quòd, vbi fatalis ad-
.utem earum, quā ἀμετάϛροφον
:m dicere poſſumus, quóque
iitatem tantùm, verùm etiam
ruantiam inducendos munus
tionibus firmam preſtent in-
libro circa finem Plato diffe-
ım ſtellarum orbe multa. La-

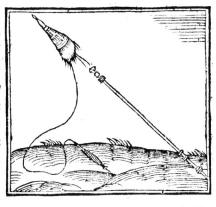

*An quòd
Iouis & The-
midis filiæ
perhibetur.*
λαγχάνω,
*fortior, quia
omniū for-
tes modera-
tur: Atro-
pos qui mu-
tari aut ver
ti nequitur
Clotho* ,

vt ſuperiorem fabulam apertiùs interpretemur) in cuius ſtellis *quòd omnia*
contineantur. Clotho verò Planetarum cœtum, in euoluendis *coordinet.*
ſtrarem. Atropon denique Saturnum, qui ſtabilitate ſua eductas *κλώτω, neo,
glomero, fi-*
onfirmet : quæ quoniam latè apud eos diſputantur, à me nunc *lum ſcilicet*
μίτοy.

D E

Fig. 18. G. P. Valeriano Bolzani, *Heiroglyphica*, Lyon, 1602

The Fates spun, and it was the assigned fate of mortal women to spin. Representations of women spinners in prints produced in early modern Europe reveal the contradictory values assigned to the distaff and spindle, in models of ideal femininity but also in comic or frightening images that acknowledge the potentially dangerous power of women who spin. Many images, predictably, encourage spinning by linking it to other female virtues. Spinning was linked to piety, particularly in Dutch genre paintings of old wives and widows. In Gerhard Dou's "Reading the Bible," an old woman bends over the Scriptures she reads to her husband while her spinning wheel stands prominently to the viewer's right; in Dou's "Old Woman Saying Grace," the female sitter prays at a table directly adjacent to a large spinning wheel.[78] The spinning wheel also signaled attachment to home rather than to wandering the countryside, as in the English woodcut used to illustrate both "The Housewife and the Hunter" in the Roxburghe Ballads and the 1630 edition of the Griselda story (fig. 51, chapter 9) and in a Dutch engraving of a woman standing on a tortoise, a creature which always keeps its house on its back, against a background in which a woman spins in the doorway to the left and a man digs at the right, an illustration for Johan van Beverwijck's *Van de wtnementheyt des vrouwelicken geslachts* (Dordrecht, 1639) (Fig. 19).

But the distaff and wheel were also represented as dangerous in the hands of actual rather than exemplary women, most comically in scenes of the world turned upside down, where they were depicted as a woman's improvised weapon. In Israhel van Meckenem's engraving "The Angry Wife" (North Germany, c. 1500) a young wife egged on by a laughing devil threatens her husband with a distaff laden with

Fig. 19. Johan van Beverwijck, engraving, *Van de wtnementheyt des vrouwelicken geslachts*, Dordrecht, 1639

flax (Fig. 20).[79] They are, in fact, battling over supremacy in the household, and she has discarded the trappings of wifely modesty. The tools of spinning were also associated with flirtation and courtship, as in van Meckenen's print "The Visit to the Spinner," in which a plume-bedecked dandy looks hopefully at a young women sitting at her distaff.[80] More bluntly, through allegory or visual suggestion, spinning tools implied ungovernable female sexuality. The printmaker Daniel Heinsius represented a scene of a fashionably dressed woman eyeing Cupid as he sits spinning at her wheel in an emblem from *Nederduytsche Poemata* (Leiden 1621);[81] Marina Warner points out how the phallic shape and angle of the distaff disturbs the image of a virtuous housewife in an anonymous engraving printed in Leiden in 1624, which illustrates a riddle about the distaff as the object of the spinner's desire, held in her fingers and between her legs.[82] Such prints register an attitude very different from the humanists' claim that domestic service to husbands and sexual purity could be guaranteed by women's devotion to spinning. In social classes in which women's threadmaking was recognized as a valuable product, spinning was associated with potentially threatening feminine will and power.

German prints of *Spinnstuben*, the public spinning rooms in which the women of a

Fig. 20. Israhel van Meckenem, engraving, *The Angry Wife*, c. 1500

village met to spin and talk, suggest anxiety over the power of female gossip and the sexual energies unleashed when men entered that semi-private sphere. The comic details of Barthel Beham's "Spinnstube" woodcut of 1524, in which a woman in a back corner leaves her distaff standing as a behatted man lurches on top of her and another woman at the center of the scene points her distaff like a weapon toward a rowdy couple ahead of her, were probably largely imaginary (Fig. 21). Alison Stewart relates many of Beham's motifs to proverbs and literary conventions, although she also suggests that the woodcut comically exaggerates behavior of genuine concern to town councils, such as Nuremberg's, which published mandates against the "vices and frivolity" that ensued when men joined such gatherings.[83]

Hans Medick records a less comic episode in the village of Laichengen. When a weaver journeyman on a visit to a *Spinnstube* tried to hug a resistant woman, broke her spindle in the process, and refused to pay for it, he was attacked by all the women present, who beat him so severely with their distaffs that he spent three weeks in bed, between life and death.[84] At the town trial, however, the women claimed that their reaction was their "good right" and that, in spite of the damage they had done him, "they should have injured him even more" (331). Another instance of women's use of distaffs as weapons was an uprising in which the women of Delft, protesting an increase in the tax on grain, attacked a government official in the town square on 2 August 1616. The scene was documented by Matthäus Merian in a print bristling with household implements, printed in a book entitled *Theatrum europaeum* (Frankfurt am Main, c. 1640).[85] Such prints suggest that the fear of women spinners was based not only on the mythical association between them and the lethally powerful Atropos but on real outbreaks of female violence.

The distaff could also suggest lasciviousness linked to magic. Albrecht Dürer's engraving from about 1500 of a naked witch clutching a distaff and riding backward on a goat draws together female nudity, the association between goats and lechery, and the belief that witches rode on broomsticks or distaffs (Fig. 22).[86] An empty distaff forked at the top, used not to spin at home but to roam abroad, identifies a naked woman as a witch in the left foreground of a woodcut used to illustrate Johann Wier's questioning of witchcraft, *De Praestigiis Daemonum*, published in Frankfurt in 1586 (Fig. 23).[87] An enormous distaff to which many full bobbins are attached is held by an aged crone in a 1532 woodcut illustrating a German translation of Petrarch's *De Remediis utriusque fortunae* (Fig. 24).[88] The ambiguity of the spinning woman is sharply delineated in the different interpretations art historians have offered of this figure. Early critics identified the old woman as a witch calling down celestial powers in a forest at night. Walther Scheidig, however, reading the image in relation to the literary text, identifies her as an allegory of "Virtue" (*die Tugend*), surviving old age and rough landscapes through uninterrupted devotion to womanly textile duty.

But the negative association between women's textile work and sorcery predominated in texts designed to have concrete social outcomes, in the witchhunts of seventeenth-century England, for example. In the first book of James I's defense of the reality of witchcraft, his *Daemonologie*, the character Epistemon gives two examples of "unlawful charmes" cast by "dafte wiues": their preserving of valued goods by "knitting roun-trees [rowan-tree leaves] vpon them" and, more alarmingly, their "staying married folkes, toe have naturallie adoe with other (by knitting so manie knottes vpon a poynt [a lace used to attach a man's hose to his doublet and to

Fig. 21. Hans (Barthel) Beham, woodcut, *Eine Spinnstube*, 1524

Fig. 22. Albrecht Dürer, engraving, *The Witch Riding Backward on a Goat*, 1511

Fig. 23. Woodcut from Johann Wier, *De Praestigiis Daemonum*, Frankfurt, 1586

Fig. 24. Woodcut illustrating Virtue, from *Von der Artzney bayder Glück*, Augsburg, 1532

Fig. 25. Woodcut from *Les Imperfections de la femme*, Paris, c. 1650

tie up a codpiece] at the time of their mariage)."[89] The reverse side of the distaff and spindle as emblems of virtue was the fantasy linking textile work to the nocturnal wandering and revelry of wild sorceresses and to women's control over male potency.

The power and danger attributed to spinning women are violently recast in a seventeenth-century printmaker's woodcut of a woman holding a distaff, from a pamphlet entitled *The Imperfections of Women*.[90] The caption is: "Si tu la cherche[s] la voicy" (If you're looking for her, here she is). Its meaning is that the ideal woman – a good spinner and a silent companion – can be achieved only by cutting off a real woman's head (Fig. 25). Renaissance ideologies worked to turn the material value of poor women's daily spinning into an emblem of feminine virtue, but the complexities repressed in that equation return in the beheading of the spinner, now an automaton capable of producing the textile staple of life but cut off in one blow from the ingenuity and power over men's fates embodied in Penelope and the Three Fates. This reversal suggests that anxiety about the spinner focuses not on her working hands but on her mind and her mouth. The silent anonymity of the thousands of spinners who clothed their families and transformed the raw material of sheep's wool into the basic substance of the wool trade is reinscribed in this woodcut as the enforced silence of the mastered, obedient wife.

Yet through Penelope and the Fates, refashioned and recirculated throughout the Renaissance, the making of life and death was powerfully inscribed in the humblest and most poorly paid form of female labor: spinning. For spinning remained the fundamental material process of a cloth culture. Spinning produced the thread that itself produced the social: the domestic and international cultures of wool, flax, silk, and cotton. In the next chapter we will see how women exploited a different form of fabrication – embroidery – to manage and interpret the *topoi* of textile work in their own interests.

6 The needle and the pen: needlework and the appropriation of printed texts

In this chapter we explore the habit of needlework assigned to high-ranking women as a form of virtuous femininity. We argue that even as a woman bent over her sewing appeared to be fulfilling the requirement of obedient domesticity, she could be materializing a counter-memory for herself, registering her links to other women and to the larger world of culture and politics. Women stitched themselves into public visibility by negotiating among the ideological and commercial versions of needlework that they found in diverse and often conflicting sources: in family conduct manuals, which demanded that women efface themselves in the private sphere through sewing and silence; in printed advertisements, books, and embroidery patterns that brought the international public sphere into the needleworker's home; and in prints dealing with topical issues, which raised the possibility of stitching political meanings into sewn texts. Looking closely at needlework done by early modern Englishwomen, we will show that thread and cloth were materials through which they could record and commemorate their participation not in reclusive domestic activity but in the larger public world.

In the households of the rich throughout early modern Europe, embroidery was such a frequent activity for women that to speak of "work" in relation to a woman of high rank was to mean needlework. (Embroidery, in fact, is a later term. "Broderers" was the Elizabethan term for male professionals who decorated cloth with fine stitchery. Women doing fine stitchery at home, whom we in modern terms call amateur embroiderers, thought of themselves as doing needlework.) The high social status of fancy needlework is foregrounded in one of a set of poems written to accompany New Year's gifts to Queen Elizabeth and her ladies-in-waiting in London in 1602. The twenty-fifth couplet of the set, presenting a case for a pair of scissors to one of the ladies-in-waiting, juggles "work" and "play" in a compliment that plays on the voluntary nature of women's fine stitchery, a hobby rather than a wage-earning necessity. At the same time, however, this little poem's vocabulary of "housewifery" signals the heavy investment that early modern gender ideology maintained in all women's textile work, regardless of their rank or wealth. The lady is praised because, in spite of her birth into a leisured class, she is devoted to needlework:

> A Lottery Proposed before Supper at the Lo[rd] Chief Justice
> his House, in the First Entrance to Hir Majestie,
> Ladies, Gentlewomen and Straungers, 1602
>
> La[dy] Newton. A sizer [scissor] case.
>
> This sizer doth your huswifry bewray:
> You love to work, though you be borne to play.[1]

134

Although women of the gentry and the aristocracy were summoned to much more luxurious forms of work than the kind performed by poor spinners and seamstresses, they, too, were the recipients of injunctions to fill their spare time attending to textiles. But rather than spinning thread, they decorated cloth. Applying silk, woolen, and sometimes gold- and silver-wrapped thread to linen, silk, and satin, they monogrammed shirts and bedclothes; they stitched designs onto smocks, caps, and gloves; and they composed samplers, book covers, casket covers, mirror frames, and pictures to decorate tables or be hung on walls. In sum, they clothed their households with needleworked cloth.

Pattern books for needlework

While spinning was a time-honored skill invoked by moralists and advice-book writers to prevent idleness, fancy needlework was potentially more problematic. A woman decorating cloth rather than spinning thread destabilized traditional male/female oppositions. In Xenophon's and Aristotle's ideal couple, resuscitated in the family theory of Leon Battista Alberti, among others, the husband was to be active in the public sphere and the wife to preserve his acquisitions at home.[2] Needlework, however, meant creating new objects through subtle forms of imitation and putting them on display: it approached other kinds of public artistry.

Fine needlework also belonged to the world of fashion. An early passage from John Taylor's introduction to his popular book of embroidery patterns, *The Needle's Excellency* (1624, in its twelfth edition by 1640), advertises the varieties of needlework techniques and fancy stitches diagrammed in the book as alluring novelties:

> For Tent-worke, Raisd-worke, Laid-Worke, Frost-worke, Net-worke,
> Most curious Purles, or rare Italian Cutworke,
> Fine Ferne-Stitch, Finny-stitch, New-stitch and Chain-stitch,
> Braue Bred-stitch, Fisher-stitch, Irish-stitch and Queene-stitch,
> The Spanish-stitch, Rosemary-stitch and Mow-stitch,
> The smarting Whip-stitch, Back-stitch and the Cros-stitch:
> All these are good, and these we must alow,
> And these are everywhere in practise now.[3]

Humanist writers, rather than providing up-to-date patterns for fine sewing, scanned contemporary history for models of moral virtue, linking women's needlework to narratives about ideal daughters, wives and queens. By praising royal or aristocratic women as needleworkers, they implied that they should be taken as models by women of lower status as well, collapsing class differences under an umbrella of generalized female duties – although in a way that shifted downward the cross-class sweep of recommendations that all women should spin. Jakob Wimpheling, writing in southern Germany, praised the handiwork of Margaret, the daughter of the Duke of Bavaria and the wife of the Elector Palatine, and stressed the participation of other women in her exemplary work: "She was active during her whole life with feminine occupations, consisting mainly of . . . sewing and all sorts of embroidery, which she did together with her entire female retinue."[4] A similar scene is sketched by Ronsard in his "Discours à Monsieur le Duc de Savoie," celebrating Henri's sister Marguerite de France as a needlewoman:

> Aucunesfois avec ses Damoiselles,
> Comme une fleur assise au milieu d'elles,

> Tenoit l'aiguille, et d'un art curieux
> Joignoit la soie et l'or industrieux
> Dessus la toile.[5]

> Often, with her ladies-in-waiting,
> Sitting like a flower in their midst,
> She held the needle, and with painstaking skill
> Joined silk and carefully wrought gold
> Upon her cloth.

As a girl, Elizabeth I of England famously covered book covers with needlework as gifts for her father and her stepmother Katherine Parr, although in later life she became the receiver rather than the donor of presents of fine stichery.[6]

John Taylor, in the sonnets that make up "The Praise of the Needle" in *The Needle's Excellency*, composed mini-histories of Katherine of Aragon, Mary Tudor, Queen Elizabeth, and Mary Countess of Pembroke as exemplary needlewomen. He downplays Queen Katherine's Spanish identity by informing his readers that her "excellent memorials," that is, her worked hangings, can still be seen in the Tower of London (Sonnet 2, B1v). In Mary Tudor, too, he stresses private virtue translated into a public model rather than her hostility to Elizabeth and the Protestantism she reinstated. Of Mary he writes:

> Her Greatnesse held it no dis-reputation,
> To take the Needle in her Royall hand:
> Which was a good example to our Nation,
> To banish idleness from out her Land.   (Sonnet 3, B2r)

While Mary is held up as a mirror of virtue for England for sharing the textile duties of women of all ranks, Elizabeth, whose needlework Taylor links to her captivity under Mary (being moved "From Jayle to Jayle, by Maries angry spleene"), is celebrated for her final triumph as "Englands Peerelesse Queene." For her, Taylor explains, fine stichery was a companion in duress:

> Yet howsoever sorrow came or went,
> She made the Needle her companion still:
> And in that exercise her time she spent,
> As many living yet, doth know her skill.   (Sonnet 4, B2v)

The ending of this sonnet, like Taylor's praise of the recently deceased Mary Countess of Pembroke in the next poem, privileges each woman's needlework over her status as queen or author. From Taylor's point of view, fame comes from the needle, not the scepter or the pen. Of Elizabeth he concludes that whatever the rise and fall of her political fortunes, she was constant in her use of the needle:

> Thus was she still a Captive, or else Crown'd,
> A Needle-woman Royall, and renown'd.

Predictably, Taylor praises the wall hangings worked by Mary Sidney Herbert rather than her translations from Italian and Hebrew, of which he says nothing. The "workes" that impress him as proof of her "vertuous industry, and studious learning" are textile, not textual:

> Brave *Wilton*-house in *Wiltshire* well can show,
> Her admirable workes in Arras fram'd . . .
> She wrought so well in Needle-worke, that she,
> Nor yet her workes, shall ere forgotten be.   (Sonnet 5, B3r)

Taylor's desire to sell his embroidery patterns is an obvious motive for his assessments of these women, as is the patriotic link he establishes between their fame as needlewomen and Englishness as a local and national identity: Mary Sidney Herbert's county, Mary Tudor's nation, even Katherine of Aragon's Tower of London are all called upon as sites that witness Englishwomen's skill.

English textile virtuosity, however, turns out to be a strikingly hybrid practice. Throughout *The Needle's Excellency*, Taylor calls attention to the exotic provenance of his designs for embroidery and lace. In the list of sewing styles on display in the book, he includes Irish, Spanish, and Italian stitches; and he advertises that his patterns are valuable to his countrywomen precisely because they bring the rest of the world's riches to England. He begins with the ambitious and intriguing claim that a needleworker can represent anything in the world: "There's nothing neere at hand, or farthest sought, / But with the Needle, may be shap'd and wrought" (A3). He then offers "all sorts of workes" from Europe, which he promotes as follows:

> . . . for this Kingdomes good are hither come,
> From the remotest parts of Christendome.
> Collected with much paines and industry,
> From scorching *Spaine*, and freezing *Moscovye*,
> From fertill *France*, and pleasant *Italy*,
> From *Poland*, *Sweaden*, *Denmarke*, *Germany*.   (A4)

The appeal of European-wide fashion was exploited as a lure to buyers of other pattern books, too, such as Cesare Vecellio's patterns for lace, *La Corona delle Nobili et Virtuose Donne* (Venice, 1591, followed by many further editions), which includes "cuffs worn by French ladies," "Flemish-style rosettes," and bedspread designs "used by Greek ladies."[7] But Taylor claims to have ventured farther, to continents and cultures beyond Europe:

> And some of these rare Patternes have been fet
> Beyond the bounds of faithlesse *Mahomet*:
> From spacious *China*, and those Kingdomes East,
> And from great *Mexico*, the Indies West.   (A4r)

If needlework demonstrates Englishwomen's capacities, it does so by absorbing Middle Eastern, Far Eastern and New World designs, and by empowering the needlewoman to represent anything in the world. This internationalism appears clearly in the sixteenth- and seventeenth-century samplers collected by Douglas Goodhart and catalogued at Montacute House in Somerset. The catalogue of these samplers identifies Romanian, Florentine, Gobelin [French], Algerian, Hungarian, and Cretan stitches in them, French knotwork, and borders imitated from Italian pattern books, including that of Federico Vinciolo – of whom more shortly.[8] The London gentlewoman sitting at home at her needlework was in fact being constituted by the textile practices of far-flung nations and faiths.

Other men writing to promote practical handbooks, that is, collections of embroidery patterns, represented high-ranking women for reasons similar to Taylor's. The images on their title pages, aimed at buyers who could afford diagrams collected into expensive large-format volumes but who were not necessarily literate, played on the desires of middle-ranking women to rise in the social hierarchy. The German pattern collector Peter Quentel implicitly offered upward mobility to his customers by opening his book of patterns, *Ein neu künstlich Modelbuch* (first published in Cologne in 1527), with a engraving depicting well-dressed bourgeois

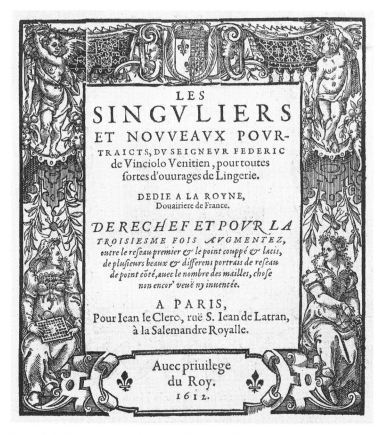

Fig. 26. Title-page engraving from *Les Singuliers et Nouveaux Portraicts,
du Seigneur Federic de Vinciolo Venetien*, Paris, 1612

women, one stitching on a frame, one stitching on a cloth on her lap, and one
working at a small table loom. The message implied by this title-page is "Work as
they do, be their social equal."[9] A more glamorous appeal to the upwardly mobile
consumer is made on the title-page of the French version of Federico Vinciolo's
pattern book (first edition Paris, 1587) through the dedication to the French queen
Catherine de Medici and the images, at lower left and right, of a court lady working
on *filet brodé*, or darned netting, and another sewing on her lap (Fig 26).[10] The title
page to *The Needle's Excellency* combines allegorical figures with high-fashion
costume and an elaborate garden landscape to suggest both virtue and elegance.
Wisdom, in a brocade gown and high ruff, reads a devotional manual (judging from
its small size) while Industrie works on a cushion (she has apparently already
completed the petticoat to her right). Follie, empty-handed, tries to distract them.
(Fig. 27).[11]

   Taylor, indeed, celebrates needlework as the basis for all kinds of clothing,
especially new styles of neckwear and women's headgear. His list moves from the
bibs and caps of childhood to the sunbonnet-like headdresses, fine hoods, net caps,
and forehead veils ("Cros-cloathes") fashionable for women. He also lists the
constantly changing styles of collars worn by both sexes, which shifted from the

Fig. 27. Title-page engraving from John Taylor, *The Needle's Excellency*, London, 1631

upright ruff of the late sixteenth century to the seventeenth-century "falling band," a long collar designed to descend from the neck rather than stand up around it like the starched ruff. The richness of Taylor's list, like the garments it names, demonstrates that sewing assists not only modesty but the desire for splendor:

> And thus without the Needle we may see,
> We should without our Bibbs and Biggings be;
> No shirts or smockes, our nakednesse to hide,
> No garments gay, to make us magnifyde;
> No Shadowes, Shapparoones, Caules, Bands, Ruffes, Cuffes,
> No Kerchiefs, Quoyfes, Chin-clouts, or Mary Muffes.   (A2r)

Taylor's praise for the lively variety of patterns in his book extends to the mental agility they permit to young needlewomen, whom he describes, via an unexpected simile of a sprightly squirrel, as far less stable than the contained, sober, stay-at-home matrons praised by moralists. Moreover, in Taylor's vision, mothers and governesses share pleasures – even the pleasures of flightiness – with their young charges rather than keep them under immobilizing surveillance:

> Here Practise and Invention may be free ,
> And as a *Squirrell* skips from tree to tree,

> So Maides (from their Mistresse, or their Mother)
> Learne to leave one worke, and to learne another.
> For here they may make choyce of which is which,
> And skip from worke to worke and stitch to stitch.   (A4v)

The arguments of some family theorists – paradoxically, according to the logic whereby domestic stitchery was praised because it kept women at home rather than wandering outside their houses – resembled Taylor's claims that needlework could lead to renown: women were promised public fame for the "private" virtue of sewing. Federigo Luigini, in his mid-sixteenth-century *Libro della bella donna* (Venice, 1554), insisted that the needle belongs to "all women, both high and low, not only to low, mechanic and plebeian females," but he then moves up the class scale to represent clothwork as a badge of honor for aristocratic women: "where the poor find only utility in these arts, the rich, the noble, and the beautiful lady wins honour also."[12] The work of Giovanni Ciotto, a collector of embroidery and lace-making patterns, was presented in England by a bookseller who exploited traditional sexual oppositions to serve his own commercial interest by promising women that fine needlework could help them rise socially. An English translation of Ciotto, *A Booke of Curious and strange Inventions, called the first part of Needleworkes*, was printed for the bookseller William Barley in 1596. Barley dedicated it to the Countess of Rutland, whose "excellent skill in curious needlework is made known by many other personages." His single page of rhymed text begins with what looks like a deprecating comparison of men's and women's capacities. Men sail the seas, experiment in alchemy and study the liberal arts, all activities that require stamina unavailable to women:

> But farre unfit for tender women kinde,
> Such toylesome studies altogether be:
> Although their wits most sharp and swift we finde,
> Yet with their strength these things do not agree:
> Their milke white hands the needle finer fits
> With silke and gold to prove their pregnant wits.[13]

The poem goes on, however, to insist that needlework requires knowledge and that it reveals "a fine conceit." Like the Italian pattern books, this one encourages young women to see embroidery as a path to fame: "Come then sweet gyrles and hereby learne the way / With good report to live another day." The writer even suggests that expertise in needlework can be the basis of a courtly profession, raising a young woman into an aristocracy of merit:

> For many maidens but of base degree,
> By their fine knowledge in the curious thing:
> With Noble Ladies oft companions be,
> Sometimes they teach the daughter of a King:
> Thus by their knowledge, fame and good report
> They are esteemd among the noblest sort.

Perhaps suspecting fine stitchery's potential for encouraging vanity and ambition, Tudor Englishmen of a humanist bent declared their suspicion of fine sewing as a way of filling time. In fact, they argued that sewing allowed women's wits too free a rein. Richard Hyrde, the son-in-law of Thomas More, condemned the mental wandering encouraged by textile work in order to defend women's reading as a hedge against it. In his dedicatory letter to Margaret More's translation of Erasmus, he remarks: "While [women] sit sewing and spinning with their fingers, they may cast and compass many peevish fancies in their minds."[14] Juan Vives, in the first book of *The Instruction of a Christian Woman*, suggested writing as a better discipline for the feminine mind: "Whilst we are writing, the mind is diverted from the thought of frivolous or improper objects."[15] By writing, Vives means copying out classical *sententiae*: pupils should be set "some weighty little opinion which it will be helpful to learn thoroughly, for by frequently writing out such things, they will necessarily be fixed in the mind." Although Vives does not mention samplers, this was a form of needlework that corresponded precisely to his desire to focus the mind on proper objects: working pious maxims in thread drew both kinds of activity together. A young girl was being trained not only in stitches and patterns but in habits of humility and orderliness as she stitched these lines on a seventeenth-century English sampler:

> I AM A MAID BVT YOUNG MY SKILL
> IS YeT BVT SMALL BVT GOD
> I HOP[E] WILL BLeS Me SO I MAY LIVe
> TO MeND THIS ALL RACHEL LOADer
> WROVGHT THIS SAMPLeR BeING
> TWeLVE YEARS OVLD THE TENTH
> DAY DeSeMBeR 1666 HL [16]

Vives's recommendation that women read and write rather than sew reverses a more usual opposition: the needle *versus* the pen. Text after text throughout Europe insisted on the division of these two kinds of labor: the useful industry of the private woman could save her from aspiring to the dangerous self-display of the woman in print. Giovanni Bruto, in his 1555 essay against humanist education for women, *La institutione di una fanciulla nata nobilmente* (1555, translated and expanded by Thomas Salter as *The Mirrhor of Modestie*, London, 1579), sets up the notoriety of ancient women poets, Sappho and Corinna, among others, as a counter-model to the chaste modesty of the daughter he is constructing for the present:

seeing . . . that in such studies as yieldeth recreation and pleasure . . . they will as well learn to be subtle and shameless lovers and cunning and skillful writers of ditties, sonnets, epigrams and ballads, let them be trained to the care and government of a family . . . how much more convenient . . . the needle and spindle were for them, with a good and honest reputation, than the skill of well using a pen or writing a lofty verse.[17]

Not surprisingly, women penned protest against such assignments. Lucy Hutchinson, whose husband was a Nottinghamshire Parliamentarian, narrated her exceptional private education in a passage of her autobiography that ends in sharp resentment at the requirement of needlework, contrasting the reading she preferred to the ladylike accomplishments of music, dancing, and fine stitchery:

When I was about seven years of age, I remember I had at one time eight tutors in several qualities, languages, music, dancing, writing and needlework; but my genius was quite averse from all but my book . . . As for music and dancing, I profited very little in them, and would never practise my lute or harpsichords but when my masters were with me; and for my needle, I absolutely hated it.[18]

A similar opposition to gendered social assignments was stated by Anne Bradstreet in the opening to her collection of poems written in New England, *The Tenth Muse Lately Sprung up in America* (London, 1650), in which she predicted the hostility she expected – or hoped to forestall – from her public:

> I am obnoxious to each carping tongue
> Who says my hand a needle better fits;
> A poet's pen all scorn I thus should wrong.[19]

Not all audiences were as critical of women wielding pens as Bradstreet expected her readers to be, however. Some men, often court poets writing in the hope of patronage from noblewomen, reversed the hierarchy of needlework over writing. In *Orlando Furioso* Ariosto praised the women poets of Italy for leaving "the needle and the cloth" for the fountain of Aganippe on Parnassus, proving that Italy could produce more poets like Vittoria Colonna.[20] Charles de Sainte-Marthe in his funeral oration for Marguerite de Navarre celebrated her independence from women's handiwork: "even in the absence of the King of Navarre, her husband, when she was alone in her bedroom, you would have seen in her hands a book instead of the distaff, a pen instead of the spindle, and the flap of her writing-desk rather than the needle."[21] William Greenhill, a minister dedicating a sermon to Princess Elizabeth, the daughter of Charles I, recommended that she follow the example of a Venetian girl "whose delight was not in wool, but in books, not in the . . . needle, but in the pen."[22] Such elevations of the pen were also written to encourage women of lower status than princesses and queens. In England, prefacing a sequel to Philip Sidney's *Arcadia* written by the gentlewoman Anna Weamys, the poet Francis Vaughan exhorted Weamys's women readers to take her as a model:

> Lay by your Needles, Ladies, take the Pen
> The only difference 'twixt you and men . . .
> Good wine does need no Bush, pure Wit no Beard
> Since all Souls equal are, let all be heard.[23]

Other Englishmen writing poetry represented needlework in ways that aligned it with their own work, elevating fine stitchery into a kind of textuality with analogies to epic and religious verse. In George Chapman's translation of *Hero and Leander* (1616) he contrasts the "conceited scarfe" worked by Hero with images of Leander to nobler (that is, less erotic) forms of representation by the needle, drawing a parallel between women's virtue and their stitchery as both the practice and representation of self-restraint. In these lines likening poets' meters to needleworkers' patterns ("numbred silks"), the poet's concern over women's idleness and the dangerous thoughts their "yeasty" minds may brew leads him to prescribe needlework on fine linen as a pictorial, even architectural, discipline of epic dimensions:

> O what sweet formes fayre Ladies soules doe shrowd,
> Were they made seen & forced through their blood,
> If through their beauties like rich work through lawn,
> They would set forth their minds with vertues drawn,
> In letting graces from their fingers flie,
> To still their yeasty thoughts with industrie:
> That their plied wits in numbred silks might sing
> Passions huge conquest, and their needels leading
> Affection prisoner through their own-built citties,
> Pinnioned with stories and Arachnean ditties.[24]

A similar interpretation of needlework as a medium capable of building a second nature shapes a long passage in Giles Fletcher's poem *Christs Victorie in Heaven* (1610). Fletcher grounds his fantastic allegorical description of the figure of Mercy in concrete needlework vocabulary, making the goddess into a celestial version of a virtuous and virtuoso needlewoman. Mercy here wears a world drawn and sewn with her own hands. Fletcher represents her as a partner to God as the architect of the universe and to himself as the poet-painter of heaven:

> Her upper garment was a silken lawne,
> With needle-woorke richly embroidered,
> Which she her selfe with her own hand had drawne,
> And all the world therein had pourtrayed,
> With threads so fresh, and lively colored
>   That seem'd the world she newe created thear,
>   And the mistaken eye would rashly swear
> The silken trees did growe, and the beasts living wear [were] . . .
>
> So curiously the underwork did creepe,
> And curling circlets so well shadowed lay,
> That afar off the waters seem'd to sleepe,
> But those that neere the margin pearle did play
> Hoarcely [harshly] enwaved wear with hastie sway,
>   As though they meant to rocke the gentle eare
>   And hush the former that enslumbred wear,
> And here a dangerous rocke the flying ships did feare.   (stanzas 53, 56)[25]

A much simpler yet still powerful language of stitchery is ascribed to the heroine of an anonymous sonnet about a jilted bride, recorded in a commonplace book. The heroine uses her sampler to publish an accusation against men for their infidelity:

> A Gentlewoman that married a Young Gent., Who after Forsooke Hir,
> Whereuppon She Tooke Hir Needle, In Which She Was Excellent, And
>   Worked upon Hir Sampler Thus:
> Come, give me needle, stitch cloth, silke, and chaire,
>   That I may sitt and sigh, and sow and singe,
> For perfect coullour to discribe the aire,
>   A subtile p[i]ersinge changinge constant thinge.
> No false stitch will I make, my hart is true,
>   Plaine stitche my sampler is for to complaine,
> How men have tongues of hony, harts of rue.
>   True tongues and harts are one, men makes them twaine.
> Give me black silk, that sable suites my hart,
>   And yet some white, though white words do deceive,
> No green at all, for youth and I must part,
>   Purple and blew, fast love and faith to weave.[26]

Yet the final couplet the poet assigns to this embroiderer suggests that planning stitchery as a form of revenge has become a satisfying substitute for the lost husband:

> Mayden, no more sleepeless Ile go to bedd,
> Take all away, the work works in my head.

The speaker's apparent simplicity finds an equivalent in her choice of "plaine stitch" and a palette limited to only four conventionally symbolic colors. But her designing of these details – the "work working in her head" – replaces her simplicity with a firmly self-legitimating textile rhetoric. The poem subversively imagines needlework as the public exposure of the imperfections of the male sex.

One sort of opposition to needlework arose from class hostility toward fine stitchery as a privilege of women in wealthy families. Silk thread was expensive, as were the tools of fine needlework. Accordingly, moralists writing for the middling sort linked decorative stitchery to vices contrary to the thrifty industry that needlework was made to signify in conduct books and sermons. Suspicion of luxury clearly motivates Thomas Milles's rejection of fashionable sewing as vanity in his *Treasure of Ancient and Moderne Times* (1613), a collection of commonplaces in which he sternly warns girls, "Fear God and learn woman's housewifery, / Not idle samplery or silken folly."[27] The same sort of suspicion is spelled out in specific needlework vocabulary by Thomas Powell in his *Art of Thriving, or the plaine pathway to preferment* (London, 1635), a book addressed to "the private gentleman," that is, to fathers of modest means. Powell associates expensive needlework with the reading of romances and reading with frivolous writing, all equally unsuited to bourgeois daughters:

It makes no matter for working in curious Italian purles [twists of silver or gold wire] or French borders, it is not worth the while. Let them learn of plain works of all kinds . . . Instead of song and music, let them learn cooking and laundry, and instead of reading Sir Philip Sidney's *Arcadia*, let them read the grounds of good housewifery. I like not a female poetess at any hand.[28]

Even Biblical subjects for needlework, if it was highly intricate, could become a target for male criticism. In Jasper Mayne's 1636 play *The City Match*, he gives to his character the fashionable Aurelia a speech mocking her Puritan maid's obsession with religious subjects in her fancy work:

> Nay Sir, she is a Puritan at her needle too . . .
> She workes religious Petticoats; for flowers
> She'l make Church Histories; her needle doth
> So sanctify my Cushionets, besides,
> My smock-sleeves have such holy imbroderies,
> And are so learned, that I feare in time
> All my apparell will be quoted by
> Some pure instructor.[29]

Intricate stitchery, then, was taken as a target by Puritan advice-givers and anti-Puritan wits alike, men otherwise occupying opposite sides of the religious controversy.

   In the long run, as such contradictions suggest, domestic ideology could not sustain an unambiguous celebration of needlework as a habit guaranteeing feminine virtue. The conflicting viewpoints in writings on needlework show that the gender prescriptions shaping guidebooks for fathers and husbands, sermons, and courtesy manuals aimed at constructing ideal women were running aground on the increasing numbers of pattern books providing consumer-needlewomen with a range of practical visual vocabularies. Early modern women found themselves in a market-place where conduct manuals defining feminine virtue as containment within the household circulated along with how-to books encouraging women to demonstrate their textile virtuosity in public. This new system of print culture was fed by more or less explicit advertisements for incompatible groups – humanists and moralists at court, pattern salesmen blazoning their commodities, defenders of different religions, city poets satirizing contemporary fashions. The crazy-quilt of conservative gender theory and new technical practices opened up unpredictable possibilities for the design and display of textile work by women. The needle could *be* a pen.

The needle and the pen

Written and sewn records suggest that many gentlewomen, even those whose interests lay outside the household sphere, adopted needlework as a sign and practice of virtue. But women also interpreted good stitchery as evidence of quick under-standing and aesthetic intelligence. Passages in texts written by women emphasize the sharp, engaged concentration that needlework required of its practitioners, as well as the mutually respectful woman-to-woman bonds enacted and preserved in needlework. One case in point is the autobiography of a Tudor woman, Lady Grace Mildmay (1552–1620). Early in her text, she describes the various subjects taught to her by her beloved governess Mistress Hamblyn, a woman who obviously saw no contradiction between girls' reading and writing, on one hand, and fine stitchery on the other:

> I had experience of a gentlewoman . . . brought up by my mother from her childhood . . . and all good virtues that might be in a woman were constantly settled in her . . . I delighted so much in her company that I would sit with her all the day in her chamber . . . And when she did see me idly disposed, she would set me to cipher with my pen . . . and to write a supposed letter to this or that body concerning such and such things . . . and sometimes set me to some curious work (for she was an excellent needlewoman in all kinds of needlework, and most curiously she would perform it).[30]

Often alone during her married life, Lady Mildmay claims that she enjoyed privacy partly because her governess, like her mother, had warned her against the dangers of "feasts, marriages and plays." Among her pastimes were reading (the Bible and books of home medicine) and needlework, which she suggests gave her pleasure of several kinds: she invented her own designs rather than following patterns, she enjoyed concentrating on what she was stitching, and she performed better than her innate talent led her to expect:

> Also every day I spent some time in works of my own invention without sample of drawing or pattern before me, for carpet or cushion work . . . All which variety of exercises did greatly recreate my mind, for I thought of nothing else but that I was doing in every particular one of these said exercises. And though I was but meanly furnished to be excellent in any one . . . , they did me good in as much as I found in myself that God wrought with me in all.[31]

Admiration for another woman's textile skill and for the native ingenuity it signaled also shapes a comment in the biography of Elizabeth Cary written by one of her daughters, Anne or Lucy, around 1635. At the end of a long paragraph on her mother's intellectual accomplishments, including her written translations of Seneca, the daughter adds, "She was skilful and curious in working, [but] never having been helped by anybody; those that knew her would never have believed she knew how to hold a needle unless they had seen it."[32] Like Mildmay, this writer sees needlework as a field for independent invention, a sign of cleverness worthy of praise in the same context as intellectual work.

The themes of women keeping each other company and of textile skill as a publicly appreciated aspect of feminine identity are combined in a scene from Mary Wroth's *Urania* (1621). In the first book of Wroth's romance, Parselius, one of the many heroes, travels through Morea and comes upon the castle inhabited by the princess Dalinea. Wroth sets the scene for Parselius's meeting and infatuation with Dalinea by emphasizing the rich hangings of her room and the needlework and reading she shares with her ladies-in-waiting. The magnificence of the setting is produced partly through the close focus governing the description of the gold and silver stitchery worked into Dalinea's royal canopy, a verbal and textile *tour de force* that allows Wroth to elevate her heroine by means of a luxurious textile framework:

... here was Dalinea sitting under a Cloth of Estate, of Carnation Veluet, curiously and richly set with Stones, all ouer being Embroidered with purle of Siluer, and Gold, the Golde made in Sunnes, the Siluer in Starres, Diamonds, Rubies, and other Stones plentifully and cunningly compassing them about, and plac'd as if for the Skye where they shin'd; but she standing appeard so much brighter, as if all that had beene, but to set forth her light, so farre excelling them, as the day wherein the Sunne doth shew most glorious, doth the drowsiest day.[33]

Wroth employs sumptuous professional embroidery (of the kind that had been in rich supply in the wardrobe and room decorations of Elizabeth I, for example) as visual confirmation of Dalinea's identity as an imposing princess. But she also familiarizes the scene by relating it to a women's world of sewing and reading, in this case, court ladies being read to as they work with the needle:

Her Ladies who attended her, were a little distant from her in a faire compasse Window, where also stood a Chaire, wherein it seemed she had been sitting, till the newes came of his arriuall. In that Chaire lay a Booke, the Ladies were all at worke; so as it shewed, she read while they wrought. (124)

The closing focus on the volume that Dalinea has been reading to her circle shifts the scene from visual splendor to an intimate social gathering, affirming Jacobean noblewomen's habitual pleasure in the needle, the book, and one another's company. Indeed, historical sources record just such behavior among English-women. Mary Stuart kept her canopied estate cloth, richly embroidered in France, and sat under it as she received her Scottish subjects in Edinburgh Castle in 1578, and Anne Clifford reports in her *Diary* that she had Montaigne's *Essays* and Ovid's *Metamorphoses* read out loud to her by ladies-in-waiting as she sat plying her needle.[34]

At the courts of Elizabeth and James I, the pen and the needle were spectacularly combined in the work of Esther Inglis, a professional calligrapher born in France and married to a Scotsman, Bartholomew Kello, employed as official writer of state documents by the king.[35] Inglis copied printed texts by hand, often in tiny books, and then embroidered rich covers for them, as for a commentary on the Psalms that she dedicated in 1608 to Henry Prince of Wales. The book is covered in red velvet intricately decorated with silver thread and seed pearls.[36] In her drawn and painted self-portraits and her emblem, a pair of crossed pens cut from Scottish thistles, however, Inglis emphasized writing over needlework. She apparently relished the fact that she was transgressing gender constraints by putting herself in the public eye as a calligrapher and as the subject of her own drawings and miniature paintings. Dedicating a collection of Psalms in 1599 to Maurice of Nassau, doing battle for the Protestant cause, she likened him to Alexander the Great, her tiny book to the *Iliad*, and herself to a queen of the Amazons: "Having almost immodestly chased away feminine fearfulness and taken on the spirit of a queen of the Amazons, I have boldly turned to my Alexander, only to beg you to receive with a welcoming eye this little book written by my hand."[37]

When Inglis posed for a portrait in oil in 1595 by an unknown artist, she was quite likely presenting herself as a needleworker and calligrapher to the queen at the same time (Fig. 28).[38] The flowers in the painting echo those preferred by Elizabeth, to

Fig. 28. Anonymous painter, *Esther Inglis Mrs. Kello*, 1595

whom Inglis had dedicated a manuscript *Discours de la foy* in 1591. She wears a stomacher embroidered with Tudor roses and English acorns, and two emblematic flowers, not her characteristic Scottish thistle but the pink or gillyflower and the honeysuckle often embroidered on Queen Elizabeth's dresses, are intertwined at her upper right. Inglis was penwoman and needlewoman both. Some of her coverings for books are of near-professional quality, and the elegance with which she clothed the books she presented to members of the royal family was an important part of their value as gifts and as evidence of her double skill. In the oil portrait she holds a small book with dimly visible embroidery on its cover. As Susan Frye points out,

Inglis gave her name to precisely those aspects of the book that popular printing was making invisible – calligraphy, binding, covers – to the materiality that is etymologically present but ideologically erased in the word "text."[39] She is the author, that is, the maker, of every element of her books.

No doubt, one function of the conflation of needle and pen was to reassure readers of women's texts of their authors' respectability. Public eloquence could be justified if it was framed by a narrative that demonstrated the writer's domestic virtue as a needlewoman. Louise Labé carried out this kind of compensatory maneuver in her "Elégie III," in which she pens the claim that as a girl, she combined the talents mythically harmonized in the goddess Minerva: she was equally able "to paint with the needle," recalling Ovid's description of Arachne, and "to march proudly with weapons."[40] A similar tactic opens and closes the biography written to introduce Moderata Fonte's dialogue *Il merito delle donne* (Venice, 1601). Fonte's uncle Giovanni Doglioni describes her as a child prodigy, amazingly quick to learn languages, music, and math. Then he adds: "She was also a superb needlewoman, and without any kind of pattern or sketch to guide her, she could embroider any subject or design that was suggested to her, bringing it to life with her needle before the eyes of the amazed lookers-on."[41] Only after this description of the poetess's manual and pictorial dexterity does Doglioni begin to list the literary texts she produced: a romance, a religious epic, the dialogue itself. He sums up her life as a perfect balance of literary and domestic skill. Her method of composition, he says, was to go to sleep with a subject in mind and to rise with many stanzas already composed. Even so, "as a woman, she had to attend to womanly tasks like sewing, and she did not wish to neglect those labors because of the false notion, so widespread in our city today, that women should excel in nothing but the running of the household" (39). Arguing against repressive gender ideology by acceding to some of it, Doglione defends Fonte as a writer by invoking her impeccable domesticity.

The needle as a pen

Any clear distinction between public and private, inner and outer spaces, was undone in material ways by English needlewomen. Whatever repressive and isolating effects stitchery as a disciplinary apparatus might have been intended to produce, women used it to connect to one another within domestic settings and to connect with the outer world, as well. Hannah Wolley, the writer of household manuals such as *The Gentlewoman's Companion* (1675), recommended handworked clothing as a public sign of a woman's skill and virtue. Rather than wearing professionally embroidered clothes, she writes, "It is more commendable a great deal to wear ones own Work, . . . and besides it argues that Person not to be idle, but rather a good Housewife."[42] Wolley's remark dissolves the private/public opposition so central to humanist family handbooks. Her "good Housewife" does fine stitchery at home, but by wearing her needlework, she displays her virtuosity in public. The same pleasure in display is evident in a fictional account of a gentlewoman who worked at home to be known abroad: she "beautified the House with Cusions, Carpets, stools and other devices of needle worke, as at such time divers will doo, to have the better report made of their credite among their servant friends in the Country."[43]

Needlework on caps, coifs, and scarves as well as samplers, cushions and wall hangings was hardly a private habit; rather, it encouraged buyers of pattern books to choose among publicly printed designs and combine them in their own way. In practice, needleworkers combined patterns from various books, as the stitchery on a woman's shift now at the Victoria and Albert Museum shows. The needlewoman may well have used Richard Shorleyker's 1624 book of patterns, *A Scolehouse for the Needle*. One page of this book offers simple flower and animal forms, including a peapod and double snail motif, top and center, that we will see again (Fig 29). A second page, this time offering designs in white on black, shows fifteen kinds of birds, including an owl, a peacock, and a turkey (Fig. 30).[44] If we look at the patterns worked into the smock, we see, at the center far left of the detail, a peapod and snail motif exactly like Shorleyker's (Fig. 31).[45] But the embroiderer's owl and crowned parrots are quite different from Shorleyker's birds of the same type. The needleworker combined a variety of forms from a variety of sources; her "private" undergarment is actually a record of her take on visual vocabularies circulating in the public world of print.

Materials and subjects for needlework ranged from the simple and pious to the hedonistic and expensive. Scenes from the Bible were a frequent topic. In one fairly simple canvas pillow cover of about 1600, worked only in red and black silk, four Old Testament scenes are straightfowardly presented in drawing-like outline: Adam and Eve, the sacrifices of Cain and Abel, Cain killing Abel, Noah building the Ark (Fig. 32).[46] In contrast, luxury and fancifulness are obvious in a 1670s' satin cover for a box, stitched in multi-colored silks, in which a lady holding a flower is surrounded by spot motifs, free-floating designs of various scales (Fig. 33).[47] Each detail is interesting on its own, rather than subordinated to a central narrative or consistent perspective. The Western and Eastern palaces on each side at the top are the same size as the unicorn and the stag at the bottom, large birds gaze inward at the central figure, an immense tulip fills the space between the unicorn and the smiling fish swimming in a grotto-surrounded pond at the center bottom. *Copia*, symmetry, and variety are the principles of composition, rather than narrative detail.

Classical mythology provided more learned subjects for embroidery, but needle-women still worked freely in scale and detail to narrate well-known myths, as in a mid-seventeenth-century silkwork picture of Diana and Actaeon (Fig. 34).[48] At the left, two of Diana's nymphs, in profile, eye Actaeon in an alarmed way; at the lower right, he is shown, with antlers, trying to defend himself against a hound, and then above, in completed metamorphosis, as a deer ravaged by hounds. Here, too, figures are freely proportioned in relation to one another. The needlewoman seems to have been most interested in the four large female figures at the left; Actaeon, drawing his bow from behind the trees above them, is a much smaller figure. And a wealth of non-narrative details surrounds the three action scenes: an intricate castle is set at the upper left, above a solitary bird and a three-dimensional butterfly; an immense iris and rose divide Diana's nymph from the startled Actaeon. The entire picture freely adapts the narrative to a flat surface and fills its empty spaces with the flora and fauna that printed pattern books made available to embroiderers.[49]

Needlewomen copied designs from many sources, not only those intended for them, using texts directed to a range of public interests: emblem books, zoological studies of plants and animals, printers' insignia on the title pages of books, prints recording contemporary paintings, political cartoons, and books about colonial explorations of the New World.[50] A mid-seventeenth-century needlewoman juxta-

Fig. 29. Page from Richard Shorleyker, *A Scolehouse for the Needle*, London, 1624

Fig. 30. Animal motifs from *A Scolehouse for the Needle*

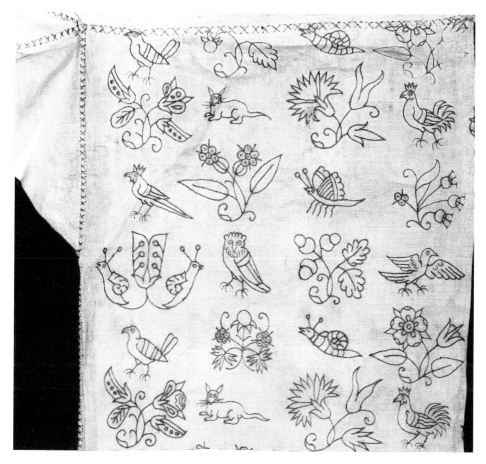

Fig. 31. Detail from a linen shirt, 1620s

posed ancient and contemporary time frames in a raised-work satin panel of Pallas and Paris, combining figures from classical mythology with newly minted allegories of the four continents. She probably intended to cut the sections apart to make a frame for a mirror: she would have positioned Athene, in her plumed helmet, and Paris, in a Renaissance plumed hat, at the top and the bottom of the. mirror (Fig. 35).[51] The four women at the corners of this panel symbolize the four continents. They are modeled on female allegories circulating on the title pages of books recounting travels to the New World, and also published separately, for example, in a set of prints by William Marshall.[52] Europe, at the upper right, wears a crown and holds a book and scepter; Asia, at the lower right in a conical headdress and veil, holds an incense burner; Africa, at the lower left, barebreasted and wearing a skin cloak, looks at a celestial globe; America, at the upper left, semi-nude in a feather headdress, holds a bow and arrow. Here, then, domestic needlework records European representations of the larger world of global travel and conquest.

Other political realities were directly addressed by needlewomen, who sometimes worked together to represent their struggles and loyalties. A scene of intimacy between girls was constructed by Shakespeare in *A Midsummer Night's Dream* in the

Fig. 32. Pillow cover, silk on linen, scenes from Genesis, c. 1600

Fig. 33. Satin cover for a box, lady in a garden, c. 1675

speech in which Helena reminds Hermia of their friendship, condensed into a memory of shared textilework:

> We Hermia, like two Artificiall gods,
> Haue with our needles, created both one flower,
> Both on one sampler, sitting on one cushion,
> Both warbling of one song, both in one key;
> As if our hands, our sides, voices, and mindes
> Had beene incorporate.[53]

This speech, like Giles Fletcher's figure of Mercy, celebrates the inventive power of the needleworkers: they are like "artificiall gods." What is also striking is that Helena's recollection of the time she spent at her needle with Hermia is articulated not as the accomplishment of the virtuous wife or wife-to-be but as the means by which women are made incorporate, "one flesh," with each other. She appropriates the language of the marriage service (the incorporation of the hands, bodies, voices, and minds of a man and a woman) to describe the shared work by which woman is incorporated with woman.

Shakespeare's collaborating flower-stitchers had a historical counterpart in two famous sixteenth-century needlewomen, Mary Queen of Scots and Bess of Hardwick, Mary's companion for fifteen years during her captivity in England. As queen, Mary was often observed at her needle, perhaps because she recalled the strategy of Catherine de Medici at the French court, who had listened intently to the conversations around her as she worked with silk thread in the evenings.[54] In 1561 Elizabeth's envoy to Scotland, Thomas Randolph, reported: "I was sent for into the Council

Fig. 34. Silkwork picture, *Diana and Actaeon*, c. 1650

Chamber, where she herself [Mary] ordinarily sitteth the most part of the time, sowing some work or other."[55] This scene is particularly interesting because it suggests that Mary refused to separate her fine stitchery from her political appearances.

Or from political action. In one of Mary's most famous pieces of needlework, she made a statement understood by her contemporaries as a political complaint and a threat to Elizabeth's sovereignty. A central panel of a wall hanging worked by Mary, now at Oxburgh Hall, pictures a hand descending from heaven with a pruning hook, cutting down a vine, with the motto "Virescit Vulnere Virtus" ("virtue grows strong by wounding").[56] Contemporary Englishmen read the motto as referring to Mary's determination to survive her imprisonment by Elizabeth. Lisa Klein, following Margaret Swain, points out a directly subversive use Mary made of this emblem by sending an identical panel on a cushion to the Duke of Norfolk, whom she saw as a possible husband and who was to join the northern Catholics in their 1569 revolt against Elizabeth. The meaning of such a gift would have been simultaneously erotic and political, encouraging Norfolk's ambitions for marriage to Mary and his resistance to the Protestant queen. The cushion cover was identified as Mary's handiwork in the testimony of her ambassador John Lesley, and it was used as evidence against Norfolk at the trial that led to his execution.[57] And the historian William Camden mentions that Mary's needlework was used as evidence against her, too, when she was put on trial for fomenting the northern rebellion.[58]

Fig. 35. Silk and satin raised-work picture, *Paris, Pallas and the Four Continents*, c. 1650

Some of Mary's smaller needlework pieces also contained political implications critical of Elizabeth, William Drummond, an expert on emblems, affirmed in a 1614 letter to Ben Jonson – for example, her panel of two women on the wheel of Fortune, and her eclipses of moon and sun.[59]

During the 1570s, the first decade that Mary spent under house arrest at the country house of Elizabeth Talbot, the Countess of Shrewsbury (later known as Bess of Hardwick Hall), the two women did needlework together. Bess's official role toward Mary was to support her third husband George Talbot, the Earl of Shrewsbury, Elizabeth's warden and therefore Mary's jailer, and she eventually ended on very bad terms with her. But in the early years of their cohabitation, they each stitched octagonal medallions about a foot across, which were later combined on several wall hangings displayed in the public rooms of Bess's country house, Hardwick Hall.[60] Mary suggested designs and *imprese* for Bess's needlework, including panels for a wall hanging commemorating her dead husband William Cavendish. The queen and the countess sat together "devising workes," as the Earl of Shrewsbury reported, studying pattern sources from France and Germany, including emblem books by Guillaume Paradin and Bernard Salomon and Conrad Gessner's 1560 book of woodcuts illustrating birds, beasts, and fish.[61] They used their ciphers, MASR (Marie Stuart Regina) and ES (Elizabeth of Shrewsbury), to identify themselves as the producers of the individual pieces of needlework later assembled into large composite hangings. On the "Marian Hanging" now at Oxburgh Hall, Mary's cipher is set above the central "Virescit Vulnere Virtus" panel and Bess's cipher is directly below it.[62] In Bess's panel commemorating William Cavendish, her cipher is placed above a central panel of falling tears; below, at the lower left, is Mary's embroidery of a "Byrde of America," with her initials MR (Maria Regina) beneath the bird's feet.[63] The placement of Bess's needlework and initials together with Mary's is a material record of her collaboration with her foreign "captive" as a needlewoman, though not as a political sympathizer, and of their shared desire to assert their identities in work that would be preserved in the public rooms of Bess's great houses.

Needlewomen less highly placed than Mary and Bess also worked to take a place in history by sewing their names into their work. Legally, women were excluded from the dominant memory system of inheritance. They were central to the production of genealogies, yet marginal to those genealogies, which privileged fathers and sons. By stitching their names, however, they sewed themselves into a different memory system, a subculture recorded in physical objects that were nearly always transmitted among women. In 1603, for example, Mary Hulton made a pillow cover celebrating the accession of King James in 1603 (Fig. 36).[64] At the center is the new royal coat of arms, with I R for "Jacobus Rex" at either side of the crown. But this apparently adulatory image is emphatically framed at the lower left and right with its maker's first and last name. Thus Mary Hulton made a place for herself in history.

Samplers, too, began to record their makers' names in the seventeenth century, as well as the names of girls or women for whom they were made.[65] One sampler stitched by Jane Bostock in 1598 announces the name of its maker on the top line of lettering (with "Bostocke" emphasized by tiny pearls) and announces the name of its recipient, a new-born girl named Alice Lee, in larger letters in the second line.[66] One might read this sampler as a rather grim copy-book page for little Alice, imposing a

Fig. 36. Mary Hulton, pillow cover, silk and wool on canvas, c. 1603

manual and moral discipline upon her. But it was, in fact, a generous present from Jane Bostock (possibly a godmother to Alice), supplying her with patterns that would otherwise have been available only in unaffordably expensive pattern books.[67] Many other samplers also dramatize connections between women. Girls dedicate them to mothers, aunts, and female friends; and by putting what they have learned from other women about stitchery and design onto cloth that can be passed down through their families, they make these knowledges available to female relatives in the future.

As the silkwork panel picturing Diana and Actaeon suggests, one source of embroidery subjects was Ovid. Among the mythological subjects derived from *The Metamorphoses* was the story of Philomela and Procne, represented in a set of elaborate bed valances produced by a late-sixteenth-century noblewoman probably working in collaboration with a professional embroiderer. Ovid's tale of Philomela and Procne stages the entire problematic we have been discussing here: the official recommendation of textilework to silence and enclose women in inner rooms of the house versus women's use of the needle to establish female bonds within doors, to create material histories, and to transgress domestic boundaries through the "publication" and transmission of their work.

In Book 6 of *The Metamorphoses*, textilework speaks for a woman who has been deprived of her tongue. Ovid tells how the Thracian king Tereus first married Procne, then raped her sister Philomela and cut out her tongue, imprisoning her behind stone walls so that she could not tell her sister or a larger public of citizens and gods what he had done. Ovid's Philomela weaves a tapestry in "purple signs on a white background" (line 577), narrating "the story of her wrongs," and when her single servant, an aged woman, takes the tapestry to Procne, she understands at once what her sister's message means.[68] Multiple revenge follows: the two women kill Procne's son by Tereus, Itys, and serve the boy to his father at a feast. Enraged, the king turns into a hoopoe and the sisters into the swallow and the nightingale.

In the bed valance, the noblewoman collaborating with the embroiderer recast this story in the medium of her own craft. Philomela tent-stitches a message into a piece of canvas on a frame, while the old woman, holding a distaff and spindle (emblems of lower-class textilework, in contrast to Philomela's needlework), waits to carry the message out of the walled prison garden (Fig. 37).[69] This image rewrites both Ovid and the conduct books of the Renaissance. Weaving becomes needlework and needlework encodes resistance to the invisible silence of women that the habit of sewing is supposed to ensure.

More often than needlewomen chose Ovid as a source for subjects, however, they worked episodes from the Old Testament. In these images, too, it is possible to read resistance to repressive contemporary lessons in femininity. Three Biblical heroines who frequently appear in women's sewn pictures were known for the violent punishments they meted out to men: Judith, the beheader of Holofernes; Jael, who, as Deborah prophesied, killed the enemy general Sisera; and Esther, whose intervention on behalf of the Jews led Ahasuerus to hang Haman.

Esther was represented more than any other Biblical heroine, usually at the moment when Ahasuerus stretches out his hand or his scepter to signal that he has granted her request for her people, the Jews, the right to self-defense.[70] One example is a 1648 canvas panel, which pictures the king, under a canopy and coat of arms, assenting to Esther's appeal; Esther, at his right, is accompanied by two ladies-in-

Fig. 37. Bed valance, wool and silk on canvas, *Story of Philomela* (detail), c. 1600

waiting carrying her train.[71] Liz Arthur identifies the source of this panel as an engraving by the Netherlandish artist Maarten van Heemskerck, in order to argue that the particular details added to the panel are evidence that the woman who embroidered it intended to give it a clear political meaning – her allegiance to Charles I – by analogy to Esther, the member of another threatened minority. The needlewoman added the arms of the Crispe family of Suffolk (an area represented by Oliver Cromwell in Parliament, and one in which Royalists suffered particularly badly during the war) above the king and worked the date 1648, the year of the second civil war, in seed pearls. Like Mary Stuart's emblems, this needlewoman's reworking of a printed source signaled her political position.

A frequent site for Biblical figures was the small caskets covered with satin worked by girls in their early teens and used to hold writing utensils, cosmetics, and jewelry.[72] Generically, such caskets broke down the needle–pen opposition: decorated with silken needlework, they contained pens and ink. For the front doors of her casket, the twelve-year-old Hannah Smith stitched an image of Deborah handing a commission to her general Barak and another of Jael pounding a nail into Sisera's temple. As Lisa Klein points out, Jael's violent gesture is embroidered right next to the keyhole, into which the owner of the casket would frequently be inserting a metal object in a gesture uncannily like Jael's.[73]

A similarly uncanny detail can be seen in a Stuart wall panel representing Judith in Holofernes' tent after she has beheaded him (Fig. 38).[74] At her left, his decapitated neck and trailing arm are visible, based on an engraving by Gerard de

Fig. 38. Raised-work panel, silk on satin, *Judith with the Head of Holofernes*, after 1650

HIC IN CONCLAVI CV SOLO SOLA RELICTA, FVNEREO STERNIT EBRIA MEBRA TORO

Fig. 39. Gerard de Jode, engraving. *Judith and Holofernes,* from *Thesaurus Sacrarum Historiarum Veteris Testamenti,* Antwerp. 1585

Jode in the *Thesaurus Sacrarum Historiarum Veteris Testamenti* (Fig. 39). But the head itself, probably sewn three-dimensionally over a wooden mold and held in Judith's left hand, has disappeared: material history has separated the villainous general's head from his body for good. Militant, active in the public sphere, celebrated for destroying men who threatened their people, Jael and Judith were selected as models of feminine power very different from the meek domestic virtue that needlework was supposed to enforce.

Another frequently represented Biblical heroine was the Queen of Sheba, bearing gifts to Solomon. Because the stories of the Queen of Sheba and of Esther both bring together a queen and a powerful king, needlework experts sometimes confuse the two heroines. The Queen of Sheba, however, is usually shown offering gifts, including a crown, to the king, and she is often shaded by a parasol held by a servant, a prominent detail in Gerard de Jode's published print of the subject.[75] The Queen of Sheba was potentially a figure with more radical implications than Esther: her act was not that of a wife but of an independent political figure claiming the public authority to legitimate Solomon's wisdom (she was also read typologically as the soul converted to Christianity). Her servants, her long train, her rich gifts all emphasize her wealth and sovereignty. On the right front door of a casket worked by Rebecca Plaisted in 1668, the manservant standing behind the queen carries a roll of dark velvet embroidered with pearls, probably a case for jewels (Fig. 40).[76] If so, Plaisted was making a witty play on her own jewel case as the platform for her representation of the Queen of Sheba's gift.

Needlewomens' choice of figures such as Esther and the Queen of Sheba, and their use of internationally circulating prints as models for designs, typify the appropriation of public visual discourses through which they took part in the production of political and national histories. In sewn pictures with explicit topical meanings, intended for display in public rooms of their houses rather than for concealment in private bedchambers, women aligned themselves with particular positions toward contemporary events. Their needlework, laid on tables or hung on the inner walls of their houses, constituted a kind of family livery, declaring the household's loyalty to one or another leader. England's troubled relationship with Spain was one topic on which needlewomen took stands; another was the civil wars of the seventeenth century.

In the early seventeenth century Dorothy Selby, of the parish of Ightham in Ipswich, laid hands on an engraving based on a design by the Ipswich preacher Samuel Ward.[77] The engraving, printed in Amsterdam in 1621, represents two earlier triumphs of Protestant England against political and religious opponents: the defeat of the Armada (the ships in a crescent formation at the left) and the Gunpowder Plot, signaled by the papal conclave in the center with the devil at the center and the figure of Guy Fawkes approaching Parliament on the right (Fig. 41). A bolt of lightning containing the words "Video Rideo," translated into English in small letters as "I see and smile" and into Dutch at the point of the ray ("Ick sie en lach"), symbolizes that the discovery of the Catholic conspiracy was divinely ordained. In Dorothy Selby's embroidered picture, she carefully reproduced the same three scenes.[78] Her Armada ships are less intricate than the printmaker's, as are the panes of the windows of Parliament, probably a result of the technical difficulty of working such fine lines on canvas. One change the needleworker made was to increase the size of the letters making up the names of two conspirators,

Fig. 40. Rebecca Stonier Plaisted, casket with scenes from the Old Testament, silk, satin weave, 1668

Catesby and Percy, which she made highly visible above the roof of Parliament. Thus Dorothy Selby joined in the Protestant patriotism reinforced by anti-papist satire and the denunciation of Catholic enemies to her state.

What did stitching such a picture mean in 1621, sixteen years after the Gunpowder Plot? It is highly likely that Selby's at-home stitchery, like Ward's print, was an intervention in contemporary politics, a critique of leanings toward Spain at court and the new specter of Catholicism triumphant in a royal marriage with Spain. Indeed, the Spanish Ambassador to James I complained about Ward's publication of the print, and Ward was arrested and imprisoned as a result.[79] Engraver and embroiderer alike were clearly taking the same side in the recycling of an earlier political crisis.

Selby's public-spirited needlework is celebrated on her monument in the village church, on which the design for her picture is carved. In a poem inscribed on the

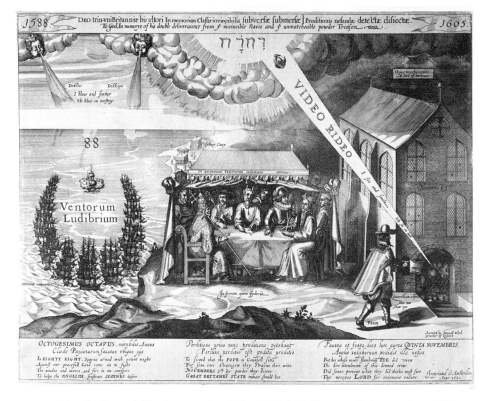

Fig. 41. Samuel Ward, engraving, "The Double Deliverance," Amsterdam, 1621

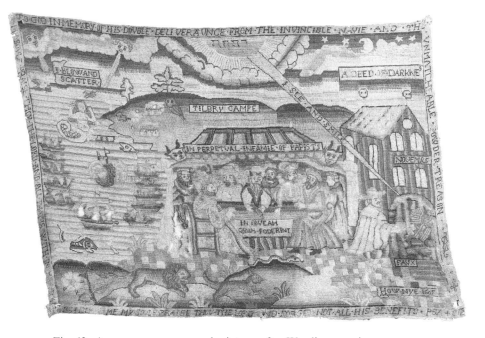

Fig. 42. Anonymous canvaswork picture, after Ward's engraving

stone, the stonecarver gave Dorothy Selby the name "Dorcas" after a New
Testament heroine, a Christian convert and maker "of coats and garments" (Acts 9:
36), and he collapsed the sewing/writing opposition by calling her needle "a steele
pen":

> She was a Dorcas,
> Whose curious Needle turn's the abused Stage
> Of this leud world into the Golden Age,
> Whose Pen of Steele and silken inck enroll'd
> The Acts of Jonah in Records of Gold.[80]
> Whose arte disclos'd that Plot which, had it taken,
> Rome had tryumph'd and Britain's walls had shaken.[81]

Commemorated as a needlewoman in an epitaph that also celebrated the defeat of
the Gunpowder Plot, Dorothy Selby broke down the private woman/public man
division not only during her life but after it had ended.

The Dutch print of the Double Deliverance interested another needlewoman, as
well, whose canvaswork picture based on Ward's design is now in the embroidery
collection of the Lady Lever Gallery in Port Sunlight, Cheshire (Fig. 42).[82] This
unknown woman's variations on the print take the image in a more popular and
more woman-focused direction. Making the meaning of the events more accessible,
she translated most of the Latin and Dutch, working an English "I see and smile"
into the ray from God's sun and rendering the Latin tag on the canopy above the
Fawkes conspirators as "In perpetual infamie of Papists." She also added a dark-
horned devil at each side of the roof and framed the piece on the left side and the
bottom with the opening verses from Psalm 103: "My soule praise thou the Lord
and all that is within me praise his holy name[;] my soule praise thou the Lord and
forget not all his benefits." And she added emblematic animals at the bottom of the
piece, where a lion (the English monarchy?) pursues a fox (punning on "Fawkes," or
"Faux," as Ward spells Fawkes's name, with a play on the French word for "false"),
itself pursuing a white lamb (Protestant innocence?).[83] This needlewoman also
considerably enlarged the small label "Tilbry Camp" above the conspirators' tent in
Ward's engraving. She gives her "Tilbry Campe" a full, hilly landscape that includes
an oak tree and an owl (Elizabeth's Minervan wisdom?); she identifies the site in
large letters emphasized by a white background and elaborates it with two military
tents. These added details may celebrate Queen Elizabeth's famous address to her
troops before the battle of the Armada, a high point of the female monarch's
visibility and power.[84]

Needlewomen positioned themselves on both sides of the Civil War. Given the
aristocratic status of many mid-seventeenth-century needleworkers, it is not surprising that their work sometimes declares Royalist loyalties more or less openly.
The caterpillars and butterflies so popular in sixteenth-century English stitchery
came to represent Charles, the son of the beheaded Charles I, whom Royalists
expected to bring the monarchy to life again.[85] Royalist needlewomen also celebrated the monarchy by working covers for mirror frames and caskets with portraits
of Charles I and Henrietta Maria and of Charles II and Catherine of Braganza. And
several caskets' interior representations of a peacock probably gave visual form to
the political vocabulary whereby loyalty to the martyred but to-be-resurrected king
was declared by swearing "by the Peacock."[86]

One Royalist Englishwoman materialized the desire for a restored monarchy by

Fig. 43. William Marshall, engraving, frontispiece of *Eikon Basilike*, 1649

juxtaposing two different public images circulating some time after 1649. She had seen an engraving by William Marshall, published by the supporters of Charles I immediately after his execution, an image that circulated widely on its own and later as the frontispiece to *Eikon Basilike, The Pourtraicture of his sacred Majestie in his Solitudes and Sufferings* (Fig. 43).[87] Marshall represents the king kneeling at an altar, taking the martyr's crown of thorns in his hands while he looks up to a heavenly crown and spurns the worldly crown inscribed with "Vanitas" at his foot. Outside the chapel, a palm tree, an emblem of the king, displays his motto, "Crescit sub pondere virtus" (Virtue grows by being weighed down); a smaller palm stands to the left. The embroiderer copied the scene of the king in the chapel onto the right side of her canvas, in a simplified form that emphasizes the three crowns (Fig. 44).[88] On the left, between two palm trees, she inserted a portrait of Charles II as a boy in armor, occupying the position of the central palm in the engraving so that he embodies royal virtue in a way that literally illustrates his replacement of his father. The caterpillar at his left has turned into the triumphant prince; two angels crown him. Three larger angels' heads and wings decorate the arches that unite the two scenes, so the framing of the royal pair asserts a divinely ordained succession from the dead king to the living prince. Picturing the Restoration on canvas, this

Fig. 44. Embroidered picture, silk on satin, *Charles I and Charles II*, after Marshall's engraving, c. 1650

needlewoman used silk and canvas to declare her participation in her fellow Royalists' vision of the future.

But needlework was also produced on the Parliamentarian side of the Civil War. In a raised-work picture worked by Damaris Pearse in the 1670s, the drowning of the Pharaoh in the Red Sea is vividly represented. Damaris, the daughter of a Nonconformist minister of Dover, was commemorated in a book published by her father in 1683, four years after she died at the age of twenty: *A Present for Youth and an Example for the Aged: or the Remains of Damaris Pearse*. The book praises her for her almost spontaneous learning, exhibited in both her needlework and her reading:

Concerning her endowments and attainments, besides her skill in, and her ingenious dexterity, ready invention, quick dispatch, and curious putting out of hand, the choicest sort of needleworks and most other kinds of fine work, such as young women are exercised in whether with silk, thread or other materials, so great variety, and plenty, and so excellently done, as is scarce credible of one so young, as when by her made and finished; and as in these, so she was skilled in writing (right spelling), reading, and of good understanding, and all learnt by little instruction.[89]

Damaris Pearse is presented as a model of balance between sewing and reading. Her father quotes her as saying, "I have many good books and I made many shifts (that is according to the flesh) to get them" (18). She probably meant shifts literally, that is, women's undergarments, smocks that she handworked for sale. Her father

Fig. 45. Damaris Pearse, silkwork on satin, *The Drowning of Pharaoh in the Red Sea*, c. 1670

Fig. 46. Gerard de Jode, *The Drowning of Pharaoh*, from *Thesaurus Sacrarum Historiarum Veteris Testamenti*, Antwerp, 1585

explains that his daughter "privately earned some small matter with her needle (when able) and it was to bestow it in books, as she did every penny thereof."

Damaris Pearse's reading predictably included the Old Testament. Her father quotes a comment she made on Exodus, on the passage in which Aaron, Moses's brother, departs from the commandment forbidding idols and makes a golden calf, to suggest that she brought egalitarian (and quite likely anti-monarchical) views to bear on her interpretations of the Bible:

> Once she talked long concerning the Israelite bondage in Egypt . . . As she proceeded besides other hints, she made some observation on Aarons making the Molten Calf, both condemning the sin, and likewise, showing how people now living should improve it, that it should teach all to be watchful against sin, not only in inferiors, but also those in high place and dignity: Considering what Aaron was, and yet how grievously he sinned. (66)

In this context, Xanthe Brooke convincingly suggests that Moses in the embroidery carries a political connotation familiar to anti-Royalist thinkers, who associated Moses with Cromwell.[90] Acccording to this logic, the drowning of Pharaoh alludes to the execution of Charles I, celebrated as the liberation of the true believers – the Israelites, understood as types of seventeenth-century supporters of the Commonwealth.

At the left in Damaris Pearse's picture, Aaron and Moses, pointing with his rod to heaven, look on as Pharaoh sinks in his chariot, drawn by two horses tossing their heads and gripped by helmeted soldiers, all surrounded by sinking pennants and weapons; at the lower left the Israelites celebrate their arrival on dry land (Fig. 45).[91] Damaris Pearse may have used a print from Gerard de Jode's collection of religious engravings as a model (Fig. 46).[92] Her bearded king's position, with arm stretched back, scepter held at an angle, and upflung foot, resembles the pose of de Jode's pharaoh, and the positions of her horses' heads also resemble his. But Pearse's pharaoh is dressed in Renaissance clothes, and she adds a wealth of everyday social detail: packages and barrels of goods float in her sea, in addition to shields and quivers for arrows. She increases the number of the defeated enemy, too. To de Jode's three soldiers, she adds five: two at one horse's head, one directly behind the chariot, one holding onto it, one floating face up; at the right, further off, standards with banners are held by drowning soldiers and a charioteer. Pearse's Parliamentarian loyalties may explain why her pharaoh is less classically ennobled than de Jode's and why her version emphasizes how many men were punished alongside the evil ruler.

Renaissance women whose needlework has been preserved, then, refused to be enclosed in a realm of anonymous private handiwork. They turned the habit of domestic stitchery into a public practice, recording their engagement with one another and communicating their responses to the larger world of culture, commodities and politics. In worked texts they recorded their ingenuity, their reading, their collaboration and their loyalties to causes beyond their families and houses. They plied the needle to materialize their views of the world and to be remembered as makers of objects that commemorated themselves, their families and their country's triumphs.

Needlework as a record of women's resistance to histories that obliterate them is at the center of a scene in Beaumont and Fletcher's play, *The Maids Tragedy*. In the second act, Aspatia, a woman disappointed in love, says to her lady-in-waiting Antiphila, "Show me the peece of needle worke you wrought."[93] Antiphila, it turns out, has been stitching a picture of Ariadne, abandoned by Theseus. Aspatia tells her to represent the Ovidian tale differently, to depict the shipwreck that Theseus ought to have suffered: "in this place worke a quick-sand, / And over it a shallow smiling water." Antiphila protests, "Twill wrong the storie." To this Aspatia replies that the story should be told more truly, that is, with a more just ending than the Ovidian tale, which follows Theseus on to further triumphs and, like him, abandons Ariadne on her island. Antiphila's revisionary needlewrought narrative "will make the story wronged by wanton Poets, / Live long and be beleev'd." Then, shifting from the hero of the story to the heroine, Aspatia asks, "where's the Lady?" We have been arguing that the lady is everywhere: in needleworked clothing, cushions, furnishings, wall hangings, and table pictures. Needlewomen clothed themselves, their intimate furnishings, and their public spaces with textiles that challenge any simple opposition between public and private, the domestic and the political, material labor and "immaterial" memory.

Part 3
Staging clothes

7   The circulation of clothes and the making of the English theater[1]

Alice had once described a play to him in which several actresses shared the role of
the heroine. After half an hour the powerful matriarch removed her large coat from
which animal pelts dangled and she passed it, along with her strength, to one of the
minor characters. In this way even a silent daughter could put on the cloak and be
able to break through the chrysalis into language. Each person had their moment
when they assumed the skins of wild animals, when they took responsibility for the
story.   Michael Ondaatje, *In the Skin of a Lion*[2]

Liveried servants

Professional actors, those most notorious of shape-shifters, were also liveried
members of aristocratic households.[3] James I's household included the King's Men,
the theatrical company to which Shakespeare belonged, and each member of the
company received every second year at Easter a livery consisting of three yards of
bastard scarlet for a cloak and a quarter yard of crimson velvet for a cape. In 1627,
the allowance for the cloak was increased from three to four yards, although it
remained only three for the Queen's Men until 1630.[4] At one level, this livery was
something of a legal fiction. Shakespeare's company was hardly a regular part of the
royal household, and its sharers earned their most significant income from the public
and private playhouses of the suburbs and the City of London. As John Stephens
said in his portrait of "A common Player," "howsoever he pretends to haue a royall
Master, or Mistresse, his wages and dependance proue him to bee the servant of the
people."[5] But legal fictions are never mere fictions. In being given royal livery, the
King's Men were given protection from the City fathers, who were constantly
troubled by the civil disturbances, the economic disruption, and the immorality
which they attributed to this new industry.[6]

The London professional theater was situated at the juncture of the court and the
city guilds, although both literally and symbolically at a distance from both. If the
actors' survival depended upon their incorporation as liveried servants, the theaters
also utilized the guild system. The training of boy actors, as Stephen Orgel has
argued, depended upon an apprentice system, and since there was no theatrical
guild, at least some of the shareholders of the company had to gain or retain
membership of other guilds so as to act as masters to the young apprentices.[7] This
meant that, from a legal point of view, the boy actors were not theatrical trainees
but apprentice bricklayers, butchers, drapers, goldsmiths, and so on.

At the same time, playwrights and actors alike were drawn into the elaborate
pageants of the guilds. Their presence was particularly striking in the Drapers'
Company, for whom Anthony Munday wrote *Metropolis Coronata*, Thomas

Middleton *Sun in Aries*, *The Triumph of Integrity*, and *The Triumph of Health and Prosperity*, and Thomas Heywood *Porta Pietatis* and *Londini Status Pacatus*. Munday and Middleton are both referred to on title pages as Drapers. Munday also wrote *The Triumphs of Reunited Britannia* and *Troia Nova Triumphans* for the Merchant Taylors, for whom John Webster wrote *Monuments of Honour*. On the title page of *Monuments of Honour*, Webster is described as himself a Merchant Taylor.[8]

Webster had been admitted to the Merchant Taylors company through patrimony, his father having been a member, and his brother Edward was also apprenticed to the company.[9] Webster's own estimate of the significance of the Merchant Taylors pageant in 1624 may be inferred both from the fact that its elaborate costumes and staging meant that it cost "at least ten times all the sum of [his] previous productions" and from its title-page motto, which he had quoted several times before but never in relation to his own work: "*Non norunt haec monumenta mori*" ("these monuments do not know how to die").[10] Like Middleton, Munday, and Heywood, Webster was proudly and actively involved in one of the guilds associated with the clothing trade.

The theaters incorporated the contradictory implications of household and guild livery. To the theater's critics, though, it was only in so far as the actors were absorbed by their livery into aristocratic households that they could be deemed worthy of respect. John Stow wrote in his *Annales* for the year 1583:

Comedians and stage-players of former time were very poore and ignorant in respect of these of this time, but being now grown very skilfull and exquisite actors for all matters, they were entertained into the service of great lords, out of which companies were xii of the best chosen at the request of Sir Francis Walsingham, they were sworne the Queenes servants, and were allowed wages and liveries as groomes of the chamber.[11]

Actors, in other words, were not attacked for their servitude but for their liberties. In so far as they were perceived as "free" men, they were imagined as dangerously transgressive vagrants. Above all, they were attacked for *shifting* liveries.

The theater and the clothes trade

To shift clothes, the actors had to have clothes. Theatrical historians have drawn attention to the extraordinarily lavish outlay on costumes. Our suggestion, which will no doubt seem counter-intuitive, is that the commercial theater was crucially shaped by the market in clothes. Or, to put it another way, the theater was a new and spectacular development of the clothing trade.

The centrality of clothes to the medieval guild theater that preceded the professional playhouse has become increasingly apparent in recent years through the publication of the *Records of Early English Drama*.[12] The guilds paid for costumes to be made; they rented them out, stored them, repaired them, dismantled them and reused the cloth for new costumes. In Coventry, the Weavers' Rentgatherers' Book for 1564 records: "Item paid for settyng one of Ihesus sleues ijd"; "Item paid for solyng of Iesus hose jd"; the Drapers' Accounts for 1563 records: "Itm payde for a Coate for god and for A peyre of gloues ffor hym iijs"; "Itm payde for blacckyng of the Sowles facys vjd."[13] On January 3, the Cappers made an inventory of their costumes and properties. A striking feature of these lists is the way in which the costumes take on a life of their own. God or the Holy Ghost, as much as Adam or Eve, take on a local habitation and a name as a coat, a glove, a beard:

Itm pylates dublit ij curtaynes the spirate of godes cote godes cotes and the hose pylates heade fyve maries heades one coyffe mary maudlynes goune iij beardes gods head the spirites heade sixe pensils iiij Rolles iij marye boxes one play boke.
    The giandes head and clubbe pylates clubbe hell mowth iiij standynge iij small stremars adams spade Ives distaffe ij angels awbes one dore for a seate.[14]

Beyond any particular performance, the specific items of costume retain not only a specific and enduring financial value (which is carefully noted), but also the vivifying magic which attaches both to a theatrical part and to the figure which the part embodies.

It is because the costume can endure after the performance is ended that it can take a curious precedence over the actor, as if through the donning of a costume the actor puts on Christ, or Satan, or a Roman soldier, or whomever. Indeed, the guild accounts suggest the ability of the clothes to absorb the very identity of the actors. Sometimes, it is true, we find records like these, from the 1584 Smiths' Accounts, paying for a production of the *Destruction of Jerusalem*: "to Jhon Bonde for playenge of Justus, Ananus, Eliazar and the Chorus, vj s viij d . . . to Jhon Hoppers for playenge of Jesus and Zacharyas, iij s."[15] Here, it is the actual labor practices of the guild members which are attended to. John Bond, who doubles in four parts, is paid 6s. 6d.; John Hopper, who doubles in two, is only paid 3s., despite the fact that one of his roles is Christ. But it is equally common to find records in which the money is paid to what we would think of as a part rather than a person. Thus, the Chester records of the Smiths, Cutlers, and Plumbers for Midsummer 1575 record payments to "litle god" of 20d. and to "oure marye" of 18d.; and the Coventry accounts of the Drapers in 1572 record: "pd to god iijs iiijd."[16] More complexly, the Coventry Smiths' accounts of 1499 record money paid "to Dame Percula for *his* wages" and "to pylatts wyffe for *his* wages," the formulation insisting both upon the absorption of the actor into the costume and upon the distance between male actor and female costume.[17]

The extraordinary expense and care given to clothes suggests that the guild theatricals that both preceded and were contemporary with the professional theaters were crucially concerned with the making and maintenance of costumes. What we argue here is that the professional London companies were equally organized around costumes, costumes that were now part of a more general circulation of clothing.

For such an argument to be plausible, it is first necessary to understand the value of clothes. Costumes were often the most expensive part of a production. As G. E. Bentley puts it:

Every new play was a gamble; it might fail miserably and the sum paid its author would constitute a total loss for the company. A fine costume, on the other hand, could be used for years and for many different plays, whether the production for which it had originally been purchased was a long-running success or a complete failure.[18]

In other words, in contrast to our retrospective view, clothes retained their value better than plays. New plays cost twice as much to see on opening nights, and though old plays were constantly restaged, comparatively large sums of money were spent to rewrite them and keep them up to date. Although clothes needed care and alteration, the materials themselves retained much of their value.

Clothes were an enormous investment. As Bentley notes, "the greatest expense of any company of players in the period was the purchase of costumes."[19] A play usually cost about £6, although the cost varied and was gradually pushed up in the seventeenth century. By comparison, Edward Alleyn lists a single, admittedly expensive "black velvet cloak with sleeves embroidered all with silver and gold" as costing £20. 10s. 6d.[20] S. P. Cerasano, drawing on E. K. Chambers's calculations, notes that "the contents of the tiring house of the Rose Playhouse . . . seem to have been worth as much, or slightly more than the cost of the playhouse itself."[21]

Because of the value of their clothes, the professional companies employed specialists, in the form of tiremen and wardrobe keepers, to look after them. In 1634, Thomas Crosfield recorded in his diary that the company at Salisbury Court had seven sharers and two "clothes keepers," Richard Kendall and Antony Dover, and one of the boys' companies seems also to have had two clothes keepers in the early seventeenth century.[22] The clothes keepers were usually tailors or apprentices to tailors, and no doubt they altered, mended, and sometimes made the costumes. Significant sums could be spent on mending alone. In July 1601, Philip Henslowe paid out 6s. 7d. to repair a tawny coat "which was eatten with the Rattes."[23] In addition to the clothes-keepers, Henslowe "apointed a man to the seeinge of his accomptes in byinge of Clothes (hee beinge to have vi^s. a weeke)."[24] And Henslowe also made independent payments on behalf of the actors to tailors, mercers, a milliner, lacemakers, and a "sylke man."[25] In other words, a labor force grew up around the theater because of the value of its clothes.

The scale of that value is suggested by Andrew Gurr, who writes:

A pair of silk stockings might cost £2 or £4, depending on quality and purchaser. A woman's gown might cost anything from £7 to £20 or more. The Earl of Leicester paid £543 for seven doublets and two cloaks, at an average cost for each item rather higher than the price Shakespeare paid for a house in Stratford.[26]

Gurr's comparative figures are staggering. Whatever we might think about the price of an Armani suit, we could not equate its cost with the price of a house. We should not be surprised, then, that Sir Thomas Cullum spent an average of £77 a year on clothes for his family and servants between 1624 and 1641, more than his average yearly rent and more than twice as much as his average for other "household stuff."[27] Edward Alleyn, having made his fortune in the theater, spent an average of £11 a year on apparel between 1618 and 1622, and in the latter year he spent the immense sum of £78. 18s. 8 1/2 d. on clothes.[28]

The above accounts are, of course, of aristocrats and wealthy entrepreneurs. But Margaret Spufford notes how carefully even peasants and artisans itemized their clothes. In 1599, Richard Linge, a Norfolk chapman, had his clothes valued as follows: two cloaks (an old one at 6s. 8d.; one with broad buttons at £1); three pairs of breeches at 2s. each; hose, doublet, and jerkin, at £1; two pairs of stockings, each at 4d.; two shirts at 1s. 6d. each (this included two old-fashioned ruffs and two falling bands); two nightcaps at 2d. each. Some of these sums are small, but the chapman's best cloak and his hose, doublet, and jerkin would represent significant outlays for a servant being paid an annual salary of £2.[29]

The extraordinary value that the clothes of even relatively modest citizens might have in the Renaissance is suggested by the 1623 inventory of Vermeer's parents. Vermeer's father was a caffa worker by profession, caffa being an expensive silk-satin fabric. John Montias writes:

[Their] clothing, as usual in those days, was very expensive. Reynier and his wife Digna each owned eight shirts valued at twenty-four guilders; a mantle priced at thirty-six guilders; Digna's hooded cape at thirty-six guilders; a silk apron at thirty-six guilders; a satin bodice at twenty guilders; and a few more ordinary items. The real magnitude of these prices may be gauged from the fact that apprentices and journeymen, who made up the bulk of the population, earned on an average less than one guilder a day.[30]

From the full inventory of Vermeer's parents, we can draw the following, to us surprising, scale of value: 19 paintings were worth less than 8 pairs of sheets and 2 green curtains; the 8 sheets and 2 curtains were worth less than a silk apron and a satin bodice; and the apron and bodice were worth more than a workman's wages for 56 days.[31]

The value of clothes meant that the lives and deaths of theatrical companies were often dependent upon the accumulation and dispersal of costumes. When Francis Langley built the Swan in 1586, he spent £300 on new apparel for his players. Henslowe established Worcester's Men at his new theater, the Fortune, in 1600 by advancing them money for apparel and playbooks.[32] And when Henry Evans established a second boys' company at the Blackfriars, he joined up with Edward Kirkham, Yeoman of the Revels and in charge of the Revels wardrobe, to supply him with clothes, and he later paid out £200 for apparel.[33] If companies collapsed, they made what they could by selling their costumes. Pembroke's Men were in trouble in 1593, so they sold costumes to the value of £80, which was divided among the six sharers. When Lady Elizabeth's Men fell out with Henslowe in 1615, the financial wrangling particularly concerned costumes and cloth. Henslowe was accused of having sold "tenn poundes worth of ould apparrell" that was the company's; of having valued apparel bought from one Rosseter at £63 when it was really only worth £40; of having held onto arras curtains for which the company had paid £40. Similarly Christopher Beeston was accused during the breakup of the Queen's Players in 1617 of embezzling costumes, selling some to other companies, and converting others to his own use.[34]

One role of the theaters in the circulation of clothes is suggested by the 1635 will of John Shank, one of the King's Men. Shank begins his will by asserting his double life as actor and as guild member: he is both "one of his Majesties servants the Players" and a "Cittizen and weaver of London." And he requires the company to give his widow £50 for his share of the costumes and books as well as to repay "Sixteene Pounds and Twelve shillings which they owe mee for Two gownes."[35] To run a theater was not only to build playhouses but also to own, lend, and sell costumes or to lend the money with which to acquire them.

We note further the striking connections between the theater and the clothing industry. John Rastell (1475–1536) was the owner of a theater and of clothes for hire, as well as being a stationer, a playwright and a printer.[36] Francis Langley, who built the Swan, was a member of the Drapers' Company, and in 1585 he was appointed as alnager to the Court of Aldermen to check the quality, size, and weight of woolen cloth.[37] Philip Henslowe was a member of the Dyers' Company when he financed the building of the Rose in 1587 and the Fortune in 1600. He also manufactured starch and worked as a pawnbroker. Shakespeare had complex familial and professional ties to the cloth trade. His father was a glover and "also bought and sold wool on a large scale."[38] It is further worth noting that the first attempt at a "collected" edition of Shakespeare was made by Thomas Pavier in 1619: Pavier was originally a draper, who, along with eleven other drapers (two of whom also published plays by Shakespeare), was translated into the Stationers' Company in 1600.[39] The retail of books and of cloth overlapped in interesting ways.

But it was clothing, not the stationers' trade, that was central to the putting on of plays. We learn about Rastell's wardrobe from his prosecution of his former friend, Henry Walton, in the 1520s. Rastell, who owned a stage at Finsbury, had a collection of clothes worth twenty marks, he claimed, including "a player's garment of green sarcenet lined with red tuke and with roman letters stitched upon it of blue and red sarcenet lined with red buckram," a garment "for a priest to play in," and "a garment of red and green Say, paned and guarded with gold skins, and fustians of Naples black, and sleeved with red, green, yellow, and blue sarcenet." Rastell left these clothes with Walton when he traveled to Europe. When he returned, he discovered that Walton had "let out the the same garments to hire to stage-plays and interludes sundry times" ("above three or four score times") and had made considerable money. Rastell claimed that the clothes had been damaged in the process. Walton responded that the clothes were already "worn and torn players' garments." The details of each and every garment were presented in court. Whatever the rights and wrongs of the case, the fundamental economic significance of clothes to Rastell's theater is striking. Such clothes were worth an extended legal battle.[40]

Actors both off and on the stage were, indeed, noted for the splendor of their clothes. That is the point of the prologue to Henry Medwall's *Fulgens and Lucres*, which John Rastell published c.1515. "A" thinks that "B" is "oon / Of them that shall play" by his "apparell." He is wrong only because now gallants wear as "nyce aray" as actors.[41] Rastell in fact had practical knowledge of the economic relations between the writing of plays and the materials of their performance. In 1527, he was employed (together with Holbein) to devise a pageant for the French ambassadors. He was paid a modest 3s. 4d. for writing the interlude of *Love and Riches* and Mercury's Latin address to the king, but he was paid the substantial fee of £26. 9s. 11d. for his designs for the pageant.[42]

In the actors' calculus of profit and loss, they had to work out how much they could afford to spend for magnificent apparel which might lead to a runaway success but which might also land them in deep debt. On the other hand, if they didn't spend enough on costumes, they were in danger of undermining one form of the magic upon which theatrical profits depended. By all accounts, Fletcher's *The Faithful Shepherdess* was a flop when it was first staged. But when it was put on over twenty years later at Somerset House before Charles and Henrietta Maria, its success seems partly attributable to "the clothes the Queen had given Taylor the year before of her own pastoral."[43] Costumes that had been seen too often, though, could bring a masque, in which novelty and surprise were at a premium, into disfavor. The Office of the Revels made an inventory of masquing costumes and of materials that had already been "often translated" into different costumes. Many were finally retired from service both because they were "forworne" and because they were "to[o] much knowen."[44] The masque that Francis Bacon paid for Gray's Inn and the Inner Temple to stage for James on February 18, 1613 was, Chamberlain thought, likely to be a flop when it was restaged. The first performance had been cancelled shortly after it had begun because the king was tired, "[b]ut the grace of their masque is quite gone when their apparel hath been already showed and their devices vented, so that how it will fall out God knows, for they are much discouraged and out of countenance."[45]

After the Restoration, John Downes's records suggest that splendor of costumes might take precedence over a company's acting skills: *The Adventures of Five Hours* was "Cloath'd so Excellently Fine in proper Habits," and only secondarily "Acted so justly well." Companies, though, had to work out a balance between staging new costumes to draw spectators and saving expenses by drawing upon stock. And Downes suggests how delicate that balance was. *Ulysses*, being "all new Cloath'd, and Excellently well perform'd," had "a Successful run" and thus presumably recouped the investment in the costumes. On the other hand, *Iphigenia*, "a good Tragedy and well Acted," "answer'd not the Expences they were at in Cloathing it." Similarly, *The Fairy Queen*, for which new clothes, scenes and music cost the staggering sum of £3,000, was well received "but the Expences in setting it out being so great, the Company got very little by it."[46]

The economic calculations on good box-office receipts meant that companies needed at times to risk large investments in clothes. We can trace some of these investments in Henslowe's accounts. In November 1602, for instance, Henslowe lent John Duke £5 for the making of a single satin suit for *Lady Jane*.[47] When the Admiral's Men staged the first part of *Cardinal Wolsey*, Henslowe paid out £35 for costumes and other properties, and he paid another £11. 6s. for costumes for the second part. The black satin suit bought for £5. 2s. for the performance of *2 Black Dog of Newgate* by Worcester's Men was perhaps not serviceable when they staged *A Woman Killed with Kindness*, for which they bought another black satin suit for 10s. as well as a woman's black velvet gown for £6. 13s.

Given the cost of clothes, the restaging of an old play saved very little if it required new costumes. When the Admiral's Men purchased the previously performed *Vayvode* in 1598–9, new apparel cost them £17. 4s. And Worcester's Men, restaging the Admiral's Men's *Sir John Oldcastle* in 1602–3, paid 50s. for revisions to the play but £15. 10s. for new costumes.[48] Like the Office of the Revels, Henslowe records many of the textiles that the companies buy for costumes. He lends money for them to buy 8 yards of cloth of gold; to buy taffeta and tinsel for a woman's gown and for making a bodice and a pair of sleeves; for taffeta and satin; for "lace" (mainly copper); to buy satin to make two doublets; to make coats for giants. And he lends money to pay the bills of the lace man and the tailors.[49] The theaters, as capitalist investors in the clothing trade, were a contributing factor to the extraordinary growth of the fashion industry from the mid-sixteenth century to the early seventeenth century.

Secondhand clothes and the theater

The players were crucially dependent upon the accumulation and circulation of clothes. But where did they get their clothes? Recent theater historians have tended to minimize Henslowe's career as a pawnbroker and as a dealer in secondhand clothes.[50] There has been a concerted attempt to rescue Henslowe from the contempt with which he was treated in the nineteenth century. Fleay, for instance, attacked Henslowe for his "selfish hand-to-mouth policy" and described him as a "pawnbroking, stage-managing, bear-baiting usurer."[51] But the modern "rescuing" mission of Henslowe rests, we suggested in chapter 1, on a misunderstanding of the crucial role that pawnbroking and the trade in clothes and jewels played for rich and poor alike before the advent of modern banking systems.

The suggestion, for instance, that Henslowe's pawnbroking business was a form of charity goes against all the evidence.[52] Civic pawnbroking "charities" did indeed exist in Italy, as a direct consequence of the anti-semitic diatribes of Franciscan preachers.[53] But even in Italy, where these "charities" were intended at first for the relief of the poor, they came with greater or lesser rapidity to be used by every class of society and by the governing bodies themselves. Jews had been officially expelled from England in 1290, and pawnbroking and moneylending were largely practiced by English gentiles or (on a larger scale) by Lombards. (Lombard Street, right at the financial heart of the City of London, recalls their earlier presence). The Lombards in fact set up businesses all over Europe. It may be the relative lack of a Jewish presence in England that prevented the establishment of "charities" like the *Monte di Pietà*, as there was less focus for the violent anti-semitic discourse that led to the founding of "charitable" civic pawnbrokers in Italy. No such charities were established in England.

We should not be surprised that Henslowe rarely mentions the interest he charges, given that the rates of usury had been set at 10 percent by the Act Against Usury of 1571.[54] That Henslowe *did* charge interest is clear. Neil Carson's claim that "there is no suggestion that [Henslowe] was guilty of usury" rests, we believe, upon a misunderstanding.[55] Any rate over 10 percent was considered usurious, even if pawnbroking was not officially covered by the 1571 Act. And it is clear that Henslowe was charging interest rates of 40 to 300 percent and more on a regular basis. The smaller the pledge, the higher the rate of interest. He charged 8d. a month (8s. a year) on a loan of 2s. 6d. for two coarse smocks (over 300 percent a year); but he charged the same 8d. a month for a gown valued at 10s. (80 percent a year), for a bible and ten pieces of linen valued at 10s. (80 percent a year), and for eleven pieces of a child's bed-linen valued at 20s. (40 percent a year). An interest rate of about 40 percent may have been average for pledges of £1 and over: Henslowe charged 14d. a month for clothes valued at 33s. 2d., and 9d. a month for clothes valued at 22s. 8d.[56] Henslowe, then, was undoubtedly charging usurious rates, even if these were the rates at which pawnbrokers typically operated.

The second reason for minimizing the significance of Henslowe's trade in second-hand clothes arose from the attempt to distinguish "clothes" from "costumes."[57] The distinction has been motivated partly by the surviving drawing of *Titus Andronicus*, partly by the players' inventories, and partly by a reaction to the assumption that the professional actors wore *only* contemporary dress. It is true that the *Titus* drawing depicts Titus in tunic, toga, and sandals, while the Goths appear in a version of Roman dress. But, as Susan Cerasano notes, there is no one style of dress in the drawing. Tamora's gown is similar to women's gowns of the 1590s, while Titus's sons (if that is who they are) wear contemporary clothes. The drawing depicts a "medley," that, as Cerasano persuasively argues, is partly determined by economics.[58] Only a few new clothes could be afforded for each new production, others being drawn from stock.

We would question whether many plays (as opposed to masques) required special *costumes* as opposed to special clothes. The complaints against the actors repeatedly refer to the splendor of their dress, or at least to their simulated splendor, not to their exoticism. And the theatrical inventories record all the usual items of contemporary dress: gowns, women's gowns, cloaks, doublets, jerkins, bodices, shirts, farthingales, breeches, venetians, French hose, stockings. The "foreign" fashions in the inventories are usually French, Spanish, and Italian – in other words, the "foreign" fashions that were an established part of London tailoring. There are important exceptions, as in the suites of plays on Robin Hood, or on "paynims," or on classical myth, or on classical history, or plays set in Asia. But even here, new costumes had to be mixed with the existing stock of clothes. In *Julius Caesar*, as Cerasano notes, Casca refers to Caesar's doublet (1. 2. 265 [TLN 369]). Certainly, as we argued above, specific costumes could take on a specific name and character: Tamberlaine's coat with copper lace; Vortigern's robe of rich taffeta; Henry V's velvet gown and his satin doublet embroidered with gold lace; a russet cloak with copper lace "called Guydoes clocke"; Robin Hood's suit; one green gown for Maryan; a bodice for Alice Pierce; Longshank's suit; Juno's coat; Dido's robe.[59] But this needs to be set against the piecemeal nature of Renaissance clothing. The actors again and again took existing clothes and "translated" them.

There was an important element of continuity, in other words, between the clothes trade in general and the players' wardrobes.[60] And in his business with the players, Henslowe profited both directly and indirectly from the trade in clothes. In the grievances of Lady Elizabeth's Men, probably dating from 1615, the players complained that Henslowe had retained ownership of their costumes and playbooks as securities for the money he had lent them. In other words, his relation to them was that of a pawnbroker, lending money upon the security of pledges. The players calculated that they would be able to pay off their debt over a period of three years, but, they claimed, Henslowe had deliberately broken up the company before they could repay him, so as to keep the stock of clothes and playbooks.[61]

If Henslowe made most of his money from the theater by renting the buildings themselves and by taking a share of the profits, there is one record that shows that he was also capable of charging interest upon costumes. On 6 December 1602, Henslowe bought four cloaks for Worcester's Men for £4 each. He charged the company 5s. interest for each cloak, so that he made a profit of £1 on the deal.[62] It may be true, as Carson claims, that this was an unusual charge, but, given what we noted about the questionable legality of high interest rates above, we should recall that Henslowe usually concealed the interest he charged. Another garment for which it seems that Henslowe was charging interest was "a damaske casock garded with velvet" which he records buying for 18s. in his "Note of all suche goodes as I have bought for the Companey of my *Lord Admirals men*, since the 3 of Aprell, 1598." On 7 April 1598 he "Lent vnto the company to by a damask cassocke garded wth velluet," which must surely be the same garment. But now he bills the company for 20s., making a profit of 2s. or 10 percent.[63]

The list of the goods that Henslowe bought for the company after 3 April, 1598 suggests that he was working as a fripper or secondhand clothes dealer. The clothes are fully made-up, which means that, with the possible exception of a pair of woolen stockings, they are secondhand. The list also shows that he was buying clothes for the company on a larger scale than his *Diary* records. There are 18 items of clothing on the list, 9 bought from Henslowe's son-in-law, Edward Alleyn. Of the 18 items, only the damask cassock is clearly identifiable from his other accounts as one that he lent the company money to buy. Two other garments have possible matches in Henslowe's diary. But Henslowe is also spending substantial sums on clothes for the company of which no account remains. Somewhere between the purchase and their theatrical use, the clothes disappear from the records, so it is perhaps appropriate that one of the garments was "a robe for to goo invisbell," bought, together with a "gown for Nembia," for £3. 10s. The clothes in all cost £53. 11s., but we don't know how frequently Henslowe was making such purchases.

As contemporary comments show, secondhand clothes dealers and pawnbrokers constantly overlapped. Frippers or fripperers, dealing in cast-off apparel, were not clearly distinguished from brokers in the Renaissance. Francis Bacon, attacking the transmission of knowledge through "impostures" and "counterfeit merchandises," compares the mass of words that Lully uses to "a fripper's or broker's shop, that hath ends of everything, but nothing of worth."[64] George Whetstone rebukes "idle persons" who pledge "their owne or their maisters apparell" at "Brokers, or fripperers" for a shilling in the pound every month. Whetstone goes on to claim that there are "two or three of these pettie brokers, or *cherish-theeues*" in "euerie streate and lane" in London.[65] And John Florio defines a *recateria* as "a fripperie or brokers shop" and a *recatière* as "a fripper, a broker."[66]

In *Your Five Gallants*, the pawnbroker is given the name of Fripper, while the character named "Fripper" in Chapman's *Monsieur D'Olive* describes his trade as "*Fripperie . . .* or as some tearme it, *Petty Brokery.*" Part of the trade of Chapman's Fripper is said to be burning gold lace so as to regain its metal content. To D'Olive, frippery and broking are interchangeable professions: "Farwell *Fripper*, Farewell *Pettie Broker.*" D'Olive assumes that Fripper wants to become his follower because "the Vulture smels a pray":

not the Carcases, but the Cases of some of my deceassed Followers; S'light, I thinke it were my wisest course, to put tenne pounds in stocke with him, and turne pettie Broker . . . [I]f we be but a day or two out of towne heele be able to load euerie day a fresh Horse with Satten suites, and send them backe hither.[67]

Like usurers and brokers, frippers were treated with ambivalence at best. The "frippery" they sold assumed antithetical meanings: showy finery, and even fashionable dress; worthless trumpery and trash. Ambivalence towards frippery rubbed off on the players, who mingled new finery and cast-off clothing, gold lace and copper lace.

Henslowe himself was, we suggest, both fripper and pawnbroker. And while he lent the companies money for the buying of costumes, he also, at least with Lady Elizabeth's Men, kept effective control of those costumes. Was this true of his earlier relations with the Admiral's Men? In March 1598, Henslowe and his son-in-law, Edward Alleyn, made inventories of the costumes and properties belonging to the Admiral's Men.[68] To us, they look like impressive lists, including "13 doublets, 10 suits, 4 jerkins, 20 gowns, 25 capes, and 23 coats."[69] But what is striking about the inventories, as Neil Carson has observed, is that "the Company maintained a surprisingly *small* stock" (our emphasis).[70] There is, for instance, no trace of many of the costumes which, according to Henslowe's records, he had officially lent money to the company for them to buy. What happened to them? The sharers occasionally divided the clothes among themselves, and they could then resell them, rent them out, or pawn them. As we noted above, Christopher Beeston was accused of appropriating company costumes. The actor Thomas Downton also pawned two cloaks, which may or may not have been his own, and Henslowe lent him £12. 10s. to get them out of pawn.[71]

One possible explanation for the disappearing costumes is that the company sold the clothes back to Henslowe when they had no further use for them or when they were in financial difficulties. This would explain the puzzling records of September 1602, when Henslowe estimated that the players owed him £718. 12s. 10d., a truly fabulous sum of money, and one that we have no reason to believe the players could pay. At Christmas, Henslowe scaled down his estimate to £226. 16s. 8d. and an extra £50 lent to Jones and Shaa. And finally, less than a year later, Henslowe claims that he had discharged all his debts except for £24.[72] Carson speculates that the players sold their costumes to raise cash but it is equally possible that the debt was never a real one in the first place. Instead, to avoid the charge of lending illegally at usurious rates, Henslowe could have lent money for the companies to "buy" clothes which he nevertheless expected to be returned to him. While the clothes were in the actors' possession, he could charge them to their account for fear of loss through damage, theft, or fire, in which case the company would be accountable. But if the costumes were returned, the debt would be cancelled. This is undoubtedly a speculative explanation. What is *not* speculative is that the theaters, like the society as a whole, turned money into clothes and clothes back into money, using textiles, jewelry, and trimming as economic currency.

Henslowe lent money both for materials to make costumes (and to pay tailors) and for specific items of clothing. Here are two consecutive records that give a sense of the difference between the two kinds of entry:

Lent vnto Thomas dowton the 31 of Janeway 1598 *to bye tafetie for ij womones gownes* for the ij angrey wemen of abengton the some of . . . . ix li

Layd owt for the company the 1 of febreyare 1598 to bye *A blacke velluet gercken layd thicke wth blacke sylke lace & A payer of Rownd hosse of paynes of sylke layd wth sylver lace and caneyanes of clothe of sylver* at the Requeste of Robart shawe the some of . . . .iiij li x s[73]

What are we to make of this distinction between lending money for *textiles* (taffeta) and for buying *clothes* (a black velvet jerkin with black silk lace, etc.)? The crucial point is that there were virtually no ready-made clothes in Renaissance England (except for certain forms of underwear, stockings, and some loose gowns). Named pieces of clothing like the jerkin and the canions above are almost certainly *second-hand* clothes.

It's just possible that the company went to great lengths to describe a garment to Henslowe that they wanted to make up or had already made up. But that seems unlikely, particularly in view of the repeated emphasis on the theaters' secondhand clothing in plays, pamphlets, and satires. Henslowe was lending money not only for new fabrics but also for a wide variety of made-up, that is, secondhand, clothes: an embroidered waistcoat; "a flame coler satten dublett"; a long, tawny cloak made of wool; a white satin doublet; a damask cassock with a decorative border of velvet; a pair of hose, decorated with bugles [ornamental glass beads], paned with cloth of silver; a rich cloak from "mr. langley."[74] These clothes could scarcely be described so specifically unless they were already made up, which suggests that they were secondhand.

Henslowe also records two kinds of clothing purchase which are more difficult to interpret. First, he lends money on occasions when it is not at all clear whether the clothes are to be made up or to be purchased secondhand, for instance "to by a sewte and a gowne" or "to bye wemenes gown[s] and other thinges." Second, Henslowe records payments for the translation of old clothes through the addition of other (new or old?) materials, as when he lends money for two skirts of white satin to be made into a woman's gown, decorated with white lace, or for the cloth of a silver skirt to be translated into a woman's gown.[75]

At the same time, Henslowe bought and sold clothes and jewels directly to the players and to the theater companies, as well as to others. The theatrical materials he bought included copper lace for 10s. 8d. and a short velvet cloak embroidered with bugles for £3. He sold the same short velvet cloak to the Admiral's Men. He also sold "A manes gowne of Pechecoler In grayne" for £3 to Richard Jones; "a manes gowne of purpell coller cloth faced wth conney & layd on the sleues wth buttenes" for £2. 3s. 4d. to James Donstall; a black cloak embroidered with silk lace for £1. 6s. 8d. to Thomas Towne; a pair of crimson silk stockings for £1. 4s. to Thomas Downton; one pound and two ounces of copper lace for 14s. to Richard Bradshaw; a gold jewel for 8s. (to be paid for at the rate of 6d. for the first five weeks, 12d. for the sixth and seventh weeks, and 2s. for the eighth week) to William Sly; a doublet, venetians and biliment lace (a kind of lace braid) for 16s. to Steven Maget, the tireman for the Admiral's Men, and, on a later occasion, a cloak of sad green for 18s.; his "owne" clothes (probably unredeemed pledges, given that they included not only venetian hose, fustian breeches, and a doublet, but also a kirtle and a woman's gown) for £3. 17s. to Goody Watson, one of his pawnbroking agents. And he also sold clothing materials to Richard Jones.[76]

Finally, Henslowe acted as a pawnbroker to the actors. He lent £2 to Richard Jones upon the pledge of four rings; £1 to Thomas Towne upon a gold ring with a green stone and 10s. upon a pair of silk stockings; 6s. to Gabriel Spenser upon a jewel; 10s. to William Birde upon two gold jewels. And he lent money to actors to redeem clothes that they had pawned to him or to other brokers: to Thomas Downton the princely sum of £12. 10s. to redeem two cloaks that he had pawned, and £3 to Downton, Jones, Robert Shaa, and William Birde to redeem a "Riche clocke."[77] The accounts of actors dealing with the pawnbrokers are peculiarly revealing of the contradictory needs of men and women to raise ready cash (through pawning) and to maintain and assert their status and identity (through buying or renting clothes). When the theatrical company to which he belonged was about to tour Europe, Richard Jones wrote to Edward Alleyn, asking for a financial loan to repurchase his pawned clothes: "J have asut of clothes and acloke [a cloak] at pane [pawn] for three pound and if it pleas you to lend me so much to release them J shalbe bound to pray for you so long as J leve, for if J go over and have no clothes J shall not be esteemed of."[78] The clothes were the precondition of "estimation." In *The Fable of the Bees*, in the early eighteenth century, Bernard Mandeville complained that the trade in secondhand clothes had totally obscured social hierarchy:

The poorest Labourer's Wife in the Parish, who scorns to wear a strong wholsom Frize, as she might, will half starve her self and her Husband to purchase a secondhand Gown and Petticoat, . . . because, forsooth, it is more genteel. The Weaver, the Shoemaker, the Tailor, the Barber, and every mean working Fellow, that can set up with little, has the Impudence with the first Money he gets, to Dress himself like a Tradesman of Substance.[79]

The expansion in the secondhand clothes trade, however, did not begin in the eighteenth century but in sixteenth-century London. It depended upon the increased accumulation of secondhand clothes that needed to find a market and upon the increase in unredeemed clothes that had been pawned. What were the reasons for this increase in stocks of clothes? As Lawrence Stone has noted in *The Crisis of the Aristocracy*, the late sixteenth century witnessed the explosion of the London "season," the renting or buying of houses by the gentry in London, and a phenomenal increase in the speed with which fashions in clothing changed. Monarchs and aristocrats accumulated and disposed of clothes at an ever increasing pace. The number of haberdashers and merchant tailors increased rapidly, as did the quantity of imported luxury cloth (silk, satin, fine linen, lace).

Given this accumulation of clothes, it was to be expected that frippers, brokers, and anyone with luxury clothes for sale looked for new outlets. The theater was one such outlet. It was a strikingly novel one, which solved a particular problem. There were real limits to what frippers and pawnbrokers could do with the most splendid of the clothes that they had acquired, because of the sumptuary laws, ineffectual as they usually were, that regulated what specific classes could wear. But the professional theaters were founded upon the flouting of the sumptuary laws and upon the circulation of clothes from aristocrats to commoners who, if they had not been defined as household servants, would have been classified as vagrants.

That players were repeatedly associated with the pawnbrokers with whom they dealt is not surprising, considering their dependency upon the circulation of clothes. John Stephens, in his satire on "a common Player," argues that "[t]he Statute hath done wisely to acknowledge him a Rogue: for his chief Essence is, *A dayly Counterfeite*." But that "dayly Counterfeite," in which the actor "professes himselfe (beeing vnknowne) to bee an apparant Gentleman," is, according to Stephens, composed of the hybrid wares of the pawnbroker. The actor's

thinne Felt, and his Silke Stockings, or his foule Linnen, and his faire Doublet, doe (in him) bodily reveale the Broaker: So beeing not sutable, he prooues a *Motley*: his minde obseruing the same fashion of his body: both consist of parcells and remnants: but his minde hath commonly the newer fashion, and the newer stuffe: hee would not else hearken so passionatly after new Tunes, new Trickes, new Devises: These together apparrell his braine and vnderstanding, whilest hee takes the materialls vpon trust, and is himselfe the Taylor to take measure of his soules liking.[80]

The player in this account is simultaneously a trickster who tailors himself and a "motley" being, tailored from the "parcells and remnants" of others. His clothing from the broker gives Stephens the language to describe how the player's "braine and vnderstanding" are formed. The only difference between the composition of his mind and his body is that his mind is made from the more recent fashionings of the playwright, the balladeer, and the actors themselves, whereas his body shows the wear of older "stuffe." But the thin felt and foul stockings are juxtaposed with the silk stockings and fair doublet. Even clothes that come from the broker can sometimes pass as "fashion."

The companies' circulation of secondhand clothes is only one way that the theaters functioned as engines of fashion. The actors provided a constant demand for clothes, but so too did the audiences who attended the theaters. Before the repeal of the sumptuary laws in 1604, it could be a risky undertaking to wear "unsuitable" clothes, particularly in church or the workplace, where one was most liable to surveillance and arrest. The sumptuary laws in England were more honored in the breach than the observance, but they were not completely without teeth. A Fellow of King's College was committed to prison in 1576 after a formal dispute with the Provost, when it was discovered that he was wearing "a cut taffeta doublet . . . and a great pair of galligastion hose" under his gown. And it was suggested that an attorney who appeared before the Privy Council in 1592 with a gilt sword, huge ruffs, and other "unseemly apparel" be dismissed from the Court of Common Pleas.[81] But in the theaters, it was virtually impossible to regulate who wore what.[82]

This accounts for the one of the central attacks upon the theaters: that audiences used the liberty of the theatrical space to rival the actors themselves in their dress. William Harrison noted that "few of either sex come thither, but in theyr hol-dayes appareil, and so set forth, so trimmed, so adorned, so decked, so perfumed, as if they made the place the market of wantonnesse."[83] And in his *Characters*, Thomas Overbury describes "A Phantastique" as one who "withers his clothes on a Stage, as a Sale-man is forc't to doe his sutes in Birchin-lane; and when the Play is done, if you marke his rising, 'tis with a kind of walking Epilogue between the two candles, to know if his suit may passe for currant."[84] Henry Fitzgeoffrey, after decrying the unpatriotic luxury of an audience whose fashions come from Turkey, Spain, and France, denounces the luxury that bankrupts a young gallant:

> Enter *Tissue slop*
> Vengeance! I know him well, did he not drop
> Out of the *Tyring-house*? Then how (the duse)
> Comes the misshapen *Prodigall* so spruce,
> His year's *Revenewes* (I dare stand unto't,)
> Is not of *worth* to purchase such a *Sute*.[85]

Attacks upon the acting companies combined a critique of the actors as shape-shifters with an awareness that the theaters staged and marketed new fashions in clothes through actors and audience alike.

No one was more aware, or more scornful, of the audience's clothes as a rival theatrical attraction than Ben Jonson. In "The Dedication to the Reader" for *The New Inn*, Jonson complains of the fastidious gallants who have decried his play:

> What did they come for, then? thou wilt aske me. I will as punctually answer: To see, and to bee seene. To make a generall muster of themselues in their clothes of credit: and possesse the Stage, against the Play.[86]

And the plot of *The Devil is an Ass* is driven by Fitzdottrell's desire to cut a figure in the theater. Fitzdottrell's insistence upon fine clothes for his wife means that he has to furnish himself from the pawnbroker, Ingine. In a wonderful metatheatrical touch, Fitzdottrell has "a hyr'd suite" from Ingine to go to a play called . . . "the Diuell is an Asse."[87] But when Wittipol offers him his new cloak, which cost £50, in exchange for a quarter of an hour's conversation with his wife, Fitzdottrell cannot resist the offer, even if it means renting out his wife. The cloak (of plush, velvet and lace) will become, as Wittipol puts it, Fitzdottrell's "Stage-garment," in which he will be as much a spectacle as the actors. Fitzdottrell explains his transaction to Frances, his wife, by saying:

> Heere is a cloake cost fifty pound, wife,
> Which I can sell for thirty, when I ha' seene
> All London in't, and London has seene mee.
> To day, I goe to the Black-fryers Play-house,

> Sit i' the view, salute all my acquaintance,
> Rise vp between the Acts, let fall my cloake,
> Publish a handsome man, and a rich suite
> (As that's a speciall end, why we goe thither,
> All that pretend, to stand for't o' the Stage)
> The Ladie aske who's that? (For they doe come
> To see vs, Love, as wee doe to see them).

In the play, as among actors and audience, clothes constantly circulate. Fitzdottrell wears Wittipol's cloak and imagines pawning or reselling it, and he rents clothes from the broker Ingine. Everill's clothes "[a]re all at pawne," and even Pug, the wretched devil, participates in the process of circulation, appearing as a human by stealing the clothes of Ambler, the gentleman usher of Lady Tailbush.[88] Ben Jonson presents this circulation with a mixture of irony, contempt, and delight. Although, like the anti-theatricalists, he scorned the mingle-mangle of social life, he himself depended upon the spectacle of the theater, as his plays constantly remind us. Even Venetian visitors who could not understand a word of English were entertained by "gazing at the very costly dresses of the actors."[89]

There were different ways in which the actors could make a sumptuous display. First, like other servants, they could inherit the clothes of their masters as perks or favors. They were not regular household servants, though, so they were unlikely to be treated with the intimacy of domestics. Nevertheless they could and did acquire either new or cast-off clothing from the court. In 1634, when a French company of players visited the English court, they not only earned "two hundred pounds at least" through their performances but "besides many rich clothes were given them."[90] Payment, as we argued in chapter 1, frequently took the form of material things.

But the actors also purchased aristocratic clothing either directly or indirectly. Ben Jonson mocks the gallant who, changing his clothes three times a day, teaches

> each suit he has, the ready way
> From *Hide-Parke* to the Stage, where at the last
> His deare and borrow'd Bravery he must cast.

John Donne also remarks on the passage of clothes from court to playhouse. Satirizing courtiers, he writes:

> As fresh, and sweet their Apparells be, as bee
> The fields they sold to buy them; "For a King
> Those hose are," cry the flatterers; And bring
> Them next weeke to the Theatre to sell.[91]

These literary anecdotes can be compared with the account by the Swiss traveler Thomas Platter. After visiting England in 1599, he wrote:

The actors are most expensively and elaborately costumed; for it is the English usage for eminent lords or Knights at their decease to bequeath and leave almost the best of their clothes to their serving men, which it is unseemly for the latter to wear, so that they offer them then for sale for a small sum to the actors.[92]

In Platter's version, the trade between court and stage is not as immediate as Jonson and Donne suggest. The clothes first pass from aristocrat to servant, and then on to the playhouse. The one thing to doubt in Platter's account is his claim that the clothes would be sold "for a small sum." We know from Henslowe's accounts that clothes made from expensive materials and dyes could be pawned for substantial sums, and there is no reason why servants would have sold their perquisites to the actors for less money than they could have got by pawning them to Henslowe.[93] But the most striking aspect of Platter's account is the suggestion that it was primarily to actors that clothes of any station or gender could safely be rented or sold.

That the most extravagant of clothes and fabrics ended up in the theater can be demonstrated from Henslowe's 1598 inventories of the Admiral's Men and from Edward Alleyn's undated inventory of theatrical apparel. The inventories include cloth-of-gold gowns, coats, venetians, and hose; a cloth-of-silver coat, jerkin, pair of venetians, pair of hose; a scarlet cloak with two broad gold laces and gold buttons; "a crymasin sattin case [doublet or jerkin] lact wt gould lace all over"; a pair of red velvet venetians and a pair of green velvet venetians both "lact wt gould spanish"; and a satin doublet "layd thycke with gowld lace." Although there are some repeats between Henslowe's and Alleyn's lists, there are 13 records of cloth of gold or cloth of silver; 32 records of garments with gold or silver lace; and a number of other garments recorded as having gold or silver trappings (fringes, spangles, etc.) or with gold or silver buttons.[94]

There is even a crimson robe, striped with gold and faced with ermine.[95] This is remarkable not so much for the extravagant gold and crimson but for the ermine. Ermine was one of the most costly imports from Russia and Scandinavia; it was also a fur "principally used for ceremonial garments within royal and aristocratic circles."[96] The coronation portrait of Elizabeth I shows her in a magnificent gown lined throughout with ermine and with a collar of ermine.[97] In the "Ermine" portrait of Elizabeth, a white ermine, spotted with black, rests upon her left arm, a gold crown around its neck.[98] It is not only the crown that asserts the regal nature of this ermine, though. Ermines were in fact white, the only black being on the tip of their tails. Sumptuary legislation limited the use of these tails to the monarch alone. The white skins were "powdered" (as it was termed) by the furrier, who pulled the black tails through slits that he or she had made and sewed them in. The black-spotted ermine on Elizabeth's sleeve thus materializes the monarch herself – the only person who can be "powdered" with their black tails.[99] The player's robe, of course, has no such tails sewn in; but a crimson robe, striped with gold and faced with ermine, is clearly a magnificent aristocratic garment which the theater had acquired second-hand from the court.

In such transmissions of clothes, liveried inscriptions upon the body were radically displaced. This displacement mirrored the theater's translations of the rituals of court and city alike from their "proper" locations to the Liberties to the north and south of London, from which distance the players could, as Steven Mullaney has shown, interrogate the solemnities of rule together with an audience which included the politically disenfranchised.[100] And it dis-located those rituals by making them nakedly dependent upon a cash nexus. Not having the deep pockets of many courtiers and merchants, players had to make do as best they could, so they intermingled their own fabrications with the cast-off paraphernalia of courtiers and citizens.

A striking example of such fabrications is to be found in the copper lace that players added to their costumes.[101] As we noted above, gold and silver lace was a major item of expense for the aristocratic and wealthy, often costing as much as or more than the garments that it adorned. The players, on the other hand, while they bought secondhand garments of cloth of gold and cloth of silver and secondhand garments richly embroidered with gold and silver lace, could rarely afford to buy such garments new. Yet they needed to display the finery of the court, and, particularly in city comedies, they staged the latest extravagances of London fashion. They did this by intermixing costumes containing gold and silver with garments faced and embroidered with copper lace. Copper lace was made in the same way as gold or silver, but it cost much less. It nevertheless represented a major expense for the companies. Between January and July 1599, Henslowe paid £17. 1s. 4d. for copper lace; between May and September 1601, he paid £20. 5s. 10d. for copper lace, although this was partly to account for old debts.[102]

Copper lace had a special place in the theater. Indeed, it became a metonymy for the professional players. In the "War of the Theaters," Jonson depicts the back-biter Tucca as fearing to be mocked "o' the stage":

you'll play me, they say: I shall be presented by a sort of copper-lac't scoundrels of you.[103]

Dekker responded in defense of John Marston with *Satiromastix* or "The Vntrussing of the Humorous Poet." Jonson, depicted as "Horace," will himself be exposed to ridicule in the theater. In Dekker's play, Horace (i.e., Jonson) responds to this threat by saying that he will bring his own audience to the play to "distaste" the impersonation of himself:

me ath stage? ha, ha. Ile starue their poore copper-lace workmasters, that dare play me.

Dekker's Tucca defends the players or "Stage-walkers" as "these charitable Copper-lac'd Christians." And when Henry Cross renewed Gosson and Stubbes's assault upon the theater, he attacked the players, "not fewe of them vsurers and extortioners," as "copper-lace gentelmen."[104]

Dekker glosses this conflation of the players with copper lace in *The Guls Hornebooke* where the gallant, eager to show off his clothes, pushes up onto the stage to display his "new Satten." Having attained a stool upon the stage, he "examine[s] the play-suits' lace, and perhaps win[s] wagers vpon laying tis copper."[105] But the gallant can lay such a wager only because of the hodge-podge of new and old, of gold lace and of copper simulating gold lace, that the theater presented.

The undoing of clear boundaries between the court, the city, and the theater is further demonstrated by an earlier record from the Office of the Revels. In 1572, Thomas Giles formally complained that the Revels was renting out its costumes. Giles was undoubtedly right. The previous year, among several other rentals, "yello clothe of golde gownes" were rented to Gray's Inn and to the Horsehead Tavern; black and white gowns were rented for the marriages of Edward Hind and Mr. Martin; copper "cloth of gold" gowns were rented for the marriage of Lord Montague's daughter; and red cloth of gold gowns were rented for a tailor's marriage. Giles, in his complaint, attributes an identity to the clothes themselves. He argues that they have suffered from the "soyll of the wereres/ who for the most parte be of the meanest sort of mene" and that this soiling was "to the grett dyscredytt of the same aparell."[106] Here, as in the accounts of the guild theaters, the clothes themselves assume an identity, one which comes from their aristocratic point of origin. The clothes can thus be dishonored, soiled by circulation among "the meanest sort of mene." Giles was himself a haberdasher who lent out clothes and he was in competition with the Office of the Revels in the secondhand clothes trade. But despite his own business, he was alarmed by a circulation of clothes that unstitched apparel from social status, an unstitching that the theater both staged in its fictions and encouraged in its audience.

The dislocations that Giles attacked appear even more dramatic if we turn from the court to the church. The church had always been involved in theatrical spectacle, and its vestments had been used in the Miracle plays.[107] But the Reformation dramatically altered the church's relation to its own clothes. As Stephen Greenblatt argues, "When the Reformation in England dismantled the histrionic apparatus of Catholicism, they sold some of its gorgeous properties to the professional players."[108] The majority of the elaborate garments which the church owned could no longer be worn. No longer having any use for Catholicism's sacred clothes, the Protestant churches rented them out or sold them. Thus, in 1560, the Church of the Holy Trinity, Chester, sold "the best cope and the vestment & appurtenances" to the mayor. But they also sold three vestments for 8s. to Thomas Shevynton's son and Thomas Dycher's son "to make players garments."[109] At Chelmsford, the church-wardens hired out clothes to visiting actors for up to £2. 19s. 0d. until 1574, when the wardrobe was sold for £6. 12s. 4d. St. Mary the Virgin in Tewkesbury regularly rented out players' costumes between 1567 and 1585, charging between 1d. and 5s., depending upon what was taken. Its "players Apparell" consisted of eight gowns, seven jerkins, four green silk caps, eight heads of hair for the apostles, ten beards, and "a face or vysor for the devyll."[110]

The case of St. Mary the Virgin is, of course, somewhat different from the other cases we have quoted. The church was, after all, renting out apparel which had always been used for acting. Far more radical in its implications was the restaging of actual ecclesiastical garments upon the secular stage. This is what St. John's College, Cambridge, did in 1540–1, when it turned two green vestments, an old silk cope, and "halfe a decones cote" into theatrical costumes.[111] At King's College, the transformation of clothes from ecclesiastical garb to players' clothes and back again took on a Monty Pythonesque absurdity when the liturgical garments that had been made into playing gear under Edward VI were turned back into priests' robes under Mary, only, presumably, to be turned back into players' clothes again after her death a few years later.[112]

Most interesting of all in revealing the relations between the church, the second-hand clothes trade, and the professional theater companies is a note by Sir Henry Herbert, the Master of the Revels, in his office book:

I committed Cromes, a broker in Long Lane, the 16 of February, 1634, to the Marshalsea for lending a church robe with the name of JESUS upon it to the players in Salisbury Court to present a Flamen, a priest of the heathens. Upon his petition of submission, and acknowledgment of his fault, I released him the 17 February, 1634.[113]

Given how few detailed records have survived, we should particularly note that the players are here renting clothes from a secondhand clothes dealer. Long Lane, where Cromer worked, was recorded by John Stow in his *Survey of London* as "now lately builded on both the sides with tenements for brokers, tiplers, and such like."[114] The brokers and secondhand clothes dealers of Long Lane and Houndsditch provided dramatists and pamphleteers with an inexhaustible supply of satirical attacks on the very trade in which they were themselves involved. In *The Puritaine*, an old soldier's weapons are "in *Long-lane* at Pawne, at Pawne"; in Dekker and Webster's *West-Ward Hoe*, Mistress Birdlime hires "three Liueries in Long-lane"; in their *North-*

Ward Hoe, Doll tells Hornet that "if the Diuel and all the Brokers in long lane had rifled their wardrob, they wud ha beene dambd before they had fitted thee thus"; and in their *The Wonder of a Kingdome*, a broker is said to have "a *long lane* of hellish Tenements/ Built all with pawnes."[115] And in Dekker's pamphlets, he writes satirically of "Vsurers and Brokers" who "dwell in the *long-lane* of hell" and of "all the Brokers in Long-Lane, Hounsditch, or elsewhere, with all the rest of their Colleagued Suburbians, that deale vpon ouerworne commodities."[116]

Jibes at the Long Lane of hell were outdone by ingenious word-play upon Houndsditch. Stow soberly noted that

[f]rom Aldgate Northwest to Bishopsgate, lieth the ditch of the Cittie, called Houndes ditch, for that in olde time when the same lay open, much filth (conueyed forth of the Citie) especially dead Dogges were there layd or cast.

Now, he writes, the houses "be for the most part possessed by Brokers, sellers of olde apparell and such like."[117] In Beaumont and Fletcher's *The Woman's Prize*, Bianca commands Livia not only to swear that they will remain faithful to each other "like a race of noble *Amazons*" who will "depise base men" but also to swear to having "more knavery, and usury / And foolery, and brokery, then doggs-ditch." In Middleton's *Michaelmas Term*, Rearage, a London gallant, sneers at Andrew Lethe as

> One that ne'er wore apparel but, like ditches,
> 'Twas cast before he had it, now shines bright
> In rich embroideries.

Rearage plays upon "casting" as meaning both the discarding of clothes and the clearing of ditches, but the two meanings are conflated in Houndsditch, simultaneously the ditch of dead dogs and the market of discarded clothes.

In *Three Weekes, three daies, and three houres Obseruations and Trauel*, John Taylor describes a woman who defends the "honesty of brokers" as if she herself "like a desperate pawn had lain seven years in lavender onsweeting in Long Lane, or amongst the dogged inhabitants of Houndsditch."[118]

The journey of the ecclesiatical robe from the church to the pawnbrokers at Long Lane to the theater was a series of translations in which a sacred garment from the theater of God came to represent a "heathen" religion on the secular stage. In the theater itself, the unstitching and restitching of clothes by tailors and brokers was often represented ambivalently as materializing the unstitching and restitching of the social fabic. But the unstitching and restitching of the social that Stephen Greenblatt has brilliantly analyzed in the professional playhouses was intrinsic to the piecemeal nature of the players' clothes.[119] The clothes, new and cast-off alike, were translated across geographical divisions, across class divisions, across gender divisions, across "national" divisions. These boundary crossings provided a rich repository of stories for theatrical scripts.

Staging clothes

The circulation of clothes (including their pawning and their theft) is repeatedly referred to in Renaissance drama, sometimes as a central aspect of the plot, sometimes as a mundane aspect of personal finances. Middleton's *Your Five Gallants* begins in a pawnshop with Frippery (the "broker-gallant," his very name testifying to the centrality of clothes in pawnbroking) going over his stock of gowns, petticoats, jackets, suits. The opening scene emphasizes the significance of pawn-broking in the play as a whole. Goldstone (the "cheating-gallant") steals the cloak of Fitzgrave ("a gentleman") and pawns it to Frippery, who then wears it himself; Goldstone also pawns a diamond and a sapphire; Tailby (the "whore-gallant"), losing at gambling, pawns his weapons, his hat, and his satin doublet; Bungler tries to pawn his grandfather's seal-ring (engraved with a "great codpeice, with nothing int" to Frippery; and, at the end of the play, Pursenet (the "pocket-gallant") gives Tailby the pledge of a chain of pearl to rent masquing costumes.[120]

The play revolves around the circulation of this pearl chain. It changes hands no less than twelve times, and its migrations illuminate the social life of other forms of clothing and jewelry as they move from being gifts and material memories to commodities that can be cashed in. At the beginning of the play, Fitzgrave (the "gentleman") has given the chain to Katherine ("a wealthy orphan") as the material form of his love. The pearls are "The hallowed beades, whereon I iustly kept / The true and perfect number of my sighs." The chain is stolen by Pursenet's Boy, who gives it to Pursenet. Pursenet gives it to the First Courtesan, who in turn gives it to Tailby. Tailby, losing at gambling, wants to pawn the chain, but he doesn't have it with him. Pursenet takes the chain back, and attacks the First Courtesan for allowing it to be "wound on a strangers arme." Pursenet pawns the chain, but later pays £40 to redeem it, only to drop it on the ground. Goldstone picks it up, mistakenly thinking it belongs to Mistress Newcut and that she "dropt it from her arme / For a deuice to toale me to her bed." Tailsby then confronts Goldstone for stealing the chain, but it is in fact restored to Pursenet. Pursenet pawns it again to Frippery (whom he calls "Iewe") as a security for the furnishing of masquing suits. Frippery gives it to Katherine in an attempt to woo her, but she declares that it is "[t]he very chaine of Pearl was filcht from me!" And so the chain is returned to Katherine, to whom it had been given at the beginning of the play. As the chain changes hands, it changes its meaning, but its own persistence as a materialized relation between giver and receiver challenges any clear opposition between "love" and "lust" (between Fitzgrave and Katherine, Pursenet and the First Courtesan, the First Courtesan and Tailby, Fripper and Katherine) or between memorial object and exchangeable commodity.[121]

We do not need to read Fripper as an allegory of Philip Henslowe to note that the circulation of clothes that was necessary to the formation of the professional theaters was also an irresistible topic for dramatists. But the theaters were never more ambivalent than in their representations of brokers, frippers, and the circulation of secondhand clothes. In Jonson's *Every Man in His Humour*, Brain-worm begins by disguising himself as a soldier with clothes purchased from a broker He later steals the clothes of Justice Clement's clerk and pawns them to raise cash. And when he promises aid to Matthew and Bobadill, they raise the necessary money by pawning a jewel, silk stockings, and a pair of boots.[122] Clothes are a banking system, moveable objects to be stolen, and the materials out of which an identity is constructed.

If the theaters staged the circulation of clothes via the pawnbroker, they also paraded their own function as renters of clothes. In Jonson's *The Alchemist*, Face tells Drugger to rent the costume of Hieronimo (the hero of Kyd's *The Spanish Tragedy*) from the players:

> Thou must borrow,
> A *Spanish* suite. Hast thou no credit with the players?
> DRUGGER: Yes, sir, did you neuer see me play the foole?
> FACE: I know not, NAB: thou shalt, if I can helpe it.
> HIERONYMO's old cloake, ruffe, and hat will serue,
> Ile tell thee more, when thou bringst 'hem.

The costume itself appears an act later, when Subtle announces to Face, "Here's your HIERONYMO's cloake, and hat," and it migrates again when Lovewit puts on the costume for his marriage to Dame Pliant.[123] The costume here hovers between a fetishized identity from the past (the specific role of Hieronimo) and its new possibilities once it has been appropriated, that is, its generalized nature as a disguise and as a sign of "Spanishness."

There's a further joke in this recirculation of the clothes of Hieronimo from *The Spanish Tragedy*. For Jonson himself had, according to Dekker, played the part of Hieronimo: "thou hast forgot," says Tucca to Horace (i.e. Jonson) in *Satiromastix*, "how thou amblest (in leather-pilch) by a play-wagon, in the high way, and took'st mad Hieronimoes part, to get seruice among the Mimickes."[124] Dekker derides Jonson as a strolling player who will "weare anything," including "a Plaiers old cast Cloake." Having played the part of a Hieronimo, run mad for the death of his son, he is said to have borrowed "a gowne of *Roscius* the stager" and sent it back "lowsie."[125] No doubt, many actors did indeed supplement their personal wardrobes both from other players and from the companies' stocks, despite the prohibitions against the latter practice.

But the implication that "a Plaiers old cast Cloake" is worthless frippery is itself a self-conscious mockery of the illusions that the theater performed and exposed. In fact, the clauses drawn up by theatrical entrepreneurs and sharers in the professional companies show that their "frippery" was far from worthless. Henslowe drew up Articles of Agreement between himself and Robert Dawes, specifically stating that Dawes should not at any time after the play is ended

depart or goe out of the [howse] with any [of their] apparell on his body, or if the said Robert Dawes [shall carry away any propertie] belonging to the said company, or shal be consentinge or privy to any other of the said company going out of the howse with any of their apparell on his or their bodies, he . . . shall and will forfeit and pay unto the said Philip and Jacob . . . the some of ffortie pounds of lawfull [money of England].[126]

The circulation of clothes was a theme for comedy, history, and tragedy alike. But it was also a carefully controlled economic practice, for the theaters were founded upon the regulated vagrancy of these moveable goods.

Fashioning "character"

We have been arguing that the theater was a direct and indirect growth out of the trade in clothes: direct, in that the companies and the theatrical entrepreneurs used the theaters as places to stage and profit from the currency of clothes; indirect, in that the players were supported both by their legal status as liveried servants and by their acquisition of aristocratic clothing. In conclusion, we suggest that the economic relations of the theater to the clothing trade help to illuminate both the repertory of the companies and the process by which roles and identities were defined on the stage.

The relation between costume and repertory has been persuasively argued by Jean MacIntyre.[127] She notes, for instance, that suites of plays relate not only to the attempt to cash in on a successful first run but also upon the need to get a return on expensive outlays on costumes. Thus, the Admiral's Men made up "paynim" costumes, which they then reused for a series of plays figuring "paynims." Similarly, they mounted a run of Iberian plays starting in 1596, of classical myths from 1598–1600, of plays on ancient British history from 1598. The different runs required differentiated costumes which could not be let go to waste. The quite extraordinary costume expenses of *Cardinal Wolsey* probably suggested the need for Rowley's Henry VIII play, *When You See Me You Know Me*, which also added a part for Will Summers. The incorporation of Summers did not, perhaps, depend entirely upon the development of a good part for a clown, since the play already has a substantial part for another clown. Was one motive for the part the fact that the Admiral's Men had "Will. Sommers sewtte" in stock, as their inventory of 1598 shows?[128]

Costumes were often prior to any particular play. The stock from a previous production could shape both the subject matter and the number of plays that might be necessary to recoup the financial outlay. At the same time, the occasional storing up of a specific named costume may imply the power of the theater to bring the dead back to life through the permeated life of their clothes. Will Summers was dead, but he survived in the clothes that bore his presence and could be made to walk again in the theatrical costume that was made to awaken him from the grave.

The professional theaters could reawaken a dead clown through his clothes; they could also appropriate the clothes of aristocrats to circulate as fetishized but displaced talismans within the theatrical marketplace. In 1624, Chamberlain wrote to Carleton about Middleton's *A Game at Chess*, which satirically portrayed the Spanish courtier Gondomar: "They counterfeited his person to the life, with all his grace and faces, and had gotten (they say) a cast [discarded] sute of his apparell for the purpose."[129] And if a person's actual clothes could not be staged in this marketing of sympathetic magic, they could be simulated. In 1599, for instance, Rowland Whyte saw a production of a play about the overthrow of Turnholt in which the actor who played the part of the still living Sir Francis Vere "got a beard resembling his, and a watchet Satin Doublet, with Hose trimmed with silver lace."[130]

There is a curious doubleness in such theatrical spectacles. If clothes retained or simulated the identity of former wearers, they were also transmissible: that is, they could be detached from their former wearers and appropriated for commercial gain. By the Restoration, the identities with which transmitted clothes had been haunted were, we would argue, beginning to withdraw from them. Clothes were increasingly merely fashions, merely commodities. And yet it is striking how attached theatrical representation remained to the appropriation of extra-theatrical magics. John Downes records that Betterton played the part of Prince Alvaro in Charles II's coronation robes, while Joseph Price wore the robes of the Earl of Oxford. When the Earl of Orrery's version of *King Henry the 5th* was staged in 1664 and 1666, the play "was Splendidly cloath'd: The King, in the Duke of York's Coronation Suit: Owen Tudor, in King Charles's: Duke of Burgundy, in the Lord of Oxford's, and the rest all new."[131] The theory of the "king's two bodies" may be more literal than Kantarowitz realized. That is, the immortal body of the king was materialized in the crown, the robes, the orb and scepter that survived any monarch's specific body. The clothes themselves incorporated the magic of kingship.

But, on the cusp between a patronage system and a capitalist economy, the theater interrogated the meaning of all magics, even as it staged them. One of the new magics that the theater both staged and popularized was the magic of fashion. This magic is energetically and troublingly presented in *Volpone*. In Act 3, scene 7, Corvino and Mosca exit, leaving Celia alone with Volpone. Then, as the stage direction reads, Volpone "leaps off from his couch" and proceeds to conjure up an extraordinary vision of polymorphous perversity. His desire for Celia has, he declares, already "rays'd" him "in severall shapes." But now Celia, the fixed star of his gaze, can herself enter into the play of metamorphoses,

> Whilst we, in changed shapes, act OVIDS tales
> Thou, like EUROPA now, and I like JOVE,
> Then I like Mars, and thou like ERYCINE,
> So, of the rest, till we have quite run through
> And weary'd all the fables of the gods.
> Then will I have thee in more moderne formes,
> Attired like some sprightly dame of *France*,
> Brave *Tuscan* lady, or proud *Spanish* beauty;
> Sometimes, unto the *Persian Sophie*s wife;
> Or the grand-*Signior's* mistress; and, for change,
> To one of our most artfull courtizans,
> Or some quick *Negro* or cold *Russian*.
> And I will meet thee, in as many shapes.[132]

In this exuberant and imperialist vision of fashion, clothes can conflate human and animal (Europa and the bull), human and divine (Mars and Erycine, Jove and Europa), different nations (Spanish, Tuscan, Persian, Russian), different continents (Europe, Asia, Africa), and different classes (the Persian Sophie's wife, a Venetian courtesan.)

Such hybridization is made possible by the transformations of the world system which Venice, where *Volpone* is set, itself helped to initiate. In the process, the aristocracy becomes no more than one possible kind of style: a style which one can adopt or drop according to the extent of one's wardrobe. In Volpone's vision, one might locate a mercantilist view of what capitalism can do. And a new political economy would later provide the very conceptual tools through which the new social order would view both itself and its prehistory: tools like "individual," "identity," "choice." These conceptual tools brought with them a new regime for regulating the relation between clothes and bodies. The body was prior, the clothes secondary; the body was essential, the clothes supplementary. If the Renaissance professional theater partly initiated that new conception, it resisted it equally powerfully. For, as Scott McMillin argues, costume preceded and defined role in the Elizabethan theater.[133] Each part was a costume or set of costumes, an expensive "prop" which the actor himself would prop up.

The simplest, and most theatrical, way of thinking about how many characters there are in any one play is to ask how many costumes the play requires. The significance of costumes begins with the centrality of doubling in the Renaissance professional theaters. From the "plot" of Peele's *The Battle of Alcazar*, for instance, we find that Samuel Rowley, the actor and dramatist, "played 1) a Moorish Attendant, 2) Pisano (a captain), 3) a Messenger, 4) a Moorish Ambassador, 5) a

Devil, 6) a Captain of Tangier, 7) Death, 8) a Portuguese soldier."[134] *Mucedorus* shows that ten actors can easily play all the parts, which means that ten actors will have time to put on as many costumes as the parts require, and a single actor can play Comedy, a Boy, an Old Woman, and Ariena.[135] We know from the plot of *2 The Seven Deadly Sins*, probably revived in the 1590s, that Burbage was to perform two parts, Cowley eight, Duke six, Pallant six, and Holland five. We also know from the 1631 promptbook of Massinger's *Believe as You List* that single parts could be divided up between two or three players.[136] To put it another way, Renaissance theatrical conventions might require both that one body wear many different costumes and that many bodies fit into a single costume.

Now what most theatrical historians argue, quite rightly, is that the more prominent the part, the less likely the player was to double. But we could put this a different way: the prominent parts were usually already doubled. That is, if doubling is above all about the timing required to get an actor off stage and into another costume before he can return, then Lear, say, or Cordelia or Edgar are doubled parts. For the prominent actor is usually divided up amongst a set of costumes, just like any other doubling actor. And the change of costume is always a change of identity. The King, divested of his crown and of his train, is merely Lear; Edgar, divested of the clothes of an aristocratic son and heir, will say "Edgar I nothing am" and be transformed by his nakedness and the blanket round his loins into Tom of Bedlam; Cordelia, invested in royal robes, becomes Queen of France; Kent, divested of his aristocratic robes, will lose his name, or belatedly take on the name of Caius.

Twelfth Night presents perhaps the most radical vision of the centrality of clothes to the fashioning of a person. Indeed, so radical is that vision that, as Phyllis Rackin and Stephen Orgel have brilliantly shown, it is one of Shakespeare's least known plays.[137] That is, although the play is frequently read, taught, and performed, its plot remains in a significant sense unknown. What *is* familiar enough to critics and playgoers alike is the transformation of Viola into Cesario. The boy actor who played Viola on the Renaissance stage appears first as "Ladie" and "Madam." He becomes Cesario through the putting on of "*mans attire*" (1. 4 S. D. [TLN 250]). In fact, as we later learn, this is not *any* man's attire. Olivia begins the play in "sad remembrance" (1. 1. 31 [TLN 38]) of her dead brother; Viola begins the play by *becoming* her brother in memory of him. That is, although she does not take her brother's name (as, in the source for the play, Barnabe Rich's Silla takes the name of her brother, Silvio), she dresses up as him, as we later learn:

> he went
> Still in this fashion, color, ornament,
> For him I imitate.   (3. 4. 381–3 [TLN 1902–4])[138]

Viola enacts her own "sad remembrance" of her brother, presumed drowned, resurrecting him by wearing his "fashion, color, ornament."

What is less familiar to modern readers is the "failure" of Cesario to be transformed back into Viola. In fact, the name "Viola" occurs in the performed text for the first time only in the last scene of the play, as Anne Barton has noted.[139] And even in the last act, the name is given only to be withdrawn. Sebastian says that he *would* call Cesario Viola "Were you a woman" (5. 1. 239 [TLN 2405]). And while Cesario repeats the name "Viola," he/she withholds it from him/herself:

VIO If nothing lets to make vs happie both,
    But this my masculine vsurp'd attyre:
    Do not embrace me, till each circumstance,
    Of place, time, fortune, do co-here and iumpe
    That I am *Viola*, which to confirme,
    Ile bring you to a Captaine in this Towne,
    Where lye my maiden weeds.   (5. 1. 249–55 [TLN 2415–21], our italics)

The embrace that will restore sister to brother, brother to sister, is elaborately held back by the eruption, at this last gasp of the play, of a whole new narrative, the narrative of Viola's "maiden weeds." And this narrative radically reshapes the ending of the play.

Cesario will become Viola when, and only when, her maiden weeds have been restored to her. And here nearly all modern readers and audiences fail at the most simple level to get the plot. What happens toward the end of *Twelfth Night*? Malvolio is recalled and he exits swearing revenge. But why is he recalled? For the simple reason that he is responsible for the imprisonment of the Captain with whom the play began. And the Captain has Viola's clothes, the clothes that Orsino calls for so that Cesario can be transformed back into Viola:

DU Giue me thy hand,
    And let me see thee in thy womans weedes.
VIO The Captaine that did bring me first on shore
    Hath my Maides garments; he vpon some Action
    Is now in durance, at *Maluolio's* suite,
    A Gentleman, and follower of my Ladies.
OL He shall inlarge him: fetch *Maluolio* hither . . .   (5. 1. 272–8 [TLN 2439–45])

Malvolio, in other words, is brought back on stage in the vain hope that he will release the Captain, so that the Captain can give Cesario his "Maides garments," so that Cesario can become Viola.

In fact, Malvolio returns only to depart again in anger. Why does Orsino send after him to try to smooth things over? It is because Malvolio *still* holds the Captain, and consequently Viola's clothes, captive.

DU Pursue him, and entreate him to a peace:
    He hath not told vs of the Captaine yet . . .   (5. 1. 380–1 [TLN 2550–1])

Because the Captain is still in prison, Cesario is without the clothes that will translate him into Viola. And it is with the *failure* of Cesario to become Viola that the play concludes:[140]

DU   *Cesario* come
    (For so you shall be while you are a man:)
    But when in other habites you are seene,
    Orsinos Mistris, and his fancies Queene.   *Exeunt*   (5. 1. 385–8 [TLN 2555–8])

Here, *Twelfth Night* departs from its source, Barnabe Rich's "Of Apolonius and Silla." In Rich's version, as in Shakespeare's, the sister dresses up as a man. But Silla takes the name of her brother, and her masculine attire is composed from "the sondrie sutes of Apparell that were the Captaines" after a shipwreck. Taking a man's clothes, Silla, like Viola, is transformed into "he." In the conclusion of Rich's tale, Silla (as Silvio) reveals him/herself to the widow Julina,

loosyng his garmentes doune to his stomacke, and shew[ing] *Iulina* his breastes and pretie teates, surmountyng farre the whitnesse of Snowe it self, saiyng: Loe Madame, behold here the partie whom you haue chalenged to bee the father of your childe, see I am a woman the daughter of a noble Duke.[141]

Unlike Shakespeare's Cesario, Rich's Silla displays his/her body. But Rich's story is as resistant to a modern reader as Shakespeare's. For Silla reveals "*his* breastes and pretie teates"; as in *Twelfth Night*, the name and the gender follow the clothes, not the body. Silla *is* Silvio, wearing man's clothes, just as Viola *is* Cesario. But in "Of Apolonius and Silla," Apolonius provides a resolution, giving Silla "sondrie sutes of sumpteous [women's] apparell."[142] In *Twelfth Night*, there is no such resolution. The failure to persuade Malvolio to release the Captain from prison leads to the failure to translate Cesario back into Viola. Viola remains Cesario because her clothes still inscribe her as "a man."

Clothes have the power to imprint their wearers because they are a form of material memory. In *Cymbeline*, the doltish but dangerous Cloten, sneering at Imogen's husband Posthumus, calls him "[a] hilding for a livery, a squire's cloth."[143] Imogen responds to Cloten's insult, not by claiming that Posthumus transcends or is better than his clothes, but by dwelling upon the value that his clothes have for her, particularly now that he is absent:

> His mean'st Garment,
> That euer hath but clipt his body; is dearer
> In my respect, then all the Heires aboue thee,
> Were they all made such men.[144]

All modern editions have followed F 2 in changing "Heires" to "haires" ("hairs" in F 3 and F 4), but the F 1 reading seems equally plausible (although with a quibble on "hairs" and "airs"). The point that Imogen would then be making is that the lowliest clothing that has touched and embraced her lover is worth more than even heirs more rightful than Cloten, who is only the stepchild of the monarch. Touching Posthumus, Posthumus's clothes have absorbed him into themselves.

For Cloten, as much as for Imogen, Posthumus's clothes come to embody meaning. To take revenge, Cloten plans to take Posthumus's place not only by becoming Imogen's lover but also by assuming Posthumus's clothes. He asks Pisanio: "Hast any of thy late Masters Garments in thy possession?" The suit which Cloten takes is the last one that Posthumus wore before he left England, and, in wearing it, Cloten attempts to erase him. He intends to do this by transforming the meaning of the clothes: "the very Garment of *Posthumus*," which Imogen held "in more respect, then my Noble and naturall person," will be transformed into the clothes of her rapist ("I will execute [the rape] in the Cloathes that she so prais'd") (3. 5. 123–4, 135–6, 142–3 [TLN 2039–40, 2051–3]). It is as if the clothes will keep Posthumus, imagined as dead, alive so that, in the remaining form of his suit, he can witness Imogen's rape, while, simultaneously, the suit, and thus Posthumus, will be both defiled and appropriated by Cloten.

Wearing Posthumus's clothes, though, Cloten erases himself. In one of the play's most bizarre jokes, Cloten, dressed in Posthumus's clothes, says to Guiderius: "Know'st me not by my Cloathes?" And yet, in an ironically inverted form, Posthumus is indeed absorbed into Cloten, as Cloten is absorbed into him. When Imogen finds the headless body of Cloten, she says:

> A headlesse man? The Garments of *Posthumus*?
> I know the shape of's Legge: this is his Hand:

His Foote Mercuriall: his martiall Thigh
The brawnes of *Hercules* . . .   (4. 2. 81, 308–11 [TLN 2350, 2630–3])

The passage is extraordinary, because, seeing the garments of Posthumus, Imogen reads the body of Cloten as Posthumus. If these are Posthumus's clothes, then this is his hand, and this his leg, foot, thigh, and brawn. No doubt one implication is that Posthumus's betrayal of Imogen has reduced him to an identity with Cloten. But we must also understand how, in the Renaissance, clothes can be imagined as retaining the identity and the form of the wearer. It is Imogen, after all, who would embrace Posthumus's meanest garment, even as that garment had embraced him ("clipt his body"). The garment bears quite literally the trace and the memory of its owner.

Cymbeline, like the theater as a whole with its "borrowed robes," makes the question of the ownership of clothes profoundly problematic. Clothes and bodies merge and separate in perverse and vagrant fashion. While Posthumus's suit migrates from him to Cloten, Posthumus himself migrates to Italy, or, in terms of the theatrical spectacle, into "these Italian weedes," which align him with the treacherous courtiership of Iachimo and of England's invaders. Returning to England again, he "disrobe[s]" himself, thus distancing himself from Iachimo, and redresses to appear, like Cymbeline's outlaw sons, as "a *Britaine* Pezant" (5. 1. 1 [TLN 2858]). Here, as Jean-Christophe Agnew puts it in a different context, "to redress [is], in effect, to redress."[145] But the scene in which Posthumus makes this last transformation simultaneously stages cloth not as a guise which can be shifted without trace, but as memory, the living embodiment of a dead past. Posthumus's opening line in the scene is "Yea bloody cloth, Ile keep thee," as he holds the cloth which Pisanio has sent as a token of his killing of Imogen (5. 1. 1 [TLN 2858]). It is as if the "Senselesse Linnen" of Posthumus's handkerchief as he parted from Imogen at the beginning of the play has been incarnated, now that she is dead, as the sentient material of the cloth which has "clipt" her (1. 3. 7 [TLN 272]). Having killed Imogen, Posthumus is forced to learn the value of the trace: the dearness of the "mean'st Garment." He will keep the bloody cloth.

There is a further unsettling twist. The bloody cloth bears a purely theatrical inscription, invented by Pisanio. Imogen is not dead, the blood is not her blood, and it is clear that the cloth is in no way connected with her. This returns us to the point we mentioned above: the theater seems to stage cloth as the site of a crisis, in which meaning is simultaneously profoundly asserted and denied. It can be asserted so powerfully because clothing *did* carry the absent body, memory, genealogy, as well as literal material value. But in the Renaissance professional theater, the social life of these things is a life of rupture and crisis. Through the transmission of clothes, there is a transmission of identity, but a transmission which is staged as constantly undoing the mutual dependencies materialized in the gift of cloth.

At the same time, clothing often exchanges hands in the form of detached parts or fragments. At one level, this reminds us of the piecemeal nature of Renaissance clothes. In Act 4, scene 4 of *Troilus and Cressida*, Troilus gives his sleeve to Cressida as a token of his love. Gifts like this are hard to understand unless one recalls that sleeves were detachable parts of overgarments, fastened on with laces or pins. Philip Gawdy sends his sister from London "a paire of truncke sleeves."[146] The Stowe Inventory of Elizabeth's clothes and jewels in 1600 records "a paire of sleeves of Lawne of the Irish facion embroidered with silver owes and knotts of silver plate," while a letter describing Mary, Queen of Scots in 1567 comments on her "sleeves tied with points."[147] And Henslowe accepted a pair of sleeves as a pledge.[148] Janet Arnold illustrates such detachable sleeves, attached by lacing through eyelet holes, in her *Patterns of Fashion*.[149] But on the stage, these fragmentary parts often take on the power of relics, their dismembered form already inscribing loss.

In the first line of the first scene of *Troilus and Cressida*, Troilus had said "I'll unarm again" (1. 1. 1 [TLN 36]). There, he took off his armor; here in Act 4, he "unarms" again. But this unarming is both literally and symbolically closer to his own arm, his own flesh, his own identity, which he takes off and gives away. When Cressida, herself given away by Troy, gives away the sleeve to Diomedes, the transaction is so prominent as to have disturbed editors, who have added stage directions so that, to quote the Arden editor, the sleeve does not "change hands with ludicrous frequency."[150] But it is precisely the extraordinary value which has been attached to the cloth and which is embodied within it that accounts for its complex back and forth exchange. As Cressida says of the sleeve, in Q1, "He that takes that doth take my heart withal," or, in the Folio, "He that takes that, rakes my heart withall" (5. 2. 82 [TLN 3069]). Q1 captures the power of a piece of clothing magically to absorb its wearer; F1 captures the power of clothing to dispossess its owner's self when the clothing is transferred. Into the sleeve which passes from hand to hand, which has no secure owner or origin, are woven the identities of both Troilus and Cressida. Diomedes, who wears the sleeve on his helmet, appropriates both lovers. And in imagining himself destroying Diomedes, Troilus imagines destroying the token of himself: "That Sleeue is mine, that heele beare in his Helme: / Were it a Caske compos'd by *Vulcans* skill, / My Sword should bite it" (5. 2. 169–71 [TLN 3166–8]). Troilus, in fighting Diomedes, attacks his own sleeve, and hence himself. The material of cloth matters so much because it operates on, and undoes, the margins of the self.

Troilus and Cressida may also remind us of the curious erotic charge which attaches so frequently to the transmission of clothes in the Renaissance. And if this eroticism comes sometimes from the specific relation of a piece of clothing to the remembered lover (Imogen's attachment to Posthumus's clothes), it can equally spring from the hybridization of bodies made possible by the circulation of clothes: the boy in woman's dress, the woman in man's clothing, the adulterous lover in the husband's garments, a man or woman's body sexualized by a transposition of class. In Middleton's *The Widow*, Martia, a woman, cross-dresses as Ansaldo. It is the "man" Ansaldo to whom Phillippa is violently attracted. But, as Susan Zimmerman observes, the attraction is to a "man" indeterminately dressed, since s/he has been stripped of her clothes down to a shirt: "I think it was a shirt," says the maid; "I know not well / For gallants wear both [i.e. shifts or shirts] now-a-days."[151] Phillippa proceeds to dress Martia/Ansaldo in an old suit of her husband's. It is as if the eroticism comes not from the body "beneath", but rather from the shifting, clothed surfaces. The eroticism of these surfaces, though, is established by the fetishized oscillation between sameness and difference, between Martia/Ansaldo imagined as man/woman, lover/husband, cuckolder/cuckolded. Desire cannot be detached from the power of clothes to inscribe.

The power of clothes to define, to produce genealogy and dependence as well as desire, is fully apparent in the care with which specific items of clothing are transmitted in Renaissance wills. Particularly among the aristocracy, the leaving of clothes is often an assertion of the power of the gift-giver and the dependency of the recipient. Such domestic power is the chilling implication of the Earl of Dorset's bequest of his wife's own clothes to her in 1624: "Item I doe give & bequeath to my deerlye beloved wife' all her wearing apparel and such rings and jewels as were hers on her marriage and the rocke rubye ring which I have given her." His own apparel Dorset divided among his servants, with the exception of some rich apparel that he left to his brother and one embroidered suit delivered to Captain Sackville.[152]

The will of Dorset's wife, Anne Clifford, on the other hand, is far more detailed in its association of clothes with memory: she leaves to her grandchildren "the remainder of the two rich armors which were my noble father's, to remaine to them and their posterity (if they soe please) as a remembrance of him." And to her "deare daughter," she leaves

my bracelett of little pomander beads, sett in gold and enamelling, containing fifty-seven beads in number, which usually I ware under my stomacher; which bracelett is above an hundred yeares old, and was given by Philip the Second, King of Spaine, to Mary, Queene of England [and by her?] to my greate grandmother, Anne, Countesse of Bedford: and also two little peices of my father and mother, sett in a tablett of gold, and enamelled with blew; and all those seaven or eight old truncks and all that is within them, being for the most part old things that were my deare and blessed mother's, which truncks commonly stand in my owne chamber or the next unto it.

Finally, Anne Clifford left

[t]o Mrs. Elizabeth Gilmore (whoe formerly served me for many yeares together) 20 l. and my fugard sattin mantle lyned with a white furr mixt, with haire collar; and to her daughter, Mrs. Elizabeth Kelloway, 10 l., and my best riding coate of haird colloured sattin. My weareing apparell to my servants, and my linnen to my daughter. 100 l. to be bestowed in mourning blacks att my death for some of my frinds and servants.

Here, the transmission of clothes is a transmission of wealth, of genealogy, of royal connections, but also of memory and of the love of mother for daughter (the trunks which she gives to her own daughter contain "old things that were my deare and blessed mother's, which truncks commonly stand in my owne chamber or the next unto it").[153]

It was not only aristocrats who bequeathed their clothing with such care. A typical legacy of a master to his apprentice was the gift of clothes. Augustine Phillips, an actor and sharer in the King's Men, left bequests upon his death in 1605 not only to fellow sharers like Henry Condell and William Shakespeare, but also to the boy actor who had trained under him:

Item, I give to Samuel Gilborne, my late apprentice, the sum of forty shillings, and my mouse-colored velvet hose, and a white taffeta doublet, and black taffeta suit, my purple cloak, sword, and dagger, and my bass viol.[154]

Bequests of clothes recur in actors' wills. Thomas Pope, another actor in the King's Men, wrote in his will in 1604: "I give and bequeath to Robert Gough and John Edmans all my wearing apparel, and all my arms, to be equally divided between them."[155] William Bird, a leading actor in the Earl of Pembroke's Men and then with the Lord Admiral's Men, wrote on January 30, 1623: "I doe bequeath vnto my eldest sonne William Byrd my Ash cullor suite and cloake of cloth laced with sattin lace . . . I give and bequeath vnto my third sonne Thomas Burde my Ash cullor suite and cloake trimmed with greene silke and siluer lace."[156] Philip Henslowe himself, while he traded professionally in secondhand clothes, participated in the circulation of material ghosts – the clothes of his dead brother, Edmond, who left him "a gold ring with a pearl, and a black cloak."[157] The clothes are preserved; they remain. It is the bodies that inhabit them that change.

Memories are literally *worn*. This is quite explicit in Renaissance wills, even when new clothing and jewelry are called for. Pieces of jewelry (and in particular rings) were, in fact, the most frequent form of explicit memorial. The actor, Thomas Bass, left money in his will in 1634 to nine friends to buy "each of them a Ring of the value of tenn shillings a peece to weare in remembrance of him."[158] Similarly John Hemminges, the sharer in the King's Men, bequeathed "vnto every of my fellowes and sharers his Mats servants . . . the somme of tenn shillinges apeece to make them ringes for remembrances of me." But William Browne left twenty shillings to his company "to buy them blacke ribbons to weare in remembrance of me." And the buying of memorial clothes is clearly implied in Nicholas Tooley's will of 1624: "Item I doe giue vnto her [Mrs. Cuthbert Burbage's] daughter Elizabethe Burbadge als Maxey the summe of tenn pounds to be paied vnto her owne proper hands (therwithall to buy her such things as shee shall thincke most meete to weare in remembrance of mee)."[159]

What implications can we draw out from the wills that bequeathed clothes? First, clothes have a life of their own; they both *are* material presences and they *absorb* other material and immaterial presences. In the transfer of clothes, identities are transferred from an aristocrat to an actor, from an actor to a master, from a master to an apprentice. Such transfers are, of course, staged within the theater in the many scenes where a servant dresses as his or her master, a lover dresses in the borrowed garments of another lover, a skull inhabits the clothes which have survived it. In *Twelfth Night*, brother is transformed into sister and sister into brother through the costume identified as Cesario/Sebastian. We here move closer to the narrower meaning of "transvestism" as the term is used today, to imply cross-gendering. But what we want to emphasize is the extent to which the Elizabethan theater, and the culture more generally, was fixated upon clothes in and of themselves. This fixation was part of a larger interest in what Arjun Appadurai has called the social life of things.[160]

In fact, the things that have most power to haunt upon the Renaissance stage are usually parts or fragments: a handkerchief, a glove, a sleeve, a shoe. As the tokens of partings or deaths, they haunt the wearer, making present an absence. When Rafe in Dekker's *The Shoemaker's Holiday* is conscripted to fight in France, he gives his wife a pair of shoes:

> Now gentle wife, my louing louely *Iane*,
> Rich men at parting, giue their wiues rich gifts,
> Iewels and rings, to grace their lillie hands,
> Thou know'st our trade makes rings for womens heeles:
> Here take this paire of shooes cut out by *Hodge*,
> Sticht by my fellow *Firke*, seam'd by my selfe,
> Made vp and pinckt, with letters for thy name,
> Weare them my deere *Iane*, for thy husbands sake,
> And euerie morning when thou pull'st them on,
> Remember me, and pray for my returne,
> Make much of them, for I haue made them so,
> That I can know them from a thousand mo.[161]

The shoes commemorate the collaborative work of the guild, the cut-out name of his wife, and his own love. They materialize memory: "euerie morning when thou pullst them on, / Remember me."

And such material memories can themselves shift, like the Ghost of Hamlet, from the neuter "it" to haunting life. Cressida, taking back Troilus's sleeve from Diomedes, talks to it and kisses it, as she imagines Troilus kissing the glove that she has given him:

> O prettie, prettie pledge;
> Thy Maister now lies thinking in [Q1, on] his bed
> Of thee and me, and sighes, and takes my Gloue,
> And giues memoriall daintie kisses to it;
> As I kisse thee.   (5. 2. 77–81 [TLN 3062–6])

Similarly, Emilia describes Desdemona as kissing and talking to the handkerchief that Othello has given her:

> This was her first remembrance from the Moore . . .
>   . . . she so loues the Token,
> (For he coniur'd her, she should euer keepe it)
> That she reserues it euermore about her,
> To kisse, and talke too. (3. 3. 295–300 [TLN 1926–31])

But in *The Shoemaker's Holiday*, in *Troilus and Cressida*, in *Othello*, the tokens of remembrance are above all *detachable*. That is, if they conjure up presence, they equally invoke loss. They are turned into imitable patterns (like Jane's shoes and Desdemona's handkerchief); they are lost or transferred from one person to another (like Troilus's sleeve and Desdemona's handkerchief); they are absorbed into new narratives or deprived of all narrative.

The handkerchief in *Othello* is striking in this respect. It is initially presented to the audience not as a "first remembrance" but as a piece of cloth that is inadequate for its function. "Your Napkin," Othello tells Desdemona, "is too little" (3. 3. 291 [TLN 1922]). Only when the napkin is lost and Emilia picks it up does it gather a story around it. Or rather, several stories: of Othello's love for Desdemona; of Iago's desire for Emilia to steal it; of Emilia's intention to imitate its design. And as the handkerchief is transferred from Emilia to Iago, from Iago to Cassio, from Cassio to Bianca, it will absorb ever new stories: as the silk that Iago claims he saw Cassio "wipe his Beard with" (3. 3. 446 [TLN 2088]); as the imagined sign of Cassio's betrayal of Bianca; as the "lost" narrative of Othello's own origins. Even in that last guise, it will tell competing and contradictory stories. In the first version that Othello gives, the handkerchief was sewed by a Sibyl of "hallowed" silkworms and it was "dyde in Mummy, which the Skilfull / Conseru'd of Maidens hearts":

> That Handkerchiefe
> Did an Aegyptian to my Mother giue:
> She was a Charmer, and could almost read
> The thoughts of people. She told her, while she kept it,
> 'T would make her Amiable, and subdue my Father
> Intirely to her loue: But if she lost it,
> Or made a Guift of it, my Fathers eye
> Should hold her loathed, and his Spirits should hunt
> After new Fancies. She dying, gaue it me,
> And bid me (when my Fate should haue me Wiu'd)
> To giue it her.   (3. 4. 53–73 [TLN 2203–24])

But when Othello returns to the story of the handkerchief in the final act, there is no mention of the Sibyl, or of the maiden's hearts, or of the Egyptian woman who was a "Charmer" and who gave it to his mother. The handkerchief is now "an Antique Token," and it was given to his mother not by a woman of supernatural powers but by his father.

The ability of the handkerchief to absorb so many different narratives lends itself to semiotic analysis, to an analysis that would repeat the transformation of memory systems into the theatrical props of the characters' fictions. Such an analysis is encouraged by the "evacuation of the real" that the innovatory professional theaters encouraged. *This* handkerchief is, indeed, infinitely imitable and replaceable; it can be imitated and replaced at every new production of the play, or whenever the theatrical prop is lost.

But to think of the handkerchief only in this way is to collude with Thomas Rymer's notorious assessment of *Othello*, since there is little to choose between imagining the handkerchief as semiotic device and as a trifling piece of cloth. Both perspectives erase the materiality of the making of memory, a materiality that inevitably includes the contingent and the fraudulent. The handkerchief is, no doubt, like the souvenir that Susan Stewart so brilliantly describes, "an object arising out of the necessarily insatiable demands of nostalgia." The inability of "narrative to be one with its object," Stewart argues, opens up a nostalgia that is "hostile to history and its invisible origins, and yet long[s] for an impossibly pure context of lived experience at a place of origin."[162] But to reduce the material bearers of memory to pure narrative is to erase their power. As Walter Benjamin wrote in *The Origin of German Drama*:

If the object becomes allegorical under the gaze of melancholy, if melancholy causes life to flow out of it and it remains dead, but eternally secure, then it is exposed to the allegorist, it is unconditionally in his power. That is to say it is now quite incapable of emanating any meaning or significance of its own.[163]

The handkerchief in *Othello* stages the evacuations of nostalgia (as in its transformation, in Othello's account, from token of female magical powers to paternal gift), but it equally presents the haunting of materiality itself. In the Renaissance theater, "character" is always haunted by clothes that give a name or that have conversed with other bodies. They stage the otherness that materializes the impossibility of self-possession. If we do not understand these clothes, we do not understand the action, or the actors, or the theater itself. But that theater, far from reproducing the orderly transmissions of a cloth economy, obsessively staged the misunderstanding of clothes, clothes as a site of crisis from which nostalgia for a lost time of splendid armor could offer no reprieve. The transmission of clothes figures the formation and dissolution of identity, the ways in which the subject is possessed and dispossessed, touched and haunted by the materials it inhabits.

8 Transvestism and the "body beneath": speculating on the boy actor

This chapter starts from a puzzle: what did a Renaissance audience see when boy actors undressed on stage?[1] The puzzle could, of course, be resolved by a simple (and, for our argument, damaging) move. The boy actor doesn't undress, or, at least, doesn't undress to the point of disturbing the illusion; the audience sees nothing. Against such a move, we want on the one hand to think bluntly about the prosthetic devices, and above all the clothes, through which gender is rendered visible upon the stage. In that sense, the visible is an empirical question (although a question to which we seem to have surprisingly few answers). But on the other hand, we want to suggest the degree to which the Renaissance spectator is required to speculate upon a boy actor who undresses, and thus to speculate upon the relation between the boy actor and the woman he plays. This speculation depends upon a cultural fantasy of sight, but a fantasy that plays back and forth between sexual difference as a site of indeterminacy (the undoing of any stable or given difference) and sexual difference (and sexuality itself) as the production of contradictory fixations, fixations articulated through a fetishistic attention to particular items of clothing, particular parts of the body of an imagined woman, particular parts of an actual boy actor. On the Renaissance stage the demand that the spectator see is at its most intense in the undressing of the boy actor, at the very moment when what is seen is most vexed, being the point of intersection between spectatorship, the specular, and the speculative.

The prosthetic body

One of the most substantial theatrical properties of the professional theaters was a bed. It is a property which is called for in play after play, mainly in tragedy, but also in history and comedy. *Volpone* revolves around the bed in which Volpone simulates death, the bed from which he rises in his attempted rape of Celia; *Cymbeline* hinges upon Iachimo spying upon Imogen while she lies asleep in bed; in *The Maid's Tragedy*, Evadne ties the king to the bed in which they have made love before she kills him; in *Othello*, the bed bears the bodies of Desdemona, Emilia and Othello in the final scene. One becomes accustomed to stage directions like: "King a bed";[2] "Enter Othello, and Desdemona in her bed"; "Enter Imogen, in her Bed, and a Lady."[3] The bed becomes a focal point of scenes of sleep, of sex, of death. But bed scenes also focus upon facts so obvious that they resist interpretation as we hasten on to find out what these scenes are about: they draw attention to undressing or being undressed, to the process of shedding those garments through which class and gender were made visible and staged. They stage clothes as material signs which can be put on and taken off.

At the same time, bed scenes foreground the body: the body which is either literally or symbolically about to be exposed. And here we come to a peculiar problem. The consensus of recent scholars on Renaissance transvestism has been that it is self-consciously staged mainly in comedy. Lisa Jardine, in her important work on the the boy actor, states what has now become a commonplace: the eroticism of the boy player is invoked in the drama whenever it is openly alluded to. These allusions appear mainly in comedy, where role-playing and disguise are often central. In tragedy, the willing suspension of disbelief, it is usually argued, extends to the acting of the female parts by boy players; taken for granted, it is rarely analyzed.[4] What are we to make, though, of those repeated bed scenes in Renaissance tragedy when we begin to witness an undressing or we are asked to see or to imagine an undressed (or partially undressed) body in the bed? What is it we are being asked to see?

If we take *Othello* as our starting point, we may reach some curious conclusions. As Lynda Boose has argued, the "ocular proof" that Othello demands is reworked in the play as the audience's voyeuristic desire to see, to "grossely gape" (3. 3. 395 [TLN 2042]).[5] But what are we to gape at? From the beginning of the eighteenth century, as Michael Neill has shown, illustrators of *Othello* were obsessively concerned with the depiction of the final bed scene. Even as Desdemona's "Will you come to bed, my Lord?" (5. 2. 24 [TLN 3265]) was cut from theatrical productions, illustrators focused upon the dead Desdemona lying in bed.[6] And what the illustrators above all reveal (requiring that the spectator grossly gape) are the bedclothes and clothing pulled back to show a single exposed breast.[7] The bed scene, then, is taken by the illustrators as an opportunity for the display of the female body, and in particular of a woman's breast.

Although we cannot take such illustrations as reflecting eighteenth-century stage productions, we do, in fact, find the exposure of the female breast recurrently called for by stage directions after the introduction of women actors to the the stage in the previous century. On the Renaissance stage, actual boys played seeming "boys" who were "revealed" to be women – Ganymede as Rosalind, Cesario as Viola.[8] But on the Restoration stage, women played boys who were revealed to be women. And they were often revealed as women by the exposure of their breasts.

In fact, the commonest technique for the revelation of the "woman beneath" after the Restoration was the removal of a wig, whereupon the female actor's "true" hair would be seen. In Boyle's *Guzman* (1669), for instance, a woman disguised as a priest is exposed when "Francisco pulls off her Peruque, and her Womans Hair falls about her ears."[9] This, of course, can depend upon the interplay of prostheses, an interplay which would have been perfectly possible on the Renaissance stage. The audience would have no means of knowing (any more than we do today) whether the hair beneath the wig was the hair of the actor or another wig. The play of difference (male wig/female hair) had no necessary relation to the anatomical specificities of the actor's body. If, then, the distinction of the sexes is staged as a distinction of hair (and above all of hair length), it will be constantly transformed by changes in hair styles. Sexual difference may, in this case, seem essentially prosthetic: the addition (or subtraction) of detachable (or growable/cuttable) parts.

It is precisely such a prosthetic view which William Prynne denounced in *The Unlovelinesse of Lovelockes* (1628). There, he elaborates at length on St. Paul: "Doth not even nature itself teach you, that, if a man have long hair, it is a shame unto him? But if a woman have long hair it is a glory to her" (I Corinthians 11. 14–15). From Prynne's perspective, the problem is precisely that "nature" doesn't seem to have taught its lesson thoroughly enough. Cavalier men flaunt their long hair (and, from 1641, were to ridicule their opponents as "Roundheads," in reference to their close-cropped hair). Prynne asserts that gender is defined by "the outward Culture of [our] Heads, and Bodies,"and that the long hair of men and the short hair of women erases sexual difference.[10] We live, he claims, in "Unnaturall, and Unmanly times: wherein . . . sundry of our Mannish, Impudent, and inconstant Female sexe, are Hermaphrodited, and transformed into men" because they "unnaturally clip, and cut their Haire."[11] Asserting hair as a sign of natural difference, Prynne is particularly fierce in his denunciation of wigs: "the wearing of counterfeite, false, and suppositious Haire, is *utterly unlawfull*."[12] In making the putting on and taking off of wigs a marker of gender difference, the Restoration stage turned Prynne on his head. "Natural" signs became the artifices of malleable gender.

But, as we noted above, the Restoration theater used a second, overlapping method of revealing the "woman beneath": the exposure of the female actor's breasts. The methods are overlapping because they could be used together: in Wycherley's *The Plain Dealer* (1676), when Fidelia, in disguise, confesses that she is a woman, Vernish "Pulls off her peruke and feels her breasts"; and in Hopkins's *Friendship Improv'd* (1699), Locris, refusing to fight with her lover, says: "Here's my bare Breast, now if thou dar'st, strike here. (*She loosens her robe a little, her Helmet drops off, and her Hair appears*)."[13] Here, the stage directions are ambiguous: even if Vernish feels Fidelia's breast and Locris "loosens her robe," we cannot be sure what it was that an audience was supposed actually to see.

The revelation of the female actor's breasts, though, is central to the staging of Aphra Behn's *The Younger Brother; Or, the Amorous Jilt* (1696). In that play, there is an elaborate bed scene in which Mirtilla, in love with the cross-dressed Olivia, says "Come to my Bed" (stage direction: "*She leading him* [sic] *to her Bed*"), while the Prince, who is in love with Mirtilla, breaks in upon the scene. The prince grabs hold of the cross-dressed Olivia, and the stage direction reads: "*The* Prince *holding* Olivia *by the Bosom of her Coat, her Breast appears to* Mirtilla." Mirtilla: "Ha! what do I see? – Two Female rising Breasts. / By heav'n, a Woman." The Prince, however, has not seen these signs of Olivia's gender, so the revelation is repeated by Mirtilla who, as a later stage direction reads, "*Opens* Olivia's *Bosom, shows her Breasts*."[14] It is worth remarking that Aphra Behn uses the revelation convention to play with the relation between woman and woman (it is Mirtilla who first sees Olivia's breasts, it is she who opens Olivia's bosom).[15]

But there can be little doubt that such stagings of the female actor's breasts were usually constituted for the arousal of the heterosexual male spectator. (A more extended discussion of this point would need to look at the significant position of the Restoration theater in the construction of the "heterosexual male spectator.") According to Colley Cibber, the very presence of female actors upon the stage helped to constitute a new audience (or rather new spectators): "The additional Objects then of real, beautiful Women, could not but draw a portion of new Admirers to the Theatre."[16] In the Epilogue to Nathaniel Lee's *The Rival Queens* (1677), the actors protest that if their male spectators continue to lure female actors away from the stage, they will return to using boy actors:

For we have vow'd to find a sort of Toys
Known to black Fryars, a Tribe of chopping Boys.
If once they come, they'l quickly spoil your sport;
There's not one Lady will receive your Court:
But for the Youth in Petticoats run wild,
With oh the archest Wagg, the sweetest Child.
The panting Breasts, white hands and little feet
No more shall your pall'd thoughts with pleasure meet.
The Woman in Boys Cloaths, all Boy shall be,
And never raise your thoughts above the Knee.[17]

The threat to replace women with boy actors is not imagined here as a general loss but as a loss to the male spectator alone. The female spectator, on the contrary, is imagined as running wild after the "Youth in Petticoats." The boy actor is thus depicted as particularly alluring to women, a possibility that has been subtly analyzed by Stephen Orgel.[18]

But the grammar of the Epilogue is strangely playful about the crucial question: the difference between a boy actor and a female actor. "The panting Breasts, white Hands and little Feet" seem at first to follow directly on from, and thus to be the attributes of, the archest wags, the sweetest children; but this possibility is retracted in the next line: "No more" shall such breasts, hands, and feet be seen when boy actors return. Yet the feet of the boy actor would seem to be adequate enough for his female role, if we are to take literally that he will "never raise your thoughts above the Knee." The crucial point of that latter line, of course, is what the boy actor does not have: implicitly a vagina; explicitly breasts.

It is that explicit absence upon which we want to dwell here. For recent criticism has been particularly concerned with the "part" that the boy actor has which is not in his part.[19] (That part is sometimes peculiarly distorted [and enlarged] by being thought of as a "phallus," as if a boy's small parts weren't peculiarly – and interestingly – at variance with the symbolic weight of *the* phallus.) Criticism has thus been concerned with what Shakespeare calls the "addition" that the boy actor brings to a female role. But in bed scene after bed scene, what is staged is a tableau in which we are about to witness the *female body* (and most particularly the female breast), even though it is a *boy* who is undressing. Indeed, there seems to be something so odd about this fact that it has usually been overlooked.[20]

So let us declare first of all what the puzzles are to which we have no solution. Did boy actors wear false breasts? There seem to be no records of such a practice, but the female fury at the beginning of *Salmacida Spolia* was presumably played by a professional actor whose "*breasts hung bagging down to her waist.*"[21] Or did boys use tight lacing to gather up their flesh so as to create a cleavage? Or were they simply flat-chested, or . . . ? While John Rainoldes denounces Achilles's trans-vestism, which William Gager had used in defense of the academic stage, he notes that Achilles had learned from Deidamia "howe *he must hold his naked brest.*"[22] A further question: in undressing scenes, how far did the boy actor go in actually removing his clothes or, if he was in bed, how much of his flesh was revealed? These questions we shall not be attempting to resolve.

We want less to suggest a resolution than to express the dimensions of the problem. Kathleen McLuskie argues for a conventional view of the boy actor.[23] To support her view, she draws upon R. A. Foakes's *Illustrations of the English Stage*, which reproduces title pages and illustrations to play quartos in which women are represented with their breasts fully or partially exposed.[24] McLuskie appears to conclude that this is how we are meant to think of the boy actors: within the convention, we can imagine them fully as women. But Foakes's *Illustrations* are themselves puzzling when we try to relate them to the practices of the English Renaissance stage and to the boy actor. Only one of the illustrations to which we will refer can, in our view, be thought of as in any way an illustration of the *stage*; the others are illustrations (some presumably reuses of woodcuts made for other purposes) for a *reader* of play quartos, a very different matter.

How do these illustrations depict the female body, and, in particular, women's breasts? There is no one answer to this. To start with the three different title pages to *If You Know Not Me, You Know Nobody* in 1605, 1623, and 1639: all depict Elizabeth I conventionally enough in an elaborate gown with a low-cut bodice.[25] But there is no suggestion of a cleavage, and only in the 1605 woodcut do two loops of pearls suggest the shape of her breasts. If a boy actor wanted to imitate such an appearance, he would have no difficulty in doing so with the help of costume alone. And the same is true for the women represented on the title pages of *The Fair Maid of the West* (1631) and of *Englishmen for my Money* (1616), in which the attributes of gender are hair and costume, and the bodices in these cases extend up to the neck.[26] But the title page of William Alabaster's *Roxana* (1632) is more complicated. It is famous for the fact that in one of its panels it shows actors upon a stage.[27] The woman on the stage is clearly depicted as having swelling breasts. Another panel of the title page shows a couple in classical clothes, the man touching the woman's breasts, which are clearly depicted, as is her right nipple. At the furthest extreme, there are the title pages of Beaumont and Fletcher's *Philaster* (1620) and Sir William Lower's *The Enchanted Lovers* (1658), both of which depict women with fully exposed breasts.[28] (On 30 May 1668, Pepys went to see *Philaster*, "where it is pretty to see how I could remember almost all along, ever since I was a boy, Arethusa, the part which I was to have acted at Sir Robert Cookes's; and it was very pleasant to me, but more to think what a ridiculous thing it would have been for me to have acted a beautiful woman."[29] Some play quartos, then, draw attention to the specificities of women's bodies in ways which would be extremely difficult (if not impossible) to represent upon the stage.

Now this whole discussion would be irrelevant if we assumed that the convention of the boy actor meant that the physical body of the boy was subsumed by the conventions of femininity signified by costume and gesture. That such subsumptions are, indeed, one feature of Renaissance theatrical and non-theatrical texts is a point to which we shall return. But what we want to emphasize here is the extent to which such subsumptions were also played with to the point of their undoing. That they *could* be played with has something to do with systematic dislocations between visual and linguistic systems of representation in the Renaissance. We noted above the extent to which visual representations of women in play quartos move between representations which depend upon costume/hair/gesture and those which also depend upon a display of the naked body, and in particular of the naked breast. The displayed breast is a metonymy for woman. Since for us, both "breast" and "bosom" are always already gendered, this comes as little surprise. But in the Renaissance, both "breast" and "bosom" are used interchangeably for men and women. ("Pap," on the other hand, was usually applied to women.) "Bosom," indeed, seems to be more frequently gendered as masculine. After the 1611 translation of the Bible introduced the Hebraic "wife of thy bosome" and "husband of her bosome," it was only the former expression which became current, thus reemphasizing the bosom as male. The language of breasts and bosoms tended to be either ungendered or absorbed into the power of the patriarch. To "toy" with breasts verbally, then, had no obvious implications for the relation of the boy actor to his female role.

But this indeterminacy of gender at the verbal level was radically opposed by the visual codes in which the breast was insistently gendered as female. What remains extraordinary is the extent to which this female-gendered breast is staged by the boy actor. In Jonson's *The Devil is an Ass*, for instance, as Wittipol approaches "[t]hese sister-swelling brests" of Frances Fitzdottrell, the stage direction reads: "*he growes more familiar in his Courtship, plays with her paps, kisseth her hands, &.*"[30] But the boy actor's "female body" is most commonly the object of attention in tragedy and tragicomedy. There, we are asked not to imagine the boy actor as he is dressed up, but literally to gaze at him while he undresses.

This staging of the undressing boy is particularly striking in death scenes and bed scenes that draw attention to the boy actor's "breast." In Ford's *Love's Sacrifice*, the Duke says to Bianca "Prepare to dye," and she responds:

> I doe; and to the point
> Of thy sharpe sword with open brest I'le runne
> Halfe way thus naked.[31]

Even more striking is the way in which Shakespeare in both *Antony and Cleopatra* and *Cymbeline* changes his sources so as to draw attention to the boy actor's breasts. In Plutarch, Cleopatra attaches an asp to her *arm*. Shakespeare retains this, but only after she has already placed an asp upon her *breast*. And Cleopatra/the boy actor, who has already imagined seeing "[s]ome squeaking *Cleopatra* Boy my greatnesse" (5. 2. 218 [TLN 3463]), focuses attention upon a nursing breast that is at the furthest remove from the breast of the boy actor: "Dost thou not see my Baby at my breast, / That suckes the Nurse asleepe" (5. 2. 309–10 [TLN 3562–3]).[32] An audience seems to be required to observe the splitting apart of what later critics have assumed to be a stable "convention." Indeed, later critics have used the presence of the boy actor to argue that Renaissance dramatists deliberately avoided drawing attention to the female body. Enobarbus's description of Cleopatra is thus taken as a technique of avoidance, by which the audience is spared the embarrassment of gazing at a transvestite boy. But what becomes of such explanations when, again and again, we find Renaissance dramatists going beyond their sources to demand that we witness the boy actor at the very point which a later audience has ruled unimaginable?

In *Cymbeline*, for instance, as Iachimo observes Imogen asleep in bed, he fetishizes both the chamber, the bracelet which will represent her lost honour, and a "mole Cinque-spotted" upon "her left brest" (2. 2. 37–8 [TLN 944–5]). This last detail, like the asp on Cleopatra's breast, is truly astonishing. It has been argued that Shakespeare used *Frederyke of Jennen* as a source for *Cymbeline*, and in that pamphlet John of Florence notes not a mole on the *breast*, but a wart on the *arm* of Ambrose's wife: "it fortuned that her lefte arme lay on the bed; and on that arme she had a blacke warte."[33] But Shakespeare replaces the wart with a mole (following Boccaccio's version of the story), a mole which is given a precise but imaginary location upon the body of the boy actor. To make the left breast the object of this voyeuristic scene is to focus our attention on one of the sites of the cultural differentiation of gender. But that site produces antithetical readings: Imogen's swelling breast; the breast of a boy actor. It is as if within the dramatic fiction, the fetishized signs of the female body are forced to confront the absences which mark the boy actor's body. Or perhaps we might rather say that two contradictory realities are forced to peer into each other's faces. In *Cymbeline*, at the very moment where a later audience would expect a discrete effacement of the theatrical means by which gender is produced, those means are verbally and visually displayed.

The specifically erotic charge of such bed scenes is suggested by Aphra Behn, even as she attempts to defend herself against the supposed indecency of her own plays. Accused of staging lewd revelations of the actor's body ("they cry, *That Mr.* Leigh *opens his Night Gown, when he comes into the Bride-chamber*"), she responds that the best plays are full of such things:

Valentinian all loose and ruffld a Moment after the Rape . . . , the *Moor of Venice* in many places. The *Maids Tragedy* – see the Scene of undressing the Bride, and between the *King* and *Amintor*, and after between the *King* and *Evadne*.[34]

It is striking that Behn, in thinking of the erotics of the theater, thinks on the one hand of Rochester's *Valentinian*, a Restoration play which explicitly stages homo-eroticism,[35] and on the other of Renaissance plays in which the undressing of the bride was performed by a boy. Behn, of course, would have seen the Renaissance plays performed with female actors, but she still empasizes the extent to which these plays reveal the body.

We need to conceptualize the erotics of Renaissance drama in totally unfamiliar ways if we are to make sense of these queer stagings of the boy actor, stagings that insist that we see what, visually, we cannot see.[36] Think, for instance, of the end of *Othello*, where Desdemona says to Emilia: "Prythee to night / Lay on my bed my wedding sheetes" (4. 2. 104–5 [TLN 2806–7]). Between the command and the on-stage arrival of the bed itself, we are asked to witness the boy actor prepare for bed. This preparation is itself an act of transvestism – a crossing from day to night, from the public clothes of a Venetian noblewoman to the private, if no less splendid, nightgown. And such "closet" scenes are frequently – and strangely – marked by an explicit movement from formal to informal dress. Even ghosts obey this convention, if we are to believe the first quarto of *Hamlet*, where Hamlet Senior, appearing to his son in Gertrude's closet, has put off his armor and put on his nightgown. Both in *Othello* and *Hamlet*, the body seems to be simultaneously sexualized and made vulnerable. But in *Othello*, the movement from one set of clothes to another is curiously truncated. Desdemona's command to Emilia, "Giue me my nightly wearing" (4. 3. 16 [TLN 2985]), is followed some twenty lines later by Emilia's inquiry, "Shall I go fetch your Night-gowne?" (4. 3. 34 [TLN 3004]), to which Desdemona answers "No." In fact, the absence of the nightgown makes all the more insistent the fact that we are witnessing Desdemona / a boy actor undress. The undressing is the more present as a strip-tease because of the absence of any substitute clothing. "Prythee vn-pin me," Desdemona says, and later, rejecting the night-gown, "No, vn-pin me here" (4. 3. 21, 34 [TLN 2990, 3005).[37]

Before we return to this moment of voyeuristic suspense when the staged body prepares to split into the unpinned clothes and the body beneath, we should note how the scene as a whole stages a series of splittings or – to put it another way – a series of radical crossings of perspective. First, there is the presentation to the audience of Emilia's impressively relativistic view of sexual morality, a view which threatens to re-present the whole play as grotesque farce, the absurd magnification of "a *small* vice." Curiously, and to the disturbance of many critics, the "sport" which Emilia commends seems to migrate into the language of Desdemona:

> DES.   vn-pin me here,
>   This *Lodouico* is a proper man.
> *Aemil.* A very handsome man.
> DES. He speakes well.
> EMIL. I know a Lady in Venice would haue walk'd barefoot to Palestine for a touch
>   of his nether lip.   (4. 3. 34–9 [TLN 3005–10])

As Desdemona is unpinned, Othello is displaced by that "proper man," Lodovico. At the same time, Desdemona herself takes on the voice of a maidservant called Barbary.[38] The willow song is the song of that maid, whose name is itself a curious transposing of Iago's slur against Othello as he goads Brabantio: "you'll have your daughter cover'd with a Barbary horse; you'll have your nephews neigh to you." Barbary: the name for a bestial male sexuality; the name for a maid betrayed in love – "poor Barbary." A single signifier slides between male and female, animal and human, betrayer and betrayed, and at the same time between opposed notions of the "barbarian" as oppressor and as victim.

These slippages within the signifier provide one possible model through which we could read the undressing of Desdemona. On such a reading, the closure of the play would be unsettled by a startling moment of indeterminacy when we are held in suspension between cultural antitheses and, at the same time, between the fiction of Desdemona and the staging of the boy actor. But is "indeterminacy" an adequate way of thinking about these moments? Are we not rather forced into contradictory attitudes about both sexuality and gender: on the one hand, gender as a set of prosthetic devices, in which case, the gendered body is absorbed into the play of those devices; on the other, gender as the "given" marks of the body – the breast, the vagina, the penis – which (however analogous in Galenic medicine) are read as the signs of an absolute difference – in which case, sexuality, whether between man and woman, woman and woman, or man and man, tends to be organized through a fixation upon the supposedly essential features of gender. But on the Renaissance stage, even these "essential" features are located – whether prosthetically or at the level of the imaginary – upon another body, the body of a boy.

In comedy, the relation between the boy's body, the female role and erotic play is at times explicitly articulated. In the anonymous *The Taming of a Shrew*, the Lord says to the boy in the first scene:

> And dresse yourselfe like some lovelie ladie,
> And when I call see that you come to me,
> For I will say to him thou art his wife,
> Dallie with him and hug him in thine armes,
> And if he desire to goe to bed with thee,
> Then faine some scuse and say thou wilt anon.[39]

And Sly puts "*the boy in Womans attire*" on his knee and says that "she and I will go to bed anon."[40] In Shakespeare's *The Taming of the Shrew*, the Lord requires of the boy that he greet Sly not only with "kinde embracements" but with "tempting kisses," and there is an expanded invocation of the pleasures of the bed:

Wee'l have thee to a Couch,
Softer and sweeter then the lustfull bed
On purpose trim'd vp for Semiramis.   (Ind. 1. 116 [TLN 129], Ind. 2. 38–40 [TLN 190–1])

Sly's invitation to bed is also amplified: "Madam vndresse you, and come now to bed" (Ind. 2. 118 [TLN 271]). In both plays, any undressing or bed scene is explicitly circumvented, and this draws attention to the fact that in bed scenes (such as the ones we have looked at above) female clothes and boy actor are separated out.

But even here we can note a radical oscillation between a sense of the absolute difference of the boy from his role and the total absorption of the boy into the role. In other words, if Renaissance theater constructs an eroticism that depends upon a play of differences (the boy's breast / the woman's breast), it also equally conjures up an eroticism which depends upon the total absorption of male into female, female into male. In the printed text of Shakespeare's *The Shrew* in 1623, the boy is named as "Bartholmew my Page" (Ind. 1. 103 [TLN 115]) and yet, in changing into the clothes of a woman, he is entirely subsumed into her role. Where in *A Shrew*, the stage direction reads "*Enter the boy in Womans attire*," in *The Shrew* it reads: "*Enter Lady with Attendants*" (Ind. 2. 99 [TLN 252]). Moreover, the speech prefixes are all for "*Lady*" or "*La.*" The text thus accomplishes what John Rainoldes warns against in *Th' Overthrow of Stage-Playes*: "beware of beautifull boyes *transformed into women* by putting on their raiment, their feature, lookes and facions."[41] This transformation is carefully erased by a modern editor like Brian Morris, who emends the stage direction to read "*Enter* [PAGE *as a*] *lady*" and changes the speech prefixes to read "*Page.*"[42] In the Folio *The Shrew*, we are thus presented with a wild oscillation between contradictory positions: the plot of the induction demands that we remain aware of Bartholomew *as* Bartholomew, while the language of the text simply cuts Bartholomew, replacing him with "Lady."

Such wild oscillations are peculiarly resonant upon the stage precisely because of the boy actor. But comparable shifts are also characteristic of non-dramatic texts. In the anonymous romance *Frederyke of Jennen*, as soon as "Ambroses wyfe" takes on the name of "Frederyke," she becomes "he." Where a modern text would want to register the body beneath (i.e. "she dressed as he"), *Frederyke* inscribes the transformation of female into male through name and clothes. But, on the other hand, the transformation of Frederick back into Ambrose's wife does depend upon the revelation of the body beneath:

in the meane whyle went the lorde Frederyke secretly away, and came into the chamber, where she did vncothe her al naked saving a clothe before her membres, and than came into the hall before the kyng and al his lordes.[43]

Yet this revelation itself suggests no simple hierarchical relation of "reality" between what would later be read as "disguise" and the "true" body: dressed in men's clothes, he is "lorde Frederyke"; naked, she is "the woman" and then "his [Ambrose's] wyfe."

This oscillation of gender within a single sentence is even more striking in Barnabe Rich's tale "Of Apolonius and Silla": Silla dresses in men's clothes and assumes the name of her brother, Silvio. When accused by Julina of impregnating her, Silvio/ Silla reveals "his" body, here with all loosing his garmentes doune to his stomacke, and shewed *Iulina* his breastes and pretie teates, surmountyng farre the whitenesse of Snowe it self, saying: . . . see I am a woman the daughter of a noble Duke.[44]

Silvio shows "*his*" breasts which show that he is a woman (but also, curiously, that he is a nobleman's daughter). The phrase "his breastes and pretie teates" thus enacts the very cross-gendering at the grammatical level which the sentence is undoing at the level of narrative. The garments which are "his" – the social inscriptions of masculinity – retain, however briefly, their power to name a body which is equally powerfully asserted as *hers* ("I am a woman"). And the body which is "hers" is in turn reinscribed as "his" through the name of father and husband ("the daughter of a noble Duke," "Ambroses wyfe").

The power of clothes, like language, to do things to the body is suggested in both these romances, and it is this power of clothes which is so insistently asserted by antitheatricalists. Although Calvin, in his sermons on Deuteronomy, sometimes thinks of clothes as manifesting sexual difference, he equally thinks of them as creating difference: "God intended to shew us that every bodies attyring of themselves ought to be such, *as there may be a difference betweene men and women*."[45] Similarly, Prynne thinks of women who "mimic" masculinity as "Hermaphrodited and transformed into men" (1628: A3) and of male actors "metamorphosed into women on the Stage" (1633: 171).[46] And he follows Calvin in arguing that "a mans attyring himselfe in womans array . . . perverts one principall use of garments, *to difference men from women*."[47]

The antitheatricalists thus feared the power of clothes to produce new subjects, to metamorphose boy into woman, commoner into aristocrat. John Rainoldes's powerful attack upon the academic stage (and, by extension, upon all theatrical activity) was provoked in the first instance by the almost magical properties of transvestism.[48] Rainoldes, one of the greatest scholars of his day, had cross-dressed in his youth himself and in *Th' Overthrow of Stage-Plays* he admits that "he did play a womans part upon the same stage, the part of Hippolyta."[49] But what exactly is the danger of transvestism? Here, Rainoldes's citations are frequently opaque, as, for instance, the following from Dionysius Carthusianus:

the apparell of wemen (saith he) *is a great provocation of men to lust and leacherie: because a womans garment being put on a man doeth vehemently touch and move him with the remembrance and imagination of a woman; and the imagination of a thing desirable doth stir up the desire*.[50]

What does Rainoldes's translation imply? That the woman's body is imprinted upon or within the clothes? That women's clothes, when they touch and move the male wearer, will awaken the desire for women (whom he will remember and imagine) or the desire to be a woman? Will the desire be homo- or hetero-erotic and will it be directed toward another or toward the self?

The Renaissance theater was thus the site for the prosthetic production of the sexualized body through the clothing of the body and the mimed gestures of love. But it was also the site where that prosthetic production was dramatically staged and speculated upon, as the boy actor undressed, as the fixations of spectators were drawn back and forth between the clothes which embodied and determined a particular sexual identity and contradictory fantasies of the body beneath – the body of a woman, the body of a boy; a body with and without breasts.

The transvestite body[51]

The interplay between clothing and undressing on the Renaissance stage organized gender around a process of fetishizing, which is conceived both as a process of fixation and as indeterminable.[52] If the Renaissance stage demands that we "see" particular body parts (the breast, the penis, the naked body), it also reveals that such fixations are inevitably unstable. The actor is both boy and woman, and he/she embodies the fact that sexual fixations are not the product of any categorical fixity of gender. Indeed, all attempts to fix gender are necessarily prosthetic: that is, they suggest the attempt to supply an imagined deficiency by the exchange of male clothes for female clothes or of female clothes for male clothes; by displacement from male to female space or from female to male space; by the replacement of male with female tasks or of female with male tasks. But all elaborations of the prosthesis which will supply the "deficiency" can secure no essence. On the contrary, they suggest that gender itself is a fetish, the production of an identity through the fixation upon specific parts. The imagined truth of gender which a post-Renaissance culture would later construct is dependent upon the disavowal of the fetishism of gender, the disavowal of gender as fetish. In its place, post-Renaissance culture would put a fantasized biology of the "real."

But this notion of the "real" seems to be dramatically undone in undressing scenes, as in *Othello* when Desdemona / the boy actor is unpinned. Lynda Boose has demonstrated how the play itself demands both concealment (of the sexual scene, of the bed and its burden which "poisons sight") and exposure (the stimulated desire that we should see, should "grossly gape").[53] But, as we have argued, what we should see is radically uncertain. It is not so much a moment of indeterminacy as of contradictory fixations. On the one hand, the clothes themselves – the marks of Desdemona's gender and status – are held up to our attention; on the other, we teeter on the brink of seeing the boy's breastless but "pinned" body revealed. It is as if, at the moments of greatest dramatic tension, the Renaissance theater stages its own transvestism.

Contradictory fixations, though, are precisely what mobilize *Othello*. Think, for instance, of how Iago constructs the narrative of Desdemona's betrayal so that Othello can approach the "gross gaping" of her being "topp'd." Iago does it by casting himself in the role of Desdemona:

> I lay with *Cassio* lately . . .
> In sleepe I heard him say, sweet *Desdemona*,
> Let us be wary, le us hide our Loves,
> And then (Sir) would he gripe, and wring my hand:
> Cry, oh sweet Creature: then kisse me hard,
> As if he pluckt up kisses by the rootes,
> That grew upon my lippes, laid his Leg ore my Thigh,
> And sigh, and kisse.
> (3. 3. 419–31)

It is these contradictory fixations (Desdemona and/as the boy actor, Desdemona and/as Iago) which a later theater would attempt to erase, precisely because the site of the audience's sexual fixation is so uncertain.

This uncertainty is, paradoxically, most powerfully felt by antitheatrical writers. They oscillate between seeing the boy actor as woman, as neither woman nor man, as alluring boy, as male prostitute (or "dogge," to use Rainoldes's term). Prynne, for instance, incorporates Cyprian's account of how the theater taught "how a man might be effeminated into a female, how their sex might be changed by Art."[54] But he can also think of actors as those who, "by unchaste infections of their members, effeminate their manly nature, being both effeminate men and women, yea, being neither men nor women."[55] Yet the uncertainty of what antitheatricalists saw in no way inhibited the obsessive fixity of their (imaginary) gaze. What they gazed at was a theater imagined as a bedroom, a bedroom which spills off the stage and into the lives of players and audience alike:

> O . . . that thou couldest in that sublime watch-tower insinuate thine eyes into these Players secrets; or set open the closed dores of their bed-chambers, and bring all their innermost hidden Cels unto the conscience of thine eyes . . . [M]en rush on men with outragious lusts.[56]

So writes Prynne, translating Cyprian. And Phillip Stubbes sees the actors as contaminating the spectators so that "these goodly pageants being done, every mate sorts to his mate . . . and in their secret conclaves (covertly) they play *the Sodomits*, or worse."[57] But what antitheatricalists saw in the "secret conclaves" of the theatrical bedroom constantly shifted, thus mimicking the shifting perspectives of the Renaissance stage itself.

For the bed scenes and undressing scenes with which we have been concerned produce moments of dizzying indeterminacy. It was such moments that Freud attempted to describe in his essay on "Fetishism," where the fetish stands in for and mediates between the marks of sexual difference.[58] Freud writes:

> In very subtle instances both the disavowal and the affirmation of the castration (of woman) have found their way into the construction of the fetish itself. This was so in the case of a man whose fetish was an athletic support-belt which could also be worn as bathing drawers. This piece of clothing covered up the genitals entirely and concealed the distinction between them. Analysis showed that it signified that women were castrated *and* that they were not castrated; and it also allowed of the hypothesis that men were castrated, for all these possiblities could equally well be concealed under the belt.[59]

The athletic support-belt, through its concealments, supports contradictory hypotheses. But for Freud, all these hypotheses must be grounded in the fantasy of castration. Why? Because Freud needs to find a fixed point (and a *male* point) outside the play of fetishism, a point to which all other fetishes will teleologically point. The fetishist is, Freud suggests, someone whose interest "*comes to a halt half-way, as it were . . .* Thus the foot or shoe owes its preference as a fetish – or a part of it – to the circumstance that the inquisitive boy peered at the woman's genitals from below, from her legs up."[60] The fetish is, for Freud, but part of the larger category of perversions. "Perversions," he writes in the *Three Essays on Sexuality*, are sexual activities which either a) extend, in an anatomical sense, beyond the regions of the body that are designed for sexual union, or b) linger, over the intermediate relations to the sexual object which should normally be traversed rapidly on the path towards the sexual aim.[61] The very notion of the perverse, like that of the fetish, can only emerge in relation to a) the parts of the body which are "naturally" sexual and b) a teleological path towards the genitals.

But the transvestite theater of the Renaissance does not allow for any such distinction between the "perverse" and the normal teleological path. From a Freudian perspective, it "comes to a halt half-way, as it were." It does so because it resists the sexual and narrative teleologies which would be developed in the eighteenth and nineteenth centuries. But that resistance is less a matter of indeterminacy than of the production of contradictory fixations: the imagined body of a woman, the staged body of a boy actor, the material presence of clothes. Freud's brilliant insight was to see that the "real person" was itself a displacement of fetishism:

> The progressive concealment of the body which goes along with civilization keeps sexual curiosity awake. This curiosity seeks to complete the sexual object by revealing its hidden parts. It can, however, be diverted ("sublimated") in the direction of art, if its interest can be shifted away from the genitals on to the shape of the body as a whole.[62]

"The body as a whole," then, is itself a fantasy, a sublimation. But for Freud, the real tends to reappear behind or beneath that fantasy, a real which always tends towards the formation of sexual difference. In the "mingle-mangle," the "hodge-podge," the "gallimaufry" of Renaissance tragedy, though, contradictory fetishisms (body parts, costumes, handkerchiefs, sheets) are staged not in the play of pure difference but in the play between indeterminacy and fixation.

9 (In)alienable possessions: Griselda, clothing, and the exchange of women

In the previous chapter, we explored the making and unmaking of gender in the dressing and undressing of the boy actor. In this chapter, we turn to Boccaccio's tale of Griselda in *The Decameron*, a story which presents successive scenes of the undressing and redressing of a young woman. In the first scene of reclothing, an aristocratic husband strips the peasant Griselda of her russet gown so as to redress her in the courtly garments that will make her a suitable wife.[1] This redressing is an act of "translation" – the technical term in Renaissance England both for linguistic metamorphosis and for the act of reclothing. In the livery companies, "translation" meant the incorporation of a member through investiture with livery into the guild; in the language of tailors, to "translate" a garment was to reuse its materials for a new garment. In the Griselda story, because Griselda has no dowry, her reclothing by Gualtieri seems to incorporate her into an aristocratic household not only as wife but also as subject and servant. Her new clothes mark her ennoblement, but they also materialize her absolute dependence upon the patronage of her husband.

In this redressing, however, Griselda's dependence exists in tension with the possibility of a limitless circulation of the female body, a circulation which women may themselves control. This counter-discourse within the tale is both effaced and elaborated in later retellings. Francesco Petrarca, for instance, wrote to Boccaccio that his translation was a "reclothing" of the tale in chastened Latin. He simultaneously distances the story from the vulgar tongue and from the "vulgarity" of Griselda's nudity by minimizing the stripping of Griselda. Petrarch also allegorizes Griselda as a figure of *masculine* Christian virtue and edits out Boccaccio's ironic conclusion, in which the narrator imagines an alternative Griselda whose cuckolding of her husband is figured as her ability to find her own clothes for herself. But the triumphant success of Petrarch's retelling (which increasingly displaced Boccaccio's version in Renaissance Europe) paradoxically led in turn to its re-"vulgarization" – its translation back into the European vernaculars, frequently with accompanying woodcuts which work against the purifying abstraction of Petrarch's allegory.

This "vulgarization" was particularly striking in England, where Chaucer's translation of Petrarch was succeeded by ballads, chapbooks, and popular plays. In these English versions, Gualtieri's control of Griselda through his livery is juxtaposed to the counter-display of her "russet garment," a display which culminates in its being hung up on the stage in *Patient Grissill*, a play performed by the Admiral's Men in 1600. It operates there as an alternative livery which calls into question the power of the husband and the court. Moreover, in the conclusion to this play, Griselda is not reclothed in her husband's "livery." The final image of Griselda wearing a crown but still in working clothes troubles the reassertion of her union with Gualtieri. These rerobings of the story materialize conflicts of status and gender through "translations" of clothing, "translations" that enact the power of clothes to shape and to resist social identities.

Translating Boccaccio

In the last story of the last day of *The Decameron*, Boccaccio recounts the tale of Gualtieri and "patient" Griselda. The 1620 English translator of the tale, possibly John Florio, summarizes the tale as follows:

The Marquesse of Saluzzo, named Gualtiero, being constrained by the importunate solliciting of his Lords, and other inferiour people, to joyne himselfe in marriage; tooke a woman according to his owne liking, called Grizelda, she being the daughter of a poore Countriman, named Janiculo, by whom he had two children, which he pretended to be secretly murdered. Afterward, they being grown to yeres of more stature, and making shew of taking in marriage another wife, more worthy of his high degree and Calling: made a seeming publique liking of his owne daughter, expulsing his wife Grizelda poorely from him. But finding her incomparable patience; more dearely (then before) received her into favor againe, brought her home to his owne Pallace, where (with her children) hee caused her and them to be respectively honoured, in despight of al her adverse enemies.[2]

Strikingly omitted in this abstract are precisely those aspects of the story which most interested Renaissance printers and artists: the undressing and reclothing of Griselda. Take, for instance, the woodcuts that accompany a 1473 German translation of Petrarch's retelling of the tale. Griselda appears at first spinning with distaff and spindle (Fig. 47).[3] Behind her are her sheep, as Gualtiero ("Waltherus") approaches on horseback with his hounds. But the rest of the woodcuts focus on Griselda's reclothing. After Gualtiero/Waltherus proposes marriage to Griselda, he strips her naked and reclothes her in the courtly costume which he has had prepared for her (Fig. 48). When he casts her off, after having pretended to kill her daughter and son, she divests herself of her courtly clothes (Fig. 49). And it is only after she has asked for some clothing to cover her nakedness that, in a simple smock, she returns to her father, bare-headed and bare-footed. At her father's house, she is reclothed in "the same poore garments" (Boccaccio 1620, 305) that she had worn before her marriage (Fig. 50). And it is in those same clothes that she is ordered back to court so as to see to the preparations for her husband's remarriage. Finally, after Gualtieri/Waltherus has "revealed" his new bride as his own daughter, Griselda is reclothed as his aristocratic wife.

Early in 1373, Petrarch, who was in Padua, received a copy of the *Decameron*. Noting that it was written for the "vulgus," he only glanced through it. He justifies its lasciviousness on account of the youth of the author and the "lowness" of the tale's intended audience – those who read only in the vulgar tongue and, in Boccaccio's staging of the tales, specifically women. But Petrarch was captivated by the final tale, which, he thought, "differ[ed] entirely from those that precede[d] it" and, having already learned it by heart, he decided to translate it into Latin, thus directing it toward an elite audience.[4] By translation, Petrarch had something quite radical in mind. "Translatio" could refer not only to a linguistic metamorphosis but also to a specific metamorphosis through clothing (thus Chaucer, translating Petrarch's version of the tale, describes Griselda as being "*translated*" by her new clothes[5]). Petrarch announced in a letter to Boccaccio that accompanied his translation that, having written in another style (*alio stilo*), he had, perhaps, "beautified it by changing

Fig. 47. Woodcut from *Historia Griseldis*, trans. Heinrich Steinhöwel, Ulm, 1473

Fig. 48. Woodcut from *Historia Griseldis*, trans. Heinrich Steinhöwel, Ulm, 1473

Fig. 49. Woodcut from *Historia Griseldis*, trans. Heinrich Steinhöwel, Ulm, 1473

Fig. 50. Woodcut from *Historia Griseldis*, trans. Heinrich Steinhöwel, Ulm, 1473

its garment,"[6] a change which effectively submerged both Boccaccio and his audience (who, in Petrarch, become *legentes* rather than *matronae*[7]).

In fact, despite Petrarch's admiration for the tale, his feelings toward Boccaccio were complex. Boccaccio had written to him that he should give up the scholar's life so as not to wear himself out in his old age, and Petrarch had not been pleased by the letter (*vehementer tamen a meis sensibus abhorrentes*).[8] So there may have been some malice in Petrarch's turn from reclothing Boccaccio's tale to reclothing Boccaccio himself. In his will, Petrarch left Boccaccio 50 gold florins to buy him "a winter robe suitable for his studious vigils."[9] In reclothing Boccaccio as a studious scholar, Petrarch implicitly reproved the licentious "clothing" of the *Decameron*, asserted his power to refashion Boccaccio in his own image, and implicitly restored his position as *magister* rather than mere translator.[10]

Petrarch's refashioning of Boccaccio repeats at the level of male rivalry Gualtieri's refashioning of Griselda. Petrarch also "chastizes," to use Stephanie Jed's term, Boccaccio's text.[11] That is, he restages the stripping of Griselda so as to efface both the violence and the sexualization of Boccaccio's version. Boccaccio writes as follows:

Then Gualtieri took [Griselda] by the hand, led her outside, and in the presence of his entire company and all others present, he had her stripped naked and the garments he had prepared for her brought forward; then he immediately had her dress and put on her shoes, and upon her hair, dishevelled as it was, he had a crown placed.[12]

This becomes, in Petrarch's reclothing of the text:

Then, lest she bring into her new home any trace of her former condition, he ordered her to be undressed, and to be clothed from head to foot in new garments. This was carried out discreetly and speedily by the ladies in waiting, who vied in cuddling her in their bosom and on their lap. Thus this girl was dressed; her dishevelled hair was combed and braided by their hands, and she was adorned for the occasion with jewels and a crown, and, as it were, suddenly transformed so that the people could hardly recognize her.[13]

Petrarch is clearly embarrassed by the public display of Griselda's nakedness, which he rightly perceives as being unmotivated in Boccaccio. So he modestly surrounds Griselda with court ladies. He also finds unacceptable Boccaccio's description of a crown being placed on Griselda's "*dishevelled*" hair; his Griselda has her hair gathered up and arranged before she is crowned.

The tension between the displayed and the hidden Griselda, between the dishevelled and the "combed and braided" Griselda, and thus between Boccaccio and Petrarch's versions of the tale,[14] is inscribed in fifteenth-century visual representations on *spalliere* (wall panels), *cassoni* (marriage chests) and in murals.[15] In *cassoni* depictions of the undressing of Griselda by Pesellino (Francesco di Stefano) and by Apollonio di Giovanni, the undressing scene is pushed to the extreme right-hand side of the panel while, at the same time, it is the culmination of the narrative sequence. In both panels, the left-hand side depicts Gualtieri discussing marriage with his courtiers, while the center is taken up with Gualtieri and his male followers and with their horses and dogs (i.e. with preparations for hunting). On the right-hand side of both panels, Gualtieri encounters Griselda, who is in simple peasant garb, a pitcher upon her head; and, on the extreme right, a naked or semi-naked Griselda is betrothed with a ring to Gualtieri, her father standing between them, his rural dwelling behind them.

But despite the striking similarity of narrative sequence in the two panels, there are significant differences in the depictions of the undressing of Griselda. In the Pesellino panel, as in Boccaccio's tale, Griselda's hair is dishevelled (Fig. 51). In the Apollonio panel, her hair is neatly tied up with linen, suggesting reliance upon Petrarch's version (Fig. 52). In the Pesellino, as in Boccaccio, Griselda is unescorted, although the painter has added a single peasant woman on the right-hand side (is this the mother, absent in both Boccaccio and Petrarch?); in the Apollonio, Griselda is surrounded by a group of women, as in Petrarch's version, although, as in the Pesellino, these are peasants, not court ladies. Finally, there is a striking difference in the depiction of Griselda's nakedness. In the Pesellino, Griselda's head hangs down, her eyes to the ground; her body is turned sideways, her left arm raised to receive the ring, thus concealing her breasts; her thighs and hips are swayed back, as if in modest withdrawal. In the Apollonio, despite the fact that with her left hand Griselda holds a transparent cloth across her genitals, her body is turned toward the viewer, her thighs and hips swaying forward toward Gualtieri.

The tension between modest withdrawal from the eyes of the beholder and display of the naked body of Griselda is not merely a tension between Boccaccio and Petrarch's versions. For Petrarch's own attempt to construct a scene of modesty is curiously contradictory: while the court ladies conceal Griselda from the imagined scene of the male gazer, the reader hears of the court ladies who vie "in cuddling her in their bosom and on their lap." That the undressing of Griselda was both problematic and prominent for narrators, as for painters, of the tale is further

Fig. 51. Francesco di Stefano (Pesellino), *cassone* painting, Griselda story, Tuscany, c. 1450, detail

Fig. 52. Apollonio di Giovanni, *cassone* painting, Griselda story, Tuscany, c. 1460, detail

suggested by Chaucer's translation of Petrarch's translation in *The Clerk of Oxford's Tale*. Chaucer, despite usually following Petrarch quite closely, suppresses the ladies' pleasure in touching Griselda. On the contrary, he suggests that in taking off her garments, they fear contamination from them:[16]

> And for that nothyng of hir olde gere
> She sholde brynge into his hous, he bad
> That wommen sholde dispoillen hire right there;

> Of which thise ladyes were nat right glad
> To handle hir clothes wher-inne she was clad;
> But nathelees this mayde, bright of hewe,
> Fro foot to heed they clothed han al newe.
>
> Hir heris han they kembd, that lay untressed
> Ful rudely, and with hir fyngres smale
> A corone on hire heed they han y-dressed,
> And sette hire ful of nowches grete and smale.
> Of hire array what sholde I make tale?
> Unnethe the peple hire knew for hire fairnesse,
> Whan she translated was in swich richesse.[17]

Chaucer's ladies thus fear handling the clothes of which they have, in a curiously violent image, *despoiled* her. But Chaucer follows Petrarch in asserting that Griselda has been "translated" by her new clothes.[18] This translation is simply absent in the *cassoni* panels. There, the agreement between Gualtieri and Griselda's father, the stripping of Griselda, and the betrothal are condensed into a single image, while the reclothing of Griselda is not even suggested by the presence of a retainer bearing her courtly garb. Yet this frozen moment of nakedness is overseen in both panels by the father. Given that *cassoni* had a prominent position within the newlyweds' bedchamber, it may be that the reinscription of the story by Pesellino and Apollonio was meant to mirror the undressing of the bridal couple, and the father's approval of that undressing.

Yet when the Master of the Griselda Story painted his *spalliera* panel of the story, it is the translation operated by the new clothes which, quite literally, occupies the center of the panel. As with the two *cassoni* panels, the *spalliera* panel depicts the undressing of Griselda on the right hand side, but unlike them, extraordinary prominence is given both to the clothes that have been taken off and to the clothes in which she will be redressed. On the ground in front of her lie her dress, her shift, and her bodice; to her side, Gualtieri gestures to the new shift and gown which an attendant holds forward (Fig. 53). (So troubling was the nakedness of Griselda to a later "restorer" that drapery was painted over her sometime around 1874.) The *spalliera* thus foregrounds the act of translation. Griselda moves from the gray homespun of her woolen peasant gown to the splendid embroidered cloth of gold gown and scarlet cloak which she has assumed for the ring ceremony in the center. Yet to mark the persistence of the peasant Griselda even in this scene of transformation, her hair is still disheveled (as in Boccaccio and in the Pesellino panel) and her eyes are modestly downcast as in the undressing scene on the right.

What all the paintings emphasize is the contrast between fully clothed men and the naked (and sometimes reclothed) Griselda. Yet the very question of the gendering of Griselda (and of the status of obedience) is at stake in Petrarch's translation of Boccaccio. Petrarch entitled the published version of his letter to Boccaccio, with the Latin version of the story, *De Insigni Obedientia et Fide Uxoris* ("Concerning the Remarkable Obedience and Faithfulness of a Wife").[19] He concludes his version, though, by asserting that Griselda is less a model for women, who will, he says, be unable to imitate her, than for constant men who suffer "without a murmur for [their] God what this little peasant woman suffered for her mortal husband."[20] Given the violent humiliations which Griselda is forced to undergo, Petrarch does at least reassign her exemplary suffering to his transvestite

Fig. 53. Master of the Story of Griselda, wooden panel, "Marriage of Griselda and Gualtieri," Sienna, c. 1500, detail

male reader, now dressed as a patient Griselda before God. But the extraordinary analogy which Petrarch thereby draws between Gualtieri and God allegorizes Gualtieri's tyranny out of existence. Boccaccio's narrator, Dioneo, tells the story as one of "insane cruelty": "I would never advise anyone to follow [Gualtieri] as an example, for I consider it a great shame that he derived any benefit from it at all."[21] Petrarch's allegory also erases the criticism of Gualtieri with which Boccaccio's narrator, Dioneo, concludes the final tale of *The Decameron*: "Al quale [Gualtieri] non sarebbe forse stato male investito d'essersi abbattuto a una che quando, fuor di casa, l'avesse fuori in camiscia cacciata, s'avesse sì a un altro fatto scuotere il pilliccione che riuscito ne fosse una bella roba" ("It might have served Gualtieri right if he had run into the kind of woman who, once driven out of her home in nothing but a shift, would have allowed another man to warm her wool in order to get a nice-looking dress out of the affair").[22] In allegorizing the tale, Petrarch leaves the shifts of Griselda's clothes behind; in ironizing the tale, Dioneo suggests that the smart way for Griselda to have treated Gualtieri in return would have been to cuckold him. And cuckolding is imagined both as a justified redressing (*investito*) of Gualtieri and as an acquisition of new clothing (*una bella roba*) which a woman herself can control.[23]

But by shifting clothes, by translating her shift (*camiscia*) into a pretty dress (*una bella roba*), a woman, it is implied, would herself *become* a *bella roba*: that is, as Cotgrave puts it in his dictionary, "good stuffe, sound lecherie; a round, fat, plumpe wench."[24] In *Henry IV Part 2*, Shallow brags that "wee knew where the *Bona-Roba's* were, and had the best of them all at commandement" and he talks nostalgically of Jane Nightwork as a "*Bona-Roba*."[25] But Dioneo imagines Gaultieri's nemesis as a woman who changes clothes not to denigrate the woman but to mock the tyrannical rule of Gualtieri. That is, while the prince wishes to control both the identities and the desires of his subjects, and above all of his wife, through the giving and taking away of livery, the very fact that livery can be put on and put off implies the "shifts" through which the subject can masquerade and evade the prince's interpellations. These interpellations were radically rewritten in the London professional theater in a play called *The Pleasant Comodie of Patient Grissill*, probably staged by the Admiral's Men in the early months of 1600.

"This russet braverie of my owne"

The play of *Patient Grissill* performed by the Admiral's Men, like the pictorial tradition of Griselda, gives extraordinary attention to her clothes. Henslowe records that, on January 26, 1600, he paid 20s. "to buy a grey gowne for gryssell."[26] In the fall of 1599, he had prepaid Chettle 20s. for a play on "gryssell"; on 19 December he paid £3 to be split between Chettle, Dekker, and Haughton; and he paid the three of them another £6 on 26 December. There were final small payments of 5s. to Dekker on the 28th and of 5s. to Haughton on the 29th.[27] The play that Chettle, Dekker, and Haughton wrote, *The Pleasant Comodie of Patient Grissill*, effected a peculiar inversion of Boccaccio's tale. Boccaccio, and Petrarch after him, organized his story around two scenes of undressing and redressing: first, when Griselda is stripped naked and reclothed before her marriage; second, when she is stripped of her court clothes, given only a smock to cover her, and sent back to her father's house. To the court of Gualtieri, she brings nothing of her own or of her family's. This lack, as we noted above, is given particular stress in Petrarch's retelling: "Then, lest she bring into her new home any trace of her former condition, he ordered her to be undressed, and to be clothed from head to foot in new garments."[28] In Chettle, Dekker, and Haughton's play, though, Grissill is metonymically represented by a single russet gown. The emphasis is thus placed less upon her shifting of costume than upon a garment that persists, a garment, moreover, which is given striking visual prominence.

Grissill is wearing the russet gown when she meets the Marquess of Salucia; it accompanies her when she goes to court, despite the fact that she has been redressed in aristocratic clothing. At court or, rather, in the public theater where the Admiral's Men performed the play, this russet gown was hung up in full view of the audience. The Marquess himself repeatedly draws attention to the gown's presence (along with Grissill's pitcher, which she was carrying when he met her, and her hat):

> See woman heere hangs vp thine auncestrie,
> The monuments of thy nobillitie,

> This is thy russet gentrie, coate, and crest:
> Thy earthen honors I will neuer hide,
> Because this bridle shall pull in thy pride.[29]

Or again:

> I rob'd my wardrop of all precious robes,
> That she might shine in beautie like the Sunne,
> And in exchange, I hung this russet gowne,
> And this poore pitcher for a monument,
> Amongst my costliest Iemmes: see heere they hang,
> *Grissill* looke heere, this gowne is vnlike to this?   (3. 1. 81–6; see also 4. 1. 168–73)

If we recall that the Griselda of Boccacio and Petrarch was explicitly detached from genealogy and dowry alike, the insistence of the Marquess in the play upon the ironic signs of Grissill's status is all the more remarkable. Mockingly, he calls the russet coat, the pitcher, and the hat "the monuments of [her] nobilitie," her "russet gentrie, coate, and crest." The armor, the helm, the ancient coat of arms that constituted a gentleman's honor are displaced by "monuments" of cloth and clay, which stage the disjunction between the peasant Grissill and her aristocratic husband.

The Marquess hangs up these "monuments" as markers of humiliation: they are there as a "bridle" to "pull in [Grissill's] pride." They are there to point to the distance between Grissill's "beggerie" and the "rich abiliments" in which the Marquess has clothed her. Robes of humiliation were not, of course, unknown in Renaissance England, where penance was enacted by the wearing of a white gown. And in Spain, not only were offenders against the Inquisition forced to wear the *sambenitillo* or garment of reconciliation, they could also be forced to hang those garments up in the church with their names upon them and to replace them when they decayed, as lasting signs of their disgrace.[30] But in the Admiral's Men's play of *Patient Grissill*, the russet gown is given a totally different significance both by Grissill and by her family. For them, it is an emblem of their resistance to the shifts of the court. As Grissill's father says, her dowry is not "silkes" but "thrid-bare russets" (1. 2. 48), but the russet gown is defiantly opposed to the silken "liverie" (2. 2. 63) which incorporates and subjects Grissill to the Marquess. Unlike the "rich abiliments" which the Marquess gives her, "this russet brauerie" she claims as "my owne" (2. 2. 74). To herself, Grissill seems "more rich in a course gowne of gray" (3. 1. 49).

We should perhaps explain at this point what at first appears puzzling. Henslowe records buying a *gray* gown for the play: the only certain new expense is the "grey gowne for grysell" (which may mean the play, not the character), bought in what seems an unusually complicated transaction: Henslowe advances to Shaw the rather large sum of 20s. to give to a tailor who would buy, not make it.[31] In the play, Grissill speaks of her "course gowne of *gray*." Similarly, in the 1620 translation of *The Decameron*, Boccaccio's description of Griselda in "suoi panicelli romagnuoli e grossi" becomes "in her gowne of Countrey gray" (Boccaccio 1620, 306). But the play insistently focuses upon her *russet* gown. In fact, depite the fact that the word "russet" was derived from the Old French *rousset*, a diminutive of *rous[x]*, meaning red, the word entered English as a marker of class rather than a color. "Russet" defined a coarse homespun woolen cloth, which was sometimes indeed dyed a reddish-brown, but was often dyed gray or another neutral color, depending upon the availability and cheapness of the dye. Thus, in *Piers Plowman*, Langland writes of Charity as being as "gladde of a goune of graye russet / As of a tunicle of tarse or of tyre scarlet."[32] One of the texts that the play by the Admiral's Men probably draws upon is a ballad registered to John Wolf in 1593. Although the earliest extant version of the ballad is of c. 1600 and it was collected into Thomas Deloney's *The Garden of Good-Will* only in 1631, the ballad "Of Patient Grissel and a Noble Marquess" shows one significant resemblance to the play, a resemblance not to be found in any other previous version of Griselda: an emphasis upon Grissel's "country russet," which is exchanged for "silk and velvet."[33] In the ballad, when the Marquess strips Grissel of her "velvet gown," she is redressed in her "russet gown" of "homely gray."[34] Samuel Richardson, himself a printer, was perhaps influenced by this ballad, reprinted throughout the seventeenth and eighteenth century, when he rewrote the Griselda story as *Pamela*. Redressed by Mr. B in the aristocratic dress of his dead mother, Pamela yearns "for my grey russet again, and my poor honest dress, with which [my parents] fitted me out for going to this place, when I was not twelve years old."[35]

"Russet" thus defined both a class position and a sometimes patronizing approval of rustic simplicity. Lyly writes in *Euphues*, "Disdaine not those that are base, thinke with your selues that russet coates haue their Christendome."[36] But if, in the ballad, Grissel's russet gown is put on her "with many a scoff,"[37] the cloth could also be politicized; in fact, it was to become symbolic of the opposition to the Cavalier court. Thus, Oliver Cromwell wrote in September 1643, preferring a loyal soldier of the middling sort over a nobleman by birth: "I had rather have a plain russet-coated Captain who knows what he fights for, and loves what he knows, than that which you call a gentleman and is nothing else."[38] And it was the theater's radical juxtaposition of russet with the court that Joseph Hall decried in his satires:

> A goodly *hoch-poch*, when vile *Russettings*,
> Are match't with monarchs, & with mighty kings.[39]

Hall's satires were published in 1597, but the "matching" of russeting and aristocracy is literalized in the Chettle, Dekker, and Haughton play, where Grissill's russet gown hangs as a counter-heraldry to the Marquess's tyranny.

The Marquess himself, when he sees Grissill at the beginning of the play, contrasts "rich robes" unfavorably with her "poore abiliments":

> Me thinkes her beautie shining through those weedes,
> Seemes like a bright starre in the sullen night.
> How louely pouertie dwels on her backe,
> Did but the proud world note her as I doe,
> She would cast off rich robes, forsweare rich state,
> To cloth them in such poore abiliments.   (1. 2. 174–9)

The Marquess eroticizes Grissill's poverty, but the language in which he does so is interesting. He describes Grissill's clothes, although poor, as "abiliments," an unusual expression, which Dekker uses elsewhere to suggest both splendor and warfare: he writes of being "Habilimented gloriously for warre." Although the word is related to the French *habit* (clothing), it was also associated with "able," "ability." "[H]abiliments" rendered fit, enabled, and and the word could explicitly refer to one's qualifications or capacity. Thus John Ford writes in *The Broken Heart*:

"Neuer liu'd Gentleman of greater merit, / Hope or abiliment to steere a king-dome."[40] Grissill's working clothes are indeed seen as enabling.

They are contrasted to "rich robes," the latter word deriving from the Old French *robe*, meaning spoil or booty – that which has been robbed. This derivation is exploited by the Marquess himself later in the play, when he says in relation to his reclothing of Grissill:

> I rob'd my wardrop of all precious robes
> That she might shine in beautie like the Sunne.   (3. 1. 81–2)

If the Marquess here claims that he has robbed himself, the etymological implication is that the rich have robbed to attain such robes. In fact, although the word "robes" was used to signify a person of high estate (often being set in opposition to "rags"), it opened up a critical discourse on the means by which such hierarchies were constructed. As the Tuscan Renaissance proverb has it, "chi ha roba, ruba" ("he who has property/robes is a thief").

The play upon "robe" and "rob" was, in fact, part of a larger Renaissance discourse on the relation between clothes and theft. Thus, Scipione Mercurio, translating Laurent Joubert's book on popular errors, notes that humans, although the most noble of animals, are born without "vestimenti." To clothe themselves, they plunder the rest of the animal world: "per procacciarsene, e provedersi di quanto avaramente gli fu dalla Natura negato, a guisa di pubblico ladrone, toglie a questo animale la pelle, a quell'altro la lana, in somma ne spoglia molti per vestir se stesso."[41] And Lear articulates the sense of clothes as stolen when, using Tom o' Bedlam as his model, he strips himself on the heath:

Is man no more than this? Consider him well. Thou ow'st the Worme no Silke; the Beast, no Hide; the Sheepe, no Wooll; the cat, no perfume . . . Off, off you Lendings.[42]

In rejecting "lendings," what has been taken from the backs of others, Lear rejects what has been "sophisticated" (both what has been elevated and what has been mixed with another substance).

But in *The Pleasant Comodie of Patient Grissill*, clothes both enable ("abiliments") and enslave. In stripping Grissill, the Marquess attempts to strip her of her abilities and to reclothe her in his livery. The act of stripping in Boccaccio can be seen as an act of theft. Indeed, the Italian *spogliare* means both to undress and to despoil, to plunder. When Chaucer translates Petrarch's description of Walter stripping Griselda, he writes, as we noted above:

> And for that nothyng of hir olde gere
> She sholde brynge into his hous, he bad
> That wommen sholde *dispoillen* hire right there.   (lines 372–4, p. 191)

And the act of reclothing is equally an attempt to despoil Grissill of her history, to incorporate her as the Marquess's wife by first making her a *tabula rasa*. In this reclothing, if Grissill's clothes are those of a bride, they are also livery. Clothed in the clothes of another, as Sir Thomas Overbury says, a servant "is not his owne man. He tells without asking who ownes him, by the superscription of his Livery."[43] And Boccaccio's tale goes to great lengths to conflate the roles of wife and servant in the single figure of Griselda, most disturbingly of all when she is recalled to the palace in her working clothes to deck it out for the arrival of the new bride. After she is despoiled of her clothes as Marchioness, her old clothes as family worker assign her to humiliating service to the court.

The Pleasant Comodie of Patient Grissill, however, sets up a powerful counter-interpellation to Boccaccio's tale of the Marquess's stripping and reclothing of Griselda: the persistent image of the gray gown which Henslowe bought for 20s. for the Admiral's men. The gray gown asserts a counter-naming for Grissill: like gristle, the indigestible food which the Marquess puns upon ("*Grissills* bones" [2. 3. 92]), Grissill cannot be fully assimilated as long as her gray russet gown hangs there, asserting her distance from the court, from the exchange of wealth and alliance which characterizes aristocratic marriages, from the oppressive genealogies and lineages that impose the rules of primogeniture. Despite Gualtieri's claim to his brother, the Marquess of Pavia, that he will "[b]y loues most wondrous Metamor-phosis . . . turne this Maide into your Brothers wife" (1. 2. 232–4), Grissill's gray gown conjures up a possession which, though detachable, is symbolically inalienable and which the Marquess conspicuously fails to metamorphose. The gray gown materializes a counter-history, a counter-memory.

"Apparaill to my body belonging": *cassoni* and paraphernalia

In Italy, the problem of the (in)alienability of elite women's goods was dramatically staged through the exchange of gifts which accompanied betrothals and weddings. Certain records from Florence indicate that *cassoni* (large gilded and painted wooden chests) used to contain a bride's trousseau were sometimes carried through the streets in a public procession to her husband's house. The splendor of the chests and the paintings demonstrated the prestige of the wife's family, although they were partially a displacement of the display of the gifts and counter-gifts which sumptuary laws attempted to regulate. Although the story of Griselda was sometimes repre-sented on these *cassoni*, Cristelle Baskins, in an important study, remarks that the story was in fact represented very infrequently.[44] This is not, perhaps, surprising: to paint the story of Griselda on the surface of a wedding chest would set up a stark contradiction between the social meaning of the chest and the topic with which it was decorated. For there is no equivalent in the Griselda story of the economic exchange enacted by the carrying of the trousseau chest from the bride's house to the husband's. Griselda brings no trousseau or dowry at all to Gualtieri; his ceremony of undressing and reclothing her insists upon the lack of any contribution to the marriage from her or her father. The Marquess, receiving neither trousseau nor dowry, makes himself the sole source of Griselda's dress – and undress; she becomes his property entirely. In the Griselda story, all clothes come from the husband; in a *cassone*, clothes were brought to the husband from the bride.

Cassoni, in fact, were a typical part of the elaborate processes of exchange which preceded and structured the financial arrangements of elite marriages. The betrothal itself, according to Antonio Landi in the sixteenth century, "seems like a sale of leather or clothes, there is so much bargaining."[45] After the betrothal (which depended upon agreement upon the dowry), three to six months commonly intervened before the wedding. This was the time necessary to prepare the lavish clothes of the bride and groom and their families, to have their wedding furniture and chamber built and decorated, and to prepare the two *cassoni* (they were invariably designed as a pair). The *cassoni* themselves required the work of carpenters and gilders as well as painters. During this period, there was an implicit shift from the bride's family's gifts to the groom's family as gift-givers. The groom's family usually paid for the *cassoni* and the groom was expected to send dresses, jewels, and headdresses.[46] This potentially hostile competition between giver and recipient found its most violent manifestation in the denial of all exchange, as in the marriage between Gualtieri and Griselda. Thus, the humanist Marco Altieri likens all weddings to the rape of the Sabine women, and he describes the groom's escort for the bride as a *brigata* (a raiding party).[47] Gualtieri's sudden marriage erases the typically long period of gift-giving between the betrothals and marriages of the elite, and his rejection of indebtedness to Griselda's family parallels the seizure that was the counter-fantasy to the complex rituals of exchange.

The physical placing of *cassoni* after the wedding would have reinforced the groom's possession of the bride. The *cassoni* were usually put in the marriage chamber of the husband's house, where, juxtaposed to the bed, they reaffirmed that what was hers was now contained in his wooden enclosures. And it was the *cassoni* themselves, not the bride's trousseau, which would have been displayed in the elaborate marriage processions of the elite, in which the bride made the journey from the house of her father to that of her new husband. Her own family's contribution of the trousseau quite literally disappeared into, or was consumed by, the chest of the groom's family. This "burial" of the bride is exaggerated in the Griselda story: taken by her husband with nothing, she shares his aristocratic dwelling without even a marriage chest to hold the linens and clothes supplied by her own family.

Boccaccio's fiction of a husband's omnipotent ownership of his wife had a historical parallel in the fantasy of ownership inscribed in the wedding gifts that Italian husbands gave their brides. In her study of Florentine marriage customs in the fourteenth century, Christiane Klapisch-Zuber argues that such gifts actually constituted a counter-dowry.[48] The husband, to avoid being overwhelmingly indebted to his wife's family as a result of her dowry, would give her clothes, jewels, and bedchamber decorations equal in value to as much as half of her dowry, thus righting the imbalance set up between the two families. The counter-gifts were largely symbolic, however; they actually established further rights of property over the wife, who typically found, after the wedding, that the sumptuous dress and rings she had worn for the public exchange of vows were not gifts but loans, rapidly retrieved from her body and restored to the coffers of her new kinsfolk by marriage.

By erasing the bride's dowry, Boccaccio's story makes Gualtieri's counter-dowry of clothes the only economic exchange, an exchange which represents the bride as irrevocably indebted. Having given all, the husband claims the right to take back all. Since Griselda's father supplies no dowry in the first place, Gualtieri claims absolute power over his wife, unchallenged by any obligation to her family. The story thus legitimates the legal system by erasing the ambivalence of ownership in marriage exchanges. In emphasizing Griselda's poverty, the story foregrounds the husband's dressing of his wife as signaling the rights he has acquired over her. Her putting on of his ring and gown, as she puts on his name (the wedding makes her the Marchioness of Sanluzzo), has a ritual significance which marks a striking imbalance between gift-giver and gift-receiver: Griselda, bringing nothing with her to the marriage, is represented as losing her entire prior identity and being invested with Gualtieri's alone.

The principle of absolute husbandly possession in the story clarifies the logic according to which clothes given by a Florentine husband to his wife remained his family's property, not hers. Only if a widow's husband had left gowns and jewels specifically to her in his will was she allowed to take them away with her after his death; and a husband was more likely to forbid than to permit his wife to keep such finery, whether the widow returned to her father's household or married another man. Klapisch-Zuber cites the case of a Tuscan widow who implored her children and children-in-law, as she was preparing to return to her family of birth, "Give me a way to be dressed" – that is, "out of kindness, allow me the dresses and jewels your father gave me during his lifetime – which you, not I, have inherited from him."[49] Griselda, lacking a dowry and a trousseau (this is the point Gualtieri makes by taking her naked), is totally dispossessed.

But what was the legal context for Griselda's story when it was Englished? In the Roman law that was so influential on the Continent, moveable and wearable goods, including "ornaments of the person," were called *paraphernalia*. *Paraphernalia* included household furniture and clothing as forms of property over which the husband could exercise no rights without his wife's consent. But in English common law,

> under which all personal or moveable property of a wife was vested *ipse jure* in the husband, the *paraphernalia* became restricted to such purely personal belongings . . . as dress, jewels, and the like. These latter were regarded as, in a sense, appropriated to the wife, and on the husband's death they were not treated as part of his succession.[50]

Although a bewildering variety of customs for the disposition of *paraphernalia* existed throughout Europe, English common law attempted to limit the share of personal property or gifts that a wife could own independently. During his lifetime a husband could sell the jewels that his wife wore; they were also vulnerable to seizure by his creditors. In his will he could give all her possessions away except "her necessary clothes" and her *paraphernalia*; but if he could not will them away, neither did his wife have absolute rights over them while he was alive. She was entitled to wear what was "on her back," but she could not dispose of her *paraphernalia* without her husband's consent.

This legal structure explains two striking features of wills. First, husbands sometimes specifically left their wives' own clothes to them in their wills. Thus, Richard Sackville writes on 26 March 1624:

> Item I doe give & bequeath to my deerlye beloved wife all her wearing apparel and such rings and jewels as were hers on her marriage and the rocke rubye ring which I have given her.[51]

Sackville asserts his ownership not only of what he has given Anne Clifford but also of her trousseau – the clothes and jewels which she brought with her into the marriage. In other words, he makes the claims of Boccaccio's Gualtieri and Petrarch's Walter to total ownership, but in a more vexed and complicated legal situation. Anne Clifford brought not only *paraphernalia* into the marriage but also land, and she spent her marriage successfully defending herself against Sackville's attempts to appropriate what had been left to her in trust and to claim those lands after he died. But Sackville's will to his "deerlye beloved wife" reasserts his legal entitlement even to his wife's clothes.

Second, because husbands could claim control of their wives' clothes and jewels, wives were supposed by law to invoke their husbands' permission when they made their own wills – wills which women were supposed to make only for their moveable goods if their husbands were alive, since they were *femmes coverts*. Henry Swinburn, the Yorkshire church court judge who wrote *A Brief Treatise of Testaments and Last Wills*, explained why "A Married woman by the lawes and Statutes of this Realm can not make her Testament of any Mannors, lands or hereditaments," that is, of immoveable property. As long as she was married, she was subject to her husband, who could therefore force her to make over all her land to him alone; thus, her incompetence as testator was intended to protect her and her children. Swinburn clarifies as follows: "by how much the husband were more cruell, and the wife more timorous; he crafty, she credulous, by so much more were the lawfull heire in danger to be disherited, and the cruell and deceitful husband in hope to be unworthily enriched and advanced."[52] But the wife's control over even the limited possessions allowed her as paraphernalia could also be restricted as a result of her subordination to her husband:

Of goods and catells the wife cannot make her testament, without the license or consent of her husband . . . because by the laws and customes of this Realme, so soone as a man and a woman be married, all the goods and cattels personal that the wife had at the time of her spousals . . . belong to the husband, by reason of the said mariage: and therefore with good reason she cannot give that away which was hers, without the sufferance or graunt of the owner.[53]

Even that "sufferance" had limits when it came to clothes. T. E., the author of *The Lawes Resolution of Womens Rights*, justifies sartorial controls over wives with metaphors drawn from political and astronomical hierarchies:

But the prerogative of the Husband is best discerned in his dominion over all externe things in which the wife by combination devesteth her selfe of proprietie in some sort, and casteth it upon her governor . . . If a woman taketh more Apparrell when her husband dyeth then is necessarily for her degree, it makes her Executrix *de son tort demesne*, 33. H. 6. A wife how gallant soever she be, glittereth but in the riches of her husband, as the Moone hath no light but it is the Sunnes. Yea, and her Phoebe borroweth sometime her owne proper light from Phoebus.[54]

A formula acknowledging that the husband controls even the possessions granted by custom to the wife opens a will written in 1506 by a gentlewoman, Alice Love:

I, Alice Love, the wife of Gyles Love of Rye, by the speciall license of my said husband, asked and opteyned bequeath my parapharnalle – that is to seye, myn apparaill to my body belonging . . . Item, to my moder my graye furred gowne with a long trayne; also a gowne clothe of russet, not made.[55]

One of Alice Love's bequests confirms that in England, as in Gualtieri's Salucia, a husband's gifts were understood as always temporary. Indeed, a second husband even comes into possession of the gifts given to his wife by her first husband: Alice Love also asks her husband's permission to pass on to her son a gift from her first marriage: "Item, to Thomas Oxenbridge my best gilt gyrdell that my [first] husband Thomas Oxenbridge bought me to my wedding."[56] As a widow, a woman could eventually make what will she chose; but what she had to leave was supposedly determined by her husband's desires during his lifetime.

The situation was in fact far more complex and malleable than legal theorists usually allowed. Women could and did appeal for various property rights to the equity courts (Chancery, Requests etc.), to the ecclesiastical courts, to customary law, as well as to common law.[57] As Amy Erickson has shown, many women made wills and sued successfully for the rights in the goods that they inherited. At the same time, Erickson gives further support for one of the central arguments of this book: the extraordinary value of moveable goods, including clothes. She argues that although women tended to inherit goods rather than lands, the value of the goods that daughters inherited was often comparable to land that their brothers inherited, so that the distribution of property by parents tended to work against the monopoly of sons and of the first-born son in particular.[58] In England, then, Griselda's total lack of property in entering marriage and her total lack of rights in relation to her husband could perhaps have been seen as aspects of a patriarchal absolutism that was alien to English "liberties."[59]

But attempts to circumscribe women's rights in England had found a well-motivated advocate in Henry VIII. The limits upon a wife's rights to use the form of a will to circumscribe her husband's ownership were restated by the Act of 34 and 35 Henry VIII (c. 5), published in 1542: the "Explanation of the Statute of Wills." The "Explanation" "declared and enacted"

> that wills or testaments made of any manors, lands, tenements or other hereditaments by any woman covert, or person within the ages of 21 years, or by any person *de non sane memory*, shall not be taken to be good or effectual in the law.[60]

This act followed on Henry's continued battle to enforce his ownership and control of the property of his divorced wife, Katherine of Aragon. This was a battle which he could not fail to win on the central issues of land and property, but which Katherine resisted, although within the language of submission, when it came to making a list of bequests on her deathbed. In this list, dictated to Chapuys in 1536, perhaps by way of insisting that she was still married to Henry, she requested his permission for her final distribution of money and possessions, at the same time that she reminded him that he still owed her an unpaid part of her pension:

> I, Katherine, &c. supplicate and desire King Henry VIII. my good Lord, that it please him of his grace, and in alms, and for the service of God, to let me have the goods which I do hold, as well in gold and silver as other things, and also the same that is due to me in money for the time passed, to the intent that I may pay my debts and recompense my servants for the good service they have done unto me . . . Item, I ordain that Mr. Whiller be paid of expense about the making of my gown, and besides that of xx £ sterling . . . Item, it may please the King my good Lord, that the house ornaments of the church to be made of my gowns, which he holdeth, for to serve the convent thereat I shall be buried. And the furs of the same I give for my daughter.[61]

The document as a whole suggests that Katherine was behaving less obediently than her opening request implies. That is, she asserts her right to give away the money, gowns and furs that she is simultaneously asking Henry to give to her.

Her supporters represented her similarly, as subtly exposing the injustice of Henry's demands and winning the allegiance of his courtiers precisely by behaving with what appeared to be exemplary humility and obedience – as, in fact, another Griselda. In 1558 William Forrest, the chaplain to Mary Tudor, presented Mary with a long manuscript poem entitled *The History of Grisild the Second*. Bound in laced satin suitable for a princess, the book had as its topic what Forrest called "Youre Mothers meeke life." In this verse narrative of Katherine and Henry's divorce, Forrest spells out the analogy between the English queen and Petrarch's heroine as follows:

> Her I heere lyken to *Grysilde* the goode,
> As well I so maye, for her great patience; . . .
> Your noble Father working like pretence

As *Walter* to *Grysilde*, by muche unkyndnes,
By name of *Walter* I dooe hym expresse.[62]

One parallel between the Petrarchan and historical plots, Forrest points out in his prose summary, is the husband's sending to Rome for a bill of divorce; another is the wife's being uncrowned and sent away. Forrest insists that Katherine, as Griselda the Second, "neaver wolde cursse or blame her mysfortune . . , lamentinge muche rather others daungers ensuying then her owne" (Forrest, 17). In other passages, he emphasizes womanly virtues like Griselda's but adjusts them to fit the queen's rank: she is busy not with the lowly spinner's distaff but with "stoole and needyl" (Forrest, 28); she attends matins at Greenwich dressed as simply but more formally than Griselda in her smock: "in devotyon kneelinge, / A mantyll about her whiche was no riche thynge" (Forrest, 47). In fact, Katherine, like Chettle, Dekker, and Haughton's Grissill, demonstrated her ambivalence toward court culture through her dress. Where Grissill emphasizes her russet gown even when dressed as the Marchioness of Salucia, Katherine put on the coarse habit of the third order of St. Francis under her court dress.[63]

Thus, like Petrarch's Griselda, Forrest's suffers meekly and patiently, but his, he claims, has the force of fact rather than fable:

> For of her great Patience theare is no dowbte,
> Her factes in present remembraunce dothe reigne;
> The *Firste* howe her doynges weare brought abowte,
> To us in theis dayes they are uncertayne;
> Many imagine that Petrarke dyd but fayne;
> Howe much the *Seconde* is true, that yee have herde,
> So muche before *thother* shee is too bee preferde.   (Forrest, 132)

Griselda can be appropriated by Forrest as an empowering figure precisely through her exemplary humility. He uses her to model Christian charity and faith in a text designed to support Katherine against her husband and to insist on the legitimacy of Henry's first daughter.

Inscribing Henry as Walter, Forrest also explicitly rejects Petrarch's allegorization of the tale, which makes Walter an analogy for God. On the contrary, what defines Forrest's Henry/Walter is his "muche unkyndnes" (Forrest, 5). Henry's "unkyndnes" was nowhere more clear than in his dealings with the paraphernalia of Katherine and her daughter Mary. Days after the birth of Elizabeth, Henry deprived Mary of her title as princess and ordered that her followers should be deprived of their coats, embroidered with her device in gold. In their place, they were given coats embroidered with the arms of the king.[64] Previously, after the coronation of Anne Boleyn as queen, Henry had sent to his now bastardized daughter demanding her jewels, which he no doubt intended to give to Anne or her expected children. Mary's chamberlain, Lord Hussey, claimed that he did not know of any jewels apart from those which Mary wore. In other words, he appealed to Mary's paraphernalia as the "clothes on her back" and therefore inalienable. On the king's insistence, Hussey asked Lady Margaret Pole, Mary's governess, to draw up an inventory of the jewels, but Pole refused to hand over the inventory. In other words, Mary and Margaret Pole, like Forrest, rejected the king's legal claims, casting them as the unreasonable demands of a tyrant.[65] They, like Forrest, represented the monarch as "commyttynge offense" against his wife and child (Forrest, 132).

Even more shocking than Henry's demand for his daughter's jewels was his order that Katherine should give up the "triumphal cloth" that she had brought with her from Spain as part of her dowry. She had wrapped her infants in the cloth at their baptisms. Now, Henry wanted it in anticipation of the birth of Anne Boleyn's child. As Walter in Boccaccio's story insists upon Griselda's welcoming the wife who will displace her, so Henry implicitly insists upon Katherine's symbolic attendance at the birth of the child who will displace her own daughter. Katherine simply refused to send the cloth, responding, "It has not pleased God that she should be so ill-advised as to grant any favour in a case so horrible and abominable."[66] The child on whose behalf Henry threatened to appropriate Katherine's paraphernalia was, of course, Elizabeth.[67]

Elizabeth displaced the Virgin Mary in Protestant hagiography, and she was also to be cast, and to cast herself, as Patient Griselda, the role in which Forrest had cast Katherine of Aragon. About 1630 (the date is conjectural since it has been cropped from the title page of the only surviving copy), John Wright published a chapbook entitled *The Pleasant and Sweet History of patient Grissell*. No doubt the printer (E. P.) used the woodcuts that were available to him to illustrate the pamphlet: on the right-hand side, there is a typical scene frequently used in a variety of versions to illustrate chapbook retellings of Petrarch's Griselda story: men hunting and a woman spinning (Fig. 54).[68] This scene is transferred to the stage in John Phillip's 1565 *Plaie of Pacient Grissell*: after Politicke Perswasion's prologue, the first stage direction reads: "Heare let ther be a clamor, with whouping and halowinge, As thoughe ye weare huntinge, or chasinge the game. Enter *Gautir* . . . ";[69] the second stage direction reads: "Heare enter Grissell, Syngyng and Spynning" (lines 216–17).

But on the left-hand page of *The Pleasant and Sweet History of patient Grissell*, opposite the title, E. P. has placed a woodcut of Elizabeth I (Fig. 55). Whatever the material preconditions which made the reuse of this woodcut practicable, the effect is both to split Grissell into Gloriana and humble spinster and to recast Elizabeth, implausible as it may seem, as the patient, obedient, and down-trodden Grissell. There is, though, another way to contextualize this woodcut of Elizabeth. In the British Museum copy, the title page which announces the chapbook's title is preceded by a page which repeats the woodcut of the men hunting and the woman spinning, but the page names the story *The History of the Noble Marques*. While the picture of Elizabeth faces the "Grissell" title page, and thus seems to assimilate the monarch, by gender, to the woman spinning, the previous title suggests the possibility of assimilating her, by rank but cross-gendered, with the "Noble Marques." Indeed, if one takes the figure riding in the right-hand woodcut to be Walter, then the analogy between Walter and Elizabeth is suggested by their exaggerated headdresses and feathers and the size of their ruffs. Elizabeth can thus be read both as Walter and as Grissell.

In fact, Elizabeth had appropriated both roles herself in her confrontation with the House of Commons in 1566. The topic of angry debate at that time was the queen's marriage and the succession question. These are the very topics of debate which open Boccaccio's tale of Gualtieri and Griselda. In Boccaccio's story, Gualtieri has rejected marriage and children, and, when badgered by his subjects "to match himselfe with a wife, to the end, that he might not decease without an heire" (Boccaccio 1620, 296), Gualtieri at first resists and finally agrees to marry only if he can do so on his own terms, without any constraints on his choice. Like Gualtieri's courtiers, Elizabeth's House of Commons petitioned her, announcing that "we may despair of your marriage, we may despair of your issue."[70] Indeed, Elizabeth's subjects had gone further in their attempts at persuasion than Gualtieri's: "certain lewd bills [were] thrown abroad against the Queen's Majesty for not assenting to have the matter of succession proceed in Parliament."[71] In her first outraged draft of a speech responding to what she saw as Parliament's interference with her prerogative, she assumed the role of a horseman over an unruly animal: "I marvel not much that bridleless colts do not know their rider's hand, whom bit of kingly rein did never snaffle yet."[72]

When Elizabeth delivered the speech to Parliament on 5 November 1566, she proclaimed that she did indeed hold the "kingly rein," and that she was invested with all the power of her father, Henry VIII:

And though I be a woman, yet I have as good a courage, answerable to my place, as ever my father had. I am your anointed Queen. I will never be by violence constrained to do anything.[73]

Like Gualtieri, she accepts the request that she marry: "I will marry as soon as I can conveniently."[74] But, like him, she asserts her absolute power to decide when and to whom and refuses any "constraint." This assertion, though, is dramatically undone by her next sentence:

I thank God I am endued with such qualities that if I were turned out of the realm in my petticoat I were able to live in any place in Christendom.[75]

Here, she shifts roles from that of a male ruler who will marry as he pleases to that of the banished wife stripped bare, or almost bare, by her husband. What is the meaning of this extraordinary and unexpected casting of herself as Griselda? Rhetorically, it immediately allows her to cast her advisors as tyrants, as unjust thieves of her rights and her dignity. But even as she casts herself as the abject outcast, she, like the Grissel of the Admiral's Men, asserts her endurance.

Indeed, the very assaults upon her dignity are rewritten as the means by which she will reveal those qualities that will make her welcome anywhere in Europe. These are hardly the moral qualities of humility and patience that Forrest attributed to Katherine of Aragon, and Elizabeth has no intention of being driven from her position as her "stepmother" Katherine had been. By laying a rival claim to be a second Griselda, she simultaneously shames Parliament and appeals for pity from her hearers. At the same time, she claims an identity that cannot be shifted by her subjects' unclothing or clothing of her. Perhaps the subtlest of her reinscriptions of Boccaccio's Griselda is her claim that the petticoat is hers ("if I were cast out of the kingdom in *my* petticoat"). Gendering herself as woman and her subjects as the husbandly controllers of the *king*dom, Elizabeth nevertheless rejects a central feature of Boccaccio's tale: that, stripped bare and sent away by her husband, Griselda has to entreat for a smock from him. Boccaccio's Griselda has to beg for even the most valueless of things, a smock which inscribes her husband's power and her own powerlessness. Elizabeth, in contrast, represents her petticoat not as a gift, implying her dependence upon a superior, but as an emblem of her inalienable self-possession.

(In)alienable possessions: smock and gown

Elizabeth's assertion that the petticoat is hers illuminates a striking difference between the play by the Admiral's men and earlier versions of the tale of Griselda.

THE PLEASANT
AND SWEET HISTORY
of patient Griffell.

Shewing how fhe from a poore mans
Daughter, came to be a great Lady in *France*,
being a patterne for all vertuous
VVomen.

Tranflated out of *Italian*.

London printed by E.P. for Iohn Wright, dwelling

Fig. 54. Woodcut, title page to *The Pleasant and Sweet History of patient Grissell*, London, 1630

Fig. 55. Woodcut, Queen Elizabeth, frontispiece to *The Pleasant and Sweet History of patient Grissell*, London, 1630. By permission of the British Library

In Boccaccio, and even more in Petrarch, the taking away of every single item of Griselda's clothes is explicitly a stripping away of her will, her desires, her liberty. This is clearly expressed in Chaucer's translation of Petrarch, in which, when Walter says that he is going to take away her son, Griselda responds:

> "Ye been oure lord, dooth with youre owene thyng
> Right as yow list, – axeth no reed at me,
> For as I lefte at hoom al my clothyng,
> Whan I first cam to yow, right so," quod she,
> "Left I my wyl, and al my libertee,
> And tooke your clothyng; wherfore I yow preye,
> Dooth youre plesaunce, I wol your luste obeye."[76]
>
> (Petrarch: "You are my lord and theirs, use your right over your property, and do not seek my consent. For the moment I entered your house, as I laid aside my clothes, I laid aside my wishes and feelings, and put on yours.")[77]

To wear one's own garments, or the garments of anyone but one's husband, would be to put on desires that were, from the husband's perspective, foreign bodies. In the Boccaccio and Petrarch versions of the tale, even a dowry is seen as a form of contamination – the incorporation of a threatening otherness into the husband's domain.

And as Gualtieri takes Griselda naked, so he threatens to send her away naked. With cruel irony, he says: "I intend to have thee no longer my Wife, but will returne thee home to thy Fathers house, with all the rich Dowry thou broughtest me" (Boccaccio 1620, 303). Griselda fully brings out the irony of Gualtieri's dismissal when she responds:

You command me, to carry home the marriage Dowry which I brought with me; there is no need of a Treasurer to repay it me, neither any new purse to carry it in, much lesse any Sumpter to be laden with it. For (Noble Lord) it was never out of my memory, that you tooke me stark naked, and if it shall seeme sightly to you, that this body which hath borne two children, and begotten by you, must againe be seene naked; willingly must I depart hence naked. But I humbly beg of your Excellency, in recompense of my Virginity, which I brought you blamelesse, so much as in thought: that I may have but one of my wedding Smocks, onely to conceale the shame of my nakednesse, and then I depart rich enough. (Boccaccio 1620, 304)

The smock in which Griselda is sent away is thus crucially not hers: it is a wedding smock, given to her as part of Gualtieri's counter-dowry. Even as she is stripped, then, she is still marked as belonging to him, marked by his humiliating livery. But in neither Boccaccio nor Petrarch is it represented as humiliating livery.

Yet that is exactly how all the clothes which the Marquess gives Grissill are viewed in the play by the Admiral's Men. As Grissill herself puts it:

> Poore *Grissill* is not proud of these attires,
> They are to me but as your liuerie.   (2. 2. 68–9)

Her own "brauerie," as we saw above, is the gray russet gown, which stands in stark antithesis to the Marquess's insistence upon his right to give clothing and to take it back. And the russet gown is explicitly staged as part of her counter-history:

> See woman heere hangs vp thine auncestrie,
> The monuments of thy nobillitie,
> This is thy russet gentrie, coate, and crest.   (2. 2. 63–5)

Not only does the gown assert the Marquess's failure to incorporate Grissill; it also derides him.

At the same time, the gray gown acts as a counter-interpellation to the play's audience. Against the splendor of court clothes that the professional theaters so wantonly display, it asserts Grissill's anti-dowry, an anti-dowry which actively enacts what the Marquess fears:

> that speckled infamie
> Sits like a screech-owle on my honored breast,
> To make my subjects stare and mock at me.   (2. 2. 54–5)

But the Marquess conjures up as humiliation what the professional theaters delighted in: the "match[ing]" of "vile Russettings" with "mighty kings." Indeed, in the public theater, Grisill remains in her russets to the end of the play. Not being reliveried in the silks and velvets of court attire, she stands in striking contrast to her aristocratic husband. The class difference between them is asserted through their clothes, even as they are rejoined as husband and wife.

This is in striking contrast to Boccaccio's tale, where the reunion of Griselda and Gualtieri is figured through the reclothing of Griselda:

the ladies arose jocondly from the tables, and attending on Grizelda to her Chamber, in signe of a more successful augury to follow, tooke off her poor contemptible rags, and put on such costly robes, which (as Lady Marchionesse) she used to weare before. (Boccaccio 1620, 308)

Petrarch: Quickly the ladies, surrounding her joyfully and graciously, took off her lowly clothing and put on what she used to wear.[78]

In the play by the Admiral's Men, on the contrary, the power of the Marquess to give and take away clothes, and thus to assert the power of his livery to name and unname, is interrogated to the end. When the play's Grissill is brought back to court, she returns with her father (Ianicola), her brother (Laureo), and the clown and servant to Ianicola (Babulo). The Marquess commands that the father and brother be reclothed in celebration of his supposed second wedding:

> *Furio* bring *Laureo* from the Porters lodge,
> Take in *Ianicola*, and cloath them both
> In rich abiliments.   (5. 2. 138–40)

But when Furio reenters with father and son, they are, as the stage direction informs us, "*striuing about attyre*" (5. 2. 157 SD). Paradoxically, it is Ianicola, the father, who is reliveried and thus subjected to the prince: "load me, for to beare is my desire" (5. 2. 162). Laureo, on the contrary, spurns both his prince and his father: "Giue him [i. e. Ianicola] his silkes they shal not touch my back"; "I will not weare proud trappings like a beast" (5. 2. 158, 160). The play thus reasserts the impotence of the patriarch before the tyrannical husband. But the tyranny of the husband is openly resisted by Grisill's brother, Laureo, an unemployed intellectual, and implicitly contested by Grisill retaining her russet gown. Grisill's "vile russeting" persists as a challenge to husbandly and princely livery.

"Russeting," it is true, was used to mark "appropriate" class distinctions, consigning the poor to their place within a sumptuary hierarchy. It was to enforce such hierarchy that the "Homily against Excess of Apparel" asserted that

every man [should] behold and consider his own vocation . . . Which if it were observed, many one doubtless should be compelled to wear a russet-coat, which now ruffleth in silks and velvets, spending more by the year in sumptuous apparel, than their fathers received for the whole revenue of their lands.[79]

But "russeting" was also a materialization of resistance to the dominant order, whether in Langland's investiture in russet, or in the russet of religious radicals, whose beliefs a conservative derided as being "a russet religion, good for none but russet cotes, & such as fauour popular gouernment."[80] Grissill's russet robe in the public theater is profoundly ambivalent, a materialization both of social subordination and of resistance to the violent hierarchies of the livery system.

10   Of ghosts and garments: the materiality of memory on the Renaissance stage[1]

The materiality of ghosts

In 1891, a short piece in *Light: A Journal of Psychical, Occult and Mystical Research* addressed the question of the clothing of ghosts. Skeptics, it argued, never fail to wear a "self satisfied grin" when they ask: "what clothes do Ghosts wear?":

We are asked triumphantly if we sincerely think that great-coats have "spirits," if we believe that there is such a thing as a ghost of a coat and a pair of trousers, of a chimney-pot hat and a pair of boots. But the matter is not so simple. The double in "Lily's" account is clothed in that spirit drapery familiar to us in spirit photographs. When Miss Eva Fay was tested in Mr. Crookes' laboratory by being "tied by a current of electricity," the hand which passed out a book to Serjeant Cox through the door that led from the laboratory in which Miss Fay was to the adjoining room in which the observers sat was attached to an arm which was covered with the sleeve of Miss Fay's dress. There was a duplication of dress as well as of hand. Yet the galvanometer testified that the medium had not moved from her place. When the "double" of certain persons has been observed it has usually been clothed as the person was – "in his habit as he lived," like the ghost of Hamlet's father.[2]

What the modern technology of the camera captures is a visible invisibility, an immaterial materiality. But the *materiality* of that immateriality became an increasing embarrassment in the nineteenth century. As the writer of the piece in *Light* observes, skeptics mock the absurd notion that there are spirits of coats or trousers or boots or chimney-pot hats. And as the materiality of ghosts' clothes became embarrassing, so too did the materiality of stage ghosts. The more that theatrical companies attempted to capture the spookiness and other-worldliness of the Ghost in *Hamlet*, the more uncomfortably material appeared the Ghost's body, clothes, voice, which no amount of complex lighting or voice-distortion could erase.

This embarrassing materiality of the immaterial Ghost is wonderfully captured in Dickens's account of Mr. Woppsle's *Hamlet* in *Great Expectations*:

The late king of the country not only appeared to have been troubled with a cough at the time of his decease, but to have taken it with him to the tomb, and to have brought it back. The royal phantom also carried a ghostly manuscript round its truncheon, to which it had the appearance of occasionally referring, and that, too, with an air of anxiety and a tendency to lose the place of reference which were suggestive of a state of mortality. It was this, I conceive, which led to the Shade's being advised by the gallery to "turn over!" – a recommendation which it took extremely ill. It was likewise to be noted of this majestic spirit that whereas it always appeared with an air of having been out a long time and walked an immense distance, it perceptibly came from a closely contiguous wall.[3]

It is particularly absurd that the Ghost should not have properly memorized his lines because a spirit should be beyond the vulgar materialities of theatricality itself. Dickens's ghost, as if not embarrassed enough at having to appear at all, brings with him an all-too-material cough. And the Ghost whose fixed command is "Remember me" is in fact an actor who cannot remember his lines. The theatrical staginess of the Ghost had in fact already been unintentionally paraded by Tabitha Bramble in Smollett's *Humphrey Clinker*. Tabitha, in praising the actor James Quinn, exposes the mechanics of the theatrical supernatural:

"Mr. Gwynn [Quinn] . . . I was once vastly entertained with your playing of the Ghost of Gimlet at Drury-lane, when you rose up through the stage, with a white face and red eyes, and spoke of *quails upon the frightful porcofine* – Do, pray, spout a little of the Ghost of Gimlet."[4]

The Ghost, who in *Hamlet* could "a tale vnfolde" and make Hamlet's hair stand on end like "quils vpon the fearefull Porpentine"[5] (1. 5. 20 [TLN 705]), becomes in Tabitha's account an actor who spouts not of hair standing on end like a porcupine's quills but of a mythical beast (a porker?) surmounted by birds. In both *Great Expectations* and *Humphrey Clinker*, the supernatural takes on an all too local habitation and place.

   More recently, John Gielgud has addressed the problem of the Ghost's materiality upon the stage. The play calls for the Ghost to wear armor at first, but, he writes, "[i]t seems to be an impossibility to design silent armour for the Ghost, and consequently he is always dressed extremely vaguely and underlighted almost out of recognition." Gielgud confesses that he has never seen the part played to his satisfaction:

In spite of the elaborate care with which he is described in the text, he is never dressed in full armour, and his vanishing is usually poorly contrived in a blackout . . . I imagine that his disappearance down a trap – which would, I suppose, be laughed at by a modern audience – gave point, long lost today, to the lines about the "cellerage" and "old mole."[6]

In fact, it is as laughter increasingly threatens the Ghost that he starts to be staged not in armor but in some form of "spirit drapery." The frontispiece to the first illustrated edition of the play, edited by Nicholas Rowe in 1709, shows the Ghost in full armor, as does the painting by Francis Hayman of the 1747 production at Drury Lane, an engraving of the 1780 production at Drury Lane, and the engraving of Mr. Stewart's Ghost in William Macready's 1849 performance of *Hamlet* at the Haymarket. But Tom Mead's Ghost in Henry Irving's *Hamlet* in 1874 wore "spirit drapery," as did the Ghost in Forbes Robertson's 1897 production and the Ghost in Frank Benson's 1900 production. In 1844, George Cruikshank etched the Ghost in full armor rising through the trap door – but as a figure of derision (Fig. 56). The mechanics of the supernatural are fully exposed as we see the stage hand beneath winding the platform up.[7]

   Yet the implausibility of Cruikshank's Ghost is perhaps no greater than the theological specters (Catholic or Protestant, revenant or demon, according to taste) who haunt the pages of John Dover Wilson, Eleanor Prosser, et al. Greg, who was more honest than most modern critics, still seems to have been over-optimistic when he claimed that "our gorge rises at [the Ghost]." Why should our gorge, rather than our laughter, rise at what he himself describes as "a grotesque fresco," "a thing we ridicule"?[8] Ridicule, rather than fear, has been the usual lot of Hamlet's Ghost. It was no doubt to avoid such ridicule that Jean François Ducis simply excised the Ghost from his adaptation of the play in 1769, an adaptation that was to hold the stage in France for over forty years.[9] And other devices have been used on the modern English stage to dispose of the Ghost. In Jonathan Pryce's performance, for

Fig. 56. George Cruikshank, etching, "Alas, poor Ghost!" London, 1844

instance, the Ghost spoke through the body of the son, thus evading the separate embodiment and costuming of the Ghost.

We are faced here with a striking paradox: at the historical point at which ghosts themselves become increasingly implausible, at least to an educated elite, to believe in them at all it seems to be necessary to assert their immateriality, their invisibility. The grosser the signs of materiality, the more the observers are likely to detect fraud and imposture, as do the skeptics who ask "what clothes do Ghosts wear?" The drapery of ghosts must now, indeed, be as spiritual as the ghosts themselves. This is a striking departure both from the ghosts of the Renaissance stage and from the Greek and Roman theatrical ghosts upon which that stage drew. The most prominent feature of Renaissance ghosts is precisely their gross materiality. They appear to us conspicuously clothed. Not only are they clothed, but after they leave the stage, their clothes, having a vulgar material value, are carefully stored away or resold. The inventory of the Admiral's Men taken in 1598 thus records "j payer of yelow cotton sleves, j gostes sewt, and j gostes bodeyes" as well as "j gostes crown."[10] Ghosts' clothes are just as substantial and recordable as yellow cotton sleeves, although we are left in the dark as to what their materials or colors were. Ghosts, as much as living persons, required suits or bodices.

The clothes of the ghost in the Renaissance theater are, in a quite literal sense, prior to the ghost. The actor has to assume the costume; the costume names (and, in the case of Edgar, for instance, continuously renames) the player as man or woman, monarch or jester, Italian or Persian. Think, for a moment, of the ghost's bodice. The ghost's bodice in the records of the Admiral's Men gives to the ghost a body, a local habitation, and a shape. The material clothes, indeed, have the ability to conjure up the dead and to materialize them upon the stage. The same inventory of the Admiral's Men contains a whole section on "Antik sutes," including "Will. Sommers sewtte" (318). It is possible that the first part of *Wolsey*, a play which the company acted in 1598, was partly written to stage Will Summers, Henry VIII's fool, in the actual costume which the historical fool had worn.[11] If so, the costume may have come from the actors who performed Nashe's *Summer's Last Will and Testament* in 1592 at Croydon. But whether or not the suit of Will Summers which the Admiral's Men owned was actually that of Henry VIII's fool and whether or not it came from Nashe's play, his play itself stages the crucial relation between clothes and the coming into being of a ghost. For *Summer's Last Will and Testament* opens with the ghost of Will Summers in the process of getting dressed, as if the actor can only become a ghost by the assumption of the clothes of the dead clown. The opening stage direction reads:

Enter Will Summers in his fooles coate but halfe on, comming out.[12]

The stage Summers, both in emphasizing the "turmoyle of getting [his] fooles apparell" on and in dressing himself "without," that is, in front of the audience, displays the very act of ghostly materialization that a later age would attempt to evade. This ghost becomes a ghost not through an act of spiritualization but through the material presentation of the "fooles coate." The Renaissance theater brought the dead back to life through the permeated life of clothes. If Will Summers was dead, he survived in the clothes that bore his presence and that could be made to walk again.

The particular power of clothing to effect this magic was, as we have been arguing

throughout this book, closely associated in the Renaissance with two almost contradictory aspects of its materiality: its ability to be permeated and transformed by
maker and wearer alike; its ability to endure over time. As a result, clothing tended
to be powerfully associated with memory. In *King John*, Constance's grief for her
son Arthur is physically located in the places that make present his absence: her grief
"fils the roome vp of my absent childe," "[l]ies in his bed," "[s]tuffes out his vacant
garments with his forme."[13] Indeed, "vacant garments" are often imagined as
retaining a person's "forme" in and of themselves. And the scattered body of the
dead is also present in the fragments that survive him. As John Kerrigan notes,
Thomas Kyd's *The Spanish Tragedy* traces a scarf which Bel-Imperia gives as a love-
token to Andrea. When Andrea is killed, his friend Horatio takes the scarf in
remembrance of him. Similarly, after Horatio is murdered, his father, Hieronimo,
dips his son's handkerchief into his blood to create a material memorial both of his
life and of his death. And Antony presents the dead emperor to the people by
showing them his rent mantle, "Our *Caesars* Vesture wounded" (*Julius Caesar* TLN
1732).[14] In *Twelfth Night*, Viola memorializes the brother she believes dead by
having her clothes cut in imitation of his (TLN 1902–4). Material ghosts, in fact,
can be seen as the logical extension of the material remains (rings, scarves,
handkerchiefs, jewels, shoes) that are so frequently staged in the Renaissance
theater. Ghosts testify simultaneously to death's undoing of the body and to the
materiality of survival.

Paradoxically, the ghost of the Renaissance stage is more fully materialized for us
than any other role for the simple reason that the scripts often contain detailed
descriptions, particularly in the stage directions. This is, no doubt, because there is a
crucial uncertainty about what clothes a ghost will wear. Will a ghost wear burial
clothing (a winding sheet) or will it appear in "his habit as he liued"? In Robert
Greene's *Alphonsus, King of Aragon*, the ghost of Calchas rises "*in a white Cirples
and a Cardinals Myter*," thus ironically declaring his former status as pagan
prophet.[15] But in *The White Devil*, Brachiano's ghost enters "In his leather Cassock
& breeches, bootes, a coule," suggesting more his present status as a ghost.[16] We
also often know just where ghosts materialize. Banquo's ghost "*sits in Macbeths
place*" (3. 4. 37, TLN 1299). And in Marston's *Antonio's Revenge*, when Maria goes
to bed, mourning for her dead husband, Andrugio, the stage direction reads: "*Maria
draweth the courtaine: and the ghost of* Andrugio *is displayed, sitting on the bed*."[17]
After sending Maria to bed, the ghost carefully "*draw[s] the Curtaines*" before
repossessing its shroud and returning to the grave. These ghosts conspicuously
interact with the material world; they are, indeed, as materialized themselves as any
part of the world around them. They have local habitations and costumes.

But why should these ghosts be so precisely clothed and situated? It is, mundanely,
so that they will be known. If a ghost says, above all, "remember me," remembrance
is materialized through the physical attributes that named the person when alive.
And those attributes are above all *superficial*: they lie on the surface, they can be
displayed to the eye (Andrugio's ghost is "*displayed*"). If a ghost is a mnemonic, the
Renaissance ghost is often remembered by what it wears, what is most visible and
tactile – its clothes. Interiority is equally literalized, but in terms of unnaming. That
is, if a later regime of individuality will try to trace its most fundamental forms in an
interior subjectivity, the interiority of Renaissance tragedy is displayed in the fully
material skull beneath the skin. And what characterizes the skull is anonymity. The

body, given over to death, could be anyone's: the skull may be Alexander's or Yorick's or anyone's. Without a memorial or a gravestone or a gravedigger to tell you whose the skull was, you don't know. But if the depths of the body display only the workings of anonymous death, the surfaces of the body trace the insignia of identity.

In an aristocratic society the most privileged markings of identity are those of the knight, and they are to be found less within the body than in the heraldic signs that adorn it. Medieval and Renaissance tombs that display the armored body above and the cadaver below make explicit this relation between surface and depth. The surface (the armored body) is elaborately identified through complex heraldic devices; it is identified, of course, not as an "individual" but as a genealogical body, a body marked, on the shields that surround it, by its kinship connections. The cadaver beneath is unidentified, unidentifiable; it is simply food for worms, which are sometimes literally depicted eating away any unique characteristics, laying bare the anonymous bones. One recognizes Hamlet's father, in death as in life, by his armor. The Ghost wears, or we might almost say *is*, were it not for his raised visor, a suit of armor. Not any suit of armor but "the very Armor he had on" when he fought with Fortinbras (1. 1. 60 [TLN 76]).

Now it is exactly such suits of armor that were transmitted as the markers and, indeed, creators of genealogy. In other words, the ghost of Hamlet's father, when it first appears, is uncanny less because of its spectral quality than because this suit of armor, which would, of course, have survived the father's death, moves, and because from this armor issues the father's voice. The Ghost in *Hamlet* thus activates a specific memory system: the transmission of property, including armor, as the material "remember me's" which mark the heir as the living embodiment of his father, Hamlet as Hamlet. If the father dies, his material identity survives in the helm and crest, the target or shield, the coat of arms which heralds carried in front of the coffin at his funeral. The aristocratic funerals of Renaissance England testify to the attempt to make memory and inheritance two sides of the same coin. For the principal mourner had to be of the same sex and status as the deceased. Thus, for all the literary demands that the wife should grieve for her dead husband, widows were in reality completely marginalized within the social processes of mourning. As Clare Gittings notes, "only the eldest of any of the sons could act as mourner to a dead father."[18] And the rite of mourning was itself a ritual transmission of the father's armor to his son. At the church, the chief mourner gave money to the church, after which the coat of arms was carried to the altar and given to the church. The function of the chief mourner's financial offering was to insure that the armor, now technically the church's, would be immediately handed back to him. Thus did the heir step into the shoes, uncomfortably metallic as they may have been, of his father.

Funerals, then, asserted the materiality of memory, and so equally did the aristocratic wills in which fathers bequeathed their armor to their sons. Such bequests remained a striking feature of aristocratic wills. They are, as one would expect, common enough in the Middle Ages. In 1368, Sir Michael de Poynings left "to my heir," "all my armour"; in 1368, the Earl of Suffolk left "to William, my eldest son, my sword, which the King gave me in name of the Earldom"; in 1369, the Earl of Warwick gave "to Thomas, my son and heir, . . . the coat of mail sometime belonging to that famous Guy of Warwick, and . . . all my harness, weapons, and such like habiliments [to] be equally divided between my two sons Thomas and

William."[19] But one equally finds precise instructions as to the disposition of armor in the sixteenth century. In his will, dated 16 January 1580, Wistan Browne left to his son and heir "my armour and weapons in Weald Hall and Rookewood Hall; all which I will shall remain in such studies, galleries and other rooms as they now be to the use of my son"; in 1579, Richard Cook left "To my son Anthony my armour and weapons at Gidea Hall"; in 1578, Clement Sysley left to his son and heir, Thomas "my armour and furniture of armour, my guns, dags, pikes, bills, targets and crossbows, and they are to remain as standards and implements of household to him and his heirs forever at Eastbury." [20] In 1582, Robert Camocke left to his wife Mary "my new bible of the greatest volume for life, and my household stuff." But he explicitly excludes his armor "which I give to my son Thomas" and which is "to remain in my house to my heirs."[21] What is striking in these four sixteenth-century wills is the explicit attempt to prevent the armor from becoming a moveable possession, to ground it in a specific house, even in specific rooms. This is even more extreme in the will of Richard Kynwelmarshe: he leaves his armor not to a person but to a place: "to the manor [Newton Hall]."[22] Such wills make clear that the identity of the gentry is not the same as individuality. It is shaped from the outside by the value and the honors it can absorb into itself.

Armor was often a form of haunting, whether or not it was activated by a ghost. It remained as a memorial system within the house. In *2 Henry VI*, as Phyllis Rackin notes, Iden, having killed "that monstrous traitor" Jack Cade, transforms his deed "from a defense of private property to a heroic victory in defense of his king" by elevating his sword as "a historical monument":[23]

> Sword, I will hallow thee for this thy deede,
> And hang thee o're my Tombe, when I am dead.   (4. 10. 67–8 [TLN 2972–3])

The material survival of armor asserts the continued presence of an absent body or line of bodies and of their martial status. Sometimes, the armor will be activated by, and in turn activate, another body – the father's heir, for instance. Sometimes, it was hung up in the church as a memorial. The helm of Sir Nichols Heron used to be above his monument in Croydon church until it was removed to the Museum of London, and the helm of Sir John St. John, who died in 1594, is still next to his tomb at Lydiard Tregoz in Wiltshire. Sir Roger Manwood's tomb in St. Stephen's, Canterbury, is surmounted by a helm and crest, a pair of gauntlets, and a mourning sword, dating from his funeral in 1592. And the most complete remaining set of armor in a church dates from an even later period, hanging above Sir William Penn, who was buried in St. Mary Redcliffe, Bristol, in 1670. "The coat, complete with tassels, is above the memorial, then, in order of ascendancy, the breast-plate with attached leg-guards, the helm and crest, and the painted wooden target behind which is tucked the sword."[24] Such displays of the armor of the dead were frequently planned in advance and set down in wills.

But although armor was a crucial memorial bequest of clothes amongst the aristocracy, the Ghost of Hamlet's father is unusual, if not unique, in returning in his armor. When the Renaissance stage ghost returned clothed, it had a striking range of clothes at its disposal, from the white surplice and cardinal's mitre of Calchas, to the leather cassock, boots and cowl of Brachiano, to the armor, and later bedgown, of Hamlet's father. In the Induction to *A Warning for Faire Women*, a play belonging to the King's Men and probably performed by them a year or so before *Hamlet*, Comedy mocks Tragedy, sneering that she stages ghosts with tattered outfits:

> [A] filthie whining ghost,
> Lapt in some fowle sheete, or a leather pelch,
> Comes skreaming like a pigge halfe stickt,
> And cries *Vindicta*, reuenge, reuenge.[25]

A pelch or pilch was an outer garment made of skin, such a garment as Brachiano wears. The "fowle sheete," on the other hand, is related to the sheet that is the familiar garb of modern ghosts. Yet the sheet of the Renaissance ghost has nothing in common with the "spirit drapery" of a later age. It is as material as the Ghost's armor. But whereas armor displays the continuity of aristocratic identity, the sheet marks the dissolution of any identity. For the "sheet" is, of course, the winding sheet in which the dead body is buried. It is this winding sheet, or shroud, which Andrugio imagines repossessing as he flees the coming day, and it is probably the remains of a winding sheet which scarcely conceal the naked body of the Ghost depicted in Stephen Batman's *Doom Warning Judgment* (1581).

John Donne strikingly displays his winding sheet in what was probably then, as now, the most famous English monument of the early seventeenth century. The monument portrays Donne, still in his winding sheet, standing up, although his knees are partially bent, as he rises out of the urn which symbolically contains his ashes (Fig. 57). Isaac Walton gives a (disputed) account of the preparations for the memorial:[26]

A monument being resolved upon, Dr. Donne sent for a carver to make for him in wood the figure of an urn, giving him directions for the compass and height of it; and to bring with it a board, of the just height of his body. These being got, then without delay a choice painter was got to be in readiness to draw his picture, which was taken as followeth:– Several charcoal fires being first made in his large study, he brought with him into that place his winding-sheet in his hand, and having put off all his clothes, had this sheet put on him, and so tied with knots at his head and feet, and his hands so placed as dead bodies are usually fitted, to be shrouded and put into their coffin or grave. Upon his urn he thus stood, with his eyes shut, and with so much of the sheet turned aside as might show his lean, pale, and death-like face, which was expressly turned towards the east, from whence he expected the second coming of his and our Saviour Jesus. In this posture he was drawn at his just height; and when the picture was fully finished, he caused it to be set by his bedside, where it continued and became his hourly object till his death, and it was then given to his dearest friend and executor, Dr. Henry King . . . , who caused him to be thus carved in one entire piece of white marble, as it now stands in that church.

The epitaph, which Donne wrote, further testifies to the significance of clothing, even in, or especially in, death: "DECANATU HUJUS ECCLESIAE INDUTUS XXVII. NOVEMBRIS, MDCXXI. EXUTUS MORTE ULTIMO DIE MARTII MDCXXXI" ("Having been invested [*indutus*] with the Deanery of this Church, 27 November 1621, he was stripped [*exutus*] of it by Death on the last day of March 1631").[27] Here, it is the disrobing of the body, its unnaming in death, which is staged. But this is done for the sake of a renaming – not by the final disappearance of clothes but by the taking on of new clothes. This process of rerobing is proclaimed in the epigraph attached to the engraving of Donne in his funeral shroud: *Corporis haec Animae sit Syndon, Syndon Jesu* ("may this shroud of the body be the shroud of the soul, the shroud of Jesu") (Fig. 58).[28] Donne strips himself of his clothes so that he will be re-membered in Christ's shroud. But in St. Paul's Cathedral, it is his own material winding sheet

Fig. 57. Nicholas Stone, monument to John Donne,
St. Paul's Cathedral, 1631

Fig. 58. Engraved frontispiece to "Deaths Duell," John Donne's
final sermon, London, 1630

which is remembered, the "fowle sheet" in which his face, the eyes still closed,
appears – both the face of the dying Donne, just before his dissolution,[29] and the
face that is turned toward the east, at the moment of rematerialization, the
resurrection.

Donne's monument both reasserts the literalness of the sheet in which the dead
body is bound and powerfully stages the antithesis of the armored body. These two
contradictory images (the armored body, the shrouded body) are brought together
in the many two-decker monuments that present the armored, aristocratic body
above, the anonymous, decaying cadaver below, body and winding sheet alike eaten
by worms. In the body above, it is as if the armor that sheathes the body has also
had the power to sheathe the face, which is preserved in stone, unreachable by

death. But neither face nor body will live long in the tomb, as both the cadaver below and the gravedigger in *Hamlet* remind us. The armor alone will endure. This ironic relation of living armor to dead body is captured in the famous monument to Engelbert II of Nassau and his wife, Cimburga of Baden, begun in 1526. Below, husband and wife lie naked, in their winding sheets; above, the empty, separated parts of Engelbert's armor are displayed. Yet here, even though the armor is preserved, it no longer creates a whole body. Scattered, empty, it lives on in a twilight world, both deathless and dead.[30]

Ghosts of both the armored and the shrouded body are in fact present in the most influential of all ghost plays, the play which profoundly influenced Seneca and, through him, Renaissance drama: Euripides's *Hecuba*. From the perspective of Renaissance tragedy, a striking feature of Greek tragedy is the absence of staged ghosts. There are none in Sophocles, and Aeschylus has only the ghost of Darius in the *Persae* and of Clytemnestra in the *Eumenides*. But neither of these ghosts was as influential as the ghost of Polydorus, Hecuba's son, as he appears in the Prologue to Euripides's play. Polydorus's ghost stands at the opposite extreme from Hamlet's. Polydorus has been murdered by his protector, Polymestor, and his body thrown into the sea:

> Here, pounded by the surf, my corpse still lies,
> carried up and down on the heaving swell of the sea,
> unburied and unmourned.[31]

Polydorus's body bears the marks of this death; as a corpse, he wears a gown (*peplos*), which, although he is described as a "naked corpse," is sufficient to identify him to Agamemnon as a Trojan ("what's that Trojan corpse beside the tents?/ I can see from his *peplos* that he's not a Greek" [lines 734–5]). The crucial point, though, is that Polydorus's ghost appears to be marked by the ravages of death.[32] This is in striking contrast to the ghost of Achilles, which, although never physically staged, is seen by Polydorus "stalking on his tomb" (line 37). According to the Chorus, Achilles appears with "armor blazing" (line 111, literally, with "golden arms"). Polydorus, in other words, is materialized as a vulnerable body; Achilles is materialized "in his habit as he lived," the most heroic of warriors.

Both conceptions of the revenant are equally materialist and both emphasize the clothing of the body. But whereas in the ghost of Polydorus we are confronted with the corruptible body and the decaying shroud, in the ghost of Achilles we witness the splendid armor of the soldier in his prime. It is the corruptible body that Cornelia, in Kyd's *Cornelia*, sees in the ghost of her former husband:

> And loe (me thought) came glyding by my bed
> The ghost of *Pompey*, with a ghastly looke,
> All pale and brawne-falne, not in tryumph borne
> Amongst the conquering Romans, as he vs'de . . .
> But all amaz'd, with fearefull, hollow eyes,
> Hys hayre and beard deform'd with blood and sweat,
> Casting a thyn course lynsel ore hys shoulders,
> That (torne in peeces) trayl'd vpon the ground;
> And (gnashing of his teeth) vnlockt his iawes,
> (Which slyghtly couer'd with a scarce-seene skyn) . . .[33]

Like the ghost of Polydorus, Pompey's ghost undergoes the material corruption of the body: his skin is pale and scarcely covers his jaws; his flesh is falling away; his hair is "deform'd" by blood and sweat. Even the shroud ("lynsel," from the French *linceul*, a winding sheet) has undergone decay and is "torne in peeces."

The Ghost in *Hamlet* is in striking contrast to Pompey's ghost. Like Achilles, it is unmarked by death. In his moment of death, the Ghost relates,

> a most instant tetter barkt about
> Most Lazerlike with vile and lothsome crust
> All my smooth body . . .
> (1. 5. 71–3 [TLN 756–8])

But when the Ghost returns he is "Armed at poynt, exactly *Capapea* [F1: *Cap a Pe*]", "[f]rom top to toe," "from head to foot" "in compleat steele."[34] His "canoniz'd bones," having "burst their cerements," revisit the earth in their most martial guise (1. 4. 47–8 [TLN 632–3]). This Ghost looks "like the King," has a "faire and warlike forme," is "Maiesticall" (1. 1. 43, 47, 142 [TLN 55, 60, 142]). There is thus no sign of the corrupting and corrupted body, no mark of the agony of his murder. This ghostly body is in contrast not only to Pompey's ghost but to most descriptions of theatrical ghosts. In *2 Henry VI*, Warwick speaks of ghosts as being "Of ashy semblance, meager, pale, and bloodlesse"; and Reginald in Heywood's *The English Traveller* describes a murdered ghost as appearing with "His body gasht, and all ore-struck with wounds."[35] But *Hamlet*'s Ghost's previously "smooth body" is not wounded but further smoothed and hardened into a carapace of "compleat steele," a carapace which, like Achilles's armor, bears his memory in a way that no mere body could do. The "mirror stage," Lacan writes, manufactures a "succession of phantasies that extends from a fragmented body-image to a form of its totality that I shall call orthopaedic – and, lastly, to the assumption of the armour of an alienating identity."[36] But "the armour of an alienating identity" was a perfectly normal feature of a knightly aristocracy. That is, its identity crucially depended upon what Derrida calls both "*a prosthetic body*" and "a technical body or an institutional body."[37] This prosthetic body is given shape by the work of the armorer and by the emblems of genealogical identity. Assuming armor, the Ghost erases the memory of his fragmented body. The body that confronts Hamlet is monumentalized. Clad in the "very Armor he had on" when he defeated Fortinbras, the Ghost is fixed in the habit of triumphalism, even as he tells of his own overthrow. The armor brings with it its own memory system; it is itself the alienated but material ghost of the royal body.

Armor and alienation

Armor as a form of clothing is at the furthest remove from the pliancy and absorbency of cloth. In the Renaissance, it was both a protective carapace and a worked and engraved mnemonic system, inscribing aristocratic genealogy. The fantasy of armor was that unlike cloth it would not decay. Moreover, armor, unless it is given by the gods, is imagined as both the work and the wear of men. If women spin thread and life alike, armor is forged, not spun. But one of the ironies of Renaissance armor is that it was always already belated. The more glorious its ceremonial forms, the more pointless its promise of material preservation in the age of gunpowder. Moreover, not only does armor rust, and therefore like cloth decay, but, like cloth, it is transferrable from body to body.

The alienability of armor is already inscribed in the fate of Achilles. In Euripides's

Hecuba, as we noted above, Achilles appears in "golden arms." Like the Ghost of Hamlet, Achilles comes back in his most heroic guise. But if armor is seen as conferring heroic identity, it is also detachable. For all the fantasy that armor will confer absolute identity – name and fame – the fate of Achilles's armor is in fact to be alienated. In the *Iliad*, Achilles's first suit of armor was given by the gods to his father, Peleus, from whom he inherited it. It is thus both a mark of the blessings of the gods and of the assimilation of the son to the father. Yet in Book 16, Patroclus becomes the *therapon* or symbolic substitute for his friend, and, as he takes Achilles's place, he takes his armor. Patroclus is wearing Achilles's armor when he is killed. And it is Achilles's armor that Hector takes by stripping Patroclus. At first, Hector puts the armor of his great enemy in a chariot to have it taken back to Troy. But then, changing his mind, he puts it on himself. As Gary Wills puts it:

The whole matter of shifts in identity, whereby men kill themselves over and over, is worked out . . . through the passage of Achilles's first set of armor . . . to Patroclus and then to Hector . . . [T]he Achilles who goes out in his divinely supplied second armor already fights as a dead man: and when he confronts his own armor, now carried on Hector, he kills himself a second time.[38]

Not only is Achilles dispossessed of his armor, but his power is temporarily transferred to Hector. Even as Zeus prophesies the death of Hector, he bends the armor to fit Hector, who, in turn, literally grows to fit the armor:

>   he made fit his lim
> To those great armes, to fill which vp the Warre god entred him,
> Austere and terrible: his ioynts and every part extends
> With strength and fortitude . . .
>   . . . He so shin'd that all could thinke no lesse
> But he resembl'd euery way great-soul'd Aeacides [Achilles].[39]

In so far as Achilles is absorbed into his own armor, he is detachable from himself, able to enter into his friend Patroclus or to be entered by Hector.

The detachability of armor enables it to reach out beyond a single body and to take hold of other bodies. Its detachability is, for instance, what enables it to join father to son. But it is also that detachability that makes it alienable. The vision of Achilles in "golden arms," then, is a nostalgic myth that erases the passage of his armor from body to body. It is the literal transference of armor that Shakespeare dramatizes in *Troilus and Cressida*. In the final act of the play, a stage direction reads "*Enter one in armour*" (5. 6. 26 [TLN 3462]). But the "one" is never identified, or only as a "Most putrified core" (5. 8. 1 [TLN 3497]), and his "goodly armour" is the cause of his death. Hector kills him so as to "be maister of it" (5. 6. 30 [TLN 3467]). And it is when Hector has unarmed, prior to his putting on of the anonymous knight's armor, that he is struck down by Achilles and his Myrmidons. Indeed, martial combat had the dispossession of armor written into it. In the *Iliad*, Hector, having defeated Patroclus, takes his armor; in *Troilus and Cressida*, Hector kills a man so as to possess his armor; in Kyd's *The Spanish Tragedy*, the armor of the defeated Balthazar is awarded to Horatio.[40]

Not only does armor change hands; for all its power to endure, it grows old, falls out of fashion, rusts. In fact, the hanging of real armor on the walls above tombs was becoming increasingly rare because it was an expensive "waste" and because the armor was liable to be stolen. Funeral armor was sometimes made of wood, and even when steel armor was used, it was often composed of mismatched and disposable parts from different periods.[41] And the professional theaters of Renaissance England played their own part in the transformations of the material ghosts of chivalry. Henry Peacham's drawing of *Titus Andronicus* shows six of the seven actors on stage wearing some kind of armor. The theater itself had become a collector and renter of armor, transforming the insignia of martial prowess into money-making display. But the theatrical stagings often suggested that armor was outmoded. One of Titus's sons, according to Martin Holmes, is wearing a "Gothic cuirass of about 1480, that had found its way eventually to a theatrical wardrobe."[42] *Hamlet* itself, for all the Ghost's armor, marks the outdatedness of this martial attire. If Old Hamlet fought in armor and with a sword, his son will fight without armor and with a rapier.[43] If clothes are often mocked for their fashionable innovations, armor is often suggestive of the antiquated. In *Measure for Measure*, Claudius talks of the unenforced laws as having "(like vn-scowr'd Armor) hung by th' wall" (1. 2. 167 [TLN 260]). In *Troilus and Cressida*, Ulysses argues that to rest on one's reputation is

> to hang
> Quite out of fashion, like a rustie male,
> In monumentall mockrie.   (3. 3. 152 [TLN 2004–6])

The rusty chain-mail is, at the same time, a hero whose time has gone by, an out-of-date male.

In *Pericles*, "rustie male" and "vnscowr'd Armor" are literally staged. When Pericles has been washed ashore in a storm, bereft "of all his fortunes," the fishermen give him "a rusty Armour."[44] It is this rusty armor that enables Pericles to participate in the tournament that Simonides holds for his daughter, Thaisa's, birthday, and it is thus the precondition for his wooing and wedding of Thaisa. But the armor's decay marks him out to the spectators as *"the meane Knight"* (sig. C4v [2. 2. 58 S.D.]). Pericles's armor is indeed the subject of mockery: the First Lord sneers that "by his rustie outside, he appeares, / To haue practis'd more the Whipstocke, then the Launce" (sig. C4v [2. 2. 49–50]); and the Third Lord jests that Pericles has "let his Armour rust" so that it will be scoured in the dust when he is dismounted (sig. C4v [2. 2. 53–4]). But Simonides rebukes them with a curiously garbled version of the conventional piety that the clothes are not the person:

> Opinion's but a foole, that makes vs scan
> The outward habit, by the inward man.   (sig. C4v [2. 2. 55–6])

From Steevens onwards, editors have emended the line to make it conform to the notion that we cannot judge inward "being" from outward "seeming." But we should note how distant this view is from Pericles's own. For it is the armor that is both the identifier of his status, however decayed, and, at the same time, the material mnemonic that joins him to his father. Having lost his armor along with all his other possessions in the storm, he says: "What I haue been, I haue forgot to know" (sig. C 2v [2. 1. 71]). Without the support of his material memory systems, he has no identity.

He is in fact rescued by the fishermen, one of whom clothes him ("I haue a Gowne heere, come put it on, keepe thee warme" [sig. C3 (2. 1. 78–9)]), thus conferring a new identity and set of obligations upon him. And it is the fishermen who draw out of the sea the armor with which Pericles will "repaire [him] selfe" (sig. C3v [2. 1.

121]). Not only does this armor enable him to participate in Simonides's tournament, it also repairs his memory and his name:

> it was mine owne part of my heritage,
> Which my dead Father did bequeath to me,
> With this strict charge, euen as he left his life,
> Keepe it my *Perycles*, it hath been a Shield
> Twixt me and death . . .
> It kept where I kept, I so dearely lou'd it.   (sig. C3v [2. 1. 122–9])

As in so many aristocratic wills, as in the case of Achilles, Pericles's armor has been transmitted to him by his father. For Pericles, indeed, the armor comes to stand in for his father ("It kept where I kept, I so dearely loued it"). But the armor is not clearly his. For it is through the fishermen's labor that the armor is recovered and their labor entitles them to lay claim to it. As the Second Fisherman says, "'twas wee that made vp this Garment through the rough seames of the Waters" (sig. C3v [2. 1. 147–9]). The language of the Second Fisherman recalls the language of tailoring, of those artisanal rather than aristocratic labors through which the armor first came into being. For it was craftsmen, not gods, who "made vp this Garment." The fisherman thus opens up the question of ownership and entitlement. Even Pericles is aware of the fishermen's entitlement and has to "begge" of them "this [not "his"] Coate of worth" (sig. C3v [2. 1. 135]).

The scene is an extraordinary one in showing the Prince as being literally "made vp" through the labors of the poor. The fishermen first clothe Pericles and then restore his armor to him, and they also give up their own clothes to prepare him for the tournament. For after the armor is given to him, Pericles is still "vnprouided of a paire of Bases" (sig. C4 [2. 1. 159–60]). "Bases" were the pleated skirts of velvet or rich brocade attached to the doublet and reaching from the waist to the knee. And even these bases will be provided by the fishermen. As the Second Fisherman says:

> Wee'le sure prouide, thou shalt haue
> My best Gowne to make thee a paire.   (sig. C4 [2. 1. 161–2])

When one recalls the extraordinarily high percentage of the wealth of the poor that was stored in the few clothes that they possessed, one recognizes that in giving away his "best Gowne," the fisherman is giving away much of his wealth. The fisherman asks for a single thing in return for his gifts: "I hope sir, if thou thriue, you'le remember from whence you had them" (sig. C3v [2. 1. 150–1]). Indebtedness will take the form of memory itself, the right of the fishermen to enter the social memory system, along with Pericles's father and Pericles himself.

But Pericles does not remember the fishermen. They disappear from the play, having given up their best clothes and their richest catch, never to be heard of again. It is the productions of armorers and, in *Pericles*, of fishermen that create the material supports of aristocratic memory. But as the aristocrats consume those productions, they also consume the memories of those who made them. The aristocrats are, in fact, the "rich Misers" whom the First Fisherman denounces; hoarding their own memories, they erase the remembrance of the poor. Like whales, "[t]he great ones eate vp the little ones." For armor and clothes tell a history of their producers different from that of their consumers. As in the writing of history itself, it is the proud possessors who are commemorated. History, Sir Walter Ralegh wrote, "hath made us acquainted with our dead Ancestors; and, out of the depth and darkness of the earth, delivered us their memory and fame." [45] But whose memory and fame are rescued? As the prefatory letter to Edward Hall's *The Union of the Two Noble and Illustre Famelies of Lancastre & Yorke* puts it: "What diuersitie is betwene a noble prince and a poore begger . . . if after their death there be left of them no remembrance or token?"[46] The remembrances and tokens of the fishermen are taken by Pericles, but not so as to record their memory. As their possessions and labor are alienated from them, so is Pericles's memory of them. And yet, in the play itself, the fishermen's gifts of armor and clothes are staged as the material preconditions that haunt the story of "*the meane Knight*."

Hauntings

Who gets to be a ghost in the first place? Who gets to make the demand: "remember me"? Who gets to haunt? One of the strangest things about haunting is the word itself. It appears that the word was first used in relation to ghosts in the drama of the 1590s. The *Oxford English Dictionary* (not, of course, that it is always reliable on these questions) gives *Midsummer Night's Dream* as the first occurrence of "haunt" meaning "to visit frequently or habitually with manifestations of [the] influence and presence of imaginary or spiritual beings, ghosts etc.": "O monstrous. O strange. We are haunted. Pray masters: fly masters: helpe."[47] When Oberon reiterates "haunted" a scene later, it is surely in the older sense of the word, although it will not be interpreted that way by most modern readers. Oberon says to Puck: "How now, mad spirit?/ What night rule now about this haunted grove?" (3. 2. 5). Oberon, the king of the fairies, is not worried about ghosts; rather, he is referring to the over-population of the grove by mortals. But the new sense of haunting in reference to spirits that *Midsummer Night's Dream* records seems above all to have emerged in the professional theater of the late sixteenth century. The next two references that the *Oxford English Dictionary* gives to this new sense are from *Richard II* ("Some haunted by the Ghosts they haue depos'd" [3. 2. 158]) and from Marston's *Antonio's Revenge* ("Bug-beares and spirits haunted him" [3. 2]). Prior to the 1590s, the word simply meant to practice or to use habitually, to resort to a place habitually, to associate with someone habitually ("Diuers and sundry goldes . . . yee may reduce into your vsuall money, such as you daily haunt [i. e. 'use']"; "I haue charg'd thee not to haunt about my doores"; "Their populous and great haunted cities"; "Africke hath euer beene the least knowen and haunted parte in the worlde.")

It is fascinating to note that as the theaters conjured up the hauntings of spirits, they were increasingly attacked as familiar "haunts" of ill resort. Gosson wrote in 1579 that "the abuse of such places [theaters] was so great, that for any chaste liuer to *haunt* them was a black swan, and a white crowe."[48] Similarly, William Prynne derides "play-*haunters* upon common playes and maskes in our publicke theaters" and Milton attacks the "Animadverter" as one who "*haunts* Playhouses and Bordelloes."[49] The theater itself ironically incorporated this sense of itself as a dangerous haunt. In *The Devil is an Ass*, Merecraft tells Everill that he has been undone by "haunting / The *Globes*, and *Mermaides*!"[50] On the one hand, "haunting" seems to be one of those antithetical words which Freud analyzed in his essay on "The Uncanny." He noted there that the word *heimlich* could mean both "homely," "familiar" and exactly the opposite: "unhomely," "unfamiliar" – "haunted," one might say.[51] "Haunting" splits in antithetical directions: from an action that suggests familiarity and habit to an action that suggests profound disturbance and the shattering of habit; from the desire to repeat to terror at the unfamiliar ("flye masters: helpe"). But, on the other hand, these antithetical senses of "haunting" start to inhabit each other. For those who attacked the theaters saw them both as over-popular (like "populous and great haunted Cities") and as "Devil-haunted," that is, both as places of over-familiarity and as the disuption of all familiarity.

We would note, though, that the haunting of ghosts emerges as part of a theatrical apparatus. That is, it is manifestly contrived: it requires the costumes, the trap-doors, the special effects of the new professional theater,[52] a theater which, as Steven Mullaney has argued, profoundly dis-places the familiar *topoi* or places of the dominant culture. "Haunting" thus parallels the later "phantasmagoria" which, as Terry Castle has shown, is first used to describe the specters created by magic lantern shows at the beginning of the nineteenth century.[53] In both cases, the uncanny is produced through spectacular technologies.[54] This sense of ghosts as theatrical productions is explicit in John Gee's critique of the "Apparitions of two new female Ghosts" in *New Shreds of the old Snare* (1624). Gee argues that Catholicism itself is merely an imitation of the theater, and an expensive one at that:

The *Jesuites* being or having *Actors* of such dexteritie, I see no reason but that they should set up a company for themselves, which surely will put down The *Fortune*, *Red-bull*, *Cock-pit*, & *Globe* . . . *[T]hey make their spectators pay to[o] deare for their Income.* Representations and apparitions from the dead might be seen farr cheaper at other Play-houses. As for example the Ghost in *Hamblet, Don Andreas Ghost* in *Hieronimo*.[55]

But if Renaissance ghosts are seen to emerge from the machinery of professional entertainment, their demand to be remembered depends upon their paradoxical claim that they have been displaced. Murdered and cast out from their homes (the places they haunted when alive), they return to reclaim what has been taken away from them, to reassert the property/propriety which the professional theaters dislocated for commercial gain. For within the staged fictions, ghosts produce terror so as to memorialize their rights to what they consider to be their own. As Jane Cooper asks in "Being Southern": "When is memory transforming? when, a form of real estate?"[56]

For something to be your own, you have to own it. And the question of ownership casts an unexpected light on the ghosts of the Renaissance theater: with important exceptions, these ghosts are materially and legally entitled, even though performed by actors who are tenuously entitled at best. Most stage ghosts have active stakes in inheritance, which is both about the ownership of the future and about the control of memory. Most of these ghosts are the revenants of men and of aristocratic men at that: Andrea in *The Spanish Tragedy*; Andrugio in *Antonio's Tragedy*; Hamlet in *Hamlet*; Banquo in *Macbeth*; Alonzo in *The Changeling*; Brachiano in *The White Devil*. They return to claim a future that they "properly" own and that has been taken away from them. There is nothing given about this predominance of male ghosts. Of Aeschylus's two ghosts, one was a woman: Clytemnestra. And Seneca's (or at least the pseudo-Seneca's) one non-prologue ghost was Agrippina in *Octavia*. But the Renaissance theaters did not, on the whole, follow this precedent.

More striking still is the fact that in the 1590s, there was a wave of female ghosts in narrative poetry. These ghosts stemmed from the extraordinary if belated influence of Thomas Churchyard's poem on Jane Shore, the mistress of Edward IV, printed in the 1563 edition of the *Mirror for Magistrates*. Jane Shore, though, is the antithesis of the "inheritance" ghosts of the Renaissance stage: not only was she a commoner, being a citizen's wife, but she was a woman. What did it mean to bring back such a person from the dead? What could be her claim to be remembered? When Samuel Daniel reused the form of the female complaint for *The Complaint of Rosamond* in 1592, he did so self-consciously to memorialize the unremembered, to bring back to life a woman whose memory had been erased. Rosamond was, according to legend, the mistress of Henry II and, according to Daniel's poem, her tomb at Godstowe nunnery had been destroyed by a bishop (Smith, 106; lines 25–8). It is this very erasure of name and fame which raises the ghost of the dead woman, who appeals to the poet to be remembered, having been immured in a castle when alive and forgotten when dead. Daniel's poem was immensely popular and created a vogue for female complaints spoken by women commoners: Thomas Lodge's Elstred, Anthony Shute's Jane Shore, ballads in Deloney's *Garland of Good Will* on Rosamund, Jane Shore, and Elstred, Churchyard's rewritten Jane Shore, all published or registered in 1593, and Michael Drayton's and Richard Barnfield's Matildas, both published in 1594.[57] At the very time when ghosts were stalking the professional stage, then, there was a vogue for the ghosts of women commoners in narrative poetry.

The revenge plays, though, usually turned their backs upon both the avenging Clytemnestra of Greek tragedy and the revenants of women commoners like Jane Shore. They more commonly staged the ghosts of the patriarchal father and the husband/lover. This father or husband, though maimed in death, returns to claim the inheritance of the future. Banquo's progeny will rule even "till the crack of doom." But Banquo's ghost is unique in this regard. No other revenge ghost so successfully restores his inheritance to its supposedly rightful owner. In *Antonio's Revenge*, Antonio, the most successful of stage revengers, is spurred on by the ghost of his father, but having achieved his ends, he refuses to take back the kingdom and, turning from his patrimony to mourn for his beloved Mellida, he withdraws to a monastery. In other words, he rejects rule, inheritance and the control of the future in favor of private grief. Moreover, he memorializes not the father who demands to be remembered but the "th'immortal fame of virgin faith" (5. 3. 178).

Nowhere is the demand for patriarchal remembrance more insistent and yet more thwarted than in *Hamlet*. The problems begin with how to name a ghost who claims paternal authority. To Marcellus, Barnardo, and Horatio, the Ghost is "it": "speake to it *Horatio*"; "Marke it"; "It is offended." But to the son, the Ghost, because dressed in his father's armor, cannnot be "it" although it is only questionably "he": "Ile *call* thee *Hamlet*, / King, Father, Royall Dane" [our emphasis].[58] And if Hamlet can ascribe the name "King" to this apparition, that appellation is given to Claudius alone in stage directions and speech prefixes alike. When he first enters in Q2, which is the only text in which the name "Claudius" occurs, the stage direction calls him "*Claudius, King of Denmarke*" (1. 2 [TLN 176]), and although the first speech prefix reads "*Claud.*" (1. 2. 1 [TLN 179]), he is uniformly "*King*" thereafter. Old Hamlet, on the other hand, however physically present in his suit of armor, is never fully interpellated through his name (he is, simply, "*Ghost*") and never fully interpellates the son whom he haunts, despite having given Hamlet his name. As Janet Adelman notes, Hamlet's memory of his father is constantly subsumed by his disgust at his mother's remarriage.[59] The Ghost's constant demand that Hamlet should "remember" is equally constantly rewritten as a memory of the bed on which the king and queen, that is Claudius and Gertrude, lie. Hamlet's memory is thus of the physical displacement of his father's body by his uncle's.

But it is also a memory of the scandal of his mother still sleeping in his father's bed. For the rules of inheritance, in the England of the Globe theater, if not in the Denmark of Hamlet, increasingly laid down that the bed of the father should become the bed of the eldest son, as the armor of the father became the armor of the son. That is, while widows had, at least in the sixteenth century, usually been allowed bench right, or a third of the profits from their husband's estates for their own lifetime, they were commonly excluded from the house and from the bed which they had occupied with their husbands. As far as the goods of the house were concerned, widows could only officially claim "paraphernalia," as we noted in chapter 9, which in common law was limited to their dress, jewels, and immediate personal belongings. And even these a widow could not legally bequeathe without her husband's permission. They were officially hers only while she lived, to be returned after her death to the heir. The widow kept her clothes; the heir got the father's bed.

The significance of the bed lay partly in its literal cost. As Amy Louise Erickson observes, "of household items, the most valuable piece of furniture was the bed." In 1616, one Sussex yeoman unusually left his best featherbed with all its "appurtenances" to his wife, Agnes Mockford, but he did so only on the condition that she sign a "dede of release in the law of all hir dower" with the exception of £3 a year. The bed was thus thought to be equivalent in value to a dower. In analyzing the inventories of working people in the seventeenth century, Erickson notes that a cottage could be bought for the price of five to ten beds, whereas today a modest house would cost the price of at least eighty luxurious beds.[60] Of course, the aristocracy owned much more, and their beds accounted for a smaller proportion of their household valuables. Yet their beds were both extraordinarily costly and symbolically charged as the site of patrilineal inheritance.[61] As Sasha Roberts points out in an important article on English Renaissance beds, the inventories of Charles I's domestic goods in 1651 valued his Raphael cartoons at £300; his bed, with its rich furnishings, was valued at £1,000.[62] The economic value of the bed materialized its significance as a site of memory.

In *The Odyssey*, the connection between the bed and family "roots" is literalized: Odysseus carves his bed out of a rooted tree and his home is built around it. And the power of the bed as a materialization of the relation between husband and wife and as a site of crisis is worked out in *Othello*, as well as in other plays after 1600 that increasingly used the bed as an important theatrical prop.

The connection between the best bed and patrilineal inheritance is implied in Shakespeare's own will, which contains the famous phrase: "I gyve vnto my wief my second best bed with the furniture." The best bed, together with his sword, would have gone to his son Hamnet, if he had survived. Given the absence of a male heir, the bed, together with the Stratford house itself, went to his daughter, Susanna Hall, and to "her heires for ever". His dead son, Hamnet, is indirectly conjured up in the gift of 26s. 8d. to "Hamlett Sadler," the probable godfather of Hamnet, to buy a mourning ring. More striking and unusual is the emphatic expression of the intent to take back the property from the female heirs and give it to male heirs.[63] The will goes to extraordinary lengths to insist upon male inheritance. The majority of the property is to be left to Susanna Hall "for & during the terme of her naturall lief,"

& after her Deceas to the first sonne of her bodie lawfullie yssueing & to the heires Males of the bodie of the saied first Sonne lawfullie yssueing, & for defalt of such issue to the second Sonne of her bodie lawfullie issueing and (so [deleted]) to the heires Males of the bodie of the saied Second Sonne lawfullie yssueinge, & for defalt of such heires to the third Sonne of the bodie of the saied Susanna Lawfullie yssueing and of the heires Males of the bodie of the saied third sonne lawfullie yssueing, And for defalt of such issue the same soe to be & Remaine to the ffourth (sonne [deleted]) ffyfth sixte and Seaventh sonnes of her bodie lawfullie issueing one after Another & to the heires Males of the bodies of the said fourth fifth Sixte & Seaventh sonnes lawfullie yssueing, in such manner as yt ys before Lymitted to be & Remaine to the first second and third Sonns of her bodie and to the heires Males; And for defalt of such issue the said premisses to be & Remaine to my sayd Neece Hall & the heires males of her bodie Lawfullie yssueing, and for defalt of issue to my daughter Judith & the heires Males of her bodie lawfullie yssueing.

There is a certain comedy to this document in which a man without lawful male heirs tried (unsuccessfully, as it turned out) to write male heirs into his future. Having failed of lawful male heirs himself, Shakespeare bequeathed his sword outside the family, to his Stratford neighbor, Thomas Combe.[64] What is not at all comic about the will is the active dispossession of the wife, the second daughter, and the granddaughters, along with second sons and any illegitimate children.[65] They are to have no part in the property which (like the sword and the mourning ring) is a *memory system* – a mnemonic to attach father to eldest son, father to eldest son, even till the crack of doom. Cast out of the best bed and out of the house, the widow is detached from the place and the things in which her own memories are stored.

This situation is almost exactly reversed in *Hamlet*. Here, there is a male heir but he does not inherit the best bed. There is a widow but she is not cast out of the house; indeed, she continues to sleep in the best bed, as if in deliberate defiance of Ralegh's axiom: "If thy wife love again let her not enjoy her second love in the same bed wherein she loved thee."[66] The dead patriarch is left with the widow's lot: namely, his paraphernalia – a suit of armor and a nightgown. It is Gertrude who inherits and who thus remains at the center of the memory system from which widows were increasingly excluded.[67] The father's bed becomes that of the mother, the father's sheets those of the mother. This disposition of goods is in striking opposition to the patrilineal fantasy inscribed in Sir Thomas Hungerford's will, where his beds, "all wayes as long as the said beddes will endure," will "remayne from heire to heire in worship and memory of my lord, my father, Walter, Lord Hungerford, that first ordeyned them and paid for them."[68] In *Hamlet*, in a wonderful reversal of the customary rules of inheritance, the father is excluded. "Must I remember?" exclaims Hamlet. But what he has to remember is that the material bearers of the memory of his father are either disposed of (like Gertrude's mourning clothes) or in the hands of his mother (like his father's bed):

> Must I remember . . .
> A little month or ere those shooes were old
> With which she followed my poore fathers bodie
> Like *Niobe* all teares . . .
> She married, o most wicked speede; to post
> With such dexteritie to incestious sheets . . .   (Q2, 1. 2. 147–57 [TLN 331–41])

It is Gertrude and Claudius who now possess (who *haunt* in its older sense of "habitually use," "habitually occupy") what the Ghost calls "the royall bed of Denmark" (1. 5. 82 [TLN 767])[69] and what Hamlet, deprived of the idealized but thoroughly material memories of patriarchal inheritance, reimagines as "an in-seemed bed" (3. 4. 92 [TLN 2469]) with "incestious sheets."

The more powerful the imagination of the queen's haunting of "the royall bed of Denmark," the less powerful the hauntings of the dead father. The Ghost enters for the last time at the moment when Hamlet, yet again, is magnifying his father at his uncle's expense. Claudius is, he declaims,

> A slaue that is not twentieth part the kyth
> Of your precedent Lord, a vice of Kings,
> A cut-purse of the Empire and the rule,
> That from a shelfe the precious Diadem stole
> And put it in his pocket.   (Q2, 3. 4. 97–101 [TLN 2476–80])

But Hamlet's speech, while denigrating Claudius, dethrones his father. His father, the monarch, does not wear the crown: the crown simply sits on a shelf for any cut-purse to lift. "The precious Diadem" is the material sign both of Claudius's acquisition of the monarchy and, in his pocket, of his power to soil state and marriage bed through his marriage to the queen. The revenant father is thus stripped of armor, of crown, of wife, and finally of the monopoly of memory itself. Revenge takes place as if by accident, and in the absence of the Ghost. It is Gertrude, widow, wife, mother, queen, who remains to haunt Hamlet, to assert, against the monopoly of male inheritance, the material place of women in the system of memory.

In fact, the dislocation of paternal inheritance is prefigured by the failure of the son to resemble the father, despite the identity of name. This failure of resemblance is quite literal. The son wears an inky cloak and suit of solemn black at the beginning of the play, and he moves toward an increasingly unarmored state. He visually refuses his father's legacy: he does not do the very thing that an aristocratic funeral enacts – inherit his father's armor. Although Hamlet takes upon himself the Ghost's demand, although he reiterates, and reverses, his father's conflict with Fortinbras, although he is buried as a soldier with "[t]he Souldiours Musicke, and the rites of Warre," he never becomes his armored father (5. 2. 399 [TLN 3900]).

It is as if the solidity of the armored father transforms his son into a ragged creature, like those ghosts who return from the grave maimed and wearing their winding-cloths. Indeed, the Ghost, clad "in compleat steele," seems to materialize at the expense of the dematerialization of his observers, who are "distil'd / Almost to gelly" (1. 2. 205 [TLN 396]). Hamlet, "the glasse of fashion, and the mould of forme, / Th'obseru'd of all obseruers" (3. 1. 153–4 [TLN 1809–10]), is displaced by a pale figure clad only in his shirt. He appears to Ophelia:

> with his doublet all vnbrac'd,
> No hat vpon his head, his stockins fouled,
> Vngartred, and down gyued to his ancle,
> Pale as his shirt, his knees knocking each other,
> And with a looke so pittious in purport
> As if he had been loosed out of hell
> To speake of horrors.   (2. 1. 74–81 [TLN 973–80])

It is this image of Hamlet, stripped to his linen like madman or ghost, that stuck in the imagination of those who recalled the play: Hamlet less as a man of words than as an unclothed revenant. The hero of Anthony Scoloker's 1604 poem *Diaphantus*, for instance,

Puts off his cloathes; his shirt he onely weares,
Much like mad-*Hamlet*.[70]

In Dekker's appropriation of Hamlet as figure for a "counterfet mad man," the man's clothes are torn like a Bedlamite:

furious *Hamlet* woulde presently eyther breake loose like a Beare from the stake, or else so set his pawes on this dog that thus bayted him, that with tugging and tearing one anothers frockes off, they both looked like mad *Tom* of Bedlam.[71]

When Hamlet returns from England, he writes to Claudius in a curiously ambiguous phrase that he is "*set naked on your Kingdome*" (4. 7. 43–4 [TLN 3054–5]). It seems, in other words, as if Hamlet gets ever more distant from the armor which his father wears, but ever more like a ghost as it was customarily imagined, "naked" and dishevelled. At the same time, in putting an "antic disposition" on, Hamlet becomes the fool or court jester. And it is the court jester, Yorick, not his father, whom Hamlet most fondly recalls: "he hath borne me on his backe a thousand times: And how abhorred in my Imagination is, my gorge rises at it. Heere hung those lipps, that I have kist I know not how oft" (5. 1. 185–89 [TLN 3374–6]). The lips that he has kissed: the lips not of the father but of the jester.

As we noted above, one of the striking features of Alleyn's inventory of the costumes of the Admiral's Men in 1598 is a list of "Antik sutes." It is not entirely clear whether "antik" here means antique or belonging to the jester, since the two words were usually written alike. Perhaps "antik" means both, since the list includes both cloth of gold and of silver and "will somers cote."[72] If the suit had belonged to Will Summers, it was both "antique" and "antic," a memorial to the power of the fool to reach out with his mocking legacy into the present. Though Yorick is dead, his skull memorializes the legacy he leaves, a legacy which includes the "antic disposition" which Hamlet, his illegitimate heir, puts on. In striking contrast to *The Spanish Tragedy*, where the ghost returns gloatingly to conclude the plot, the Ghost of *Hamlet* simply disappears after Act 3.[73] One might say that the ghost of the jester displaces the ghost of the soldier-king.

But if we are to believe the so-called "bad" Q1, the soldier-king had been displaced even before Act 3. In the bedchamber scene, as Hamlet berates his mother, the stage direction reads "Enter the ghost in his night gowne" (3. 4. 101 [TLN 2482]). Nearly all editions delay this entry by a single line, the line where Hamlet says: "A King of shreds and patches" (3. 4. 102 [TLN 2483]). Moved to this position, the line can refer only to Claudius (especially if, as in many modern productions, the Ghost is still wearing armor). But in its earlier position in Q1, Q2, and F1 alike, the line seems to hover between the mock king who rules and the dead king who returns, no longer clad in complete steel, but in a robe of undress, a nightgown. "A King of shreds and patches": the father, like the son, *as* jester, denuded of his armor, yet still "[m]y Father in his habite, as he liued" (3. 4. 135 [TLN 2518]). The bedchamber scene, in fact, suggests the unnaming and renaming of father and mother alike. Hamlet, the old king, returns for the last time, vulnerable now, no longer the warrior hero, as if the relative impermanence of cloth prefigures his own impermanence.

Yet when Hamlet fantasizes the transformation of his own body, it is not into steel. On the contrary, he wants his "too too sallied [F1, solid] flesh" to "melt / Thaw and resolue it selfe into a dewe" (1. 2. 129–30 [TLN 313–14]). Nor does he figure memory in terms of monumentalizing brass or stone but in terms of a commonplace book or the assumption of clothes. At the beginning of the play, it is true, Hamlet emphasizes the insufficiency of clothes as memory: they are "but the trappings and the suites of woe" (1. 2. 86 [TLN 267]). His claim, though, at least in Q2, is that it is not "*alone*" his "incky cloake" or "customary suites of solemne blacke" that can "*deuote*" [F1, "denote"] him truly (1. 2. 77–8 [TLN 258–9]). Having cast off her mourning clothes, Gertrude has ceased to devote herself to the memory of her dead husband. Retaining his mourning clothes, and thus refusing to celebrate the remarriage of his mother, Hamlet attempts to perpetuate his father's memory, even if his clothes alone are inadequate for the work of mourning. He reiterates the significance of clothing when, attacking the "frailty" of Gertrude, he claims that, between the funeral and the marriage, it has been

> A little month or ere those shooes were old
> With which she followed my poore fathers bodie.   (1. 2. 147–8 [TLN 331–2])

Taking off her mourning shoes, Gertrude takes her feet out of the past. She casts off Old Hamlet, just as she asks Hamlet to "cast [his] nighted color off" (1. 2. 68 [TLN 248]). For the material memory of mourning devotes its wearer to the ghosts of the past.

   And it is in terms of clothing that Hamlet demands of his mother that she remake herself:

> Assume a vertue if you haue it not,
> That monster custome, who all sence doth eate
> Of habits deuill, is angell yet in this
> That to the vse of actions faire and good,
> He likewise giues a frock or Liuery
> That aptly is put on.   (3. 4. 160–5 [TLN 2544–9])

Virtue is figured as a garment that can be put on; the more frequently put on, the more it will be a livery that will dedicate its wearer to "actions faire and good." The costume of custom habituates one to the habits (both dress and customary behavior) of good and evil alike.[74] And the clothing of habit "almost can change the stamp of nature" (3. 4. 168 [TLN 2546]). It is, Hamlet claims, Gertrude's ability to be permeated, like cloth, that can (almost) undo the "stamp" that Nature, like a seal or a press, has imprinted upon Gertrude's wax or paper.[75] Although here the livery of custom is opposed to the stamp of nature, Hamlet had previously envisaged "the stamp" of a defect as itself "Natures liuery" (1. 4. 31–2 [TLN 636–7]), as if clothes were themselves a seal that imprinted their wearer. While Hamlet imagines the body as stamped, Gertrude imagines her soul as dyed. Turning her eyes into her soul, Gertrude sees "such blacke and grained spots, / As will not leaue their Tinct" (F1, 3. 4. 90–1 [TLN 2466–7]).[76] "Tinct" is from the Latin *tingere*, to dye or stain. And the spots that Gertrude sees in F1 are both black and red, since the technical meaning of "grained" is dyed in scarlet.[77] The dyeing or imprinting of clothing, though, is not to be undone by the revelation of "naked" Truth, but by a new imprinting or permeation by it.

   As Margreta de Grazia observes, *Hamlet* "is pervaded by images of permeable materials and matter, specifically textile materials and corporeal matter."[78] Old Hamlet's Ghost seems finally both too immaterial ("[t]his bodilesse creation,"

Gertrude calls it [3. 4. 139 (TLN 2521)]) and too armored to be memorable. The heart can only be moved, Hamlet tells Gertrude,

> If damned custome haue not brasd it so,
> That it be proofe and bulwark against sence.   (3. 4. 37–8 [TLN 2419–20])

Covered with brass, the heart becomes "proofe" – that is, like proof armor, or armor of tested strength and quality. For the heart to be invulnerable, it must become as unbending as armor. Hamlet, though, invokes his mother's heart as "made of penitrable stuffe" (3. 4. 36 [TLN 2418]), made, that is, of material that can be stained.[79] In *Hamlet*, as on the Renaissance stage more generally, it is less the armor of the father than "penitrable stuffe" that is the material of haunting.

Conclusion: the end(s) of livery

In *Renaissance Clothing and the Materials of Memory*, we have attempted to understand two conflicting aspects of clothes: clothes as material memories, constitutive of the subject; clothes as a currency whose circulation unmakes and remakes the subject. As we argued in our introduction, the modern sense of "fashion" no longer captures the root sense of clothes as the making or fashioning of a person. We moderns consequently have difficulty in understanding the myth of origin that so preoccupied early modern Europe. Genesis, to which Renaissance commentators returned again and again, begins with an extraordinary meditation upon clothes. Adam and Eve are given food and a place to live by God. They are not given clothes. From the reader's perspective, this nakedness is simultaneously primary and derivative: primary, because it is presented as the original human condition; derivative, because nakedness is the marked term in the narrative, because the receivers of this narrative see it from their own clothed state (the unmarked, unremarkable state). Indeed, so exceptional did Tyndale think the naked state to be that he imagined creation itself as coterminous with clothing; translating Genesis 2.1, he wrote, "[t]hus was heauen & erth fynished wyth all their *apparell*." What later translators will call the "hosts of heaven" here become the necessary clothing of heaven and earth.[1] It is as if Tyndale cannot imagine anything as complete or fully fashioned until it has been clothed.

Tyndale's version makes the nakedness of Adam and Eve all the more marked. They are "naked" (in contrast to both heaven and earth, and to "us," who are clothed); they are "not ashamed" (with the implication that "we," "naturally" clothed subjects, would be ashamed). But then Adam and Eve eat a fruit that their landlord has reserved for himself, and this food transforms them. They become self-conscious, vulnerable to the eyes of another. They try to free themselves from subjection to those eyes by making their own clothes. That, in fact, is the immediate effect of the Fall. Not lamentations, not even at first mutual accusations, but the knowledge of being naked and of the need for clothes:

Then the eyes of them bothe were opened, & they knewe that they were naked, and they sewed figtre leaues together, and made them selues breeches. (3.7)[2]

The first innovative act of Adam and Eve is eating forbidden food; their second act is learning how to make clothes. They sew. Is this their first act of sweated labor? Their loincloths are fig leaves transformed by their own manu-facture.

The vegetable clothes of Adam and Eve, though, do not protect them from the eye of their lord. He sees them and curses them. But then he reclothes them: "Vnto Adam also and to his wife did the Lord God make coates of skinnes, and clothed them" (3.21). Adam and Eve are the first makers of clothing; but their lord now asserts his right to be their tailor. In chapter 3, we quoted Barnabe Rich's complaint that tailors now "make the whole world with their new inuentions." Tailors, he laments, have become "*Body-makers*" who are "more sought vnto then he that is the *Soule-maker*."[3] But in Genesis, God is himself a body-maker and tailoring is a role he assumes in his attempt to refashion his unruly subjects.[4]

In making clothes for Adam and Eve, God gives them his livery. His livery is both a form of protection and a threat. Fig leaves, the clothes that Adam and Eve made for themselves, are minimal and temporary. These vegetable forms will wear out. In contrast, animal skins give greater warmth and have a longer shelf life. But they also inscribe upon the bodies of Adam and Eve the first deaths in Eden. For animal skins become clothing through the deaths of the animals. In asserting their independence from God, Adam and Eve clothe themselves. In reclaiming them as his subjects, God reclothes them in his livery – a livery of protection, but also a livery haunted by death.

For fallen humans, clothes are the necessary prostheses that re-member the self, reminding us who we are. To be unnamed, whether in death or through ritual humiliation, is to have one's clothes taken away. Michael Neill persuasively argues in *Issues of Death* that the shame of death in the Renaissance was intimately connected to the disgrace of nakedness. As we argued in the previous chapter, Renaissance double-decker tombs powerfully represented the shock of the naked corpse. The clothed body of the elite was a body memorialized through the markings of heraldry, armor, and letters. These were the prostheses that transformed the naked body into an identifiable person. Stripped of these prostheses, the body returned to shameful anonymity.

This point is made in an Italian *novelle* that Neill retells. A furrier from Lucca goes to the public baths but, surrounded by unidentifiable naked bodies, he is afraid to undress for fear that he will lose himself. He attaches a straw cross to his shoulder, a material mark through which he can keep hold of himself. But a man suddenly takes his cross, saying "[n]ow I am you; begone, you are dead."[5] The tale ironically brings together two of the most culturally potent images of dressing and undressing. The furrier repeats as his profession the initiating rite of clothing: God's clothing of Adam and Eve in the skins of dead animals. But the cross that he puts upon himself recalls Christ's naked body, the stripping of God at the crucifixion. When the furrier's cross is taken from him, he is, so to speak, doubly dead, no longer just stripped of self so as to conform to the stripping of Christ, but stripped of Christian identity as well. If, as the Renaissance proverb had it, "[w]e are all Adams sons, silk onely distinguisheth us,"[6] take all clothing away and we are even less than Adam's sons.

As we noted in chapter 1, the institution of clothing was regarded by Renaissance commentators as a form of material memory. In his new clothing (and Eve is often forgotten in these commentaries, a point to which we shall return), Adam puts on "new life, by *putting on the Lord Jesus Christ*, Rom. 13.14. and the *garments of salvation*, wherwith God clotheth his church."[7] That is, even as Adam is clothed to remind him of his sin, he is also remade as a figure of Christ. Similarly, Abraham Rosse, while repeating the commonplace that these first clothes were "to teach vs sobrietie; for those were Skinnes, not Silke, Purple, or Cloth of Gold, which are not worne so much for necessitie, as for pride," goes on to extol them as the material memory of what was yet to come. This investiture was carried out so that the first *Adam* might in some sort be a type of the second *Adam*, ɪᴇsᴠs: for this was cloathed with the skinnes of dead beasts, so Christ with our dead sinnes; for he became sinne for vs, that we might be made the righteousnesse of God in him.[8]

But even as these skins become, as Milton argued, a "robe of righteousness" with which the "Father of his Familie" liveried his household,[9] they are also the memorials of mortality.

Wearing carnal as opposed to vegetable clothes, Adam and Eve wear the memories of their own deaths, the deaths that the Fall initiates. Martin Luther argued:

God himself gave Adam and Eve clothes to remind them of their wretched Fall . . . God clothed them with skins of slain animals to remind them that they were mortal and lived in (*constant*) danger of death. They were also to remind them of their sins, present as well as future, and of the misery which sin causes.

Luther continues:

Such reminders are necessary for men who forget both the bad and the good, as St. Peter writes, "But he . . . hath forgotten that he was purged from his old sins" (2 Peter 1:9). In verse 12 he continues, "Wherefore I will not be negligent to put you always in remembrance of these things, though ye know them, and be established in the present truth."[10]

"Knowing" is not enough, Luther claims. One must be *put* in remembrance through the material memory that one wears every day, the memory that one is mortal and lives in constant danger of death. Similarly, Andrew Willet concludes his analysis of Genesis 3.21 by remarking that Adam's livery "put[s] him in minde of mortalitie, by his cloathing of dead beastes skinnes."[11]

But for all this emphasis upon memory, it is as if the skins in which God clothes Adam and Eve do not memorialize enough for the tastes of Renaissance commentators. Above all, they do not "remember" the need for clothes that will mark the distinction between man and woman. Hence, the elision of Eve in so many of these accounts. It is, paradoxically, as if Adam is the only clothes-horse in Eden, Eve never coming into visibility because she has not been adequately marked as a woman. But the attempts to literalize these originary garments make problematic the relations between clothes, memory, gender, and religion. According to one Jewish tradition, the skins that Adam and Eve wear are the skins of the sacrifices that they offer up to God. As the Bishop of Ely wrote,

The *Jewish* Doctors have carried this Matter so far, as to say, That *Adam* being a Priest, these were his Priestly Garments. The Skin indeed of the Burnt-Offering under the Law, is given to the Priest, *Lev*. ᴠɪɪ.8. but not to make him Cloaths: And *Eve*, if this were true, must have been a Priest also; for she had a Coat made of Skins, no less than *Adam*. Who, they fansie, left this Coat to his Posterity; so that *Noah*, *Abraham*, and all the rest of the *Patriarchs* (as *Abel* they say did) sacrificed in the very same Coat.[12]

In other words, the more memorial these initial liveries become, the more they threaten the distinction between man and woman, between the male priesthood and the woman prohibited from wearing "Priestly Garments."

While God's clothing of Adam and Eve figures the materiality of memory, it also prefigures the disruptions of patrilineage. Clothes can be put on, but they can also be taken off, transferred from one person to another. Clothes mark, but they also re-mark and un-mark. Rebekah, the wife of Isaac, has twin sons, Esau and Jacob, but she favors Jacob, the younger son. She helps Jacob to get his blind father's blessing as eldest son by three acts of "translation":[13] she translates kid's meat into the

Geneva version's "pleasant" and the Authorized's "sauoury" dish (27.17) that will taste like the venison that Esau has promised his father; she translates Jacob's arms with the skin of the kids so that he will be, like Esau, a "rough" (Geneva) or "hairy" (Authorized) man (27.11); she translates Jacob himself into Esau by dressing him in his brother's clothes (27.15).[14] The taste of kid is transformed into the taste of venison; the feel of Jacob's body is transformed into the feel of Esau's body; the smell of Jacob is transformed into the smell of Esau:

> Afterwarde his father Izhak said vnto him, Come nere now, and kisse me, my sonne.
>   And he came nere and kissed him. Then he smelled the sauour of his garments, & blessed him, and said, Beholde, the smel of my sonne is as the smel of a field, which ye Lord hathe blessed. (27.26–7)

Wearing his elder brother's clothes, smelling like him, Jacob will steal not only the "smel of a field, which ye Lord hath blessed" but the field itself. Dressed as his brother, Jacob appropriates his brother's blessing and his inheritance. Against the patriarch and the rules of primogeniture, wife and younger son use the transmission of clothes to refigure inheritance.

But patriarchs can themselves refigure inheritance through the circulation of clothes. Jacob, the younger son who has now himself become a patriarch, loves his own younger son, Joseph, more than all his elder brothers.[15] He materializes his love by giving Joseph "a coate of many colors" (37.3).[16] Joseph's elder brothers violently reassert the norms of primogeniture when they strip Joseph of his coat and throw him into a well. Like Esau's clothes, Joseph's coat, detached from Joseph, will now tell its own story. Dipped in the blood of a kid, it "tells" Jacob that his son is dead. And Jacob rematerializes the imagined destruction of Joseph by the destruction of his own clothes:

> It is my sonnes coat: a wicked beast hathe deuoured him; Ioseph is surely torne in pieces.
>   And Iaakob rent his clothes, & put sackcloth about his loynes. (37.33–4)

Jacob tries to make Joseph like himself by marking him with his favor; the patriarch rematerializes himself as his supposedly dismembered younger son. As the son is supposedly rent in pieces, so the father rends his clothes and refuses to be comforted. Jacob marks his grief through the mnemonic of textiles.

Throughout *Renaissance Clothing*, we have explored clothes as material memory systems. The clothes of Adam and Eve materialize both their deaths and their salvation; mourning clothes materialize Jacob's grief; the sackcloth which Jacob wears upon his loins materializes the death of Joseph, his "seed." But clothes do not necessarily tell "true" stories, as the story of Jacob reminds us. Detached from their wearer, Posthumus's clothes will tell Imogen, falsely, that Posthumus is dead; detached from its bearer, Desdemona's dropped handkerchief will tell Othello, falsely, that she is false. The detachability of clothes thus conjures up the alienability and reconfiguration of memory itself. This is a repeated motif of Joseph's story. Joseph is twice stripped of his clothes, and both times his clothes will tell stories that are false. The first time his bloody coat of many colors proclaims that he is dead. The second time, Potiphar's wife, desiring Joseph, embraces him; but, fleeing, "he left his garment in her hand" (39.12). She then "layed up [Joseph's] garment by her, vntil her lord came home" (39.16). It is thus Joseph's own garment that testifies against him, that makes visible, falsely, that his body, like his clothes, has been "layed up" beside Potiphar's wife.

But the detachability of clothes, their ability to lie, does not lead in these narratives away from clothes, or toward a fantasy of immaterial memory. On the contrary, the strippings of Joseph are not a movement toward the "naked" truth. The first stripping leads to his being sold into slavery (as if the stripping of his coat already prefigured a stripping of any cultural and social identity); the second stripping prefigures his being cast into prison. Restoration in both cases depends upon the reassumption of livery. He is rescued from slavery by the assumption of Potiphar's livery; he is rescued from prison through the assumption of Pharaoh's livery.

When Pharaoh commands the imprisoned Joseph to interpret his dreams, Joseph's first acts are to shave himself and to change his raiment (41.14). He then succeeds in his dream-interpretations and Pharaoh materializes his bequest of power and favor to Joseph by reclothing him:

And Pharaoh toke of his ring from his hand, and put it vpon Iosephs hand, and araied him in garments of fine linen and put a golden cheine about his necke. (41.42)[17]

As we have seen so often in Renaissance drama, the changing of clothes leads to a changing of name:

And Pharaoh called Iosephs name Zaphnath-paaneah: and he gaue him to wife Asenath ye daughter of Poti-pherah prince of On. (41.45)

Joseph, the Israelite, is reclothed as an Egyptian, renamed as an Egyptian, married to an Egyptian. Indeed, in the concluding verse of Genesis, Joseph will be mummified and buried as an Egyptian ("and they enbaumed him & put him in a chest in Egypt" [50.26]). But this ending is in tension with the previous verse, in which Joseph takes an oath with the children of Israel that "ye shal cary my bones hence" (50.25). And in Exodus, Moses will carry Joseph's bones with him (13.19). In death as in life, Joseph is split: he is a settler and has a fixed burial place, he is a nomad and his bones will wander; he is Zaphnath-paaneah, he is Joseph; he is an Egyptian, he is an Israelite. The split is inscribed in his conflicting liveries. He is marked as the favored son of Jacob by the coat of many colors; he is marked as the favored "son" of Pharaoh because he wears his ring, his linen, his chain of gold. The clothes, like the forms of burial, like the acts of naming, are attempts to stitch together past and future, to constitute genealogy and identity. But for Joseph/Zaphnath-paaneah, they stitch together radically conflicting pasts and futures, radically different genealogies and identities.

The end or aim of livery is to to mark the body with its debts – debts of love, of solidarity, of servitude, of obedience. Liveries are material "remember me's." It is for this reason that God tells Moses:

Speake vnto the children of Israel, and byd them that thei make them fringes vpon ye borders of their garments throughout their generacions, and put vpon the fringes of the borders a rybande of blewe silke.
    And he shal haue the fringes, that when ye loke vpon them, ye may remember all the commandements of the Lord, & do them. (Numbers 15.38–9)

God commands his people to livery themselves as his. Looking upon the fringes of their garments, they will see and do his commandments. They will inhabit godliness by being habited in his livery.

As we have argued throughout *Renaissance Clothing*, the material "remember me's" of livery were still central in early modern Europe, even as they were coming under increasing pressure from an emergent notion of "fashion." No doubt, a nostalgic resistance to this new sense of fashion helps to account for the extra-ordinary popularity of the story of Patient Griselda in early modern Europe. For the story of Griselda, as we saw in chapter 9, is above all a story about livery. Griselda is constituted and unconstituted by being dressed and undressed, moving between the livery of a peasant and of a prince. What is far more surprising is that a refashioned Griselda was to be the most popular fictional character of the eighteenth century – as if the problem of livery were still the crucial question of what it meant to be a person.

Griselda, a peasant, wears a dress of gray russet, a dress of what in eighteenth-century France would be called *grisette*. *Grisette* meant both an inferior grey fabric and a seamstress or working-class woman. And the story of a servant woman who longs to be reclothed in "gray russet"[18] was the literary sensation of the eighteenth century. In fact, Samuel Richardson's *Pamela* was more than a literary sensation; it was a major social event, being taken up (and denounced) as a radical political tract, as a model of how to write letters, as a treatise on Christian virtue. At the same time, the book created a market in Pamela paintings, prints, playing-cards, fans, snuff-boxes, wax figures, translations, imitations, continuations, rebuttals (of which Fielding's *Shamela* is perhaps the most famous). In France, the book was turned into a play by both Voltaire and Goldoni. The measure of *Pamela*'s power to shock is suggested by the fact that both Voltaire and Goldoni raised the heroine's status so as to make her genteel marriage more decorous. *Pamela*'s cultural centrality is shown by the fact that, more than fifty years after its first publication in 1740, Goldoni's translation became an official subject of debate in the French Revolution. In 1793, the Committee of Public Safety censured Goldoni for transforming Pamela's father from a ditch digger into a count.[19]

At the center of *Pamela*, as of the story of Griselda, is the question of what clothes a woman should wear. In the Renaissance story, a prince marries Griselda, having first stripped her of her previous clothes and then marked her as his by reclothing her. After the marriage, the prince proceeds to take everything away from her again, reducing her to her smock. Finally, he takes her back and reclothes her. *Pamela* both rehearses and reverses this story. Like Griselda, Pamela starts out in "grey russet"; like Griselda, she ends wearing aristocratic finery; like Griselda, Pamela constantly changes her clothes. But unlike Griselda, Pamela refuses to wear the clothes of her master, Mr. B, as a form of livery. Moreover, unlike Griselda but like the women we examined in chapter 6, Pamela works with her needle. Not only does she "work very hard with [her] needle, upon [Mr. B's] linen" but she is also engaged in "flowering him a waistcoat."[20] Moreover, as Pamela fashions Mr. B's clothes, she also refashions him as a person. That is, while Griselda is made and unmade by Gualtieri, Pamela unmakes and remakes Mr. B, transforming him from libertine to model Christian husband. But she is able to do this to the very extent that she refuses the material and moral dependence that her livery implies. Indeed, she asserts her independence by an elaborate process of distinguishing the clothes in which she can be "free" from the clothes that mark her subservience. In doing so, she differentiates between the different mnemonic systems that her clothes materialize.

As she prepares to leave Mr. B, Pamela divides her clothes into three bundles. The first bundle is composed of the clothes that her dead mistress has given her; the second bundle is composed of the clothes that Mr. B has given her; the third bundle is composed of the clothes that she has bought and made for herself. Each bundle materializes different forms of social relations. Pamela will reject the first two bundles as unacceptable forms of livery. They are not, of course, livery in the narrowest sense of that term, that is, a marked form of servant's livery. As we saw in chapter 1, such marked forms were already on the decline in the Renaissance, and although they were still widely used in the eighteenth century, they were increasingly resisted as humiliating. In 1752, a gentleman wrote to a friend looking for a servant that "no servant which can, will wear Livery." And in 1751, Daniel Darbyshire, riding through a Middlesex village, was mocked by a young man for wearing livery: "I wear my own Coat, and you wear your Master's." Darbyshire was so outraged that he shot and killed the young man. His outrage seems to have been generated by the shame that attached to his livery.[21] In contrast, Pamela shows an acute awareness that even the gift of unmarked clothes is a form of livery. The "gift" is a form of incorporation.

Rejecting the first bundle of clothes, the gifts of her former mistress, Pamela writes:

Those things there of my lady's I can have no claim to, so as to take them away; for she gave them me, supposing I was to wear them in her service, and to do credit to her bountiful heart. But since I am to be turned away, you know, I cannot wear them at my poor father's; for I should bring all the little village upon my back: and so I resolve not to have *them*. (111)

However much Pamela loved her mistress, these clothes still inscribe the hierarchical relation between them. If she was to wear them, it should only be "in her service." Worn back in her home village, they will imply that Pamela is absurdly pretending to the status of a lady.

Pamela could, of course, sell these clothes. But here the difference between the "gift" of clothes and the payment of a salary becomes a pressing question. Mr. B, the son of Pamela's previous mistress, has also given her clothes, the clothes that will make up her second bundle:

My master . . . has given me a suit of my lady's clothes, and half a dozen of her shifts, and six fine handkerchiefs, and three of her cambric aprons, and four Holland ones. The clothes are fine silk, and too rich and too good for me, to be sure. I wish it was no affront to him to make money of them, and send it to you [her parents]: that would do me more good. (49–50)

To the extent that the clothes are material reminders, it is an "affront" to treat them as exchangeable commodities. Indeed, when Pamela itemizes her lady's clothes in the first bundle, she intermingles her accounting with "blessings . . . on my lady's memory" (110). But Mr. B teaches Pamela the violent lesson that such "gifts" have strings attached. In the process, the novel imagines the advantages of money over permeated objects that enforce memories of obligation and indebtedness. It is from the perspective of a salary (payment for labor) that one can critique the mystified economics of a master's "gifts," an economics in which labor appears as "gratitude." Pamela, still thinking that she will be allowed to go home, hears rumors that the two bundles that she has rejected may be sent after her. She reasserts that she "can't wear them," but now she does indeed think that she "will turn them into money" (121).

As she thinks in terms of money and of the owning of her "own" clothes, Pamela thinks through the founding concept that would overthrow the long regime of livery: the concept of the individual. Indeed, one could define the ideology of the "individual" as the conceptual system in which a person is prior to his or her wardrobe. From that conceptual system, a person who emerges through and subsequent to his or her wardrobe will increasingly appear as an exception, an anachronism, a non-individual. Exceptions include uniformed soldiers, whose status is visibly inscribed through clothes and badges. Anachronisms include monarchs, whose position is materialized through the assumption of coronation livery. Non-individuals include children, whose clothes are bought for them and who cannot vote. *Pamela* is an extraordinary book because it attempts to imagine the individual in its least imaginable form: the individual as servant and as woman. That is, it imagines the emergent individual in the form of a person most fully subordinated by the livery system.

But *Pamela* is able to conjure up the conceptual field of the individual only through an act of negation. Pamela *rejects livery*; she does not take the bundles of clothes that came from her dead mistress and from her living master. Having rejected the material traces that mark her as another's, she emerges as owner of herself through a fantastically detailed listing of the clothes that she herself owns:

"Now comes poor Pamela's bundle, and a little one it is, to the others. First, here is a callico night-gown, that I used to wear o' mornings. It will be rather too good for me when I get home; but I must have something. Then there is a quilted calimanco coat, and my straw hat with green strings; and a piece of Scots cloth, which will make two shirts and two shifts, the same I have on, for my poor father and mother. And here are four other shifts; and here are two pairs of shoes; I have taken the lace off, which I will burn, and this, with an old silver buckle or two, will fetch me some little matter at a pinch . . . Here are two cotton handkerchiefs and two pairs of stockings, which I bought of the pedlar"; (I write the very words I said) "and here too are my new-bought mittens: and this is my new flannel coat, the fellow to that I have on. And in this parcel pinned are several pieces of printed callico, remnants of silks, and such-like, that, if good luck should happen, and I should get work, would serve for robings and facings, and such-like uses. And here too are a pair of pockets, and two pairs of gloves. Bless me!" said I, "I did not think I had so many good things!" (110–11)

Here are the materials out of which Pamela will new-mint herself: clothes that she has bought, clothes that she has made or will make, the "piece of Scots cloth" in which she will clothe (and thus "livery"?) her own parents. Pamela rejects the implication that she is liveried, but she remakes herself out of the same materials that constituted the livery system. Standing at the end of the livery system, she is intensely aware of the materials that construct the self either as subject or as individual.

If there is something comic for us about Pamela's list of clothes and accessories, this is partly because we fail to see that her clothes are the materialization of her labor. In a historical record of such a materialization, a New England mill worker, herself professionally engaged in the production of cloth, recorded her own life in the quilt she made. She wrote in *The Lowell Offering* in 1845:

how many passages of my life seem to be epitomized in this patchwork quilt. Here . . . are remnants of that bright copperplate cushion that graced my mother's chair . . . Here is a piece of the first dress I ever saw, cut with what were called "mutton-leg" sleeves. It was my sister's . . . , and here is a fragment of the first gown that was ever cut for me with a bodice waist . . . Here is a fragment of the first dress which baby brother wore when he left off long clothes . . . Here is a piece of the first dress which was ever earned by my own exertions! What a feeling of exultation, of self-dependence, of *self-reliance*, was created by this effort.[22]

"Annette" (probably Harriet Farley or Rebecca Thompson), like Pamela, details the materials of her self-construction. Like Pamela, Annette emphasizes the extent to which she herself has been constituted through her family (a piece of material that covered her mother's chair, a piece of her sister's dress). Like Pamela, Annette celebrates that she is the owner of her own clothes, the materials of her wage-labor. "Here is a piece of the first dress which was ever earned by my own exertions! What a feeling of exultation, of self-dependence, of *self-reliance*, was created by this effort."

Livery ends at the moment when one wears one's own clothes. From the perspective of that moment of "self-dependence," the connections between livery and more violent forms of servitude appear more clearly. In *Incidents in the Life of a Slave Girl*, Harriet Jacobs writes:

I have a vivid recollection of the linsey-woolsey dress given me every winter by Mrs. Flint. How I hated it! It was one of the badges of slavery.[23]

"Fashion," by contrast, was one of the badges of her freedom. On 4 July 1835, the *American Beacon* published an advertisement for the capture of Harriet Jacobs:

Being a good seamstress, she has been accustomed to dress well, has a variety of very fine clothes, made in the prevailing fashion, and will probably appear, if abroad, tricked out in gay and fashionable finery.[24]

Jacobs's clothes are here the mark of her own work, her own self-constitution. They are "gay and fashionable" in contrast to the livery of a "linsey-woolsey" dress, the "gift" of slave-owner to slave.

In *If This Is a Man*, Primo Levi captures the power of clothes to make and unmake a person. In the concentration camp at Buna, he writes, "[w]e will be given shoes and clothes – no, not our own – other shoes, other clothes . . . We are naked now."[25] Stripped naked and reclothed in the clothes of another, Levi learns "for the first time" how a person is demolished:

In a moment, with almost prophetic intuition, the reality was revealed to us: we had reached the bottom. It is not possible to sink lower than this; no human condition is more miserable than this, nor could it conceivably be so. Nothing belongs to us any more; they have taken away our clothes, our shoes, even our hair. (32–3)

In Buna, Levi discovers the ways in which the self is constituted through clothes, shoes, hair.

The shock of that discovery suggests as its unconscious ground the fantasy of an individual who is not fashioned by "mere" things. But our clothes, as Levi writes, may become "almost like limbs of our body," a "personification and evocation of our memories" (33). The liberating effects of the end of livery are compromised by the emptiness of the new concept of a person. From this new perspective, it comes as a shock to recall the etymology of "person" in *persona* – the mask through which an actor assumes a name and a being. In that earlier formulation, a person comes into being through the "second body" – the mask, the clothes – that they put on. As Renaissance clothes marked and unmarked status, they also fashioned and un-fashioned a person. To rethink clothes as habits is to rethink what it means to be a person, to rethink both the materiality of social hierarchy and the materiality of memory.

Notes

INTRODUCTION: FASHION, FETISHISM, AND MEMORY IN EARLY MODERN ENGLAND
AND EUROPE

1 Elizabeth Wilson, *Adorned in Dreams: Fashion and Modernity* (Berkeley: University of California Press, 1987), 3.

2 All quotations from Shakespeare are from *The First Folio of Shakespeare: The Norton Facsimile*, ed. Charlton Hinman (New York: Norton, 1968) and are followed by act, scene, and line numbers keyed to *The Riverside Shakespeare*, ed. G. Blakemore Evans (Boston: Houghton Mifflin, 1974) and then to the through line numbers (TLN) of Hinman's *First Folio*. William Shakespeare, *Loues Labour's Lost*, 4. 2. 18 (TLN 1169); *Much Adoe About Nothing*, 3. 3. 124 (TLN 1450), 3. 3. 141 (TLN 1457); *The Tragedie of Cymbeline*, 3. 4. 53 (TLN 1722).

3 Thomas Dekker, *The Seuen Deadly Sinnes of London* (1606) in *The Non-Dramatic Works of Thomas Dekker*, ed. Alexander Grosart (London: privately printed, 1885), vol. 2, 59–60.

4 Shakespeare, *Loues Labour's Lost*, 5. 2. 413 (TLN 2345).

5 William Tyndale, trans., *The New Testament* (1526), St. Luke 12.56; Thomas Bowes, *De La Primaudayes French academie* (London, 1594), vol. 2, 394.

6 *The Bible* (Geneva, 1560), Job 10. 8; Psalm 119.73; Psalm 33.15. On "fashioning," see also Stephen Greenblatt, *Renaissance Self-Fashioning: From More to Shakespeare* (University of Chicago Press, 1980), 2–3.

7 As Stephen Orgel observes: "What allows boys to be substituted for women in the theater is not anything about the genital nature of boys and women, but precisely the costume, and more particularly, cultural assumptions about costume" (*Impersonations: The Performance of Gender in Shakespeare's England* [Cambridge University Press, 1996], 103–4). We are deeply indebted to Orgel's insights and suggestions.

8 Quoted in Nicholas Thomas, *Entangled Objects: Exchange, Material Culture, and Colonialism in the Pacific* (Cambridge, Mass.: Harvard University Press, 1991), 21.

9 *Hamlet* 1. 2. 76–7 (TLN 257–8). See also Hal's later disavowal of the significance of investiture in *Henry V* (4. 3. 26–7 [TLN 2270–1]): "It yernes [grieves] me not, if men my Garments weare; / Such outward things dwell not in my desires."

10 Phillip Stubbes, *The Anatomie of Abuses* (London, 1583), sigs. B6, B7v.

11 Stubbes, *The Anatomie of Abuses*, sig. G1.

12 Anthony Gilby, *A Pleasaunt Dialogue betweene a Souldior of Barwicke and an English Chaplaine* (London?, 1566), sig. K4v. Gilby was one of the translators of the Geneva Bible. For the controversy, see M. M. Knappen, *Tudor Puritanism: a chapter in the history of idealism* (Gloucester, Mass.: P. Smith, 1939), 187–216; Patrick Collinson, *Godly People: Essays on English Protestantism and Puritanism* (London: Hambledon Press, 1983), 325; and *The Elizabethan Puritan Movement* (London: Cape, 1967), "That Comical Dress," 71–83 and "The People and the Pope's Attire," 92–7.

13 Gilby, *A Pleasant Dialogue*, sig. C4v. Miles insists that the surplice, stole and tippet that Parker attempted to impose must be cast away as "a menstruous cloth" and as "Antichristes Garmentes" that imprint "Idolatricall slauerie" (sig. K5, I5, K6v). "Christes lieuerie garmentes," in contrast, are the preaching of the word and purity of life (sig. K8v).

14 Knappen, *Tudor Puritanism*, 214, 205, 187.

15 Stubbes, *The Anatomie of Abuses*, sig. C5v.
16 For a later denial that the wearing of vestments and other "superstitious practices" were things indifferent, and therefore could be imposed by the state, see George Gillespie, *A dispute against the English-popish ceremonies obtruded vpon the Church of Scotland* (London?, 1637). Gillespie attacks the surplice and other forms of "idolatry" as "the wares of *Rome*, the baggage of *Babylon*, the trinkets of the Whoore, the badges of Popery, the engines of Christs enemies, and the very Trophies of Antichrist" (Part 3, 35).
17 Edmund Spenser, *A View of the State of Ireland*, ed. Andrew Hadfield and Willy Maley (Oxford: Blackwell, 1997), 72–3.
18 John Milton, *The Reason of Church Government* (London, 1641), 247.
19 John Milton, *Areopagitica*, in *John Milton: Complete Poems and Major Prose*, ed. Merritt Y. Hughes (New York: Macmillan, 1957), vol. 4, 348.
20 Stubbes, *The Anatomie of Abuses*, sigs. C1^v–C2^v.
21 The significance of Boemus's book may be gauged from the fact that between 1536 and 1611 it went through twenty-three reprints and revisions in five languages (nine in Latin, five in Italian, four in French, three or four in English, and one in Spanish). See Margaret T. Hodgen, *Early Anthropology in the Sixteenth and Seventeenth Centuries* (Philadelphia: University of Pennsylvania Press, 1964), 131–43.
22 Daniel Defert, "Un Genre ethnographique profane au XVIe: les livres d'habits," in *Histoires de l'Anthropologie (XVIe-XIXe Siècles)*, ed. Britta Rupp-Eisenreich (Paris: Klincksieck, 1984), 27 (our translation).
23 Defert, "Un Genre ethnographique," 28.
24 These instances of the anticlerical proverb are cited under "Cowl" in *The Oxford Dictionary of English Proverbs*, 3rd edn. (Oxford: Clarendon Press, 1982), 152. See Shakespeare, *The Life of King Henry the Eight* (3. 1. 23 [TLN 1643]).
25 For an account of the "excellencyes" of Eastern textiles, see the instructions which Charles I gave to the painter Nicholas Wilford when he was sent to Persia. He was particularly requested to "take notice" of the manufacture of "Cloth of Gould Silke with its colors and dies" (R. W. Ferrier, "Charles I and the Antiquities of Persia: The Mission of Nicholas Wilford," *Iran* 8 [1970]: 51).
26 All the materials for these three paragraphs are drawn from Jennifer Wearden, "Siegmund von Herberstein: An Italian Velvet in the Ottoman Court," *Costume* 19 (1985): 22–9. See also John Nevinson, "Siegmund von Herberstein: Notes on Sixteenth-Century Dress," *Waffen und Kostümkunde* (1959): 86–93, and Patricia L. Baker, "Islamic Honorific Garments," *Costume* 25 (1991): 25–35 on the presentation of clothes as honorific gifts. Baker notes that Muhammad supposedly gave his own cloak to a poet as a mark of respect. This cloak was used by the Abissad caliphate (750–1258) as the caliphal investiture robe. "After the 1517 Ottoman conquest of Mamluk Egypt and Syria, such a garment passed into the royal Ottoman treasury. On the fifteenth day of Ramadan each year, the garment was washed and the water, now containing *baraka* (blessings), was saved to fill phials for imperial distribution as gifts" (25).
27 It is perhaps surprising that trade with Asia, Africa, and the Americas was ideologically so prominent, given that the majority of trade was still between different regions of Britain and between Britain and Europe.
28 Daniel Miller, *Material Culture and Mass Consumption* (Oxford: Blackwell, 1987), 18.
29 Our thinking on subjects and objects in the Renaissance has been deeply shaped by Margreta de Grazia. See also the introduction to *Subject and Object in Renaissance Culture*, ed. Margreta de Grazia, Maureen Quilligan, and Peter Stallybrass (Cambridge University Press, 1995), 1–13.
30 See Karl Marx, "The Fetishism of the Commodity and Its Secret," in *Capital*, vol. 1, trans. Ben Fowkes (New York: Vintage, 1976), 163–77. For Marx's assertion of the *necessity* of "alienation" in the positive form of the imbuing of objects with subjectivity through our work upon them and of the imbuing of the subject with objectivity through our materializations, see his *On James Mill*, in *Karl Marx: Selected Writings* (Oxford University Press, 1977), ed. David McLellan, 114–23.

31 On the movement of objects in and out of commodification, see Igor Kopytoff, "The Cultural Biography of Things: Commoditization as Process," in *The Social Life of Things: Commodities in Cultural Perspective*, ed. Arjun Appadurai (Cambridge University Press, 1986), 64–91.

32 Marcel Mauss, *The Gift: Forms and Functions of Exchange in Archaic Societies*, trans. Ian Cunnison (New York: Norton, 1967), 55, 22. For developments and critiques of Mauss's theory, see Chris Gregory, "Kula Gift Exchange and Capitalist Commodity Exchange: A Comparison," in *The Kula: New Perspectives on Massim Exchange* (Cambridge University Press, 1983), 103–17; Annette Weiner, "Inalienable Wealth," *American Ethnologist* 12 (1985), 210–27; Appadurai, *The Social Life of Things*, "Introduction: Commodities and the Politics of Value," 3–63; Marilyn Strathern, *The Gender of the Gift: Problems with Women and Problems with Society in Melanesia* (Berkeley: University of California Press, 1988); Thomas, *Entangled Objects*; Jacques Derrida, *Given Time: 1. Counterfeit Money*, trans. Peggy Kamuf (University of Chicago Press, 1992), 34–70.

33 Kopytoff, "The Cultural Biography of Things," 64.

34 William Pietz, "The Problem of the Fetish, I," *Res* 9 (1985), 5–17; "The Problem of the Fetish, II," *Res* 13 (1987), 23–45; "The Problem of the Fetish, IIIa," *Res* 16 (1988), 105–23. See also his "Fetishism and Materialism: The Limits of Theory in Marx," in *Fetishism as Cultural Discourse*, ed. Emily Apter and William Pietz (Ithaca: Cornell University Press, 1993), 119–51.

35 Pietz, "Fetish, I," 5.

36 Pietz, "Fetish, II," 24–5.

37 Pietz, "Fetish, II," 35.

38 Pietz, "Fetish, I," 10.

39 Pietz, "Fetish, II," 23.

40 Pieter de Marees, "A Description and Historicall Declaration of the Golden Kingdome of Guinea," in Samuel Purchas, *Haklytus Posthumus, or Purchas His Pilgrimes* (Glasgow: MacLehose, 1905), vol. 6, 280–1, quoted in Pietz, "Fetish, II," 39. De Marees' "Description" was published in Dutch in 1602 and published in English translation in 1625.

41 De Marees, "A Description," 319, quoted in Pietz, "Fetish, II," 43–4.

42 For attacks upon images in the Netherlands, see P. Mack Crew, *Calvinist Preaching and Iconoclasm in the Netherlands, 1544–1569* (Cambridge University Press, 1978) and David Freedberg, *Iconoclasm and Painting in the Revolt of the Netherlands, 1566–1609* (New York: Garland, 1987); for England, see J. Phillips, *The Reformation of Images: Destruction of Art in England, 1535–1660* (Berkeley: University of California Press, 1973); Margaret Aston, *England's Iconoclasts*, vol. 1, "Laws Against Images" (Oxford: Clarendon Press, 1988); and Eamon Duffy, *The Stripping of the Altars: Traditional Religion in England, c.1400–c.1580* (New Haven: Yale University Press, 1992).

43 On Protestantism and (de)materialization, see Stephen Greenblatt, "Remnants of the Sacred in Early Modern England," in *Subject and Object in Renaissance Culture*, ed. Margreta de Grazia, Maureen Quilligan, and Peter Stallybrass (Cambridge University Press, 1995), 337–45.

44 Duffy, *The Stripping of the Altars*, 384.

45 Aston, *England's Iconoclasts*, vol. 1, 467.

46 Nicolas Villault, *Relation des Costes d'Afrique, Appellées Guinée* (Paris: Thierry, 1669), 261, quoted in Pietz, "Fetish, IIIa," 110n.

47 Pietz, "Fetish, IIIa," 110.

48 John Atkins, *A Voyage to Guinea, Brasil, and the West Indies* (London, 1737), quoted by Pietz, "Fetish, IIIa," 110.

I THE CURRENCY OF CLOTHING

1 Statistics drawn from Steve Rappaport, *Worlds within Worlds: Structures of Life in Sixteenth-Century London* (Cambridge University Press, 1989), 394–9. There was an equally dramatic rise in the number of men and women admitted to the Haberdashers

company. On average, 23 were enrolled in the company each year from 1530–1539, compared to 106 a year from 1600–1609, and the decades in between show a steady increase in enrollments. Between 1530 and 1609, 4,904 men and women were enrolled in the Clothworkers, which had traditionally been associated with England's main industry. But during the same period, the Clothworkers were outstripped by the Haberdashers, who enrolled 5,114 men and women, and the Merchant Taylors, who enrolled 6,895. While it should be remembered that a man or woman who entered into the livery could then practice any trade ("drapers" and "butchers" might and did work as booksellers), each company nevertheless tried to protect its turf. On the acrimonious disputes between the Clothworkers and the Merchant Taylors in the sixteenth century, see Rappaport, 113–14, 246–7. On the small number of women admitted to the London companies in the sixteenth century, see Rappaport, 36–42. This can be contrasted with women's relative freedom of access to the companies in some other cities. See K. D. M. Snell, *Annals of the Labouring Poor* (Cambridge University Press, 1987), and Stephen Orgel, *Impersonations: The Performance of Gender in Shakespeare's England* (Cambridge University Press, 1996), 72–4.

2 Anon., *Muld Sacke: or The Apologie of Hic Mulier* (London, 1620), sig. B3v–4.

3 Sir Thomas Overbury, *A wife now the widdow of Sir T. Overbury . . . Whereunto are added many witty characters* (London: A. Crooke, 1638), "A Servingman," sig. G.

4 John Milton, *Samson Agonistes*, in *John Milton: Complete Poems and Major Prose*, ed. Merritt Y. Hughes (New York: Macmillan, 1957), 590, lines 1616, 1622; Joseph Hall, *The Righteous Mammon* (London, 1618), 60.

5 Francis Bacon, *Historie of the raigne of king Henry the seventh* (London, 1622), 58. We are grateful for Michael Macdonald's criticism here: to characterize Elizabethan society as a livery society without making clear that "livery" was not necessarily identifiable as such is misleading. On livery, in the narrow sense under the Tudors, see David Starkey, "The Age of the Household: Politics, Society and the Arts c. 1350–c. 1550," in *The Later Middle Ages*, ed. Stephen Medcalf (New York: Holmes and Meier, 1981), 224–90, especially 264–73, and Kate Mertes, *The English Noble Household 1250–1600: Good Governance and Political Rule* (Oxford: Blackwell, 1988), 132–3.

6 E. K. Chambers, *The Elizabethan Stage* (Oxford: Clarendon Press, 1923), vol. 1, 52.

7 Janet Arnold, *Queen Elizabeth's Wardrobe Unlock'd* (Leeds: Maney, 1988), 99–108.

8 Arnold, *Wardrobe*, 107.

9 Arnold, *Wardrobe*, 107

10 William Shakespeare, *Loues Labour's Lost*, in *The First Folio of Shakespeare: The Norton Facsimile*, ed. Charlton Hinman (New York: Norton, 1968), 4. 1. 99 (TLN 1080). Unless otherwise noted, all quotations from Shakespeare are from this edition and references are to the act, scene, and line numbers of *The Riverside Shakespeare*, ed. G. Blakemore Evans (Boston: Houghton Mifflin, 1974), followed by the through line numbers (TLN) of Hinman's *First Folio*.

11 Arnold, *Wardrobe*, 106.

12 Arnold, *Wardrobe*, 105.

13 Arnold, *Wardrobe*, 349–50.

14 Gifts of clothing still constituted an important form of social and economic life in the eighteenth century. See Daniel Roche, *The Culture of Clothing: Dress and Fashion in the "Ancien Régime"* (Cambridge University Press, 1994), 89. Roche writes of eighteenth-century Paris: "Charitable gifts of clothes are attested at all levels of society. They were part of the gift economy, and probably by no means unimportant, both in their direct financial and their indirect social consequences; whether by resale or charitable distribution, the clothes of one group were made available to another."

15 For an account of the significance of non-monetary goods in the Marx household, see Peter Stallybrass, "Marx's Coat," in *Border Fetishisms: Material Objects in Unstable Spaces*, ed. Patricia Spyer (London: Routledge, 1997), 183–207.

16 *Robert Loder's Farm Accounts 1610–1620*, ed. G. F. Fussell, Camden Society, 3rd series, vol. 53 (London: Camden Society, 1936), xxviii–xxx.

17 Alan Macfarlane, *The Family Life of Ralph Josselin, a Seventeenth-Century Clergyman: An Essay in Historical Anthropology* (Cambridge University Press, 1970), 45–6.

18 Dorothy Marshall, *The English Domestic Servant in History* (London: The Historical Association, 1949), 16, 27.

19 Frances Parthenope Verney, *Memoirs of the Verney Family during the Civil War* (London: Longmans, Green, and Co., 1892), vol. 2, 227–8.

20 Sara Mendelson and Patricia Crawford, *Women in Early Modern England* (Oxford: Clarendon Press, 1998), 223.

21 H. M. Colvin, D. R. Ransome, and John Summerson, *The History of the King's Works*, vol. 3, 1485–1660 (Part 1) (London: Her Majesty's Stationery Office, 1975), 110–20.

22 The account book of Sir John Nicholas, Folger MS v. a. 420, n.p. One should note, however, that Nicholas also gave other gifts of money to his servants at different points in the year.

23 Marcel Mauss argues for the centrality of objects in *pre*capitalist economies in *The Gift: Forms and Functions of Exchange in Archaic Societies*, trans. Ian Cunnison (New York: Norton, 1967).

24 *The Geneva Bible* (Geneva, 1560), Genesis 3. 21.

25 John Milton, *Paradise Lost* (London, 1674), Book 10, lines 211–23. We are grateful to Michael Neill for bringing this passage to our attention. See his *Issues of Death: Mortality and Identity in English Renaissance Tragedy* (Oxford: Clarendon Press, 1997), 8. His account of "shameful death" (8–13 and 66–7) illuminates the significance of clothing in the constitution of identity.

26 Gervase Babington, *Certaine Plaine, briefe, and comfortable Notes vpon euerie Chapter of Genesis* (London, 1592), fol. 21. We write about the significance of Genesis 3. 21 at greater length in our conclusion, "The end(s) of livery."

27 Lancelot Andrewes, *Apospasmatia Sacra* (London, 1657), 330, 333.

28 Lawrence Stone, *The Crisis of the Aristocracy 1558–1641* (Oxford: Clarendon Press, 1965), 563.

29 Stone, *The Crisis of the Aristocracy*, 564–5.

30 Menna Prestwich, *Cranfield: Politics and Profits under the Early Stuarts* (Oxford: Clarendon Press, 1966), 228–9. There are two sets of figures for the years 1612–15. The higher figures are: £65,999. 2s 2d., £46,032. 0s. 4d., and £41,317. 16s. 6d. The year 1612–13 was particularly expensive because of Princess Elizabeth's marriage to the Elector Palatine.

31 Prestwich, *Cranfield*, 228, 229, 260, 263.

32 Stone, *The Crisis of the Aristocracy*, 585–6.

33 See Rappaport, *Worlds within Worlds*, 394–9.

34 On court culture and conspicuous consumption, see Norbert Elias, *The Court Society*, trans. Edmund Jephcott (Oxford: Basil Blackwell, 1983) and Werner Sombart, *Luxury and Capitalism*, trans. W. R. Dittmar (Ann Arbor: University of Michigan Press, 1967).

35 Janet Arnold, *Patterns of Fashion: The Cut and Construction of Clothes for Men and Women c.1560–1620* (London: Macmillan, 1985), passim, especially ills. 87, 151, 163, 164, 174, 309, 312, 328, 329, and the drawings on 53, 55, 59, 72, 77, 84, 103, 108, 109, 113.

36 Verney, *Memoirs*, vol. 2, 229. Mary Verney's nineteenth-century editor writes in surprise that women so capable of running households should be "so very helpless about dressing themselves" (229). But this shows her unfamiliarity with what dressing entailed in the Renaissance.

37 [Thomas Tomkis], *Lingua* (London, 1607), 4. 6, sig. I2v.

38 M. Channing Linthicum, *Costume in the Drama of Shakespeare and his Contemporaries* (Oxford: Clarendon Press, 1936), 279. Linthicum's indispensable book has an excellent chapter on "Costume Fastenings," to which we are indebted.

39 Thomas Middleton and William Rowley, *The Old Law*, ed. Catherine M. Shaw (New York: Garland, 1982), 2. 1. 63–5.

40 Anon., *Dick of Devonshire* (Oxford: Malone Society, 1955), lines 1356–62.

41 Arnold, *Wardrobe*, 327–33. That buttons might cost more than the clothes they adorned is

implicit in the will of Thomas Radcliffe, third Earl of Sussex, dated 1 April 1583. Sussex left his apparel to his brother, *except* for those clothes with buttons "enriched with stone or pearl." These buttons were to be put with his chains, collars, and georges to pay for his funeral and for "the performance of my will." See F. G. Emmison, *Elizabethan Life: Wills of Essex Gentry and Merchants* (Chelmsford: Essex County Council, 1978), 3, 2.

42 The Inventory of Lady Jane Stanhope's apparel, made on 20 November 1614, Folger MS. x. d. 522, nos. 1–2 (a rough draft, followed by a fair copy).

43 *Henslowe's Diary*, ed. R. A. Foakes and R. T. Rickert (Cambridge University Press, 1961), 142, 113, 118, 149, 115; 112, 116, 161, 255. Henslowe also records clothes that are "missing" parts, such as two cloaks *without* linings (145).

44 We are indebted here to Carol Pech, whose forthcoming dissertation at Johns Hopkins University includes a fascinating analysis of gold and silver thread in seventeenth-century England. She drew the significance of "lace" to our attention and supplied us with references. See also her analysis of silver and fetishism in "'His Nuts for a piece of Metal': Fetishism in the Monetary Writings of John Locke." For an analysis of attempts to regulate the wearing of gold and silver in Italy, see Catherine Kovesi Killerby, "Practical Problems in the Enforcement of Italian Sumptuary law, 1200–1500," in *Crime, Society and the Law in Renaissance Italy* (Cambridge University Press, 1994), ed. Trevor Dean and K. J. P. Lowe, 99–120, especially 115. She records accusations against even children for wearing gold ribbons and silver buttons.

45 Arnold, *Wardrobe*, 100, 103.

46 Horace Stewart, *History of the Worshipful Company of Gold and Silver Wyre-Drawers* (London: The Leadenhall Press, 1891), 3–4.

47 See J. J. Scarisbrick, *Henry VIII* (London: Eyre and Spottiswoode, 1968), 74–80 and A. F. Pollard, *Henry VIII* (London: Jonathan Cape, 1970), 112–15.

48 Stewart, *Gold and Silver Wyre-Drawers*, 19–21.

49 Arnold, *Wardrobe*, 100–1.

50 On the import of lace as opposed to cloth of gold and silver, Lawrence Stone writes: "[I]mports of gold, silver, and copper lace were negligible in 1560, but by 1594–5 about 2 1/2 tons a year were coming in. Twenty-odd years later the home market was estimated, admittedly by an optimistic projector, to be capable of absorbing an English output of 400 lb. a week, or about 10 tons a year, besides considerable imports" (*Crisis of the Aristocracy*, 585).

51 Stewart, *Gold and Silver Wyre-Drawers*, 17–18, 22, 26, 27–35, 38.

52 *Henslowe's Diary*, 258, 259, 111.

53 *The Diary of Anne Clifford 1616–1619: A Critical Edition*, ed. Katherine O. Acheson (New York: Garland, 1995), 81, 165.

54 Margaret Mitchell, *Gone with the Wind* (New York: Warner Books, 1993), 535. The fact that Scarlett's dress is "incomparable, so rich and handsome looking and yet so dignified" does not alter the fact that it is a (successful) ruse, exposing her poverty to the reader even as it hides it from the eyes of Rhett Butler (557, 564).

55 Arnold, *Wardrobe*, 98, 175, 100–3, 174.

56 Quoted in Arnold, *Wardrobe*, 174. Arnold notes that Scaramelli was exaggerating: there were a "mere" 1,900 items in Elizabeth's wardrobe in 1600.

57 E. T. Bradley, *Life of the Lady Arabella Stuart* (London: Richard Bentley, 1889), vol. 2, 195. We are indebted to Carol Levin for this reference.

58 Albert Feuillerat, ed., *Documents Relating to the Office of the Revels in the Time of Queen Elizabeth I* (Louvain: Uystpruyst, 1908), 19.

59 Robert Lopez, "The Dawn of Medieval Banking," in *The Dawn of Modern Banking*, Center for Medieval and Renaissance Studies, University of California, Los Angeles (New Haven: Yale University Press, 1979), 1–24, especially 4.

60 On European pawnbroking, see Brian Pullan, *Rich and Poor in Renaissance Venice: The Social Institutions of a Catholic State, to 1620* (Oxford: Blackwell, 1971); Frederic C. Lane and Reinhold C. Mueller, *Money and Banking in Medieval and Renaissance Venice*, vol. 1, *Coins and Moneys of Account* (Baltimore: The Johns Hopkins University Press, 1985);

Reinhold C. Mueller, *The Venetian Money Market: Banks, Panics, and the Public Debt, 1200–1500* (Baltimore: The Johns Hopkins University Press, 1997); Carol Bresnahan Menning, *Charity and the State in Late Renaissance Italy: The Monte di Pietà of Florence* (Ithaca, NY: Cornell University Press, 1993). On the problems of Christians charging interest, see Jacques Le Goff, "The Usurer and Purgatory," in *The Dawn of Modern Banking*, Center for Medieval and Renaissance Studies, University of California, Los Angeles (New Haven: Yale University Press, 1979) 25–52; and Richard A. Goldthwaite, *Banks, Palaces and Entrepreneurs in Renaissance Florence* (Aldershot: Variorum, 1992), 31–9. On the Lombards as bankers/pawnbrokers, see Michael Prestwich, "Italian Merchants in Late Thirteenth and Early Fourteenth Century England," in *Modern Banking*, 77–104; and Raymond de Roover, *Money, Banking and Credit in Mediaeval Bruges: Italian Merchant-Bankers, Lombards, and Money-Changers: A Study in the Origins of Banking* (Cambridge, Mass.: The Mediaeval Academy of America, 1948), especially 113–65. On goldsmiths and early banking in England, see R. D. Richards, *The Early History of Banking in England* (London: Frank Cass, 1958), especially 24–35.

61 Roover, *Money, Banking and Credit*, 134.

62 Prestwich, "Italian Merchants," 86–7.

63 Yvonne Hackenbroch, *Renaissance Jewellery* (London: Sotheby Parke Bernet, 1979), 298–303.

64 J. W. Gough, *Sir Hugh Middleton: Entrepreneur and Engineer* (Oxford: Clarendon Press, 1964), 3, 5, 7.

65 Anthony F. Upton, *Sir Arthur Ingram, c. 1565–1642: A Study of the Origins of an English Landed Family* (Oxford University Press, 1961), 57.

66 Prestwich, "Italian Merchants," 597.

67 Prestwich, "Italian Merchants," 228–32; 75; 480–3.

68 Stone, *Crisis of the Aristocracy*, 509.

69 There were, though, different kinds of conspicuous consumption. A horde of Renaissance writers contrasted wealth distributed as "charity" and neighborliness to the wealth "eaten up" in personal displays of prodigality. And *Timon of Athens* gives a profoundly skeptical view of even the "charitable" distribution of wealth as a means to assure continuing "credit."

70 Stone, *Crisis of the Aristocracy*, 506.

71 He was in fact almost immediately released from prison and his fine was reduced.

72 Prestwich, "Italian Merchants," 597, 72–6, 480–1, 483, 594–600.

73 Stone, *Crisis of the Aristocracy*, 517.

74 Verney, *Memoirs*, vol. 1, 145.

75 Jean Sutherland Boggs, *Picasso and Things* (Cleveland Museum of Art, 1992), 12–13.

76 Thomas Middleton, *Your Five Gallants (1607), A Critical Edition*, ed. Clare Lee Colegrove (New York: Garland, 1979), [1.1], lines 98–9; Robert Greene, *A Quip for an Vpstart Courtier* (1592) in *The Life and Complete Works in Prose and Verse of Robert Greene*, ed. Alexander B. Grosart, vol. 11 (privately printed, 1881–3), 243–4. It appears to have been common for pawnbrokers to store clothes in lavender. In *Newes from Hell* (London, 1606), Thomas Dekker writes of the linen of brokers and usurers lasting longest because "it comes commonly out of Lauender & is seldom worn" (sig. E2). In Dekker and Webster's *The Wonder of a Kingdome* (1636), the "lame legg'd Souldier," brother of the "gorgeously attyred" Torrenti, describes the Broker who has taken even his false leg as interest payment as

> A moath that eates up gowns, doublets and hose,
> One that with Bills, leads smocks and shirts together
> To linnen close adultery, and upon them
> Strowes lavender, so strongly, that the owners
> Dare never smell them after.

(*The Dramatic Works of Thomas Dekker*, ed. Fredson Bowers [Cambridge University Press, 1958], vol. 3, 4. 2. 47–51.) "Out of Lauender" meant "out of pawn" (see Thomas Dekker, *The Honest Whore, Part 2*, *Dramatic Works*, ed. Bowers, vol. 2, 2. 1. 4).

77 Greene, *A Quip*, 245–6.

78 Jeremy Boulton, *Neighbourhood and Society: A London Suburb in the Seventeenth Century* (Cambridge University Press, 1987), 88–9. See also Neil C. Carson, *A Companion to Henslowe's Diary* (Cambridge University Press, 1988), 23. Carson calculates that Henslowe normally charged sixpence or eightpence in the pound per month, which would work out as an annual interest rate of around 30 percent.

79 Melanie Tebbutt, *Making Ends Meet: Pawnbroking and Working-Class Credit* (Leicester University Press, 1983), 9.

80 Roover, *Money, Banking and Credit*, 121.

81 Home brought a lawsuit, complaining that the interest of 43 1/3 percent was exorbitant, but he lost the case. The interest rate was the standard one (*ad usum banchi nostri*), even though it was never spelled out. See Roover, *Money, Banking and Credit*, 131–3.

82 See Carol Chillington Rutter, ed., *Documents of the Rose Playhouse* (Manchester University Press, 1984): "Over a period in which they repaid Henslowe some £92 from the gallery receipts, the Admiral's Men took loans of £142 in thirty-seven payments. They spent nearly twice as much on costumes (£88. 1*s*) as on playbooks (£45. 10*s*), partly because they had reached an agreement with Francis Langley about the costumes he had evidently been withholding since Pembroke's Men decamped from the Swan in the summer of 1597, partly because they 'exsepted into the stocke' two expensive cloaks that had been in pawn since the previous November, and partly because they spent heavily on costumes for Drayton and Dekker's *Civil Wars in France* trilogy: in the second week of October, £10 for *Part I* and in late November, £20 for *Part II* just about the time *Part III* was being commissioned. Lavish costumes were likewise bought for Chapman's *Fount of New Fashions . . .* By 14 November £17 had been spent to costume that play. Some of these costumes were enormously costly. Langley's 'Riche clocke' cost £19" (152–3). The outlay for costumes was not, as Rutter notes, always so large, but it was invariably a substantial part of performance costs.

83 Carson, *A Companion*, 22–3; Boulton, *Neigbourhood and Society*, 88–91.

84 The figures are drawn from Boulton, *Neigbourhood and Society*, 91.

85 Tebbutt, *Making Ends Meet*, 33. On the crucial significance of pawnbroking, particularly to the poor, see also Kenneth Hudson, *Pawnbroking: An Aspect of British Social History* (London: The Bodley Head, 1982) and Stallybrass, "Marx's Coat."

86 Carson, *A Companion*, 23.

87 *Henslowe's Diary*, 151, 149, 151, 158.

88 *Henslowe's Diary*, 159, 259, 152, 156.

89 Middleton, *Your Five Gallants*, [1. 1].

90 Natasha Korda, "Household Property/Stage Property: Henslowe as Pawnbroker," *Theater Journal* 48 (1996): 185–95, 187–8, 191–3.

91 The figures cannot be exact, since the people with whom he did business may be recorded under more than one name. Is, for instance, the "lorde" whose cloak and silver hose Henslowe held as a pledge (145) the same as "my lorde Burte," whose long black coat was pawned? We have recorded them separately, but they may well be the same person. On the other hand, we have recorded "mrs barterman" and "goodwiffe Buterman" as the same person. We have also attributed the gender of at least one of the customers ("Jude merecke") upon the nature of the pledges. The women we've recorded Henslowe as doing business with (excluding agents or *revendeuses* like Goody Watson, Mrs. Grant, and Ann No[c]kes) are: "A womon dwellinge in londitche"; "Mrs floode"; "goody whitacker"; "A chapmanes wiffe"; "A poor womon dwellnge in theveng lane"; "the buchers wiffe in greenes Alley"; "Jane clarke"; "a buchers wiffe in gardenares alley"; "good wiffe Browne"; "goodwife harysone"; "goodwife streate"/"elyzabeth strete"; "mrs northe"; "mrs wayght"; "mrs palle"; "goodwife williames"; "ellen evdell"; "Katrene tenche"; "mrs Ratlefe"; "mrs Joanes"; "amayde in chanell Rowe"; Frances, his nephew's, "wife"; "goodwiffe atkines"; "mrs barterman"/ "goodwiffe Buterman"; "Goody nalle"; "her dawghter"/"gooddy nalles dawghter"; "goody diers"; "goody harese"; "goody Breaye"/ "goody Braye"; "goody cadmanes mother"; "mrs Rysse a tayllers wiffe"; "Jude merecke";

"the womone wch selles earbes in the market"; "goody haryson"; "the womon wch sealles Reasones" [sic; presumably, raisins]; "mrs northe"; "a taylers wife in tutell strete"; "mrs spenser"; "mrs palle"; "mrs bedell"; "mother Kempe"; "mrs Hunte"; "goody newbereye"/ "mrs newbery"; "mrs marten"; "the midwiffes dawter"; "mrs prisse"/"Ketren prisse"; "good wiffe allene"; "beasse bucher"; "the strangers wiffe"; "mary adames"; "mrs neler"; "a womone dwellinge by the cocke in tuttel streate"; "mrs atkinsone"; "elysabeth marnar"; "mrs adyse"; "goody whittlocke"; "goody s Tvcke" [sic]; "mrs combers."

The men we've recorded (excluding Henslowe's nephew Philip) are: "goodman Baggete"; "wm covnde"; "mr Toogood"; "edwardes hellode"; "a chapmanes"; "wm harbarte"; "mr Johnes"; "dornacke"; "A footmane"; "the drawer"; "captaine swane"; "angiell goodyere"; "Robarte cadbery dwelinge in sothwarke in the iij cvpes alley"; "mr dorington"; "leanard Borowdes"; "my lorde"; "captayne hamame" or "Haname"; "a man of charles williames"; "thomas lewknore"; "my lord Burtes man"; "williame davies"; "mr hvssey"; "harye ssheffelde"; "Jonne Boothe"; "a coper in theuenglane"; "my lord Burte"; "mr. Burde"; "mr spencer"; "mr hare"; "goodman hvlle"; "mr Crowche" ["vpon his wiffes gowne"]; "my tenent tomsones"; "goodman cadman"; "John hecke;" "a Joyner."

Customers whom we cannot or have not included in the above lists are "Johen pettet" ["John" or "Joan"?] and "ower tenentes."

92 Quoted by William Ingram, *The Business of Playing: The Beginnings of the Adult Professional Theater in Elizabethan London* (Ithaca, NY: Cornell University Press, 1992), 58.
93 Sue Wright, "'Churmaids, Huswyfes and Hucksters': The Employment of Women in Tudor and Stuart Salisbury," in *Women and Work in Pre-Industrial England*, ed. Lindsay Charles and Lorna Duffin (London: Croom Helm, 1985), 100–21, 111.
94 See Roche, *The Culture of Clothing*, 346–7.
95 On the preponderance of women's clothes as pledges in the nineteenth century, see Tebbutt, *Making Ends Meet*, 34 and chapter 5; Ellen Ross, *Love and Toil: Motherhood in Outcast London 1870–1918* (Oxford University Press, 1993), 46–8 and 81–4; and, for anecdotal evidence, Stallybrass, "Marx's Coat," 196–8. For a fine account of women's pledges in the twentieth century, see Annelies Moors, "Wearing Gold," in *Border Fetishisms: Material Objects in Unstable Spaces*, ed. Patricia Spyer (London: Routledge, 1997), 208–23.
96 See Amy Louise Erickson, *Women and Property in Early Modern England* (London: Routledge, 1993), particularly 17–20, 61–78, 223–36. Erikson's account not only challenges the view that women did not inherit property but also establishes the financial value of the moveable goods that women owned and circulated.
97 Margaret Cavendish, Marchioness of Newcastle, "The Epistle Dedicatory," *Poems and Fancies* (London, 1653), sig. A2r-v; see also Sylvia Bowerbank, "The Spider's Delight: Margaret Cavendish and the 'Female' Imagination," in *Women in the Renaissance: Selections from "English Literary Renaissance*," ed. Kirby Farrell, Elizabeth H. Hageman, and Arthur F. Kinney (Amherst: University of Massachusetts Press, 1990), 187–203.
98 Samuel Richardson, *Pamela; Or, Virtue Rewarded* (Harmondsworth: Penguin 1980 [1740, 1801]), 49–50).

2 COMPOSING THE SUBJECT: MAKING PORTRAITS

1 James Howell, *Paroimiographia* (London, 1659), 13.
2 Nicholas Hilliard, *A Treatise Concerning the Arte of Linning*, ed. R. K. R. Thornton and T. G. S. Cain (Manchester: Carcanet Press, 1992), 54.
3 Patricia Fumerton, *Cultural Aesthetics: Renaissance Literature and the Practice of Social Ornament* (University of Chicago Press, 1991), 79–80.
4 Edward Norgate, *Miniatura or the Art of Linning*, ed. Martin Hardie (Oxford University Press, 1919), 20.
5 V. J. Murrell, "The Art of Limning," in Roy Strong, *Artists of the Tudor Court: The Portrait Miniature Rediscovered 1520–1620* (London: Victoria and Albert Museum catalogue, 1983), 16.

6 Murrell, "The Art of Limning," 16.

7 As Murrell notes, "the beauty of Hilliard's pearls and diamonds is now so often marred by the inconstancy of the silver, which has tarnished to a jet black color" (16).

8 Strong, *Artists*, 133–4.

9 Strong, *Artists*, 134–5.

10 Strong, *Artists*, 166–7.

11 Quoted in ms. notes to William Larkin's portrait of Richard Sackville, third Earl of Dorset, in the Ranger's House, Greenwich, London.

12 Roy Strong, *William Larkin: Icons of Splendour* (Milan: Franco Maria Ricci, 1995), 34.

13 Peter and Ann Mactaggart, "The Rich Wearing Apparel of Richard, 3rd Earl of Dorset," *Costume* 14 (1980), 44–7.

14 Strong, *Artists*, 148.

15 Strong, *Artists*, 148. See Sir Guy Laking, *Catalogue of the Armoury of Windsor Castle* (London: Bradbury and Agnew, 1904), nos. 786 and 802.

16 Christine Junkerman, "Constructing Gender: The Meaning of Dress in Renaissance Patrician Venice," paper delivered at UCLA, 23 April 1992. We are indebted to Junkerman's work throughout this paragraph.

17 *The Diary of Samuel Pepys*, ed. Robin Latham and William Matthews, vol. 10 (London: Bell and Hyman, 1983), 98.

18 John Michael Montias, *Vermeer and His Milieu: A Web of Social History* (Princeton University Press, 1988), 46, 50–51.

19 *Calendar of the Manuscripts of the Marquess of Bath preserved at Longleat*, vol. 5, "Talbot, Dudley and Devereux Papers 1533–1659," ed. G. Dyfnallt Owen, Historic Manuscripts Commission 58 (London: Her Majesty's Stationery Office, 1980), 204, 207, 221, 222; Erna Auerbach, *Nicholas Hilliard* (Boston: Boston Book and Art Shop, 1961), 227.

20 Auerbach, *Hilliard*, 5–10, 169, 224.

21 Auerbach, *Hilliard*, 7.

22 Auerbach, *Hilliard*, 170.

23 John Rowlands, *Holbein: The Paintings of Hans Holbein the Younger* (Boston: David Godine, 1985), 89.

24 Hilliard, *Arte*, 48.

25 Yvonne Hackenbroch, *Renaissance Jewellery* (London: Sotheby Parke Bernet, 1979), 272. In Holbein's will, one gets a further sense of the interconnected trades of armorer, goldsmith, and painter. His witnesses were "Anthoney Schnecher, armerer, Mr John of Antwarpe, goldsmythe before said, Olrycke Obynger, merchaunte and Harry Maynert, panter" (Rowlands, *Holbein*, 122).

26 Hackenbroch, *Jewellery*, 276, 271.

27 Maryan Ainsworth, " 'Paternes for phisioneamyes': Holbein's Portraiture Reconsidered," *The Burlington Magazine* 132 (1990): 173–86. No official record of Holbein's assistants exists since, as a foreigner, he was technically not permitted to employ any. However, it is clear from the number of copies of "his" paintings and from the slowness which his methods necessitated that he must have employed several assistants.

28 Jane Roberts, *Holbein and the Court of Henry VIII: Drawings and Miniatures from the Royal Library, Windsor Castle* exhibition catalogue (Edinburgh: National Galleries of Scotland, 1993), 72–3. See also Stella Mary Newton, "Some Notes on the Dress in Holbein's Portraits," in *Holbein and the Court of Henry VIII*, exhibition catalogue (London: The Queen's Gallery, Buckingham Palace, 1978–9), 20–2.

29 Roberts, *Holbein*, 73; Queen's Gallery, *Holbein*, 49, 99, 36, 84.

30 Roberts, *Holbein*, 59, 50, 38; Queen's Gallery, *Holbein*, 79, 91, 93.

31 Hilliard, *Arte*, 52, 80, 70, 72, 74.

32 Susan Foister, "Foreigners at Court: Holbein, Van Dyck and the Painter-Stainers Company," in *Art and Patronage in the Caroline Courts: Essays in Honour of Sir Oliver Millar*, ed. David Howarth (Cambridge University Press, 1994), 32–50.

33 Hilliard, *Arte*, 72–74. Smalt was made "from pulverised glass which had been colored by oxide of cobalt" (Hilliard, 38); blue bice, also known as blue ashes, was made from copper

salts (Daniel V. Thompson, *The Materials and Techniques of Medieval Painting* [New York: Dover, 1956], 152–3).

34 Michael Baxandall, *Painting and Experience in Fifteenth-Century Italy*, 2nd edn (Oxford University Press, 1988), 2.

35 Baxandall, *Painting*, 6.

36 Baxandall, *Painting*, 11.

37 Marcia B. Hall, *Color and Meaning: Practice and Theory in Renaissance Painting* (Cambridge University Press, 1992), 33.

38 Hall, *Color*, 35.

39 Quoted in Baxandall, *Painting*, 16.

40 Strong, *Artists*, 166.

41 Oliver Millar notes that Van Dyck's portraits typically cost about £20, although his largest and most elaborate ones of the monarch might cost as much as £100. See his "Van Dyck in London," in *Anthony van Dyck*, ed. Arthur K. Wheelock, Susan J. Barnes, et al. (New York: Abrams, 1990), 53. In 1638, Van Dyck submitted a list of his paintings to Charles I with prices attached. In three cases where Van Dyck had valued portraits of Henrietta Maria at £20, Charles had himself crossed out the valuation and substituted £15. He also revalued one of Van Dyck's most magnificent compositions, *Roi à la Chasse*: according to Van Dyck, it was worth £200; Charles thought it was worth £100. See Christopher Brown, *Van Dyck* (Ithaca, NY: Cornell University Press, 1983), 164–5.

42 Carol Christensen, Michael Palmer, and Michael Swicklik, "Van Dyck's Painting Technique, his Writings, and Three Paintings in the National Gallery of Art," in *Anthony van Dyck*, ed. Wheelock, Barnes, et al., 48.

43 John H. Munro, "The Medieval Scarlet and the Economics of Sartorial Splendour," in *Cloth and Clothing in Medieval Europe: Essays in Memory of Professor E. M. Carus-Wilson*, ed. N. B. Harte and K. G. Ponting, Pasold Studies in Textile History (London: Heinemann Educational Books, 1983), 13–70, 39.

44 Munro, "Scarlet," 17, 54–8, 39–52, 32, 63, 64.

45 Judith H. Hofenk-De Graaff, "The Chemistry of Red Dyestuffs in Medieval and Early Modern Europe," in *Cloth and Clothing in Medieval Europe: Essays in Memory of Professor E. M. Carus-Wilson*, ed. N. B. Harte and K. G. Ponting, Pasold Studies in Textile History (London: Heinemann Educational Books, 1983), 71–9, especially 75.

46 Christensen, et al., "Van Dyck's Technique," 45–52.

47 Christensen, et al., "Van Dyck's Technique," 50–1.

48 Christensen, et al., "Van Dyck's Technique," 47.

49 Strong, *Larkin*, 31–2.

50 Christensen, et al., "Van Dyck's Technique," 47–8.

51 G. H. Villiers, *Hans Holbein: The Ambassadors*, National Gallery Books, no. 18 (London: Percy Lund Humphries, n.d.), 10–11.

52 John Rowlands, *Holbein*, 83.

53 Mary F. S. Hervey, *Holbein's "Ambassadors": The Picture and the Men* (London: Bell, 1900). We are indebted to Hervey's book in this and later paragraphs.

54 Hervey, *"Ambassadors,"* 235.

55 Hervey, *"Ambassadors,"* 199.

56 Hervey, *"Ambassadors,"* 207.

57 Kurt Erdmann, *Seven Hundred Years of Oriental Carpets*, ed. Hanna Erdmann, trans. May H. Beattie and Hildegard Herzog (Berkeley: University of California Press, 1970), 20, 22. See also Hülye Tezcan, *The Topkapi Saray Museum: Carpets*, trans., expanded, and ed. J. M. Rogers, New York Graphic Society (Boston: Little, Brown and Company, 1987), 31–8. So popular were Turkish carpets that they provoked English imitations. The Leicester Inventory of 1588 records a "Turqoy carpett of Norwiche work," according to Eric Mercer, *English Art 1553–1625* (Oxford: Clarendon Press, 1962), 141.

58 Cesare Vecellio, *Habiti antichi, et moderni di tutto il mondo* (Venice: Sessa, 1598), reprinted and abridged as *Vecellio's Renaissance Costume Book* (New York: Dover, 1977), 128–9.

59 See Hervey, "*Ambassadors*," 241–2.

60 Holbein was himself directly affected by the Reformation. He had early commissions in Basel for religious paintings both for Catholic churches and for private Catholic devotional use and some of his paintings were destroyed by Protestant iconoclasts on Shrove Tuesday, 1529; on his first visit to England in 1526, he was associated with the circle of Sir Thomas More, for whom he designed a crucifix, as well as painting his portrait. Yet during his second stay in England, from 1532 until his death in 1543, he became painter to a Protestant court, particularly associating at first with the Protestant circles around Anne Boleyn, his main patron from before her coronation in 1533 (Rowlands, *Holbein*, 31–66, 79, 67–72, 87–8).

61 Hervey, "*Ambassadors*," 228–30.

62 For a fine analysis of the political disharmonies registered in Holbein's painting, see Lisa Jardine, *Worldly Goods: A New History of the Renaissance* (London: Macmillan, 1996), 425–36.

63 John Berger, *Ways of Seeing* (London: BBC/Penguin, 1972, rpt. 1985), 91. He comments, "there is not a surface in this picture which does not make one aware of how it has been elaborately worked over – by weavers, embroiderers, carpetmakers, goldsmiths, leather workers, mosaic makers, furriers, tailors, jewellers – and of how this working-over and the resulting richness of each surface has been finally worked-over and reproduced by Holbein the painter" (90).

64 E. K. Chambers, *Sir Henry Lee: An Elizabethan Portrait* (Oxford: Clarendon Press, 1936), 185–6. For a color reproduction of the painting, see *Dynasties: Painting in Tudor and Jacobean England 1530–1630*, ed. Karen Hearn (London: Tate Publishing, 1995), 177, with useful commentary, 176. See also Christopher Highley's discussion of Lee as "English from the waist up" and Irish "from the thighs down" in *Shakespeare, Spenser and the Crisis in Ireland* (Cambridge University Press, 1997), 91, though in fact Lee's conical helmet and round, fringed shield mark him as Irish above the waist, too. Hiram Morgan also offers an analysis of the portrait in "Tom Lee: The Posing Peacemaker," in *Representing Ireland: Literature and the Origins of Conflict, 1534–1600*, ed. Brian Bradshaw, Andrew Hadfield, and Willy Maley (Cambridge University Press, 1993), 132–65. Morgan comments in useful detail on Lee's writings about Ireland, but his conjecture that Lee had himself painted bare-legged to show his desirability as a husband seems farfetched, given the gender conventions of Renaissance portraiture.

65 Chambers, *Sir Henry Lee*, cites de Bruyn as source, 191; Roy Strong cites Boissard, in *The English Icon: Elizabethan and Jacobean Portraiture* (London: Mellon Foundation for British Art/Routledge and Kegan Paul, 1969), 279. For an English drawing of 1540–7, showing the full-sleeved linen shirt and bare legs of the Irish kern, see Mairead Dunlevy, *Dress in Ireland* (New York: Holmes and Meier, 1989), 53, fig. 37.

66 Roy Strong, "Elizabethan Painting: An Approach through the Inscriptions of Marcus Gheeraerts the Younger," *The Burlington Magazine* 105 (1963), rpt. in *The English Icon*, 350. On Henry Lee as tilt choreographer, see also Richard McCoy, *The Rites of Knighthood: The Literature and Politics of Elizabethan Chivalry* (Berkeley: University of California Press, 1989), 44–5, 145–6; on the Ditchley entertainment, see Chambers, *Sir Henry Lee*, appendix D, and Frances Yates, *Astraea, the Imperial Theme in the Sixteenth Century* (London: Routledge and Kegan Paul, 1975), 99–100, 103–5.

67 Chambers supplies this and the following biographical data, *Sir Henry Lee*, 186–91.

68 Chambers, *Sir Henry Lee*, 191 n. 2.

69 This company regularly ordered its travelers to learn the secrets of Persian industry, including carpet coloring (T. S. Willan, *The Early History of the Russia Company* [Manchester University Press, 1955], 148–9).

70 Quoted in M. Channing Linthicum, *Costume in the Drama of Shakespeare and His Contemporaries* (New York: Russell and Russell, 1936, 2nd edn. 1963), 9–10.

71 C. A. Bayly, ed., *The Raj: India and the British 1600–1947* (London: Pearson/National Portrait Gallery, 1990), 67–8.

72 Cecilia, Countess of Denbigh, *Royalist Father and Roundhead Son* (London: Methuen,

1915), 76, cited in Gregory Martin, *The Flemish School circa 1600–1900* (London: The National Gallery, 1970), 54.

73 Bayly, *The Raj*, 73; Martin, *The Flemish School*, 52–5; Oliver Millar, *Van Dyck in England* (London: National Portrait Gallery, 1982), 56–7.

74 Martin, *The Flemish School*, 54, citing Col. H. Yule, ed., *The Diary of William Hedges, Esq.*, in *The Hakluyt Society*, vol. 75 (1878), 344 ff.

75 Martin, *The Flemish School*, 54, citing H. R. Robinson.

76 See, for examples of feathers as ornaments, Stephen Orgel and Roy Strong, *Inigo Jones: The Theater of the Stuart Court* (London and Berkeley: Sotheby Parke Bernet/University of California Press, 1973), vol. 2, 490, fig. 88; 491, figs. 224 and 225; Allardyce Nicoll, *Stuart Masques and the Renaissance Stage* (London: George Harrap, 1937), 196–8, figs. 170–4; and Margaret Ferguson, "Feathers and Flies: Aphra Behn and the Seventeenth-Century Trade in Exotica," in *Subject and Object in Renaissance Culture*, ed. Margreta de Grazia, Maureen Quilligan, and Peter Stallybrass (Cambridge University Press, 1995), 235–59.

77 Martin, *The Flemish School*, 53. On the popularity of such hats, see Linthicum, *Costume in Shakespeare*, 228–9. Beaver skins came from North America and also from Russia during this period. See Janet Martin, *Treasure of the Land of Darkness: The Fur Trade and Its Significance for Medieval Russia* (Cambridge University Press, 1986), chap. 4, esp. 99; William Roberts, "The Fur Trade of New England in the Seventeenth Century," Ph.D. dissertation, University of Pennsylvania, 1958, 68–71; and J. Frederick Fausz, "'To Draw Thither the Trade of Beavers': The Strategic Significance of the English Fur Trade in the Chesapeake, 1620–1660," in *Le Castor Fait Tout: Selected Papers of the Fifth North American Fur Trade Conference*, ed. Bruce Trigger, Toby Morantz, and Louise Dechène (Montréal: La Société, 1987), 55–61.

78 Linthicum, *Costume in Shakespeare*, 229.

79 Millar, *Van Dyck*, 56.

80 Vecellio, *Costume Book*, 142, figs. 450 and 451; "A Group of Servants at the Outskirts of the Camp of some Great Personage," Bayly, *The Raj*, 51, fig. 25. Drawings of Persian headgear in the sixteenth and early seventeenth centuries in Claudia Müller, *The Costume Timeline: Five Thousand Years of Fashion History* (London: Thames and Hudson, 1993), show high, rounded, diagonally tied turbans as the norm for Persian dress, in contrast to the smaller, pointed turbans of India. Cf. Inigo Jones's drawing of "A Turk," in Orgel and Strong, *Inigo Jones*, vol. 2, 699, fig. 378.

81 Martin, *The Flemish Schoool*, 55.

82 Kim Hall, in *Things of Darkness: Economies of Race and Gender in Early Modern England* (Ithaca, NY: Cornell University Press, 1995), includes a section, "Male Portraits, Property and Colonial Might," relevant to the Denbigh portrait. She points out that Europeans often confused Indian and African peoples in the seventeenth and eighteenth centuries. Of the portrait she says, "The Indian here is used not so much to juxtapose dark and light skin as to heighten the exoticism of the landscape . . . [he is] subtly associated with exotic foreign commodities [the coconut and parrot]," 231–2.

83 Martin, *The Flemish Schoool*, 53; Millar, *Van Dyck*, 56.

84 Alastair Laing, *In Trust for the Nation: Paintings from National Trust Houses* (London: The National Trust, 1995), cat. 2, 20.

85 Samuel Pepys was clearly "orientalizing" on 21 November 1666, when he went to see Sir Philip Howard in a nightgown and a Turkish turban. Pepys also had himself painted in an "Indian" gown, which he had hired for the purpose. See Diana de Marly, "Pepys and the Fashion for Collecting," *Costume* 21 (1987): 34–43, 42.

86 On surface inscriptions and/as deep makings, see our Introduction, and, on the presentation of clothes as honorific gifts, Patricia L. Baker, "Islamic Honorific Garments," *Costume* 25 (1991): 25–35.

87 As we note in our Introduction, Charles I instructed the painter Nicholas Wilford to attend to the "excellencyes" of the Persian "Cloth of Gould Silke with its colors and dies." See R. W. Ferrier, "Charles I and the Antiquities of Persia: The Mission of Nicholas Wilford," *Iran* 8 (1970): 51–6, 51.

88 Philip D. Curtin, *Cross-Cultural Trade in World History* (Cambridge University Press, 1984), 149.

89 Nicholas Canny, "The Permissive Frontier: The Problem of Social Control in English Settlements in Ireland and Virginia 1550–1650," in *The Westward Enterprise: English Activities in Ireland, the Atlantic, and America 1480–1650*, ed. K. R. Andrews, N. P. Canny, and P. E. H. Hair (Liverpool University Press, 1979), 17–44, 19.

90 Thomas Fuller, *The Worthies of England* (1662), ed. John Freeman (London: Allen and Unwin, 1952), 572.

91 Wheelock, Barnes, et al., *Anthony van Dyck*, 155.

92 Wheelock, Barnes, et al., *Anthony van Dyck*, 155.

3 YELLOW STARCH: FABRICATIONS OF THE JACOBEAN COURT

1 We are deeply indebted to David Underdown for sending us a copy of his paper, "Yellow Ruffs and Poisoned Possets: Placing Women in Early Stuart Political Debate," presented at the conference "Attending to Women," University of Maryland, College Park, 1994. For a further account of the politics of scandal in the Stuart court, see his *A Freeborn People: Politics and the Nation in Seventeenth-Century England* (Oxford: Clarendon Press, 1996), 28, 33, 57, 62–7.

2 This list includes only some of the secrets of James I's reign that Michael Sparke claims to bring to light in *Truth Brought to Light and Discovered by Time or A Discourse and Historicall Narration of the first XIIII yeares of King Iames Reigne* (London, 1651), sig. Av.

3 Sparke, *Truth Brought to Light*, title page.

4 On Jonson's part in the celebration of the Somerset marriage, as well as on the festivities more generally, see David Lindley's "Embarrassing Ben: The Masques for Frances Howard," *English Literary Renaissance* 16, 2 (1986): 343–59, and his *The Trials of Frances Howard: Fact and Fiction at the Court of King James* (London: Routledge, 1993), 123–31. Lindley's is the most incisive account of the Overbury affair, although in his fine critique of the misogyny of the trials, he tends to overlook the extent to which (however problematically) they also opened up a radical critique of the court.

5 Sir Edward Peyton, *The Divine Catastrophe of the Kingly Family of the House of Stuarts* (London, 1652), 353.

6 Robert Codrington, *The Life and Death of the illustrious Robert, Earl of Essex* (1646), in *The Harleian Miscellany* (London: John White, 1808), vol. 1, 219.

7 Overbury's *A Wife* may well have already been in print in 1611, long before Frances Howard's marriage had been annulled. Ben Jonson, in any case, claimed that Overbury had written the poem in an attempt to seduce the Countess of Rutland. See James E. Savage, *The "Conceited Newes" of Sir Thomas Overbury and His Friends* (Gainesville, Fla.: Scholars Press, 1968), xiv.

8 As David Underdown notes, the Overbury scandal was only one of several scandals that rocked the court: "In 1617 the families of the Earl of Exeter and the Secretary of State, Sir Thomas Lake, exchanged wild accusations about crimes which included incest and poisoning. In the same year the enforced marriage of Sir Edward Coke's daughter to the deranged brother of the rising royal favorite, George Villiers, later Duke of Buckingham, led to some dramatic public quarrels. Finally, there were allegations of popish and other malign influences levelled at Buckingham's female relatives" ("Yellow Ruffs"; see note 1).

9 Robert Bancroft, "To Sir Thomas Overbury, on his Wife," in *Two Bookes of Epigrammes and Epitaphs* (London, 1639), 112.

10 On the importance of anti-Catholic sentiment in seventeenth-century politics, see in particular Peter Lake, "Anti-popery: The Structure of a Prejudice," in *Conflict in Early Stuart England: Studies in Religion and Politics 1603–1642*, ed. Richard Cust and Ann Hughes (London: Longman, 1989), 72–106.

11 Anon., *A Cat May Look upon a King* (London, 1652), 53–9, 43, and 90; Peyton, *The Divine Catastrophe*, 352.

12 Sparke, *Truth Brought to Light*, 4; Peyton, *The Divine Catastrophe*, 351 and 369; Francis Osborne, *The True Tragicomedy Formerly Acted at Court*, ed. Lois Potter (New York: Garland, 1983), 34.

13 Peyton, *The Divine Catastrophe*, 336–7, 344, and 348.

14 Anon., *A Cat May Look upon a King*, 40; Francis Osborne, *The Works of Francis Osborne* (London, 1682), 476–7.

15 The attacks on James's court in the 1650s were, in fact, building upon the widespread satires and libels on court scandals that circulated in the 1610s and 1620s. On the latter, see James L. Sanderson, "Poems on an Affair of State: The Marriage of Somerset and Lady Essex," *Review of English Studies* 16, no. 65 (1966): 57–61; Thomas Cogswell, "England and the Spanish Match," in *Conflict in Early Stuart England*, ed. Cust and Hughes, 107–33; Alastair Bellany, "'Raylinge Rhymes and Vaunting Verse': Libellous Politics in Early Stuart England, 1603–1628," in *Culture and Politics in Early Stuart England*, ed. Kevin Sharpe and Peter Lake (Stanford University Press, 1993), 285–310.

16 Robert Anton, "The Philosophers Third Satyr of Iupiter," in *The Philosophers Satyrs* (London, 1616), 25.

17 *The Widdow* (London, 1653), sig. H3.

18 Joseph Allen Matter, *My Lord and Lady of Essex: Their State Trials* (Chicago: Henry Regnery, 1969), 935.

19 James Howell,"To my Father upon my first going beyond Sea," March 1, 1618, in *Epistolae Ho-Elianae: The Familiar Letters of James Howell*, ed. Joseph Jacobs (London: David Nutt, 1892), 20–1. For a brilliant reading of the relation between yellow starch and *Hic Mulier* to which we are deeply indebted, see Stephen Orgel, *Impersonations: The Performance of Gender in Shakespeare's England* (Cambridge University Press, 1996), chapter 5, "Masculine Apparel," 83–105. We are also indebted to David Underdown for his "Yellow Ruffs."

20 Sir Simonds D'Ewes, *The Autobiography and Correspondence of Sir Simonds D'Ewes*, ed. James Orchard Halliwell (London: Richard Bentley, 1845), vol. 1, 79.

21 John Castle to James Miller, November 1615, in Thomas Birch, *The Court and Times of James the First* (London: Henry Colburn, 1848), vol. 1, 377.

22 Sparke, *Truth Brought to Light*, sig. A2.

23 Humphrey Mill, *A Nights Search: Discovering the Nature and Condition of Night-Walkers with their Associates* (London, 1640), 241.

24 Karen Newman, *Fashioning Femininity and English Renaissance Drama* (University of Chicago Press, 1991), 65–6.

25 We are indebted to conversations with John Guillory on the relation between fashion, faction, and fetishism.

26 Richard Niccols, *Sir Thomas Overburies Vision* (London: The Hunterian Club, 1873), 31. Compare Barnabe Rich, *The Irish Hubbub, or the English Hue and Crie* (London, 1618), where the yellow of the starch is figured as the singeing of the collars by hellfire. How, Rich inquires, can men "walke the streets with one of these base, odious, vgly, beastly bands, this new diuellish inuented fashion, looking as though they had scaped from the Diuell in hell, and there had scorched his band" (40–1)?

27 Thomas Dekker, *The Seuen Deadly Sinnes of London* (1606), in *The Non-Dramatic Works of Thomas Dekker*, ed. Alexander Grosart (London: privately printed, 1885), vol. 2, 59–60. Quoted in Newman, *Fashioning Femininity*, 125.

28 Henry Fitzgeoffrey, *Notes from the Blackfryers* (1617), sigs. Fv–F2.

29 Mairead Dunlevy, *Dress in Ireland* (New York: Holmes and Meier, 1989), 54; Ada Kathleen Longfield, *Anglo-Irish Trade in the Sixteenth Century* (London: Routledge, 1929), 180.

30 Dunlevy, *Dress in Ireland*, 54.

31 Edmund Spenser, *A View of the State of Ireland*, ed. Andrew Hadfield and Willy Maley (Oxford: Blackwell,1997), 65.

32 Fynes Moryson, *An Itinerary containing his ten yeeres travel through . . . Germany . . . England, Scotland and Ireland* (London, 1617) (Glasgow: MacLehose, 1907), vol. 2, 236.

33 *Calendar of State Papers Venetian*, 4 (1527–33), no. 693, cited in H. F. McClintock, *Old Irish and Highland Dress* (Dundalk: Dundalgan Press, 1943), 68.

34 McClintock, *Old Irish Dress*, 53.

35 William Camden claimed that the fashion for yellow starch came from France and had been invented to set off sallow faces to advantage. See Matter, *My Lord and Lady of Essex*, 160.

36 Thomas Stoughton, *The Christians Sacrifice* (London, 1622), 166. See also Richard Brome, *The Damoiselle*, in *The Dramatic Works of Richard Brome* (London: John Pearson, 1873), vol. 1, act 5, scene 1, p. 456, where Frances says:

> formerly the Saffron-steeped Linnen,
> By some great man found usefull against Vermine,
> Was ta'ne up for a fashionable wearing.

37 All the references in this paragraph are to Longfield, *Anglo-Irish Trade*, 113, 117, 130.

38 John Stow, *Annales of England*, continued by Edmund Howes (London, 1632), sigs. Dddd1v–2; quoted in Newman, *Fashioning Femininity*, 115. It is worth noting that Philip Henslowe, pawnbroker, moneylender, and theatrical entrepreneur, was also, among his innovatory practices, a manufacturer of starch (see Peter Thomson, *Shakespeare's Theater* [London: Routledge and Kegan Paul, 1983], 27. Among the preconditions for the making of the new professional actor were up-to-date clothes and a ready supply of starch.

39 See Joan Thirsk, *Economic Policy and Projects: The Development of a Consumer Society in Early Modern England* (Oxford: Clarendon, 1978), 85.

40 Phillip Stubbes, *The Anatomie of Abuses* (London, 1583), sigs. D7v–D8.

41 Phillip Stubbes, *The Anatomie of Abuses*, ed. Frederick J. Furnivall, The New Shakespeare Society, series 6, no. 4 (London: Trübner, 1877–9), 71–2.

42 Ben Jonson, *The Devil is an Ass, Ben Jonson*, eds. C. H. Herford, Percy and Evelyn Simpson (Oxford: Clarendon Press, 1950), vol. 6, 5. 8. 75.

43 See Steve Rappaport, *Worlds within Worlds: Structures of Life in Sixteenth-Century London* (Cambridge University Press, 1989), 13. For the proclamation of 31 July, 1596, see Paul L. Hughes and James F. Larkin, eds., *Tudor Royal Proclamations* (New Haven: Yale University Press, 1969), vol. 3, 188, 166.

44 See Thirsk, *Economic Policy*, pp. 88–90 and Linda Levy Peck, *Northampton: Patronage and Policy at the Court of James I* (London: George Allen and Unwin, 1982), 67.

45 Peck, *Northampton*, p. 68; *Commons Debates 1621*, ed. Wallace Notestein, Frances Helen Relf, and Hartley Simpson (New Haven: Yale University Press, 1935), vol. 7, 441. To compensate Northampton for the revocation of his starch monopoly, the crown granted him £4,000 a year for twelve years.

46 John Chamberlain, *The Letters of John Chamberlain*, ed. Norman Egbert McLure (Philadelphia: The American Philosophical Society, 1939), vol. 1, 586–7.

47 Thomas Tomkis, *Albumazar: A Comedy*, ed. Hugh G. Dick, University of California Publications in English (Berkeley: University of California Press, 1944), 2. 1, lines 576, 588–9, 590–1.

48 Thomas Middleton and William Rowley, *The World Tost at Tennis* (London, 1620), sig. D2.

49 Middleton and Rowley, *The World*, sig. D2v.

50 Middleton and Rowley, *The World*, sig. D3v.

51 For other aspects of Middleton's relation to the Somerset affair, see Lindley, *Trials of Frances Howard*, "The Philosophers Third Satyr," particularly 78–9, 114–15, 120–1, 124, 128; Margot Heinemann, *Puritanism and Theatre: Thomas Middleton and Opposition Drama under the Early Stuarts* (Cambridge University Press, 1980), 107–13; and A. A. Bromham and Zara Bruzzi, *"The Changeling" and the Years of Crisis, 1619–1624: A Hieroglyph of Britain* (London: Pinter Publishers, 1990), 18–36. We would argue that Middleton's *Women Beware Women* was also tied in to the Somerset scandal. When it was first published together with *More Dissemblers besides Women* in 1657, the two plays were prefaced by a single poem on *Women Beware Women* by Nathaniel Richards. Richards writes that "Drabs of State vext, / Have Plots, Poysons, Mischief that seldom miss." The

"Drabs of State" had earlier in Richards's writing clearly been Frances Howard and Anne Turner. In the satires which he appended to *The Celestial Publican* (London, 1630), Richards attacked the court, court women, Jesuits, and "The Vicious Courtier." He particularly reviled the "Court *Concubines*" who "ne'r kill, but with delight" (sig. H), and who, "by Sugar Candid Poysons" had murdered "the sad most Lamented Knight" (sig. G6v). He continues: "A *Drab* of *State* is a consuming Flame" (sig. H2). Richards returned to what was for him the obsessive topic of the powerful and monstrous "*Smocke-statist*" (*The Celestial Publican*, sig. H2) in *The Tragedy of Messalina* (London, 1640). Messalina, "a drab / Of state, a cloth of Silver slut," had been frequently invoked in relation to Frances Howard. See Nathaniel Richards, *The Tragedy of Messalina*, ed. A. R. Skemp (Louvain: A. Uystpruyst, 1910), 68.

52 The fears of Ananias and Sir Poule are largely taken over by Jonson from Stubbes's *Anatomie of Abuses*. See above.

53 Samuel Harsnet, *A Discouery of the Fraudulent Practices of Iohn Darrel* (London, 1599), 120.

54 Jonson was followed in his attack on the attack on yellow starch by Henry Hutton, who write in *Follies Anatomie: or satyres and satyricall epigrams* (London, 1619) against a "Timist" who

> Censures base whoredome, with a Mustard face,
> With a sowre pis-pot visage, doth disgrace
> A Ruffled Boote, and will in no case stand,
> In view of a (sir reuerence) yellow band.
> He rayles on Musick, pride, and wines excesse,
> And from an Organ-pipe himselfe doth blesse.
> Abhorres a Sattin suit, or veluet cloake,
> And sayes Tobacco is the Diuells smoake.   (sigs. A7–A7v)

The Timist who cannot stand "a (sir reuerence) yellow band" may well be modeled on Robert Anton, who in 1616 had raged against the "*sur-reuerence fashion*" of "*yellow bands.*" See Robert Anton, "The Philosophers Third Satyr of Iupiter," in *The Philosophers Satyrs* (London, 1616), 24–5. Hutton also mocks a glutton for "Rayling on cloakebagge, breeches, yellow bands" (sig. B5).

55 It is notoriously difficult to pin down Jonson's politics. Throughout his Jacobean writings, he swung wildly between court and anticourt rhetorics, partly depending upon where he was looking for patronage. His early court writings praised the man-woman, in the form of the "virtuous amazon" for whom he wrote: Queen Anne, the patron of his *Masque of Blackness* and the *Masque of Queens*. Equally, with James in view, he elaborately supported the union of England and Scotland in *Hymenaei*, the masque he had written for Frances Howard's first marriage to the Earl of Essex. Jonson's *court* writings, then, often positioned him as "feminist" and "unionist." But these writings have to be set against his violent attacks both on the power of court women and on the Scots. In 1609, he attacked first Cecilia Bulstrode in an epigram as a "pucell" (whore) of "Tribade lust" (lesbian desire) and "epicoene fury." He went on to attack Arbella Stuart, in his misogynist farce *Epicoene; or, The Silent Woman*, as a transvestite "mistris *Epicoene*." Jonson himself feared that his attack upon Cecilia Bulstrode had cost him the support of the queen, while the Venetian ambassador reported that the attack upon Lady Arbella had led to the suppression of the play. Equally, despite his support for union with Scotland in his court masques, Jonson is more famous for his opposition to any such union in his plays for the public theater. In 1605, he had collaborated on *Eastward Ho* with Chapman and Marston, in which a gentleman in a comic Scots accent refers to his thirty-pound knights, a clear attack upon James and his Scottish followers. Jonson and Chapman were arrested and it was rumored that they would have their ears and noses cut off. In fact, while Jonson's participation in this attack may look like a sign of daring independence from the court, it was probably part of a concerted factional move by Jonson's patron, the Earl of Pembroke, leader of the Protestant, anti-Scottish faction, possibly with the support of the queen, who was dismayed by the influence of the Scottish favorites. And, despite the fact

that Jonson wrote *The Irish Masque* to celebrate the marriage of Somerset to Frances Howard, his relations with the Howards were not good. After the staging of *Sejanus* in 1603–4, Northampton, Frances Howard's uncle, called Jonson before the council, accusing him "both of popperie and treason," no doubt partly to deflect interest away from his own Catholic sympathies. Jonson stated in 1619 that Northampton had been "his mortall enemie for brauling on a St. Georges day one of his attenders." Jonson had also fallen out with Suffolk, Frances Howard's father: in *Eastward Ho*, not only had he attacked the Scots at court but he had failed to submit the play to Suffolk, then Lord Chamberlain, before the performance. This makes it all the more surprising that Jonson does not seem to have joined in the celebrations of the fall of the Howards. On Jonson's patrons and for the passages quoted above, see David Riggs, *Ben Jonson: A Life* (Cambridge, Mass.: Harvard University Press, 1989), passim.

56 Rich, *Hubbub*, A2–A2v.
57 Rich, *Hubbub*, 8. Rich had denounced yellow starch even before the trial of Mrs. Turner. In *The Honestie of this Age* (London, 1614), he had written: "amongst all the rest of these ill becomming follies, that are now newly taken vppe (me thinkes) these yellow starcht bandes should bee euer best suited, with a yellow *Coate*" (35).
58 Rich, *Hubbub*, 49.
59 Rich, *Hubbub*, 40.
60 See M. Channing Linthicum, *Costume in the Drama of Shakespeare and his Contemporaries* (New York: Russell and Russell, 1963), 156–7.
61 Richard Niccols, "Epig. XII. *In Tubrionem*" and "Epig. XIIII. *In Verrem*," in *The Furies. With Virtues Encomium. Or, the Image of Honour* (London, 1614), C8 and C8v. Niccols capitalized on his early attack on yellow bands in *Sir Thomas Ouerburies Vision* (see above).
62 Richard Brathwait, "Upon the Generall Sciolists or Poettasters of Brittaine. A Satyre," in *A Strappado for the Diuell* (London, 1615), sig. C3/p. 21.
63 Richard Brathwait, "The Ape of Fashion," in *An Excellent Piece of Conceipted Poetry* (London, 1658), sig. K6v.
64 Anton, "Philosophers Third Satyr," 24, 25.
65 John Heath, "*In Lusiam*," in *The House of Correction: or, Certayne Satyricall Epigrams* (London, 1619), sig. A5v.
66 Joseph Martyn, "39. To *Flaua* of her yellow Band," in *New Epigrams, and a Satyre* (London, 1621), sig. C1.
67 See Graham Reynolds, "Elizabethan and Jacobean," in *Costume of the Western World: Fashions of the Renaissance*, ed. James Laver (New York: Harper and Brothers, 1951), 146. For a detailed reading of the relation between what Queen Anne is wearing and "manlike apparel," see Orgel, *Impersonations*, 83–105. See also Lindley, *The Trials of Frances Howard*, 6–12.
68 Randle Holme, in *The Academy of Armory* (Chester, 1688), Book 3, 15, claims that "in the beginning of the raigne of King Charles the first, Yellow Bands were much used, which were Dyed with Safron, and Supported round the neck by a Picadill." But the use of saffron for yellow starch is absent from the wardrobe accounts after 1625. See Linthicum, *Costume*, 117, fn. 5.
69 B.M. Egerton MS 1269, f. 33; B.M. Egerton MS 1264, f. 22; B.M. Egerton MS 3039, f. 20.
70 Attributed to William Larkin, "George Villiers, 1st Duke of Buckingham (1592–1628)," c. 1616.
71 See Roger Lockyer, *Buckingham: The Life and Political Career of George Villiers, First Duke of Buckingham 1592–1628* (London: Longman, 1981), 16–29.
72 Cogswell, "England and the Spanish Match," 107–33; 124.
73 Bellany, "Raylinge Rhymes," 303.
74 Bellany, "Raylinge Rhymes," 305.
75 Orgel, *Impersonations*, 84. He cites the *Letters of John Chamberlain*, ed. Norman E. McClure (Philadelphia: The American Philosophical Society, 1939), vol. 2, 286–7.
76 D'Ewes, *Autobiography*, vol. 1, 170.

77 On these contradictory aspects of conservative republican ideology, see Peter Stallybrass, "The World Turned Upside Down: Inversion, Gender, and the State," in *The Matter of Difference: Materialist Feminist Criticism of Shakespeare*, ed. Valerie Wayne (Ithaca, NY: Cornell University Press, 1991), 201–20.

78 Thomas Tuke, *A Treatise against Painting and Tincturing of Men and Women* (London, 1616), 24.

79 Tuke, *A Treatise*, 52.

80 Tuke, *A Treatise*, 57, 59.

81 Matter, *My Lord and Lady of Essex*, 175.

82 W. Sanderson, *Aulicus Coquinariae* (London, 1650).

83 Osborne, *The Works*, 476.

84 Stoughton, *The Christians Sacrifice*, 168.

85 Barnabe Rich, *The Honestie of this Age*, 35.

86 Barnabe Rich, *Riche his farewell to Militarie Profession* (London, 1581), 159–60.

87 Lindley, *The Trials of Frances Howard*, fig. 5, a and b.

88 Richard Niccols, *The Furies* (London, 1614), A6v.

89 George Gascoigne, *The Steele Glas* (London, 1576), sig. Ii v.

90 John Williams, *A Sermon of Apparell* (London, 1619), 7, 20–22.

91 "*Hic Mulier*: or, The Man-Woman" (1620), in *Three Pamphlets on the Jacobean Antifeminist Controversy*, ed. Barbara Baines (Delmar, New York: Scholars' Facsimiles, 1978), title page.

92 Stoughton, *The Christians Sacrifice*, 169.

93 Lindley, *The Trials of Frances Howard*, 11.

94 "Muld Sacke: or The Apologie of *Hic Mulier*" (1620), in *Three Pamphlets on the Jacobean Antifeminist Controversy*, ed. Baines, sig. B1. "Hic Mulier" is here denouncing the inadequacy of the definition of the man-woman in the *Hic Mulier* pamphlet.

95 For a fine account that challenges the conventional connection between women's breasts and the "feminine" and analyzes how that connection begins to be formulated in the seventeenth century, see Phyllis Rackin, "Dating Shakespeare's Women," *Shakespeare Jahrbuch* 134 (1998): 29–43.

96 *Hic Mulier*, sigs. A4–4v.

97 *Hic Mulier*, sigs. B–Bv.

98 William McElwee claims that Anne Turner "was a court dressmaker and she had made a considerable reputation by collaborating with Inigo Jones in the preparation of costumes for masks" (*The Murder of Sir Thomas Overbury* [London: Faber and Faber, 1952], 48–9). We have not found any sources that confirm this claim.

99 Osborne, *The True Tragicomedy*, 2. 1, S.D., 67.

100 Osborne, *The True Tragicomedy*, 9–10.

101 See Lois Potter's commentary in Osborne, 10 fn.1.

102 Richard Brathwait, "Upon our Ages MESSALINA, insatiat Madona, the matchless English-COROMBONA," in *An Excellent Piece of Conceipted Poetry* (London, 1658), sigs. G2–G3.

103 John Webster, *The White Diuel*, *The Complete Works of John Webster*, ed. F. L. Lucas (Boston: Houghton Mifflin, 1928), vol. 1, 5. 6. 261–2. Several critics have connected Webster's plays with the events of the Jacobean court. See, for instance, J. W. Lever, *The Tragedy of State* (London: Methuen, 1971), 86–8, and John Russell Brown's edition of *The Duchess of Malfi*, the Revels Plays (Cambridge, Mass.: Harvard University Press, 1964), xxxviii–xli. On Webster's active hand in the expansion of the "characters" in Sir Thomas Overbury's *A Wife* after Overbury's death, see Charles R. Forker, *Skull Beneath the Skin* (Carbondale: Southern Illinois University Press, 1986), 120–3.

104 Lindley, *Trials of Frances Howard*, 179–85.

105 *State Papers* 14/83/20, quoted in Lindley, *Trials of Frances Howard*, 184; Dr. Whiting's report on his conference with Anne Turner, November 11, 1615, *Calendar of State Papers, Domestic*, vol. 83 (1858), 327; John Castle to James Miller, at Southampton, November 1615, in Thomas Birch, *The Court and Times of James the First* (London: Henry Colburn, 1848), vol. 1, 377.

106 Lady Anne recorded in her diaries that the Countess "was much pitied by all beholders" (*The Diaries of Lady Anne Clifford*, ed. D. J. H. Clifford [Wolfeboro Falls, New Hampshire: Alan Sutton, 1991], 35).

107 *Calendar of State Papers, Domestic*, vol. 83 (1858), 327.

108 *Muld Sacke*, sig. B.

109 Curiously, Elizabeth I was attended by "the Laundress of the Body": the laundress's functions were entirely related to cleaning the queen's underwear, not to what we would call her body. See Anne Somerset, *Ladies-in-Waiting* (New York: Alfred Knopf, 1984), 96.

110 Rich, *The Honestie of this Age*, 20.

4 ARACHNE'S WEB: VELÁZQUEZ'S *LAS HILANDERAS*

1 See, however, Merry Wiesner's citation of a German religious reformer's remark that male spinners reversed gender expectations in uneasy ways. Sebastian Franck, after visiting the villages around Ulm and Augsberg, wrote, "Not only women and maids, but also men and boys, spin. One sees contradictions; they work and gossip like women, yet are still vigorous, active, strong and quarrelsome people, the kind any area would want to have" (*Women and Gender in Early Modern Europe* [Cambridge University Press, 1993], 91).

2 For the history of the painting, see Maria Caturla, "El coleccionista madrileño Don Pedro de Arce, que poseyó 'Las Hilanderas' de Velázquez," *Archivo Español d'Arte* 21 (1948): 292–304; Vicente Lleò, cited by Jonathan Brown, *Velázquez, Painter and Courtier* (New Haven: Yale University Press, 1988), 302, fn. 34; Enriqueta Harris, *The Prado: Treasure House of the Spanish Royal Collection* (New York: The Studio, 1940): 85. Brown discusses the painting in *Velázquez*, 252–3 and notes.

3 For detailed description and illustrations of wool spinning, see Eliza Leadbeater, *Spinning and Spinning Wheels* (Princes Risborough, Bucks.: Shire Publications, 1979), 24–30. For an overview of flax and wool spinning throughout Europe, see Irena Turnau, "The Organization of the European Textile Industry from the Thirteenth to the Eighteenth Century," *The Journal of European Economic History* 17 (Winter 1988), 586, 589–2, 594–6.

4 On the wool industry in Spain, see James La Force, Jr., *The Development of the Spanish Textile Industry* (Berkeley: University of California Press, 1965) and K. G. Ponting, *The Wool Trade, Past and Present* (Manchester: Columbine Press, 1961), chap. 3.

5 Brown, *Velázquez*, 251–3.

6 Madlyn Kahr, *Velázquez: The Art of Painting* (New York: Harper & Row, 1976), 211.

7 For an account of Rubens's lost painting and an illustration of his surviving oil sketch, see Svetlana Alpers, *The Decoration of the Torre de la Parada*, Corpus Rubenianum, vol. 9 (New York: Phaidon, 1971), 156, 160, cat.3, 3a, figs. 60–2.

8 See Brown, *Velázquez*, 256, fig. 323.

9 Brown, *Velázquez*, 253. In fact, this subordination of narrative to genre is not unique in Velázquez's work. See also his *Kitchen Scene with Christ in the House of Martha and Mary* (1618) and *Kitchen Maid with the Supper at Emmaus* (also known as *The Black Servant*), in both of which the kitchen scene is in the foreground and Christ is seen in the background through a hatch. See David Davies and Enriqueta Harris, *Velázquez in Seville*, exhibition catalogue (Edinburgh: National Gallery of Scotland, 1996), cat. 21 and 22. The extent to which the foreground dominates the background (and to which the latter is *not* the key to the former) is suggested by a second version of the *Kitchen Maid with the Supper at Emmaus* (The Art Institute of Chicago), in which the religious scene has simply been eliminated (see cat. 23). On problems of foreground and background in these paintings, see Norman Bryson, *Looking at the Overlooked: Four Essays on Still Life Painting* (Cambridge, Mass.: Harvard University Press, 1990), 150–5.

10 Albert F. Calvert, *The Spanish Royal Tapestries* (New York: John Lane, 1921), 32–6.

11 W. G. Thompson, *A History of Tapestry*, 3rd edn. (East Ardsley, UK: EP Publishing, 1973), 236–7; Calvert, *Spanish Royal Tapestries*, 11.

12 Women spinners in Spain in fact protested their exclusion from the public work sphere in this period, in uprisings analyzed by Marta Vicente, "Images and Realities of Work: Women and Guilds in Early Modern Barcelona," in *Spanish Women in the Golden Age*, ed. Magdalena Sanchez and Alain Saint-Saens (Westport, Conn.: Greenwood Press, 1996), 127–37.

13 On linen fiber as a women's product, see La Force, *Spanish Textile Industry*, 23–5, and on its production throughout preindustrial Europe, William Miller, "The Linen Manufactures of the Olden Time," in Alex J. Warden, *The Linen Trade*, 3rd edn. (London: Cass, 1967), including descriptions of various stages of linen making (3–40).

14 For detailed instructions about the labor-intensive domestic growing, treatment, and spinning of flax, see Gervase Markham, *The English Hus-wife* (London, 1615), ed. Michael Best (Montreal: McGill/Queen's University Press, 1986), 146–65.

15 Antonio Palomino y Velasco, *El museo pictorico y la escala optica*, 3 vols. (Madrid, 1715–24); trans. Zahira Veliz, in *Artists' Techniques in Golden Age Spain: Six Treatises in Translation* (Cambridge University Press, 1986), 148.

16 We have used the Loeb edition of Ovid's *Metamorphoses*, ed. and trans. Frank Justus Miller, 3rd edn., rpt. (Cambridge, Mass.: Harvard University Press, 1984), vol. 2, 289–99, Book 6, lines 19–23. Further line numbers are given in our text.

17 Leonard Barkan, *The Gods Made Flesh: Metamorphosis and the Pursuit of Paganism* (New Haven: Yale University Press, 1986), 3. See also William S. Anderson, ed., *Ovid's Metamorphoses, Books 6–10* (Norman, Okla.: University of Oklahoma Press, 1972), who remarks of the two tapestries, "As can be recognized, the composition of the goddess' work is flawlessly classical, perfectly centered, balanced, and framed, highly moral and didactic in content . . . Inasmuch as Ovid refuses to give it the victory, he may – having probably changed the story to produce this ambivalent result – be suggesting the value of Arachne's kind of composition: freer, more mannered, more dramatic and distorted, less specifically didactic" (160, note to lines 70–102). Frederick Ahl argues not only for sympathy but for a specific parallel between Ovid, banished from Rome, and Arachne: "Arachne is Ovid's artistic double . . . The kinds of motifs she represents are very similar to . . . the heavenly tales Ovid himself tells. And she, like Ovid, suffers for her outspoken criticism" (*Metaformations: Soundplay and Wordplay in Ovid and Other Classical Poets* [Ithaca, NY: Cornell University Press, 1985], 227).

18 George Sandys, *Ovid's Metamorphosis Englished, Mythologized, and Represented in Figures by George Sandys* (Oxford, 1632, ed. K. K. Hulley and S. T. Vandersall [Lincoln, Neb.: University of Nebraska Press, 1970]), 217. We have adjusted Sandys's punctuation for clarity here.

19 Anderson points out that ivy was regularly associated with poets in ancient Greece and Rome and suggests, "Possibly Ovid is seeking a floral symbol with connotations to rival those of Minerva's olive" (*Metamorphoses*, 167, note to lines 127–8).

20 For the many contrasting meanings assigned to ivy as an emblem, see Beverly Ormerod, "The Ivy Emblem in Scève's *dizain* 150," *Australian Journal of French Studies* 17, 1 (January–April 1980): 58–84.

21 Cited by Richard McCoy, *The Rites of Knighthood: The Literature and Politics of Elizabethan Chivalry* (Berkeley: University of California Press, 1989), 40–1.

22 George Turberville, *Epitaphes, Epigrams, Songs and Sonets* (London, 1567), 13.

23 Joseph Beaumont, *Psyche in XXIV Cantos*, canto 4, verse 51, in Joseph Beaumont, *The Complete Poems of Dr. Joseph Beaumont*, ed. Alexander B. Grosart (Blackburn: Edinburgh University Press, 1880), 64. See also Sir John Harington, *Orlando Furioso in English Heroical Verse* (London, 1607), Book 7, verse 21, 50:
> the chambers furniture could not be mended [improved],
> It seemd *Arachne* had the hangings wrought.

24 Thomas Storer, *The Life and Death of Thomas Wolsey Cardinal* (London, 1599), sig. A2.

25 John Beaumont, "To the Authour," in Francis Beaumont, *Salamacis and Hermaphroditus* (London, 1602), sig. A3.

26 William Browne, "The Third Song," in *The Whole Works of William Browne*, ed. W. Carew Hazlitt (London: Roxburgh Library, 1868), lines 293–314.

27 Thomas Moffet, on the other hand, in his georgic in praise of the cultivation of silkworms, claims that after the Fall humans should wear only fallen clothes rather than linen (""[c]leane, knotlesse, straight, spotlesse, vpright, and fine""), the latter being reserved for the priesthhood. He argues that Arachne spun flax "onely for the sacrificers weede" (*The Silkewormes, and their Flies* [London, 1599], 3–4).

28 Brown, *Velázquez*, 191.

29 Ovid, *Metamorphoses*, 6. 19–22, cited earlier in our text.

30 Moffet, *The Silkewormes*, 4. See also the descriptions of Arachne as a spinner by Joseph Beaumont and William Browne above.

31 Lisa Jardine, *Worldly Possessions: A New History of the Renaissance* (London: Macmillan, 1996), 26.

32 Jardine, *Worldly Possessions*, 391–6.

33 R. Malcolm Smuts, *Court Culture and the Origins of a Royalist Tradition in Early Stuart England* (Philadelphia: University of Pennsylvania Press, 1987), 131.

34 Brown, *Velázquez*, 251–2.

35 Brown, *Velázquez*, 250.

5 THE FATE OF SPINNING: PENELOPE AND THE THREE FATES

1 Alice Clark, *The Working Life of Women in the Seventeenth Century* (London: Routledge and Sons, 1919; rpt. London: Frank Cass, 1968), 94. For a sense of how much work was involved for a housewife in bringing flax and wool to the point of being spinnable and in the winding and finishing of thread, see Gervase Markham's detailed instructions in chapter 5, "Of wool, hemp, flax, and cloth . . . with all the knowledges belonging thereunto," in *The English Housewife* (1631), ed. Michael Best (Montreal: McGill/Queeen's University Press, 1986), 146–65.

2 On weavers' demand for spun wool, see Susan Cahn, *The Industry of Devotion: The Transformation of Women's Work in England, 1500–1660* (New York: Columbia University Press, 1987), 55. E. Lipson, in *A Short History of Wool and Its Manufacture* (London: Heinemann, 1953), gives the figure of six spinners' work needed by one weaver, as does Elizabeth Ewing, in *Everyday Dress 1650–1900* (London: B.T. Batsford, 1984), 11. Merry Wiesner gives a much higher figure for seventeenth-century Germany, where up to twenty carders and spinners were needed to supply one weaver using a technologically advanced loom (*Women and Gender in Early Modern Europe* [Cambridge University Press, 1995], 97).

3 Kenneth Ponting, *The Woollen Industry of South-west England* (Bath: Adams and Dart, 1971), 25. The figure for artisans' wages is from Andrew Gurr, *The Shakespearean Stage 1574–1642*, 3rd edn. (Cambridge University Press, 1992), 12.

4 Gurr, *The Shakespearean Stage*, 12.

5 Clark, *Working Life of Women*, 134. On decreases in the demand and price paid for raw wool throughout the seventeenth century, which negatively affected the price clothiers were willing to pay spinners, see Peter Bowden, *The Wool Trade in Tudor and Stuart England* (London: Macmillan, 1962), 7.

6 Clark, *Working Life of Women*, 95.

7 Clark, *Working Life of Women*, 107–10. For discussion of the poverty and dependency established by clothiers' exploitation of poor flax spinnners, see Enid Gauldie, *Spinning and Weaving* (Edinburgh: National Museums of Scotland, 1995), 24–6, and Wiesner, *Women and Gender*, 97–100. For comments on the status of spinners throughout Europe from the thirteenth to the eighteenth century, see Bonnie Anderson and Judith Zinsser, *A History of Their Own*, I (New York: Penguin Books, 1988), 99–102, 132–3.

8 Pierre Bourdieu first defined *habitus* in ""Champ intellectuel et projet créateur,"" *Les Temps modernes* (November 1966), 865–906. For a translation, see "Intellectual Field and Creative Project," in *Knowledge and Control*, ed. Michael F. D. Young (London: Collier Macmillan, 1971), 161–88. For commentary on the concept, see Randal Johnson, "Editor's Introduction," in Pierre Bourdieu, *The Field of Cultural Production: Essays on*

Art and Literature, ed. Randal Johnson (New York: Columbia University Press, 1993), 4–6.

9   For illustrations of wool-spinning wheels, see Eliza Leadbeater, *Spinning and Spinning Wheels* (Princes Risborough, Bucks.: Shire Publications, 1979, rpt. 1992). For the flax bobbin-winding wheel, see Isaac van Swanenburgh's "Spinning and Weaving," painted for the town of Leiden between 1594 and 1612, reproduced in Linda A. Stone-Ferrier, *Images of Textiles: The Weave of Seventeenth-Century Dutch Art and Society* (Ann Arbor, Michigan: UMI Research Press, 1985), chap. 1, fig. 5; and Patricia Baines, *Flax and Linen* (Princes Risborough, Bucks.: Shire Publications, 1985), 10–11.

10   Leadbeater, *Spinning*, 12. See also Eric Kerridge, *Textile Manufactures in Early Modern England* (Manchester University Press, 1985), who points out that only handspun wool was accepted for warp threads until the fifteenth century. He adds, "Wheelspun tops [long fibers] suited many purposes, but the wheel could never spin as tightly and finely as the rock [distaff], which was sometimes preferred on that account alone" (6).

11   On textile workshops in the Middle Ages, see David Herlihy, *Opera Muliebra: Women and Work in Medieval Europe* (New York: McGraw Hill, 1990), 77–92.

12   Natalie Davis, "Women in the Crafts in Sixteenth-Century Lyon," in *Women and Work in Preindustrial Europe*, ed. Barbara A. Hanawalt (Bloomington: Indiana University Press, 1986), 179.

13   Cited in Davis, "Women in the Crafts," 179.

14   *Les Evangiles des quenouilles*, ed. Madeleine Jeay (Montreal: Presses Universitaires, 1985), 104; 92; 144; 97 and 129.

15   "Die Schickerlinge," no. 156 in *The Grimms' German Folk Tales*, trans. Francis Magoun and Alexander Krappe (Carbondale: Southern Illinois University Press, 1960), 521.

16   "Spindel, Weberschifften und Nadel," no. 188 in *Grimms' Folk Tales*, 607–10.

17   Jack Zipes, *Fairy Tale as Myth, Myth as Fairy Tale* (Lexington: University Press of Kentucky, 1994), 68.

18   "Die drei Spinnerinen," in *The Grimms' Folk Tales*, 55–7.

19   Maria Tatar, *The Hard Facts of the Grimms' Fairy Tales* (Princeton: Princeton University Press, 1987), chap. 5, "Spinning Tales: The Distaff Side," 123. We thank Elizabeth Harries for referring us to this book. For a similar view that the tale suspends two different attitudes toward spinning, see Ruth Bottigheimer, *Grimms' Bad Girls and Bold Boys: The Moral and Social Vision of the Tales* (New Haven: Yale University Press, 1987), 118–20. But see also the critique of this piece by Jack Zipes in *Fairy Tale as Myth*, chap. 2, "Rumpelstiltskin and the Decline of Female Productivity," in which he argues that early versions of tales collected by the Grimm brothers demonstrate how highly women of all classes regarded spinning as a skill until it was taken from them by entrepreneurs using spinning machines. For a conflicting interpretation of spinning tales as registering hostility toward the craft, resulting from competition over land use between farmers and flax producers, see Jane Schneider, "Rumpelstiltskin's Bargain: Folklore and the Merchant Capitalist Intensification of Linen Manufacture in Early Modern Europe," in *Cloth and Human Experience*, ed. Annette B. Weiner and Jane Schneider (Washington, D.C.: Smithsonian Institution Press, 1989), 177–213.

20   Tatar, *Grimms' Fairy Tales*, 131.

21   Ruth Kelso, *Doctrine for the Lady of the Renaissance* (Urbana: University of Illinois Press, 1956; rpt. 1978), 46.

22   Kelso, *Doctrine for the Lady*, 46–7.

23   Juan Luis Vives, *Instruction of a Christian Woman*, cited in Kelso, *Doctrine for the Lady*, 69. For an analysis of this kind of assignment as it was made in German and Dutch writing and art, see Cordula Grewe, "Shaping Reality through the Fictive: Images of Women Spinning in the Northern Renaissance," *RACAR: Revue d'art canadienne/Canadian Art Review* 19, 1–2 (1992): 6–19. We thank Claudia Lazzaro for referring us to this article.

24   Thomas Salter, *A Mirrhor mete for all Mothers, Matrones and Maidens, intituled the Mirrhor of Modestie* (London: Edward White, 1579), C8v.

25 John Taylor (?), *The Women's Sharp Revenge* (London: John Okes, 1640), in *The Women's Sharp Revenge: Five Women's Pamphlets from the Renaissance*, ed. Simon Shepherd (New York: St. Martin's Press, 1985), 170. Shepherd argues convincingly that John Taylor wrote this pamphlet as a rejoinder to his own *A Juniper Lecture* and *Divers Crabtree Lectures*, published the previous year.

26 Taylor may be drawing, however, on a long tradition of women's complaints about the distaff and spindle as emblems of housework, including Louise Labé's call to other women citizens of Lyon to "raise their minds a bit above their distaffs and their spindles" and write for publication. Louise Labé, "Epistre dédicatoire," *Euvres* (Lyon, 1555), in *Oeuvres complètes*, ed. François Rigolot (Paris: Flammarion, 1986), 42. For a study of feminist protest against the distaff and spindle, see Anne R. Larsen, "Reading/Writing and Gender in the Renaissance: The Case of Catherine Des Roches," *Symposium* 41 (Winter 1987–8): 292–307, esp. 294–5. As early as the *Greek Anthology*, poems written by men in women's voices celebrated the choice of Cypris (Venus) over Athena through jubilant farewells to spinning and weaving, as in an anecdote said to be by Nicarchus:

> Nicarete, who formerly was in the service of Athene's shuttle, and stretched out many a warp on the loom, made in honour of Cypris a bonfire in front of her house of her work-basket and bobbins and her other gear, crying, "Away with thee, starving work of wretched women that have power to waste away the bloom of youth." Instead the girl chose garlands and the lyre, and a gay life spent in revel and festivity.

The Greek Anthology, Books 1–6, trans. W. R. Paton (Cambridge, Mass.: Harvard University Press, 1916; rpt. 1993), Book 6, no. 288, 451–2. We thank Justina Gregory for this reference.

27 Jacob Cats, *Houwelyck. Dat ist de gansche gelegentheyt des echten staets* (Middelburg, 1625; 4th edn., The Hague, 1632), chap. 4, cited and trans. by Wayne Franits, *Paragons of Virtue: Women and Domesticity in Seventeenth-Century Dutch Art* (Cambridge University Press, 1993), fn. to 71, 216. Italics ours. For a series of six Dutch prints in which Maarten van Heemskerck depicted the good wife of Proverbs spinning and selling her cloth, see Ilya Veldman, "Lessons for Ladies: a selection of sixteenth and seventeenth-century Dutch Prints," *Simiolus* 16, 2–3 (1986): figs. 2–7, 115–16. We thank Larry Silver for lending us Veldman's article.

28 Francesco Barbaro, *De re uxoria* (Florence, 1416), trans. as "On Wifely Duties" in *The Earthly Republic: Italian Humanists on Government and Society*, ed. Benjamin Kohl and Ronald G. Witt, with Elizabeth B. Welles (Philadelphia: University of Pennsylvania Press, 1978), 216. We have adjusted the translation from "an ordinary shoe" to "a household slipper," following Guillaume Bouchet's paraprase of Plutarch's description (also Barbaro's source) of "les patins [slippers] de ceste Caia, et sa quenouille," in *Les Serées* (Poitiers, 1584), "Troisième Serré," 113, cited in Sara Matthews Grieco, *Ange ou diablesse: la représentation de la femme au XVIe siècle* (Paris: Flammarion, 1991), 452, n. 156. For a study of ancient Roman gender ideologies and representations of spinning women, see Nathalie Kampen, *Image and Status: Roman Working Women in Ostia* (Berlin: Mann, 1981), 68–123.

29 Patricia Crawford, "'The only ornament in a woman:' Needlework in Early Modern England," in *All her Labours: Two, Embroidering the Framework* (Sydney: Hale and Ironmonger, 1984), 10. We are indebted to this thoughtful, detailed study throughout the discussion that follows.

30 Richard Brathwait, *The English Gentlewoman* (London, 1631), cited in Crawford, "'The only ornament,'" 10.

31 Anthony Fitzherbert, *The Book of Husbandrie* (London, 1555), cited in Clark, *Working Life of Women*, 48–9.

32 John Evelyn, *Diary*, ed. E. S. de Beer (Oxford University Press, 1959), 831.

33 Merry Wiesner, "Spinsters and Seamstresses: Women in Cloth and Clothing Production," in *Rewriting the Renaissance: The Discourses of Sexual Difference in Early Modern Europe*, ed. Margaret Ferguson, Maureen Quilligan, and Nancy Vickers (University of Chicago Press, 1986), 202.

34 F. W. Tickner, *Women in English Economic History* (London: Dent, 1923), 93. Cf. *Oxford English Dictionary*, "Spinninghouse."

35 Wiesner, "Spinsters and Seamstresses," 202.

36 Franits, *Paragons of Virtue*, 30. Cordula Grewe makes a similar point about other Dutch paintings, including Maarten van Heemskerck's representation of a fantastic dolphin-shaped wheel in his "Portrait of a Lady with Spindle and Distaff" ("Images of Women Spinning," 9.)

37 Cornelia Niekus Moore, "Books, Spindles and the Devil's Bench or What Is the Point in Needlepoint?" in *Barocker Lust-Spiegel: Studien zur Literatur des Barock (Festschrift für Blake Lee Spahr)* (Amsterdam: Rodopi, 1984), 321.

38 Publius Ovidius Naso, *Heroides 1*, in *Heroides and Amores*, rev. edn., ed. G. P. Goold, trans. Grant Showerman (Cambridge, Mass.: Harvard University Press, 1977), lines 10, 11.

39 See Nancy Felson-Rubin, *Regarding Penelope: From Character to Poetics* (Princeton University Press, 1994), 17, 41–2, and throughout. For a summary of critical disagreements about Penelope as character, see also Marylin Katz, *Penelope's Renown: Meaning and Indeterminacy in the "Odyssey"* (Princeton University Press, 1991), chap. 4, "What Does Penelope Want?".

40 John J. Winkler, "Penelope's Cunning and Homer's," in *The Constraints of Desire: The Anthropology of Sex and Gender in Ancient Greece* (New York: Routledge, 1990), 156.

41 Felson-Rubin, *Regarding Penelope*, fn. 9, 151–2.

42 Katz, *Penelope's Renown*, 77.

43 I. D. Jenkins, "The Ambiguity of Greek Textiles," *Arethusa* 18, 2 (1985): 115.

44 For discussion of woolworking in ancient Greece, including Helen of Troy as spinner in *The Odyssey*, see Elizabeth Wayland Barber, *Women's Work: The First 20,000 Years* (New York: Norton, 1994), 273–83.

45 David Herlihy argues that women's exclusion from the cloth trades began as early as the twelfth century in *Opera Muliebra*, chap. 4, "Spinners, Weavers, Dyers." See also Clark, *Working Life of Women*, 102–6, but also the critique of Clark by Barbara Hanawalt in *Women and Work in Preindustrial Europe*, xiv–xvii, and by Martha Howell in *Women, Production and Patriarchy in Late Medieval Cities* (University of Chicago Press, 1986), 30–41. Wiesner confirms Clark's view of women's exclusion from guild work in "Spinsters and Seamstresses" and *Working Women in Renaissance Germany* (New Brunswick, NJ: Rutgers University Press, 1986), 152ff. See also Mary Prior, "Women and the Urban Economy: Oxford 1500–1800," in *Women in English Society*, ed. Mary Prior (New York: Methuen, 1985), 110–11. For a contrasting history of women's ongoing participation in large-scale cloth production in Holland, see Stone-Ferrier, *Images of Textiles*, chaps. 1 and 2, and, more generally, Judith M. Bennett, "'History that stands still': women's work in the European past," *Feminist Studies* 14 (1988): 269–83.

46 *Tottel's Miscellany (1557–1587)*, ed. Hyder Rollins, rev. edn. (Cambridge, Mass.: Harvard University Press, 1965), vol. 1, 219.

47 Peter Colse, *Penelope's Complaint: or, A Mirrour for wanton Minions* (London: H. Jackson, 1596), title page.

48 For the dating of the European spinning wheel, probably an import from India, see Eliza Leadbeater and D. C. Coleman, "Textile Growth," in *Textile History and Economic History: Essays in Honour of Miss Julia de Lacy Mann*, ed. N. B. Harte and K. G. Ponting (Manchester University Press, 1973), 5–6. For linen as an Egyptian import to Greece, see Barber, *Women's Work*, chap. 8, and Jenkins, "Ambiguity," 120.

49 Joan Pong Linton, *The Romance of the New World: Gender and the Literary Formations of English Colonialism* (Cambridge University Press, 1998), 68.

50 Linton, *Romance of the New World*, 69–70.

51 On the techniques of carding in England, see Kerridge, *Textile Manufactures*, 3–4.

52 Robert Greene, *Penelopes Web*, in *The Life and Complete Works in Prose and Verse of Robert Greene, M.A.*, ed. Alexander Grosart (New York: Russell and Russell, rpt. 1964), vol. 5, 151. Greene's citation from Ovid is from *Remedia amoris*, line 139. See *The Remedies of Love*, trans. J. H. Mozley, in *Ovid*, vol. II (Cambridge, Mass.: Harvard

University Press, 1929; rev. edn. 1979), 187. For an excellent study of Greene's text and related visual representations of Penelope, see Georgianna Ziegler, "Penelope and the Politics of Women's Place in the Renaissance," in *Gloriana's Face: Women, Public and Private, in the English Renaissance*, ed. S. P. Cerasano and Marion Wynne-Davies (Detroit: Wayne State University Press, 1992), 23–46.

53 Michael Drayton, "Lady Geraldine to the Earl of Surrey," *Heroicall Epistles*, in *The Works of Michael Drayton*, vol. 2, ed. J. William Hebel (Oxford: Blackwell, 1961), 292. For more on Drayton's adaptation of Ovid's Penelope, see Deborah Greenhut, *Feminine Rhetorical Culture: Tudor Adaptations of Ovid's "Heroides"* (New York: Peter Lang, 1988), 96–114.

54 For an account of the association of spinning with storytelling in the Mother Goose tradition, in which large-footed female figures like Mother Goose herself resemble lifelong spinsters with their treadle-enlarged feet, see Tatar, *Grimms' Fairy Tales*, 107–14.

55 Ben Jonson, *Hymenaei*, *Ben Jonson*, ed. C.H. Herford, Percy and Evelyn Simpson (Oxford: Clarendon Press, 1941), vol. 7, 211.

56 John Jones, *The Arte and science of preserving bodie and soule* (London, 1579), cited in Kelso, *Doctrine for the Lady*, 112.

57 On this decline, see Lipson, who places the height of the wool industry under the early Tudors (*Wool and Its Manufacture*, 12). Bowden pinpoints a first decline in the middle sixteenth century. He argues that under Elizabeth and then James, trade in rough wool almost ended, woolen exports were sluggish, and only the production of worsted fabrics grew, a development in the interest of the rich clothiers but one that cut out wool growers and middlemen (*Wool Trade*, chap. 7).

58 Gervase Markham, *The English Hus-wife* (London, 1615, 1631), ed. Michael Best (Montreal: McGill/Queen's University Press, 1986), 3–4. For an excellent analysis of the gaps between prescriptions and the practical realities of work in England during the sixteenth and seventeenth centuries, see Michael Roberts, " 'Words they are women, and deeds they are men': Images of Work and Gender in Early Modern England," in *Women and Work in Preindustrial England*, ed. Lindsey Charles and Lorna Duffin (London: Croom Helm, 1985), 122–80.

59 Cahn, *Industry of Devotion*, fn 9, 206–7.

60 See Linton for an analysis of the English turn to the New World as a market for the woolen goods that were not being successfully sold in Europe (*Romance of the New World*, 64, 75–83).

61 Detail, pillow cover, scenes from Genesis, reproduced in *The Victoria and Albert Museum's Textile Collection: Embroidery in Britain from 1200–1750* (New York: Canopy Books, 1993), fig. 38, 53.

62 Fifteenth-century painting from the Rhine, reproduced in Erich Neumann, *The Great Mother: An Analysis of the Archetype* (New York: Pantheon, 1955), plate 97.

63 Sue Welsh Reed, "Jacques Bellange," entries 194 and 193 in *The French Renaissance in Prints from the Bibliothèque Nationale de France*, ed. Karen Jacobson (Los Angeles: Grunwald Center for the Graphic Arts, University of California, Los Angeles, 1994), 460, 459.

64 "Heilige Elisabeth," reproduced in *Hans Baldung Grien: Das graphische Werk*, ed. Matthias Mende (Unterschneidheim: Alfons Uhl, 1978), plate 409.

65 Barber, *Women's Work*, 238.

66 For an illustration of the drop spindle, from a Greek vase c. 490 B.C., see Barber, *Women's Work*, 38.

67 Plato, *The Republic*, trans. Francis M. Cornford (Oxford University Press, 1967), 355.

68 Aeschylus, *Prometheus Bound*, in *Three Greek Tragedies*, trans. David Grene (University of Chicago Press, 1956), 55; Aeschylus, *Eumenides*, in *Aeschylus I: Oresteia*, trans. Richmond Lattimore (University of Chicago Press, 1953), 169.

69 Catullus, *Carmina 4*, ed. and trans. G. P. Goold (London: Duckworth, 1983), 159–63.

70 See Susan Saward, *The Golden Age of Maria de' Medici* (Ann Arbor, Mich.: UMI Research Press, 1982), 7.

71 Hendrik Goltzius, "The Three Fates," in *The Complete Engravings and Woodcuts*, ed. Walter Strauss (New York: Abaris Books, 1977), plate 251, 431.

72 Muller's engraving of Goltzius's drawing is reproduced by Saward, *The Golden Age*, plate 25.

73 Hans Baldung Grien, "Die drei Parzen," *Das graphische Werk*, plate 32.

74 Saward, *Golden Age*, 25. She mentions as another version of Clotho/Aphrodite Raphael's painting of the three Fates for the loggia of the Vatican, in which a winged cupid helps Clotho with her distaff.

75 David Acton, "The School of Paris and the Dissemination of the Fontainebleau Style," in *The French Renaissance in Prints*, 299.

76 Acton cites a drawing by Guido Calza of Roman tomb frescoes at Ostia Antica as a possible source for Rosso ("School of Paris," 300, fn 7).

77 G. P. Valeriano Bolzani, *Hieroglyphica* (Lyon, 1602), ed. Stephen Orgel (New York: Garland Publishing, 1976), 515.

78 Dou's "Reading the Bible" is reproduced in Olwen Hufton, *The Prospect before Her: A History of Women in Western Europe*, I (London: HarperCollins, 1995), fig. 46, facing p. 465. For his "Old Woman Saying Grace," see Franits, fig. 147, p. 171.

79 Israhel van Meckenem, "The Angry Wife," from *The Scenes of Daily Life* series. Reproduced by Diane H. Russell in *Eva/Ave: Women in Renaissance and Baroque Prints* (Washington, DC: National Gallery of Art and New York: The Feminist Press at the City University of New York, 1990), fig. 125; commentary, 194.

80 See Russell, *Eva/Ave*, fig. 115; commentary, 184–5. Grewe suggests an opposing interpretation – that the young woman's spinning signifies her resistance to the man's courtship ("Images of Women Spinning," 11) – but Russell's reading is more persuasive to us, given the context of other eroticized images of spinners.

81 Daniel Heinsius, emblem from *Nederduytsche Poemata*, reproduced in Stone-Ferrier, *Images of Textiles*, fig. 39.

82 Anonymous engraving from *Enigmata sive emblemata amatoria* (Leiden, 1624), reproduced in Marina Warner, *From the Beast to the Blonde: On Fairy Tales and Their Tellers* (New York: Farrar, Strauss and Giroux, 1994), 137; discussion, 136.

83 Alison Stewart, "The First 'Peasant Festivals': Eleven Woodcuts Produced in Reformation Nuremberg … to 1535," Ph.D. dissertation, Columbia University, 1986, 276–80. Beham's "A Spinnstube" is reproduced in Hans Medick, "Village Spinning Bees: Sexual Culture and Free Time Among Rural Youth in Early Modern Germany," in *Interest and Emotion: Essays on the Study of Family and Kinship*, ed. Hans Medick and David Warren Sabean (Cambridge University Press and Paris: Maison des Sciences de l'Homme, 1984), 320.

84 Medick, "Village Spinning Bees," 331.

85 For a reproduction of Merian's print, see Grieco, *Ange ou diablesse*, 338, with useful discussion, 336–9.

86 Reproduced in *The Complete Engravings, Etchings and Drypoints of Albrecht Dürer*, ed. Walter L. Strauss (New York: Dover, 1973), plate 46.

87 For a reproduction of Wier's illustration, see Marta Weigle, *Spiders and Spinsters: Women and Mythology* (Albuquerque: University of New Mexico Press, 1982), 139.

88 See, for a summary of earlier interpretations and the argument that the old woman represents virtue, Walther Scheidig, *Die Holzschnitte des Petrarca-Meisters zu Petrarcas Werk "Von der Artzney bayder Glück, des guten und widerwartigen," Augsburg 1532* (Berlin: Henschelverlag, 1955), 54–5. This print is reproduced with the title "The Witch" in Weigle, *Spiders and Spinsters*, 28.

89 King James I, *Daemonologie* (1597), ed. G. B. Harrison (London: John Lane, The Bodley Head Ltd., 1924), 11–12. We thank Laura Levine for pointing out this passage.

90 Woodcut frontispiece of *Les Imperfections de la femme*, reproduced by Françoise Borin, "Judging by Images," in *A History of Women in the West, III: Renaissance and Enlightenment Paradoxes*, ed. Natalie Zemon Davis and Arlette Farge (Cambridge, Mass.: Harvard University Press, 1993), 218.

6 THE NEEDLE AND THE PEN: NEEDLEWORK AND THE APPROPRIATION OF PRINTED
TEXTS

1 "A Lottery Proposed before Supper at the Lo:[rd] Chief Justice his House, in the First
Entrance to Hir Majestie, Ladies, Gentlewomen, and Straungers," in *Early English Poetry
and Ballads and Popular Literature of the Middle Ages*, Percy Society Reprints, vol. 15, ed.
J. O. Halliwell (London: T. Richards, 1845), *Poetical Miscellanies*, II, 8. We thank Juliet
Fleming for calling our attention to this poem. More generally, we are deeply indebted to
Lisa M. Klein, whose "Needlework and the Fashioning of a Renaissance Woman," a
workshop paper for the "Attending to Women" conference at the University of Maryland
in November 1990, introduced us to the materialization of ideology and resistance to it in
women's embroidery. See the summary of the workshop in *Attending to Women in Early
Modern England*, ed. Betty Travitsky and Adele Seeff (Newark: University of Delaware
Press, 1994), 200–3.

2 For a genealogy of the public husband and private wife, see Lorna Hutson, *The Usurer's
Daughter: Male Friendship and Fictions of Women in Sixteenth-Century England* (London:
Routledge, 1994), 19–24. We thank Karen Newman for this reference.

3 John Taylor, *The Needle's Excellency* (London: James Boler, 1624; 3rd edn. 1631),
A4–A4v. Further quotations from Taylor refer to this edition. For a modern reprint of
"The Praise of the Needle," see Gertrude Whiting, *Old-Time Tools and Toys of Needlework*
(New York: Dover, 1971; rpt. of *Tools and Toys of Stitchery* [New York: Columbia
University Press, 1928], 341–8.

4 Quoted by Merry Wiesner, "Spinsters and Seamstresses: Women in Cloth and Clothing
Production," in *Rewriting the Renaissance: The Discourses of Sexual Difference in Early
Modern Europe*, ed. Margaret Ferguson, Maureen Quilligan, and Nancy Vickers (Chicago
University Press, 1986), 191.

5 Pierre de Ronsard, "Discours à Monsieur le Duc de Savoie," *Oeuvres complètes*, ed. Paul
Laumonnier (Paris: Droz, 1937), vol. 9, 171.

6 For an important study of gifts by and to Elizabeth, and of Elizabethan women circulating
their embroideries to forge alliances, see Lisa M. Klein, "Your Humble Handmaid:
Elizabethan Gifts of Needlework," *Renaissance Quarterly* 50 (1997): 459–93.

7 Cesare Vecellio, *La corona delle nobili e virtuose donne* (Venice, 1617), trans. as *A Pattern
Book of Renaissance Lace* (New York: Dover, 1988), 23, 24, 36.

8 The National Trust, *Montacute House: Goodhart Collection of Samplers*, entries 1–31.

9 Peter Quentel, *Ein neu künstlich Modelbuch* (Cologne, 1527), reproduced in Roszika
Parker, *The Subversive Stitch: Embroidery and the Making of the Feminine* (London: The
Women's Press, 1984; rpt. New York: Routledge, 1989), 66. To this pathbreaking book,
we, like all recent students of women's needlework, are deeply indebted.

10 *Les Singuliers et nouveaux pourtraicts, du Seigneur Federic de Vinciolo Venitien* (Paris,
1606), reproduced in Parker, *The Subversive Stitch*, 66.

11 Reproduced by Suzanne Hull, *Chaste, Silent and Obedient: English Books for Women,
1475–1640* (San Marino, Calif.: Huntington Library, 1982), 47. For comments on Taylor's
book and an argument much like mine about women as embroiderers, see Susan Frye,
"Sewing Connections: Elizabeth Tudor, Mary Stuart, Elizabeth Talbot, and Seventeenth-
Century Anonymous Needleworkers," in *Maids and Mistresses, Cousins and Queens:
Women's Alliances in Early Modern England*, ed. Susan Frye and Karen Robertson
(Oxford and London: Oxford University Press, 1999).

12 Federigo Luigini, *Il libro della bella donna* (Venice, 1554), quoted by Ruth Kelso, *Doctrine
for the Lady of the Renaissance* (Urbana: University of Illinois, 1965; rpt. 1978), 121.

13 Giovanni Ciotto, *A Booke of Curious and strange Inventions, called the first part of
Needleworkes*, expanded edition (London: William Barley, 1596). Cited by Hull, *Chaste,
Silent and Obedient*, 46.

14 Richard Hyrde, Introduction to Margaret More Roper's 1524 translation of Erasmus's
Precatio dominica in septem portiones distributa, in *Vives and the Renascence Education of
Women*, ed. Foster Watson (New York: Longmans, Green, 1912), 167.

15 Juan Luis Vives, *The First Book of the Instruction of a Christian Woman*, trans. Foster Watson, in *Vives*, 41.

16 Reproduced in Averill Colby, *Samplers Yesterday and Today* (London: Batsford, 1964), 166.

17 Thomas Salter, *A Mirrhor mete for all Mothers, Matrones and Maidens, intituled the Mirrhor of Modestie* (London, 1579), B8v–C1.

18 Lucy Hutchinson, "The Life of Mrs. Lucy Hutchinson, Written by Herself," in *The Memoirs of the Life of Colonel Hutchinson*, ed. James Sutherland (Oxford University Press, 1973), 288.

19 Anne Bradstreet, "The Prologue," *The Tenth Muse Lately Sprung Up in America*, in *The Works of Anne Bradstreet*, ed. Jeannine Hensley (Cambridge, Mass.: Harvard University Press, 1967), 4. Quoted in Parker, *The Subversive Stitch*, 105.

20 Ludovico Ariosto, *Orlando Furioso*, ed. Lanfranco Caretti, 2nd edn. (Milan: Ricciardi, 1962), Canto 37, ottavo 14:

> Et oltre a questi et altri ch'oggi avete,
> che v'hanno dato gloria et ve la danno,
> voi per voi stesse dar ve la potete;
> poi che molte, lasciando l'ago e 'l panno,
> son con le Muse a spegnersi la sete
> al fonte d'Aganippe andate, e vanno;
> e ne ritornan tai, che l'opra vostra
> è più bisogno a noi ch'a voi la nostra.

(And in addition to these and other men whom you have [as admirers today] who have given and now give you fame, you can give it to yourselves; for many of you, leaving the needle and cloth behind, have gone and now go with the Muses to quench your thirst at Aganippe's fountain; and you return so [inspired] that we need your works more than you need ours.) (Our translation)

21 Cited by Anne R. Larsen, "Reading/Writing and Gender in the Renaissance: The Case of Catherine Des Roches (1542–1587)," *Symposium* 41, 4 (Winter 1987–8): 305, fn 15.

22 William Greenhill, *An Exposition of the first five chapters . . . of Ezekiel* (London, 1645). Quoted in Crawford, "Needlework," 14.

23 Anna Weamys, *A Continuation of Philip Sidney's Arcadia* (London, 1651), ed. Patrick Cullen (New York: Oxford University Press, 1994), 11.

24 George Chapman, *Hero and Leander, Completed by George Chapman*, in *Elizabethan Minor Epics*, ed. Elizabeth Donno (New York: Columbia University Press, 1963), "Fourth Sestyad," lines 112–21, 99. For a study of Chapman's attitude toward textile work as an analogy to poetry, see Judith Dundas, "'Arachnean Eyes': A Mythological Emblem in the Poetry of George Chapman," *John Donne Studies* 6, 2 (1987): 275–83.

25 Giles Fletcher, *Christ's Victorie in Heaven*, Book I, in *The Poetical Works of Giles and Phineas Fletcher*, ed. Frederick Boas (Cambridge University Press, 1908), vol. 1, 31–2.

26 From *Poetical Miscellanies*, Percy Society Reprint, vol. 15, 11. Thanks again to Juliet Fleming.

27 Quoted by Colby, *Samplers*, 54.

28 Thomas Powell, *The Art of Thriving, or the plaine path-way to preferment* (London, 1635), 113–14.

29 Jasper Mayne, *The City Match* (Oxford, 1659), 2. 2 (p. 13), quoted in Colby, *Samplers*, 58.

30 Lady Grace Mildmay, *Autobiography*, in *With Faith and Physic: The Life of a Tudor Gentlewoman, Lady Grace Mildmay 1552–1620*, ed. Linda Pollock (London: Collins and Brown, 1993), 26.

31 Mildmay, *Autobiography*, 35.

32 Anne [?] Cary, *The Lady Falkland: Her Life*, in Elizabeth Cary, *The Tragedy of Mariam*, ed. Barry Weller and Margaret Ferguson (Berkeley: University of California Press, 1994), 186.

33 Lady Mary Wroth, *The Countess of Montgomeries Urania* (London: 1621), ed. Josephine Roberts (Binghamton, New York: Medieval and Renaissance Texts and Studies, 1995), 124.

34 Margaret Swain, *The Needlework of Mary Queen of Scots* (London: Van Nostrand Reinhold, 1973; rpt. Carlton, Bedford: Ruth Bean, 1986), 48; Anne Clifford, *Diary, 1616–1619*, quoted in Frye, "Sewing," 30, fn. 19.

35 On Esther Inglis, see Jonathan Goldberg, *Writing Matter: From the Hands of the English Renaissance* (Stanford: Stanford University Press, 1990), 146–53, a study that includes two of her penned self-portraits (figs. 19 and 20). For thought-provoking analyses of the interplay between Inglis's crafts, see Susan Frye, "Esther Inglis and Early Seventeenth-Century Print Conventions of Authorship," a paper for the Shakespeare Association of America meeting, Albuquerque, 1994, and Georgianna Ziegler, "Hand-Ma(i)de Books: The Manuscripts of Esther Inglis, Early-modern Precursors of the Artists' Book," forthcoming in *English Manuscript Studies*, 2000. See also Peter Beal, who argues that Inglis translated needlework into calligraphy, in *In Praise of Scribes* (Oxford University Press, 1998), 14, fn 65.

36 Esther Inglis, *Argumenta Psalmorum Davidis*, cover reproduced in Frederick Bearman, Nati Krivatsy, and J. Franklin Mowery, *Fine and Historic Bookbindings from the Folger Shakespeare Library* (Washington, DC: Folger Shakespeare Library, 1993), 133. For an argument that Inglis embroidered her own book coverings, see 132.

37 Quoted in Inglis's French by Goldberg, *Writing Matter*, 149.

38 From Rosalind Marshall, *Costume in Scottish Portraits 1560–1830* (Edinburgh: Scottish National Portrait Gallery, 1986), 35. On the "copintank" hat, see M. Channing Linthicum, *Costume in the Drama of Shakespeare and his Contemporaries* (New York: Russell and Russell, 1936, rpt. 1963), 215.

39 Frye, "Esther Inglis," 1.

40 Louise Labé, "Elégie III," in *Oeuvres complètes*, ed. François Rigolot (Paris: Flammarion, 1986), lines 33, 38 (116). For an extended analysis of Labé's comparisons of herself to Minerva, see François Rigolot, *Louise Labé Lyonnaise ou la Renaissance au féminin* (Paris: Champion, 1997), chap. 3, "Faire taire Pallas et parler Arachné."

41 Moderata Fonte, *Il merito delle donne* (Venice: Domenico Imberti, 1600), ed. Adriana Chemello (Mirano: Eidos, 1988), 6. We cite from the recent translation by Virginia Cox, *The Worth of Women* (University of Chicago Press, 1997), 36.

42 Hannah Wolley, *A Supplement to the Queen-like Closet* (London, 1674), 81. Quoted in Crawford, "Needlework," 18.

43 Quoted in Carroll Camden, *The Elizabethan Woman: A Panorama of English Womanhood, 1540–1640* (London: Cleaver-Hume, 1952), 256.

44 Both pages from Shorleyker's *Scholehouse for the Needle* (London, 1624) are reproduced in *The Victoria and Albert Museum's Textile Collection: Embroidery in Britain from 1200 to 1750* (New York: Canopy Books, 1993), fig. 62, p. 66.

45 *V and A*, fig. 63, p. 67.

46 *V and A*, fig. 38, p. 53.

47 *V and A*, fig. 69, p. 70.

48 Reproduced in Xanthe Brooke, *Catalogue of Embroideries: The Lady Lever Art Gallery* (Phoenix Mill, Glos.: Alan Sutton and Trustees of the National Museums and Galleries on Merseyside, 1992), 35.

49 For a rich discussion of floral motifs and their printed sources, see Thomasina Beck, *The Embroiderer's Flowers* (Newton Abbot, Devon: David and Charles, 1992; rpt. 1993), especially chaps. 1 and 2.

50 For studies of the various sources of embroidery patterns, see John L. Nevinson, "Peter Stent and John Overton, Publishers of Embroidery Designs," *Apollo Magazine* 24 (1936): 279–83; his "English Domestic Embroidery Patterns of the Sixteenth and Seventeenth Centuries," *Walpole Society Publications* 28 (1939–40): 1–13; and Swain, *The Needlework of Mary Queen of Scots*, chaps. 9 and 12.

51 Reproduced in Brooke, *Lady Lever Embroideries*, 66. The four figures were identified in ink by the embroiderer.

52 Marshall's print as the source for a similar piece of needlework is identified in a Christie's sale catalogue, 23 June 1987, lot 168, plate 8.

53 William Shakespeare, *A Midsommer Nights Dreame*, in *The First Folio of Shakespeare: The Norton Facsimile*, ed. Charlton Hinman (New York: Norton, 1968), 3. 2. 203–8 (TLN 1230–5).

54 Pierre de Bourdeille, Abbé de Brantôme, a long-time observer of the French court, wrote of Catherine de Medici, "She energetically spent her evenings after dinner working on her silken embroideries, at which she was as perfect as it was possible to be," in *Les Vies des dames illustres françoises et étrangères*, ed. Louis Moland (Paris: Garnier, 1841), "Discours II: Catherine de Médicis," 45 (our translation.)

55 Swain, *Needlework of Mary Queen of Scots*, 32.

56 Mary Stuart, Norfolk panel, in Swain, *Needlework of Mary Queen of Scots*, plate 42.

57 Lisa Klein, "Needlework"; Swain, *Needlework of Mary Queen of Scots*, 74. Lesley's testimony during his 1571 interrogation in the Tower is cited by Francis de Zulueta, *Embroideries by Mary Stuart and Elizabeth Talbot at Oxburgh Hall, Norfolk* (Oxford University Press, 1923), 7.

58 Jennifer Summit quotes Camden's remarks from his *Annales, or the History of the Most Renowned and Victorious Princess Elizabeth, Late Queen of England*, 3rd edn. (London, 1635), in "'The Arte of a Ladies Penne': Elizabeth I and the Poetics of Queenship," *ELR* 26, 3 (Autumn 1996): 419, fn 59.

59 Zulueta cites Drummond's letter (July 1, 1614) in *Embroideries*, 5–6.

60 For an excellent photo of six of Bess's needleworked octagons, see Santina Levey, *Elizabethan Treasures: The Hardwick Hall Textiles* (London: National Trust, 1998), fig. 52, 59.

61 The Earl of Shrewsbury's remark is quoted in Swain, *Embroideries of Mary Queen of Scots*, p. 63. For comparisons of Gessner's prints and panels embroidered by Mary and Bess, see Swain, *Needlework of Mary Queen of Scots*, 64–73.

62 Swain, *Needlework of Mary Queen of Scots*, plate 55, p. 100.

63 Swain, *Needlework of Mary Queen of Scots*, plates 56 and 85.

64 Mary Hulton, cushion cover, first quarter of the seventeenth century, *V and A*, fig. 34, p. 51.

65 Parker discusses the shift from anonymous to named samplers in *The Subversive Stitch*, 86–8.

66 The Jane Bostock Sampler is reproduced in *V and A*, fig. 47, p. 57.

67 We are indebted to Patricia Warner, textile historian at the University of Massachusetts, Amherst, for the reminder that samplers functioned for girls of the middling sort as pattern books did for the far fewer rich women who could afford them. See, on this topic, Pamela Claeburn, *Samplers* (Princes Risborough, Bucks.: Shire Publications, n.d.), 3.

68 Ovid, *Metamorphoses*, Book 6, trans. Frank Justus Miller (Cambridge, Mass.: Harvard University Press, 1916, rpt. 1971), in *Ovid*, vol. 3, 328–9.

69 Bed valance (detail), Untermeyer Collection, Metropolitan Museum, New York. The valance as a whole is reproduced in Yvonne Hackenbroch, *English and Other Needlework, Tapestries and Textiles in the Irwin Untermeyer Collection* (Cambridge, Mass.: Harvard University Press, 1960), fig. 27. This detail is reproduced in Thomasina Beck, *Embroidered Gardens* (New York: Viking, 1979), 15.

70 Liz Arthur, *Embroidery 1600–1700 at the Burrell Collection* (Glasgow: John Murray and the Glasgow Museums, 1995), 92. Arthur cites the survey by Charlotte Mayhew, "The Effects of Economic and Social Development in the Seventeenth Century upon British Amateur Embroideries," M.A. thesis in Literature, University of St. Andrews, 1988. See also Susan Frye's comments on the figure of Esther, in "Sewing Connections."

71 This panel is reproduced in Arthur, *Burrell Collection*, plate 64; discussion, 89–92.

72 For the discussion that follows we are indebted to Lisa Klein, "Fashioning of a Renaissance Woman," and Arthur, *Burrell Collection*, 62–8.

73 For a discussion of Hannah Smith's casket, now in the Whitworth Gallery, Manchester, UK, see Klein, "Fashioning of a Renaissance Woman," final section, 2.

74 Judith with the head of Holofernes, Stuart embroidery, silk on satin, Brooke, *Lady Lever Embroideries*, 72.

75 For a discussion of de Jode as a source for figures of the Queen of Sheba, see Brooke, *Lady Lever Embroideries*, 44–5. Arthur also traces embroideries based on de Jode's prints, for example, Rebecca at the well (*Burrell Collection*, figs. 59, 60).

76 Christa C. Mayer Thurman, *Textiles in the Art Institute of Chicago* (Chicago Art Institute, 1992), 73. For the various meanings assigned to the Queen of Sheba, see Marina Warner, *From the Beast to the Blonde: On Fairy Tales and Their Tellers* (New York: Farrar, Strauss, and Giroux, 1994), chaps. 6–8.

77 "The Double Deliverance" is reproduced in Nevinson, "Embroidery Patterns," fig. vɪa, and in Brooke, *Lady Lever Embroideries*, 18.

78 Dorothy Selby's wall picture is reproduced in Nevinson, "Embroidery Patterns," fig. vɪb.

79 Brooke thus summarizes an unpublished study of Ward's political activities and imprisonment by John Blatchly, "Samuel Ward's 'Double Deliverance' and Thomas Scott's *vox populi*: an anti-Spanish Partnership in Ipswich," intended for *Studies in Ipswich History* (*Lady Lever Embroideries*, 18, fns. 1–3).

80 Selby also embroidered a picture of the acts of Jonah, which is represented in her portrait at Ightham Mote. See Katharine Esdaile, "Gunpowder Plot in Needlework: Dame Dorothy Selby, 'Whose Arte Disclos'd that Plot,'" *Country Life* (June 1943): 1094–6.

81 Quoted in Nevinson, "Embroidery Patterns," 10.

82 Brooke, *Lady Lever Embroideries*, 19; color plate 1, p. 116.

83 Thanks to Barbara Kellum and Larry Silver for suggesting that the animals might be read emblematically, in a discussion at the Women's Studies Research Center, Dickinson House, Mount Holyoke College, September 1994.

84 Thanks to Kathleen Swaim for this observation.

85 Parker, *Subversive Stitch*, 95.

86 This oath is quoted by E. Bryding Adams, entry 55, in *The Stuart Legacy: English Art 1603–1714*, ed. Walter R. Brown (Birmingham, Ala.: Birmingham Museum of Art, 1991), 88.

87 Nevinson, "Embroidery Patterns," fig. vɪɪa. For an interesting discussion of Marshall's print, see Marshall Grossman, "The Dissemination of the King," in *The Theatrical City: Culture, Theatre and Politics in London, 1576–1649*, ed. David Smith, Richard Streier, and David Bevington (Cambridge University Press, 1995), 272–6. Thanks to Kathleen Swaim for sending us a copy of this piece in its early form as a paper for the Milton seminar at the University of Massachusetts, spring 1994.

88 Nevinson, "Embroidery Patterns," fig. vɪɪb.

89 William Pearse, *A Present for Youth and an Example for the Aged: or the Remains of Damaris Pearse* (London, 1683), cited in Brooke, *Lady Lever Embroideries*, 59–60.

90 Brooke, *Lady Lever Embroideries*, 61. She cites John Morill, "The Stuart Period," in *The Oxford Illustrated History of Britain*, ed. Kenneth O. Morgan (Oxford University Press, 1984), as a source for the Moses–Cromwell association.

91 "The Drowning of Pharaoh in the Red Sea," Brooke, *Lady Lever Embroideries*, 60, and color plate 7.

92 Gerard de Jode's print is reproduced by Brooke, *Lady Lever Embroideries*, 61, fig. 14.

93 Francis Beaumont and John Fletcher, *The Maids Tragedy*, ed. Andrew Gurr (Berkeley: University of California Press, 1969), 2.2.43. We thank Gabriele Jackson for mentioning this passage to us.

7 THE CIRCULATION OF CLOTHES AND THE MAKING OF THE ENGLISH THEATER

1 This chapter is indebted to the invaluable suggestions of David Scott Kastan, Margreta de Grazia, Randy Nakayama, and Karen Newman, and to criticisms of an earlier version of the piece by Michael Macdonald and Carol Rutter.

2 Michael Ondaatje, *In the Skin of a Lion* (Harmondsworth: Penguin, 1987), 157.

3 For a brief but stimulating account of what such livery did and did not mean, see Stephen Orgel, "Making Greatness Familiar," in *The Power of Forms in the English Renaissance*, ed. Stephen Greenblatt (Norman, Okla.: Pilgrim Books: 1982), 41–8, especially 44, 46.

4 G. E. Bentley, *The Jacobean and Caroline Stage* (Oxford: Clarendon Press, 1941), vol. 1, 247. One finds substantial gifts of livery to visiting English trumpeters by Duke Charles at the court of Nyköping in Sweden in 1591, including embroidered English cloth, heavy velvet, silk taffeta, Geldern cloth, stockings, and linen. See Erik Wikland, *Elizabethan Players in Sweden 1591–92: Facts and Problems* (Stockholm: Almqvist and Wiksell, 1962), 124–5.

5 John Stephens, *Satyricall Essayes* (London, 1615), 246. We are grateful to Crystal Bartolovich for this reference.

6 For the importance of such protection, see Mary A. Blackstone, "Patrons and Elizabethan Dramatic Companies," *The Elizabethan Theatre* 10 (1988): 112–32.

7 Stephen Orgel, *Impersonations: The Performance of Gender in Shakespeare's England* (Cambridge University Press, 1996), 65–70.

8 See M. C. Bradbrook, *John Webster: Citizen and Dramatist* (New York: Columbia University Press, 1980), 180.

9 Bradbrook, *John Webster*, 1.

10 Bradbrook, *John Webster*, 166.

11 John Stow, *Annales*, continued by Edmund Howe (London, 1615), 697.

12 On the crucial dramatic significance of costumes and changes of costumes in the guild theaters, see Richard Southern, *The Staging of Plays before Shakespeare* (London: Faber and Faber, 1973), particularly 132–42; and David M. Bevington, "'Blake and wyght, fowll and fayer': Stage Picture in *Wisdom*," in *The "Wisdom" Symposium*, ed. Milla Cozart Riggio, Papers from the Trinity College Medieval Festival (New York: AMS Press, 1986), 18–38. For an admirably full account of the function of costumes on the Elizabethan and Jacobean stage, see Jean MacIntyre, *Costumes and Scripts in the Elizabethan Theatres* (Edmonton: University of Alberta Press, 1992).

13 *Coventry*, ed. R. W. Ingram, Records of Early English Drama (University of Toronto Press, 1981), 226, 224.

14 *Coventry*, 334–5.

15 *Coventry*, 308.

16 *Chester*, ed. Lawrence M. Clopper, Records of Early English Drama (Toronto University Press, 1979), 105; *Coventry*, 259.

17 *Coventry*, 93.

18 G. E. Bentley, *The Profession of Dramatist in Shakespeare's Time, 1590–1642* (Princeton University Press, 1971), 88–9fn.

19 Bentley, *Profession*, 88.

20 Andrew Gurr, *The Shakespearean Stage 1574–1642*, 2nd edn. (Cambridge University Press, 1980), 178.

21 S. P. Cerasano, "'Borrowed Robes,' Costume Prices, and the Drawing of *Titus Andronicus*," *Shakespeare Studies* 22 (1994): 45–57, 51. We are throughout indebted to Cerasano's fine account.

22 Bentley, *Profession*, 91, 90.

23 *Henslowe's Diary*, ed. R. A. Foakes and R. T. Rickert (Cambridge University Press, 1961), 184. For an excellent edition of the Henslowe documents associated with the Rose, see *Documents of the Rose Playhouse*, ed. Carol Chillington Rutter (Manchester University Press, 1984).

24 *Henslowe Papers*, ed. Walter W. Greg (London: A. H. Bullen, 1907), 90.

25 *Henslowe's Diary*, 168–9, 178, 179, 180, 169–70, 179, 185–6, 97, 133; Neil Carson, *A Companion to Henslowe's Diary* (Cambridge University Press, 1988), 38–9.

26 Gurr, *The Shakespearean Stage*, 13.

27 See Alan Smith, *The Wealth of the Gentry 1540–1669: East Anglian Studies* (Cambridge University Press, 1961), 124–5. Cullum had made his fortune by a combination of legacies, loans, and wages, but he increased his capital by buying and selling indigo and cochineal (he made £29 from the latter scarlet dye in 1617), by reselling his cloak for £3, and by reselling a red cloth for over £19 that he had bought for £10 (118).

28 Cerasano, "Borrowed Robes," 49.

29 Margaret Spufford, *The Great Reclothing of Rural England: Petty Chapmen and their Wares in the Seventeenth Century* (London: The Hambledon Press, 1984), 127. The main focus of Spufford's study is on the increase of "luxury" goods among the poor in the later seventeenth century.

30 John Michael Montias, *Vermeer and His Milieu: A Web of Social History* (Princeton University Press, 1989), 57.

31 The statistics are drawn from Montias, *Vermeer*, 55–7.

32 Gurr, *The Shakespearean Stage*, 44, 47.

33 Gurr, *The Shakespearean Stage*, 50.

34 Gurr, *The Shakespearean Stage*, 57–8; Bentley, *Stage*, vol. 2, 367.

35 Bentley, *Stage*, vol. 1, 646–7.

36 See A. W. Reed, *Early Tudor Drama: Medwall, the Rastells, Heywood, and the More Circle* (London: Methuen, 1926), and Janette Dillon, "John Rastell's Stage," *Medieval English Theater* 18 (1996): 5–45.

37 William Ingram, *A London Life in the Brazen Age: Francis Langley, 1548–1602* (Cambridge, Mass.: Harvard University Press, 1978), 51–65.

38 E. A. J. Honigmann, " 'There Is a World Elsewhere': William Shakespeare, Businessman," in *Images of Shakespeare*, ed. Werner Habicht, D. J. Palmer, and Roger Pringle, Proceedings of the Third Progress of the International Shakespeare Association, 1986 (Newark: University of Delaware Press, 1988), 40.

39 See Gerald D. Johnson, "The Stationers Versus the Drapers: Control of the Press in the Late Sixteenth Century," *The Library*, sixth series, 10, 1 (1988): 16.

40 The lawsuit is printed in Alfred W. Pollard, *Fifteenth Century Prose and Verse, An English Garner* (Westminster: Constable, 1903), 307–21, but it has recently been re-edited by Janette Dillon in "John Rastell v. Henry Walton," *Leeds Studies in English*, n.s. 28 (1997), 57–75. See also her "John Rastell's Stage," and William Ingram, *The Business of Playing: The Beginnings of the Adult Professional Theater in Elizabethan London* (Ithaca: Cornell University Press, 1992), 71.

41 Henry Medwall, *Fulgens and Lucres*, in *Tudor Interludes*, ed. Peter Happé (Harmondsworth: Penguin, 1972), 82.

42 Reed, *Early Tudor Drama*, 17–19.

43 See Bentley, *Profession*, 259.

44 Albert Feuillerat, *Documents Relating to the Office of the Revels in the Time of Queen Elizabeth I* (Louvain: Uystpruyst, 1908), 22. At the same time, the inventory shows the extraordinary value of the materials, which are carefully recorded by material (cloth of gold, cloth of "Copper gold," cloth of silver, velvet, sarsenet, satin, damask, taffeta, tinsel) and by color (crimson, purple, tawny, black, yellow, carnation, red, orange, etc.) (23–36). These materials are translated again and again, with the addition and subtraction of a variety of facings so as not to be "to[o] much knowen." Six masquing costumes of Turkish magistrates made out of red cloth of gold are translated first into masquing costumes of astronomers and then of barbarians before being too often "translated and shewen forworne and knowen" (20).

45 *The Chamberlain Letters*, ed. Elizabeth McClure Thomson (London: Murray, 1965), 75.

46 John Downes, *Roscius Anglicanus*, ed. Judith Milhous and Robert D. Hume (London: Society for Theatre Research, 1987), 53, 101, 94, and 89.

47 *Henslowe's Diary*, 219.

48 *Henslowe's Diary*, 97, 213, 214, 216. See also Roslyn Lander Knutson, *The Repertory of Shakespeare's Company, 1594–1613* (Fayetteville: University of Arkansas Press, 1991), 35–7.

49 *Henslowe's Diary*, 132, 122, 92, 102, 97. On a single folio (f. 95–95v, 184–6), Henslowe recorded lending money for six payments to "the littell tayller," which were also to cover his expenses in buying buckram, taffeta, sarsenet, and "diverse thinges." On the same folio, he lent money for 12 yards of velvet, for unspecified "cloth," for "a head tyer," and for dyeing an embroidered cloak.

50 An important exception to this remark is the work of Natasha Korda, whose independent

analysis of Henslowe's accounts in many ways parallels our own. We have drawn upon her fine work in revising this chapter. See her "Household Property/Stage Property: Henslowe as Pawnbroker," *Theatre Journal* 48 (1996): 185–95, and also her "Household Kates: Domesticating Commodities in *The Taming of the Shrew*," *Shakespeare Quarterly* 47, 2 (1996): 109–31.

51 Frederick Fleay, *Chronicle History of the London Stage 1559–1642* (London: Reeves and Turner, 1890), 94. See Korda's excellent account of the critical handling of Henslowe in "Household Property/Stage Property," 185–9.

52 Rutter, in *Documents of the Rose*, writes of Henslowe's pawnbroking business as "an acceptable charity" and claims that Henslowe "could have made small profit from [his neighbours'] pitiful, contaminated pawns" (5). We are nevertheless deeply indebted to Dr. Rutter for detailed and thorough criticism of our previous account of Henslowe.

53 The long and tangled relations between civic authorities allowing and forbidding Jews and Christians to lend at interest is described in Brian Pullan, *Rich and Poor in Renaissance Venice: The Social Institutions of a Catholic State, to 1620* (Oxford: Blackwell, 1971), especially 443 ff. and 605–21; Frederic C. Lane and Reinhold C. Mueller, *Money and Banking in Medieval and Renaissance Venice*, vol. 1, *Coins and Moneys of Account* (Baltimore: The Johns Hopkins University Press, 1985), especially 75–8; Reinhold C. Mueller, *The Venetian Money Market: Banks, Panics, and the Public Debt, 1200–1500* (Baltimore: The Johns Hopkins University Press, 1997), especially 26–7, 89–90, 240, and 571–5; Carol Bresnahan Menning, *Charity and the State in Late Renaissance Italy: The Monte di Pietà of Florence* (Ithaca, NY: Cornell University Press, 1993), especially 1–17. On the problems of Christians charging interest, see Jacques Le Goff, "The Usurer and Purgatory," in *The Dawn of Modern Banking*, Center for Medieval and Renaissance Studies, University of California, Los Angeles (New Haven: Yale University Press), 25–52; and Richard A. Goldthwaite, *Banks, Palaces and Entrepreneurs in Renaissance Florence* (Aldershot: Variorum, 1992), 31–9. On the Lombards as bankers/pawnbrokers, see Michael Prestwich, "Italian Merchants in Late Thirteenth and Early Fourteenth Century England," in *The Dawn of Modern Banking*, 77–104; and Raymond de Roover, *Money, Banking and Credit in Mediaeval Bruges: Italian Merchant-Bankers, Lombards, and Money-Changers: A Study in the Origins of Banking* (Cambridge, Mass.: The Mediaeval Academy of America, 1948), especially 113–65. On goldsmiths and early banking in England, see R. D. Richards, *The Early History of Banking in England* (London: Frank Cass, 1958), especially 24–35, although Richards shows little awareness of the significance of pawnbroking.

54 See Norman Jones, *God and the Moneylenders: Usury and Law in Early Modern England* (Oxford: Basil Blackwell, 1989).

55 Carson, *A Companion*, 30. Carson nevertheless gives a good analysis of Henslowe's customary interest rates (22–4), as does Korda in "Household Property/Stage Property," 192.

56 *Henslowe's Diary*, 156 (f. 79), where Henslowe atypically records the interest he charges. Sometimes, he records charging interest without stating the amount. Next to the pledge of a white satin doublet, for which he lent his nephew Frances £1 on 10 March, 1593, he notes "the vse pd vnto the 16 of desemb[er] 1593." On 19 June, he lent Anne Nockes, one of his agents or a *revendeuse* who did business with him, 6s. for a ring of gold, a silver whistle, and a child's coral set in silver, and he notes, rather oddly, that "about" 15d. had been "pd for vsse for this." Even if this was a yearly rate of interest, which seems highly unlikely, as opposed to interest for a number of months, the rate was more than 20 percent (109, 255). See also Jeremy Boulton, *Neigbourhood and Society: A London Suburb in the Seventeenth Century* (Cambridge University Press, 1987), 89.

57 For a fine account that attends to the complex relations between "clothes" and "costumes," see Cerasano, "Borrowed Robes."

58 Cerasano, "Borrowed Robes," 48–52.

59 *Henslowe Papers*, 113–21.

60 On the similar costs of clothing and of "costumes," see Cerasano, "Borrowed Robes," 52.

61 Carson, *A Companion*, 31–2.

62 *Henslowe's Diary*, 220. See also Bernard Beckerman, "Philip Henslowe," in *The Theatrical Manager in England and America*, ed. Joseph W. Donohue (Princeton University Press, 1971), 19–62, 41 n. 33, and Carson, *A Companion*, 27.

63 *Henslowe Papers*, 122; *Henslowe's Diary*, 88. The lists of the costumes of the Admiral's Men were recorded by Malone, but they no longer survive. We see no reason, however, to doubt their authenticity.

64 Francis Bacon, *The Advancement of Learning*, ed. Arthur Johnston (Oxford: Clarendon Press, 1974), 135, 138–9.

65 George Whetstone, *A Mirour for Magestrates of Cyties* (London, 1584), sig. Kv.

66 John Florio, *A World of Wordes* (London, 1598), 313, under "*Recateria*" and "*Recatière.*" As definitions of the latter word, he also gives "huckster," "retailer," "regrater," and "forestaller."

67 Middleton, *Your Five Gallants*; George Chapman, *Monsieur D'Olive*, ed. Allan Holaday, in *The Plays of George Chapman: A Critical Edition*, general ed. Holaday (Urbana: University of Illinois Press, 1970), 3. 2. 76, 81, 88–9, 169–75.

68 *Henslowe Papers*, 113–33; *Henslowe's Diary*, 316–25. The inventories, recorded by Edmund Malone, were later lost.

69 Carson, *A Companion*, 52.

70 Carson, *A Companion*, 52.

71 *Henslowe's Diary*, 73.

72 *Henslowe's Diary*, 207, 209–10; Carson, *A Companion*, 29.

73 *Henslowe's Diary*, 104 (our emphasis).

74 *Henslowe's Diary*, 77, 81, 86, 88, 89, 98. Was the "mr. langley" Francis Langley, draper, alnager, and proprietor of the Swan theater?

75 *Henslowe's Diary*, 97, 101, 94, 199.

76 *Henslowe's Diary*, 84, 102, 35, 37, 52, 81, 165, 35–6, 37, 50, 44, 49.

77 *Henslowe's Diary*, 44, 61, 79, 82, 73, 68, 98.

78 *Henslowe Papers*, 33.

79 Bernard Mandeville, *The Fable of the Bees: Or Private Vices, Publick Benefits* (London: J. Roberts, 1714; Oxford: Clarendon Press, 1957), 127–8. See also Beverly Lemire, *Fashion's Favourite: The Cotton Trade and the Consumer in Britain, 1660–1800* (Oxford University Press, 1991), 15.

80 Stephens, *Satyricall Essayes*, 244–5.

81 N. B. Harte, "State Control of Dress and Social Change in Pre-Industrial England," in *Trade, Government and Economy in Pre-Industrial England: Essays Presented to F. J. Fisher*, ed. D. C. Coleman and A. H. John (London: Weidenfeld and Nicolson, 1976), 147.

82 For a fine account of the "idolatry" of clothes in the theater, see Jean Howard, "'Satan's Synagogue': The Theater as Constructed by its Enemies," *The Stage and Social Struggle in Early Modern England* (London: Routledge, 1994), 22–46.

83 Quoted in Andrew Gurr, *Playgoing in Shakespeare's London* (Cambridge University Press, 1987), 234.

84 Sir Thomas Overbury, *A wife now the widdow of Sir T. Overbury . . . Whereunto are added many witty characters* (London: A. Crooke, 1638), M4; Gurr, *Playgoing*, 228.

85 Henry Fitzgeoffrey, *Satyres: and Satyricall Epigrams: With Certaine Observations at Black-Fryers* (London: Miles Patrich, 1617), F2v; Gurr, *Playgoing*, 231–2.

86 Ben Jonson, *The New Inn* (acted 1629), in *Ben Jonson*, ed. C. H. Herford, Percy and Evelyn Simpson (Oxford: Clarendon, 1938), vol. 6, 397.

87 For the play's dependence upon old costumes, even as it emphasizes Fitzdottrell's craving for the new, see MacIntyre, *Costumes and Scripts*, 309.

88 Ben Jonson, *The Devil is an Ass* (acted 1616), in *Ben Jonson*, ed. Herford, vol. 6, 1. 4. 16–25, 1. 6. 187, 1. 6. 28–38, 3. 3. 19.

89 Quoted in Bentley, *Jacobean and Caroline Stage*, vol. 1, 136.

90 *The Dramatic Records of Sir Henry Herbert, Master of the Revels 1623–1673*, ed. Joseph Quincy Adams (New Haven: Yale University Press, 1917), 61.

91 Ben Jonson, "An Epistle to a Friend, to Persuade Him to the Wars," no. 15, *The Vnder-wood*, in *Ben Jonson*, ed. Herford, vol. 8, lines 107–10; John Donne, "Satire IV," in *The Satires, Epigrams, and Verse Letters*, ed. W. Milgate (Oxford: Clarendon Press, 1967), lines 180–4. We are indebted to Susan Cerasano for both these references. See her "Borrowed Robes," 55.

92 Clare Williams, *Thomas Platter's Travels in England, 1599* (London: Jonathan Cape, 1959), 167. See also Orgel, "Making Greatness Familiar," 44.

93 This is not to deny that secondhand clothes cost much less than new clothes. See Cerasano, "Borrowed Robes," 50.

94 *Henslowe Papers*, 52–5 and 113–23.

95 *Henslowe Papers*, 53.

96 Valerie Cumming, "'Great vanity and excesse in Apparell': Some Clothing and Furs of Tudor and Stuart Royalty," in *The Late King's Goods: Collections, Possessions and Patronage of Charles I in the Light of the Commonwealth Sale Inventories*, ed. Arthur MacGregor (London: Alistair McAlpine, 1989), 322–50, 328.

97 Roy Strong, *Portraits of Queen Elizabeth I* (Oxford: Clarendon Press, 1963), 56, P. 7 (plate IV). See also P. 93 (the frontispiece), P. 87, M. 1, D. and I. 7, D. and I. 12, E. 8, W. 2, W. 7.

98 Strong, *Portraits*, 86, plate XXI (b) (which is mislabeled as referring to p. 85).

99 By the mid seventeenth century, however, Vermeer owned a yellow satin jacket with a trim of white fur, powdered with black fur. This was either powdered ermine or a simulation of it in lamb's wool. The jacket is recorded in the inventory of Vermeer's possessions (see Montias, *Vermeer*, 221, 340), and it appears in several of Vermeer's paintings. See Albert Blankert, John Michael Montias, and Giles Aillaud, *Vermeer* (New York: Rizzoli, 1988), 113, 131, 132, 133, 144.

100 Steven Mullaney, *The Place of the Stage: License, Play and Power in Renaissance England* (University of Chicago Press, 1988).

101 We are indebted to Gil Harris for drawing our attention to the significance of copper lace and for providing references. See also MacIntyre, *Costumes and Scripts*, 93–5, although her claim that copper lace was "inexpensive" is surely contradicted by the fact that, as she notes, a single purchase of copper lace of £3. 18s. 4d. was used on a single gown and a single suit. Clothes were often bought for less than the price of the copper lace with which they were embroidered.

102 *Henslowe's Diary*, 121–2 and 169–82. On 3 July 1601, Henslowe paid the copper lace man £4 for an "owld deate" (176), and on 6 July of the same year he settled "the wholle deat" for £12. 2s. 10d. (177).

103 Ben Jonson, *Poetaster*, *Ben Jonson*, ed. Herford, vol. 4, 3. 4. 197–8.

104 Thomas Dekker, *Satiro-Mastix, or the Vntrussing of the Humorous Poet* (London, 1602), ed. Hans Scherer (Louvain: Uystpruyst, 1907), lines 409–12, 2010–12; Henry Cross, *Vertues Common-wealth* (1603), quoted in Rutter, *Documents*, 216.

105 Thomas Dekker, *The Guls Horne-booke* (London, 1609), 28–9.

106 Feuillerat, *Documents*, 409, 410. See also Ingram, *The Business of Playing*, 69–72.

107 Glynne Wickam, *Early English Stages, 1300–1660* (New York: Columbia University Press, 1963), vol. 2, part 1, 1576–1660, 37.

108 Stephen Greenblatt, *Learning to Curse: Essays in Early Modern Culture* (New York: Routledge, 1990), 162. Greenblatt's fine chapter on "Resonance and Wonder" (161–83) has shaped our argument.

109 Wickham, *Early English Stages*, 3.

110 *Cumberland, Westmoreland, Gloucestershire*, ed. Audrey Douglas and Peter Greenfield, Records of Early English Drama (University of Toronto Press, 1986), 335–9.

111 *Cambridge*, ed. Alan H. Nelson, Records of Early English Drama (University of Toronto Press, 1989), vol. 1, 123.

112 *Cambridge*, ed. Nelson, vol. 1, 189; vol. 2, 756.

113 Bentley, *Profession*, 179.

114 John Stow, *A Survey of London*, ed. Charles Kingsford (Oxford: Clarendon Press, 1908),

vol. 2, 28. In his additions to Stow, John Strype wrote that Long Lane was a "Place of Note for the sale of Apparel, Linen, and Upholsters Goods, both Second-hand and New, but chiefly for Old, for which it is of note" (John Stow, *A Survey of the Cities of London and Westminster . . . Corrected, Improved, and very much Enlarged by John Strype* [London: A. Churchill et al., 1720], Book 2, 122).

115 Thomas Dekker and John Webster, *West-Ward Hoe* (1607), in *The Dramatic Works of Thomas Dekker*, ed. Fredson Bowers (Cambridge University Press, 1958), vol. 2, 2. 2. 45–6; Thomas Dekker and John Webster, *North-Ward Hoe* (1607), in *The Dramatic Works of Dekker*, vol. 2, 2. 1. 13–15; Thomas Dekker and John Webster, *The Wonder of a Kingdome* (1636), in *The Dramatic Works of Dekker*, vol. 3, 4. 2. 56–7 (our emphasis); W. S., *The Puritaine or The Widdow of Watling-streete* (1607) in *The Shakespeare Apocrypha*, ed. C. F. Tucker Brooke (Oxford: Clarendon Press, 1918), 2. 1. 7–8.

116 Dekker, *The Wonderfull Yeare*, in *The Dramatic Works of Dekker*, vol. 2, 12 (our emphasis); Dekker, *Newes from Hell* (London, 1606), sig. F4v. See also Anon., *Muld Sacke*: "This [broker] is so cruell, that he will incroch vpon the very garments that shelter the poore and fatherlesse. I doe know (*Clinias*) a poore Widdow dwelling by me, neere Long-lane, that hath foure young Children, who for want hath beene forced to engage (to one of those Cormorants) the Couerlet of her bed, for twelue pence, and comming at night to haue it backe, she could not haue it without fourteene pence, and so in defect of two pence, shee and her Children were exposed to the extremitie of cold" (sig. B4).

117 Stow, *A Survey of London*, vol. 1, 128–9.

118 Francis Beaumont and John Fletcher, *The Woman's Prize, or The Tamer Tamed*, ed. Fredson Bowers, in *The Dramatic Works in the Beaumont and Fletcher Canon*, general ed. Fredson Bowers (Cambridge University Press, 1979), 2. 2. 37–9, 53–4; Thomas Middleton, *Michaelmas Term* (1607), ed. Richard Levin, Regents Renaissance Drama (Lincoln: University of Nebraska Press, 1966), 1. 1. 63–5; John Taylor, *Three Weekes, three daies, and three houres Obseruations and Trauel* (1617) in *The Works of John Taylor, the Water Poet*, ed. Charles Hindley (London: Reeves and Turner, 1876), 1. In Jonson's *Every Man in His Humour*, Brainworm disguises himself as a soldier, down on his luck, getting his clothes from "a *Hounds-ditch* man, sir. One of the devil's neere kinsmen, a broker" (in *Ben Jonson*, ed. Herford, vol. 3, 2. 3 and 3. 5. 31–2). See also Samuel Rowlands's *Doctor Merry-man: or, Nothing but Mirth* (London, 1616), where a "professed Courtizan" mocks those who "goe to Houns-ditch with their Cloathes / To pawne for Money lending" (sig. C4); and Rowlands's "Satyre 2" in *The letting of humours blood in the head-vaine* (1611), in which he depicts a gentleman bowing to his "Liuing-griper":

> And farre to fetch the same I will not goe,
> But into *Hounds-ditch*, to the Brokers row:
> Or any place where that trade doth remaine,
> Whether at *Holborne Conduit*, or *Long-lane*:
> If thyther you vouchsafe to turne your eye,
> And see the Pawnes that vnder forfayte lye,
> Which are foorth comming sir, and safe enough
> Sayes good-man Broker, in his new print ruffe:
> He will not stand too strictly on a day,
> Encouraging the party to delay,
> With all good wordes, the kindest may be spoke,
> He turnes the Gentleman out of his Cloake.   (sig. D2v)

119 See Stephen Greenblatt, *Renaissance Self-Fashioning: from More to Shakespeare* (University of Chicago Press, 1980); *Learning to Curse*, particularly 161–83; and *Shakespearean Negotiations: The Circulation of Social Energy in Renaissance England* (Berkeley: University of California Press, 1988).

120 Middleton, *Your Five Gallants* (1607), [1. 1] lines 2–6; [4. 1] 1915–31; [4. 2] 1946–53; [2. 3] 1141–8 and 1176; [2. 3] 1200–13; [4. 6] 2569–73.

121 Middleton, *Your Five Gallants*, [1. 2] 366–7 and 414–15; [2. 1] 619 and 806; [2. 3]

1138–40; [3. 5] 1749; [4. 6] 2290–1, 2319–20, 2341–8, 2412, 2432–7, and 2569–73; [5. 2] 2920–2.

122 Ben Jonson, *Every Man in His Humour* (acted 1598, 1616 text) in *Ben Jonson*, ed. Herford, vol. 3, 3. 5. 31–2, 4. 9. 45–50.

123 Ben Jonson, *The Alchemist* (acted 1610), in *Jonson*, ed. Herford, vol. 5, 4. 3. 63–73, 5. 4. 68, 5. 4. 84–8. We are indebted to Michael Warren for drawing this passage to our attention.

124 Thomas Dekker, *Satiromastix*, in *The Dramatic Works of Thomas Dekker*, ed. Fredson Bowers (Cambridge University Press, 1953), vol. 1, 4. 1. 129–32.

125 Dekker, *Satiromastix*, 1. 2. 352–8.

126 *Henslowe Papers*, 125.

127 MacIntyre emphasizes both the differences between the costumes for the revels and for the professional companies and the increasing outlays for costumes by the professional companies during the seventeenth century, as the theaters attempted to rival the court masque in extravagance. As she notes, this extravagance led to difficulties for all the companies and was responsible for the collapse of some companies (*Costumes and Scripts*, 322).

128 *Henslowe's Diary*, 318.

129 Quoted in Gurr, *Playgoing*, 235.

130 Bentley, *Profession*, 189.

131 Downes, *Roscius Anglicanus*, 52, 61.

132 Jonson, *Volpone* in *Ben Jonson*, ed. Herford, vol. 5, 3. 7. 221–33.

133 Scott McMillin, *The Elizabethan Theatre and "The Book of Sir Thomas More"* (Ithaca, NY: Cornell University Press, 1987), 53–4.

134 G. K. Hunter, "Flatcaps and Bluecoats: Visual Signals on the Elizabethan Stage," *Essays and Studies* (1980): 40–1 fn.

135 Hunter, "Flatcaps," 40–1 fn.

136 Bentley, *Profession*, 230, 231.

137 Phyllis Rackin, "Androgyny, Mimesis, and the Marriage of the Boy Heroine on the English Renaissance Stage," *PMLA* 102 (1987): 29–41, especially 38; Orgel, *Impersonations*, 33–34, 104. On the relation of clothes to gender, see Lisa Jardine, *Still Harping on Daughters* (Brighton: Harvester, 1983), and, on the partial homology between women and boys, Jardine's "Twins and Travesties: Gender, Dependency and Sexual Availability," in *Erotic Politics: Desire on the Renaissance Stage*, ed. Susan Zimmerman (New York: Routledge, 1992), 27–38. On the homoerotics of *Twelfth Night* (with particular attention to the relation between Viola and Olivia), see Valerie Traub, *Desire and Anxiety: Circulations of Sexuality in Shakespearean Drama* (London: Routledge, 1992), 117–44. Our account of *Twelfth Night* is also indebted to conversations with Margreta de Grazia, Lisa Jardine, John Kerrigan, Stephen Orgel, Phyllis Rackin, and Valerie Traub.

138 We are grateful to John Kerrigan for drawing this passage to our attention.

139 For a lucid account of the significance of naming in *Twelfth Night*, see Anne Barton, *The Names of the Comedy* (Oxford: Clarendon Press, 1990), 137–9.

140 See Rackin, "Androgyny," 38.

141 Barnabe Rich, *Riche his Farewell to Militarie Profession* (London, 1581), sig. K1.

142 Rich, *Riche his Farewell*, sig. L3v, L4.

143 On clothes in *Cymbeline*, see David Bevington, *Action Is Eloquence: Shakespeare's Language of Gesture* (Cambridge, Mass.: Harvard University Press, 1984), 63–4.

144 William Shakespeare, *Cymbeline*, in *The First Folio of Shakespeare: The Norton Facsimile*, ed. Charlton Hinman (New York: Norton, 1968), 2. 3. 133–6 (TLN 1111–14).

145 Jean-Christophe Agnew, *Worlds Apart: The Market and the Theater in Anglo-American Thought, 1550–1750* (Cambridge University Press, 1986), 35.

146 *Letters of Philip Gawdy 1579–1616* (London: J. B. Nichols, 1906), ed. Isaac Herbert Jeayes, 49.

147 Arnold, *Wardrobe*, 274, 162 n. 337.

148 *Henslowe's Diary*, 142.

149 Arnold, *Patterns of Fashion*, 44, ill. 312. See also the details of how a sleeve was laced into a doublet on 72, ill. 11B.

150 *Troilus and Cressida* (5. 2. 65–106 [TLN 3049–96]); *Troilus and Cressida*, ed. Kenneth Palmer, The Arden Shakespeare (London and New York: Methuen, 1982), 273.

151 Middleton, *The Widow*, in *The Works of Thomas Middleton*, ed. A. H. Bullen (London: John Nimmo, 1885), vol. 5, 3. 3. 24–8; see Susan Zimmerman, "Disruptive Desire: Artifice and Indeterminacy in Jacobean Comedy," in *Erotic Politics*, 50–1.

152 George C. Williamson, *Lady Anne Clifford, Countess of Dorset, Pembroke, and Montgomery, 1590–1676: Her Life, Letters and Work* (Kendal: Wilson, 1922), 460, 462.

153 Williamson, *Lady Anne Clifford*, 467, 468, 469. On Anne Clifford's construction of a "matrilineal dynasty," see Alice T. Friedman's fine analysis, "Constructing an Identity in Prose, Plaster and Paint: Lady Anne Clifford as Writer and Patron of the Arts," in *Albion's Classicism: The Visual Arts in Britain, 1550–1660*, ed. Lucy Gent (New Haven: Yale University Press, 1995), 359–76.

154 Bentley, *Profession*, 20.

155 Bentley, *Profession*, 130.

156 S. P. Cerasano, "New Renaissance Players' Wills," *Modern Philology* 82, 158 (1985): 300–1.

157 S. P. Cerasano, "Revising Philip Henslowe's Biography," *Notes and Queries* 230 (1985): 68.

158 Bentley, *Jacobean and Caroline Stage*, vol. 3, 631.

159 Bentley, *Jacobean and Caroline Stage*, vol. 3, 644, 637, 649.

160 *The Social Life of Things: Commodities in Cultural Perspective*, ed. Arjun Appadurai (Cambridge University Press, 1986).

161 Thomas Dekker, *The Shoemaker's Holiday* (1600), *The Dramatic Works of Thomas Dekker*, ed. Fredson Bowers, vol. 1 (Cambridge University Press, 1953), 1. 1. 224–35.

162 Susan Stewart, *On Longing: Narratives of the Miniature, the Gigantic, the Souvenir, the Collection* (Baltimore: The Johns Hopkins University Press, 1984), 135, 23.

163 Walter Benjamin, *The Origin of German Drama*, trans. John Osborne (London: New Left Books, 1977), 183–4.

8 TRANSVESTISM AND THE "BODY BENEATH": SPECULATING ON THE BOY ACTOR

1 Much of this chapter is a response to the work and comments of Jonathan Dollimore, Marjorie Garber, Lisa Jardine, Stephen Orgel, Phyllis Rackin, and Susan Zimmerman. We are also indebted for ideas, references, and challenges to Lynda Boose, Greg Bredbeck, Linda Charnes, Jean Howard, David Kastan, Michael Shapiro, and Valerie Traub.

2 Francis Beaumont and John Fletcher, *The Maid's Tragedy*, ed. Andrew Gurr (Berkeley: University of California Press, 1969), 5. 1. 12 S.D.

3 William Shakespeare, *Othello*, 5. 2 S.D. (TLN 3239) and *Cymbeline*, 2. 2 S.D. (TLN 903) in *The First Folio of Shakespeare: The Norton Facsimile*, ed. Charlton Hinman (New York: Norton, 1968). All further quotations from Shakespeare are from the First Folio and are followed by act-scene-line numbers keyed to *The Riverside Shakespeare*, ed. G. Blakemore Evans (Boston: Houghton Mifflin, 1974) and to the Through Line Numbers (TLN) of Hinman's *First Folio*.

4 Lisa Jardine, *Still Harping on Daughters: Women and Drama in the Age of Shakespeare* (Brighton: Harvester, 1983), 23. For important revisions to Lisa Jardine's earlier work, see her "Twins and Travesties: Gender, Dependency and Sexual Availability in *Twelfth Night*," in *Erotic Politics: Desire on the Renaissance Stage*, ed. Susan Zimmerman (New York: Routledge, 1992), 27–38.

5 Lynda Boose, "'Let It Be Hid': Iago, Renaissance Pornography, and *Othello*'s 'Grossly Gaping' Audience," unpublished MS (1987). We are deeply indebted to Professor Boose for showing us this paper.

6 Michael Neill, "Unproper Beds: Race, Adultery, and the Hideous in *Othello*," *Shakespeare Quarterly* 40, 4 (1989): 383–412.

7 See the illustrations by Boitard (1709), Loutherbourg (1785), Metz (1789), and Leney (1799) in Neill, "Unproper Beds," 386–9.

8 On the occasional presence of women on English stages prior to the Restoration, see, for instance, John Stokes, "The Wells Cordwainers Show: New Evidence Concerning Guild Entertainments in Somerset," *Comparative Drama* 19, 4 (1985–6): 332–46; G. E. Bentley, *The Jacobean and Caroline Stage*, vol. 1 (Oxford: Clarendon Press, 1941), 25; and Suzanne Gossett, "'Man-maid, begone!': Women in Masques," in *Women in the Renaissance*, ed. Kirby Farrell, Elizabeth Hageman, and Arthur Kinney (Amherst: University of Massachusetts Press, 1990), 118–35.

9 Quoted in John Harold Wilson, *All the King's Ladies: Actresses of the Restoration* (University of Chicago Press, 1958), 84.

10 William Prynne, *The Unlovelinesse of Lovelockes* (London, 1628), sig. A3v.

11 Prynne, *Lovelockes*, sigs. A3, G2.

12 Prynne, *Lovelockes*, sig. C4v (original emphasis).

13 See Wilson, *All the King's Ladies*, 84–5.

14 Aphra Behn, *The Younger Brother; Or, the Amorous Jilt*, in *The Works of Aphra Behn*, ed. Montague Summers (New York: Phaeton, 1967), 5. 2, vol. 4, 390.

15 Curiously, it seems that it was for the revelation of the *male* body that Behn was most violently criticized: taxing her with indecency, her critics claim, she writes, "*That Mr. Leigh opens his Night Gown, when he comes into the Bride-Chamber*; if he do, which is a Jest of his own making, and which I never saw, I hope he has his Cloaths on underneath? And if so, where is the Indecency?" Behn goes on to imply that the charge of indecency is specifically levelled against her as a woman writer: "had the Plays I have writ come forth under any Mans Name, and never known to have been mine; I appeal to all unbyast Judges of Sense, if they had not said that Person had made as many good Comedies, as any one Man that has writ in our Age; but a Devil on't the Woman damns the Poet." See *The Lucky Chance; Or, An Alderman's Bargain*, in *The Works of Aphra Behn*, ed. Summers, vol. 3, 186, 184.

16 Colley Cibber, *An Apology for the Life of Colley Cibber*, ed. B. R. S. Fone (Ann Arbor: University of Michigan Press, 1968), 55.

17 Nathaniel Lee, *The Rival Queens*, in *The Works of Nathaniel Lee*, ed. T. B. Stroup and A. L. Cooke (New Brunswick: Scarecrow Press, 1954), 282.

18 Stephen Orgel, *Impersonations: The Performance of Gender in Shakespeare's England* (Cambridge University Press, 1996), 71–82.

19 For an analysis of the relation between the actor's part and prosthetic body parts, see Marjorie Garber, "Fetish Envy," in *Vested Interests: Cross-Dressing and Cultural Anxiety* (New York: Routledge, 1992), 118–27.

20 An important exception, to which we are deeply indebted, is Michael Shapiro, "Crossgender Casting, Crossgender Disguise, and Anxieties of Intimacy in *Twelfth Night* and Other Plays," paper given at the Shakespeare Association of America meeting, Philadelphia, 1990. For an earlier attempt to deal with this subject, see Marvin Rosenberg, *The Masks of Othello* (Berkeley: University of California Press, 1971), 17, 19.

21 Gossett, "'Man-maid, begone!'," 134.

22 John Rainoldes, *Th' Overthrow of Stage-Playes* (London, 1599), 17.

23 Kathleen McLuskie, "The Act, the Role, and the Actor: Boy Actresses on the Elizabethan Stage," *New Theatre Quarterly* 3, 10 (1987): 120–30.

24 R. A. Foakes, *Illustrations of the English Stage 1580–1642* (London: Scolar Press, 1985).

25 Foakes, *Illustrations*, 91–3.

26 Foakes, *Illustrations*, 130, 166.

27 Foakes, *Illustrations*, 73.

28 Foakes, *Illustrations*, 118, 146.

29 Samuel Pepys, *Pepys on the Restoration Stage*, ed. H. McAfee (New Haven: Yale University Press, 1916), 94–5.

30 Ben Jonson, *The Devil is an Ass* (acted 1616), in *Ben Jonson*, ed. C. H. Herford, Percy and Evelyn Simpson (Oxford: Clarendon, 1954), vol. 6, 2. 6. 71. Michael Shapiro gives other striking examples of such play with the boy's "paps" in "Crossgender Casting."

31 John Ford, *Loues Sacrifice* (London, 1633), 5. 1, sig. K2v.

32 For other accounts of Cleopatra and/as the boy actor, see Phyllis Rackin, "Shakespeare's Boy Cleopatra, the Decorum of Nature, and the Golden World of Poetry," *PMLA* 87 (1972): 201–12; Michael Shapiro, "Boying Her Greatness: Shakespeare's Use of Coterie Drama in *Antony and Cleopatra*," *Modern Language Review* 77, 1 (1982): 1–15; and William E. Gruber, "The Actor in the Script: Affective Strategies in Shakespeare's *Antony and Cleopatra*," *Comparative Drama* 19, 1 (1985): 30–48.

33 Anon., *Frederyke of Jennen* (1560), in *Cymbeline*, ed. J. M. Nosworthy, the Arden Shakespeare (London: Methuen, 1955), 197.

34 Behn, *The Lucky Chance*, 186.

35 See John Wilmot, Earl of Rochester, *Poems On Several Occasions with Valentinian* (London, 1696). Act 5, scene 5 of *Valentinian* opens with "Valentinian *and the* Eunuch *discovered on a Couch*." Valentinian says:

> Oh let me press these balmy Lips all day,
> And bath my Love scorch'd Soul in thy moist Kisses.
> Now by my Joys thou art all sweet and soft,
> And thou shalt be the Altar of my love;
> Upon thy Beauties hourly will I offer,
> And pour out Pleasure and blest Sacrifice,
> To the dear Memory of my Lucina . . .   (215)

36 For a fine early study of the ways in which the boy actor created "a liminal moment when gender definitions were open to play," see Phyllis Rackin, "Androgyny, Mimesis, and the Marriage of the Boy Heroine on the English Renaissance Stage," *PMLA* 102 (1987): 29–41, 38. For another important account, see Jean Howard, *The Stage and Social Struggle in Early Modern England* (London: Routledge, 1994), 93–128.

37 John Russell Brown has pointed out to us that, in the dominant theatrical tradition, the "unpinning" refers to Desdemona's *hair*. That there is no Renaissance warrant for this is suggested by the *Oxford English Dictionary*, which actually quotes Desdemona's lines as referring to the unpinning of *clothes*, but gives no examples for the unpinning of hair.

38 We are here indebted to Raima Evans's unpublished work on this scene.

39 Anon., *The Taming of a Shrew* (1594), in *Narrative and Dramatic Sources of Shakespeare*, ed. Geoffrey Bullough, vol. 1 (London: Routledge and Kegan Paul, 1957), 71.

40 Anon., *The Taming*, 72.

41 Rainoldes, *Th' Overthrow of Stage-Playes*, 34 (our emphasis).

42 *The Taming of the Shrew*, ed. Brian Morris, the Arden Shakespeare (London: Methuen, 1981), 168.

43 Anon., *Frederyke of Jennen*, 202.

44 Barnabe Rich, "Of Apolonius and Silla" (1581), in *Twelfth Night*, ed. J. M. Lothian and T. W. Craik, the Arden Shakespeare (Methuen: London and New York, 1975), 177.

45 Jean Calvin, *The Sermons of M. John Calvin Upon . . . Deuteronomie*, trans. Arthur Golding (London, 1583), 773 (our emphasis).

46 Prynne, *Lovelockes*, sig. A3; Prynne, *Histrio-Mastix* (London, 1633), 171.

47 Prynne, *Histrio-Mastix*, 207 (original emphasis).

48 See Frederick S. Boas, *University Drama in the Tudor Age* (Oxford University Press, 1914), 231–4; K. Young, "William Gager's Defence of the Academic Stage," *Transactions of the Wisconsin Academy of Sciences, Arts, and Letters* 18 (1916): 593–638; J. W. Binns, "Women or Transvestites on the Elizabethan Stage?: An Oxford Controversy," *Sixteenth Century Journal* 5, 2 (1974): 95–120; Jardine, *Still Harping on Daughters*, 14–17.

49 Boas, *University Drama*, pp. 105–6; Rainoldes, *Th' Overthrow of Stage-Playes*, 45.

50 Rainoldes, *Th' Overthrow of Stage-Playes*, 96.

51 Our account of transvestism, and of the boy actor in general, is deeply indebted to Jonathan Dollimore's "Subjectivity, Sexuality, and Transgression: The Jacobean Connection," *Renaissance Drama* n.s. 17 (1986): 53–81. See also his "Early Modern: Cross-Dressing in Early Modern England," in *Sexual Dissidence: Augustine to Wilde, Freud to Foucault* (Oxford University Press, 1991), 284–306.

52 On the eroticism of clothes in the Renaissance, see Stephen Greenblatt, "Erotische

Provokation im Elizabethanischen Theater," *Shakespeare Jahrbuch* 124 (1988): 56–61; and Richard Levin, "The Economics and Erotics of Cross-Class Dressing in Early Modern (formerly Renaissance) English Drama," *Journal of Theatre and Drama* 3 (1997): 93–101. Levin emphasizes the eroticism of class as opposed to gender in the fetishizing of clothes in the Renaissance.

53 Boose, " 'Let It Be Hid.' "
54 Prynne, *Histrio-Mastix*, 169.
55 Prynne, *Histrio-Mastix*, 169.
56 Prynne, *Histrio-Mastix*, 135.
57 Phillip Stubbes, *The Anatomie of Abuses* (1583), ed. Frederick J. Furnivall, New Shakespeare Society (London: Trübner, 1877–79), 144–5.
58 Our account of fetishism is deeply indebted to Marjorie Garber. See *Vested Interests*, particularly 118–27.
59 Sigmund Freud, "Fetishism" (1927), in *The Standard Edition of the Complete Psychological Works of Sigmund Freud*, trans. James Strachey (London: The Hogarth Press,), vol. 21 (1961), 149–57, 156.
60 Freud, "Fetishism," 155 (our emphasis).
61 Sigmund Freud, "The Sexual Aberrations," in *Three Essays on the Theory of Sexuality* (1905), in *The Standard Edition of the Complete Psychological Works of Sigmund Freud*, trans. James Strachey (London: The Hogarth Press), vol. 8 (1953), 153–5.
62 Freud, "The Sexual Aberrations," 169.

9 (IN)ALIENABLE POSSESSIONS: GRISELDA, CLOTHING, AND THE EXCHANGE OF WOMEN

1 We are particularly indebted in this chapter to conversations with and the work of Margaret Rose Jaster and David Wallace. See Jaster's chapter "Painted Puppets: Dressing and Undressing in Early Modern England," in "Fashioning the Minde and Condicions: the Uses and Abuses of Apparel in Early Modern England," Ph.D. thesis, University of Maryland, College Park, 1992.
2 Giovanni Boccaccio, *The Decameron* (trans. into English 1620), ed. W. E. Henley (New York: AMS Press, 1967), 295. All further references to this translation are in our text.
3 The woodcuts were printed in Petrarca, *Historia Griseldis*, trans. Heinrich Steinhöwel (Ulm: Johann Zainer, 1473).
4 For Petrarch's letter on the subject, see James H. Robinson, *Petrarch, the First Modern Scholar and Man of Letters* (New York: Putnam, 1898), 191–6.
5 *The Works of Geoffrey Chaucer*, ed. Alfred W. Pollard et al. (London: Macmillan, 1965), "The Clerk of Oxford's Tale," line 385, p. 191. For a fine analysis of the divergent "translations" of Boccaccio in Petrarch and Chaucer, see David Wallace, " 'Whan She Translated Was': Humanism, Tyranny, and the Petrarchan Academy" in *Chaucerian Polity: Absolutist Lineages and Associational Forms in England and Italy* (Stanford University Press, 1997), 261–98.
6 Francis Petrarch, *Letters of Old Age: Rerum Senilium Libri I-XVIII*, vol. 2 (Books X–XVIII), trans. Aldo S. Bernardo, Saul Levin, and Reta A. Bernardo (Baltimore: The Johns Hopkins University Press, 1992), 656. The Latin version of the tale, with Italian translation, appears in *Opere Latine di Francesco Petrarca*, vol. 2, ed. Antonietta Bufano (Turin: Unione Tipografico, 1975), 1312–39.
7 *Opere Latine*, vol. 2, 1336.
8 "Sen. XVII.1" in Ernest H. Wilkins, *Petrarch's Later Years* (Cambridge, Mass.: The Medieval Academy of America, 1959), 243.
9 Petrarch, "Testamentum" in *Opere Latine*, vol. 2, 1352.
10 The notion that the *magister* should be appropriately dressed to step into the role is suggested by Machiavelli's famous letter on the composition of *The Prince*. He wrote to Francesco Vettori in 1513 that, in the afternoons, he would retire to the woods with Dante or Petrarch or a "minor" poet like Ovid, and read of amorous love. Then, after a slanging

match with peasants in the local inn, "I return home and go into my study. On the threshold I strip off my muddy, sweaty, workaday clothes, and put on the robes of the court and palace, and in this graver dress I enter the antique courts of the ancients and am welcomed by them" (Letter of 10 December 1513, *The Literary Works of Machiavelli*, ed. J. R. Hale [London: Oxford University Press, 1961], 138). We are grateful to Dominick La Capra for drawing the relevance of this letter to our attention.

11 Stephanie Jed, *Chaste Thinking: the Rape of Lucretia and the Birth of Humanism* (Bloomington: Indiana University Press, 1989). On the implications of Petrarch's involvement with Milanese absolutism in his rewriting of Boccaccio, see Wallace, *Chaucerian Polity*, 270–86.

12 Giovanni Boccaccio, *The Decameron*, trans. Mark Musa and Peter Bondanella (New York: New American Library, 1982), 674.

13 Petrarch, *Letters of Old Age*, vol. 2, 660.

14 In 1355, Petrarch responded to a letter from Francesco Nelli that, he claimed, had the "appearance" of a "rather dishevelled lover." Wallace notes that Petrarch treats Boccaccio's tale as itself "dishevelled," in need of reclothing in "the *ornatus difficilis* of humanist Latin" (283, 285).

15 Our analysis of *spalliere* and *cassoni* is deeply indebted to Cristelle L. Baskins, "Griselda, or the Renaissance Bride Stripped Bare by Her Bachelor in Tuscan *Cassone* Painting," *Stanford Italian Review* 10. 2 (1991): 153–75; Irene Fizer, "Rocabianca's Griselda: Boccaccio and his Illustrators" (an unpublished paper, which Irene Fizer generously shared with us); Brucia Witthoft, "Marriage Rituals and Marriage Chests in Quattrocento Florence," *Artibus et Historiae* 5 (1982): 43–59; Suzanne L. Wofford, "The Social Aesthetics of Rape: Closural Violence in Boccaccio and Botticelli," in *Creative Imitation: New Essays on Renaissance Literature in Honor of Thomas M. Greene*, ed. David Quint, Margaret W. Ferguson, G. W. Pigman III, and Wayne A. Rebhorn (Binghamton, NY: Medieval and Renaissance Texts and Studies, 1992), 189–238; Ellen Callmann, *Apollonio di Giovanni* (Oxford: Clarendon Press, 1974); Anne R. Barriault, *Spalliera Paintings of Renaissance Tuscany: Fables of Poets for Patrician Homes* (University Park: Pennsylvania State University Press, 1994); Jaster, "Painted Puppets." We are also grateful to Pat Simons for her caveat about the presence of *cassoni* in all wedding processions.

16 On this "threat of contamination" in Chaucer's version, see Jaster, "Painted Puppets."

17 Chaucer, "The Clerk of Oxford's Tale," lines 372–85 (191).

18 Wallace notes that Petrarch's account of the "translation" of Griselda by Walter parallels his own translation and chastisement of Boccaccio's vernacular story (*Chaucerian Polity*, 285).

19 *Opere Latine*, vol. 2, 1312.

20 Petrarch, *Letters of Old Age*, vol. 2, 668; *Opere Latine*, vol. 2, 1336–8.

21 *Decameron*, trans. Musa and Bondanella, 672.

22 Giovanni Boccaccio, *Il Decamerone* in *Tutte le opere di Giovanni Boccaccio*, ed. Vittore Branca (Milan: Arnaldo Mondadori, 1976), vol. 4, 954; *Decameron*, trans. Musa and Bondanella, 681.

23 Wallace persuasively argues that Dioneo's tale is a deliberate subversion of the topic of the tenth day's tales: liberality and magnificence (*Chaucerian Polity*, 278, 280). The tyrannical Gualtieri is the antithesis of liberality and magnificence; it is he, not Griselda, who requires "translation."

24 Randle Cotgrave, *A Dictionarie of the French and English Tongues* (London, 1611).

25 William Shakespeare, *Henry IV, Part Two*, in *The Norton Facsimile: The First Folio of Shakespeare*, ed. Charlton Hinman (New York: Norton, 1968), 3. 2. 23 (TLN 1555–7) and 3. 2. 205 (TLN 1740).

26 *Henslowe's Diary*, ed. R. A. Foakes and R. T. Rickert (Cambridge University Press, 1961), 130; Cyrus Hoy, "Commentary" to *Patient Grissill*, in *Introductions, Notes, and Commentaries to Texts in "The Dramatic Works of Thomas Dekker,"* ed. Fredson Bowers (Cambridge University Press, 1980), vol. 1, 130.

27 *Henslowe's Diary*, 125, 128, 129; Hoy, "Commentary," 130.

28 Petrarch, *Letters of Old Age*, vol. 2, 660.

29 Thomas Dekker, *Patient Grissill*, in *The Dramatic Works of Thomas Dekker*, ed. Fredson Bowers (Cambridge University Press, 1953), vol. 1, 2. 2. 63–7. All further references to the play are given in our text.

30 See Henry Kamen, *Inquisition and Society in Spain in the Sixteenth and Seventeenth Centuries* (London: Weidenfeld and Nicolson, 1985), 122–3.

31 *Henslowe's Diary*, p. 130.

32 William Langland, *The Vision of William Concerning Piers the Plowman: The Crowley Text; or Text B*, ed. Walter W. Skeat (Oxford University Press, 1869), Passus 15. 162. In Passus 8. 1, Langland describes himself as "yrobed in russet."

33 Thomas Deloney, "Of Patient Grissel and a Noble Marquess," in *The Garland of Good-Will*, ed. James Henry Dixon, in *Early English Poetry, Ballads, and Popular Literature of the Middle Ages*, Percy Society vol. 30 (London: Percy Society, 1852), 83.

34 Deloney, "Grissel," 87.

35 Samuel Richardson, *Pamela; Or, Virtue Rewarded* (1740, 1801; Harmondsworth: Penguin, 1980), 57.

36 John Lyly, *Euphues: the Anatomy of Wit* (1580), ed. Edward Arber (Westminster: Constable, 1895), 443.

37 Deloney, "Grissel," 87.

38 Oliver Cromwell, letter written at Cambridge, September 1643, in *The Letters and Speeches of Oliver Cromwell*, ed. Thomas Carlyle (London: Methuen, 1904), vol. 1, 154.

39 Joseph Hall, "Satyre 1.3," in *The Poems of Joseph Hall*, ed. Arnold Davenport (Liverpool University Press, 1969), 15.

40 John Ford, *The Broken Heart* (London, 1633), 5. 2, sig. I 5.

41 Scipione Mercurio, *De gli errori popolari d'Italia. Libri sette* (Padua: Francesco Bolzetta, 1645), 182. We are grateful to Mary Galucci for this and other references and for her analysis of *spogliare*.

42 William Shakespeare, *The Tragedie of King Lear*, in *The First Folio of Shakespeare*, ed. Hinman, 3. 4. 103–8 (TLN 1882–8).

43 *A wife now the widdow of Sir Thomas Overbury . . . Whereunto are added many witty characters* (London: A. Crooke, 1638), sig. G.

44 Baskins, "Griselda," 156.

45 Witthoft, "Marriage Chests," 44.

46 Witthoft, "Marriage Chests," 55, fn. 21.

47 See Witthoft, "Marriage Chests," 47; Wofford, "The Social Aesthetics of Rape," 199.

48 Christiane Klapisch-Zuber, *Women, Family and Ritual in Renaissance Italy* (Chicago University Press, 1985), 224–5.

49 Klapisch-Zuber, *Women, Family and Ritual*, 227, fn. 49.

50 Sir Frederick Pollock and Frederic William Maitland, *The History of English Law*, vol. 2 (Cambridge University Press, 1968), 405–6.

51 George C. Williamson, *Lady Anne Clifford, Countess of Dorset, Pembroke, and Montgomery, 1590–1676: Her Life, Letters and Work* (Kendal: Wilson, 1922), 460. See also the will of Thomas Radcliffe, third Earl of Sussex, dated 1 April 1583: "I freely give to the Lady Frances my wife (if she overlive me) the jewels, billiments, chains, buttons, aglets and other ornaments whatsoever dressed with precious stones or pearls or without which have been known to have been for the most part in her custody and use; with her apparel and other ornaments belonging to her person, saving one great table diamond, one great table ruby, one great pointed diamond" (F. G. Emmison, *Elizabethan Life: Wills of Essex Gentry and Merchants* [Chelmsford: Essex County Council, 1978], 1–2).

52 Henry Swinburn, *A Brief Treatise of Testaments and Last Wills* (London, 1611), 49–51.

53 Swinburn, *Testaments and Last Wills*, 52.

54 T. E., *The Lawes Resolution of Womens Rights* (London, 1632), 129–30.

55 Virgil M. Harris, *Ancient, Curious and Famous Wills* (Boston: Little, Brown, and Company, 1911), 36.

56 Harris, *Ancient Wills*, 36.

57 See Tim Stretton, *Women Waging Law in Elizabethan England* (Cambridge University Press, 1998), 21–42.

58 Amy Erickson, *Women and Property in Early Modern England* (London: Routledge, 1993), 61–78; 139–43; 223–36. We are grateful to Phyllis Rackin for drawing this book to our attention and discussing the significance of Erickson's findings.

59 For earlier English attitudes to the tensions between Italian republicanism and absolutism, see Wallace, *Chaucerian Polity*.

60 J. H. Baker and S. F. C. Milson, *Sources for English Legal History* (London: Butterworth and Co., 1986), 119. See also Swinburn, citing the edict, *Testaments and Last Wills*, 92.

61 Harris, *Ancient Wills*, 39.

62 William Forrest, *The History of Grisild the Second*, ed. W. D. Macray, Roxburghe Club (London: Chiswick Press, 1875), 5. All further page references are given in our text.

63 Garrett Mattingly, *Catherine of Aragon* (Boston: Little, Brown, and Co., 1941), 176.

64 Frank A. Mumby, *The Girlhood of Queen Elizabeth: A Narrative in Contemporary Letters* (Boston: Houghton Mifflin Co., 1910), 5.

65 John E. Paul, *Katherine of Aragon and her Friends* (New York: Fordham University Press, 1966), 136.

66 Paul, *Katherine of Aragon*, 136.

67 Elizabeth had her own methods of appropriation. When Mary Queen of Scots was forced to sell a prized possession, a string of pearls like "black muscat grapes," in 1563, Elizabeth secretly bought them for £3,600 and publicized her acquisition in the "Ermine" portrait of 1583, now in Hatfield House. Jane Ashelford, *A Visual History of Costume: The Sixteenth Century* (London: Batsford, 1983), 66.

68 *The Pleasant and Sweet History of patient Grissell* (London, c. 1630).

69 John Phillip, *The Play of Patient Grissell*, ed. W. W. Greg and Ronald B. McKerrow (London: Malone Society, 1909), lines 56–8.

70 J. E. Neale, *Elizabeth I and Her Parliaments 1559–1581* (London: Jonathan Cape, 1953), 133.

71 Neale, *Elizabeth I*, 133.

72 Neale, *Elizabeth I*, 146.

73 Neale, *Elizabeth I*, 149.

74 Neale, *Elizabeth I*, 147.

75 Neale, *Elizabeth I*, 149. Thanks to Miranda Haddad for first calling our attention to this passage.

76 Chaucer, "The Clerk of Oxford's Tale," lines 652–8.

77 Petrarch, *Letters of Old Age*, vol. 2, 663.

78 Petrarch, *Letters of Old Age*, vol. 2, 667.

79 "An Homily against Excess of Apparel" (1563) in *Certain Sermons or Homilies* (Oxford University Press, 1844), 276.

80 Quoted in Richard L. Greaves, *Society and Religion in Elizabethan England* (Minneapolis: University of Minnesota Press, 1981), 506.

10 OF GHOSTS AND GARMENTS: THE MATERIALITY OF MEMORY ON THE RENAISSANCE STAGE

1 We are particularly indebted to the work and comments of Margreta de Grazia and Phyllis Rackin, and to the suggestions of John Kerrigan, Laurie Maguire, Michael Neill, and Stephen Orgel.

2 *Light: A Journal of Psychical, Occult and Mystical Research*, vol. 11, no. 537, Sat., 18 April 1891, 127. We are indebted to Pamela Thurschwell for this reference.

3 Charles Dickens, *Great Expectations*, ed. Angus Calder (Harmondsworth: Penguin, 1965), 274.

4 Tobias Smollett, *The Expedition of Humphrey Clinker*, ed. Lewis M. Knapp (Oxford University Press, 1966), 53.

5 All quotations from *Hamlet*, unless otherwise noted, are from Q2 (*The Tragicall Historie*

of Hamlet, Prince of Denmarke [London, 1604]) as reproduced in *Shakespeare's Plays in Quarto*, ed. Michael J. B. Allen and Kenneth Muir (Berkeley: University of California Press, 1981). All further quotations are followed in the text by act, scene, and line numbers keyed to *The Riverside Shakespeare*, ed. G. Blakemore Evans (Boston: Houghton Mifflin, 1974) and the Through Line Numbers (TLN) of *The Norton Facsimile: The First Folio of Shakespeare*, ed. Charlton Hinman (New York: Norton, 1968).

6 John Gielgud, "Notes on Costume, Scenery and Stage Business" in Rosamond Gilder, *John Gielgud's Hamlet* (Oxford University Press, 1937), 33, 47.

7 Raymond Mander and Joe Mitchenson, *Hamlet Through the Ages: A Pictorial Record from 1709*, ed. Herbert Marshall (London: Rockliff, 1952), 95, 28, 29, 33, 100, 34.

8 W. W. Greg, "Hamlet's Hallucination," *Modern Language Review* 12 (1917): 393–421, especially 412–13.

9 See Richard Flatter, *Hamlet's Father* (New Haven: Yale University Press, 1949).

10 *Henslowe's Diary*, ed. R. A. Foakes and R. T. Rickert (Cambridge University Press, 1961), 318, 321.

11 Fools' costumes, along with other kinds of clothing, appear in the inventories of Renaissance wonder-cabinets, so it is not implausible that Summers's clothes (or clothes that were *claimed* to have been Summers's) would have been preserved. See, for instance, John Tradescant, *Musaeum Tradescantianum: Or, A Collection of Rarities* (London, 1657), which catalogues "Little *Jeffreyes* Boots" and "Little *Jeffreyes* Masking-Suit," along with "Handkerchiffs of severall sorts of excellent needle-work," "*Henry* the 8 his Stirrups, Haukes-hoods, Gloves," and "*Anne* of *Bullens* Night-vayle embroidered with silver" and "silver knit-gloves" (47–9).

12 In *The Works of Thomas Nashe*, ed. Ronald B. McKerrow (London: A. H. Bullen, 1905), vol. 3, 233.

13 Shakespeare, *The life and death of King John*, in *The Norton Facsimile: The First Folio of Shakespeare*, ed. Charlton Hinman (New York: Norton, 1968), 3. 4. 93–7.

14 See John Kerrigan, "Hieronimo, Hamlet and Remembrance," *Essays in Criticism* 31 (1981): 105–26.

15 Robert Greene, *Alphonsus King of Aragon*, ed. W. W. Greg (Oxford: Malone Society, 1926), sig. Ev.

16 John Webster, *The White Devil* (1612), in *The Complete Works of John Webster*, ed. F. L. Lucas (Oxford University Press, 1937), vol.1, 5. 4. 118.

17 John Marston, *Antonio's Revenge*, in *The Plays of John Marston*, ed. H. Harvey Wood (London: Oliver and Boyd, 1934), vol. 1, 3. 4. 107.

18 Clare Gittings, *Death, Burial and the Individual in Early Modern England* (Beckenham, Kent: Croom Helm, 1984), 173, 175.

19 Sir Nicholas Harris Nicolas, *Testamenta Vetusta* (London: Nichols and Son, 1826), vol. 1, 73, 74, 79.

20 F. G. Emmison, *Elizabethan Life: Wills of Essex Gentry and Merchants* (Chelmsford: Essex County Council, 1978), 64, 70, 180.

21 Emmison, *Wills of Essex*, 175

22 Emmison, *Wills of Essex*, 221.

23 Phyllis Rackin, *Stages of History: Shakespeare's English Chronicles* (Ithaca, NY: Cornell University Press, 1990), 212.

24 Julian Litten, *The English Way of Death: The Common Funeral since 1450* (London: Robert Hale, 1991), 181, 184, 183.

25 Anon., *A Warning for Faire Women* (London, 1599), sig. A2v.

26 For a skeptical reading of Walton's account, see Helen Gardner, "Dean Donne's Monument in St. Paul's," in *Evidence in Literary Scholarship*, ed. René Wellek and Alvaro Ribeiro (Oxford: Clarendon Press, 1979), 29–44.

27 Edmund Gosse, *The Life and Letters of John Donne* (London: William Heinemann, 1899), vol. 2, 282.

28 For the inscription and the problem of translating it, see John Donne, *Deaths Duell*, ed. Geoffrey Keynes (Boston: David Godine, 1973), 43–4. John Sparrow suggests a different

translation: "This is my body's shroud, may my soul's shroud be that of Jesus." (Joe Farrell has independently communicated to us a similar translation.) Sparrow notes that Donne was familiar "with Alfonso Paleotti's treatise on the Sindon, or winding-sheet, of Christ preserved in Turin," in John Donne, *Devotions on Emergent Occasions*, ed. John Sparrow (Cambridge University Press, 1923), 44. See also Catherine Creswell, "Reading Subjectivity: The Body, the Text, the Author in John Donne," Ph.D. thesis, SUNY Buffalo, 1992, 109–10.

29 Or possibly after his dissolution (see Gardner, "Donne's Monument").

30 See Ethan M. Kavaler, "Being the Count of Nassau: Refiguring Identity in Space, Time, and Stone," in *Beeld en Zelfbeeld in de Nederlandse Kunst, 1550–1750*, ed. Reindert Falkenburg, Jan de Jong, Herman Roodenburg, and Frits Scholten (*Nederlands Kunst-historisch Jaarboek* 1995), 13–51. The device was copied by Maximilian Colt in the early seventeenth century for his monument to Sir Francis Vere, but Colt erases the absolute contrast by representing Vere below clothed.

31 Euripides, *Hecuba*, trans. William Arrowsmith, in *Euripides III, The Complete Greek Tragedies*, ed. David Grene and Richmond Lattimore (University of Chicago Press, 1958), lines 26–8.

32 Similarly in *The Changeling*, Alonzo's Ghost displays his own maimed body; he appears to Deflores, "*shewing him the hand whose finger he had cut off.*" Thomas Middleton and William Rowley, *The Changeling* (London, 1653), sig. F2, 4. 1 S.D.

33 Thomas Kyd, *Cornelia*, in *The Works of Thomas Kyd*, ed. Frederick S. Boas (Oxford: Clarendon Press, 1955), 3. 1. 75–86.

34 1. 2. 200 [TLN 391], 1. 2. 227 [TLN 423], 228 [TLN 424], 1. 4. 52 [TLN 637].

35 *The Second Part of Henry the Sixt*, in *The Norton Facsimile: The First Folio of Shakespeare* (New York: Norton, 1968), ed. Charlton Hinman, 3. 2. 161 (TLN 1866); Thomas Heywood, *The English Traveller* (London, 1633), sig. Ev.

36 Jacques Lacan, "The Mirror Stage as Formative of the Function of the I as Revealed in Psychoanalytic Experience," in *Ecrits*, trans. Alan Sheridan (New York: Norton, 1977), 4.

37 Jacques Derrida, *Specters of Marx: The State of the Debt, the Work of Mourning, and the New International*, trans. Peggy Kamuf (New York: Routledge, 1994), 126–7.

38 Gary Wills, "Homer Alive," *New York Review of Books* 39, 8 (23 April 1992), 42. For our account of armor in Homer, and of its relevance to Shakespeare, we are indebted to John Parker.

39 *Chapman's Homer*, ed. Allardyce Nicoll, vol. 1, *The Iliad* (London: Routledge and Kegan Paul, 1957), Book 16, lines 180–4.

40 Thomas Kyd, *The Spanish Tragedy*, in *The Works of Thomas Kyd*, ed. Frederick S. Boas (Oxford: Clarendon Press, 1955), 1. 2. 190.

41 See Nigel Llewellyn, *The Art of Death: Visual Culture in the English Death Ritual, c.1500–c.1800* (London: Reaktion Books, 1991), 68; Litten, *The English Way of Death*, 176–81.

42 Martin Holmes, *Shakespeare and His Players* (London: John Murray, 1972), 152. We are indebted to Holmes's account of stage armor throughout this paragraph.

43 On the "unrecoverable heroic world" of sword-and-buckler and "the sequestration of violence to the bureaucratic state," see Sheldon P. Zittner, "Hamlet, Duellist," in *Hamlet: Critical Essays*, ed. Joseph G. Price (New York: Garland, 1986), 123–43, especially 124–28.

44 *Pericles, Prince of Tyre*, in *Shakespeare's Plays in Quarto*, ed. Allen and Muir, sig. C3 (2. 1. 118). All further references are in our text.

45 Sir Walter Ralegh, *The History of the World* (London, 1677), "Preface," sig. Bv. We are indebted for this and the following quote to Rackin, *Stages of History*, 3–5, and, more generally, to her fine account of the emergence of "history" at the expense of the dispossessed. See, in particular, chapters 1, 4 and 5.

46 Edward Hall, *The Union of the Two Noble and Illustre Famelies of Lancastre & Yorke* (London, 1548), sig. B1.

47 *A Midsommer nights dreame* (London, 1600), in *Shakespeare's Plays in Quarto*, ed. Allen and Muir, sig. D2v, 3. 1. 107.

48 Stephen Gosson, *The Schoole of Abuse* (London, 1579), ed. Edward Arber (London: Murray and Son, 1868), 30.

49 William Prynne, *Documents Relating to the Proceedings against William Prynne*, ed. Samuel Rawson Gardiner, Camden Society n.s. vol. 18 (1877), 49; John Milton, *Apology for Smectymnus*, in *The Complete Prose Works of John Milton*, ed. Don M. Wolfe et al. (New Haven: Yale University Press, 1953), vol. 1, 886. See also Sir Henry Wotton's reference to "Haunters of theaters," *Reliquiae Wottonianae* (London, 1651), 84.

50 Ben Jonson, *The Devil is an Ass*, in *Ben Jonson*, ed. C. H. Herford, Percy and Evelyn Simpson (Oxford: Clarendon Press, 1954), vol. 6, 3. 3. 25–6.

51 Sigmund Freud, "The Uncanny," in *The Standard Edition of the Complete Psychological Works of Sigmund Freud*, ed. James Strachey (London: Hogarth Press), vol. 17 (1955), 218–52, especially 220–6.

52 For a full account of the auditory and visual materialization of the "ghostly" by thunder and lightning, see Leslie Thomson, "The Meaning of *Thunder and Lightning*: Stage Directions and Audience Expectations," *Early Theatre* (forthcoming).

53 Terry Castle, "Phantasmagoria: Spectral Technology and the Metaphors of Modern Reverie," *Critical Inquiry* 15, 1 (1988): 26–51.

54 Stephen Greenblatt has written brilliantly throughout his work about the Renaissance theater's ambivalent relation to magic and technology. See in particular *Learning to Curse: Essays in Early Modern Culture* (New York: Routledge, 1990), 161–3.

55 John Gee, *New Shreds of the old Snare* (London, 1624), 17, 20.

56 Jane Cooper, *Green Notebook, Winter Road* (Gardiner, Maine: Tilbury House, 1994), 27.

57 Hallett Smith, *Elizabethan Poetry: A Study in Conventions, Meaning, and Expression* (Cambridge, Mass.: Harvard University Press, 1952), 108–19.

58 *Hamlet*, 1. 1. 45, 43, 50 (TLN 54, 55, 63), 1. 4. 44–5 (TLN 629–30).

59 Janet Adelman, *Suffocating Mothers: Fantasies of Maternal Origin in Shakespeare's Plays, "Hamlet" to "The Tempest"* (New York: Routledge, 1992), 11–37.

60 Amy Louise Erickson, *Women and Property in Early Modern England* (London: Routledge, 1993), 65.

61 Jasper Griffin comments on the symbolic significance of Odysseus's bed: "The bed . . . turns into the vital key which allows husband and wife to find each other at last. Odysseus built it, as part of his house; unmoved and unrevealed to any outsiders, it embodies the solidity and wholeness of their union" (*Homer on Life and Death* [Oxford: Clarendon Press, 1980], 13).

62 Sasha Roberts, "Lying among the Classics: Ritual and Motif in Elite Elizabethan and Jacobean Beds," in *Albion's Classicism: The Visual Arts in Britain, 1550–1660*, ed. Lucy Gent (New Haven: Yale University Press, 1995), 327.

63 On the extent to which Shakespeare's will breaks with customary forms, see E. A. J. Honigman, "The Second-Best Bed," *The New York Review of Books* 38, 18 (November 7, 1991), 27–30; and Richard Wilson, *Will Power: Essays on Shakespearean Authority* (London: Harvester Wheatsheaf, 1993), 184–237. We are generally indebted to Wilson's suggestive account.

64 E. K. Chambers, *William Shakespeare: A Study of Fact and Problems* (Oxford: Clarendon Press, 1930), vol. 2, 170, 172, 173.

65 Shakespeare's will is not normative. The rigorous enforcement of patrilineal inheritance seems to have been resisted by most working people in early modern England. While sons normally inherited land (with the exception of Yorkshire, where daughters also inherited), land itself was so frequently bought and sold that in Terling, Essex, of a sample of twenty-one freeholds, not a single one remained in the male line during the seventeenth century. Even if daughters did not usually inherit land, "their parents tended to compensate them with a substantially larger share of moveable goods than their brothers had, in order to approximately balance all children's shares of parental wealth" (Erickson, *Women and Property*, 66, 224).

66 Quoted in Wilson, *Will Power*, 210.

67 On the diminishing rights of widows to dower in the Renaissance, see Wilson, *Will Power*,

209–10. But for more detailed analysis of the complex legal situation, see Erickson, *Women and Property*, and Tim Stretton, *Women Waging Law in Elizabethan England* (Cambridge University Press, 1998).

68 Quoted in Roberts, "Lying among the Classics," 327.

69 The public significance of the "royall bed" is frequently noted in Shakespeare's plays. In *The Winter's Tale*, Dion recommends remarriage to Leontes "to blesse the Bed of Majesty again" (5. 1. 33 [TLN 2765]); in *Richard II*, Bolingbroke accuses Richard's favorites of breaking "the possession of a Royall Bed" (3. 1. 13 [TLN 1325]); in *Henry V*, Henry speaks of the king's "Bed Maiesticall" (4. 1. 267 [TLN 2117]).

70 Anthony Scoloker, *Diaphantus, or the Passions of Loue* (London, 1604), sig. E4v.

71 Thomas Dekker, *The Dead Tearme* (London, 1608), sig. G3.

72 Greg, *Henslowe Papers*, 53, 54.

73 The significance of the *absence* of the Ghost at the conclusion of the play struck Alexandre Dumas who, for his 1847 production, rewrote the final act with the Ghost at the center of the action. Having pronounced on the deaths of Laertes, Gertrude, and Claudius, his sentence to Hamlet is: "Tu vivras!" ["You will live!"]. Dumas's version thus works in the opposite direction from Shakespeare's, toward the reconciliation of father and son. See Romy Heylen, *Translation, Poetics, and the Stage: Six French Hamlets* (New York: Routledge, 1993), 53–5.

74 Harold Jenkins notes of "habit" that "its original meaning, dress, was still the usual one; and indeed the passage beautifully illustrates how a word which at first referred to clothing can come to denote customary behaviour," in *Hamlet*, ed. Harold Jenkins, the Arden Shakespeare (London: Methuen, 1982), 521.

75 On memory, stamping and materiality, we are deeply indebted to Margreta de Grazia's unpublished paper, "Embodied Memory in *Hamlet*."

76 Q2 reads here: "And there I see such blacke and greeued spots / As will leaue there their tinc't." The curious opposition between "will not leaue" (F) and "will leaue" (Q2) is partially undone by the ambiguity of "leave," which, as Harold Jenkins observes, "means either cease, give up (F) or cause to remain behind (F)" (*Hamlet*, 324).

77 Scarlet was, by the late sixteenth century, made from cochineal beetles imported from Mexico. The beetles looked like, and were constantly mistaken for, seeds, hence the name "grain." For more on scarlet dye, see our chapter 2.

78 De Grazia, "Embodied Memory," 8.

79 "Stuff" could mean matter generally, but it was directly related to the Italian *stoffa*, a piece of rich textile fabric, and was frequently used in English both for the material for making garments and for a specific kind of woolen cloth. See the *Oxford English Dictionary*, heading 5.

CONCLUSION: THE END(S) OF LIVERY

1 William Tyndale, *The Five Books of Moses called the Pentateuch*, ed. J. I. Mombert (Fontwell, Sussex: Centaur Press, 1967). The Matthew's Bible of 1537 gives the following marginal gloss on Genesis 2.1: "The apparell of heauen is the sterres and planettes, etc."

2 *The Bible and Holy Scriptures* (the "Geneva" Bible, Geneva, 1560). All further biblical references are to the Geneva Bible unless otherwise noted. *The Holy Bible* (the King James or Authorized translation) (London, 1611) has "aprons" in place of "breeches."

3 Barnabe Rich, *The Honestie of this Age* (London, 1614), 20.

4 It should be noted, however, that many of the reformers were uncomfortable with the analogy between God and a tailor. Calvin, for instance, wrote that "we must not take [Moses'] wordes, as thoughe God were a Tawer of skinnes, or a Tailer," in *A Commentarie of John Caluine, vpon the first booke of Moses*, trans. Thomas Tymme (London, 1578), 118. And the Geneva Bible glosses the statement that God "made coates of skinnes" with the marginal "Or gaue them knowledge to make them selues coates."

5 Michael Neill, *Issues of Death: Mortality and Identity in English Renaissance Tragedy*

(Oxford: Clarendon Press, 1997), 8–9. We are grateful to Michael Neill for comments and suggestions and to Susan Snyder for drawing this passage to our attention.

6 James Howell, *Paroimiographia* (London, 1659), 13.

7 Henry Ainsworth, *Annotations upon the first book of Moses, called Genesis* (Amsterdam, 1616), sig. D2v.

8 Abraham Rosse, *An Exposition on the Fourteene first Chapters of Genesis* (London, 1626), 70.

9 John Milton, *Paradise Lost* (London, 1674), Book 10 (lines 211–23).

10 *Luther's Commentary on Genesis*, trans. J. Theodore Mueller (Grand Rapids, Michigan: Zondervan, 1968), vol. 1, 85–6.

11 Andrew Willet, *Hexapla in Genesin* (Cambridge, 1605), sig. E3.

12 Symon, Bishop of Ely, *A Commentary upon the First Book of Moses, called Genesis* (London, 1698), 80.

13 On clothing and "translation," see our chapter 9.

14 "And Rebekah took goodly raiment of her eldest son Esau, which were with her in the house, and put them upon Jacob her younger son" (27. 15). One of the more mysterious aspects of the story, as early Jewish commentators realized, was why Esau, who had two wives, stored this "goodly raiment" with his mother.

15 When Joseph is lost, presumed dead, Jacob transfers his affection to Benjamin, the son born after Joseph.

16 "A coat of many colors" is the translation of William Tyndale (1530), the Geneva Bible (1560), and the King James Bible (1611), although marginal glosses give the alternative "pieces" for "colors." Robert Alter in his 1996 translation renders *ketonet pasim* as "ornamented tunic" (see his *Genesis: Translation and Commentary* [New York: Norton, 1996], 209).

17 In the bible, rings, and in particular "signet" rings, inscribe the transference of power and favor in material form. See, for instance, Haggai 2. 24: "In that day, saith the Lord of hostes, wil I take thee, o Zerubbabel my seruant, the sonne of Shealtiel, saith the Lord, & will make thee as a signet: for I haue chosen thee, saith the Lord of hostes." But even these materializations of power are detachable. See Jeremiah 22.24: "As I liue, saith the Lord, thogh Coniah . . . were the signet of my right hand, yet wolde I pluck thee thence."

18 Samuel Richardson, *Pamela; Or, Virtue Rewarded* (London, 1740, 1801; Harmondsworth: Penguin, 1980), 56–7. All further references to *Pamela* are given in our text.

19 See Henry Seidel Canby, "*Pamela* Abroad," *Modern Language Notes* 18 (1903), 206–13; T. C. Duncan Eaves and Ben D. Kimpel, *Samuel Richardson: A Biography* (Oxford: Clarendon Press, 1971), 126. Eaves and Kimpel also note that *Pamela* had the unusual distinction for an English novel of being placed on the Catholic *Index* of forbidden books in 1744. It remained on the *Index* until 1900 (126).

20 In fact, in one of his many rewritings of *Pamela*, Richardson downplayed Pamela's own pride in her work in embroidering Mr. B's waistcoat. In the 1740 text, Pamela gives as one of her reasons for staying on for a few more days despite Mr. B's advances the fact that she has not yet completed her embroidery. Her reason for staying and her virtue were ridiculed in the anonymous *Lettre sur Pamela* (1742), and Richardson later rewrote the passage to make Mrs. Jervis put pressure upon Pamela to stay. See Richardson, *Pamela*, 519.

21 Beverly Lemire, *Dress, Culture and Commerce: The English Clothing Trade before the Factory, 1660–1800* (London: Macmillan, 1997), 149 n. 18, 7.

22 *The Lowell Offering: Writings by New England Mill Women (1800–1845)*, ed. Benita Eisler (Philadelphia: Lippincott, 1977), 152–3.

23 Harriet A. Jacobs, *Incidents in the Life of a Slave Girl*, ed. Jean Fagin Yellin (Cambridge, Mass.: Harvard University Press, 1987), 11.

24 Quoted in Jacobs, *Incidents*, 215.

25 Primo Levi, *If This Is a Man*, trans. Stuart Wolf (London: Abacus, 1979), 31. All further references are in our text.

Bibliography

Acton, David, "The School of Paris and the Dissemination of the Fontainebleau Style," in *The French Renaissance in Prints from the Bibliothèque Nationale de France*, ed. Karen Jacobson, Los Angeles: Grunwald Center for the Graphic Arts, University of California, Los Angeles, 1994, 298–300.

Adams, E. Bryding, *The Stuart Legacy: English Art 1603–1714*, ed. Walter R. Brown, Birmingham, Ala.: Birmingham Museum of Art, 1991.

Adelman, Janet, *Suffocating Mothers: Fantasies of Maternal Origin in Shakespeare's Plays, "Hamlet" to "The Tempest"*, New York: Routledge, 1992.

Aeschylus, *Eumenides*, in *Aeschylus I: Oresteia*, trans. Richmond Lattimore, University of Chicago Press, 1953.

Aeschylus, *Prometheus Bound*, in *Three Greek Tragedies*, trans. David Grene, University of Chicago Press, 1956.

Agnew, Jean-Christophe, *Worlds Apart: The Market and the Theater in Anglo-American Thought, 1550–1750*, Cambridge University Press, 1986.

Ahl, Frederick, *Metaformations: Soundplay and Wordplay in Ovid and Other Classical Poets*, Ithaca, NY: Cornell University Press, 1985.

Ainsworth, Henry, *Annotations upon the first book of Moses, called Genesis*, Amsterdam, 1616.

Ainsworth, Maryan, "'Paternes for phisioneamyes': Holbein's portraiture reconsidered," *The Burlington Magazine* 132 (1990): 173–86.

Alpers, Svetlana, *The Decoration of the Torre de la Parada*, Corpus Rubenianum, vol. 9, New York: Phaidon, 1971.

Alter, Robert, *Genesis: Translation and Commentary*, New York: Norton, 1996.

Anderson, Bonnie and Judith Zinsser, *A History of Their Own, I*, New York: Penguin Books, 1988.

Andrewes, Lancelot, *Apospasmatia Sacra*, London, 1657.

Anon., *A Cat May Look upon a King*, London, 1652.

Anon., *Dick of Devonshire*, Oxford: Malone Society, 1955.

Anon., *Frederyke of Jennen* (1560), in *Cymbeline*, ed. J. M. Nosworthy, the Arden Shakespeare, London: Methuen, 1955.

Anon., *Lettre sur Pamela*, Paris, 1742

Anon., *Muld Sacke: or The Apologie of "Hic Mulier "*, London, 1620.

Anon., *The Taming of a Shrew* (1594), in *Narrative and Dramatic Sources of Shakespeare*, ed. Geoffrey Bullough, London: Routledge and Kegan Paul, 1957, vol. 1.

Anon., *A Warning for Faire Women*, London, 1599.

Anton, Robert, "The Philosophers Third Satyr of Iupiter," in *The Philosophers Satyrs*, London, 1616.

Appadurai, Arjun, "Introduction: Commodities and the Politics of Value," in *The Social Life of Things: Commodities in Cultural Perspective*, ed. Arjun Appadurai, Cambridge University Press, 1986, 3–63.

Ariosto, Ludovico, *Orlando Furioso*, ed. Lanfranco Caretti, 2nd edn., Milan: Ricciardi, 1962.

Arnold, Janet, *Patterns of Fashion: The Cut and Construction of Clothes for Men and Women c.1560–1620*, London: Macmillan, 1985.

Arnold Janet, *Queen Elizabeth's Wardrobe Unlock'd*, Leeds: Maney, 1988.

Arthur, Liz, *Embroidery 1600–1700 at the Burrell Collection*, Glasgow: John Murray and the Glasgow Museums, 1995.

Ashelford, Jane, *A Visual History of Costume: The Sixteenth Century*, London: Batsford, 1983.

Aston, Margaret, *England's Iconoclasts*, vol. 1, *Laws Against Images*, Oxford: Clarendon Press, 1988.

Atkins, John, *A Voyage to Guinea, Brasil, and the West Indies*, London, 1737.

Auerbach, Erna, *Nicholas Hilliard*, Boston: Boston Book and Art Shop, 1961.

Babington, Gervase, *Certaine Plaine, briefe, and comfortable Notes vpon euerie Chapter of Genesis*, London, 1592.

Bacon, Francis, *The Advancement of Learning*, ed. Arthur Johnston, Oxford: Clarendon Press, 1974.

Baines, Patricia, *Flax and Linen*, Princes Risborough, Bucks.: Shire Publications, 1985.

Baker, J. H. and S. F. C. Milson, *Sources for English Legal History*, London: Butterworth and Co., 1986.

Baker, Patricia L., "Islamic Honorific Garments," *Costume* 25 (1991): 25–35.

Bancroft, Robert, "To Sir Thomas Overbury, on his Wife," in *Two Bookes of Epigrammes and Epitaphs*, London, 1639, 112.

Barbaro, Francesco, *De re uxoria* (Florence, 1416), trans. as "On Wifely Duties," in *The Earthly Republic: Italian Humanists on Government and Society*, ed. Benjamin Kohl and Ronald G. Witt, with Elizabeth B. Welles, Philadelphia: University of Pennsylvania Press, 1978, 189–228.

Barber, Elizabeth Wayland, *Women's Work: The First 20,000 Years*, New York: Norton, 1994.

Barkan, Leonard, *The Gods Made Flesh: Metamorphosis and the Pursuit of Paganism*, New Haven: Yale University Press, 1986.

Barriault, Anne R., *Spalliera Paintings of Renaissance Tuscany: Fables of Poets for Patrician Homes*, University Park: Pennsylvania State University Press, 1994.

Barton, Anne, *The Names of the Comedy*, Oxford: Clarendon Press, 1990.

Baskins, Cristelle L., "Griselda, or the Renaissance Bride Stripped Bare by Her Bachelor in Tuscan *Cassone* Painting," *Stanford Italian Review* 10. 2 (1991): 153–75.

Baxandall, Michael, *Painting and Experience in Fifteenth-Century Italy*, 2nd edn., Oxford University Press, 1988.

Bayly, C. A., ed., *The Raj: India and the British 1600–1947*, London: Pearson/National Portrait Gallery, 1990.

Beal, Peter, *In Praise of Scribes*, Oxford University Press, 1998.

Beaumont, Francis and John Fletcher, *The Maids Tragedy*, ed. Andrew Gurr, Berkeley: University of California Press, 1969.

Beaumont, Francis and John Fletcher, *The Woman's Prize, or The Tamer Tamed*, in *The Dramatic Works in the Beaumont and Fletcher Canon*, ed. Fredson Bowers, Cambridge University Press, 1979.

Beaumont, John, "To the Authour," in Francis Beaumont, *Salamacis and Hermaphroditus*, London, 1602.

Beaumont, Joseph, *Psyche in XXIV Cantos*, in *The Complete Poems of Dr. Joseph Beaumont*, ed. Alexander B. Grosart, Blackburn: Edinburgh University Press, 1880.

Beck, Thomasina, *Embroidered Gardens*, New York: Viking, 1979.

Beck, Thomasina, *The Embroiderer's Flowers*, Newton Abbot, Devon: David and Charles, 1992; rpt. 1993.

Beckerman, Bernard, "Philip Henslowe," in *The Theatrical Manager in England and America*, ed. Joseph W. Donohue, Princeton University Press, 1971.

Behn, Aphra, *The Lucky Chance; Or, An Alderman's Bargain*, in *The Works of Aphra Behn*, ed. Montague Summers, New York: Phaeton, 1967, vol. 3.

Behn, Aphra, *The Younger Brother; Or, the Amorous Jilt*, in *Works*, ed. Summers, vol. 4.

Bellany, Alastair, "'Raylinge Rhymes and Vaunting Verse': Libellous Politics in Early Stuart

England, 1603–1628," in *Culture and Politics in Early Stuart England*, ed. Kevin Sharpe and Peter Lake, Stanford University Press, 1993, 285–310.

Benjamin, Walter, *The Origin of German Drama*, trans. John Osborne, London: New Left Books, 1977.

Bennett, Judith M., "'History that stands still': Women's Work in the European Past," *Feminist Studies* 14 (1988): 269–83.

Bentley, G. E., *The Jacobean and Caroline Stage*, Oxford: Clarendon Press, 1941.

Bentley, G. E., *The Profession of Dramatist in Shakespeare's Time, 1590–1642*, Princeton University Press, 1971.

Bentley, G. E., *The Profession of Player in Shakespeare's Time, 1590–1642*, Princeton University Press, 1984.

Berger, John, *Ways of Seeing*, London: BBC/Penguin, 1972; rpt. 1985.

Bevington, David, *Action Is Eloquence: Shakespeare's Language of Gesture*, Cambridge, Mass.: Harvard University Press, 1984.

Bevington, David M., "'Blake and wyght, fowll and fayer': Stage Picture in *Wisdom*" in *The "Wisdom" Symposium*, ed. Milla Cozart Riggio, Papers from the Trinity College Medieval Festival, New York: AMS Press, 1986, 18–38.

The Bible, Geneva, 1560.

The Holy Bible, the King James or Authorized translation, London, 1611.

Binns, J. W., "Women or Transvestites on the Elizabethan Stage? An Oxford Controversy," *Sixteenth Century Journal*, 5. 2 (1974): 95– 120.

Birch, Thomas, *The Court and Times of James the First*, London: Henry Colburn, 1848, vol. 1, 377.

Blackstone, Mary A., "Patrons and Elizabethan Dramatic Companies," *The Elizabethan Theatre* 10 (1988): 112–32.

Blankert, Albert, John Montis, and Giles Ailland, *Vermeer*, New York: Rizzoli, 1988.

Boas, Frederick S., *University Drama in the Tudor Age*, Oxford University Press, 1914.

Boccaccio, Giovanni, *Il Decamerone*, in *Tutte le Opere di Giovanni Boccaccio*, ed. Vittore Branca, Milan: Mondadori, 1976, vol. 4.

Boccaccio, Giovanni, *The Decameron (trans. into English 1620)*, ed. W. E. Henley, New York: AMS Press, 1967.

Boccaccio, Giovanni, *The Decameron*, trans. Mark Musa and Peter Bondanella, New York: New American Library, 1982.

Boggs, Jean Sutherland, *Picasso and Things*, Cleveland Museum of Art, 1992.

Bolzani, G. P. Valeriano, *Hieroglyphica* (Lyon, 1602), ed. Stephen Orgel, New York: Garland Publishing, 1976.

Boose, Lynda, "'Let It Be Hid': Iago, Renaissance Pornography, and *Othello's* 'Grossly Gaping' Audience," unpublished MS (1987).

Borin, Françoise, "Judging by Images," in *A History of Women in the West, III: Renaissance and Enlightenment Paradoxes*, ed. Natalie Zemon Davis and Arlette Farge, Cambridge, Mass.: Harvard University Press, 1993, 187–254.

Bottigheimer, Ruth, *Grimms' Bad Girls and Bold Boys: The Moral and Social Vision of the Tales*, New Haven: Yale University Press, 1987.

Bouchet, Guillaume, *Les Serées*, Poitiers, 1584.

Boulton, Jeremy, *Neighbourhood and Society: A London Suburb in the Seventeenth Century*, Cambridge University Press, 1987.

Bourdeille, Pierre de, Abbé de Brantôme, "Discours 2: Catherine de Médicis," in *Les Vies des dames illustres françoises et étrangères*, ed. Louis Moland, Paris: Garnier, 1841.

Bourdieu, Pierre, "Champ intellectuel et projet créateur," *Les Temps modernes* (November 1966): 865–906.

Bourdieu, Pierre, "Intellectual Field and Creative Project," in *Knowledge and Control*, ed. Michael F. D. Young, London: Collier Macmillan, 1971, 161–88.

Bowden, Peter, *The Wool Trade in Tudor and Stuart England*, London: Macmillan, 1962.

Bowerbank, Sylvia, "The Spider's Delight: Margaret Cavendish and the 'Female' Imagination," in *Women in the Renaissance: Selections from "English Literary Renaissance*," ed. Kirby Farrell, Elizabeth H. Hageman, and Arthur F. Kinney, Amherst: University of Massachusetts Press, 1990, 187–203.

Bowes, Thomas, trans., *De La Primaudayes French academie*, London, 1594.

Bradbrook, M. C., *John Webster: Citizen and Dramatist*, New York: Columbia University Press, 1980.

Bradley, E. T., *Life of the Lady Arabella Stuart*, London: Richard Bentley, 1889.

Bradstreet, Anne, "The Prologue," *The Tenth Muse Lately Sprung Up in America*, in *The Works of Anne Bradstreet*, ed. Jeannine Hensley, Cambridge, Mass.: Harvard University Press, 1967.

Brathwait, Richard, "The Ape of Fashion," in *An Excellent Piece of Conceipted Poetry*, London, 1658.

Brathwait, Richard, *The English Gentlewoman*, London, 1631.

Brathwait, Richard, "Upon our Ages MESSALINA, insatiat Madona, the matchless English-COROMBONA," in *An Excellent Piece of Conceipted Poetry*, London, 1658.

Brathwait, Richard, "Upon the Generall Sciolists or Poetasters of Brittaine. A Satyre," in *A Strappado for the Diuell*, London, 1615, 20–40.

Brome, Richard, *The Damoiselle*, in *The Dramatic Works of Richard Brome*, London: John Pearson, 1873.

Bromham, A. A. and Zara Bruzzi, *"The Changeling" and the Years of Crisis, 1619–1624: A Hieroglyph of Britain*, London: Pinter Publishers, 1990.

Brooke, Xanthe, *Catalogue of Embroideries: The Lady Lever Art Gallery*, Phoenix Mill, Glos.: Alan Sutton and Trustees of the National Museums and Galleries on Merseyside, 1992.

Brown, Christopher, *Van Dyck*, Ithaca, NY: Cornell University Press, 1983.

Brown, Jonathan, *Velázquez, Painter and Courtier*, New Haven: Yale University Press, 1988.

Browne, William, "The Third Song," in *The Whole Works of William Browne*, ed. W. Carew Hazlitt, London: Roxburgh Library, 1868.

Bryson, Norman, *Looking at the Overlooked: Four Essays on Still Life Painting*, Cambridge, Mass.: Harvard University Press, 1990.

Cahn, Susan, *The Industry of Devotion: The Transformation of Women's Work in England, 1500–1660*, New York: Columbia University Press, 1987.

Calendar of the Manuscripts of the Marquess of Bath preserved at Longleat, vol. 5, *Talbot, Dudley and Devereux Papers 1533–1659*, ed. G. Dyfnallt Owen, Historic Manuscripts Commission 58, London: Her Majesty's Stationery Office, 1980.

Calendar of State Papers Venetian, vol. 4 (1527–33).

Callmann, Ellen, *Apollonio di Giovanni*, Oxford: Clarendon Press, 1974.

Calvert, Albert F., *The Spanish Royal Tapestries*, New York: John Lane, 1921.

Calvin, Jean, *A Commentarie of John Caluine, vpon the first booke of Moses*, trans. Thomas Tymme, London, 1578.

Calvin, Jean, *The Sermons of M. John Calvin Upon...Deuteronomie*, trans. Arthur Golding, London, 1583.

Cambridge, ed. Alan H. Nelson, Records of Early English Drama, University of Toronto Press, 2 vols.

Camden, Carroll, *The Elizabethan Woman: A Panorama of English Womanhood, 1540–1640*, London: Cleaver-Hume, 1952.

Camden, William, *Annales, or the History of the Most Renowned and Victorious Princess Elizabeth, Late Queen of England*, 3rd edn., London, 1635.

Canby, Henry Seidel, "*Pamela* Abroad," *MLN* 18 (1903): 206–13.

Canny, Nicholas, "The Permissive Frontier: The Problem of Social Control in English Settlements in Ireland and Virginia 1550–1650," in *The Westward Enterprise: English Activities in Ireland, the Atlantic, and America 1480–1650*, ed. K. R. Andrews, N. P. Canny, and P. E. H. Hair, Liverpool University Press, 1979, 17–44.

Carson, Neil, *A Companion to Henslowe's Diary*, Cambridge University Press, 1988.

Cary, Anne [?], *The Lady Falkland: Her Life,* in Elizabeth Cary, *The Tragedy of Mariam*, ed.

Barry Weller and Margaret Ferguson, Berkeley: University of California Press, 1994, 183–275.

Castle, Terry, "Phantasmagoria: Spectral Technology and the Metaphors of Modern Reverie," *Critical Inquiry* 15. 1 (1988): 26–51.

Cats, Jacob, *Houwelyck. Dat ist de gansche gelegentheyt des echten staets*, Middelburg, 1625; 4th edn., The Hague, 1632.

Catullus, "Carmen 4," in *Carmina*, ed. and trans. G. P. Goold, London: Duckworth, 1983, 159–63.

Caturla, Maria, "El coleccionista madrileño Don Pedro de Arce, que poseyó 'Las Hilanderas' de Velázquez," *Archivo Español d'Arte* 21 (1948): 292–304.

Cavendish, Margaret, Marchioness of Newcastle, "The Epistle Dedicatory," *Poems and Fancies*, London, 1653.

Cerasano, S. P., "'Borrowed Robes,' Costume Prices, and the Drawing of *Titus Andronicus*," *Shakespeare Studies* 22 (1994): 45–57.

Cerasano, S. P., "New Renaissance Players' Wills," *Modern Philology* 82 (1985): 299–304.

Cerasano, S. P., "Revising Philip Henslowe's Biography," *Notes and Queries*, 230 (1985): 68.

Chamberlain, John, *The Letters of John Chamberlain*, ed. Norman E. McClure, Philadelphia: The American Philosophical Society, 1939.

Chamberlain, John, *The Chamberlain Letters*, ed. Elizabeth McClure Thomson, London: Murray, 1965.

Chambers, E. K., *The Elizabethan Stage*, Oxford: Clarendon Press, 1923. Chambers, E. K., *Sir Henry Lee: An Elizabethan Portrait*, Oxford: Clarendon Press, 1936.

Chambers, E. K., *William Shakespeare: A Study of Facts and Problems*, Oxford: Clarendon Press, 1930, 2 vols.

Chapman, George, *Hero and Leander, Completed by George Chapman*, in *Elizabethan Minor Epics*, ed. Elizabeth Donno, New York: Columbia University Press, 1963, 85–126.

Chapman, George, *Monsieur D'Olive*, ed. Allan Holaday, in *The Plays of George Chapman: A Critical Edition*, Urbana: University of Illinois Press, 1970.

Chapman., George, *Chapman's Homer*, ed. Allardyce Nicoll, vol. 1, *The Iliad*, London: Routledge and Kegan Paul, 1957.

Chaucer, Geoffrey, "The Clerk of Oxford's Tale," in *The Works of Geoffrey Chaucer*, ed. Alfred W. Pollard et al., London: Macmillan, 1965.

Chester, ed. Lawrence M. Clopper, Records of Early English Drama, Toronto University Press, 1979.

Christensen, Carol, Michael Palmer, and Michael Swicklik, "Van Dyck's Painting Technique, His Writings, and Three Paintings in the National Gallery of Art," in Arthur K. Wheelock, Susan J. Barnes, et al., eds., *Anthony van Dyck*, New York: Harry Abrams, 1990, 45–52.

Cibber, Colley, *An Apology for the Life of Colley Cibber*, ed. B. R. S. Fone, Ann Arbor: University of Michigan Press, 1968.

Ciotto, Giovanni, *A Booke of Curious and strange Inventions, called the first part of Needleworkes,* expanded edn., London: William Barley, 1596.

Claeburn, Pamela, *Samplers*, Princes Risborough, Bucks.: Shire Publications, n.d.

Clark, Alice, *The Working Life of Women in the Seventeenth Century*, London: Routledge and Sons, 1919; rpt. London: Frank Cass, 1968.

Clifford, Anne, *Lady Anne Clifford, Countess of Dorset, Pembroke, and Montgomery, 1590–1676: Her Life, Letters and Work*, ed. George C. Williamson, Kendal: Wilson, 1922.

Clifford, Anne, *The Diary of Anne Clifford 1616–1619: A Critical Edition*, ed. Katherine O. Acheson, New York: Garland, 1995.

Clifford, Lady Anne, *The Diaries of Lady Anne Clifford*, ed. D. J. H. Clifford, Wolfeboro Falls, NH: Alan Sutton, 1991.

Codrington, Robert, *The Life and Death of the illustrious Robert, Earl of Essex* (1646), in *The Harleian Miscellany*, vol. 1, London: John White, 1808.

Cogswell, Thomas, "England and the Spanish Match," in *Conflict in Early Stuart England: Studies in Religion and Politics 1603–1642*, ed. Richard Cust and Ann Hughes, London: Longman, 1989, 107–33.

Colby, Averill, *Samplers Yesterday and Today*, London: Batsford, 1964.

Coleman, D. C, "Textile Growth," in *Textile History and Economic History: Essays in Honour of Miss Julia de Lacy Mann*, ed. N. B. Harte and K. G. Ponting, Manchester University Press, 1973, 1–21.

Collinson, Patrick, *Godly People: Essays on English Protestantism and Puritanism*, London: Hambledon Press, 1983.

Collinson, Patrick, *The Elizabethan Puritan Movement*, London, Cape, 1967.

Colse, Peter, *Penelope's Complaint: or, a Mirrour for wanton Minions*, London, 1596.

Colvin, H. M., D. R. Ransome, and John Summerson, *The History of the King's Works*, vol. 3, 1485–1660, Part 1, London: Her Majesty's Stationery Office, 1975.

Commons Debates 1621, ed. Wallace Notestein, Frances Helen Relf, and Hartley Simpson, New Haven: Yale University Press, 1935.

Cooper, Jane, *Green Notebook, Winter Road*, Gardiner, Maine: Tilbury House, 1994.

Cotgrave, Randle, *A Dictionarie of the French and English Tongues*, London, 1611.

Coventry, ed. R. W. Ingram, Records of Early English Drama, University of Toronto Press, 1981.

Crawford, Patricia, "'The only ornament in a woman:' Needlework in Early Modern England," in *All her Labours: Two, Embroidering the Framework*, Sydney: Hale and Ironmonger, 1984, 7–20.

Creswell, Catherine, "Reading Subjectivity: The Body, the Text, the Author in John Donne," Ph.D. thesis, SUNY Buffalo, 1992.

Crew, P. Mack, *Calvinist Preaching and Iconoclasm in the Netherlands, 1544–1569*, Cambridge University Press, 1978.

Cromwell, Oliver, Letter written at Cambridge, September 1643, in *The Letters and Speeches of Oliver Cromwell*, ed. Thomas Carlyle, London: Methuen, 1904, vol. 1, 154.

Cross, Henry, *Vertues Common-wealth*, London, 1603.

Cumberland, Westmoreland, Gloucestershire, ed. Audrey Douglas and Peter Greenfield, Records of Early English Drama, University of Toronto Press, 1986.

Cumming, Valerie, "'Great vanity and excesse in Apparell': Some Clothing and Furs of Tudor and Stuart Royalty," in *The Late King's Goods: Collections, Possessions and Patronage of Charles I in the Light of the Commonwealth Sale Inventories*, ed. Arthur MacGregor, London: Alistair McAlpine, 1989, 322–50.

Curtin, Philip D., *Cross-Cultural Trade in World History*, Cambridge University Press, 1984.

D'Ewes, Sir Simonds, *The Autobiography and Correspondence of Sir Simonds D'Ewes*, ed. James Orchard Halliwell, London: Richard Bentley, 1845.

Davies, David and Enriqueta Harris, *Velázquez in Seville*, exhibition catalogue, Edinburgh: National Gallery of Scotland, 8 August–20 October 1996.

Davis, Natalie, "Women in the Crafts in Sixteenth-Century Lyon," in *Women and Work in Preindustrial Europe*, ed. Barbara A. Hanawalt, Bloomington: Indiana University Press, 1986, 167–97.

de Grazia, Margreta, "Embodied Memory in *Hamlet*," unpublished paper.

de Grazia, Margreta, Maureen Quilligan, and Peter Stallybrass, eds., *Subject and Object in Renaissance Culture*, Cambridge University Press, 1995.

de Marees, Pieter, "A Description and Historicall Declaration of the Golden Kingdome of Guinea," in Samuel Purchas, *Hakluytus Posthumus, or Purchas His Pilgrimes*, Glasgow: MacLehose, 1905, vol. 4.

de Marly, Diana, "Pepys and the Fashion for Collecting," *Costume* 21 (1987): 34–43.

de Roover, Raymond, *Money, Banking and Credit in Mediaeval Bruges: Italian Merchant-Bankers, Lombards, and Money-Changers: A Study in the Origins of Banking*, Cambridge, Mass.: The Mediaeval Academy of America, 1948.

Defert, Daniel, "Un Genre éthnographique profane au XVIe: les livres d'habits," in *Histoires de l'anthropologie (XVIe-XIXe siècles)*, ed. Britta Rupp-Eisenreich, Paris: Klincksieck, 1984, 25–39.

Dekker, Thomas, *The Dead Tearme*, London, 1608.

Dekker, Thomas, *The Gulls Horne-booke*, London, 1609.

Dekker, Thomas, *The Honest Whore, Part 2*, in *The Dramatic Works of Thomas Dekker*, ed. Fredson Bowers, Cambridge University Press, 1958, vol. 2.

Dekker, Thomas, *Newes from Hell*, London, 1606.

Dekker,Thomas, *Satiromastix*, in *The Dramatic Works*, ed. Bowers, vol. 1.

Dekker, Thomas, *Satiro-Mastix, or the Vntrussing of the Humorous Poet*, ed. Hans Scherer, Louvain: Uystpruyst, 1907.

Dekker, Thomas, *The Seuen Deadly Sinnes of London* (1606), in *The Non-Dramatic Works of Thomas Dekker*, ed. Alexander Grosart, London: privately printed, 1885, vol. 2.

Dekker, Thomas, *The Shoemaker's Holiday* (1600), in *The Dramatic Works*, ed. Bowers, vol. 1.

Dekker, Thomas, *The Wonderfull Yeare* (1603), in *The Dramatic Works*, ed. Bowers, vol. 2.

Dekker, Thomas and John Webster, *North-Ward Hoe* (1607), in *The Dramatic Works*, ed. Bowers. vol. 2.

Dekker, Thomas and John Webster, *West-Ward Hoe* (1607), in *The Dramatic Works*, ed. Bowers, vol. 2.

Dekker, Thomas and John Webster, *The Wonder of a Kingdome* (1636), in *The Dramatic Works*, ed. Bowers, vol. 3.

Deloney, Thomas, "Of Patient Grissel and a Noble Marquess," in *The Garland of Good-Will*, ed. James Henry Dixon, in *Early English Poetry, Ballads, and Popular Literature of the Middle Ages*, Percy Society, London: Percy Society, vol. 30, 1852, 82–89.

Denbigh, Cecilia, Countess of, *Royalist Father and Roundhead Son*, London: Methuen, 1915.

Derrida, Jacques, *Given Time: 1. Counterfeit Money*, trans. Peggy Kamuf, University of Chicago Press, 1992.

Derrida, Jacques, *Specters of Marx: The State of the Debt, the Work of Mourning, and the New International*, trans. Peggy Kamuf, New York: Routledge, 1994.

Dickens, Charles, *Great Expectations*, ed. Angus Calder, Harmondsworth: Penguin, 1965.

Dillon, Janette, "John Rastell's Stage," *Medieval English Theater* 18 (1996): 5–45.

Dillon, Janette, "John Rastell v. Henry Walton," *Leeds Studies in English*, n.s. 28 (1997): 57–75

Dollimore, Jonathan, "Early Modern: Cross-Dressing in Early Modern England," in *Sexual Dissidence: Augustine to Wilde, Freud to Foucault*, Oxford University Press, 1991, 284–306.

Dollimore, Jonathan, "Subjectivity, Sexuality, and Transgression: The Jacobean Connection," *Renaissance Drama*, n.s. 17 (1986): 53–81.

Donne, John, *Deaths Duell*, ed. Geoffrey Keynes, Boston: David Godine, 1973.

Donne, John, *Devotions on Emergent Occasions*, ed. John Sparrow, Cambridge University Press, 1923.

Donne, John, *Satire IV*, in *The Satires, Epigrams, and Verse Letters of John Donne*, ed. W. Milgate, Oxford: Clarendon Press, 1967.

Downes, John, *Roscius Anglicanus*, ed. Judith Milhous and Robert D. Hume, London: Society for Theatre Research, 1987.

Drayton, Michael, "Lady Geraldine to the Earl of Surrey," *Heroicall Epistles*, in *The Works of Michael Drayton*, ed. J. William Hebel, Oxford: Blackwell, 1961, vol. 2, 288–92.

Duffy, Eamon, *The Stripping of the Altars: Traditional Religion in England, c.1400–c.1580*, New Haven: Yale University Press, 1992.

Dumas, Alexandre, *Hamlet*, in Romy Heylen, *Translation, Poetics, and the Stage: Six French Hamlets*, New York: Routledge, 1993.

Dundas, Judith, "'Arachnean Eyes': A Mythological Emblem in the Poetry of George Chapman," *John Donne Studies* 6. 2 (1987): 275–83.

Dunlevy, Mairead, *Dress in Ireland*, New York: Holmes and Meier, 1989.

Dürer, Albrecht, *The Complete Engravings, Etchings and Drypoints of Albrecht Dürer*, ed. Walter L. Strauss, New York: Dover, 1973.

Dynasties: Painting in Tudor and Jacobean England 1530–1630, ed. Karen Hearn, London, Tate Publishing, 1995.

E., T., *The Lawes Resolution of Womens Rights*, London, 1632.

Eaves, T. C. Duncan and Ben D. Kimpel, *Samuel Richardson: A Biography*, Oxford, Clarendon Press, 1971.

Egerton MSS., B.M. Egerton MSS. 1269, 1264, 3039.

Elias, Norbert, *The Court Society*, trans. Edmund Jephcott, Oxford: Blackwell, 1983.

Emmison, F. G., *Elizabethan Life: Wills of Essex Gentry and Merchants,* Chelmsford: Essex County Council, 1978.

Erdmann, Kurt, *Seven Hundred Years of Oriental Carpets*, ed. Hanna Erdmann, trans. May H. Beattie and Hildegard Herzog, Berkeley, University of California Press, 1970.

Erickson, Amy Louise, *Women and Property in Early Modern England,* London: Routledge, 1993.

Esdaile, Katharine, "Gunpowder Plot in Needlework: Dame Dorothy Selby, 'Whose Arte Disclos'd that Plot,'" *Country Life*, June 1943: 1094–6.

Euripides, *Hecuba*, trans. William Arrowsmith, in *Euripides III, The Complete Greek Tragedies*, ed. David Grene and Richmond Lattimore, University of Chicago Press, 1958.

Les Evangiles des quenouilles, ed. Madeleine Jeay, Montreal: Presses Universitaires, 1985.

Ewing, Elizabeth, *Everyday Dress 1650–1900*, London: Batsford, 1984.

Fausz, J. Frederick, "'To Draw Thither the Trade of Beavers': The Strategic Significance of the English Fur Trade in the Chesapeake, 1620–1660," in *Le Castor Fait Tout: Selected Papers of the Fifth North American Fur Trade Conference*, ed. Bruce Trigger, Toby Morantz, and Louise Dechène, Montreal: La Société, 1987.

Felson-Rubin, Nancy, *Regarding Penelope: From Character to Poetics*, Princeton University Press, 1994.

Ferguson, Margaret, "Feathers and Flies: Aphra Behn and the Seventeenth-Century Trade in Exotica," in *Subject and Object in Renaissance Culture*, ed. Margreta de Grazia, Maureen Quilligan, and Peter Stallybrass, Cambridge University Press, 235–59.

Ferrier, R. W., "Charles I and the Antiquities of Persia: The Mission of Nicholas Wilford," *Iran* 8 (1970): 51–6.

Feuillerat, Albert, ed., *Documents Relating to the Office of the Revels in the Time of Queen Elizabeth I*, Louvain: Uystpruyst, 1908.

Fitzgeoffrey, Henry, *Notes from the Blackfryers*, London, 1617.

Fitzgeoffrey, Henry, *Satyres: and Satyricall Epigrams: With Certaine Observations at Black-Fryers*, London, 1617.

Fitzherbert, Anthony, *The Book of Husbandrie*, London, 1555.

Fizer, Irene, "Rocabianca's Griselda: Boccaccio and his Illustrators," unpublished paper.

Flatter, Richard, *Hamlet's Father*, New Haven: Yale University Press, 1949.

Fleay, Frederick, *Chronicle History of the London Stage 1559–1642*, London: Reeves and Turner, 1890.

Fletcher, Giles, *Christ's Victorie in Heaven*, in *Poetical Works of Giles and Phineas Fletcher*, ed. Frederick Boas, Cambridge University Press, 1908, vol. 1, 18–39.

Florio, John, *A World of Wordes*, London, 1598.

Foakes, R. A., *Illustrations of the English Stage 1580–1642*, London: Scolar Press, 1985.

Foakes, R. A. and R. T. Rickert, eds., *Henslowe's Diary*, Cambridge University Press, 1961.

Foister, Susan, "Foreigners at Court: Holbein, Van Dyck and the Painter-Stainers Company," in *Art and Patronage in the Caroline Courts: Essays in Honour of Sir Oliver Millar*, ed. David Howarth, Cambridge University Press, 1994, 32–50.

Fonte, Moderata (Modesta Pozzo), *Il Merito delle donne* (Venice: Domenico Umberti, 1600), ed. Adriana Chemello, Mirano: Eidos, 1988, trans. by Virginia Cox as *The Worth of Women*, University of Chicago Press, 1997.

Ford, John, *Loues Sacrifice*, London, 1633.

Ford, John, *The Broken Heart*, London, 1633.

Forker, Charles R., *Skull Beneath the Skin*, Carbondale: Southern Illinois Press, 1986.

Forrest, William, *The History of Grisild the Second*, ed. W. D. Macray, Roxburghe Club, London: Chiswick Press, 1875.

Franits, Wayne, *Paragons of Virtue: Women and Domesticity in Seventeenth-Century Dutch Art*, Cambridge University Press, 1993.

Freedberg, David, *Iconoclasm and Painting in the Revolt of the Netherlands, 1566–1609*, New York: Garland, 1987.

Freud, Sigmund, "Fetishism" (1927), in *The Standard Edition of the Complete Psychological Works of Sigmund Freud*, trans. James Strachey, London: The Hogarth Press, vol. 21, 1961, 152–57.

Freud, Sigmund, "The Sexual Aberrations," *Three Essays on the Theory of Sexuality* (1905), in *The Standard Edition of the Complete Psychological Works of Sigmund Freud*, trans. James Strachey, London: The Hogarth Press, vol. 7, 1953, 130–243.

Freud, Sigmund, "The Uncanny" (1919), in *The Standard Edition of the Complete Psychological Works of Sigmund Freud*, trans. James Strachey, London: Hogarth Press, vol. 17, 1955, 218–52.

Friedman, Alice T., "Constructing an Identity in Prose, Plaster and Paint: Lady Anne Clifford as Writer and Patron of the Arts," in *Albion's Classicism: The Visual Arts in Britain, 1550–1660*, ed. Lucy Gent, New Haven: Yale University Press, 359–76.

Frye, Susan, "Esther Inglis and Early Seventeenth-Century Print Conventions of Authorship," seminar paper for the Shakespeare Association of America meeting, Albuquerque, 1994.

Frye, Susan, "Sewing Connections: Elizabeth Tudor, Mary Stuart, Elizabeth Talbot, and Seventeenth-Century Anonymous Needleworkers," in *Maids and Mistresses, Cousins and Queens: Women's Alliances in Early Modern England*, ed. Susan Frye and Karen Robertson, Oxford University Press, 1999, 165–82.

Fuller, Thomas, *The Worthies of England* (1662), ed. John Freeman, London: Allen and Unwin, 1952.

Fumerton, Patricia, *Cultural Aesthetics: Renaissance Literature and the Practice of Social Ornament*, University of Chicago Press, 1991.

Garber, Marjorie, "Fetish Envy," in *Vested Interests: Cross-Dressing and Cultural Anxiety*, New York: Routledge, 1992, 118–27.

Gardner, Helen, "Dean Donne's Monument in St. Paul's," in *Evidence in Literary Scholarship*, ed. René Wellek and Alvaro Ribeiro, Oxford: Clarendon Press, 1979, 29–44.

Gascoigne, George, *The Steele Glas*, London, 1576.

Gauldie, Enid, *Spinning and Weaving*, Edinburgh: National Museums of Scotland, 1995.

Gawdy, Philip, *Letters of Philip Gawdy 1579–1616*, ed. Isaac Herbert Jeayes, London: J. B. Nichols, 1906.

Gee, John, *New Shreds of the Old Snare*, London, 1624.

Gielgud, John, "Notes on Costume, Scenery and Stage Business," in Rosamond Gilder, *John Gielgud's Hamlet*, Oxford University Press, 1937.

Gilby, Anthony, *A Pleasaunt Dialogue betweene a Souldior of Barwicke and an English Chaplaine*, Middelburg (?), 1566.

Gillespie, George, *A dispute against the English-popish ceremonies obtruded vpon the Church of Scotland*, Leiden (?), 1637.

Gittings, Clare, *Death, Burial and the Individual in Early Modern England*, Beckenham, Kent: Croom Helm, 1984.

Goldberg, Jonathan, *Writing Matter: From the Hands of the English Renaissance*, Stanford University Press, 1990.

Goldthwaite, Richard A., *Banks, Palaces and Entrepreneurs in Renaissance Florence*, Aldershot: Variorum, 1992.

Goltzius, Hendrik, *The Complete Engravings and Woodcuts of Hendrik Goltzius*, ed. Walter Strauss, New York: Abaris Books, 1977.

Gosse, Edmund, *The Life and Letters of John Donne*, London: William Heinemann, 1899, 2 vols.

Gossett, Suzanne, "'Man-maid, begone!': Women in Masques," *Women in the Renaissance*, ed. Kirby Farrell, Elizabeth Hageman, and Arthur Kinney, Amherst: University of Massachusetts Press, 118–35.

Gosson, Stephen, *The Schoole of Abuse*, ed. Edward Arber, London: Murray and Son, 1868.

Gough, J. W., *Sir Hugh Middleton: Entrepreneur and Engineer*, Oxford: Clarendon Press, 1964.

Greaves, Richard L., *Society and Religion in Elizabethan England*, Minneapolis: University of Minnesota Press, 1981.

The Greek Anthology, Books 1–6, trans. W. R. Paton, Cambridge, Mass: Harvard University Press, 1916; rpt. 1993.

Greenblatt, Stephen, "Erotische Provokation im Elizabethanischen Theater," *Shakespeare Jahrbuch* 124 (1988): 56–61.

Greenblatt, Stephen, *Learning to Curse: Essays in Early Modern Culture,* New York: Routledge, 1990.

Greenblatt, Stephen, "Remnants of the Sacred in Early Modern England," in *Subject and Object in Renaissance Culture*, ed. Margreta de Grazia, Maureen Quilligan, and Peter Stallybrass, Cambridge University Press, 1995, 337–45.

Greenblatt, Stephen, *Renaissance Self-Fashioning: From More to Shakespeare*, University of Chicago Press, 1980.

Greenblatt, Stephen, *Shakespearean Negotiations: The Circulation of Social Energy in Renaissance England*, Berkeley: University of California Press, 1988.

Greene, Robert, *A Quip for an Vpstart Courtier* (1592), in *The Life and Complete Works in Prose and Verse of Robert Greene*, ed. Alexander B. Grosart (privately printed, 1881–3), vol. 11.

Greene, Robert, *Alphonsus King of Aragon*, ed. W. W. Greg, Oxford: Malone Society, 1926.

Greene, Robert, *Penelope's Web*, in *The Life and Complete Works in Prose and Verse of Robert Greene, M.A.*, ed. Alexander Grosart, New York: Russell and Russell, rpt. 1964, vol. 5.

Greenhill, William, *An Exposition of the first five chapters... of Ezekiel,* London, 1645.

Greenhut, Deborah, *Feminine Rhetorical Culture: Tudor Adaptations of Ovid's "Heroides"*, New York: Peter Lang, 1988.

Greg, W. W., "Hamlet's Hallucination," *Modern Language Review* 12 (1917): 393–421.

Gregory, Chris, "Kula Gift Exchange and Capitalist Commodity Exchange: A Comparison," in *The Kula: New Perspectives on Massim Exchange*, Cambridge University Press, 1983, 103–117.

Grewe, Cordula, "Shaping Reality through the Fictive: Images of Women Spinning in the Northern Renaissance," *RACAR: Revue d'art canadienne/Canadian Art Review* 19.1–2 (1992): 6–19.

Grieco, Sara Matthews, *Ange ou diablesse: La Représentation de la femme au XVIe siècle*, Paris: Flammarion, 1991.

Grien, Hans Baldung, *Hans Baldung Grien: Das graphische Werk*, ed. Matthias Mende, Unterschneidheim: Alfons Uhl, 1978.

Griffin, Jasper, *Homer on Life and Death*, Oxford: Clarendon Press, 1980.

The Grimms' German Folk Tales, trans. Francis Magoun and Alexander Krappe, Carbondale: Southern Illinois University Press, 1960.

Grossman, Marshall, "The Dissemination of the King," in *The Theatrical City: Culture, Theatre and Politics in London, 1576–1649*, ed. David Smith, Richard Streier, and David Bevington, Cambridge University Press, 1995, 260–81.

Gruber, William E., "The Actor in the Script: Affective Strategies in Shakespeare's *Antony and Cleopatra*," *Comparative Drama* 19.1 (1985): 30–48.

Gurr, Andrew, *Playgoing in Shakespeare's London*, Cambridge University Press, 1987.

Gurr, Andrew, *The Shakespearean Stage 1574–1642*, 3rd edn., Cambridge University Press, 1992.

Hackenbroch, Yvonne, *English and Other Needlework, Tapestries and Textiles in the Irwin Untermeyer Collection*, Cambridge, Mass.: Harvard University Press, 1960.

Hackenbroch, Yvonne, *Renaissance Jewellery*, London: Sotheby Parke Bernet, 1979.

Hall, Edward, *The Union of the Two Noble and Illustre Famelies of Lancastre & Yorke*, London, 1548.

Hall, Joseph, "Satyre 1.3," in *The Poems of Joseph Hall*, ed. Arnold Davenport, Liverpool University Press, 1969.

Hall, Joseph, *The Righteous Mammon*, London, 1618.

Hall, Kim, *Things of Darkness: Economies of Race and Gender in Early Modern England*, Ithaca, NY: Cornell University Press, 1995.

Hall, Marcia B., *Color and Meaning: Practice and Theory in Renaissance Painting*, Cambridge University Press, 1992.

Harington, Sir John, *Orlando Furioso in English Heroical Verse*, London, 1607.

Harris, Enriqueta, *The Prado: Treasure House of the Spanish Royal Collection*, New York: The Studio, 1940.

Harris, Virgil M., *Ancient, Curious and Famous Wills*, Boston: Little, Brown and Company, 1911.

Harsnet, Samuel, *A Discouery of the Fraudulent Practices of Iohn Darrel*, London, 1599.

Harte, N. B., "State Control of Dress and Social Change in Pre-Industrial England," in *Trade, Government and Economy in Pre-Industrial England: Essays Presented to F. J. Fisher*, ed. D. C. Coleman and A. H. John, London: Weidenfeld and Nicolson, 1976.

Heath, John, "In Lusiam," in *The House of Correction: or, Certayne Satyricall Epigrams*, London, 1619.

Hedges, William, *The Diary of William Hedges, Esq.*, ed. Col. H. Yule, *The Hakluyt Society*, 75 (1878): 344–50.

Heinemann, Margot, *Puritanism and Theatre: Thomas Middleton and Opposition Drama under the Early Stuarts*, Cambridge University Press, 1980.

Henslowe Papers, ed. Walter W. Greg, London: A. H. Bullen, 1907.

Henslowe, Philip, *Henslowe's Diary*, ed. R. A. Foakes and R. T. Rickert, Cambridge University Press, 1961.

Herbert, Sir Henry, *The Dramatic Records of Sir Henry Herbert, Master of the Revels 1623–1673*, ed. Joseph Quincy Adams, New Haven: Yale University Press, 1917.

Herlihy, David, *Opera Muliebra: Women and Work in Medieval Europe*, New York: McGraw Hill, 1990.

Hervey, Mary F. S., *Holbein's "Ambassadors": The Picture and the Men*, London: Bell, 1900.

"*Hic Mulier*: or, The Man-Woman," London, 1620, in *Three Pamphlets on the Jacobean Antifeminist Controversy*, ed. Barbara Baines, Delmar, NY: Scholars' Facsimiles, 1978.

Highley, Christopher, *Shakespeare, Spenser and the Crisis in Ireland*, Cambridge University Press, 1997.

Hilliard, Nicholas, *A Treatise Concerning the Arte of Linning*, ed. R. K. R. Thornton and T. G. S. Cain, Manchester: Carcanet Press, 1992.

Hodgen, Margaret T., *Early Anthropology in the Sixteenth and Seventeenth Centuries*, Philadelphia: University of Pennsylvania Press, 1964.

Hofenk-De Graaff, Judith H., "The Chemistry of Red Dyestuffs in Medieval and Early Modern Europe," in *Cloth and Clothing in Medieval Europe: Essays in Memory of Professor E. M. Carus-Wilson*, ed. N. B. Harte and K. G. Ponting, Pasold Studies in Textile History, London: Heinemann Educational Books, 1983, 71–9.

Holme, Randle, *The Academy of Armory*, Chester, 1688.

Holmes, Martin, *Shakespeare and His Players*, London: John Murray, 1972.

"An Homily against Excess of Apparel" (1563) in *Certain Sermons or Homilies*, Oxford University Press, 1844, 276.

Honigmann, E. A. J., "The Second-Best Bed," *The New York Review of Books* 38.18 (7 November, 1991): 27–30.

Honigmann, E. A. J., "'There Is a World Elsewhere': William Shakespeare, Businessman," in *Images of Shakespeare*, ed. Werner Habicht, D. J. Palmer, and Roger Pringle, Proceedings of the Third Progress of the International Shakespeare Association, 1986, Newark: University of Delaware Press, 1988, 40–6.

Howard, Jean, *The Stage and Social Struggle in Early Modern England*, London: Routledge, 1994.

Howell, James, *Paroimiographia*, London, 1659.

Howell, Joseph Allen, "To my Father upon my first going beyond Sea," 1 March 1618, in *Epistolae Ho-Elianae: The Familiar Letters of James Howell*, ed. Joseph Jacobs, London: David Nutt, 1892.

Howell, Martha, *Women, Production and Patriarchy in Late Medieval Cities*, University of Chicago Press, 1986.

Hoy, Cyrus, "Commentary" to *Patient Grissil*, in *Introductions, Notes, and Commentaries to Texts in "The Dramatic Works of Thomas Dekker"*, ed. Fredson Bowers, Cambridge University Press, 1980, vol. 1.

Hudson, Kenneth, *Pawnbroking: An Aspect of British Social History*, London: The Bodley Head, 1982.

Hufton, Olwen, *The Prospect before Her: A History of Women in Western Europe*, I, London: HarperCollins, 1995.

Hull, Suzanne, *Chaste, Silent and Obedient: English Books for Women, 1475–1640*, San Marino, Calif.: Huntington Library, 1982.

Hunter, G. K., "Flatcaps and Bluecoats: Visual Signals on the Elizabethan Stage," *Essays and Studies* (1980): 16–47.

Hutchinson, Lucy, "The Life of Mrs. Lucy Hutchinson, Written by Herself," in *Memoirs of the Life of Colonel Hutchinson*, ed. James Sutherland, London: Oxford University Press, 1973, 278–89.

Hutson, Lorna, *The Usurer's Daughter: Male Friendship and Fictions of Women in Sixteenth-Century England*, London: Routledge, 1994.

Hutton, Henry, *Follies Anatomie: or satyres and satyricall epigrams*, London, 1619.

Hyrde, Richard, Introduction to Margaret More Roper's translation of Erasmus' *Precatio dominica in septem portiones distributa* (1524), in *Vives and the Renascence Education of Women*, ed. Foster Watson, New York: Longmans, Green, 1912, 162–73.

Inglis, Esther, *Argumenta Psalmorum Davidis*, cover reproduced in Frederick Bearman, Nati Krivatsy, and J. Franklin Mowery, *Fine and Historic Bookbindings from the Folger Shakespeare Library*, Washington, DC: Folger Shakespeare Library, 1993.

Ingram, William, *The Business of Playing: The Beginnings of the Adult Professional Theater in Elizabethan London*, Ithaca, NY: Cornell University Press, 1992.

Ingram, William, *A London Life in the Brazen Age: Francis Langley, 1548–1602*, Cambridge, Mass.: Harvard University Press, 1978.

Inventory of Lady Jane Stanhope's Apparel, made on 20 November 1614, Folger MS. X. d. 522.

Jacobs, Harriet A., *Incidents in the Life of a Slave Girl*, ed. Jean Fagin Yellin, Cambridge, Mass.: Harvard University Press, 1987.

James I of England, *Daemonologie* (1597), ed. G. B. Harrison, London: John Lane, The Bodley Head Ltd., 1924.

Jardine, Lisa, *Still Harping on Daughters*, Brighton: Harvester, 1983.

Jardine, Lisa, "Twins and Travesties: Gender, Dependency and Sexual Availability," in *Erotic Politics: Desire on the Renaissance Stage*, ed. Susan Zimmerman, New York: Routledge, 1992, 27–38.

Jardine, Lisa, *Worldly Goods: A New History of the Renaissance*, London: Macmillan, 1996.

Jaster, Margaret, "Painted Puppets: Dressing and Undressing in Early Modern England," in

"'Fashioning the Minde and Condicions': The Uses and Abuses of Apparel in Early Modern England," Ph.D. thesis, University of Maryland, College Park, 1992.

Jed, Stephanie, *Chaste Thinking: The Rape of Lucretia and the Birth of Humanism*, Bloomington: Indiana University Press, 1989.

Jenkins, Harold, "Notes," *Hamlet*, The Arden Shakespeare, London: Methuen, 1982.

Jenkins, I. D., "The Ambiguity of Greek Textiles," *Arethusa* 18. 2 (1985): 109–132.

John Evelyn, *Diary*, ed. E. S. de Beer, Oxford University Press, 1959.

Johnson, Gerald D., "The Stationers Versus the Drapers: Control of the Press in the Late Sixteenth Century," *The Library*, sixth series, 10.1 (1988): 1–17.

Johnson, Randal, "Editor's Introduction," in Pierre Bourdieu, *The Field of Cultural Production: Essays on Art and Literature*, ed. Randal Johnson, New York: Columbia University Press, 1993.

Jones, Ann Rosalind, "The Mirror, the Distaff, the Pen," in *The Currency of Eros: Women's Love Lyric in Europe, 1540–1620* (Bloomington: Indiana University Press, 1990), 11–35.

Jones, Ann Rosalind, "Nets and Bridles: Early Modern Conduct Books and Sixteenth-Century Women's Lyrics," in *The Ideology of Conduct: Essays in Literature and the History of Sexuality*, ed. Nancy Armstrong and Leonard Tennenhouse (London: Methuen, 1987), 39–72.

Jones, John, *The Arte and science of preserving bodie and soule*, London, 1579.

Jones, Norman, *God and the Moneylenders: Usury and Law in Early Modern England*, Oxford: Basil Blackwell, 1989.

Jonson, Ben, *The Alchemist*, in *Ben Jonson*, ed. C. H. Herford, Percy and Evelyn Simpson, Oxford: Clarendon Press, 1950, vol. 5.

Jonson, Ben, *The Devil is an Ass*, in *Ben Jonson*, ed. Herford, vol. 6.

Jonson, Ben, "An Epistle to a Friend, to Persuade Him to the Wars," *The Vnder-wood* no. 15, in *Ben Jonson*, ed. Herford, vol. 8.

Jonson, Ben, *Every Man in His Humour*, in *Ben Jonson*, ed. Herford, vol. 3.

Jonson, Ben, *Hymenaei*, in *Ben Jonson*, ed. Herford, vol. 7, 209–41.

Jonson, Ben, *The New Inn*, in *Ben Jonson*, ed. Herford, vol. 6.

Jonson, Ben, *Poetaster*, in *Ben Jonson*, ed. Herford, vol. 4.

Jonson, Ben, *Volpone*, in *Ben Jonson*, ed. Herford, vol. 5.

Junkerman, Christine, "Constructing Gender: The Meaning of Dress in Renaissance Patrician Venice," paper delivered at the conference Dressing the Renaissance Woman, University of California at Los Angeles, 23 April, 1992.

Kahr, Madlyn, *Velázquez: The Art of Painting*, New York: Harper and Row, 1976.

Kamen, Henry, *Inquisition and Society in Spain in the Sixteenth and Seventeenth Centuries*, London: Weidenfeld and Nicolson, 1985.

Kampen, Nathalie, *Image and Status: Roman Working Women in Ostia*, Berlin: Mann, 1981.

Katz, Marylin, *Penelope's Renown: Meaning and Indeterminacy in the "Odyssey"*, Princeton University Press, 1991.

Kavaler, Ethan M., "Being the Count of Nassau: Refiguring Identity in Space, Time, and Stone," in *Beeld en Zelfbeeld in de Nederlandse Kunst, 1550–1750*, ed. Reindert Falkenburg, Jan de Jong, Herman Roodenburg, and Frits Scholten, *Nederlands Kunsthistorisch Jaarboek* (1995): 13–51.

Kelso, Ruth, *Doctrine for the Lady of the Renaissance*, Urbana: University of Illinois Press, 1956; rpt. 1978.

Kerridge, Eric, *Textile Manufactures in Early Modern England*, Manchester University Press, 1985.

Kerrigan, John, "Hieronimo, Hamlet and Remembrance," *Essays in Criticism* 31 (1981): 105–26.

Killerby, Catherine Kovesi, "Practical Problems in the Enforcement of Italian Sumptuary Law, 1200–1500," in *Crime, Society and the Law in Renaissance Italy*, ed. Trevor Dean and K. J. P. Lowe, Cambridge University Press, 1984.

Klapisch-Zuber, Christiane, *Women, Family and Ritual in Renaissance Italy*, Chicago University Press, 1985.

Klein, Lisa M., "Your Humble Handmaid: Elizabethan Gifts of Needlework," *Renaissance Quarterly* 50 (1997): 459–93.

Klein, Lisa M., "Needlework and the Fashioning of a Renaissance Woman," workshop paper for the conference "Attending to Women," University of Maryland, November 1990, summarized in *Attending to Women in Early Modern England*, ed. Betty Travitsky and Adele Seeff, Newark: University of Delaware Press, 1994, 200–3.

Knappen, M. M., *Tudor Puritanism: A Chapter in the History of Idealism*, Gloucester, Mass.: P. Smith, 1939.

Knutson, Roslyn Lander, *The Repertory of Shakespeare's Company, 1594–1613*, Fayetteville: University of Arkansas Press, 1991.

Kopytoff, Igor, "The Cultural Biography of Things: Commoditization as Process," in *The Social Life of Things: Commodities in Cultural Perspective*, ed. Arjun Appadurai, Cambridge University Press, 1986, 64–91.

Korda, Natasha, "Household Kates: Domesticating Commodities in *The Taming of the Shrew*," *Shakespeare Quarterly* 47. 2 (1996): 109–31.

Korda, Natasha, "Household Property/Stage Property: Henslowe as Pawnbroker," *Theatre Journal* 48 (1996): 185–95.

Kyd, Thomas, *Cornelia*, in *The Works of Thomas Kyd*, ed. Frederick S. Boas, Oxford: Clarendon Press, 1955.

Kyd, Thomas, *The Spanish Tragedy*, in *Works*, ed. Boas.

La Force, Jr., James, *The Development of the Spanish Textile Industry*, Berkeley: University of California Press, 1965.

Labé, Louise, "Elégie 3," *Euvres* (Lyon, 1555), in *Oeuvres complètes*, ed. François Rigolot, Paris: Flammarion, 1986.

Labé, Louise, "Epistre dédicatoire," *Euvres* (Lyon, 1555), in *Oeuvres complètes*, ed. Rigolot.

Lacan, Jacques, "The Mirror Stage as Formative of the Function of the I as Revealed in Psychoanalytic Experience," in *Ecrits*, trans. Alan Sheridan, New York: Norton, 1977.

Laing, Alastair, *In Trust for the Nation: Paintings from National Trust Houses*, London: The National Trust, 1995.

Lake, Peter, "Anti-popery: The Structure of a Prejudice," in *Conflict in Early Stuart England: Studies in Religion and Politics 1603–1642*, ed. Richard Cust and Ann Hughes, London: Longman, 1989, 72–106.

Laking, Sir Guy, *Catalogue of the Armoury of Windsor Castle*, London: Bradbury and Agnew, 1904.

Lane, Frederic C. and Reinhold C. Mueller, *Money and Banking in Medieval and Renaissance Venice*, vol. 1, *Coins and Moneys of Account*, Baltimore: Johns Hopkins University Press, 1985.

Langland, William, *The Vision of William Concerning Piers the Plowman: The Crowley Text; or Text B*, ed. Walter W. Skeat, Oxford University Press, 1869.

Larkin, William, MS notes to William Larkin's portrait of Richard Sackville, third Earl of Dorset, in the Ranger's House, Greenwich, London.

Larsen, Anne R., "Reading/Writing and Gender in the Renaissance: The Case of Catherine Des Roches (1542–1587)," *Symposium* 41.4 (Winter 1987–8): 292–307.

Le Goff, Jacques, "The Usurer and Purgatory," in *The Dawn of Modern Banking*, Center for Medieval and Renaissance Studies, University of California, Los Angeles, New Haven: Yale University Press, 1979, 25–52.

Leadbeater, Eliza, *Spinning and Spinning Wheels*, Princes Risborough, Bucks.: Shire Publications, 1979; rpt. 1992.

Lee, Nathaniel, *The Rival Queens*, in *The Works of Nathaniel Lee*, ed. T. B. Stroup and A. L. Cooke, New Brunswick: Scarecrow Press, 1954.

Lemire, Beverly, *Dress, Culture and Commerce: The English Clothing Trade before the Factory, 1660–1800*, London: Macmillan, 1997.

Lemire, Beverly, *Fashion's Favourite: The Cotton Trade and the Consumer in Britain, 1660–1800*, Oxford University Press, 1991.

Lever, J. W., *The Tragedy of State*, London: Methuen, 1971.

Levey, Santina, *Elizabethan Treasures: The Hardwick Hall Textiles*, London: National Trust, 1998.

Levi, Primo, *If This Is a Man*, trans. Stuart Wolf, London: Abacus, 1979.

Levin, Richard, "The Economics and Erotics of Cross-Class Dressing in Early Modern (formerly Renaissance) English Drama," *Journal of Theatre and Drama* 3 (1997): 93–101.

Light: A Journal of Psychical, Occult and Mystical Research, vol. 11, no. 537 (Sat. 18 April 1891).

Lindley, David, "Embarrassing Ben: The Masques for Frances Howard," *English Literary Renaissance* 16. 2 (1986): 343–59.

Lindley, David, *The Trials of Frances Howard: Fact and Fiction at the Court of King James*, London: Routledge, 1993.

Linthicum, M. Channing, *Costume in the Drama of Shakespeare and his Contemporaries*, Oxford: Clarendon Press, 1936; 2nd edn. 1963.

Linton, Joan Pong, *The Romance of the New World: Gender and the Literary Formations of English Colonialism*, Cambridge University Press, 1998.

Lipson, E., *A Short History of Wool and Its Manufacture*, London: Heinemann, 1953.

Litten, Julian, *The English Way of Death: The Common Funeral since 1450*, London: Robert Hale, 1991.

Llewellyn, Nigel, *The Art of Death: Visual Culture in the English Death Ritual, c.1500–c.1800*, London: Reaktion Books, 1991.

Lockyer, Roger, *Buckingham: The Life and Political Career of George Villiers, First Duke of Buckingham 1592–1628*, London: Longman, 1981.

Loder, Robert, *Robert Loder's Farm Accounts 1610–1620*, ed. G. F. Fussell, Camden Society, 3rd series, vol. 53, London: Camden Society, 1936.

Longfield, Ada Kathleen, *Anglo-Irish Trade in the Sixteenth Century*, London: Routledge, 1929.

Lopez, Robert, "The Dawn of Medieval Banking," in *The Dawn of Modern Banking*, Center for Medieval and Renaissance Studies, University of California, Los Angeles, New Haven: Yale University Press, 1979, 1–24.

"A Lottery Proposed before Supper at the Lo:[rd] Chief Justice his House, in the First Entrance to Hir Majestie, Ladies, Gentlewomen, and Straungers," *Poetical Miscellanies*, II, 8, in *Early English Poetry and Ballads and Popular Literature of the Middle Ages*, Percy Society Reprints, vol. 15, ed. J. O. Halliwell, London: T. Richards, 1845.

The Lowell Offering: Writings by New England Mill Women (1800–1845), ed. Benita Eisler, Philadelphia: Lippincott, 1977.

Luigini, Federigo, *Il Libro della bella donna*, Venice, 1554.

Luther, Martin, *Luther's Commentary on Genesis*, trans. J. Theodore Mueller, Grand Rapids, Michigan: Zondervan, 1968.

Lyly, John, *Euphues: the Anatomy of Wit* (1580), ed. Edward Arber, Westminster: Constable, 1895.

Macfarlane, Alan, *The Family Life of Ralph Josselin, a Seventeenth- Century Clergyman: An Essay in Historical Anthropology*, Cambridge University Press, 1970.

Machiavelli, Niccolo, Letter of 10 December 1513, *The Literary Works of Machiavelli*, ed. J. R. Hale, London: Oxford University Press, 1961, pp. 136–41.

MacIntyre, Jean, *Costumes and Scripts in the Elizabethan Theatres*, Edmonton: University of Alberta Press, 1992.

Mactaggart, Peter and Ann, "The Rich Wearing Apparel of Richard, 3rd Earl of Dorset," *Costume* 14 (1980): 44–7.

Mander, Raymond and Joe Mitchenson, *Hamlet Through the Ages: A Pictorial Record from 1709*, ed. Herbert Marshall, London: Rockliff, 1952.

Mandeville, Bernard, *The Fable of the Bees: Or Private Vices, Publick Benefits* (London, 1714), Oxford: Clarendon Press, 1957.

Markham, Gervase, *The English Hus-wife* (London, 1615, 1631), ed. Michael Best, Montreal: McGill/Queen's University Press, 1986.

Marshall, Dorothy, *The English Domestic Servant in History*, London: The Historical Association, 1949.

Marshall, Rosalind, *Costume in Scottish Portraits 1560–1830*, Edinburgh: Scottish National Portrait Gallery, 1986.

Marston, John, *Antonio's Revenge*, in *The Plays of John Marston*, ed. H. Harvey Wood, London: Oliver and Boyd, 1934, vol. 1.

Martin, Gregory, *The Flemish School circa 1600–1900*, London: The National Gallery, 1970.

Martin, Janet, *Treasure of the Land of Darkness: The Fur Trade and Its Significance for Medieval Russia*, Cambridge University Press, 1986.

Martyn, Joseph, "39. To *Flaua* of her yellow Band," in *New Epigrams, and a Satyre*, London, 1621.

Marx, Karl, *On James Mill*, in *Karl Marx: Selected Writings*, ed. David McLellan, Oxford University Press, 1977, 114–23.

Marx, Karl, "The Fetishism of the Commodity and Its Secret," in *Capital*, vol. 1, trans. Ben Fowkes, New York: Vintage, 1976, 163–77.

Matter, Joseph Allen, *My Lord and Lady of Essex: Their State Trials*, Chicago: Henry Regnery, 1969.

Mattingly, Garrett, *Catherine of Aragon*, Boston: Little, Brown and Co., 1941.

Mauss, Marcel, *The Gift: Forms and Functions of Exchange in Archaic Societies*, trans. Ian Cunnison, New York: Norton, 1967.

Mayhew, Charlotte, "The Effects of Economic and Social Development in the Seventeenth Century upon British Amateur Embroideries," MA thesis in Literature, University of St. Andrews, 1988.

Mayne, Jasper, *The City Match*, Oxford, 1659.

McClintock, H. F., *Old Irish and Highland Dress*, Dundalk: Dundalgan Press, 1943.

McCoy, Richard, *The Rites of Knighthood: The Literature and Politics of Elizabethan Chivalry*, Berkeley: University of California Press, 1989.

McElwee, William, *The Murder of Sir Thomas Overbury*, London: Faber and Faber, 1952.

McLuskie, Kathleen, "The Act, the Role, and the Actor: Boy Actresses on the Elizabethan Stage," *New Theatre Quarterly* 3, 10 (1987): 120–30.

McMillin, Scott, *The Elizabethan Theatre and "The Book of Sir Thomas More,"* Ithaca, NY: Cornell University Press, 1987.

Medick, Hans, "Village Spinning Bees: Sexual Culture and Free Time among Rural Youth in Early Modern Germany," in *Interest and Emotion: Essays on the Study of Family and Kinship*, ed. Hans Medick and David Warren Sabean, Cambridge University Press and Paris: Maison des Sciences de l'Homme, 1984, 317–39.

Medwall, Henry, *Fulgens and Lucres*, in *Tudor Interludes*, ed. Peter Happé, Harmondsworth: Penguin, 1972.

Mendelson, Sara and Patricia Crawford, *Women in Early Modern England*, Oxford: Clarendon Press, 1998.

Menning, Carol Bresnahan, *Charity and the State in Late Renaissance Italy: The Monte di Pietà of Florence*, Ithaca, NY: Cornell University Press, 1993.

Mercer, Eric, *English Art 1553–1625*, Oxford: Clarendon Press, 1962.

Mercurio, Scipione, *De gli errori popolari d'Italia. Libri sette*, Padua: Francesco Bolzetta, 1645.

Mertes, Kate, *The English Noble Household 1250–1600: Good Governance and Political Rule*, Oxford: Blackwell, 1988.

Middleton, Thomas, *Michaelmas Term* (1607), ed. Richard Levin, Regents Renaissance Drama, Lincoln: University of Nebraska Press, 1966.

Middleton, Thomas, *More Dissemblers besides Women*, London, 1657.

Middleton, Thomas, *The Widow*, in *The Works of Thomas Middleton*, ed. A. H. Bullen, London: John Nimno, 1885–6, vol. 5.

Middleton, Thomas, *Women Beware Women*, London, 1657.

Middleton, Thomas, *Your Five Gallants (1607): A Critical Edition*, ed. Clare Lee Colegrove, New York: Garland, 1979.

Middleton, Thomas, *Your Five Gallants*, in *Works*, ed. Bullen, vol. 3.

Middleton, Thomas and William Rowley, *The Changeling*, London, 1653.

Middleton, Thomas and William Rowley, *The Old Law*, ed. Catherine M. Shaw, New York: Garland, 1982.

Middleton, Thomas and William Rowley, *The World Tost at Tennis*, London, 1620.

Mildmay, Lady Grace, *Autobiography*, in *With Faith and Physic: The Life of a Tudor Gentlewoman, Lady Grace Mildmay 1552–1620*, ed. Linda Pollock, London: Collins and Brown, 1993.

Mill, Humphrey, *A Nights Search: Discovering the Nature and Condition of Night-Walkers with their Associates*, London, 1640.

Millar, Oliver, *Van Dyck in England*, London: National Portrait Gallery, 1982.

Millar, Oliver, "Van Dyck in London," in *Anthony van Dyck*, ed. Arthur K. Wheelock, Susan J. Bernes, et al., New York: Abrams, 1990.

Miller, Daniel, *Material Culture and Mass Consumption*, Oxford: Blackwell, 1987.

Miller, William, "The Linen Manufactures of the Olden Time," in Alex J. Warden, *The Linen Trade*, 3rd edn., London: Frank Cass, 1967, 3–40.

Milton, John, *Apology for Smectymnus*, in *The Complete Prose Works of John Milton*, ed. Don M. Wolfe et al., New Haven: Yale University Press, 1953, vol. 1.

Milton, John, *Areopagitica*, in *John Milton: Complete Poems and Major Prose*, ed. Merritt Y. Hughes, New York: Macmillan, 1957.

Milton, John, *Paradise Lost*, London, 1674.

Milton, John, *Samson Agonistes*, in *Complete Poems and Major Prose*, ed. Hughes.

Milton, John, *The Reason of Church Government*, London, 1641.

Mitchell, Margaret, *Gone with the Wind*, New York: Warner Books, 1993.

Moffet, Thomas, *The Silkewormes, and their Flies*, London, 1599.

Montias, John Michael, *Vermeer and His Milieu: A Web of Social History*, Princeton University Press, 1988.

Moore, Cornelia Niekus, "Books, Spindles and the Devil's Bench or What Is the Point in Needlepoint?" in *Barocker Lust-Spiegel: Studien zur Literatur des Barock (Festschrift für Blake Lee Spahr)*, Amsterdam: Rodopi, 1984, 319–28.

Moors, Annelies, "Wearing Gold," in *Border Fetishisms: Material Objects in Unstable Spaces*, ed. Patricia Spyer, London: Routledge, 1997, 208–23.

Morgan, Hiram, "Tom Lee: The Posing Peacemaker," in *Representing Ireland: Literature and the Origins of Conflict, 1534–1600*, ed. Brian Bradshaw, Andrew Hadfield and Willy Maley, Cambridge University Press, 1993, 132–65.

Morill, John, "The Stuart Period," in *The Oxford Illustrated History of Britain*, ed. Kenneth O. Morgan, Oxford University Press, 1984.

Moryson, Fynes, *An Itinerary containing his ten yeeres travell through... Germany...England, Scotland and Ireland*, London, 1617, Glasgow: MacLehose, 1907.

Mueller, Reinhold C., *The Venetian Money Market: Banks, Panics, and the Public Debt, 1200–1500*, Baltimore: Johns Hopkins University Press, 1997.

"Muld Sacke: or The Apologie of *Hic Mulier*," London, 1620, in *Three Pamphlets on the Jacobean Antifeminist Controversy*, ed. Barbara Baines, Delmar, NY: Scholars' Facsimiles, 1978.

Mullaney, Steven, *The Place of the Stage: License, Play and Power in Renaissance England*, University of Chicago Press, 1988.

Müller, Claudia, *The Costume Timeline: Five Thousand Years of Fashion History*, London: Thames and Hudson, 1993.

Mumby, Frank A., *The Girlhood of Queen Elizabeth: A Narrative in Contemporary Letters*, Boston: Houghton Mifflin, 1910.

Munro, John H., "The Medieval Scarlet and the Economics of Sartorial Splendour," in *Cloth and Clothing in Medieval Europe: Essays in Memory of Professor E. M. Carus-Wilson*, ed. N. B. Harte and K. G. Ponting, London: Pasold Studies in Textile History, Heinemann Educational Books, 1983, 13–70.

Murrell, V. J., "The Art of Limning," in Roy Strong, *Artists of the Tudor Court: The Portrait Miniature Rediscovered 1520–1620*, London, Victoria & Albert Museum catalogue, 1983.

Nashe, Thomas, *The Works of Thomas Nashe*, ed Ronald B. McKerrow, London: A. H. Bullen, 1905.

The National Trust, *Montacute House: Goodhart Collection of Samplers*, n.d.

Neale, J. E., *Elizabeth I and Her Parliaments 1559–1581*, London: Jonathan Cape, 1953.

Neill, Michael, *Issues of Death: Mortality and Identity in English Renaissance Tragedy*, Oxford: Clarendon Press, 1997.

Neill, Michael, "Unproper Beds: Race, Adultery, and the Hideous in *Othello*," *Shakespeare Quarterly* 40.4 (1989): 383–412.

Neumann, Erich, *The Great Mother: An Analysis of the Archetype*, New York: Pantheon, 1955.

Nevinson, John L., "English Domestic Embroidery Patterns of the Sixteenth and Seventeenth Centuries," *Walpole Society Publications* 28 (1939–40): 1–13.

Nevinson, John L., "Peter Stent and John Overton, Publishers of Embroidery Designs," *Apollo Magazine* 24 (1936): 279–83.

Nevinson, John L., "Siegmund von Herberstein: Notes on Sixteenth- Century Dress," *Waffen und Kostümkunde* (1959): 86–93.

Newman, Karen, *Fashioning Femininity and English Renaissance Drama*, University of Chicago Press, 1991.

Newton, Stella Mary, "Some Notes on the Dress in Holbein's Portraits," in *Holbein and the Court of Henry VIII*, exhibition catalogue, London, The Queen's Gallery, Buckingham Palace, 1978–79.

Niccols, Richard, "Epig. XII. *In Tubrionem*" and "Epig. XIIII. *In Verrem*," in *The Furies. With Virtues Encomium. Or, the Image of Honour*, London, 1614.

Niccols, Richard, *Sir Thomas Overburies Vision*, London: The Hunterian Club, 1873.

Nicholas, Sir John, account book, Folger MS. V. a. 420.

Nicolas, Sir Nicholas Harris, *Testamenta Vetusta*, London: Nichols and Son, 1826, vol. 1.

Nicoll, Allardyce, *Stuart Masques and the Renaissance Stage*, London: George Harrap, 1937.

Norgate, Edward, *Miniatura or the Art of Limning*, ed. Martin Hardie, Oxford University Press, 1919.

Ondaatje, Michael, *In the Skin of a Lion*, Harmondsworth: Penguin, 1987.

Orgel, Stephen, *Impersonations: The Performance of Gender in Shakespeare's England*, Cambridge University Press, 1996.

Orgel, Stephen, "Making Greatness Familiar," in *The Power of Forms in the English Renaissance*, ed. Stephen Greenblatt, Norman, Oklahoma: Pilgrim Books, 1982, 41–8.

Orgel, Stephen, and Roy Strong, *Inigo Jones: The Theater of the Stuart Court*, London and Berkeley: Sotheby Parke Bernet/University of California Press, 1973.

Ormerod, Beverly,"The Ivy Emblem in Scève's *dizain* 150," *Australian Journal of French Studies* 17.1 (January–April, 1980): 58–84.

Osborne, Francis, *The True Tragicomedy Formerly Acted at Court*, ed. Lois Potter, New York: Garland, 1983.

Osborne, Francis, *The Works of Francis Osborne*, London, 1682.

Overbury, Sir Thomas, "A Servingman," in *A wife now the widdow of Sir T. Overbury... Whereunto are added many witty characters*, London: A. Crooke, 1638, sig. G.

Ovid (Publius Ovidius Naso), *Metamorphoses*, ed. and trans. Frank Justus Miller, 3rd edn., Cambridge, Mass.: Harvard University Press, 1984.

Ovid, *Heroides 1*, in *Heroides and Amores*, rev. edn., ed. G. P. Goold, trans. Grant Showerman, Cambridge, Mass.: Harvard University Press, 1977.

Ovid, *Ovid's Metamorphoses, Books 6–10*, ed. William S. Anderson, Norman, Okla.: University of Oklahoma Press, 1972.

Ovid, *Remedia amoris*, trans. as *The Remedies of Love* by J. H. Mozley, in *Ovid*, vol. 2, Cambridge, Mass.: Harvard University Press, 1929, rev. edn. 1979.

The Oxford Dictionary of English Proverbs, 3rd edn., Oxford: Clarendon Press, 1982.

Oxford English Dictionary

Palomino y Velasco, Antonio, *El Museo pictorico y la escala optica* (Madrid, 1715–24), trans. Zahira Veliz, in *Artists' Techniques in Golden Age Spain: Six Treatises in Translation*, Cambridge University Press, 1986.

Parker, Roszika, *The Subversive Stitch: Embroidery and the Making of the Feminine*, London: The Women's Press, 1984; rpt. New York: Routledge, 1989.

Paul, John E., *Katherine of Aragon and her Friends*, New York: Fordham University Press, 1966.

Pearse, William, *A Present for Youth and an Example for the Aged: or the Remains of Damaris Pearse*, London, 1683.

Pech, Carol, "'His Nuts for a piece of Metal': Fetishism in the Monetary Writings of John Locke," chapter in Ph.D. dissertation, Johns Hopkins University, forthcoming 2000.

Peck, Linda Levy, *Northampton: Patronage and Policy at the Court of James I*, London: George Allen and Unwin, 1982.

Pepys, Samuel, *Pepys on the Restoration Stage*, ed. H. McAfee, New Haven: Yale University Press, 1916.

Pepys, Samuel, *The Diary of Samuel Pepys*, ed. Robin Latham and William Matthews, London: Bell and Hyman, 1983.

Petrarca, Francesco, *Historia Griseldis*, trans. Heinrich Steinhöwel, Ulm: Johann Zainer, 1473.

Petrarch, Francis, *Letters of Old Age: Rerum Senilium Libri I-XVIII*, vol. 2 (Books X-XVIII), trans. Aldo S. Bernardo, Saul Levin, and Reta A. Bernardo, Baltimore: Johns Hopkins University Press, 1992.

Petrarca, Francesco, *Opere Latine di Francesco Petrarca*, ed. Antonietta Bufano, Turin: Unione Tipografico, 1975, 2 vols.

Petrarca, Francesco, "Sen. XVII," in Ernest H. Wilkins, *Petrarch's Later Years*, Cambridge, Mass.: The Medieval Academy of America, 1959, 243.

Petrarca, Francesco, "Testamentum," in *Opere Latine*, vol. 2, 1352.

Peyton, Sir Edward, *The Divine Catastrophe of the Kingly Family of the House of Stuarts*, London, 1652.

Phillip, John, *The Play of Patient Grissell*, ed. W. W. Greg and Ronald B. McKerrow, London: The Malone Society, 1909.

Phillips, J, *The Reformation of Images: Destruction of Art in England, 1535–1660*, Berkeley: University of California Press, 1973.

Pietz, William, "Fetishism and Materialism: The Limits of Theory in Marx," in *Fetishism as Cultural Discourse*, ed. Emily Apter and William Pietz, Ithaca, NY: Cornell University Press, 1993, 119–51.

Pietz, William, "The Problem of the Fetish, I," *Res* 9 (1985): 5–17.

Pietz, William, "The Problem of the Fetish, II," *Res* 13 (1987): 23–45.

Pietz, William, "The Problem of the Fetish, IIIa," *Res* 16 (1988): 105–23.

Plato, *The Republic*, trans. Francis M. Cornford, Oxford University Press, 1967.

The Pleasant and Sweet History of patient Grissell, London: John Wright, 1630.

Pollard, A. F., *Henry VIII*, London: Jonathan Cape, 1970.

Pollard, Alfred W., *Fifteenth-Century Prose and Verse, An English Garner*, Westminster: Constable, 1903.

Pollock, Sir Frederick and Frederic William Maitland, *The History of English Law*, Cambridge University Press, 1968.

Ponting, K. G., *The Wool Trade, Past and Present*, Manchester: Columbine Press, 1961.

Ponting, Kenneth, *The Woollen Industry of South-west England*, Bath: Adams and Dart, 1971.

Powell, Thomas, *The Art of Thriving, or the plaine path-way to preferment*, London, 1635.

Prestwich, Menna, *Cranfield: Politics and Profits under the Early Stuarts*, Oxford: Clarendon Press, 1966.

Prestwich, Michael, "Italian Merchants in Late Thirteenth and Early Fourteenth Century England," in *The Dawn of Modern Banking*, Center for Medieval and Renaissance Studies, University of California, Los Angeles, New Haven: Yale University Press, 1979, 77–104.

Prior, Mary, "Women and the Urban Economy: Oxford 1500–1800," in *Women in English Society*, ed. Mary Prior, New York: Methuen, 1985, 93–117.

Prynne, William, *Histrio-Mastix*, London, 1633.

Prynne, William, *Documents Relating to the Proceedings against William Prynne*, ed. Samuel Rawson Gardiner, Camden Society, n.s, vol. 18 (1877).

Pullan, Brian, *Rich and Poor in Renaissance Venice: The Social Institutions of a Catholic State, to 1620*, Oxford: Blackwell, 1971.

Quentel, Peter, *Ein neu künstlich Modelbuch*, Cologne, 1527.

Rackin, Phyllis, "Androgyny, Mimesis, and the Marriage of the Boy Heroine on the English Renaissance Stage," *PMLA* 102 (1987): 29–41.

Rackin, Phyllis, "Dating Shakespeare's Women," *Shakespeare Jahrbuch* 134 (1998): 29–43.

Rackin, Phyllis, "Shakespeare's Boy Cleopatra, the Decorum of Nature, and the Golden World of Poetry," *PMLA* 87 (1972): 201–12.

Rackin, Phyllis, *Stages of History: Shakespeare's English Chronicles*, Ithaca, NY: Cornell University Press, 1990.

Rainoldes, John, *Th' Overthrow of Stage-Playes*, London, 1599.

Ralegh, Sir Walter, "Preface," *The History of the World*, London, 1677.

Rappaport, Steve, *Worlds Within Worlds: Structures of Life in Sixteenth- Century London*, Cambridge University Press, 1989.

Reed, A. W., *Early Tudor Drama: Medwall, the Rastells, Heywood, and the More Circle*, London: Methuen, 1926.

Reed, Sue Welsh, "Jacques Bellange," in *The French Renaissance in Prints from the Bibliothèque Nationale de France*, ed. Karen Jacobson, Los Angeles: Grunwald Center for the Graphic Arts, University of California, Los Angeles, 1994.

Reynolds, Graham, "Elizabethan and Jacobean," in *Costume of the Western World: Fashions of the Renaissance*, ed. James Laver, New York: Harper and Brothers, 1951.

Rich, Barnabe, "Of Apolonius and Silla" (1581), in *Twelfth Night*, ed. J. M. Lothian and T. W. Craik, the Arden Shakespeare, London: Methuen, 1975.

Rich, Barnabe, *The Honestie of this Age*, London, 1614.

Rich, Barnabe, *The Irish Hubbub, or the English Hue and Crie*, London, 1618.

Rich, Barnabe, *Riche his farewell to Militarie Profession*, London, 1581.

Richards, Nathaniel, *The Celestial Publican*, London, 1630.

Richards, Nathaniel, *The Tragedy of Messalina*, London, 1640, ed. A. R. Skemp, Louvain: A. Uystpruyst, 1910.

Richards, Nathaniel, "Upon the Tragedy of my Familiar Acquaintance, Thos. Middleton," in Thomas Middleton, *Women Beware Women* and *More Dissemblers besides Women*, London, 1657.

Richards, R. D., *The Early History of Banking in England*, London: Frank Cass, 1958.

Richardson, Samuel, *Pamela; Or, Virtue Rewarded* (1740, 1801), Harmondsworth: Penguin 1980.

Riggs, David, *Ben Jonson: A Life*, Cambridge, Mass.: Harvard University Press, 1989.

Rigolot, François, "Faire taire Pallas et parler Arachné," in *Louise Labé Lyonnaise ou la Renaissance au féminin*, Paris: Champion, 1997, 117–51.

Roberts, Jane, *Holbein and the Court of Henry VIII: Drawings and Miniatures from the Royal Library, Windsor Castle*, exhibition catalogue, Edinburgh: National Galleries of Scotland, 1993.

Roberts, Michael, "'Words they are women, and deeds they are men': Images of Work and Gender in Early Modern England," in *Women and Work in Preindustrial England*, ed. Lindsey Charles and Lorna Duffin, London: Croom Helm, 1985, 122–80.

Roberts, Sasha, "Lying among the Classics: Ritual and Motif in Elite Elizabethan and Jacobean Beds," in *Albion's Classicism: The Visual Arts in Britain, 1550–1660*, ed. Lucy Gent, New Haven: Yale University Press, 1995, 325–57.

Roberts, William, "The Fur Trade of New England in the Seventeenth Century," Ph.D. dissertation, University of Pennsylvania, 1958.

Robinson, James H., *Petrarch, the First Modern Scholar and Man of Letters*, New York: Putnam, 1898.

Roche, Daniel, *The Culture of Clothing: Dress and Fashion in the "Ancien Régime"*, Cambridge University Press, 1994.

Ronsard, Pierre de, "Discours à Monsieur le Duc de Savoie," *Oeuvres complètes*, ed. Paul Laumonnier, Paris: Droz, 1937, vol. 9, 164–73.

Rosenberg, Marvin, *The Masks of Othello*, Berkeley: University of California Press, 1971.

Ross, Ellen, *Love and Toil: Motherhood in Outcast London 1870–1918*, Oxford University Press, 1993.

Rosse, Abraham, *An Exposition on the Fourteene first Chapters of Genesis*, London, 1626.

Rowlands, John, *Holbein: The Paintings of Hans Holbein the Younger*, Boston: David Godine, 1985.

Rowlands, Samuel, *Doctor Merry-man: or, Nothing but Mirth*, London, 1616.

Rowlands, Samuel, "Satyre 2," *The Letting of humours blood in the head-vaine*, London, 1611.

Russell, Diane H., *Eva/Ave: Women in Renaissance and Baroque Prints*, Washington, DC: National Gallery of Art/New York: The Feminist Press at the City University of New York, 1990.

Rutter, Carol Chillington, ed., *Documents of the Rose Playhouse*, Manchester University Press, 1984.

S., W., *The Puritaine or The Widdow of Watling-streete* (1607), in *The Shakespeare Apocrypha*, vol. 2, ed. C. F. Tucker Brooke, Oxford: Clarendon Press, 1918.

Salter, Thomas, *A Mirrhor mete for all Mothers, Matrones and Maidens, intituled the Mirrhor of Modestie*, London: 1579.

Sanderson, James L., "Poems on an Affair of State: the Marriage of Somerset and Lady Essex," *Review of English Studies* 16, no. 65 (1966): 57–61.

Sanderson, W., *Aulicus Coquinariae*, London, 1650.

Sandys, George, *Ovid's Metamorphosis Englished, Mythologized, and Represented in Figures by George Sandys* (Oxford, 1632), ed. K. K. Hulley and S. T. Vandersall, Lincoln, Neb.: University of Nebraska Press, 1970.

Savage, James E., *The "Conceited Newes" of Sir Thomas Overbury and His Friends*, Gainesville, Fla.: Scholars Press, 1968.

Saward, Susan, *The Golden Age of Maria de' Medici*, Ann Arbor, Mich.: UMI Research Press, 1982.

Scarisbrock, J. J., *Henry VIII*, London: Eyre and Spottiswoode, 1968.

Scheidig, Walther, *Die Holzschnitte des Petrarca-Meisters zu Petrarcas Werk "Von der Artzney bayder Glück, des guten und widerwartigen" (Augsburg 1532)*, Berlin: Henschel-verlag, 1955.

Schneider, Jane, "Rumpelstiltskin's Bargain: Folklore and the Merchant Capitalist Intensification of Linen Manufacture in Early Modern Europe," in *Cloth and Human Experience*, ed. Annette B. Weiner and Jane Schneider, Washington, DC: Smithsonian Institution Press, 1989, 177–213.

Scoloker, Anthony, *Diaphantus, or the Passions of Loue*, London, 1604.

Shakespeare, William, *The First Folio of Shakespeare: The Norton Facsimile*, ed. Charlton Hinman, New York: Norton, 1968.

Shakespeare, William, *The Riverside Shakespeare*, ed. G. Blakemore Evans, Boston: Houghton Mifflin, 1974.

Shakespeare, William, *The Taming of the Shrew*, ed. Brian Morris, the Arden Shakespeare, London: Methuen, 1981.

Shakespeare, William, *The Tragicall Historie of Hamlet, Prince of Denmarke* (London, 1604), *Shakespeare's Plays in Quarto*, ed. Michael J. B. Allen and Kenneth Muir, Berkeley: University of California Press, 1981.

Shakespeare, William, *Troilus and Cressida*, ed. Kenneth Palmer, the Arden Shakespeare, London: Methuen, 1982.

Shapiro, Michael, "'Boying Her Greatness': Shakespeare's Use of Coterie Drama in *Antony and Cleopatra*," *Modern Language Review* 77.1 (1982): 1–15.

Shapiro, Michael, "Crossgender Casting, Crossgender Disguise, and Anxieties of Intimacy in *Twelfth Night* and Other Plays," paper for the Shakespeare Association of America meeting, Philadelphia, 1990.

Shorleyker, Richard, *A Scholehouse for the Needle*, London, 1624.

Sinfield, Alan, *Faultlines: Cultural Materialism and the Politics of Dissident Reading*, Berkeley, University of California Press, 1992.

Smith, Alan, *The Wealth of the Gentry 1540–1669: East Anglian Studies*, Cambridge University Press, 1961.

Smith, Hallett, *Elizabethan Poetry: A Study in Conventions, Meaning, and Expression*, Cambridge, Mass.: Harvard University Press, 1952.

Smollett, Tobias, *The Expedition of Humphrey Clinker*, ed. Lewis M. Knapp, Oxford University Press, 1966.

Smuts, R. Malcolm, *Court Culture and the Origins of a Royalist Tradition in Early Stuart England*, Philadelphia: University of Pennsylvania Press, 1987.

Snell, K. D. M, *Annals of the Labouring Poor*, Cambridge University Press, 1987.

Sombart, Werner, *Luxury and Capitalism*, trans. W. R. Dittmar, Ann Arbor: University of Michigan Press, 1967.

Somerset, Anne, *Ladies-in-Waiting*, New York: Alfred Knopf, 1984.

Southern, Richard, *The Staging of Plays before Shakespeare*, London: Faber and Faber, 1973.

Sparke, Michael, *Truth Brought to Light and Discovered by Time, or A Discourse and Historicall Narration of the first XIIII yeares of King Iames Reigne*, London, 1651.

Spenser, Edmund, *A View of the State of Ireland*, ed. Andrew Hadfield and Willy Maley, Oxford: Blackwell, 1997.

Spufford, Margaret, *The Great Reclothing of Rural England: Petty Chapmen and their Wares in the Seventeenth Century*, London: Hambledon Press, 1984.

Stallybrass, Peter, "Marx's Coat," in *Border Fetishisms: Material Objects in Unstable Spaces*, ed. Patricia Spyer, London: Routledge, 1997, 183–207.

Stallybrass, Peter, "The World Turned Upside Down: Inversion, Gender, and the State," in *The Matter of Difference: Materialist Feminist Criticism of Shakespeare*, ed. Valerie Wayne, Ithaca, NY: Cornell University Press, 1991, 202–20.

Starkey, David, "The Age of the Household: Politics, Society and the Arts c. 1350–1550," in *The Later Middle Ages*, ed. Stephen Medcalf, New York: Holmes and Meier, 1981, 224–90.

Stephens, John, *Satyricall Essayes*, London, 1615.

Stewart, Alison, "The First 'Peasant Festivals': Eleven Woodcuts Produced in Reformation Nuremberg... to 1535," Ph.D. dissertation, Columbia University, 1986.

Stewart, Horace, *History of the Worshipful Company of Gold and Silver Wyre-Drawers*, London: The Leadenhall Press, 1891.

Stewart, Susan, *On Longing: Narratives of the Miniature, the Gigantic, the Souvenir, the Collection*, Baltimore: Johns Hopkins University Press, 1984.

Stokes, John, "The Wells Cordwainers Show: New Evidence Concerning Guild Entertainments in Somerset," *Comparative Drama* 19.4 (1985–6): 332–46.

Stone, Lawrence, *The Crisis of the Aristocracy 1558–1641*, Oxford: Clarendon Press, 1965.

Stone-Ferrier, Linda A., *Images of Textiles: The Weave of Seventeenth-Century Dutch Art and Society*, Ann Arbor, Michigan: UMI Research Press, 1985.

Storer, Thomas, *The Life and Death of Thomas Wolsey Cardinal*, London, 1599.

Stoughton, Thomas, *The Christians Sacrifice*, London, 1622.

Stow, John, *Annales of England*, continued by Edmund Howes, London, 1632.

Stow, John, *A Survey of London*, ed. Charles Kingsford, Oxford: Clarendon Press, 1908, 2 vols.

Stow, John, *A Survey of the Cities of London and Westminster... Corrected, Improved, and very much Enlarged by John Strype*, London: A. Churchill et al., 1720.

Strathern, Marilyn, *The Gender of the Gift: Problems with Women and Problems with Society in Melanesia*, Berkeley: University of California Press, 1988.

Stretton, Tim, *Women Waging Law in Elizabethan England*, Cambridge University Press, 1998.

Strong, Roy, "Elizabethan Painting: An Approach through the Inscriptions of Marcus Gheeraerts the Younger," *The Burlington Magazine* 105 (1963); rpt. in *The English Icon: Elizabethan and Jacobean Portraiture*, London: Mellon Foundation for British Art/ Routledge and Kegan Paul, 1969, 350–51.

Strong, Roy, *Portraits of Queen Elizabeth I*, Oxford: Clarendon Press, 1963.

Strong, Roy, *The English Icon: Elizabethan and Jacobean Portraiture*, London: Mellon Foundation for British Art/Routledge and Kegan Paul, 1969.

Strong, Roy, *William Larkin: Icons of Splendour*, Milan: Franco Maria Ricci, 1995.

Stubbes, Phillip, *The Anatomie of Abuses*, London, 1583.

Stubbes, Phillip, *The Anatomie of Abuses*, ed. Frederick J. Furnivall, The New Shakespeare Society, series 6, no. 4, London: Trübner, 1877–79.

Summit, Jennifer, "'The Arte of a Ladies Penne': Elizabeth I and the Poetics of Queenship," *English Literary Renaissance* 26.3 (Autumn 1996): 395–422.

Swain, Margaret, *The Needlework of Mary Queen of Scots*, London: Van Nostrand Reinhold, 1973; rpt. Carlton, Bedford: Ruth Bean, 1986.

Swinburn, Henry, *A Brief Treatise of Testaments and Last Wills*, London, 1611.

Symon, Bishop of Ely, *A Commentary upon the First Book of Moses, called Genesis*, London, 1698.

Tatar, Maria, *The Hard Facts of the Grimms' Fairy Tales*, Princeton: Princeton University Press, 1987.

Taylor, John, "The Praise of the Needle," in *The Needle's Excellency*, London: James Boler, 1624, 3rd edn., 1631.

Taylor, John, "The Praise of the Needle," in Gertrude Whiting, *Old-Time Tools and Toys of Needlework*, New York: Dover, 1971, rpt. of *Tools and Toys of Stitchery*, New York: Columbia University Press, 1928, 341–8.

Taylor, John, *Three Weekes, three daies, and three houres Obseruations and Trauel* (1617), in *The Works of John Taylor, the Water Poet*, ed. Charles Hindley, London: Reeves and Turner, 1876.

Taylor, John (?), *The Women's Sharp Revenge* (London, 1640), in *The Women's Sharp Revenge: Five Women's Pamphlets from the Renaissance*, ed. Simon Shepherd, New York: St. Martin's Press, 1985.

Tebbutt, Melanie, *Making Ends Meet: Pawnbroking and Working-Class Credit*, Leicester University Press, 1983.

Tezcan, Hülye, *The Topkapi Saray Museum: Carpets*, trans., expanded, and ed. J. M. Rogers, New York Graphic Society, Boston: Little, Brown, and Co., 1987.

Thirsk, Joan, *Economic Policy and Projects: The Development of a Consumer Society in Early Modern England*, Oxford: Clarendon, Press, 1978.

Thomas, Nicholas, *Entangled Objects: Exchange, Material Culture, and Colonialism in the Pacific*, Cambridge, Mass.: Harvard University Press, 1991.

Thompson, Daniel V., *The Materials and Techniques of Medieval Painting*, New York: Dover, 1956.

Thompson, W. G., *A History of Tapestry*, 3rd edn., East Ardsley, UK: EP Publishing, 1973.

Thomson, Leslie, "The Meaning of *Thunder and Lightning*: Stage Directions and Audience Expectations," *Early Theatre* (forthcoming).

Thomson, Peter, *Shakespeare's Theater*, London: Routledge and Kegan Paul, 1983.

Thurman, Christa C. Mayer, *Textiles in the Art Institute of Chicago*, Chicago Art Institute, 1992.

Tickner, F. W., *Women in English Economic History*, London: Dent, 1923.

Tindale, William, trans., *The New Testament*, 1526.

Tomkis, Thomas, *Albumazar: A Comedy*, ed. Hugh G. Dick, University of California Publications in English, Berkeley: University of California Press, 1944.

[Tomkis, Thomas], *Lingua*, London, 1607.

Tottel's Miscellany (1557–1587), ed. Hyder Rollins, rev. edn., Cambridge, Mass.: Harvard University Press, 1965.

Tradescant, John, *Musaeum Tradescantianum: Or, A Collection of Rarities*, London, 1657.

Traub, Valerie, *Desire and Anxiety: Circulations of Sexuality in Shakespearean Drama*, London: Routledge, 1992.

Tudor Royal Proclamations, ed. Paul L. Hughes and James F. Larkin, New Haven: Yale University Press, 1969.

Tuke, Thomas, *A Treatise against Painting and Tincturing of Men and Women*, London, 1616.

Turberville, George, *Epitaphes, Epigrams, Songs and Sonets*, London, 1567.

Turnau, Irena, "The Organization of the European Textile Industry from the Thirteenth to the Eighteenth Century," *The Journal of European Economic History* 17 (Winter 1988): 586–96.

Tyndale, William, trans., *The Five Books of Moses called the Pentateuch*, ed. J. I. Mombert, Fontwell, Sussex: Centaur Press, 1967.

Underdown, David, *A Freeborn People: Politics and the Nation in Seventeenth-Century England*, Oxford: Clarendon Press, 1996.

Underdown, David, "Yellow Ruffs and Poisoned Possets: Placing Women in Early Stuart Political Debate," paper presented at the conference "Attending to Women," University of Maryland, College Park, November, 1994.

Upton, Anthony F., *Sir Arthur Ingram, c, 1565–1642: A Study of the Origins of an English Landed Family*, Oxford University Press, 1961.

Vecellio, Cesare, *La Corona delle nobili e virtuose donne* (Venice, 1617), trans. as *A Pattern Book of Renaissance Lace*, New York: Dover, 1988.

Vecellio, Cesare, *Habiti antichi, et moderni di tutto il mondo* (Venice, 1598), rpt. and abridged as *Vecellio's Renaissance Costume Book*, New York: Dover, 1977.

Veldman, Ilya, "Lessons for Ladies: A Selection of Sixteenth- and Seventeenth-Century Dutch Prints," *Simiolus* 16. 2–3 (1986): 113– 27.

Verney, Frances Parthenope, *Memoirs of the Verney Family during the Civil War*, London: Longmans, Green, and Co., 1892, 4 vols.

Vicente, Marta, "Images and Realities of Work: Women and Guilds in Early Modern Barcelona," in *Spanish Women in the Golden Age*, ed. Magdalena Sanchez and Alain Saint-Saens, Westport, Conn.: Greenwood Press, 1996, 127–37.

The Victoria and Albert Museum's Textile Collection: Embroidery in Britain from 1200–1750, New York: Canopy Books, 1993.

Villault, Nicolas, *Relation des Costes d'Afrique, Appellées Guinée*, Paris: Thierry, 1669.

Villiers, G. H., *Hans Holbein: The Ambassadors*, National Gallery Books, no. 18, London: Percy Lund Humphries, n.d.

Vinciolo, Federigo, *Les Singuliers et nouveaux pourtraicts, du Seigneur Federic de Vinciolo Venitien*, Paris, 1606.

Vives, Juan Luis, *Instruction of a Christian Woman*, in *Vives and the Renascence Education of Women*, ed. Foster Watson, London: Edward Arnold, 1912.

Wallace, David, "'Whan She Translated Was': Humanism, Tyranny, and the Petrarchan Academy," in *Chaucerian Polity: Absolutist Lineages and Associational Forms in England and Italy*, Stanford University Press, 1997, 261–98.

Warner, Marina, *From the Beast to the Blonde: On Fairy Tales and Their Tellers*, New York: Farrar, Strauss, and Giroux, 1994.

Weamys, Anna, *A Continuation of Philip Sidney's Arcadia* (London, 1651), ed. Patrick Cullen, Oxford University Press, 1994.

Wearden, Jennifer, "Siegmund von Herberstein: An Italian Velvet in the Ottoman Court," *Costume* 19 (1985): 22–9.

Webster, John, *The Duchess of Malfi*, ed. John Russell Brown, The Revels Plays, Cambridge, Mass.: Harvard University Press, 1964.

Webster, John, *The White Devil* (1612), in *The Complete Works of John Webster*, vol. 1, ed. F. L. Lucas, Oxford University Press, 1937.

Weigle, Marta, *Spiders and Spinsters: Women and Mythology*, Albuquerque: University of New Mexico Press, 1982.

Weiner, Annette, "Inalienable Wealth," *American Ethnologist* 12 (1985): 210–227.

Whetstone, George, *A Mirour for Magestrates of Cyties*, London, 1584.

Whiting, Dr., report on his conference with Anne Turner, 11 November 1615, *Calendar of State Papers, Domestic*, vol. 83 (1858), 327.

Wickam, Glynne, *Early English Stages, 1300–1660*, vol. 2, part 1, 1576– 1660, New York: Columbia University Press, 1963.

Wier, Johann, *De Praestigiis Daemonum*, Frankfurt, 1586.

Wiesner, Merry, "Spinsters and Seamstresses: Women in Cloth and Clothing Production," in *Rewriting the Renaissance: The Discourses of Sexual Difference in Early Modern Europe*, ed. Margaret Ferguson, Maureen Quilligan, and Nancy Vickers, University of Chicago Press, 1986, 191–205.

Wiesner, Merry, *Women and Gender in Early Modern Europe*, Cambridge University Press, 1993.

Wiesner, Merry, *Working Women in Renaissance Germany*, New Brunswick, NJ: Rutgers University Press, 1986.

Wikland, Erik, *Elizabethan Players in Sweden 1591–92: Facts and Problems*, Stockholm: Almqvist and Wiksell, 1962.

Willan, T. S., *The Early History of the Russia Company*, Manchester University Press, 1955.

Willet, Andrew, *Hexapla in Genesin*, Cambridge, 1605.

Williams, Clare, *Thomas Platter's Travels in England, 1599*, London: Jonathan Cape, 1959.

Williams, John, *A Sermon of Apparell*, London, 1619.

Williamson, George C., *Lady Anne Clifford, Countess of Dorset, Pembroke, and Montgomery, 1590–1676: Her Life, Letters and Work*, Kendal: Wilson, 1922.

Wills, Gary, "Homer Alive," *New York Review of Books*, 39.8 (April 23, 1992): 42.

Wilmot, John, Earl of Rochester, *Poems On Several Occasions with Valentinian*, London, 1696.

Wilson, Elizabeth. *Adorned in Dreams: Fashion and Modernity*, Berkeley: University of California Press, 1987.

Wilson, John Harold, *All the King's Ladies: Actresses of the Restoration*, University of Chicago Press, 1958.

Wilson, Richard, *Will Power: Essays on Shakespearean Authority*, London: Harvester Wheatsheaf, 1993.

Winkler, John J., "Penelope's Cunning and Homer's," in *The Constraints of Desire: The Anthropology of Sex and Gender in Ancient Greece*, New York: Routledge, 1990, 129–61.

Witthoft, Brucia, "Marriage Rituals and Marriage Chests in Quattrocento Florence," *Artibus et Historiae* 5 (1982): 43–59.

Wofford, Suzanne L., "The Social Aesthetics of Rape: Closural Violence in Boccaccio and Botticelli," in *Creative Imitation: New Essays on Renaissance Literature in Honor of Thomas M. Greene*, ed. David Quint, Margaret W. Ferguson, G. W. Pigman III, and Wayne A. Rebhorn, Binghamton, NY: Medieval and Renaissance Texts and Studies, 1992, 189–238.

Wolley, Hannah, *A Supplement to the Queen-like Closet*, London, 1674.

Wotton, Sir Henry, *Reliquiae Wottonianae*, London, 1651.

Wright, Sue, "'Churmaids, Huswyfes and Hucksters': The Employment of Women in Tudor and Stuart Salisbury," in *Women and Work in Pre-Industrial England*, ed. Lindsay Charles and Lorna Duffin, London: Croom Helm, 1985, 100–21.

Wroth, Lady Mary, *The Countess of Montgomeries Urania* (London: 1621), ed. Josephine Roberts, Binghamton, NY: Medieval and Renaissance Texts and Studies, 1995.

Yates, Frances, A*straea, the Imperial Theme in the Sixteenth Century*, London: Routledge and Kegan Paul, 1975.

Young, K., "William Gager's Defence of the Academic Stage," *Transactions of the Wisconsin Academy of Sciences, Arts and Letters* 18 (1916): 593–638.

Ziegler, Georgianna, "Hand-Ma(i)de Books: The Manuscripts of Esther Inglis, Early-modern Precursors of the Artists' Book," forthcoming in *English Manuscript Studies* (1999).

Ziegler, Georgianna, "Penelope and the Politics of Women's Place in the Renaissance," in *Gloriana's Face: Women, Public and Private, in the English Renaissance*, ed. S. P. Cerasano and Marion Wynne-Davies, Detroit: Wayne State University Press, 1992, 25–46.

Zimmerman, Susan, "Disruptive Desire: Artifice and Indeterminacy in Jacobean Comedy," in *Erotic Politics*, ed. Susan Zimmerman, New York: Routledge, 1992, 39–63.

Zipes, Jack, *Fairy Tale as Myth, Myth as Fairy Tale*, Lexington: University Press of Kentucky, 1994.

Zittner, Sheldon P., "Hamlet, Duellist," in *Hamlet: Critical Essays*, ed. Joseph G. Price, New York: Garland, 1986, 123–43.

Zulueta, Francis de, *Embroideries by Mary Stuart and Elizabeth Talbot at Oxburgh Hall, Norfolk*, Oxford University Press, 1923.

Index

Cambridge Studies in Renaissance Literature and Culture

General editor
STEPHEN ORGEL
Jackson Eli Reynolds Professor of Humanities, Stanford University